Philosophies of History

B

Philosophies of History

From Enlightenment to Postmodernity

Introduced and Edited by
Robert M. Burns and
Hugh Rayment-Pickard

BLACKWELL
Publishers

Copyright © Blackwell Publishers Ltd 2000. Editorial arrangement and introductions copyright © Robert M. Burns and H. Rayment-Pickard 2000

First published 2000

2 4 6 8 10 9 7 5 3 1

Blackwell Publishers Ltd
108 Cowley Road
Oxford OX4 1JF
UK

Blackwell Publishers Inc.
350 Main Street
Malden, Massachusetts 02148
USA

British Library Cataloguing in Publication Data

A CIP catalogue record for this book is available from the British Library.

Library of Congress Cataloging-in-Publication Data

Philosophies of history : from enlightenment to postmodernity / Robert Burns
    and Hugh Rayment-Pickard.
        p.   cm.
    Includes bibliographical references and index.
    ISBN 0–631–21236–1 (hb : acid-free paper) — ISBN 0–631–21237–X
(pb : acid-free paper)
    1. History—Philosophy.   I. Burns, Robert.   II. Rayment-Pickard, Hugh.

D16.7.P45   2000
901—dc21
                                                                99–056272

Typeset in 10 on 12 pt Galliard
by Ace Filmsetting Ltd, Frome, Somerset
Printed and bound in Great Britain by TJ International Ltd
Padstow, Cornwall

This book is printed on acid-free paper

Contents

Preface

This book is designed to meet the needs of History undergraduates and postgraduates who wish to develop their capacity to philosophize about History but have had little previous exposure to philosophy. We hope it will be helpful to others, including more advanced students, insofar as one of its main concerns is to make available some of the classic texts in philosophy of history which are currently difficult to find. A main aim of the book, arising out of the conviction that one can understand the present only in terms of the past, and that those who will not learn the lessons of history condemn themselves to repeat its mistakes, is to trace something of the *historical* development of the subject. Certainly, we hope to show that many theses often regarded as originating only in the late twentieth century were first articulated several generations ago, in some cases with a clarity and force not matched more recently.

The first chapter traces the historical relationship of philosophy to history, and introduces some of the issues which have emerged in the philosophical tradition in general which bear most directly on the efforts of historians. An underlying aim of this chapter is to persuade the reader that philosophical theorizing *is* relevant, and indeed indispensable to serious historical study, and that those like G. R. Elton who consider that 'a philosophical concern with such problems as the reality of historical knowledge or the nature of historical thought only hinders the practice of history' (Elton 1969, p. vii) are profoundly mistaken. In the nine remaining chapters the strategy of the authors has been to focus on nine major themes which have emerged in philosophy of history. Each chapter begins with a critical introduction which is followed by a selection of original texts. These have in many cases been edited to make them more comprehensible to students, who are warned that the originals, which it is hoped they will eventually explore, are frequently more difficult to digest. The use of ellipses in the text should, however, give some indication of the nature of the changes which we have made.[1] There is, of course, no need to read the chapters of the book consecutively, although later chapters assume a knowledge of what is contained in the earlier chapters

The book is inevitably *selective*, which implies that it reflects the values and judgments of its authors and editors. One can be sure that others would have produced a book which would tell a different story, with different emphases. The readers must

---

1 Three ellipses in the middle of a paragraph indicates that a clause/sentence or sentences have been omitted. Four ellipses at the end of a paragraph means that the original paragraph contains additional sentences beyond those provided; that the excerpt has ended in mid sentence. Three freestanding ellipses between paragraphs indicates the omission of one or more paragraphs.

themselves decide how far the plot of the our book exposes structures and trends really present in the intellectual history of the last 250 years, or reads into it patterns which are the products only of the authors' imaginations. Some of the thinkers discussed in this book suggest that the latter must be the case with regard to all history-writing. The two authors indeed disagreed with one another on various aspects of the selection. This shows up in particular in chapter 7, in which Hugh Rayment-Pickard contributes the introductory discussion and made the selection on Husserl, and Robert Burns the rest. There were differences between us on the question of the importance of Husserl in the development of the subject, and especially on the relation of Heidegger's thinking to that of Husserl. Another point of difference was the relevance to the evaluation of Heidegger's philosophy of his commitment to Nazism. Such differences arise inevitably, and in the nature of the case can never completely be overcome. Nevertheless, if there is such a thing as progress towards the truth in this field, it must lie through attempts to reconcile such differences.

But the major factor governing selection was the sheer impossibility of including all the texts and all the authors which one would have wished to include: a longer book would certainly have made room for excerpts from Droysen, Troeltsch, Spengler, Croce, Gramsci, Hempel, and Collingwood among many others. One criterion used was whether the texts in question were already easily obtainable: for instance, the ready availability of texts by and about Marx and his successors has meant that restricted coverage has been given to them in this book. Likewise little attention is paid to the contributions of 'analytical' philosophy, which flourished particularly in the English-speaking philosophical world in the middle decades of the twentieth century because primary texts and anthologies are widely available.

The two authors reviewed and commented on each other's work but remain separately responsible for the selection of texts and the commentary as indicated in the text.

Hugh Rayment-Pickard records his gratitude to George Pattison and Don Cupitt for their invaluable advice, and Robert Burns wishes to thank Irina Korovushkina for helping to compile the Index of Names. The authors are also grateful to Tony Grahame for his readily available expert attention at various stages of the book's production. They also wish to thank several years of students in 'History and Culture from Hume to Heidegger', the second-year course in History at Goldsmiths College, out of which this book has emerged.

Acknowledgements

The authors and publishers gratefully acknowledge the following for permission to reproduce copyright material:

Barthes, R., *Image Music Texts* (ed. S. Heath) (Fontana Publishing, 1977, reprinted by kind permission of HarperCollins Publishers Ltd);

Baudrillard, Jean, 'The Year 2000 Will Not Take Place', *Futur* Fall: Excursions into Post-Modernity* (ed. E. A. Grosz et al.) (Power Institute of Fine Arts, 1986);

Benjamin, W., 'Theses on the Philosophy of History', from *Illuminations* (ed. H. Arendt) (Fontana Publishing, 1973, reprinted by permission of HarperCollins Publishers Ltd);

Comte, Auguste, *Essential Comte* (ed. S. Andreski, trans. M. Clarke) (Croom Helm Ltd., London, 1974, copyright Routledge);

Dilthey, W., 'A Critique of Historical Reason' from *W. Dilthey: Selected Writings* (ed. and trans. H. P. Rickman) (Cambridge University Press, 1976);

Dilthey, W., Wilhelm Dilthey: *Selected Works, Vol. I, Vol. IV* (ed. Rudolf A. Makkreel and Fritzhof Rodi) (Princeton University Press, 1992. Copyright © 1989 & 1992 by Princeton University Press. Reprinted by permission of Princeton University Press);

Foucault, M., *The Order of Things* (Tavistock Publications, London, 1970, copyright Routledge);

Foucault, M., 'Nietzsche, Genealogy, History', from *The Foucault Reader* (ed. P. Rainbow) (Penguin Books Ltd, Harmondsworth, 1991);

Fukuyama, Francis, *The End of History and The Last Man* (Hamish Hamilton, London, 1992);

Gadamer, Hans-Georg, *Truth and Method* © copyright 1975 by Sheed & Ward. Reprinted by permission of The Continuum International Publishing Group;

Habermas, Jürgen, 'Communication and the Evolution of Society', from *The Habermas Reader* (ed. W. Outhwaite) (Polity Press, 1996, copyright Beacon Press, Boston);

Heidegger, M., *Being and Time* (trans. J. Macquarrie and Edward Robinson) (Blackwell Publishers, Oxford, 1978);

Herder, J.G., 'Yet Another Philosophy of History', from *J. G. Herder on Social and Political Culture* (ed. and trans. F. M. Barnard) (Cambridge University Press, 1969);

Humboldt, Wilhem von, *On Language* (trans. Peter Heath) (Cambridge University Press, 1988. Copyright © Freie Universität Berlin);

Humboldt, Wilhelm von, 'On the History Task' (1821) from *The Theory and Practice of History* (ed. G. C. Iggers and K. von Moltke) (Irvington Publishers, New York, 1983);

Hume, David, *Enquiries concerning Human Understanding and concerning the Principles of Morals* (Oxford University Press, ed. L. A. Selby-Bigge, 1902, second edition);

Kant, Immanuel, *Political Writings* (ed. H. Reiss, trans. H. B. Niset) (Cambridge University Press, 1969);

Kierkegaard, S., *Concluding Unscientific Postscript, Vol. I* (Princeton University Press, 1992. Copyright © 1992 Princeton University Press. Reprinted by permission of Princeton University Press);

Lévi-Strauss, Claude, *The Savage Mind* (Weidenfield and Nicholson, 1966);

Lukács, G., *History and Class Consciousness* (trans. R. Livingstone) (Merlin Press, London, 1971);

Marx, Karl, 'The Economic & Philosophical Manuscripts', from *Karl Marx: Selected Writings* (ed. D. McLellan) (Oxford University Press, 1977, reprinted by permission of Oxford University Press);

Marx, Karl, 'The German Ideology', from *Karl Marx: Selected Writings* (ed. D. McLellan) (Oxford University Press, 1977, reprinted by permission of Oxford University Press);

Nietzsche, F., *Untimely Meditations* (trans. R. Hollingdale) (Cambridge University Press, 1983);

Nietzsche, F., *The Will to Power* (trans. W. Kaufmann and R. J. Hollingdale). Copyright © 1967 by Walter Kaufmann. Reprinted by permission of Random House Inc;

Nietzsche, F., *The Gay Science* (trans. W. Kaufmann and R. J. Hollingdale). Copyright © 1974 by Random House Inc. Reprinted by permission of Random House Inc.;

Ranke, Leopold von, *The Theory and Practice of History* (ed. and trans. G. G. Iggers and Konard von Moltke) (Irvington Publishers Inc., New York, 1983);

Rickert, Heinrich, *The Limits of Concept Formation in Natural Science* (ed. trans. Guy Oakes) (Cambridge University Press, 1986);

Ricoeur, P., 'Existence and Hermeneutics', from *The Conflict of Interpretations* (trans. K. McLaughlin) (Northwestern University Press, 1975, Les Editions de Seuil);

Ricoeur, P., 'Life in Quest of Narrative', from *On Paul Ricoeur* (ed. D. Wood) (Routledge, 1991);

Schleiermacher, Frederick, *Hermeneutics: The Handwritten Manuscripts* (trans. James Duke and Jack Forstmann) (Carl Winter, Heidelberg, 1974; Scholars Press, Missoula, Montana, 1977).

Schopenhauer, Arthur. *The World as Will and Representation* (trans. Payne) (Dover Publications, 1966);

Simmel, Georg, *The Problems of the Philosophy of History* (ed. trans. Guy Oakes) (Free Press, New York, 1977);

Weber, Max, *Max Weber: Selections in Translation* (ed. W. G. Runciman, trans. E. Mathews) (Cambridge University Press, 1978);

Weber, Max, *The Methodology of the Social Sciences* (ed. and trans. E. A. Shils and H. A. Finch) (Free Press, New York, 1949);

White, Hayden, 'The Fictions of Factual Representation' from *Tropics of Discourse* (Johns Hopkins University Press, Baltimore, 1978);

White, Hayden, *Metahistory* (Johns Hopkins University Press, Baltimore, 1973);

Windelband, Wilhelm, 'History and Natural Science' (trans. Guy Oakes) *History and Theory 19* (1980);

The publishers apologize for any errors or omissions in the above list and would be grateful to be notified of any corrections that should be incorporated in the next edition or reprint of this book.

1 On Philosophizing about History

Robert M. Burns

This chapter is intended to provide History students who are not experts in philosophy with some prerequisites for grappling with the philosophical thought about history, which is presented in the subsequent chapters, and above all to enable them to start philosophizing for themselves. This chapter need not be read at the outset, if at all: some might consider that they already know enough to skip it, returning possibly at a later point when its relevance might be more apparent. Section 1.I is a sketch of the historical relationship between the traditions of philosophy and history since the origins of both in ancient Greece up to the mid-eighteenth century. The main point which emerges is that the dominant view of 'knowledge' in Western philosophy, for the first two millennia of its history, was that it consists of perceiving its objects as instances or examples of general or universal principles, effective in all times and places. The message of Herder, Humboldt, Ranke and later historicists such as Dilthey, Rickert or Simmel (see chapters 3 and 6, respectively), was that the historian must break with this presumption and that his task is to render past events, persons, and cultures intelligible in their very uniqueness, particularity and difference from other persons and epochs. They considered that 'history' had come of age as a discipline only when it understood itself in this way. The positivists of chapter 4 by contrast, by and large, continued to hold the view that knowledge or explanation always involves seeing particulars as instances of universal laws.

Section 1.II seeks to stimulate the student to begin to philosophize for herself or himself by considering a definition of the term 'philosophy' offered by R. G. Collingwood. He suggests that it is 'thinking about thinking'. Just think: you have been thinking ever since you can remember but have you ever stopped to think about it? What does 'to think about something' mean? But how can you possibly have been thinking, without thinking what you are doing, for doesn't 'thinking' imply being conscious of what you are doing? Aristotle considered (and few philosophers have subsequently disagreed) that the essential distinguishing characteristic of man, which raises him in dignity above all other animals, is his capacity to think or reason. But how *does* one think? Can one think, and do it wrong? How can one know when one is thinking correctly? Can one know that one is thinking incorrectly? And what can one hope to achieve through thinking? One only has to raise these questions to realize that 'thinking for oneself' (see 2.C.I) is easier said than done. Perhaps this is why much of the time many of us would rather do almost anything else rather than think: 'I have often felt that the sole cause of man's unhappiness is that he does not know how to stay quietly in his own room', wrote Pascal. Thinking is hard work, which helps to explain why many passages in this book will be difficult to understand the first time around. You will often have to read passages several times in order to make sense of them: on the reasons for this read Schleiermacher (3.C.II) and the comments about him in chapter 3. Remember, when discouraged, that, according to Aristotle, you are engaging in the distinctively human activity which makes you better than animals (or do you *think* he was mistaken about that?)

After reading a few sentences of the attempt to think about Collingwood's definition it should be become clear that it throws into question some widespread assumptions human beings generally make about their thoughts, especially the assumption *that through thinking one can come to a knowledge of objective reality*. All of us believe (I believe) that we are mentally in touch with reality (this is a metaphor: we do not mean by such a term being physically in touch), which is to say we perceive or think things 'truly', and so achieve 'objective' knowledge of things at least some of the time, although most of us would admit that for much of the time our thoughts are infected with various degrees of error or delusion. In recent years this issue has been high on the philosophical agenda in the English-speaking world, being frequently termed that of 'realism' versus 'non-realism', 'anti-realism' or 'relativism'; the former term means in this context, roughly speaking,[1] that the human mind can come to know what things-in-themselves are really like, the other terms are employed to refer to the denial that this is so. However, this issue is by no means new in philosophy. We shall see that the 'Neo-Kantian' philosophers assembled in chapter 6, such as Simmel and Rickert, considered 'realism' an untenable notion with reference to history, and indeed every other form of knowledge. But disputes over whether the human mind could know the real stretched right back in ancient Greece, where we find 'sceptics' who denied that human beings could ever 'know' any thing or, rather, strictly speaking, denied that one could ever know whether or not one knew. In the Hellenistic period (that is from the time of Alexander the Great until the rise of the Roman Empire), 'sceptics' had taken over the Platonic Academy, an institution which in some respects could be termed the world's first university, and they made the running in the discussion of the nature of knowledge which took place between different philosophical schools, being opposed by Stoics, Aristotelians and Epicureans who were 'realists' in their different ways. There was a revival of ancient scepticism in the late Renaissance in the thinking of figures such as Montaigne and this again was the stimulus for the thought of Descartes, whose philosophy took the form of an attempted refutation of scepticism. David Hume's philosophy too was deeply impregnated with sceptical influence. In section III, then, this central philosophical issue of realism versus and non-realism is explored by means of some references to historical and contemporary discussions.

The issue of realism versus non-realism is really that of the nature of human knowledge, which particularly dominated early modern philosophy from Descartes to Kant, the assumption being that the first thing a philosopher must do is clarify what is meant by 'knowledge' because all his other more specific efforts will be attempts to 'know' something, and his conclusions will depend on what he takes knowledge to be. This question includes topics such as *what* it is to 'know' something, *how* one comes to

---

1   Like many abstract philosophical terms, 'realism' is very slippery in its meaning: many disputes between philosophers concerning it turn out to be at least partly the result of the word being understood differently by the various parties.

know something, how one verifies that one truly knows something, whether one must be certain of something before one can be said to know it, whether there are any absolute limits to what the human mind is capable of knowing, what it is about 'mind' which enables it to know, what it is to 'explain' something, or 'understand' it, or render it 'intelligible', and so forth. Sections IV and V sketch the epistemologies (i.e., theories of knowledge) of two Enlightenment philosophers, both of whose views on history are explored in chapter 2 but whose epistemologies conditioned the subsequent development of philosophy to such a degree that no one can hope to follow it without knowing something about them.

1.1 Philosophy and History: The Universal versus the Particular

What has philosophy to do with history or history with philosophy? Not very much if one looks at the early history of the two disciplines in the Western intellectual tradition. 'Philosophy' (Greek for 'love of wisdom'), began with the so-called Pre-Socratics (*c*.600–400 BC) as an effort to understand the nature of the cosmos. The distinctive feature of their speculations compared with earlier attempts usually categorized as 'mythological' was that they sought to justify their ideas by rational argument. They presupposed in all their work both that the universe was ultimately rational and that the human mind was equipped to discover the nature of that rationality, a presupposition at first evident in the assumption that everything must have a single ultimate explanation or first cause (*arche*) such as water, air, or fire. Soon, though, the difficulty of explaining how multiple and incompatible qualities ('fire and water don't mix') could spring from a single one of them, led some to maintain instead that the cosmos resulted from the interaction of two primordial contraries (e.g., Empedocles, *c*.495–*c*.435 BC, called them Love and Strife, i.e., a drive to sameness and unity opposed by a drive to difference and multiplicity). Socrates (*c*.470 –399 BC), who was executed for corrupting the minds of the youth of Athens by encouraging them to think for themselves rather than uncritically accepting traditional *mores*, and who has ever since been reverenced as the ideal philosopher because of his single-minded pursuit of truth, turned the focus on *ethics* after spending many years engaged in cosmological speculation. According to tradition,[2] this turn was connected with the Delphic oracle's admonition 'Know thyself', which Socrates understood to mean knowledge of human nature, which he assumed must be innate in all of us, but somehow obscured. Consequently, he taught not by imparting his own theories but by interrogating his disciples to bring out their implicit assumptions as to the nature of goodness, beauty, justice, courage, styling himself merely a 'midwife' who brought to birth the truth already present in others. A major burden of his teaching seems to have been that it was wiser to confess ignorance than to make assertions which one could not rationally defend. But in the voluminous writings of his student Plato (*c*.428–348/7 BC) and *his* student Aristotle (384/3–322/1 BC) nearly all the traditional main subdivisions of the academic world

---

2 Socrates never committed himself to writing, provoking comparison with Jesus of Nazareth. The 'Socrates' with whom the philosophical tradition is most familiar is that of Plato's *Dialogues*, whom we know is not entirely historical.

take shape as subdivisions of 'philosophy': cosmology, astronomy, physics, biology, psychology, theology, ethics, political theory, literary theory, and so forth, with two conspicuous exceptions, which had begun independently, and remained so, namely medicine (regarded as a practical art rather than a theoretical discipline) and history.

Strikingly the first historians, such as Herodotus (*c.*495–425 BC), and Thucydides (*c.*471–400 BC), were not recognized as philosophers and did not regard themselves as philosophers. Aristotle, in an often-cited passage, throws light on this: he ranks history as less valuable than poetry (*poesis,* which for him includes not only the work of poets such as Homer but drama, such as the tragedies of Aeschylus and Sophocles), since 'the distinction between historian and poet . . . consists really in this, that the one describes the thing that has been, and the other a kind of thing that might be. Hence poetry is something more philosophic and of graver import than history, since its statements are of the nature rather of universals, whereas those of history are singulars' (Kelley, 1991, p. 60). The suggestion is that history is of minimal worth because it concerns itself with the fortuitous course of particular events whilst poets modify characters and events so as to make them symbols expressing abiding insights into the human condition, which is to say to raise them to *universal,* essential significance. Nevertheless, poetry is inferior to philosophy, because the latter raises the 'universal' to a fully scientific, 'conceptual' level.

Expressed here is a presumption close to the heart of classical Western philosophy. Aristotle assumes true knowledge (*episteme*) to be essentially universal, since if you point to a particular thing, and say 'What's that?' the answer will specify the *kind* of thing it is (water, a tree). Such terms are 'universals' because in principle they could be exemplified endlessly in all times and places. Moreover they imply a grasp (Aristotle assumes) of the 'nature' or 'essence' of the thing: that is, an integrated set of qualities which give it its 'form', without which it would not be what-it-is. Note that 'essence' comes from the Latin verb '*esse*' (to be), and we still mean by it the very core of the being of something. Especially when Aristotle thinks of living things, he thinks of them as animated by the purpose (never fully self-conscious except sometimes in man), of fulfilling their nature, or bringing it to perfection, as when an acorn strives to reach the goal (*telos,* the 'final cause') of becoming an oak. If you 'think away' all the 'general' qualities in any material object you are left with the underlying *material* upon which the 'form' or essence has been imposed. Material objects are therefore fusions of form and this underlying prime matter.[3] The latter never exists without some form or other, but it can lose one form and gain another (as when wood is burned, it loses the form of wood and takes on the forms of smoke and ashes). Being essentially the recipient of these qualities it must itself be devoid of them, and be itself intrinsically unintelligible (i.e., unconceptualizable), and even hostile to form, which leads Aristotle to attribute to it defects in the bodies of animals. Nevertheless the implication seems to be that matter must be the basis of the particularity of things, i.e., it allows the *same* universal forms (e.g., human nature) to be shared by *different* beings, which led the medieval Aristotelian Thomas Aquinas (1225–74) to declare matter to be 'the principle of individuation'. Much of this approach comes from Plato who in his *Timaeus* portrayed the world as having been formed when a creator God imposed the 'forms'

---

3   So-called because we can say that the material out of which a clothes peg is made is 'wood', even though, in this instance, wood is the form imposed on prime matter.

or 'ideas' on a turbulent deep. They (he was thinking primarily of the shapes of Euclidean geometry, suggesting that these were the ultimate building blocks out of which all physical things were composed) could never 'fix' this chaos completely. This understanding is largely extrapolated from everyday experience; if someone pointed out to a mathematics teacher that the internal angles of a triangle chalked on a blackboard did not add up to 180 degrees, the response would be that this was due to the recalcitrance of the materials used (the brittleness of chalk and the unevenness of the surface of the blackboard for example), and we might perhaps even say that therefore it was not a 'real' triangle. But, suggests Plato, this is always the case: geometry alone makes the shapes or structures of physical beings *intelligible*, but we have not derived our knowledge of geometry *from* them, and so always regard them as imperfect imitations of the changeless ideals to which they approximate (compare 6.E.III, and also 6.D.III and 4.B.V).[4]

Aristotle's negative assessment of history (given classic expression as late as the mid-nineteenth century by Schopenhauer: see 5.A.1) must be understood against this background, but it distorts the explicit aims of historians: Thucydides, a century earlier than Aristotle, had written that his aim was to 'provide an exact knowledge of the past as an aid to the interpretation of the future, which in the course of human things must resemble if it does not reflect it' and so be a 'possession for all time' (Kelley, 1991. pp. 34–5), and Polybius (*c*.198–117 BC) was to write that the aim of history is 'pragmatic' in the sense that 'men have no more ready corrective of conduct than knowledge of the past . . . [*Therefore*] the soundest education and training for a life of active politics is the study of History'. For him history is 'the discussion of why, how, and wherefore, each thing was done'; take away this analysis of the underlying universal principles of explanation and 'what is left is a clever essay but not a lesson, and while pleasing for the moment of no possible benefit for the future', p. 40; compare Diodorus of Sicily (*c*.90–20 BC, pp. 48–9), and Dionysius of Halicarnassus (latter part of the first century BC), who expressed the basic point more succinctly: 'History is philosophy teaching by example' (p. 54).

Nevertheless, throughout the later Hellenistic and Roman period the philosophical discounting of history as a scientific discipline continued. One might have expected that with the advent of Christianity, which elevates some alleged historical facts, especially concerning Jesus, to universal significance, concern to affirm the scientific status of history would emerge, but this did not happen. When in the twelfth and thirteenth centuries the texts of Aristotle were 'rediscovered' in Western Christendom by importing them from the Arab world, and disseminating them in universities such as Paris and Oxford, which were newly founded for this purpose, history was still given short shrift in the great scholastic philosophical systems subsequently developed. For instance, Thomas Aquinas (1225–74) defines a '*scientia*' as a systematic organization of knowledge which 'proceeds from self-evident principles known by the natural light of the intellect, such as arithmetic and geometry and the like' or from 'principles known by the light of a higher science' such as optics from geometry (*Summa Theologiae* 1a.1.2). Particular beings are simply *instances* to be explained by these sciences, which

---

4   In all these later cases the ideals are human inventions not eternally given by logical necessity as in Plato's understanding of geometry, but they are still held to be constitutive of scientific knowledge of historical fact.

are networks of logical necessity in which the first principles are self-evident, and the subordinate elements emerge as logically necessary deductions from them. What we would term 'history' could never be a 'science' for Aquinas, if only because he holds that human beings can perform non-necessary ('contingent') acts out of free will (1a.14.13). Yet he insisted that Christian theology not only was a 'science' but 'nobler' than the others, which are 'its inferiors and handmaidens' (1a. 1.5 ad 2). Moreover, 'the articles of faith', which include alleged historical facts about Jesus, 'stand in the same relation to the doctrine of faith, as self-evident principles to teaching on natural reason' (II.II. 1. 7, 8). Nevertheless Aquinas is not concerned to establish them as indisputably objective facts. He maintains that alleged facts such as the Virgin Birth and Resurrection of Jesus are not logically or physically impossible, but the criteria for assessing their factuality are uncertain, and in the end subjective, so that reasonable men can disagree about them (II.II. 1. 6). The faithful consider them to have 'greater certitude' than the principles of other sciences because their minds have been raised to supernatural certitude by the infusion of divine grace (I.II.4. 86.1).

However, a markedly different attitude emerges in the later Middle Ages. First, some philosophers were increasingly dissatisfied with earlier accounts of the nature of individuality. Duns Scotus (c.1265–1308) explicitly rejected Aquinas's doctrine that matter could be the 'principle of individuation' since something merely passive and characterless could never cause the real distinction of things from one another; instead 'something positive' in addition to a thing's 'essence' must be responsible, which additional ingredient he terms *haecceitas* (thisness) (Schoedinger, 1996, pp. 746–61). One must ask whether this *explains* individuality rather than merely bestows a name on what is left unexplained. A generation later William of Ockham (c.1280–1349) was to insist that it was absurd to suggest that knowledge could consist only of generalities because he considered that *every* real thing is a *particular* thing and knowledge has to be about realities (compare Windelband 6.B.I and Rickert 6.C.I; also Ranke, 3.E.II and Herder 3.A.I) In knowledge, according to Ockham, we therefore 'intuit' *only* particular things. We then notice *similarities* in their qualities, and we manufacture concepts to refer to these similarities, which are really *ficta* (fictions; made-up), for there are no 'real' general qualities or essences which individual things merely exemplify.

But the greater interest in history which characterizes Renaissance humanism did not flow from such metaphysical considerations, but from its effort to retrieve ancient Greek and Roman culture, which was a quintessentially *historical* activity. Moreover many Italian humanists thought of Italy as the successor of ancient Rome and looked back to its history for guidance in its present political weakness. Thus Lorenzo Valla (1407–57) counters Aristotle's disdain for history by asserting not only that it is 'more robust than poetry because it is more truthful . . . it is oriented not towards abstraction but towards truth . . . [*and*] teaching by example', but is even philosophy's superior because 'the discourse of historians exhibits more substance, more practical knowledge . . . more customs and more learning of every sort than the precepts of any of the philosophers' (Kelley, 1988, p. 749) . Similarly Machiavelli (1469–1527), echoing the ancient historians, wrote: 'Whoever considers the past and present will readily observe that all cities and all people are and ever have been animated by the same desires and the same passions; so that it is easy, by diligent study of the past to foresee what is likely to happen in the future in any republic' (Kelley, 1991 p. 294). But even some humanists were sceptical: Henry Cornelius Agrippa von Nettesheim (1486–1535) maintained that history is 'least among all arts' as a source of truth because historians 'disagree mightily among themselves and write such variable and different things about one event that it is impossible that a number of them should not be liars' (pp. 264–7). Even one of the most distinguished Renaissance historians of all, Francesco Guicciardini (1483–1540), wrote, perhaps with Machiavelli in mind: 'How wrong it is to cite the Romans at every turn. For any comparison to be valid, it would be necessary to have a city with conditions like theirs, and then to govern it according their example' (Guicciardini, 1964, p. 69), for 'unless they are similar in every respect, examples, are useless, since every tiny difference in the case may be a cause of great deviations in the effects'. For the same reason it is difficult to 'write discourses on the future, basing themselves on current events' since 'every tiny particular circumstance that changes is apt to alter a conclusion. The affairs of this world, therefore, cannot be judged from afar but must be judged and resolved day by day' (p. 70). Nevertheless he does not deny that there are essential underlying uniformities, and implies that the historian's difficult task is to discern them; 'Everything that has been in the past and is in the present will be in the future. But the names and appearances of things change, so that he who has not a discerning eye will not recognize them' (pp. 60–1; compare p. 123).

In the light of such views, it is not surprising that philosophers throughout the seventeenth century perpetuated the traditional suspicion of history: Descartes (1596–1650), the so-called father of modern philosophy, writes of how he had abandoned histories as a source of truth because of their inevitable selectivity: 'even the most accurate histories . . . almost always omit the baser and less notable events; as a result, the other events appear in a false light'. Moreover 'knight errants', cannot provide exemplars for modern conduct and there are many 'fables' in history (Descartes, 1985, p. 114), and 'hardly anything is said by one writer the contrary of which is not asserted by some other', and it is no use 'counting heads'. The only road to truth is to examine ideas which we can 'clearly and evidently intuit' or deduce with certainty', (p. 13) that is, logically self-evident ideas which each rational mind can verify for himself at all times and places. It is entirely in line with this approach that, when he began to develop a science of human nature, he makes not a single reference to historical experience as a means of gathering evidence or verifying the claims he makes (see pp. 325–404). However some contemporaries are more positive: Tommaso Campanella (1568–1639) classified historiography as 'the basis of all sciences, though it forms the fifth part of Rational Philosophy' (Kelley, 1991, p. 373), and Francis Bacon (1561–1626) divided learning into three primary categories history, poetry, and philosophy (Tinker, 1996, p. 232) Yet for both 'history' primarily means purely descriptive collections of facts which is subsequently raised to the level of science by generalization. It is not a 'science' on its own account.

However, during the seventeenth century a new[5] interest in probability judgements developed which rejected the previous assumption that true knowledge must always be flawlessly certain. Two distinct approaches emerged: on the one hand, Blaise Pascal

---

5　The only exception to this had been in the later Hellenistic period. Plato's Academy had come to be dominated by Sceptics who denied the possibility of human knowledge, and who engaged in a long controversy with Stoics who affirmed it. Eventually many on both sides came to accept that human knowledge could never be more than 'probable', but no suggestions were developed as to how one could objectively measure degrees of probability of beliefs.

(1623–62) and others explored different forms of mathematical probability judgement (see Hacking, 1975), and on the other there were those such as Pascal's contemporary Antoine Arnauld (1611–94) who argued (Arnauld, 1964, see Part IV, chs 13–16) that, because of the essentially contingent nature of human life, another essentially non-mathematical form of probability judgement must be applied to it, namely 'moral probability.'[6] The importance of the notion of moral probability judgment for history is twofold. First, according to its advocates, it offers a way of reaching a high degree of certainty in circumstances where there is no possibility of imposing the rigorous methods which can sometimes be applied in the 'exact' sciences where experiments can be repeated under controlled conditions and the data quantified. Secondly, it enables knowledge of a unique historical particular (whether an individual personality, or cultural group or course of events) to be known in its individuality rather than as an instance of a general principle. Jean Mabillon (1623–1707) the leading member of that French school of Benedictine Maurist monks, long recognized as playing a prominent role in the development of modern historical research, applied this in detail to the assessment of the authenticity of historical documents. He wrote that a person who has for years been acquainted with ancient documents could acquire the skill to make such judgements, which sometimes might reach a degree of probability tantamount to certainty, even though each and every piece of evidence in isolation might be of little weight. This is because such a judgement assesses qualitatively the general drift or overall impact of the evidence not 'considered separately but only the total interconnection of all of them' which is to say in 'all the coincidences and circumstances' (Kelley, 1991, pp. 413–17).

It was especially in England that the indispensability of the 'moral probability' judgement in all areas of life was celebrated; natural scientists such as Robert Boyle or Newton (in opposition to Descartes) maintained that even the theories of natural science ultimately must be judged true on moral probability grounds.[7] Joseph Butler (1692–1752), who wrote that 'probability is the very guide of life', stated that 'the conviction arising from [*such a*] kind of proof may be compared to what they call *the effect* in architecture or other works of art; a result from a great number of things so and so disposed and taken into one view . . . evidence arising from various coincidences, which support and confirm each other . . . [*including*] a great variety of circumstantial things also' (Butler, 1961, p. 207).[8] Thus, members of a jury might decide that an alleged event – essentially unique, and unrepeatable – had occurred 'beyond reasonable doubt' by pondering a range of facts until they see it as compelling evidence of the event because it 'hangs together' as an intelligible whole once the assumption is made that the event occurred. There will be no question of reducing the evidence to a mathematical calculation, indeed the strength of the evidence will be increased if it is of different kinds, and so incommensurable. The usual name of the faculty employed to integrate the evidence into a single picture is the 'imagination'.

6   Arnauld 1964, see Part IV, chs 13–16.
7   See Burns, 1981; Shapiro, 1969; Van Leeuwen, 1963.
8   J. H. Newman (1801–90), much influenced by Butler, wrote an entire treatise, *A Grammar of Assent* (1870) on the moral probability judgment, which he termed 'informal' or 'concrete inference' or 'personal reasoning', and which he claimed was the mode of cognition by which we arrive at almost all our decisions in life and form our deepest certitudes, including the religious beliefs which were his fundamental concern.

From Pythagoras through Plato, Roger Bacon and Descartes onwards there have been many philosophers enthralled by mathematics, and dreaming that it can provide a means of achieving objective certainty in every field, a fascination intensified by the success of the seventeenth-century scientific revolution in achieving certainty about the nature of the physical world through the specification of precisely quantified mathematical laws, which could therefore be tested empirically, who would dismiss the 'moral probability' judgement as an essentially subscientific, impressionistic 'subjective' mode of proceeding, which ideally should be replaced in history as elsewhere by methods essentially the same as those in the 'hard' physical sciences. Hume goes as far (2.A.II) as suggesting that all genuine probability judgments are at some subconscious level mathematical, and certainly implies that rigorous historical judgements must always strive to be explicitly so (see 2.A.I and II). In this, as in many aspects of his philosophy, he is the father of 'positivism' (e.g., Buckle 4.C.II). The fundamental objection to such views would be that human beings are living moral probability judgments: arguably from birth onwards we orientate ourselves in life, by making, and perpetually revising, impressionistic judgments about our own overall character and the broader world into we must fit, and in which alone we can hope to flourish. All practical 'life' decisions about how we are to act emerge out of such overall 'gestalt' judgments, which are constantly being reappraised to take account of further experience, including the 'feed back' of the results of our previous actions (see Dilthey, especially 6.A.VIII). Frequently general principles of many different kinds will be integrated into our judgments, but always because they are judged relevant to the unique circumstances or predicament which we are seeking to understand. Human history is simply (it could be maintained) the ongoing interrelationship of such judgments, made at individual and group levels, and their gradual transformation over time. If so, the historian's function is to 'shadow' them, adding an extra reflective layer of judgment to these judgments, certainly (as Simmel in particular emphasizes in 6.D.II) enormously simplifying the complexity of them by selecting for attention only those strands in the process which he finds of particular significance or importance, this latter judgment being, of course, also made by a moral probability judgment.

A modern presentation of the case that historical judgment is essentially of this kind was provided by Louis Mink (1965). He writes that the 'mode of understanding' which we find especially at work in history deals essentially with 'types of evidence to which quantitative weights cannot be assigned' and in it 'the total weight of evidence is not a function of the weights of individual evidence taken separately (p. 180). Rather it is essentially a matter of 'comprehending a complex event by "seeing things together" in a total and synoptic judgment which cannot be replaced by any analytic technique' (p. 184). This synoptic judgement is 'much like what everyone does in interpreting the meaning of a statement' (compare 3.C.II); so that the historian is seeking to discover 'the syntax of events' (p. 182). He adds that 'it would be misleading to suggest that historical inquiry consists of the indefatigable collection of facts and *then* a great swoop of synthesis', since 'the complicated connections between facts and inference' means that we are talking 'both of a characterization of the type of historical thought in the process of research and also a description of its final aim' (p. 85), so that there are no 'detachable conclusions', even if it sometimes looks as if it is so if the historian 'summarizes his conclusions', for in historical writing 'the ingredient conclusions are exhibited rather than demonstrated', and even if articulated separately 'in a grand finale, are not conclusions but reminders to the reader of the topography of events to which the entire narrative has given order' (p. 181). In the last few paragraphs we have raised issues often regarded as first articulated with the rise of 'historicism' which we shall be examining in chapters 3 and 6. The point is that some of the key features in these later developments can be traced as far back as the seventeenth century, but indeed no further.

1.II   A Definition of Philosophy: The Science of Absolute Presuppositions

Even from the brief, very selective survey in the previous section, it should be clear that 'philosophy' has meant different things to different people in different eras. But what should 'philosophy' mean for the purposes of this book? For a provisional definition one could do worse than take up the suggestion of R. G. Collingwood (1889–1943) that it is 'the science of absolute presuppositions' (Collingwood, 1940, p. 41).[9] This implicitly takes for granted another definition which he offers at the outset of *The Idea of History* that philosophy is 'thought of second degree . . . reflective thought about thought' (Collingwood, 1946, p. 1). 'First degree' thought is that directed towards some particular aspect of things; thus, historians think about events in the human past, e.g., the Fall of the Roman Empire, the Reformation, World War II. 'Second degree' thinking is thought *about* such thinking; that is, reflection about its *how, why* and *wherefore*. And this is tantamount, for Collingwood, to the suggestion that philosophising about history is seeking to clarify its operational *presuppositions* because a coherent thought can emerge only out of some presupposition or 'constellation' (p. 60) of presuppositions. We can always readily specify some of the presuppositions of our thinking. For instance, if someone asks why we have just bought a sandwich, we might reply that we presupposed that if we didn't eat one we would be short of energy a couple of hours later when we needed to work hard. Collingwood terms such easily specifiable assumptions 'relative presuppositions'. He considers however that there are other presuppositions which are 'absolute' because relative presuppositions presuppose them, but they presuppose nothing beyond themselves, but rather govern our entire attitude to life in general, or important segments of it, such as our personal relations or professional or political activities. For this reason they can be virtually impossible to acknowledge calmly. He gives the example of a pathologist who takes for granted that 'everything has a cause'. He cannot prove it, because it is the presupposition of all his proofs. Doubting it would be tantamount to doubting the worth of all his scientific activity. He therefore considers it 'inconceivable' that some things could happen without a cause. Collingwood says that everyone is 'ticklish' about his or her absolute presuppositions, and 'if you put your finger on one of his absolute presuppositions' he will be likely not to *argue* with you but 'will probably blow up in your

---

9   Actually he offers this as a definition of 'metaphysics' which however, he defines as 'first philosophy', that is philosophy at its core or summit. Note that he refuses to follow the English-speaking practice of equating 'science' with natural science, a refusal also shared by this book: he, and we, use 'science' as it would be used in German for any disciplined search for knowledge according to the means appropriate for the objects considered.

face' (Collingwood, 1940, p. 31). Much the same point came to be emphasised by a philosopher who became incomparably more influential in English-speaking philosophy in general than Collingwood, namely, Ludwig Wittgenstein (1889–1951); he argued that questioning and doubting can only take place *within* a 'frame of reference' (Wittgenstein, 1969, prop. 83), which he also terms a 'world picture' or even 'mythology' (props. 94, 95), which is not itself questioned or doubted; that is a 'system', which is 'the element in which arguments have their life' (prop. 105), which 'stands fast' (prop. 116), and is the 'substratum of all my enquiring and asserting', the 'hinge . . . on which the *questions* we raise and our *doubts* depend' (prop. 341). Applied to historical thinking, one would say that it involves raising doubts and questions, constructing arguments and counter-arguments, offering proofs or demonstrations, all of which can take place only if criteria are presupposed for assessing their adequacy which must therefore themselves be regarded as beyond proof and disproof, beyond doubt and question.

To define philosophy as the attempt to scrutinize such ultimate presuppositions certainly accords with a good deal of what has historically been termed philosophising: we have already seen that Socrates taught by critically examining the presuppositions of his students. Two thousand years later Immanuel Kant made the analysis of the basic presuppositions of human consciousness the fundamental task of philosophy (1.V). Moreover, it is nowadays a commonplace that knowing 'where someone is coming from' is the key to understanding them, and insofar as the term 'philosophy' is current in everyday life it has the meaning illustrated by Tolstoy's remark that 'everyone must have a philosophy of life', that is, some general guiding presuppositions, which they should always be ready to scrutinize.

Yet the notion is problematic. Sigmund Freud is particularly responsible for the widespread diffusion of the idea that we keep out of consciousness attitudes or drives which we cannot bear to acknowledge precisely because they dominate our psyche. In truth, while we all in theory see the point of achieving greater self-possession through being put 'in touch' with ourselves, we all have misgivings about such an enterprise: such self-scrutiny threatens to be merely subversive, destabilising and demoralising, if nothing better is to be found to put in the place of discredited assumptions. Martin Heidegger argued that escapist turning away or 'falling away' from the truth about ourselves is a pervasive feature of 'average' human existence (see 7.B.II) which constantly adopts strategies to cover over the truth about itself. He wrote, for example, of 'busyness' that is, the hustle and bustle of everyday life: we might complain of never having a minute's peace, but really the 'peace' which would allow us to confront ourselves is what above all we dread. There is 'curiosity and idle talk' which, translated into current terms would include a vast range of phenomena, not only gossiping, prurient sensationalism in the mass media, being an addict of TV soap operas, or a 'news junkie', through which we generate the illusion of being mentally engaged when in fact we are in full flight from engagement with truth. Is Heidegger simply an élitist complaining about the vulgar stupidity of the masses? No, because he extended this analysis to academic life, with his severest strictures often reserved for historians. His basic complaint was that they refuse to ask themselves with any sustained rigour why they are doing what they are doing, and how could possibly justify it, collectively conspiring (for we always turn to what 'they' think when we want to fortify ourselves in our illusions), to pretend that it is self-evidently justifiable for 'professional' historians to be paid to indulge in self-indulgent antiquarianism or the petty intrigues of competitive careerism, their social and political irresponsibility masquerading as academic neutrality or autonomy. How far, one can ask, do his strictures, intended for Germany in the 1920s, apply to the current Western historical profession? Certainly the deliberate 'tuning out' according to Novick, (1988, p. 400) by American historians of what philosophers might wish to say to them, their 'utter indifference' to 'issues of epistemology or philosophy of history'(quoting Michael Kammen), engaging doggedly in a 'matter-of-fact, antitheoretical and anti-philosophical objective empiricism' (p. 593),[10] which renders it quite unthinkable that 'the American historical community' could 'sustain a discipline-wide discussion on the meaning of the historical venture as a whole' (p. 592) would not have impressed Heidegger.

Yet there have always been voices which have challenged such calls for grimly heroic 'existential' authenticity. Erasmus's *Praise of Folly* can be commended for its delightful presentation of the thesis that human happiness, and indeed all effective social relationships, depend on sustaining the 'folly' of a mutual conspiracy of deception, in which we pander to one another's petty vanities, sensitivities, and pretensions. Shakespeare's Hamlet, who could never get round to doing anything because he was 'sicklied o'er by the pale cast of thought', is an object lesson in the futility of self-reflection. A pervasive theme of David Hume is that the relentless pushing of philosophical reflection to its ultimate conclusions only leads to 'melancholy and delirium', and the beginning of wisdom is the acceptance, with 'blind submission', that I am 'absolutely and necessarily determined to live, and talk, and act like other people in the common affairs of life' (Hume, 1978, p. 269), while Nietzsche stressed that human creative vigour depends on 'the power of forgetting' which is 'essential to action of any kind', so that 'he who acts is, in Goethe's words, always without a conscience, without knowledge' (5.C.I), which is to say without paralyzing self-reflection.

Yet, despite all of this, all of us recognize that plunging ourselves into whatever activity offers itself, in order to avoid facing up to home truths, is a temptation which should be resisted, because it is not only a fundamental duty to ourselves but to humanity in general, to scrutinize received beliefs since 'no one's belief is . . . a private matter which concerns himself alone . . . Our forms and processes and modes of thought are common property, fashioned and perfected from age to age; an heirloom . . . to be handed on . . . enlarged and purified . . . an awful privilege and an awful responsibility.'[11] The human imagination has demonstrably, over the centuries, been the victim of countless destructive delusions, so that we all must play our part in the never-ending work of weaning it away from untruth. And after all, are not the anti-philosophical positions just referred to, despite themselves, really attempts at philosophizing despite themselves? [12]

---

10   For a British equivalent see G. R. Elton who writes that his book *The Practice of History* 'embodies an assumption that the study and writing of history are justified in themselves, and reflects a suspicion that a philosophical concern with such problems as the reality of historical knowledge or the nature of historical thought only hinders the practice of history' (Elton, 1969, p. vii).
11   From W. K. Clifford's 'The Ethics of Belief' (published in his *Lectures and Essays*, 1879), reprinted (pp. 241–7) in *Readings in the Philosophy of Religion*, ed. B. A. Brody, Englewood Cliffs, NJ: Prentice-Hall, Inc. 1974.
12   Thus Elton's book (see footnote 10) largely consists of his own answers to philosophical questions; what he really meant was that what most professional philosophers wrote about history did not seem to him to be philosophically true.

Yet this is not how Collingwood puts it. In the first place he says that it is no good hoping, after rooting up our ultimate convictions, to 'ground' them rationally because they never can be 'grounded' since they are the 'ground' of everything else we be-lieve:[13] 'I deny [*that*] you can criticize them in order to find out whether they are true or false' because to treat any of our presuppositions in this way would be 'to assume that it is not an absolute presupposition but a relative presupposition'. Moreover, we simply cannot *know* them because we can never find out what is going on in the depths of our minds by 'introspection' since they are 'doing their work in darkness, the light of consciousness never falling on them' (Collingwood, 1940, p. 43). Here Collingwood challenges what has seemed to common-sense, and many philosophers in the Western tradition, a self-evident truism, i.e., that we obviously have infallible access to our own thoughts because we are immediately present to them. It is an absolutely fundamental philosophical issue with a direct bearing on central issues of philosophy of history and will be addressed at length in several sections of this book (see the next chapter. Also 4.A.IV, 4.B.I, 6.A.I. 6.A.V). For the present let us acknowledge the plausibility of Collingwood's view that since absolute presuppositions are the standpoint *from* which we look at things including ourselves, they must constitute a blind spot which we cannot get into view, and note that this seems confirmed by much everyday experi-ence: we can see often see at a glance the delusions and pretensions of others, while remaining oblivious to our own, until perhaps with the wisdom of hindsight, but often too late, our own folly becomes evident.

Accordingly, Collingwood maintains that all we can do is analyse the presupposi-tions which we perceive operative in others. For this reason 'the science of absolute presuppositions' turns out to be exclusively 'an historical science' (p. 49). His full definition of it is:

> the attempt to find out what absolute presuppositions have been made by this or that person or group of persons, on this or that occasion or group of occasions, in the course of this or that piece of thinking. Arising out of this, it will consider (for example) whether absolute presuppositions are made singly or in groups, and if the latter, how the groups are organized: whether different absolute presuppositions are made by different individu-als or races or nations or classes: or on occasions when different things are being thought about; or whether the same have been made *semper, ubique, ab omnibus* and so on. (p. 47)[14]

It should now be possible to understand how Collingwood blends history and phi-losophy together to a perhaps greater extent than anyone else except for Benedetto Croce (1866–1952) who greatly influenced him. For, on the one hand, philosophy is in its essence the exploration of past thoughts, and on the other hand, 'history' can only be 'the history of thought' because it is 'the re-enactment of past thought in the historian's own mind' (Collingwood, 1946, p. 215), so that 'historical knowledge is

---

13   As Wittgenstein puts it 'at the foundation of well-founded belief lies belief that is not founded' Wittgenstein, 1974, prop. 253).

14   The latter phrase is taken from the so-called creed of Vincent of Lérins (434), which states that the test of the genuine truth of any purported Christian doctrine is whether it has been believed always, everywhere, and by all' within the Church. H. Bettenson, *Documents of the Christian Church*, Oxford University Press, 1963, p. 84. But according to our reading of Collingwood this is not pos-sible for reasons given in the main text.

the knowledge of what mind has done in the past' (p. 218). This is because even if the historian is focusing on how the material environment has affected a given population, his ultimate interest lies not in the material factors but the human reaction to them (p. 79).

Yet the suggestion that our own absolute presuppositions must remain opaque to us seems to contradict Collingwood's own answer to the question '*What is history for?* . . . My answer is "for" . . . human self-knowledge' (Collingwood , 1946, p. 10) at least if this means the individual's knowledge of his own self, or his own generation. Of course, Collingwood is assuming that my presuppositions are historically conditioned, which is to say that I have inherited them through the cultural tradition in which I participate. Nevertheless, what historical investigation cannot bring objectively to my consciousness, according to his analysis of presuppositions, is precisely that which I need to know to achieve self-possession because I must always have a 'blind spot' for those presuppositions held millennia ago if I still hold them (or rather, they have a hold on me). A further problem is that, according to Collingwood, since I can only be conscious of anything in terms of my own 'absolute presuppositions', I could never come to grasp the presuppositions of past human beings as they were in themselves, rather than as modified by being understood in terms of my own perspectives. Collingwood's analysis therefore appears to rule out both an objective knowledge of myself, and the culture in which I participate *as well as* other, past cultures, and therefore undermines the very notion of the possibility of 're-enacting' the thoughts of others, a conclusion which he eventually works desperately to avoid by arguing that thought has a 'double character', in that it is both historical and non-historical; that is, 'every act of thought . . . happens in a context out of which it arises and in which it lives, as an organic part of the thinker's life' but is also 'an act of thought in addition to actually happening, is capable of sustaining in itself and being re-enacted or re-enacted' by the thinker himself or anyone else 'without loss of its identity' (p. 300).[15]

If something has gone wrong with Collingwood's analysis perhaps Hans-Georg Gadamer (b. 1900), who in many respects shares Collingwood's approach, can help. According to Gadamer, seeking to understand a historical reality – a culture, epoch, or person – is comparable to coming to understand another person (Gadamer, 1979, 324ff). Gadamer would say that you can never move towards understanding another except first in terms of your own prejudices (*Vorurteile*, the provocative term he likes to use of the assumptions or presuppositions which must govern our thinking; see 7.C.III). Of course, to the extent that your preconceptions differ from hers you will fail fully to understand her. To use another term Gadamer derives from Nietzsche (see 5.C.I), your prejudices will form a 'horizon' and she will, to a greater or lesser extent lie beyond it. Perhaps, though, the shock of experiencing her resistance to your preconceptions will induce in you an awareness for the first time of their limitations, and you will begin to stretch, modify, and broaden them. You will therefore be enriched and indeed the impact might be mutual. A blending (*Verschmelzung*) of your horizon and hers will then occur. You may both mutually 'come to an understanding', i.e. inhabit the same meaning. But Gadamer is adamant that you can never magically take

---

15   The idea is is that the thought 2 + 2 = 4, for example, is the same thought, and we know it to be such whether thought yesterday or in two years time by us or anyone else. Collingwood is wrestling with the same point as Rickert in writing of 'non-real meaning'. See 6.C.III.

leave of your own consciousness and transpose yourself into hers for he abandons the idea of a purely objective understanding of the other (e.g., the original 'authorial intention' of a text) as an incoherent notion of a perspectiveless standpoint, a 'view from nowhere,'[16] but holds out the hope of an, in principle, endless expansion of one's perspective through such transforming encounters .

Of course, unlike a conversation-partner, a past historical era cannot literally 'answer back', but nevertheless I come to understand a previous era not by seeking impossibly to suppress my own prejudices in order to grasp it as it was in itself (contrast Ranke 3.E.I), but operating through my prejudices I can come to a new and possibly richer understanding of it than was possible to those alive then, for my vantage-point has its own unique value. The new insight will also transform me. And although there is no 'answering back', a sensitive interpreter will always be on the look-out for aspects of the past which fail to makes sense in terms of his prejudices and adjust them. The ultimate result will not be the achievement of some definitive, absolute standpoint but simply the potentially ever-expanding realisation of a richer, fuller, deeper humanity.

Gadamer assimilates historical enquiry to the reproduction of a work such as a Shakespeare play (7.C.I). Every producer, actor or theatregoer will necessarily reinterpret the play in his own terms: there is no possibility of an 'objective' interpretation, if that means knowing what it 'meant' to Shakespeare (even if he knew), but that is not to say that the perspective he or she brings to it will not 'bring out' something always potentially in the work even though not consciously in the author's mind. Which artist ever knows fully what he has in mind before it wells out of his creative depths, and so how can even he know fully this child even when he has brought it to birth? Might not a spectator or reader understand it more fully than he? A slavishly 'authentic' Shakespeare reproduction attempting to reproduce early seventeenth-century culture in every known detail would fail because twentieth- century actors *cannot* take leave of themselves, and transport themselves back to an Elizabethan or Jacobean mentality. What they must do is expand and extend the reality of Shakespeare by making him live again in present terms. And, so too, attempts to understand the history of past eras: past human beings cannot be understood on their own terms, but only by succeeding generations in their own way. This is why every generation needs to rewrite the histories of the past for itself. Just as any Shakespeare producer will acquaint himself with past interpretations, though with slavish imitation the last thing he has in mind, the same will be true of the historian, so that a historiographical review will always form at least a preparatory element to his own work. And just as no producer of a Shakespeare play should be so absurd as to consider that he had produced the 'definitive' version of it which no one could ever improve upon, likewise it would be preposterous for anyone to assume he had written the definitive history of a past epoch. Even so, some Shakespeare productions are 'untrue' to him, and some histories, even if technically painstakingly accurate, might fail to produce the enhanced insights which can be their only ultimate aim.

Yet does Gadamer brush aside too glibly the idea of recovering the author's intention or retrieving the nature of a past historical epoch as it was in itself? In 1942 he journeyed to occupied Paris to deliver a lecture in which he lauded Herder, declaring that through him 'the word "*Volk*" achieves in German a new depth and a new power'

16 A phrase made famous by Nagel, 1986.

which now 'in contrast to the democratic slogans of the West, demonstrates the force for a new political and social order'. When later it was objected that this clearly echoed Nazi ideology, he complained that his critics had *misunderstood* his intention which had been 'purely academic' (Warnke, 1987, pp. 71–2).

I.III   Realism versus Relativism

Gadamer and Collingwood were by no means the first to emphasize the role of pre-suppositions in anything we could call knowledge. For instance in late nineteenth century Germany a group of 'Neo-Kantian' philosophers (see chapter 6) had insisted on it too. They argued that even the simplest act of cognitive consciousness – your awareness, say, of the contents of the room in which you are reading this book – is extremely *selective*; that though your senses are providing an enormous amount to which you could attend, you will remain oblivious of most of it because of lack of *interest*. For example, if you *want* to, you can become aware now of the feeling of the surface of your foot touching the inside of your shoe, of your pulse, your breathing, the noise of distant traffic or bird song, or the shadows on the walls, the colour of the flooring, the style of the window-frames, the number of electric lights, the heating installations, and so on practically ad infinitum. And we might add that when you do focus on an individual object such as a desk, what you do is *interpret* a mutating mass of sensations of coloured shapes, of sounds, of smells, and so forth *as* a 'desk'. Without having the concept of 'desk' already in your mind (*a priori* as philosophers put it, i.e., prior to having the sensations) you could not *perceive* yourself to be in a room which contains a desk, because you would not know what to 'make of' your sensations; you could not *perceive*, therefore, this object except for a highly complex active interpretational contribution by your mind to whatever sensations present themselves.

However reasonable, and perhaps unchallengeable, some of the above points might seem, they fly in the face of deeply embedded ordinary, everyday human beliefs. The common-sense man, I suspect, believes he 'knows' he is in a room with various contents simply because, when he opens his eyes and ears and other senses, the information floods in ready-made, so that he contributes nothing beyond merely passively receiving it. Of course, he would readily admit that he and everyone else makes many mistakes about what is real, but he attributes this to various specific causes, such as carelessness in observation, lack of intelligence, gullibility about what others say, the influence of drugs, or the blinding effect of prejudices. If, however, care is taken to avoid these pitfalls, he assumes that the mind naturally registers the truth, at least concerning those things of which it is immediately aware in sense-perception. These common-sense views are by no means unrepresented in philosophy. The view that knowledge is built up from information received passively through the senses is often termed 'empiricism': Locke and Hume have been among those seeking to justify it. The notion that prejudices must be removed if knowledge is to be achieved was strongly emphasized by Descartes and Bacon. The view that the human knower, *can* come to know and appreciate reality as it is in itself and not merely as it seems to him from his perspective, the mind reflecting the nature of things like a mirror, is often known in philosophy as 'realism'.

But 'realism' is slippery, like so many philosophical terms. Sometimes it refers to the notion that the human mind can transcend itself and know material (i.e., non- mental) objects truly. Its opposite is then 'idealism' (which does not imply moral idealism) which is the view that you could not possibly be conscious of something non-mental for if you think you are conscious of anything 'non-mental' it is entirely because of *thoughts* and *sensations* which you take to 'represent' the non-mental but are all 'in the mind'. Dr. Samuel Johnson reacted to the idealism of George Berkeley by kicking a stone and saying 'I refute him *thus*', but of course he had not done so, because the sense of resistance he *thought* he *felt* in his foot was felt 'in his consciousness'. But in a broader sense 'realists' can be also be idealists because the term can refer to the belief that the human mind can know reality 'as it is in itself' whether this reality is mental or not (e.g., other minds or God), as distinct from 'merely how it seems to me'. In this sense, the opposite of 'realism' is 'relativism' or 'scepticism'. Not all realists are empiricists or vice versa. Hume is always classified as an 'empiricist' (a term which, however, postdates him), but he declares that, strictly speaking, we know only impressions in the mind (e.g., sounds, shapes, smells, and such emotions which well up in the mind apparently in response to these sensations) but cannot know that they originate in objects outside the mind. This belief that, in fact, we know only what later philosophers were to term 'sense-data' is sometimes known as 'phenomenalism' (again a term unknown to Hume) because the assumption is that we are immediately conscious only of 'phenomena' or 'appearances' within the mind, and not what may or may not underlie them. Descartes, on the other hand, though an 'idealist' at least to the degree that he thinks the senses are untrustworthy as sources of knowledge about objective reality, nevertheless thought that that we have access to the truth about the non-mental reality he called 'matter' or 'extension' through a concept of it implanted in the mind by God.[17]

To clarify the issue further let us look at the version of 'realism' which (in various forms) was the standard accepted view for several centuries until the beginning of the seventeenth century, namely medieval Aristotelian scholasticism, considering in particular Thomas Aquinas's account. His realism is summed up in a definition of truth, which had long been current, that it is that it is the '*adaequatio rei et intellectus*' (*Summa Theologiae* 1a.16, art. 1 and 2) that is, we truly know when the concepts in our intellect correspond to or conform to the things to which we mean them to refer. But how does this happen? Through a process which begins when the images or likenesses (*species*) of things enter the mind through the five senses from the outside world. But the mere reception of these sensory likenesses (for instance the image on the eye's retina) does not constitute rational knowledge, for animals obviously receive them, but one would hesitate to ascribe to them purely objective knowledge of the real nature of things. Rather, it seems reasonable to assume that they merely notice them, retain them in their memories, and learn to associate them with danger, or opportunity for food etc. by blind stimulus and response habit-forming mechanisms. Thus, a

---

7 'Extension' means for Descartes simply 'three-dimensionality' and the rigorous and *a priori* science of it was already available in Euclidean geometry, which therefore is the basic science of the physical world. Because of this insistence that all science must be essentially *a priori* and mathematical, Descartes and his followers are traditionally labelled 'rationalists', and contrasted with 'empiricists' such as Locke or Hume who argue that the physical world can be primarily and properly known only through sense experience.

dog may wag its tail on hearing the sound of the front door opening because he has learned to associate it with his master's return, but there is no need to ascribe to him a purely objective, theoretical grasp of his own nature and that of his master, and their place in the real world. In contrast, when these images are received into the human mind they are worked on by a special faculty which Aquinas, following Aristotle, [18] called the 'agent intellect' which somehow 'abstracts' from the sensory data the intelligible content, forming an '*intelligible* likeness' of the thing out of the *sensible* likeness, which is none other than the rational essence of the thing.

But one perhaps has only to state such as account of cognition to register its implausibilities. For example how could I verify that my consciousness generates *real* 'likenesses' of things since it can never climb out of itself to check up? And granted that we do develop general concepts to sort out and render coherent the information received through our senses, why need these be more than gadgets to render more efficient our relationship to factors in our environment? Obviously there would be some sort of minimal correspondence between the regular structures of things in the unknowable real world and the concepts developed to handle them, but we need never flatter ourselves that our conceptual systems reveal the reality of things in themselves. This basic understanding can be found in Hume and the positivists (e.g., 4.A.I) but was particularly developed and promoted by the American Pragmatists,[19] Peirce, James and Dewey, and versions of it have become widespread in the last hundred years. Wittgenstein repeatedly uses the terms *Handlung* (practical dealing) to describe the ultimate basis of our knowledge of the world (Wittgenstein, 1969, props. 39, 110, 204, 229, 411, 422), and declares that the notions of 'agreement' or 'correspondence' with reality in the abstract have no clear application (props. 215, c. 203, 191, 199). Heidegger maintains in *Being and Time*, that we first encounter things in this world as 'tools' (*Zeuge*) or 'equipment', that is, in terms of 'the kind of dealing (*Handlung*) which is closest to us ... not a bare perceptual cognition, but rather that kind of concern which manipulates things and puts them to use' (Heidegger, 1962, pp. 67–70). We make a distinction between practical and theoretical knowledge, but the latter emerges out of the former (pp. 357–64) so that:

> There is 'truth' only in so far as Dasein[20] is and so long as Dasein is. . . . Newton's laws, the principle of contradiction, any truth whatever – these are true only as long as Dasein *is*. Before there was any Dasein, there was no truth; nor will there be any after Dasein is no more. . . . Before Newton's laws were discovered, they were not 'true'; it does not follow that they were false. . . .
>
> . . .

18   Plato is famous for developing the view that our minds are impregnated, as it were, prior to birth with general concepts of the natures of things, and it is merely when an approximation to (a copy or imitation of) one of these forms is encountered by the senses that we dredge up into consciousness the form which enables us to know what the thing was. Aristotle rejected the idea of our *a priori* possession of forms but developed the view that we 'abstract' them from sense data in order to know the natures of things, so that Aristotelianism was a form of empiricism.

19   This use of the term does not have the same connotation as the usage introduced in section 1 in relation to 'pragmatic' history; Polybius clearly meant that knowledge of the *real* truth about the past would be practically useful.

20   Heidegger prefers to refer to the human being as *Dasein* (there-being or existence) because he wants to get away from the traditional connotations of the term human.

Because the kind of Being that is essential to truth is of the character of Dasein, all truth is relative to Dasein's Being. Does this relativity signify that all truth is 'subjective'? If one Interprets 'subjective' as 'left to the subject's discretion', then it certainly does not . . . (pp. 269–70)

One reason for the emergence of this modern relativist-pragmatist view of human knowledge was the Darwinian theory of evolution with its implication that our intellect, like all other human faculties, could only have emerged by 'natural selection' as an aid to survival, rather than as a capacity to perceive absolute truth. But it has been given additional impetus by radical changes in the fundamental concepts of physics: Heidegger in the mid–1920s could still write as if Newton's laws were 'true'. Their status was soon to be reduced by Einstein to that of simplified approximations to reality. The experience of this devaluation of Newtonian science, generally regarded for the previous two centuries as secure and definitive, has provoked especially in the post-World War II period, a radical reappraisal of the history of scientific revolutions, especially that of sixteenth and seventeenth centuries. This is encapsulated in T. S. Kuhn's *Structure of Scientific Revolutions* of which it has been said that 'it would be hard to nominate another twentieth-century American academic work, which has been as widely influential; among historical books it would appear to be without serious rival' (Novick, 1988, p. 526). It seeks to show that when fundamental theoretical concepts ('paradigms') have been overthrown as when Newton displaced Descartes' notions of matter and movement, as Descartes had displaced those of Aristotle, or eventually Einstein those of Newton, it was not because former paradigms have been conclusively falsified and the new ones conclusively verified. Rather such 'revolutions' result from far more ambiguous and complex shifts, which in part can be explained only through the *historical* exploration of psycho-sociological realities.

Another factor, conditioning, perhaps even more deeply, the retreat from 'realism' has been the decline in belief in God which accelerated from the eighteenth century onwards especially among the educated; according to Nietzsche the 'death of God' (5.C.VI) is the fundamental cultural phenomenon of our epoch, not only because it undermines Christian morality, but also the conviction that the human mind could know reality objectively with, as it were God's Eye View. Heidegger's entire Dasein-centred account of knowledge and truth was an attempt to come to terms with the challenge of Nietzsche's diagnosis. According to Heidegger, the Western mentality is still so profoundly conditioned by the synthesis forged by medieval philosophy between Biblical and Platonic ideas that we still regard as 'self-evident' notions about knowledge which come from this historically conditioned source, which, because of the demise of the latter, are now indefensible. Chief among these is the conviction that every human being has the capacity to be an 'ideal subject', that is, is capable of knowing the 'absolute' truth about things as they are in themselves. In fact the whole notion is based on the assumption that the things of this world are 'creatures', i.e., products manufactured by a creator God (found both in the Bible and in Plato's *Timaeus*), and that our minds have special access into the intentions of the divine Craftsman because we are 'made in the image and likeness of God' (*Genesis* 1:26). According to Heidegger, this is a mere *'fanciful idealisation'* and it 'belongs those residues of Christian theology within philosophical problematics' which have to be radically extruded' (Heidegger, 1962, p. 272), indeed 'destroyed' (p. 44) because we cannot expect it simply to wither away, and it is blocking our access to the truth about ourselves. An examination of Aquinas's presuppositions about knowledge lends support to the claims of Heidegger and Nietzsche concerning the theological grounding of traditional views of knowledge. Aquinas assumes that the species or forms which the mind abstracts from physical realities had originally been fused with 'matter' in the act of creation. They had eternally pre-existed as 'Ideas' in the mind of God, just as a house exist in an architect's mind as a blueprint before creation (*Summa Theologiae*, 1a.q.14, art. 5, and 15 art. 2). When our mind achieves 'adequation' with things it is primarily achieving '*adaequatio*' not with the things themselves, but with the Ideas of them in the mind of God which is the ultimate cause of all things, and therefore the ultimate bridge between our minds and the things which we know. In a Platonist strain in Christian theology stemming above all from St. Augustine (354–430), which Aquinas, because of his Aristotelianism, to some extent resists, the connection between the divine and human minds is even closer: God, in the Augustinian tradition, directly and immediately causes true knowledge in the human mind by 'illuminating' it by infusing it with his Ideas so that knowledge is always participation in the mind of the divine creator (see Nash, 1969b). The same essential involvement of God in human cognition is evident at the beginning of the modern era in the thought of Descartes (see Heidegger, 1962, p. 46), who overcame the threat of 'scepticism' about our knowledge of the 'real' and the 'true' (that is the possibility that human beings might never escape their subjectivity to know things objectively) only by providing what he regarded as a proof of the existence of a good and truthful creator God, who would never allow the human mind to be deceived, provided that it took care to use its faculties properly. However, Heidegger considers that the threat of 'scepticism', which has conditioned so much of modern philosophy following the lead of Descartes, is empty, once one has realised that 'Truth' is not first and foremost God-relative, leaving us with the problem of aligning ourselves with God, but only ever Dasein-relative, an insight which Heidegger boasts transcends the conflict between 'realism' and 'idealism' (pp. 57 and 249–63). Similar claims have been made by many twentieth century philosophers in their own ways from Wittgenstein to Rorty. Unfortunately, there is a retort to it, namely that the claims of Heidegger and the others about the nature of man and truth are themselves quasi-absolute, quasi-divine.

The issue has nevertheless been a major item on the agenda of philosophy in the English-speaking world in the last couple of decades, the discussion largely centring on the question of whether the natural sciences can be regarded as achieving knowledge of the real nature of things. But what of historical knowledge? Here developments have run somewhat differently. First, the lonely genius, Giambattista Vico (1668–1744) of Naples, who was in many ways the first advocate of 'historicism' (see chapter 3) even if his influence on its later development is difficult to establish, declared that 'the true (*verum*) and the made (*factum*) are convertible'. This is a reference to that link between having produced something and knowing the truth about it which lies at the root of the connection between theology and realism just discussed. But Vico emphasises it in order to stress, first, that since we did not create the world we can never do more than make guesses at its nature because we are not privy to its creator's intention, and secondly we *can* know our own thoughts and the products of our own creativity, in which he includes all the historical developments of human culture, because they are all the products of the human imagination, so that we can come to know about them from the 'inside'. A similar notion became central to historicism (see chapters 3 and 6): the aim of history was conceived as knowing the minds of others by using our imagination to come to understand (*Verstehen*), on the assumption that our own consciousness allows us to empathise with or re-live the mentalities of other individuals and cultures. Yet this notion is suspect in the eyes of many because it seems to imply a kind of magical clairvoyance. Surely I can no more get 'inside' the mind of someone else than I can get 'inside' the structure of an inanimate object, for both are alien to my consciousness? We shall see that strenuous efforts were devoted in the historicist tradition to providing a theoretical account of such understanding which came to be known as 'hermeneutics', with Gadamer a later member of this tradition who nevertheless repudiates the aim, as we have already seen, of rediscovering the original state of mind of historical agents. However, positivists (see chapter 4) have followed the position classically stated by Hume that there is no essential difference between understanding the thinking of others and natural scientific explanation since in both cases particular phenomena are subsumed under empirically verified general laws.

The historicists assembled in chapter 3 are all 'realists' in their understanding of historical knowledge, considering that the historian can and must represent the past '*wie es eigentlich gewesen*' (how it actually, or essentially, was), meaning that he must understand past human beings 'on their own ground, in their own environment, so to speak, in their own particular inner state. . . . Our task is to penetrate them to the bottom of their existence and to portray them with complete objectivity' (Ranke, 1983, p. 42). Yet in chapter 6 are collected a group of thinkers whose aim is to defend what they consider the essential aims of the earlier historicists, but strikingly, they all abandoned 'realism', although they be no means abandoned the '*Verstehen*' ideal in all respects. It is surely no coincidence that a major difference between them and the early historicists is that they had all abandoned belief in God, but their standard argument against historical realism was that the historian could proceed only by being selective and therefore could not possibly reproduce or 'copy' reality (see especially 6.D.I).

The realist is not entirely defenseless against such arguments. In the first place, the so-called copy theory of knowledge articulated by Simmel or Rickert is something of a caricature of what thinkers such as Aquinas or Ranke maintained. Aquinas's 'intelligible likeness' is precisely not, as we have seen, a physical 'likeness', although the 'sensible' image at the back of the retina of the eye may be; only by *analogy* is it comparable to a physical likeness, that it is *like* a likeness. *Eigentlich* in Ranke's famous phrase means 'essentially' rather than 'actually' in all its infinite detail. Secondly the argument that a real thing cannot be copied in any way by the mind because it has infinite aspects depends on the presumption that one cannot know anything about something unless one knows everything about it, which is surely dubious. I can know that a certain highway is ten miles long without knowing that it passes alongside a beautiful lake, and that my friend is patient without knowing that he is in love with Sarah. Only if every aspect of everything were tightly integrated into everything else would it be really true that I could not 'abstract' from the totality without untruthful distortion. There have been philosophers – for instance, Leibniz – who thought this was so but there seems no compelling reason for agreeing with them (see Nagel, 1959) . Thirdly, 'realism' is perhaps far more deeply, indeed even *inextricably* embedded in the structure of human consciousness than many non-realists have acknowledged. They sometimes can be found arguing that *because* of some alleged fact of history (such as the fact that each generation sees the past differently from its predecessors) or natural science (such as the theory of evolution) realism is not a possible option. But it is, of course, self-contradictory to argue, for example, that because we now know that the human race has developed under evolutionary pressures, we can be sure that the human mind has only a practical survival function and cannot know 'objective' truth, because if this were true we could never know it. Something of the same inconsistency (sometimes known as a 'performative self-contradiction'), is apparent in Gadamer's complaint that the intention of his 1942 Herder lecture had been 'misunderstood' when he claims that we can never know the original intentions of others.

1.IV David Hume's Phenomenalistic Empiricism

Hume is usually regarded as the greatest British philosopher in terms of originality and historical influence. He would normally be classified as a 'non-realist' because, he maintained that, assuming that you consider yourself to be perceiving a chair, you are conscious only of a collection of 'perceptions' (shapes, colours, etc.) in your mind which persist through time, and therefore have no *rational* basis for the belief that there is anything *beyond* them which causes them, let alone that they resemble the object you assume is causing them, because you cannot get out of your consciousness and see what lies outside it. Moreover, when you close your eyes the perceptions disappear, and when you open them they reappear, which gives you no reason for believing that the object you take to be causing them continues to exist when you close your eyes. Rather you '*feign*' (Hume, 1978, p. 208) its continued existence. This predicament is insurmountable for 'no beings are ever present to the mind but perceptions; it follows that we . . . can never observe . . . a conjunction . . . between perceptions and objects' (p. 213). However, 'men are carried, by a . . . blind and powerful . . . natural instinct or prepossession, to repose faith in their senses . . . Without any reasoning we always suppose an external universe', and 'the very images, presented by the senses, to be the . . . external objects'. Yet 'the slightest philosophy destroys this faith' (Hume, 1902, p. 151).

Nevertheless some things are known for certain: 'since all actions and sensations of the mind are known to us by consciousness, they must necessarily appear in every particular what they are, and be what they appear'. Trying to maintain the opposite would be 'to suppose that even where we are most intimately conscious, we might be mistaken'(p. 190). They are therefore 'perfectly known' (Hume, 1978, p. 366) for 'consciousness never deceives' (Hume, 1902, p. 66), and 'consequently . . . there is a truth and falsehood in all propositions on this subject, and a truth and falsehood which lie not beyond the compass of human understanding' (p. 14). For this reason 'mental geography', i.e., pure descriptions of the mind as it appears to itself, constitute 'true metaphysics' (pp. 12–13). This science will be 'the only solid foundation for the other sciences' because in truth all the sciences, Newtonian physics, mathematics, or whatever are aspects of human mental activity and so 'lie under the cognisance of men, and are judged of by their powers and faculties' (Hume, 1978, p. xix). The assumption that we have immediate infallible knowledge of the way things appear in the mind has become known as 'phenomenalism'. The view that all truly scientific assertions must ultimately be reducible to assertions about these appearances or phenomena is an empiricist version of what has become known as 'foundationalism' i.e., that all knowledge must ultimately be grounded in what is infallibly known. It amounts to the claim that contrary to Collingwood, Gadamer and the Neo-Kantians, there are *pure givens* known *presuppositionlessly*.

Hume next invites his readers to verify by this supposedly infallible introspection that the mind's 'perceptions' fall into two broad categories which he terms 'impressions' and 'ideas'. There are two types of the former: 'impressions of sensation' which are given through the five senses, and 'impressions of reflection', which is to say emotions or passions, which we find well up in our minds in response to sensations, or thoughts of them. 'Impressions' are distinguished from 'ideas' by their greater 'force and liveliness' (p. 1) or 'vivacity' (p. 17). What is striking is 'the great resemblance between our impressions and ideas in every other particular . . . The one seem to be in a manner the reflexion of the other . . . When I shut my eyes and think of my chamber the ideas I form are exact representations of the impressions I felt; nor is there any circumstance of the former, which is not to be found in the other' (pp. 2–3). Therefore 'it seems a proposition which will not admit of much dispute, that all our ideas are nothing but copies of our impressions, or, in other words . . . it is impossible for us to think of anything, which we have not antecedently felt, either by our external or internal senses' (Hume, 1902, p. 62).

If all is so transparently clear how does error arise? Because 'ideas' confuse, not only because of their inherent faintness, but because our imagination can 'compound, transpose, augment, or diminish' original impressions to form fictitious ideas such as that of a golden mountain (p. 19). But Hume unveils an 'invention' which he says can render our ideas 'altogether precise and determinate'. It is simply to 'produce the impression or original sentiments, from which the ideas are copies. These impressions are all strong and sensible. They admit not of ambiguity. They are not only placed in a full light themselves, but may throw light on their correspondent ideas, which lie in obscurity' (p. 62). Thus, 'when we entertain . . . any suspicion that a philosophical term is employed without any meaning or idea (as is but too frequent), we need but enquire, *from what impression is that supposed idea derived?* (p. 22).

Hume's most famous doctrine concerns causality. After stressing that 'all reasoning concerning matter of fact seem to be founded on the relation of *Cause and Effect*'(p. 26) he argues that the only basis we have for affirming any instance of it, is repeated experiences of 'constant conjunction' between two impressions. This engenders a 'habitual' or 'customary' expectation, which is nothing more than an 'instinct implanted in us by nature' that when we experience the first the second will follow with 'the highest degree of certainty' (p. 55). For example, because we have always observed that water boils after heat is applied, we unhesitatingly expect it to continue to do so invariably, and say that we know that heat 'causes' water to boil. Our sense that there is a 'necessary connection' (p. 62) between the phenomena is, however, purely subjective. Moreover, we have no *reason* for believing that any past experiences could be any guide for the future, since that the future must be like the past is unprovable (p. 35). Thus, all our causal 'reasonings' are of the same kind as the instinctive learning from repeated experiences which we find in animals (p. 106). Natural science is merely an artificial refinement of this which is pragmatic in nature: 'the only immediate utility of all science, is to teach us, how to control and regulate future events by their causes' (p.

76). At no point does it become purely 'theoretical' as opposed to practical knowl-edge. Hume insists that this same analysis applies to explanation of human actions:

> The philosopher, if he be consistent, must apply the same reasoning to the actions and volitions of intelligent agents. The most irregular and unexpected resolutions of men may frequently be accounted for by those who know every particular circumstance of their character and situation . . . The internal principle and motives may operate in a uniform manner, notwithstanding these seeming irregularities; in the same manner as the winds, rain, clouds, and other variations of the weather are supposed to be governed by steady principles; though not easily discoverable by human sagacity and enquiry. Thus it appears . . . that the conjunction between motives and voluntary actions is as regular and uniform as that between the cause and effect in any part of nature. (p. 88)

In effect, Hume is here espousing a version of what is often called 'determinism'. Section 2.A.I shows his application of this to history.

Hume also applied his understanding of causal knowledge to belief in God with devastatingly negative results. Most traditional arguments for the existence of God depend on the assumption that the principle of causality is *known* as a rationally self-evident principle to hold for all beings, so that one must be able to trace everything up to a single first cause which transcends the universe. It was a relatively straightforward exercise for him to show that, from his point of view these were illegitimate extensions of the principle of causality (See Hume, 1902, section XI and Hume, 1947). He also demonstrated that belief in miracle stories was incompatible with his understanding of causality, which struck at the heart not only of the content of orthodox Christian doctrine but the standard arguments in is lifetime for the truth of the Christian revela-tion (see ch. 2) . He was in this way the first major philosopher since the ancient Epicureans to leave no positive role at all for the term 'God' in his theory of knowl-edge and to develop an unambiguously secular philosophy of morals. He was not an atheist, but he was an agnostic[21] and in this way, a hundred years before Nietzsche, he announced 'the death of God'.

There is space to point to make only two critical comments. First, his 'invention' has a superficial plausibility because in everyday life if, say, we are attracted to an item in a shop, and then return later, we frequently find that our imagination has begun to deceive us, and the deception cured by the return visit. Yet the comparison is invalid, since for Hume every 'impression' occurs at a particular time and then perishes, so I *cannot* 'go back' to any original impression; all I can do is *judge* the new impression to be identical with the old, and my yardstick can only be that the new impression is similar to the very 'idea' of the original impression which is supposedly suspect. Sec-ondly, the suggestion that concepts are merely after-effects of particular impressions, and must be traced back to them if their validity is questioned, ignores the fact that a crucial feature of any concept is, as we saw earlier; that they are 'universals' whilst all perceptions are particular. Hume responds to this problem by taking over from Berkeley (1685–1753) what he describes as 'one of the greatest and most valuable discoveries that has been made of late years'. It is that we get round the fact that all perceptions are particular by 'annexing' 'terms' or 'words' to one particular idea when we 'have found

---

21   A term not invented until the nineteenth century by T. H. Huxley.

a resemblance among several objects' and then 'apply the same name to all of them, whatever differences we may observe'. We then acquire a 'custom' whereby 'the hearing of that name revives the idea of one of these objects' even though all the objects in question 'are not really and in fact present to the mind' (Hume, 1978, pp. 19–20) and thus we become able to discourse generally of 'triangles' although any imagined triangle will be irreducibly different from others (e.g., it could be equilateral or right-angled, etc. but no image could cover all of them).

There are several difficulties with this account. One is that if general concepts or 'abstract ideas' are acquired only through learning one of the historico-cultural forms of expression which we term 'languages', the general terms of which are all ambiguous and mutate constantly as individuals and generations modify them in a piecemeal fashion, then we have left behind the world of inner experience with its alleged infallible immediacy. Secondly, even if we assume that by a 'word' Hume could mean some purely private internal invention by a solitary human consciousness his account presupposes that somehow or other the mind must perceive a 'similarity' prior to inventing a word to signify it. But perception of similarity is precisely what is usually meant by the formation by the mind of general concepts. Only after this key activity has taken place, could one go through the business of annexing the consciousness of similarity to a general 'term' which could function merely as a mnemonic device. So on this interpretation too Hume seems to be implicitly moving to the notion that human consciousness is not primarily the passive reception of sensory particulars but that active effort at *universalization* is part of its every essence (see Marx 8.A.II). It does not seem that Hume ever explored all these ramifications: perhaps he sensed that it would have required far too many radical changes in his entire approach. In the *Enquiry* he relegates discussion of the issue to a few sentences in the final Section (Hume, 1902, pp. 154–5), having previously given the impression that he regarded consciousness as essentially wordless.

I.V **Immanuel Kant's Transcendentalism**

By Kant's own account the revolutionary theory of knowledge expounded in his *Critique of Pure Reason* (1781) would never have been conceived but for Hume's philosophy, of which he wrote that 'no event has occurred since the beginning of metaphysics, which could have been more decisive' (Kant, 1953, p. 10) for it 'interrupted my dogmatic slumber and gave a completely different direction to my enquiries in the field of speculative philosophy' (p. 9). He described the aim of the 1781 *Critique* as 'the *working out* of Hume's problem in its greatest possible extension' (p. 5), that is, the problem of how far human knowledge extends, and whether it extends to discovery of the causes of events in the world. Hume's solution was unacceptable to Kant because of its denial of genuine knowledge of necessary causal relationships in the world. The basic defect of Hume's approach, according to Kant, is that his empiricism left him with no adequate means of completing the task of defining the limits of human knowledge which he had set himself; all that he could do was insist dogmatically that it ended where *his* experience had seemed to him to give out, which could not possibly be the absolute 'horizon' or 'determinate and necessary *limits*' of human knowledge. But Kant considered that he could show that once this fundamental mistake has been corrected, the necessary limits of knowledge could be specified precisely, and moreover it could be proved that knowable causes operated without exception in the world of experience.

Hume's mistake was to be assume that there could be any such thing as purely 'given' presuppositionless sensory experience, whereas sensations in themselves, which Kant terms the 'unsynthesized manifold', are only the 'raw material' (*Critique of Pure Reason*, A1/B2) on which thought has to work before 'experience' can result. Therefore there has to be activity on the part of the thinker which is distinct from the sensations, and not based on them as their after-effects as Hume claimed: 'without sensibility no object would be given to us, without understanding no object would be thought. Thoughts without concepts are empty, intuitions without concepts are blind. . . . These two powers or capacities cannot exchange their functions. The understanding can intuit nothing, the senses can think nothing' (B 75) The basic function of concepts, according to Kant, is *to refer our sensation to some object or other*, for until we consider ourselves confronted by an 'object' we are not conscious, for sensations in themselves are not objects. As a quick way of getting hold of the point, try to imagine being conscious of sensations given through the five senses *without* assuming they are attached to objects; that is, a world of sheer 'blooming, buzzing confusion' with no relatively stable objects at all beneath the transient sensations. This means, according to Kant, that consciousness involves interpreting sensations as manifestations of objects by the use of concepts which 'synthesise' the sensations into knowable objects. We must therefore already have the fundamental concept of an 'object' in our mind from the start (*a priori*) and apply it to sensations. More precisely, the concept of object is given in an interrelated set of concepts which he terms 'categories' which together are 'concepts of an object in general' (B 128).

At the core of the *Critique of Pure Reason* is a series of arguments purporting to prove that there are twelve, and twelve only, of these interrelated concepts needed to make sensations thinkable, that is, to transform the sensory manifold into objective experience. Among these is the concept of cause-and-effect. Putting Kant's argument very simply: to perceive an object means that I have to regard the sensory flow as *both* an order causally related to my ongoing existence as a perceiver with a specific location in space and time, *and* an order related causally to the object or objects in question, for to take my sensations as disclosing the 'object' means that I must regard them as causally related to it, i.e., as connected in an orderly manner to that object. Thus, I *must* regard the world I experience as the result of an *orderly* causal interaction between my sensory equipment and objects in the 'world', which must be an interacting system of such objects. Because I could not be conscious of objects without applying the categories or 'pure concepts of the understanding' I must regard them as 'the principles *a priori* of possible experience' and as 'at the same time universal laws of nature, which can be known *a priori*'. Together they constitute a 'logical system' which is a 'system of nature; which system precedes all empirical knowledge of nature' and 'first makes it possible' (Kant, 1953, pp. 64–5). The startling implication is that 'however exaggerated and absurd it may sound to say that the understanding is itself the source of the laws of nature . . . such an assertion is none the less correct . . . appearances take on an orderly character . . . under . . . the pure laws of understanding' (*Critique of Pure Reason*, A 127) This result, Kant proudly boasts, is nothing less than a 'Copernican Revolution' in philosophy, for 'hitherto it has been assumed that all our knowledge must conform to objects', whereas from now on we must 'suppose that objects must conform to our knowledge' (B xvi). In short, there is a guaranteed 'adequation' between the intellect and thing because our intellect half-creates the thing we know. We therefore *know* a priori that the principle of causality applies to the world of experiences, which is to say, we can 'dispose of the Humean doubt once and for all' (Kant, 1953, p. 70).

A criticism often made by modern commentators who see some strength in such 'transcendental'[22] arguments is that they might well prove that I cannot be conscious without perceiving objects in ordered causal interaction with myself as one of the physical entities with them in the world, but that does not prove that the human mind must be responsible for imposing this order. This would not satisfy Kant, however, because then any correspondence between my concepts and the object would still need explaining: it could hardly be regarded as other than being a 'pre-established harmony' achieved by some transcendent all-powerful god, in whom we could only have faith, and our 'knowledge' would then be deprived of the 'necessity' which Kant still regards as essential to true knowledge. More than that, the first *Critique* opens with a discussion (the 'Transcendental Aesthetic') which, together with some later sections of the book, analyses the many paradoxes which seem inseparable from space and time, and which have been explored at least since the pre-Socratic Zeno. Kant concludes that the paradoxes are irresolvable, and imply that space and time cannot possibly be aspects of reality-in-itself, and he concludes that the only coherent view is that space and time are 'pure forms of all sensible intuition' (A 39/B56), which is to say (to use inadequate analogies), spectacles or filters, through which we receive 'sensations' by which Kant means that, as in the case of the categories, we impose them on sensations i.e., we spatio-temporalize everything in our world of experience. However, because of their inherently logically inconsistent nature, he will not however allow that they are 'concepts', and so are not 'categories'. Kant therefore is directly opposed to the traditional 'materialist' view that *only* the spatio-temporal can be real. Space and time are however defining characteristics of the world of 'empirical reality': only 'absolute reality' is denied of them.

Is Kant's position realism or non-realism? In one sense, of course, it is non-realism because the objects perceived are appearances (*phenomena*) and not things in themselves (*noumena*). We do not create the sensations which trigger off the process of knowledge so they must come from a 'real' world out there which we can never know. The 'self' from which the activity of thinking comes forth must also belong to that real, but unknowable, world of things-in-themselves. To say that it is unknowable means that we do not know whether or not our categories apply to it, which is another way of saying that we do not know whether or not, or how far, our notion of 'object' or 'thing' applies in that world. On the other hand the world which we experience is the only one we can possibly know, and we do know it because we half-create it, precisely by imbuing it with the character of being a world of which there is 'objective' knowledge to be had.. Why should the fact that we half-create the phenomenal world lead us to deny it 'reality'? Would a creator God be unable to regard the world he created as 'real' because He had created it, i.e., it was his 'fiction'? Certainly, *within*

---

22 'Transcendental' is the term Kant uses to refer to the various *a priori* ingredients of consciousness as opposed to *a posteriori* sensations.

the world of experience we *can* and *must* distinguish between the real and the illusory (A 493/B 521, A600/B 629).

If one rejects the presupposition that the human mind has only to free itself from any presuppositions in order effortlessly to reflect reality in itself, and accepts instead that it must somehow actively apply its concepts to sensations if it is to be rationally conscious of anything, then the term 'reality' can only *mean* what is real in terms of human concepts. It was the conviction of thinkers such as Simmel and Dilthey (see chapter 6) that this must be the case which makes them 'Neo-Kantian'. The great difference between them and Kant was that they allowed that human presuppositional concepts or categories can and do change through history, and moreover that there might also be equally valid alternative conceptual schemes, there being virtually no sense in the notion of a single, absolutely correct conceptual scheme, whereas Kant maintained that his categories were the 'conditions of the possibility' of any experience whatever, and so unquestionably necessary. Essentially the same position as Simmel or Dilthey has been advocated in recent years by Hilary Putnam, one of the most influential of contemporary American philosophers, who had developed what he terms an 'internal realist' view of truth, or 'realism with a human face', to distinguish it from what he terms the absolute or metaphysical conception of truth.

One of the most paradoxical implications of Kant's position is that my 'really real' self – the source for example of all this activity of thinking – can only be *non-temporal*; I impose time on all my experience so that it is only my *phenomenal* self which has thoughts and volitions which change through time. Viewed as phenomenal beings, Kant agrees with Hume that all the actions of human beings must have complete explanations in terms of necessary scientific laws: 'all acts of rational beings, in that they are appearances (are encountered in some experience) stand under natural necessity' (Kant, 1953, p. 111). Another similarity with Hume is that Kant is sure that none of the traditional proofs of the existence of God work, because they all depend on seeking to apply categories, especially that of causality, which apply only to the phenomenal world, to a trans-phenomenal reality. However, he makes a number of moves in a rather more traditional direction when it comes to discussing the nature of morality in his second *Critique*, that of *Practical Reason* (1788). Morality for Kant springs from the fact that as rational agents we should impose on ourselves the demand that all our actions should be rational in form, and to be 'rational' for Kant as for the philosophic tradition in general, as we have seen (1.I), is to generalize or universalize (Kant, 1956, p. 33). In practice this means that as I pursue my happiness, because any rational being equipped with bodily needs and desires will, other things being equal, seek to fulfil them, I must recognize that I have no more right to pursue my happiness than any other rational agent has a right to pursue his or her happiness. I must therefore never pursue my happiness in a way which would undermine the possibility of the happiness of others, and I must coordinate my own pursuit with that of others. Kant expresses this by saying I must 'universalize' my maxims (p. 49), which is to say, never do anything contrary to the happiness of those whose right to pursue it is equal to mine. Thus, I must not break my promises because that would reduce the social world to chaos and so render sustained happiness impossible for anyone, and, generally, I must not ever use any other person merely as a means to my own happiness. This absolute moral ought Kant terms the 'categorical imperative', which it is important to note is a self-imposed law.

But 'ought' implies 'can'; if we take this moral ought seriously we must assume that we are *free* to follow its call or fail to do so. It is here that Kant deploys his phenomenal/noumenal distinction to square the circle of the determinism he affirms in human actions as phenomenal with the freedom required if the categorical imperative is to be taken seriously, arguing that there is nothing to prevent us assuming that, as noumenal beings we are free, indeed he is so convinced of this that he comes to talk of a unique knowledge of 'fact' (pp. 30–1) about the noumenal world, i.e., our own freedom. Yet the whole notion is very paradoxical indeed for, since we are timeless as noumenal beings, the implication is that our moral freedom is really actualized in one timeless decision which somehow manifests itself, refracted into the endless specific moral decisions we make in this world, which in some way are ultimately rooted in this single noumenal free act. The best Kant can do to prevent us falling into despair if, looking back over past failures, we conclude that this timeless decision must have determined us to be evil, is to suggest that if there is an overall trend of moral improvement in our lives, this might mean that our timeless freedom includes a timeless repentance for our failures (Kant, 1998, pp. 89–90). Kant is very far removed from the agnosticism of Hume. Although we do not know as a fact (in contrast to our knowledge of our freedom) that God exists, it is a 'subjective . . . moral necessity' for us in a 'pure *rational faith*' (Kant, 1956, p. 130) to posit the existence of an all-powerful and all good God who will proportion happiness to virtue (the 'highest good') in a last judgement and therefore bring to completion a perfectly moral universe, which must be the ultimate aim of all moral activity. We cannot envisage the highest good being brought about in any other way, because there is no empirical evidence that the blind operation of the laws of nature will bring it about (p. 150). If we were to cease to belief in this achievement our commitment to morality would collapse for 'the impossibility of the highest good must prove the falsity of the moral law also' (p. 118). The moral man may 'waver' in his belief in God but he can never 'fall into unbelief' (p. 151).

2 Enlightenment

Robert M. Burns

Introduction

The verb 'to enlighten' is used metaphorically in many languages to refer to the coming of truth to the mind. The term 'enlightenment' (*Aufklärung*) became widespread in eighteenth-century Germany especially (but not exclusively) with reference to the spread of the ideas of the French *philosophes*, in what was often a top-down movement promoted by 'enlightened despots' such as Frederick the Great. English absorbed the term from German to refer to eighteenth century thought only gradually from the second half of the nineteenth century onwards, and this usage has become common only in the last fifty years.

There has been a recent tendency in socio-political criticism to understand the modern age as the continuation or dénouement of 'the Enlightenment'[1] such that it becomes the key to understanding modernity and post-modernity. John Gray provides a typical example of this approach, invoking an impressive array of thinkers such as Nietzsche, Weber, Heidegger, Horkheimer and Adorno, Lyotard, MacIntyre, Derrida, and Rorty in support of the thesis that we live today 'amid the dim ruins of the Enlightenment project' (Gray, 1995, p. 145) which is 'irreversible in its cultural effect' but was 'self-undermining and is now exhausted' (p. viii). Citing MacIntyre (1981) he identifies its central thrust as the attempt to 'secularize or naturalize' traditional Western morality by 'shedding or marginalizing' its original basis in Greek metaphysics and Christian theology (p. 152), and reconstructing it on 'universal, tradition-independent rational principles' (p. 149) that is, on allegedly scientific facts about human nature. But its emphasis on a 'unitary scientific method' and the 'ascription to science of a prescriptive authority whereby other forms of knowledge can be humiliated' (p. 154) was disastrous: its emphasis on a single universal human nature was 'an assault on cultural difference,' its 'project of universal civilization' being actually 'Western cultural imperialism' (p. viii). Echoing Lyotard (1984) Gray declares it an 'an illusion that the diverse forms of human knowledge, or even of scientific knowledge, can be unified in a single system or brought under the discipline of a single method', this being 'just one of the many superstitions of enlightenment cultures' (p. 154), a remark which indicates the influence Adorno and Horkheimer (1997), one of whose main themes was that the Enlightenment's claim to transcend 'myth' scientifically is in fact one

---

1 For example, Adorno and Horkheimer, 1997; Foucault 'What is Enlightenment? ' in Rabinow 1984, 45–56; J. Habermas, 'Taking Aim at the Heart of the Present' in Hoy, 1986, 103–19.

more myth. Gray also endorses another Adorno–Horkheimer thesis, one also prominent in the thought of the later Heidegger, and earlier in Weber, that 'the legacy of the Enlightenment project, is a world ruled by calculation and willfulness which is humanly unintelligible and destructively purposeless' (p. 146). This undermines its surface liberalism because not only does its 'project of subjugating nature' threaten to produce 'ecological catastrophe on an almost apocalyptic scale', but it turns 'instrumental reason' on man himself reducing him to a mere cog in a machine. He rejects as untenable MacIntyre's attempt to turn the clock back by embracing once more the ethics of Aristotle and Aquinas, because the Enlightenment is an 'irreversible' historical process. In any case, pre-modern thought would not free us from the Enlightenment because it 'was itself an authentic development of a central Western tradition going back to Socrates and indeed beyond, to the pre-Socratics such as Parmenides and Heraclitus', namely, 'logocentrism' which is the conception that 'human reason mirrors the structure of the world' (p. 152). The Enlightenment was in fact 'a half-way house between the central, classical beliefs of the West and an as-yet-unborn culture in which those commitments had been shed'. Gray's own remedy is that we must learn to accept the 'postmodern condition of plural and provisional perspectives lacking any rational or transcendental ground or unifying world view' (p. 153), but somehow transform our own inner spiritual condition by 'letting things be rather than aiming willfully to transform them or subject them to our purposes', thereby achieving 'a new relationship with our natural environment, with the earth and other living things', inspiration here being drawn from the later Heidegger's notion of 'Gelassenheit' (p. 182; see chapter 7 in this volume).

Such views are now so fashionable that any attempt to understand 'the Enlightenment' needs to bear them in mind. Whilst a totalizing[2] historical vision of this kind satisfies a need to locate ourselves in the entire sweep of history, it is difficult to reconcile with trends among historians of eighteenth-century thought. There is no space here to provide a full critique of such views but we will note three frequently made generalizations about the Enlightenment endorsed by Gray, which are questionable. First, it has long been almost a cliché to refer to the 'secularism' of the Enlightenment; Collingwood, for instance, wrote that 'by the Enlightenment, *Aufklärung*, is meant that endeavour, so characteristic of the early eighteenth century, to secularize every department of human life and thought. It was a revolt not only against the power of institutional religion, but against religion as such' (Collingwood, 1946, p. 76). But at most this is a half-truth: Certainly, some leading French *philosophes* were atheistic materialists (e.g., D'Holbach; see Buckley, 1987) and the 'Deism' of many others not easy to distinguish from it: Condorcet's hostility to Christianity is evident in 2.B.1. But in England, where the Enlightenment can be said to have first got underway, atheists are hard to find (see Berman, 1990). 'Deists' were often accused of crypto-atheism by their contemporaries but their minimalist rationalistic theism was for the most part genuine. God played an indispensable role in Locke's ethico-political thought which so strongly influenced American Revolutionary ideology (especially through its impact on Jefferson), and Newton, Shaftesbury, Berkeley, Butler, Hutcheson and Reid were among many other British thinkers whose thinking had an important religious

2 Totalizing despite the fact that it is part of Gray's thesis that the human mind is incapable of producing 'unifying world views' on this scale.

ingredient. Hume was anti-religious, but the dogmatic atheism of some of the French philosophes was not to his taste. His position is best described as 'agnostic'. The German Enlightenment was characterized by a pervasive if unorthodox religiosity, developing towards the end of the century into a fairly widespread pantheism or panentheism. We have already noted the role of God in Kant's ethics. Only by taking the French Enlightenment to be normative for Enlightenment in general could Peter Gay characterize it as 'the rise of modern paganism' (the subtitle of volume 1 of Gay, 1966), and declare that 'the Enlightenment' regarded its humanism as 'wholly incompatible' (p. 256) with Christianity.

Secondly, the Enlightenment is often held to be characterized by optimism about the future of mankind related to activist, and indeed revolutionary political liberalism: 'the men of the Enlightenment had no doubts about their political aims. With few hesitations and only marginal disagreements, they called for a social and political order that would be secular, reasonable, human, pacific, open and free . . . with the same spirit and the same program' (Gay, 1969, p. 397). Condorcet (2.B.III) is evidence that there is some truth in this. Yet Rousseau had first become famous by arguing that the advances of civilization had produced moral decline, and there is very little optimism in Hume's assessment of the human condition; his *History of England* does sustain the thesis that very slow social amelioration has occurred in England directly connected with the increasing power of the commercial middle classes, but he nowhere indicates a belief that this is necessarily irreversible, and in many places reveals a conviction that only a relatively small élite will ever achieve intellectual enlightenment. In fact Hume was more inclined towards the cyclical view of history we find among thinkers of the ancient world than the progressivism which Condorcet expresses (see section 2.A.III). He was moreover no political liberal: one looks in vain for a doctrine of universal human rights in him, whilst Kant in 1793 wrote that 'all resistance against the supreme legislative power, all incitement of the subjects to violent expressions of discontent, all defiance which breaks out into rebellion, is the greatest and most publishable crime in a commonwealth, for it destroys its very foundations', with 'counter-resistance' even against a tyrant condemned (Kant, 1991, p. 81). He endorses the notion of human progress but only with many provisos, including the fact that it must not be '*from the bottom* upwards, but *from the top downwards*' (p. 188). He was far from optimistic about the human moral condition, explicitly endorsing a secular doctrine of the Fall or 'radical evil' (see Kant, 1999).

Thirdly, there is the charge that the Enlightenment promoted a uniform view of human nature and ignored cultural difference. Again, one could quote Collingwood as well as Gray. Each of the three thinkers excerpted in this chapter provides some supporting evidence for this notion. The historicists of chapter 3 who certainly stress the differences between, and the irreducible individuality of, persons, epochs, and nations (e.g., 3.A.I and II) are sometimes labelled 'Counter-Enlightenment' in line with this assumption. But in the next chapter we shall maintain that in fact there was rather more continuity between Enlightenment thinking and the historicists than this label suggests. Vyverberg (1989) in particular emphasizes that leading Enlightenment thinkers were far more ready to interest themselves in the moral and cultural diversity of humanity than has often been recognized. The discussion of Hume below illustrates this.

A recent study points out that in the last twenty years the view of the period as '*the* Enlightenment' if this means a 'relatively homogeneous . . . unitary phenomenon in the history of ideas' has been abandoned by historians, and that there is now little 'real interest in defining the Enlightenment in terms of a coherent intellectual programme' (Outram, p. 3). The confidence with which Gay could write in his opening words that 'there were many philosophes in the eighteenth century, but there was only one Enlightenment . . . The men of the Enlightenment united on a vastly ambitious program, a program of secularism, humanity, cosmopolitanism, and freedom' (Gay, 1966, pp. 3–4) must be challenged. Even the term 'the Enlightenment' is frequently questioned today. Kant and other contemporaries wrote of 'Enlightenment' as a process which takes place in individuals, and wrote of an 'Age of Enlightenment' not an 'Age of *the* Enlightenment': "If it . . . be asked whether we at present live in an *enlightened age*, the answer is: No, but we do live in an *age of enlightenment*. But we do have distinct indications . . . that the obstacles to universal enlightenment, to man's emergence from his self-incurred immaturity are gradually becoming fewer. In this respect our age is the age of enlightenment, the century of *Frederick*' (Kant, 1991, p. 58).

The three authors selected here are certainly not representative of Enlightenment thinking as a whole about history: Voltaire (the inventor of the term 'philosophy of history', Montesquieu (perhaps the first to stress the role of reference to 'general laws' in historical explanation; see Carrithers, 1986), and several figures from the Scottish Enlightenment (for instance Smith, Ferguson, or Millar) would deserve inclusion in a fuller treatment, but the three figures excerpted here are especially significant in contrasting ways. The central notions of the first two philosophers selected have already been discussed at some length in chapter 1 and our discussion of them here can be relatively brief.

David Hume (1711–1776) produced a six-volume *History of England* (1754–1762), which remained unrivalled for a century. Not surprisingly, his philosophical works, though completed before he took up sustained activity as a historian (which brought him the fame for which he longed, and which his philosophy had not granted him) contain lengthier reflections on historical method than can be found in any earlier philosopher. Sections 2.A.I and 2.A.II are his best-known contributions. Sections 2.A.I expresses what is often regarded as the pervasive Enlightenment assumption of the uniformity of mankind: as Collingwood scornfully expressed it, the thesis that 'human nature had existed ever since the creation of the world exactly as it existed among themselves . . . conceived substantialistically as something static and permanent, an unvarying substratum underlying the course of historical changes and human activities . . . Hume never shows the slightest suspicion that the human nature he is analysing . . . is the nature of a western European in the early eighteenth century' (Collingwood, 1946, 82–3). Certainly, his uniformitarianism means that his account of the purpose of history is identical to that of Classical or Renaissance historians; he declares history's chief use is to 'discover the constant and universal principles of human nature' in order to 'instruct us in the principles of human nature and regulate our future conduct' (2.A.I). The first thing to note about section 2.A.I. is that although the uniformity thesis is several times expressed as if it were a fact inferred from history, it in fact operates as an *a priori* presupposition of historical investigation. Hume will simply not allow that human behaviour, whatever superficial appearances might suggest to the contrary, can be anything other than ultimately uniform. This is why the historian must ultimately *discount* reports of human behaviour widely different from that which he had experienced. The particular reason why Hume believes this will become apparent on reading 2.A.II. The problem is that it forces the historian to commit the cardinal sin of anachronism, that is, of assuming that the past must be like the present. Hume however, even in this passage, far from 'never entertaining the slightest suspicion', as Collingwood puts it, of variations in human nature, concedes that one must 'make allowance for diversity' although without specifying any *rule* allowing one to abandon the presumption of uniformity for the recognition of diversity, despite the rhetoric of rigorous precision which pervades the passage. He tries to remain consistent by arguing that any diversity can be explained by the operation of the ultimately *uniform* principles of 'custom and education' but this leaves him in the, surely, very awkward position of maintaining that human beings are 'uniformly' non-uniform. As he himself rather startlingly puts it, 'we know, in general, that the characters of men are to a certain degree inconstant and irregular. This is, in a manner, the constant character of human nature . . .' (Hume, 1902, p. 88). Historicists such as Herder would consider that this unpredictable proliferation of diversity in human nature renders talk of 'uniformity' in relation to human actions beside the point.

It is clear, however, that Hume was troubled by the recognition that the facts of history fundamentally challenged his uniformitarian assumptions, which, flow, of course, from the doctrine of causality, which we have already explored in 1.IV. He returns to the question, as if aware of the inadequacy his earlier treatment, in a 'Dialogue' added to the end of the second *Enquiry* in which he acknowledges that the ancient Greeks differed in many aspects of their behaviour – incest, infanticide, homosexuality, suicide – from modern Frenchmen. Gay finds 'the germs of historicism' (Gay, 1969, p. 381) in these views. But Hume here still explains them on the basis that 'fashion, vogue, custom, and law are the chief foundation all moral determinations' as if this reconciled the facts with uniformitarianism. Ultimately we should regard them as flowing from constants in human nature: 'The Rhine flows north, the Rhone south; yet both spring from the same mountain, and are also actuated, in their opposite directions, by the *same* principle of gravity. The different inclinations of the ground, on which they run, cause all the difference of their courses' (Hume, 1902, p. 333). He then offers, as proof of such constants the fact that in all cultures 'good sense, knowledge, wit, eloquence, humanity, fidelity, truth, justice, courage, temperance, constancy, dignity of mind' (p. 334) are prized as virtues, although towards the end of the Dialogue he acknowledges that even these can be undermined in '*artificial* lives and manners' (p. 341) by which he means the unhealthy influence of religion.

But in several essays another Hume emerges fully justifying Gay's perception of his 'historicist sentiments' and his 'capacity to appreciate historical individuality' (Gay, 1969, pp. 381–2[3]) because in them, off his philosophical guard as it were, he makes assertions quite at odds with his uniformitarianism. Thus in *Of Civil Liberty* (1741) he argues that 'the world is too young to fix many general truths in politics. We have not yet had experience of three thousand years . . . It is not fully known what degree of refinement, either in virtue or vice, human nature is susceptible of; nor what may be expected of mankind from any great evolution in their education, customs, and principles . . . Such mighty revolutions have happened in human affairs, and so many events

---

3 It is however, I believe, going far too far to describe Hume as 'the most genuinely historicist of philosophers and the most subtly and profoundly philosophical of historians' (Phillipson, 1989, p. 4).

have arisen contrary to the expectation of the ancients, that they are sufficient to beget the suspicion of still further changes' (Hume, 1987, pp. 87–8). Elsewhere he writes that history surprises by showing that 'the manner, customs, and opinions, of the same species [*are*] susceptible of such prodigious changes in different periods of time' (p. 97). The most astonishing essay in this regard, however, is *Of National Characters* (1748) which only limitations of space prevent us from reproducing here, in which Hume argues against Montesquieu's position that physical causes, i.e., geographical and climatic, determine differences in national character. In his polemical enthusiasm his commitment to uniformitarianism is quite forgotten, resulting in an essay which Herder was to applaud for the 'very vivid' way in which Hume had shown that 'every class, every way of life has its customs' (Herder, 1969, p. 76). It is 'moral causes', says Hume, which are clearly responsible for human differences, by which 'I mean all circumstances, which are fitted to work on the mind as motives or reason, and which render a peculiar set of manners habitual to us', the key factor of which is that 'the human mind is of a very imitative nature' such that it is not 'possible for any set of men to converse often together, without acquiring a similitude of manners', for we have a 'propensity . . . which makes us enter deeply into each other's sentiments, and causes like passions and inclinations to run, as it were, by contagion through the whole club or knot of companions' (Hume, 1987, p. 202) . It produces 'common or national character' especially where 'the same speech or language' is shared and this is reinforced when they 'unite in one political body' (p. 202–3). It alone can explain, and certainly not geographical factors, why 'upon crossing a river or passing a mountain, one finds a new set of manners' (p. 204). He also points out that ethnic minorities such as Jews and Armenians, and religious communities such as Jesuits, can develop and sustain their own separate manners even when spread among many nations (p. 205), and that different European nations with colonies side by side in the tropics retain essentially their varying national characteristics (p. 205), whilst despite this, different nations communicating through trade etc., mutually influence one another's manners (p. 206), and each generation within a nation transforms the national character that it inherits. For instance, the English exhibit now 'the most cool indifference with regard to religious matters, that is to be found in any nation of the world' whereas in the previous century they 'were inflamed with the most furious enthusiasm', and prior to that 'were sunk into the most abject superstition' (p. 207).

Section 2.A.II is perhaps the most notorious passage in Hume's philosophical works because it attacked the credibility of miracles stories in an age when the standard view was that the New Testament miracles stories, especially that of the resurrection of Jesus, were fully adequate proofs that Jesus was truly the Son of God because no one but the Creator could set aside the laws of nature involved. The argument is therefore no piece of disengaged abstract scholarship but an attack on the credibility of Christianity. It is also an attack upon the 'moral probability' judgement as discussed at the end of 1.I, attempting to show that when legitimate, such judgements are essentially *mathematical*. The argument begins by suggesting that dependence on the testimony of others is always a matter of coming to a conclusion concerning the probable veracity of the witnesses, but note that he insists that such judgements are always based on the *number* of previously observed instances of the types of testimony in question. But in addition to this factor he suggests (as had Arnauld, Locke and others before him) that we must also assess what might be called the 'intrinsic credibility' of the event itself.

That is, if the alleged event is highly unlikely in terms of our own previous experience of the world, then even what we would regard as normally reliable testimony might still leave us legitimately sceptical. Hume's key move is then to point out that since a miracle 'is a violation of the laws of nature, and as a firm and unalterable experience has established these laws, the proof against a miracle, from the nature of the fact', i.e., its intrinsic credibility, 'is as entire as any argument from experience can possibly be established'. The quality of the testimony would have to be extremely high to overcome therefore the scepticism which the event itself would demand from reasonable men. But, he implies, human testimony is never of such a high quality because our experience is that all testimony is fallible; the testimony itself would have to be miraculously strong before we could believe a miracle story.

Contemporary critics responded (see Burns, 1981), first, that Hume presupposed an entirely fanciful capacity in the human mind to *quantify* probability judgements, which are irreducibly qualitative (see 1.I). Secondly, natural scientists frequently have no difficulty accepting reports of extremely rare phenomena which would be incredible on Hume's account. Thirdly, the crucial factor in rendering miracles credible is that the entire context (e.g., being performed by Jesus who taught a sublime moral message, showed personal integrity in his life, etc.) indicates divine providence at work. Hume responded by producing supplementary arguments and additional comments not reproduced here in which he maintained that a religious context of any kind only decreases still further the credibility of an account because, for example, religious fanaticism tends to render human beings highly biased and credulous.

Note that the argument depends upon the assumption that the *only* reason for believing any reports of others is that we have in the past observed frequent if not constant connection between testimony and the truth of the reported fact. This assumption ultimately depends on Hume's phenomenalism (see 1.IV) according to which in the last analysis all forms of scientific knowledge must be reducible to regularities between sense impressions experienced privately within my mind. But if it is decided that phenomenalism is unsustainable because all human consciousness involves the use of public languages (see 1.IV) so that my capacity to be conscious even of my own inner states is dependent on my participation in a linguistic community, then I am never in a position to be *initially* sceptical of the reports of others. It would follow that initial scepticism as to the reliability of the testimony of others is unrealistic: it would not follow from this observation that one should be indiscriminately credulous of the reports of others, but starting out with an initial belief which is discounted only for special reasons, is likely to yield very different results, not only in the case of miracle stores but historical research generally, from starting out with a sceptical stance. The question of how much reliability to place on sources is one which the historical researcher faces constantly, and there is no calculating device available which could relieve him or her of the need to make a personal overall assessment of it in each particular instance in the last analysis.

Section 2.A.III shows how far Hume was from endorsing the alleged standard Enlightenment belief in universal human progress: entirely consistently with uniformitarianism, he suggests that in different peoples there is progress, decline, revival at different times. The implication is that all such movements would be cyclical exactly as was the usual belief in classical Greece and Rome. The remarks about the 'mortality of the fabric of the world' do not imply total cosmic annihilation but rather the ancient idea of the periodical destruction of the cosmos in a great conflagration from which it will emerge again, in a cycle of eternal recurrence, particularly associated with the Stoics, but found much more widely (e.g., Plato *Statesman* 270–274) and sometimes taken to imply that every possible combination of events must have occurred and will occur on an infinity of occasions. Hume's speculations are tentative but it should be noted that he pays not the slightest account to the 'linear' view of history from Creation to the Last Judgement which had replaced the cyclical view of time to which Hume returns in what should certainly be seen as an instance of revived paganism .

The Marquis de Condorcet (1743–1794) achieved renown as a mathematician at a very early age, specializing in the calculus of probability, consciously elaborating Hume's stress just noted (Baker, 1975, p. 187), and being particularly associated with Turgot, the political economist. In 1776, at the age of 32, he became permanent secretary to the French Academy of Sciences. He became active as a radical in politics in the 1780s, and after the Revolution, became a leading member of the Legislative Assembly, being especially concerned to realize major educational reforms. Between 1793 and shortly before his death he wrote his *Sketch for a Historical Picture of the Progress of the Human Mind*. Here we find the classic expression of the Enlightenment 'grand narrative' maintaining that the human race is destined to experience unending political, moral and material progress as a result of intellectual progress, the French Revolution being the decisive event which guarantees the eventually triumph of enlightenment throughout the world. The naively enthusiastic but intelligent conviction with which it is written is moving, particularly in view of its having been composed while hiding from the Jacobins, and the fact that he was found dead in suspicious circumstances the day after his eventual discovery and arrest. It is frequently pointed out that this view of human progress constitutes a secular version of the Christian linear view of the shape of history which had supplanted the ancient Greek cyclical view (contrast 2.A.III and 5.C.VIII and 5.C.V), which had, for example, been expressed in Bossuet's (1627–1704) *Discourse on Universal History* (1681). According to Christianity the world was created by God at a particular point in time and is destined by God to achieve a consummation at the Last Judgement, which will ensure the complete triumph of good over evil, this victory having already been in principle achieved in the decisive redemptive event of the death and resurrection of Jesus. The equivalent event in Condorcet's Gospel is instead the French Revolution, depicted as an act of collective human self-redemption from evil, which evil flows from religious belief or 'superstition' in general and Christianity in particular (1.B.I) , the 'son of Mary' himself meriting only one indirect reference in the entire *Sketch*. Echoing Bossuet's eight epochs Condorcet divides history into ten stages, beginning with the first stage of primitive hunter-gatherers. The French Revolution constitutes the end of the ninth stage and the beginning of the tenth and final stage. From the start, one fundamental disease frustrated human progress to happiness: 'I refer to the separation of the human race into two parts; the one destined to teach the other made to believe. The one wishing to place itself above reason, the other humbly renouncing its own reason' (Condorcet, 1955, p. 17), that is, a fraudulent priestly caste substituted allegedly supernatural knowledge for true science. Human self-emancipation from this ignorance began in ancient Greece with the emergence of philosophy: 'the death of Socrates is an important event in human history. It was

the first crime which marked the beginning of the war between philosophy and superstition, a war which is till being waged among us between this same philosophy and
the oppressors of humanity' (p. 45). Considerable progress was, however, achieved in
the following centuries, but it was almost snuffed out by the triumph of Christianity,
most virulent of superstitions (2.B.I). The invention of printing, however, made the
ultimate triumph of rational thought inevitable, for the reason stated very clearly in
2.B.II. This provides the precondition for the ninth stage which was the period of
scientific enlightenment initiated by Bacon, Descartes and Galileo. Locke and Newton
accelerated this development but the 'superstition' and 'hypocrisy' of the English sty-
mied their contribution. But soon Enlightenment, as a triumphant revolutionary movement became the 'common faith' of the educated in 'every class of society' (2.B.III) in
every Western country. The tenth and final stage, which is already dawning, is one of
endless improvement for all mankind. Even death itself, mankind's last enemy, is as
good as conquered. In the social sphere Condorcet's 'calculus of probability' plays a
central role (2.B.IV).

With the wisdom of hindsight the weaknesses of Condorcet's account are glaring.
First, as Comte among others was to complain, the stages, apart from the first two, and
those subsequent to the invention of printing, do not emerge *causally* out of one
another, and they are often not sharply distinguishable. Rather, the ten-fold schema is
arbitrary, perhaps echoing the revolutionary project of decimalization. Secondly, the
entire argument presupposes that humanity's thirst for rational truth is so overwhelming that access to a mass medium guarantees universal enlightenment; there is no
inkling that a 'culture industry' might develop in which books and other media merely
provide escapist 'entertainment'. Thirdly, the degree to which educated Europeans
were united in a secular 'common faith' in the decades before the Revolution is much
exaggerated. Fourthly, that the 'calculus of probability' would be a panacea for most
social and scientific problems has not been vindicated by subsequent experience despite its proven utility in some fields. Finally, the assumption that scientific education
will lead to moral advance seems to have been repeatedly falsified, perhaps most obviously by the Holocaust, but also by the Terror which eliminated Condorcet himself.

It might seem strange that a man who denied the ultimate reality of time (1.V),
could take the historical process seriously, but **Immanuel Kant** (1724–1804) did
repeatedly turn his attention to historical issues. Section 2.C.I is the opening paragraph of Kant's essay '*What is Enlightenment?*' which was his contribution to a controversy which had broken out in the *Berlinische Monatschrift* in 1783 concerning the
meaning of the word '*Aufklärung*', and is evidence both that the term was fashionable
in Germany at that time, and that there was uncertainty as to its implications.

Section 2.C.II reproduces most of his Kant's main contribution to philosophy of
history, which had appeared in the *Monatschrift* one month earlier. It begins by reiter-
ating his notion that as phenomenal human actions are causally determined (see 1.V)
but then suggests, with very questionable consistency, that empirically observable human actions *can* be regarded as 'free' but that it might be possible to discern some
overall, law-like natural trend in them statistically. He then enunciates nine propositions. The first adopts a maxim that goes back at least to Aristotle; namely, that any
capacities in creatures must be intended by nature to fulfil their function. This is questionable in terms of the doctrine of the first *Critique*, which excludes 'teleological'
considerations from scientific explanation, and is also less plausible after Darwin. The

second suggests that the attainment of perfection in man's rational capacities can only be expected in the historical development of the species as a whole, which already implies the conclusion Kant intends to prove, namely that 'Nature' has predestined mankind to reach perfection. The third declares that, while this includes moral perfection because man will 'make his own conduct worthy of life and well-being', earlier generations are destined merely to be means to the end of the perfection of later generations. Kant himself expresses some misgivings about this, thereby anticipating the objections of Herder and Ranke. The fourth and fifth propositions are especially significant in terms of their impact on Hegel. The concept of mankind's 'unsocial sociability' is possibly inspired by Adam Smith's claim that national economic prosperity emerges as an unintended consequence of the pursuit of individual self-interest, and thus providentially as if by a 'hidden hand'. The sixth has provoked, perhaps, the most hostile reaction of them all in its suggestion that political society inevitably involves the setting up of a 'master' who must use force to break the will of his subjects. The seventh and eighth propositions suggest that war-making will cease as mankind learns from its mistakes, and eventually a world federation will be established. The ninth proposition defends the legitimacy of these *a priori* speculations, i.e., 'philosophical history', whilst not denying the value of empirical history.

In the 1790s, possibly in reaction to the events in France, Kant becomes distinctly more pessimistic about the possibility of the moral amelioration of mankind, writing in 1793 of the ultimately inexplicable fact of man's 'radical evil' (Kant, 1999), a philosophical equivalent of the Christian doctrine of 'original sin', which had been contemptuously rejected by many Enlightenment figures such as Voltaire. The result is that in his *Perpetual Peace* (1795), while sticking to the claim that progress will occur in political institutions, he suggests that this means only that 'man even if he is not morally good in himself' will be 'nevertheless compelled to be a good citizen. As hard as it may sound, the problem of setting up a state can be solved even by a nation of devils (so long as they possess understanding),' for such a state 'does not involve the moral improvement of man' (Kant, 1970, pp. 112–13). Warfare will cease simply because 'the *spirit of commerce* sooner or later strikes hold of every people, and it cannot exist side by side with war' (p. 114). We must not be misled by 'the homage which every state pays (in words at least) to the concept of right', for whilst, in both private and public, men 'pay [*moral*] concepts all the honour they deserve', they 'devise a hundred excuses and subterfuges to get out of observing them in practice' (p. 121), so that we would still be left 'facing the evil principle and overcoming its wiles,' for it is 'deceitful, treacherous and liable to exploit the weakness of human nature' (p. 24). However, in 1798 in 'a renewed attempt' to tackle the question 'Is the Human Race Continually Improving?' he suggests that the answer can be found in a historical fact which 'proves the existence of a *tendency* within the human race as a *whole*' (p. 181) to such improvement. Surprisingly, in view of his earlier condemnation of rebellion, he points to the French Revolution. He claims that it can provide the basis for a 'theoretical' (p. 85) proof of moral progress, even though, with something approaching equivocation, he suggests it will not affect the 'inner' nature of man 'or transform his 'basic moral capacity' (p. 188).

Selected Texts

Edited by Robert M. Burns

2.A David Hume, 1711–1776

2.A.1 The Uniformity of Human Nature[1]

. . . It is universally acknowledged that there is a great uniformity among the actions of men, in all nations and ages, and that human nature remains still the same, in its principles and operations. The same motives always produce the same actions: The same events follow from the same causes. Ambition, avarice, self-love, vanity, friendship, generosity, public spirit: these passions, mixed in various degrees, and distributed through society, have been, from the beginning of the world, and still are, the source of all the actions and enterprises, which have ever been observed among mankind. Would you know the sentiments, inclinations, and course of life of the Greeks and Romans? Study well the temper and actions of the French and English: You cannot be much mistaken in transferring to the former *most* of the observations which you have made with regard to the latter. Mankind are so much the same, in all times and places, that history informs us of nothing new or strange in this particular. Its chief use is only to discover the constant and universal principles of human nature, by showing men in all varieties of circumstances and situations, and furnishing us with materials from which we may form our observations and become acquainted with the regular springs of human action and behaviour. These records of wars, intrigues, factions, and revolutions, are so many collections of experiments[2] by which the politician or moral philosopher fixes the principles of his science, in the same manner as the physician or natural philosopher becomes acquainted with the nature of plants, minerals, and other external objects, by the experiments which he forms concerning them. Nor are the earth, water, and other elements, examined by Aristotle, and Hippocrates, more like to those which at present lie under our observation than the men described by Polybius and Tacitus are to those who now govern the world.

Should a traveller, returning from a far country, bring us an account of men, wholly different from any with whom we were ever acquainted; men, who were entirely divested of avarice, ambition, or revenge; who knew no pleasure but friendship, gener-

---

1 From Hume, 1902, pp 83–6
2 Hume does not mean by 'experiment' a laboratory test, but an 'experience' observed in the ordinary course of life. [RMB]

osity, and public spirit; we should immediately, from these circumstances, detect the falsehood, and prove him a liar, with the same certainty as if he had stuffed his narration with stories of centaurs and dragons, miracles and prodigies. And if we would explode any forgery in history, we cannot make use of a more convincing argument, than to prove, that the actions ascribed to any person are directly contrary to the course of nature, and that no human motives, in such circumstances, could ever induce him to such a conduct. The veracity of Quintus Curtius is as much to be suspected, when he describes the supernatural courage of Alexander, by which he was hurried on singly to attack multitudes, as when he describes his supernatural force and activity, by which he was able to resist them. So readily and universally do we acknowledge a uniformity in human motives and actions as well as in the operations of body.

Hence likewise the benefit of that experience, acquired by long life and a variety of business and company, in order to instruct us in the principles of human nature, and regulate our future conduct, as well as speculation. By means of this guide,we mount up to the knowledge of men's inclinations and motives, from their actions, expressions, and even gestures; and again descend to the interpretation of their actions from our knowledge of their motives and inclinations. The general observations treasured up by a course of experience, give us the clue of human nature, and teach us to unravel all its intricacies. Pretexts and appearances no longer deceive us. Public declarations pass for the specious colouring of a cause. And though virtue and honour be allowed their proper weight and authority, that perfect disinterestedness, so often pretended to, is never expected in multitudes and parties; seldom in their leaders; and scarcely even in individuals of any rank or station. But were there no uniformity in human actions, and were every experiment which we could form of this kind irregular and anomalous, it were impossible to collect any general observations concerning mankind; and no experience, however accurately digested by reflection, would ever serve to any purpose. Why is the aged husbandman more skilful in his calling than the young beginner but because there is a certain uniformity in the operation of the sun, rain, and earth towards the production of vegetables; and experience teaches the old practitioner the rules by which this operation is governed and directed?

We must not, however, expect that this uniformity of human actions should be carried to such a length as that all men, in the same circumstances, will always act precisely in the same manner, without making any allowance for the diversity of characters, prejudices, and opinions. Such a uniformity in every particular, is found in no part of nature. On the contrary, from observing the variety of conduct in different men, we are enabled to form a greater variety of maxims, which still suppose a degree of uniformity and regularity.

Are the manners of men different in different ages and countries? We learn thence the great force of custom and education, which mould the human mind from its infancy and form it into a fixed and established character. Is the behaviour and conduct of the one sex very unlike that of the other? Is it thence we become acquainted with the different characters which nature has impressed upon the sexes, and which she preserves with constancy and regularity. Are the actions of the same person much diversified in the different periods of his life, from infancy to old age? This affords room for many general observations concerning the gradual change of our sentiments and inclinations, and the different maxims which prevail in the different ages of human creatures. Even the characters, which are peculiar to each individual, have a uniformity in their influence; otherwise our acquaintance with the persons and our observation of their conduct could never teach us their dispositions, or serve to direct our behaviour with regard to them.

I grant it possible to find some actions, which seem to have no regular connexion with any known motives, and are exceptions to all the measures of conduct which have ever been established for the government of men. But if we would willingly know what judgement should be formed of such irregular and extraordinary actions, we may consider the sentiments commonly entertained with regard to those irregular events which appear in the course of nature, and the operations of external objects. All causes are not conjoined to their usual effects with like uniformity. An artificer, who handles only dead matter, may be disappointed of his aim, as well as the politician, who directs the conduct of sensible and intelligent agents.

2.A.II   Historical Method: The Case of Miracle Stories[2]

Though experience be our only guide in reasoning concerning matters of fact; it must be acknowledged, that this guide is not altogether infallible, but in some cases is apt to lead us into errors. One, who in our climate, should expect better weather in any week of June than in one of December, would reason justly, and conformably to experience; but it is certain, that he may happen, in the event, to find himself mistaken. However, we may observe, that, in such a case, he would have no cause to complain of experience; because it commonly informs us beforehand of the uncertainty, by that contrariety of events, which we may learn from a diligent observation. All effects follow not with like certainty from their supposed causes. Some events are found, in all, countries and all ages, to have been constantly conjoined together: Others are found to have been more variable, and sometimes to disappoint our expectations; so that, in our reasonings concerning matter of fact, there are all imaginable degrees of assurance, from the highest certainty to the lowest species of moral evidence.

A wise man, therefore, proportions his belief to the evidence. In such conclusions as are founded on an infallible experience, he expects the event with the last degree of assurance, and regards his past experience as a full *proof* of the future existence of that event. In other cases, he proceeds with more caution: He weighs the opposite experiments: He considers which side is supported by the greater number of experiments: to that side he inclines, with doubt and hesitation; and when at last he fixes his judgement, the evidence exceeds not what we properly call *probability*. All probability, then, supposes an opposition of experiments and observations, where the one side is found to overbalance the other, and to produce a degree of evidence, proportioned to the superiority. A hundred instances or experiments on one side, and fifty on another, afford a doubtful expectation of any event; though a hundred uniform experiments with only one that is contradictory, reasonably beget a pretty strong degree of assurance. In all cases, we must balance the opposite experiments, where they are opposite and deduct the smaller number from the greater, in order to know the exact force of the superior evidence.

3   Ibid., pp. 110–16, and p. 127.

To apply these principles to a particular instance; we may observe, that there is no species of reasoning more common, more useful, and even necessary to human life, than that which is derived from the testimony of men, and the reports of eye-witnesses and spectator. This species of reasoning, perhaps, one may deny to be founded on the relation of cause and effect. I shall not dispute about a word. It will be sufficient to observe that our assurance in any argument of this kind is derived from no other principle than our observation of the veracity of human testimony, and of the usual conformity of facts to the reports of witnesses. It being a general maxim, that no objects have any discoverable connexion together, and that all the inferences, which we can draw from one to another, are founded merely on our experience of their constant and regular conjunction; it is evident, that we ought not to make an exception to this maxim in favour of human testimony, whose connexion with any event seems, in itself, as little necessary as any other. Were not the memory tenacious to a certain degree, had not men commonly an inclination to truth and a principle of probity; were they not sensible to shame, when detected in a falsehood: Were not these, I say, discovered by *experience* to be qualities, inherent in human nature, we should never repose the least confidence in human testimony. A man delirious, or noted for falsehood and villainy, has no manner of authority with us.

And as the evidence, derived from witnesses and human testimony, is founded on past experience, so it varies with the experience, and is regarded either as a *proof* or a *probability*, according as the conjunction between any particular kind of report and any kind of object has been found to be constant or variable. There are a number of circumstances to be taken into consideration in all judgements of this kind; and the ultimate standard, by which we determine all disputes, that may arise concerning them, is always derived from experience and observation. Where this experience is not entirely uniform on any side, it is attended with an unavoidable contrariety in our judgements, and with the same opposition and mutual destruction of argument as in every other kind of evidence. We frequently hesitate concerning the reports of others. We balance the opposite circumstances, which cause any doubt or uncertainty; and when we discover a superiority on any side, we incline to it; but still with a diminution of assurance, in proportion to the force of its antagonist.

This contrariety of evidence, in the present case, may be derived from several different causes; from the opposition of contrary testimony; from the character or number of the witnesses; from the manner of their delivering their testimony; or from the union of all these circumstances. We entertain a suspicion concerning any matter of fact, when the witnesses contradict each other; when they are but few, or of a doubtful character; when they have an interest in what they affirm; when they deliver their testimony with hesitation, or on the contrary, with too violent asseverations. There are many other particulars of the same kind, which may diminish or destroy the force of any argument, derived from human testimony.

Suppose, for instance, that the fact, which the testimony endeavours to establish, partakes of the extraordinary and the marvellous; in that case, the evidence, resulting from the testimony, admits of a diminution, greater or less, in proportion as the fact is more or less unusual. The reason why we place any credit in witnesses and historians, is not derived from any *connexion*, which we perceive *a priori*, between testimony and reality, but because we are accustomed to find a conformity between them. But when the fact attested is such a one as has seldom fallen under our observation, here is a contest of two opposite experiences; of which the one destroys the other, as far as its force goes, and the superior can only operate on the mind by the force, which remains. The very same principle of experience, which gives us a certain degree of assurance in the testimony of witnesses, gives us also, in this case, another degree of assurance against the fact, which they endeavour to establish; from which contradiction there necessarily arises a counterpoise, and mutual destruction of belief and authority.

. . .

But in order to encrease the probability against the testimony of witnesses, let us suppose, that the fact, which they affirm, instead of being only marvellous, is really miraculous; and suppose also, that the testimony considered apart and in itself, amounts to an entire proof; in that case, there is proof against proof, of which the strongest must prevail, but still with a diminution of its force, in proportion to that of its antagonist.

A miracle is a violation of the laws of nature; and as a firm and unalterable experience has established these laws, the proof against a miracle, from the very nature of the fact, is as entire as any argument from experience can possibly be imagined. Why is it more than probable, that all men must die; that lead cannot, of itself, remain suspended in the air; that fire consumes wood, and is extinguished by water; unless it be, that these events are found agreeable, to the laws of nature, and there is required a violation of these laws, or in other words, a miracle to prevent them? Nothing is esteemed a miracle, if it ever happen in the common course of nature. It is no miracle that a man, seemingly in good health, should die on a sudden: because such a kind of death, though more unusual than any other, has yet been frequently observed to happen. But it is a miracle, that a dead man should come to life; because that has never been observed in any age or country. There must, therefore, be a uniform experience against every miraculous event, otherwise the event would not merit that appellation. And as a uniform experience amounts to a proof, there is here a direct and full *proof*, from the nature of the fact, against the existence of any miracle; nor can such a proof be destroyed, or the miracle rendered credible, but by an opposite proof, which is superior.[4]

The plain consequence is (and it is a general maxim worthy of our attention), That no testimony is sufficient to establish a miracle, unless the testimony be of such a kind, that its falsehood would be more miraculous, than the fact, which it endeavours to establish; and even in that case there is a mutual destruction of arguments, and the superior only gives us an assurance suitable to that degree of force, which remains after deducting the inferior. When anyone tells me, that he saw a dead man restored to life, I immediately consider with myself, whether it be more probable, that this person should either deceive or be deceived, or that the fact, which he relates, should really have happened. I weigh the one miracle against the other; and according to the superiority, which I discover, I pronounce my decision, and always reject the greater miracle. If the falsehood of his testimony would be more miraculous, than the event which he relates; then, and not till then, can he pretend to command my belief or opinion.

. . .

Upon the whole, then, it appears, that no testimony for any kind of miracle has ever

4   Footnote omitted.

amounted to a probability, much less to a proof, and that, even supposing it amounted to a proof, it would be opposed by another proof, derived from the very nature of the fact, which it would endeavour to establish. It is experience only, which gives authority to human testimony; and it is the same experience, which assures us of the laws of nature. When, therefore, these two kinds of experience are contrary, we have nothing to do but subtract the one from the other, and embrace an opinion, either on one side or the other, with that assurance which arises from the remainder. But according to the principle here explained, this subtraction, with regard to all popular religions, amounts to an entire annihilation; and therefore we may establish it as a maxim, that no human testimony can have such force as to prove a miracle, and make it a just foundation for any such system of religion.

2.A.III   The Overall Shape of History[5]

There is very little ground, either from reason or observation, to conclude the world eternal or incorruptible. The continual and rapid motion of matter, the violent revolutions with which every part is agitated, the changes remarked in the heavens, the plain traces as well as tradition of an universal deluge, or general convulsion of the elements; all these prove strongly the mortality of this fabric of the world, and its passage, by corruption or dissolution, from one state or order to another. It must therefore, as well as each individual form which it contains, have its infancy, youth, manhood, and old age; and it is probable, that, in all these variations, man, equally with every animal and vegetable, will partake. In the flourishing age of the world, it may be expected, that the human species should possess greater vigour both of mind and body, more prosperous health, higher spirits, longer life, and a stronger inclination and power of generation. But if the general system of things, and human society of course, have any such gradual revolutions, they are too slow to be discernible in that short period which is comprehended by history and tradition. Stature and force of body, length of life, even courage and extent of genius, seem hitherto to have been naturally, in all ages, pretty much the same. The arts and sciences, indeed, have flourished in one period, and have decayed in another: But we may observe, that, at the time when they rose to greatest perfection among one people, they were perhaps totally unknown to all the neighbouring nations; and though they universally decayed in one age, yet in a succeeding generation they again revived, and diffused themselves over the world. As far, therefore, as observation reaches, there is no universal difference discernible in the human species; and though it were allowed, that the universe, like an animal body, had a natural progress from infancy to old age; yet as it must still be uncertain, whether, at present, it be advancing to its point of perfection, or declining from it, we cannot thence presuppose any decay in human nature . . .

---

5   From 'Of the Populousness of Ancient Nations', in Hume 1987 (pp. 377–464), pp. 377–378.

2.B   Condorcet, Marquis de (Marie-Jean-Antoine-Nicholas Caritat), 1743–1794

2.B.I   Christianity: Enemy of Enlightenment[6]

One of the advantages of the propagation of Greek philosophy had been the destruction of the belief in popular divinities in all classes that had received any education. A vague theism, or the pure mechanism of Epicurus, was, even in Cicero's day, the ordinary belief of anyone who had cultivated his mind and of all those who directed public affairs . . .

The people of conquered nations, the misfortuned, and men of a wretched and inflamed imagination chose to attach themselves to priestly religions because the priests who controlled them, in their own interest breathed into them a belief in equality even in slavery, in the renunciation of worldly goods and in the existence of heavenly rewards for the blindly submissive, for the suffering, for those who had voluntarily humiliated themselves or endured humiliation patiently: a doctrine so seductive in the eyes of oppressed humanity! . . .

As the [*Roman*] empire weakened, the faster was the progress of [*the*] Christian religion. The degeneracy of the ancient conquerors of the world spread to their gods, who, having presided over their victories, were now merely the impotent witnesses of their defeats. The spirit of the new sect was better suited to an age of decadence and misery . . . Soon Christianity became a powerful force . . .

Disdain for the humane sciences was one of the first characteristics of Christianity. It had to avenge itself against the outrages of philosophy, and it feared that spirit of doubt and inquiry, that confidence in one's own reason which is the bane of all religious belief. The natural sciences were odious and suspect, for they are very dangerous to the success of miracles, and there is no religion that does not force its devotees to swallow a few physical absurdities. So the triumph of Christianity was the signal for the compete decadence of philosophy and the sciences.

2.B.II   Creation of World Public Opinion through Printing[7]

With printing the copies of any book can be multiplied indefinitely at little cost. Since its invention, its had been possible for anyone who could read to obtain any book that he wanted or needed; and this which made reading easier in turn increased the will to learn and the means of instruction.

. . .

. . . What formerly only a few individuals had been able to read, could now be read by a whole nation and could reach almost at the same moment everyone who understood the same language.

6   From Condorcet 1955, pp. 70–2.
7   Ibid., pp. 100–2.

Men found themselves possessed of the means of communicating with people all over the world . . . The public opinion that was formed in the way was powerful by virtue of its size, and effective because the forces that created it operated with equal strength on all men at the same time, no matter what distances separated them. In a word we now have a tribunal, independent of all human coercion, which favours reason and justice, a tribunal whose scrutiny it is difficult to elude, and whose verdict it is impossible to evade.

. . .

Any new mistake is criticized as soon as it is made, and often attacked even before it has been propagated; and so it has no time to take root in men's minds . . .

. . .

Has not printing freed the education of the people from all political and religious shackles? . . . The instruction that every man is free to receive from books in silence and solitude can never be completely corrupted. It is enough for there to exist one corner of free earth from which the press can scatter its leaves. How with the multitude of different books, with innumerable copies of each book, of reprints which can be made at a moment's notice, how could it be possible to bolt every door, to seal every crevice through which truth aspires to enter? . . .

2.B.III   Enlightenment and Revolution[8]

The sketch of the progress of philosophy and the dissemination of enlightenment, whose more general and more evident effect we have already examined brings us to the stage where the influence of progress upon public opinion, of public opinion upon nations or their leaders, suddenly ceases to be a slow, imperceptible affair, and produces a revolution in the whole order of several nations, a certain earnest of the revolution that must one day include in its scope the whole of the human race.

After long periods of error, after being lead astray by vague or incomplete theories, publicists have at last discovered the true rights of man and how they can all be deduced from the single truth, that *man is a sentient being, capable of reasoning and of acquiring moral ideas.*

They have seen that the maintenance of these rights was the sole object of men's coming together in political societies, and that the social art is the art of guaranteeing the preservation of these rights and their distribution in the most equal fashion over the largest areas . . .

. . . In the face of such principles, we see the disappearance of the belief in the existence of a contract between the people and the lawgivers, which can be annulled only by mutual consent or by the defection of the parties; and along with it there disappeared the less servile but no less absurd opinion according to which a nation was for ever chained to its constitution once this constitution had been established – as though the right to change it were not the guarantee of every other right . . .

. . .

Thus an understanding of the natural rights of man, the belief that these rights are

Ibid., pp. 127–47 and 168–9.

inalienable and indefeasible, a strongly expressed desire for liberty of thought and letters, of trade and industry, and for the alleviation of the people's suffering, for the proscription of all penal laws against religious dissenters and the abolition of torture and barbarous punishment, the desire for a milder system of criminal legislation . . . and for a simpler civil code . . . a hatred of hypocrisy and fanaticism, a contempt for prejudice, zeal for the propagation of enlightenment; all these principles gradually filtering down from philosophical works to every class of society whose education went beyond the catechism and the alphabet, became the common faith, the badges of all who were neither Machiavellians nor fools. . . .

. . .

. . . But the British government affected to believe that God had created America, as it had created Asia, for the pleasure of the inhabitants of London . . . It therefore ordered the compliant representatives of the English people to violate the rights of America, and to impose taxation on her without asking her consent. America proclaimed that this injustice released her from the obligations binding here to England, and she declared her independence.

. . . We see then for the first time, a great people deliver from all its chains, giving itself in peace the laws and the constitution what it believe most likely to bring it happiness. . . .

. . .

The American revolution . . . was about to spread to Europe; and if there existed a country where sympathy with the American cause had diffused more widely than elsewhere its writings and its principles, a country that was at once the most enlightened and the most enslaved of lands, a country that possessed at the same time the most enlightened philosophers and the most crassly and insolently ignorant government, a country whose laws were so far below the level of public intelligence that not even patriotism or prejudice could attach the people to its ancient institutions, was not this country destined by the very nature of things to start that revolution which the friend of humanity awaited with such impatience and such high hopes? It was inevitable, then, that the revolution should begin in France.

The maladroitness of her government precipitated it, her philosophers guided its principles and the power of her people destroyed the obstacles which might have stood in its way.

The revolution in France was more far-reaching than that in America and therefore more violent: for the Americans, who were content with the civil and criminal code that they had received from England; who had no vicious system of taxation to reform and no feudal tyrannies, no hereditary distinctions, not rich, powerful and privileged corporations, no systems of religious intolerance to destroy, limited themselves to establishing an authority in place of that which had been exercised up until then by the British. None of these innovations affected the ordinary people or changed the relations between individuals. In France, on the contrary, the revolution was to embrace the entire economy of society, change every social relation and find its way to the furthest links of the political chain . . .

. . .

We shall show in what ways the principles from which the constitution and laws of France were derived were purer, more precise and, more profound than those that guided the Americans; how they more successfully escaped every kind of prejudice how the equality of rights was nowhere replaced by the identity of interest, which is only a feeble and hypocritical substitute . . .

. . .

. . . The principles of philosophy, the slogans of liberty, the recognition of the true rights of man and his real interests, have spread through far too great a number of nations, and now direct in each of them the opinions of far too great a number of enlightened men, for us to fear that they will ever be allowed to relapse into oblivion. And indeed what reason could we have for fear, when we consider that the languages most widely spoken are the languages of the two peoples who enjoy liberty to the fullest extent and who best understand its principles, and that no league of tyrants, no political intrigues, could prevent the resolute defence, in these two languages, of the rights of reason and liberty?

2.B.IV   The Future[9]

Survey the history of our settlements and commercial undertakings in Africa or Asia, and you will see how our trade monopolies, our treachery, our murderous contempt for men of another colour or creed, the insolence of our usurpations, the intrigues or the exaggerated proselytic zeal of our priests, have destroyed the respect and goodwill that the superiority of our knowledge and the benefits of our commerce at first won for us in the eyes of the inhabitants. But doubtless the moment approaches when, no longer presenting ourselves as always either tyrants or corrupters, we shall become for them the beneficent instruments of their freedom.

. . .

The time will come when the sun will shine only on free men who know no other master but their reason; when tyrants and slaves, priests and their stupid or hypocritical instruments will exist only in works of history or on the stage . . .

. . .

It is easy to prove that wealth has a natural tendency to equality and that any excessive disproportion could not exist or at least would rapidly disappear if civil laws did not provide artificial ways of perpetuating and uniting fortunes; if free trade and industry were allowed to remove the advantages that accrued wealth derives from any restrictive law or fiscal privilege. . . .

We shall point out how it can be in great part eradicated by guaranteeing people in old age a means of livelihood produced partly by their own saving and partly by the saving of others who makes the same outlay, but who die before they need to reap the reward . . . It is to the application of the calculus to the probabilities of life and the investment of money that we owe the ideas of these methods which have already been successful, although they have not been applied in a sufficiently comprehensive and exhaustive fashion to render them really useful, not merely to a few individuals, but to society as a whole . . .

. . .

. . . By a suitable choice of syllabus and methods of education, we can teach the citizen everything that he needs to know in order to be able to manage his household,

Ibid., pp. 175–200.

administer his affairs and employ his labour and his faculties in freedom; to know his rights and to be able to exercise them; to be acquainted with his duties and fulfil them satisfactorily . . . [*and*] not to be in a state of blind dependence upon those to whom he must entrust his affairs or the exercise of his rights; to be in a proper condition to choose and supervise them . . .

. . .

These various causes of equality do not act in isolation; they unite, combine and support each other and so their cumulative effects are stronger, surer, and more constant. With greater equality of education there will be greater equality in industry and so in wealth; equality in wealth leads necessarily to equality in education; and equality between the nations and equality with a single nation are mutually dependant.

. . .

. . . At present even in the most enlightened countries scarcely one in fifty of the people who have natural talents, receives the necessary education to develop them; and how, if this were done there would be a proportionate increase in the number of men destined by their discoveries to extend the boundaries of science . . .

. . . This equality in education and the equality which will come about between the different nations would accelerate the advance of those sciences whose progress depends on repeated observations over a large area . . .

. . . New instruments, machines and looms can add to man's strength and can improve at once the quality and accuracy of his productions, and can diminish the time and labour that has to be expended on them . . .

A very small amount of ground will be able to produce a great quantity of supplies of greater utility or higher quality; more goods will be obtained for a smaller outlay the manufacture of articles will be achieved with less wastage in raw materials and will make better use of them. . . .

. . .

With all this process in industry and welfare . . . might there not . . . come a moment when these necessary laws begin to work in an opposite direction; when, the number of people in the world finally exceeding the mans of subsistence, there will in consequence ensue a continual diminution of happiness and population, a true retrogression, or at best an oscillation between good and bad? . . .

. . .

But even if we agree that the limit will one day arrive, nothing follows from it that is in the least alarming as far as either the happiness of the human race or its indefinite perfectibility is concerned; if we consider that, before all this comes to pass the progress of reason will have kept pace with that of the sciences, and that the absurd prejudice of superstition will have ceased to corrupt and degrade the moral code by its harsh doctrine instead of purifying and elevating it, we can assume that by them man will know that, if they have a duty towards those who are not yet born, that duty is not to give them existence, but to give them happiness; their aim should be to promote the general welfare of the human race . . . rather than foolishly to encumber the world with useless and wretched beings . . .

. . .

. . . Among the causes of the progress of the human mind that are of the utmost importance to the general happiness, we must number the compete annihilation of the prejudices that have brought about an inequality of rights between the sexes, an in equality fatal even to the party in which favour it works. It is vain for us to look for a justification of this principle in and differences of physical organisation, intellect or moral sensibility between men and women. . . .

Once people are enlightened they will know that they have the right to dispose of their own life and wealth as they chose; they will gradually learn to regard war as the most dreadful of scourges, the most terrible of crimes. . . .

Nations will learn that they cannot conquer other nations without losing their own liberty; that permanent confederations are their only means of preserving their independence; and that they should seek not power but security. Gradually mercantile prejudices will fade away . . . When at last the nations come to agree on the principles of politic and morality, when in their own better interests, they invite foreigners to share equally in all the benefits men enjoy either through the bounty of nature or by their own industry, then all the causes that produce and perpetuate national animosities and poison national relations will disappear one by one; and nothing will remain to encourage or even to arouse the fury of war.

. . .

. . . A universal language is that which expresses by signs either real objects themselves, or well-defined collections composed of simple and general ideas, which are found to be the same or may arise in a similar form in the minds of all men, or the general relations holding between these ideas, the operations of the human mind, or the operations peculiar to the individual sciences, or the procedures of the arts. So people who become acquainted with the signs . . . will be able to read it as easily as their own language. . . .

We shall show that the language, ever improving and broadening its scope all the while, would be the means of giving to every subject embraced by the human intelligence, a precision and rigour that would make knowledge of the truth easy, and error almost impossible . . .

. . .

. . . As the two most virulent causes of deterioration, misery and excessive wealth, are eliminated, the average length of human life will be increased and a better health and a stronger physical constitution will be ensured. The improvement of medical practice, . . . will mean the end of infectious and hereditary diseases and illness brought on by climate, food, or working conditions . . . Would it be absurd to suppose that the perfection of the human species might be capable of indefinite progress; that the day will come when death will be due only to extraordinary accidents or to the decay of the vital forces, and that ultimately the average span between birth and decay will have no assignable value? Certainly man will not become immortal, but will not the interval between the first breath that he draws and the time when in the natural course of events, without disease or accident, he expires, increase indefinitely . . . [*Until the*] average span of life . . . reaches a length greater than any detrimental quality we may assign to it as its limit? . . .

2.C   Immanuel Kant, 1724–1804

2.C.I   What is Enlightenment?[10]

Enlightenment is man's emergence from his self-incurred immaturity. Immaturity is the inability to use one's own understanding without the guidance of another. This immaturity is *self-incurred* if its cause is not lack of understanding, but lack of resolution and courage to use it without the guidance of another. The motto of enlightenment is therefore: *Sapere aude!* Have courage to use your *own* understanding.

2.C.II   Progress in History[11]

Whatever conception of the freedom of the will one may form in terms of metaphysics, the will's manifestations in the world of phenomena, i.e. human actions, are determined in accordance with natural laws, as is every other natural event. History is concerned with giving an account of these phenomena, no matter how deeply concealed their causes may be, and it allows us to hope that, if it examines the free exercise of the human will *on a large scale*, it will be able to discover a regular progression among freely willed actions. In the same way, we may hope that what strikes us in the actions of individuals as confused and fortuitous may be recognised, in the history of the entire species, as a steadily advancing but slow development of man's original capacities. Thus marriages, births, and deaths do not seem to be subject to any rule by which their numbers could be calculated in advance, since the free human will has such a great influence upon them; and yet the annual statistics for them in large countries prove that they are just as subject to constant natural laws as are the changes in the weather . . . Individual men and even entire nations little imagine that, while they are pursuing their own ends, each in his own way and often in opposition to others, they are unwittingly guided in their advance along a course intended by nature. They are unconsciously promoting an end which, even if they knew what it was, would scarcely arouse their interest.

. . . The only way out for the philosopher, since he cannot assume that mankind follows any rational *purpose of its own* in its collective actions, is for him to attempt to discover a *purpose in nature* behind this senseless course of human events, and decide whether it is after all possible to formulate in terms of a definite plan of nature a history of creatures who act without a plan of their own. Let us now see if we can succeed in finding a guiding principle for such a history. . . .

10   The opening paragraph of 'An Answer to the Question "What is Enlightenment?" ' (1784 translated in Kant, 1991, p. 54.
11   From 'Idea for a Universal History with a Cosmopolitan Purpose', 1784, translated in Kant 1991. pp. 41–51.

First Proposition

All the natural capacities of a creature are destined sooner or later to be developed completely and in conformity with their end. This can be verified in all animals by external and internal or anatomical examination. An organ which is not meant for use or an arrangement which does not fulfil its purpose is a contradiction in the teleological theory of nature. For if we abandon this basic principle, we are faced not with a law-governed nature, but with an aimless, random process, and the dismal reign of chance replaces the guiding principle of reason.

Second Proposition

In man (as the only rational creature on earth), *those natural capacities which are directed towards the use of his reason are such that they could be fully developed only in the species, but not in the individual.* . . . Every individual man would have to live for a vast length of time if he were to learn how to make complete use of all his natural capacities; or if nature has fixed only a short term for each man's life (as is in fact the case), then it will require a long, perhaps incalculable series of generations, each passing on its enlightenment to the next, before the germs implanted by nature in our species can be developed to that degree which corresponds to nature's original intention. . . .

Third Proposition

Nature has willed that man should produce entirely by his own initiative everything which goes beyond the mechanical ordering of his animal existence, and that he should not partake of any other happiness or perfection than that which he has procured for himself without instinct and by his own reason. For . . . Everything had to be entirely of his own making-the discovery of a suitable diet, of clothing, of external security and defence [*etc.*] It seems as if nature had intended that man, once he had finally worked his way up from the uttermost barbarism to the highest degree of skill . . . should be able to take for himself the entire credit for doing so and have only himself to thank for it. It seems that nature has worked more with a view to man's rational *self-esteem* than to his mere well-being. For in the actual course of human affairs, a whole host of hardships awaits him. Yet nature does not seem to have been concerned with seeing that man should live agreeably, but with seeing that he should work his way onwards to make himself by his own conduct worthy of life and well-being. What remains disconcerting about all this is firstly, that the earlier generations seem to perform their laborious tasks only for the sake of the later ones . . . and . . . that only the later generations will in fact have the good fortune to inhabit the building on which a whole series of their forefathers (admittedly, without any conscious intention) had worked without themselves being able to share in the happiness they were preparing . . .

Fourth Proposition

The means which nature employs to bring about the development of innate capacities is that of antagonism within society, in so far as this antagonism becomes in the long run the cause of a law-governed social order. By antagonism, I mean in this context the *unsocial sociability* of men, that is, their tendency to come together in society, coupled, how-ever, with a continual resistance which constantly threatens to break this society up. This propensity is obviously rooted in human nature. Man has an inclination to *live in society*, since he feels in this state more like a man, that is, he feels able to develop his natural capacities. But he also has a great tendency to *live as an individual*, to isolate himself, since he also encounters in himself the unsocial characteristic of wanting to direct everything in accordance with his own ideas. He therefore expects resistance all around, just as he knows of himself that he is in turn inclined to offer resistance to others. It is this very resistance which awakens all man's powers and induces him to overcome his tendency to laziness. Through the desire for honour, power or property, it drives him to seek status among his fellows, whom he cannot *bear* yet cannot *bear to leave* . . . Nature should thus be thanked for fostering social incompatibility, enviously competitive vanity, and insatiable desires for possession or even power. Without these desires, all man's excellent natural capacities would never be roused to develop. . . .

Fifth Proposition

The greatest problem for the human species, the solution of which nature compels him to seek, is that of attaining a civil society which can administer justice universally. The highest purpose of nature – i.e. the development of all natural capacities – can be fulfilled for mankind only in society. . . . Man, who is otherwise so enamoured with unrestrained freedom, is forced to enter this state of restriction by sheer necessity. And this is indeed the most stringent of all forms of necessity, for it is imposed by men upon themselves, in that their inclinations make it impossible for them to exist side by side for long in a state of wild freedom. But once enclosed within a precinct like that of civil union, the same inclinations have the most beneficial effect. In the same way, trees in a forest, by seeking to deprive each other of air and sunlight, compel each other to find these by upward growth, so that they grow beautiful and straight-whereas those which put out branches at will, in freedom and in isolation from others, grow stunted, bent and twisted. All the culture and art which adorn mankind and the finest social order man creates are fruits of his unsociability. For it is compelled by its own nature to discipline itself, and thus, by enforced art, to develop completely the germs which nature implanted.

Sixth Proposition

This problem is both the most difficult and the last to be solved by the human race. The difficulty (which the very idea of this problem clearly presents) is this: if he lives among others of his own species, man is *an animal who needs a master.* For he certainly abuses his freedom in relation to others of his own kind. And even although, as a rational creature, he desires a law to impose limits on the freedom of all, he is still misled by his self-seeking animal inclinations into exempting himself from the law where he can. He thus requires a *master* to break his self-will and force him to obey a universally valid will under which everyone can be free. But where is he to find such a master? Nowhere else but in the human species. But this master will also be an animal who needs a master. Thus while man may try as he will, it is hard to see how he can obtain for public justice a supreme authority which would itself be just, whether he seeks this authority in a single person or in a group of many persons selected for this purpose. For each one of them will always misuse his freedom if he does not have anyone above him to apply force to him as the laws should require it. Yet the highest authority has to be just *in itself* and yet also *a man*. This is therefore the most difficult of all tasks, and a perfect solution is impossible. Nothing straight can be constructed from such warped wood as that which man is made of. Nature only requires of us that we should approximate to this idea . . .

Seventh Proposition

The problem of establishing a perfect civil constitution is subordinate to the problem of a law-governed **external relationship** with other states, and cannot be solved unless the latter is also solved. . . . Nature has . . . again employed the unsociableness of men, and even of the largest societies and states which human beings construct, as a means of arriving at a condition of calm and security through their inevitable *antagonism*. Wars, tense and unremitting military preparations, and the resultant distress which every state must eventually feel within itself, even in the midst of peace – these are the means by which nature drives nations to make initially imperfect attempts, but finally, after many devastations, upheavals and even complete inner exhaustion of their powers, to take the step which reason could have suggested to them even without so many sad experiences – that of abandoning a lawless state of savagery and entering a federation of peoples in which every state, even the smallest, could expect to derive its security and rights not from its own power or its own legal judgement, but solely from this great federation (*Foedus Amphictyonum*).

Eighth Proposition

The history of the human race as a whole can be regarded as the realisation of a hidden plan of nature to bring about an internally – and for this purpose also externally – perfect political constitution as the only possible state within which all natural capacities of mankind can be developed completely. This proposition follows from the previous one. . . . The real test is whether experience can discover anything to indicate a purposeful natural process of this kind. In my opinion, it can discover *a little* . . . Civil freedom can no longer be so easily infringed without disadvantage to all trades and industries, and especially to commerce, in the event of which the state's power in its external relations will also decline. But this freedom is gradually increasing. If the citizen is deterred from seeking his personal welfare in any way he chooses which is consistent with the freedom of others, the vitality of business in general and hence also the strength of the whole are held in check. For this reason, restrictions placed upon personal activities are increasingly relaxed, and general freedom of religion is granted. And thus, although folly and caprice creep in at times *enlightenment* gradually arises . . . Eventually, war itself gradually becomes not only a highly artificial undertaking, extremely uncertain in its outcome for both parties, but also a very dubious risk to take, since its aftermath is felt by the state in the shape of a continually increasing national debt . . . and in addition, the effects which an upheaval in any state produces upon all the others in our continent, where all are so closely linked by trade, are so perceptible that these other states are forced by their own insecurity to offer themselves as arbiters, albeit without legal authority, so that they indirectly prepare the way for a great political body of the future. . . . This encourages the hope that, after many revolutions, with all their transforming effects, the highest purpose of nature, a universal *cosmopolitan* existence, will at last be realised as the matrix within which all the original capacities of the human race may develop.

3 Classical Historicism

Robert M. Burns

Introduction

Friedrich Meinecke (1862–1954), whose definition of 'historicism' (German: *Historismus)* is followed here,[1] claimed that it was 'the greatest spiritual revolution that has ever taken place in Western thought' (Meinecke, 1972, p. liv). He wrote: 'The essence of historicism is the substitution of a process of *individualising* observation for a *generalising* view of human forces in history [*without excluding*] . . . altogether any attempt to find general laws and types in human life.' Without denying 'the existence of a permanent foundation of basic human qualities', it rejects 'belief in the stability of human nature' for the notion that it 'constantly took on new and individual forms', which means that it also assumes that 'the essence of individuality . . . is revealed only in a process of development', by which is not meant merely 'perfectibility or 'progress' but recognition of 'spontaneity, plastic flexibility and incalculability' (pp. lv–lvii). Historicism therefore aims to shift Western thought away from its preoccupation with universal and timeless truth (see 1.I). This definition varies from its usual meaning in nineteenth-century Germany (e.g., 6.D.I), with which some still employ it, which equates it with historical determinism and relativism. For instance, Lentricchia writes that: 'the central commitment of historicism, old and new, is to the self as product of forces over which we exercise no control – the soul as effect, not origin' (Lentricchia, 1989, p. 241), and he deplores 'its prime antihumanist assumption that all cultural and social phenomena, especially selves, like all natural phenomena, are to be understood as effects produced by imperious agents of (cultural traditions, institutions, race, ethnicity, relations of gender, economic and physical environments, dispositions of power)' (p. 231). Meinecke explicitly rejected such relativism as defeatist,[2] taking it for granted, with Herder and Ranke (see 3.A.II and 3.E. IV) that the entire point of historical study is to *expand* one's cultural horizons, and therefore, somehow,

---

1   Others who understand the term likewise include Iggers, 1983; Meyerhoff, 1959, introduction; Berlin, 1960; Berlin, 1976. For discussions of the range of understandings of the term see Lee and Beck, 1954; Schnädelbach, 1984, pp. 33–8; Iggers, 1995; Kelley, 1998, pp. 265–72.

2   He writes of a 'positive relativism . . . backed in the last resort by a strong creative faith' expressed in 'humility and reverence in the face of the unsearchable'. Historicism 'understands the world in relative terms, recognizes 'its own conditioned status' but refuses 'to sunder itself from the mysterious springs of power which flow from a belief in absolute values'. Of course, some would dismiss this as empty rhetoric: Meinecke himself acknowledges that the 'absolute' in question 'can neither be demonstrated nor defined' (pp. 490–1); see chapter 6 for further discussion of this issue.

transcend one's historical conditioning, endorsing Ranke's remark that the historian can and must seek to understand an alien epoch 'as it actually was'. Note that the 'absolute historicism' of Benedetto Croce (1866–1952) goes much further than any of the thinkers in this chapter (including Croce's hero Hegel) who would all acknowledge a place of generalization *as well as* individualization in understanding historical reality (e.g., 2.B.II, 3.C.I, 3.E.III). Croce accused Meinecke of leaving the 'individual' and 'general' in a merely loose juxtaposition, maintaining instead that they are always fused in a 'concrete universal'[3] (Croce, 1941, pp. 66–7), such that 'history never repeats itself' (p. 267).

Yet a third usage was promoted by Karl Popper (1902–94) who sought to defend 'the view, so often attacked as old-fashioned by historicists, that *history is characterised by its interest in actual, singular, or specific events, rather than laws or generalizations*' (Popper, 1957, p. 143). We have just seen that this is virtually the central characteristic of Meineckean historicism, to say nothing of that of Croce. Yet he also writes that 'I mean by historicism an approach to the social sciences which assumes that historical prediction is their principal aim, and which assumed that this aim is attainable by discovering the 'rhythms' or the 'patterns', the 'laws' or 'the 'trends' that underlie the evolution of history' (p. 3) which will 'help to reveal the political future'(p. 42). This approximates closely not to historicism but to positivism as defined in this book, and it is no surprise that it is Comte and Mill, together with Marx who serve as his standard examples of historicists. Popper's definition is idiosyncratic but not entirely unparalleled: Mandelbaum 1971 takes 'historicism' to imply belief in a developmental process in history, and consequently writes that 'Herder, Hegel, Comte, Marx and Spencer are all generally considered to provide classic examples of it'(p. 42). But with one exception the historicists of this chapter and chapter 6 explicitly reject the notion of such developmental laws because of their stress on the

---

3   'Concrete universal' is a term Hegel uses to reject the view that the 'concept' (*Begriff*) is essentially a product of abstraction by the mind, i.e., 'the notions (*Begriffe*) of colour, plant, animal, etc. . . . are supposed to be arrived at by neglecting the particular features which distinguish the different colours, plants, and animals from each other and by retaining those common to them all'. Hegel says that 'feeling is in the right when it stigmatizes such hollow and empty notions as mere phantoms and shadows'. True universals (and there is one single ultimate cosmic universal embracing all others) are 'self-actualizing or self-specifying'. It is not really the case that 'the objects which form the content of our mental ideas come first and that our subjective agency then supervenes, and by the aforesaid operation of abstraction by colligating the points possessed in common by the objects, frames notions of them. Rather the notion is the genuine first; and things are what they are through the action of the notion, immanent in them, and revealing itself in them' (Hegel, 1975, para. 163). In short the true, concrete (*konkret*) universal concretizes itself or realizes itself in and through particulars, which are one-sided dialectical expressions of it and means towards its realization and therefore are internal to it, i.e., it is 'immanent' in them. It is the central boast of Hegelianism that it has 'overcome' (*aufgehoben*) the apparently irreconcilable opposition between 'universals' and 'particulars' which runs through our ordinary understanding of things: thinkers such as Ranke or Windelband or Rickert insist against Hegel that the means whereby the universal and particular are related in reality is unfathomable. Rickert was to write of a *hiatus irrationalis* between concept and reality which must simply be acknowledged as unfathomable. Specifically with regard to history Hegel, followed by Croce, would consider that historical events are rendered truly intelligible *not* by seeing them as instances of a universal law which can be stated abstractly and which could in principle be endlessly repeated in further essentially identical examples of its realization, but as the unique, once-for-all concretion of the cosmic rational principle for that historical moment alone.

diversity and spontaneity, unique reality, value, and dignity of each generation and each culture (see 3.A.I, II, II, VI; 3.E I, II, V). Hegel, the exception, is included here[4] because he does take from Herder the notion that humanity is differentiated into separate cultures with real and deep moral differences. But he attempts to show that, despite these differences or rather moving through them 'dialectically', there is a single progressive structure in history. Hegel's notion of the world-historical individual (3.D.V) is specifically meant to address the fact that national cultural differences are so great that there can be no smooth transition or evolution from one to the next, so that progress requires an external application of violence directed by a ruthless charismatic leader which terminates the existence of one *Volk* or state and establishes another in its place. In view of this diversity of usage, one can certainly understand the view that 'historicism . . . is a confused and confusing word which should be abandoned since it obscures more than it illuminates' (Cannon, 1988, p. 194) but, against this, general terms are indispensable in philosophical and any scholarly discourse; confusion is inevitable, but the remedy is that each user explains the intended meaning clearly and sticks to it.

Historicism is often regarded as part of a 'Counter-Enlightenment' (Berlin, 1973), but almost 70 years ago Cassirer wrote, following Dilthey,[5] that 'the common opinion that the eighteenth century was an "unhistorical" century, is not and cannot be historically justified' (Cassirer, 1951, p. 197).[6] He argued this case particularly with regard to **Johann Gottfried Herder** (1744–1803) to whom we now turn: 'Herder's break with his age was not abrupt. His progress and ascent were possible only by following the trails blazed by the Enlightenment . . . Herder's achievement is in fact one of the greatest intellectual triumphs of the philosophy of the Enlightenment' (ibid., p. 233). But far from denying Herder's originality,[7] he maintains that 'considered in its totality, his achievement is incomparable and without any real preliminaries. It seems to descend spontaneously from the Gods and to be born out nothing; it is derived from an intuition of the historical hitherto unequalled in its purity and perfection' (p. 230). Berlin's verdict is comparable; 'He is the father of the related notions of nationalism, historicism, and the *Volksgeist*, one of the leader of the romantic revolt against classicism, rationalism, and faith in the omnipotence of the scientific method' (Berlin, 1992, p. 145), whilst pointing out that this picture is 'oversimplified' because one can find anticipations and parallels in abundance in nearly all aspects of his thought in other eighteenth-century thinkers (see his survey of these pp. 147–52). Still the 'Counter-Enlightenment' element in Herder is undeniable to any reader of his indictment of Enlightenment as the mechanization of man (3.A.V), which prefigures Weber's complaints about *Zweckrationalität* (means-end rationality; see chapter 6) as the bane of modern Western civilization, and the later Heidegger's claims concerning *Technik* (see chapter 7). Again, Herder's emphasis on both the reality and the value of cultural and

---

4 Note Croce (1941) declares that Hegel, apart from Vico, is the greatest figure in the development of historicism, and criticizes Meinecke for omitting him, pp. 71–9.
5 In a 1901 essay 'The Eighteenth Century and the Historical World' in Dilthey, 1996, pp. 325–35.
5 Compare Schnädelbach, 1984, which speaks of a 'historicist Enlightenment' since 'Enlightenment and historicism are not simple opposites', p. 37. Reill 1990 also argues that the opposition between the two is based on 'unsupportable simplifications' (p. 22).
7 Elsewhere he dubs him 'the Copernicus of history', Cassirer, 1950, p. 218.

historical diversity is unprecedented[8] (3.A.I–IV). But the nature of this enthusiasm has sometimes been misunderstood; Collingwood grossly libels Herder in imputing to him 'the idea that there is a European race whose peculiar virtues render it fit to dominate the rest of the world' and that cultural differences 'are derived not from the historical experience of each race but from its innate psychological peculiarities' such that 'once Herder's theory of race is accepted, there is no escaping the Nazi marriage laws' (Collingwood, 1946, pp. 91–2). Kant, reviewing the same book on which Collingwood's remarks are based wrote: 'our author disapproves of the division of mankind into *races*, especially on the basis of inherited colour' (Kant, 1991, p. 217). Herder himself wrote:

> There is no such thing as a specially favoured nation (*Favoritvolk*) on earth. . . . there cannot, therefore, be any order of rank . . . The Negro is as much entitled to think the white man degenerate as the white man is to think of the Negro as a black beast . . . Least of all must we think of European culture as a universal standard of human values . . . Only a real misanthrope could regard European culture as the universal condition of our species. The culture of *man* is not the culture of the *European*; it manifests itself according to place and time in *every* people. (Herder, 1969, p. 24)

Although Herder was certainly of the first philosophers of nationalism, he had no intention whatever of encouraging the aggressive nationalism which emerged in later times in Germany. He deplored German contempt for Slavs, and it is not surprising that in the nineteenth century he became one of the main inspirations of Pan-Slavic nationalism. His dream was of a world in which each national tradition could flourish, rooted in a home-territory (*Heimat*). For this reason he called for the repatriation of those Germans who had settled in Transylvania, opposed colonialism in general, and was scathing in his condemnation of the slave trade. His fundamental message was an absolute respect for human difference at both the national and individual level: 'No other person has the right to constrain me to feel as he does, nor the power to impart to me his mode of perception. No other person, can in short, transform my existence and identity into his' (Herder, 1969, p. 308).

Different cultures emerge because of what he terms, a '*genetische Kraft*' (genetic force or power). This has nothing to do with modern 'biogenetics'. Herder means a formative creative drive working in each individual person or community to create a fulfilling whole or *Gestalt* out of the always differing heritage and predicament, striving to turn happenstance into happiness, to 'create one's own luck'. He was one of the first thinkers to use the term 'culture' in the plural, meaning mainly national cultures, but pointing out that every class and profession or trade has its own culture, referring to Hume as one of the first to have noted this (Herder, 1969, p. 76 see supra p. 35). But how are 'cultures' transmitted from generation to generation, and why do they differentiate themselves from one another, both sustaining their separate identities over time, and gradually mutating, so that, whilst each people has its own enduring spirit (*Volksgeist*), each generation within it manifests its own Zeitgeist? For Herder the answer lies principally in *language*. In one of his earliest publications, *On the Origin of*

---

8   Justus Möser (1720–94) is often specified as the single most important influence on Herder's notions of historico-cultural difference. See Dilthey, 1996, pp. 365–74 and Meinecke, 1972, ch. 8.

Language (1770), he moves to the view that there is no coherent thought without words. He thereby broke with the hitherto dominant Western philosophical, and perhaps common-sense view, that language is merely a means for the communication to others of originally wordless thoughts; Kant, for instance, following this traditional view, hardly ever mentions language, and we saw that except for one brief passage the same is true of Hume. Out of such attitudes developed the call for the invention of an artificial, scientific universal language such as we found in Condorcet (2.B.IV). But if there is no thinking outside languages, then human beings are *historical* to their very core because there is no language in the abstract, but only historical languages, with specific characteristics which mutate through time. Language and the national mentality (*Volksgeist*) are intertwined because speaking a common language ensures communication and reinforcement of ideas and values amongst a population whilst preventing communication with neighbours. Thus language becomes the very embodiment or organ of the national spirit. This understanding of its role provides the philosophical backbone of the historicism of Herder and of Humboldt, who took it up and carried it much further.

All our excerpts are taken from his *Yet Another Philosophy of History* (1774) in which 'historicist' themes are more forcefully presented than in the later *Ideas for a Philosophy of the History of Mankind* (1784–91), which blends with historicist themes some notion of moral progress in mankind as a whole towards a final perfection termed *Humanität*, a condition not of cosmopolitan cultural blending or political unification, but one in which diverse cultures exist peacefully side by side, and mutually enrich one another. The development of this new emphasis appears to have been largely in reaction to the doctrine of radical evil, which we have seen Kant developed in the 1790s, and which Herder along with Goethe opposed.

Wilhelm von Humboldt (1767–1835) played a leading role in building up the cultural and educational institutions of post-Napoleonic Prussia, being largely responsible for the development of the university in Berlin which now bears his name. The importance of his work on language for historicism can scarcely be exaggerated: Heidegger wrote of 'this astounding, obscure, and continually stimulating treatise which has ever since determined the course of all subsequent philology and philosophy of language' (Heidegger, 1982, p. 116). For Humboldt language (3.B.I) is 'inexplicable'. On the one hand, languages cannot be the 'product and creation' of men for they are the precondition of creative thought. Despite that, they have arisen historically. Moreover, they belong not to individuals but to communities, yet are not superindividual consciousnesses; they remain alive only so long as individuals still speak them *meaningfully*. Meaning is governed by conventions which transcend individuals, and yet everyone must come to his own sense of what the words mean, and therefore each individual appropriates his mother tongue uniquely, and transmits it to others in a modified form.

Sections 3.B.II and 3.B.III are taken from an essay published in 1822 on historical method. Section 3.B.II begins by stating that in gathering the facts about 'what actually happened', the historian is merely collecting his 'raw materials'. His real work is to pierce through them to the 'actual inner causal nexus . . . the inner truth'. This must be distinguished sharply from the causal explanations of Hume and Kant: expressing himself in Kantian terminology he writes that these apply only to the outer, phenomenal spatio-temporal appearance of events, whereas the historian penetrates to the inner psychological realities which are 'little subject to discernible laws', which 'defy calculation' and which are caused by 'Ideas' which it is the task of the historian to intuit. They are 'active forces' (Humboldt, 1983, p. 14), mysterious realities which have something transcendent, and infinite about them 'yet pervade and dominate every part of world history' (2.B.III). Every 'individuality' is rooted in an 'Idea', Humboldt meaning by 'individuality' not merely persons but nations. Sometimes the Idea takes complete possession, the individual being ready to sacrifice the whole world for his Idea, but usually it 'struggles' to become actual. The historian grasps these 'Ideas' at work in the minds of others though his 'imagination', but he cannot succeed unless there is 'an original, antecedent congruity' between himself and them, providing a 'bridge of communication'. This bridge lies in his 'heart' in which all ideas will be obscurely present. They will, however, remain mute unless the historian has been inducted into a language which can express them for 'every important language appears as a unique vehicle for the creation and communication of Ideas' (p. 22). The language of a *Volk* is the expression of its spirit, which is why Humboldt says, 'the more deeply the soul of a nation feels everything human, the greater will be its chances to produce historians in the true sense of the word' (2.B.III), for in truth the historian, like the Romantic poet will be a 'seer' or spokesman for his nation's spirit, and the world spirit.

As a first clue to what Humboldt means by 'Ideas', recall that when puzzled by the behaviour of others we might ask ourselves 'what's the idea?', and then exercise our imaginations to ponder the external evidence until we can sense the inner animating *rationale* of their activity. Past empirically observed regularities are often of little help because they would simply be the routinized after-effects, the empty husks of previous original, creative thinking. But the word 'Idea' has entered everyday usage from Platonic philosophy where, in part, it means the obscurely grasped ideals which ultimately orientate the human spirit, and when Kant turns to discuss what motivates the mind to engage in cognitive activity he adopts this Platonic meaning by suggesting that it occurs through the lure of what he terms 'transcendental ideas'. The scientist, he argues, is ultimately motivated by the aim of explaining as much as possible in the natural world by the minimum number of principles, that is, to prove the world to be a 'system' (*Critique of Pure Reason* A645/B673). No one could 'make sense' of the behaviour of scientist *simply* by observing their external 'phenomenal' activities (test tubes, microscopes, research trips, conferences) but must penetrate intuitively to this inner 'Idea', which is not a surface empirical fact because it is an ideal which has never been fully realized. Humboldt, however, believes that individual persons and nations are haunted and captivated by a far wider range of 'Ideas' than those of the natural scientist. He was associated with the Early German Romantics (*Frühromantiker*) who saw all human beings as artists, trying to turn their lives into works of art, by striving to realize the unique 'Idea' which each alone is supposed to realize, and thereby to make a unique contribution to the universe, which is an infinite work of art being organized by one supreme divine artist, and our imaginations are not hermetically sealed cellars but wells which reach down into the infinite deep of the cosmic creative imagination of God, 'languages' being mysteriously providential means by which 'ideas' can be raised out of it into the light.

Humboldt obliged the historian to take 'great care not to attribute to reality arbitrarily created ideas of his own' by 'subordinating his imagination to experience', but did not discuss the details of *how* this might be achieved. Likewise Herder calls on the historian to 'feel himself into' (3.A.I) the thinking of another *Volk*, epoch or individual person but never explained how one could ensure that one's 'feeling' of identity with them was not merely subjective fantasy. ***Friedrich Schleiermacher*** (1768–1834) set about trying to remedy this omission by developing the discipline of 'hermeneutics'. The term had been originally used by seventeenth-century German theologians to refer to the study of the rules for Scriptural interpretation, but by the time of Schleiermacher it was being extended it to mean 'the art of interpreting' the utterances of others in general. As a radical young theologian, he had been a core member of the Early German Romantic circle, in 1799 publishing *Speeches on Religion to its Cultured Despisers*, which presented a highly unorthodox, typically Romantic mystical pantheist view of religion. Later he became Professor of Theology at the new University of Berlin, producing a systematic theology which led later to his being later dubbed 'the father of modern Protestant theology'. But his scholarship ranged far beyond theology, and included between 1804 and 1828 the translation of Plato's works into German. His hermeneutics springs out of both his theological and philosophical activities, his efforts being first published posthumously in 1838.

For Schleiermacher hermeneutics must explain how the interpreter can 'put himself "inside" the author' (Schleiermacher, 1977, p. 64), or 'transform himself, so to speak, into the author' (p. 150), or 'step out of one's own frame of mind into that of the author' (p. 42). These phrases are deliberately provocative, as indeed, is perhaps also his use of the term 'divination' for this process; in this century, Gadamer, for reasons we have already begun to explore (1.II), rejected Schleiermacher's hermeneutical ideal as 'foolish . . . [a] pointless undertaking in view of the historicity of our being', for we can never dredge up the ' "original" form of the lost past' but only a 'secondary, cultural existence' (Gadamer, 1979, p. 149).[9] Schleiermacher would have responded that we take for granted that understanding the minds of others successfully occurs many times daily, however magical or miraculous it might seem. For example, you are currently assuming that by scanning black printed shapes on this page you can penetrate beyond them to my state of mind when I composed this paragraph. But Schleiermacher goes even further, maintaining that the interpreter's ultimate aim should be to 'understand an author better than he understood himself' (p. 64, cf., 69, 112). Again, this is a commonplace assumption: most of us believe we can 'see through' to aspects of the personalities of acquaintances and friends, their vanities, hang-ups and delusions, to which they would never admit and of which they are indeed not consciously aware. Likewise a historian might consider that he more fully understands what led Germans in the 1930s to embrace the Nazi ideology than they would have acknowledged at the time.

This provides a clue to Schleiermacher's entire understanding of the process of successful interpretation, because it implies that none of us necessarily have 'privileged access' to what is really going on in our own consciousnesses, and that growth in self-knowledge will be precisely a matter of coming to see myself as I might appear from the 'outside', at least to ideally sympathetic and informed observers. Schleiermacher shares with Herder and Humboldt the conviction that 'understanding' whether of others or myself arises communally, in language, because no thought is purely 'imme-

---

9   Betti, 1980, defends Schleiermacher's approach at length against Gadamer's attack.

diate' to anyone's consciousness but must be 'mediated' through language before even its author can begin to understand it. Schleiermacher says there are two distinguishable but inseparable sides to understanding any text or oral statement (3.C.I), which 'coinhere' (p. 98), like the two sides of a coin. On the one hand, understanding someone's utterance is understanding his words in terms of their established usage; that is, standard in the time and context, and taking into account the generic type of expression being employed: e.g., campaign speech, sworn deposition, poem, joke. Schleiermacher calls this the 'grammatical', 'comparative', or 'objective' side of interpretation. It can never produce final definitive certainty because the meaning of words of every language are always in flux, and relatively ambiguous, but nevertheless a high degree of certainty is often available. The other side is 'psychological', 'subjective' or 'divinatory.' Our 'divinatory' efforts always need 'corroborating' by references to the 'comparative', but this in turn arises only out of our experiences of having understood individual expressions of meaning: the two 'interpenetrate' and engage in 'interplay' at all times (3.C.I).

Schleiermacher never assumes that 'divination' is infallible or magically instantaneous; on the contrary, he repeatedly states that it remains always provisional: 'the task is unending . . . completed only by approximation' (p. 77). Above all interpretation can never be definitive because it involves a 'hermeneutical circle' (3.C.II), which consists in the fact that the parts are intelligible only in terms of the whole, but the whole can never be understood except through the parts. This applies to the meaning of any sentence; a word such as 'cat' or 'the' means nothing except in relation to a whole sentence, but this can only be known through these parts, e.g., 'The cat sat on the mat'. Likewise sentences can only be understood fully in relation to paragraphs, and these to chapters and the whole book, and the entire book in terms of the entire personality and sweep of the life of the author, and these in terms of his place in the totality of a given society and culture. However, *in fact* in pursuit of this ultimately unattainable ideal or 'transcendental idea' one 'breaks into' such apparently closed, 'vicious' circles at first roughly and even violently by making stabs at or guesses as to the meaning of the whole, and so makes some provisional sense of the parts. Next one revises one's sense of the whole in order to incorporate into it parts which remained unintelligible after the first run through. And so on, back and forth repeatedly between parts and whole. One rests content only when all the relevant parts of a text or speech appear to fall into place in terms of the overall interpretation which has gradually emerged. We are back, of course, with what we have seen was in English termed the 'moral probability judgement' (1.I).

Georg Wilhelm Friedrich Hegel (1770–1831) is counted as one of the three great 'German Idealists',[10] the other two being Fichte (1762–1814), the originator of the movement, and Schelling (1775–1854). Fichte regarded himself as a Kantian who had overcome a basic flaw in Kant, namely the duality of concept and sensory manifold (see 1.V). He asked how, if thought and sensation were ultimately different from one another, they could 'fit' together in cognition. In any case are not 'sensory manifold' and 'things-in-themselves' concepts or thoughts? How could anything within our consciousness *not* be a thought, an 'idea'? The Idealists' solution to this problem, which they saw as a new version of the mind–matter duality in Descartes, and the form–

10   In a slightly looser sense of the term, Humboldt and Schleiermacher are Idealists.

matter dualism in Aristotle, was bold; the 'sensory manifold' was to be regarded as mind in disguise, with mind playing with the thought of having encountered non-thought. Why? Here the Idealists, took up the 'Principle of Polarity' which was then very fashionable in German thought. Herder in *God: Some Conversations* (1787) argues that the great all-embracing cosmic principle is that 'opposites help and need each other; because only through the union of the two does a world come into being in every substance' (Herder, 1940, p. 151); that is, a thing persists only in so far as there is a counterbalances of oppositions in it. Thus the north and south poles are exclusive opposites yet neither could exist without the other or any planet without both, just as the inside of something is the opposite of its outside, yet there could not be one without the other. Newton's laws of gravitational attraction and inertia manifest it, as does magnetism, and electricity, but the entire cosmos is a living, dynamic interplay of opposites, with God the 'totality of all forces' (p. 141). At the human level 'are not . . . hate and love . . . both equally necessary for the formation of the whole? He who cannot hate, cannot love either, only he must learn to hate rightly and love rightly' (p. 183). J. W. Goethe's writings are full of the same notion. Both Herder and Goethe were endorsing the 'vitalism' which was becoming highly regarded in Germany as an improvement on the mechanistic physics of many French and English thinkers; Schelling declared that 'it is the first principle of a philosophical doctrine of nature to go *in search of polarity and dualism throughout all nature*', elaborating on the notion in his *Ideas for a Philosophy of Nature* (1797) (Schelling, 1988). Hegel is therefore simply drawing on a common notion when he writes: 'every actual thing involves a coexistence of opposed elements. Consequently to know or to comprehend an object is equivalent to being conscious of it as a concrete unity of opposed determinations' (Hegel, 1975, para. 48).

The Idealists (but let us limit our remarks to Hegel) applied this to the duality of mind and matter, or concepts and sensations, by reflecting that consciousness itself only emerges within contrasts or oppositions; good health is only appreciated in its absence, we can only come to know a shade of colour by setting it against contrasting shades, and therefore 'mind' can only know itself by first positing non-mind over against itself, but this of course is, ultimately, mind counterposing itself in disguise to itself. Thus, while still acknowledging the validity and the necessity of the relative opposition of 'mind' and 'matter', Hegel considers himself to have reached a higher standpoint which overcomes this duality because everything is seen as 'Idea'. He uses an everyday German verb for this move in thinking, namely, *aufheben* (noun *Aufhebung*). It literally means 'to lift up' but can mean both *cancel* (as when the EC 'lift' a ban on the sale of British beef) and *save* (as when I ask the Box Office to 'keep' some tickets for me). He also employs the term 'dialectical' to describe it because in a 'dialogue' (literally a talking-through, a conversation) one partner might propose something, and the other might then criticize it or 'negate' it. Then the first party responds by presenting a modified or improved version of his original thesis which takes account of the criticism, and which, in Hegel's phrase, is a 'a negation of the negation'.

He sees the whole history of Western philosophy as a great conversation in which later theories 'preserve-but-cancel' earlier theories resulting in evermore adequate syntheses as when Kant integrated empiricism and rationalism in a higher synthesis, and this in turn was transcended by the Idealists. Thus, there develops a 'holy chain' (Hegel, 1985, p. 10, quoting Herder) linked by a 'necessary connection' (p. 63), the result of 'the great labour of preceding generations' (p. 9), which anyone who would philoso-phize must work through so that the history of philosophy *is* philosophy (p. 88). No thought is completely 'untrue'; rather, everything is partially true and partially false, but destined to be integrated into the complete truth at the end of the process. When-ever a person 'thinks something over' he does so dialectically, even if silently and alone, because to conceive something is to de-fine it and so trespass its limitations or boundaries (i.e., its 'de-finition'), that is, 'negate' it, move over to its opposite and then eventually to a higher position which embraces both sides. Genuinely productive thinking always involves such a zigzag ascent to a fuller truth: '*Der Weg des Geistes ist der Umweg*' ('The way of Mind (or Spirit) is diversion' (p. 43)). But dialectic is not only 'the life and soul of scientific progress'. Rather 'wherever there is movement, wherever there is life, wherever anything is carried into effect in the actual world, there is Dialectic at work' for everything 'naturally veers round into its opposite'. Thus, 'in political life, as everyone knows, extreme anarchy and extreme despotism naturally lead to one another . . . In individual ethics . . . Pride comes before a fall . . . Joy seeks relief in tears' (Hegel, 1975, para. 81) In fact, the entire universe is one great Thought or Idea thinking itself through. It starts out unconscious, as merely potential con-sciousness but in a blind move, at it were, to render itself conscious, it opposes Matter to itself (3.D.III). It thinks itself through, unfolds itself, by setting up an infinite number of oppositions in order to overcome them and integrate them into itself, which is why every distinct and therefore opposite thing in the world is really related dialectically to the others. Only in philosophically undeveloped human perception does the world appear to be a series of independent things merely externally related to one another and existing side by side: 'Thus, we suppose that the moon, being something else than the sun, might ever will exist without the sun. But really the moon, as a something has its other implicit in it' (para. 92).

The entire material world is simply Idea: it is in alienated, objectified form, 'a system of unconscious thought, or to use Schelling's expression, a petrified intelligence' (para. 24). This single cosmic drive towards consciousness of the Idea or Concept Hegel can call the 'world Spirit' (*Weltgeist*) or God. He writes that 'the World-Spirit has the patience to pass through these shapes (i.e., transient finite beings) over the long pas-sage of time, and take upon itself, the enormous labour of world history, in which it embodies in each shape as much of its entire content as that shape was capable of holding' (Hegel, 1979, para. 29), and that 'the divine Idea is precisely this; to disclose itself, and to exhibit the other produced from itself, and to take it back with itself in order to become subjectivity and spirit' (Hegel, 1975, para. 257 z. 2). All of this is what Hegel means in 3.D.I by insisting that 'Reason' is the 'substance of the universe' and its 'infinite energy', and elsewhere by saying that 'the real is the rational and the rational is the real' (Hegel, 1991, p. 20; 1975, para. 6).

Hegel frequently stresses the similarities between this vision and Christianity, argu-ing that the Trinity is a pictorial expression of his doctrine of the Dialectic: the Father produces his opposite, the Son, and the two are reconciled '*aufgehoben*', in the Spirit (*Geist*). Yet there are several differences between it and traditional Christianity. 'God' is not originally conscious, and He produces the universe out of blind necessity in order to become conscious through the world, so that the creation does not result from a free decision. Moreover, the world is an essential part of His dialectical unfold-ing, which is to say, is part of God. Consciousness enters the universe, and therefore

God, in human consciousness, the full flowering of which is the recognition of the truth of the Hegelian system which 'is not only the intuition of the Divine but the Divine's intuition of itself' (Hegel, 1977, para. 795): 'the so-called humility, i.e., the limitation involved in man's [alleged] inability to know God, we must discard altogether. To know God is rather the sole aim and end of religion' (Hegel, 1985, p. 133). At this point man realizes he is one with God, and this is the truth portrayed in picture language by the doctrines of the Incarnation and the descent of the Holy Spirit at Pentecost.

Some have always found this 'demythologization' of Christianity impossible to take seriously. Solomon, for instance, writes of Hegel that 'his "Christianity" is nothing but . . . an elaborate subterfuge to protect his professional ambitions . . . in "spirit" he was anything but a Christian. He was the precursor of atheistic humanism in German philosophy' (Solomon, 1983, p. 582). It is certainly the case that his philosophy did topple over, in a dialectical conversion or translation, into atheistic humanism in the minds of Feuerbach and Marx. But there is no reason to imply that Hegel was out to hoodwink the public: the only evidence Solomon can adduce is what he said in his books and in his lectures.

Hegel made a habit of refashioning accepted meanings of terms in order to raise them to what he regarded as a fuller expression of truth: for instance he endorses the French Revolutionary view that the ultimate goal of human history is 'Freedom' (3.D.III), but insists that true freedom is rational self-possession, so 'man is not free when he is not thinking'. Random or capricious decisions are not truly free: true freedom therefore exists only in a society pervaded by truth about human nature. True 'Freedom' failed to emerge in the French Revolution because it was dominated by an abstract rationalism, which led to the Terror. The abstract 'head' of French (i.e., Latin or Romanic) rationalism needed to be synthesized with its dialectical opposite Germanic 'heart'. This is a national characteristic which has its weaknesses ('barbarian dullness, mental confusions and vagueness', Hegel, 1956, p. 352) but shows itself in the Germans' courage in the fight for freedom against the Romans, in their 'fidelity' (p. 353), 'honest truth and simplicity' and 'sincerity' (p. 414) . This was why Christianity came to its fullness not in Greek and Latin culture but with Luther's Germanic awareness of the 'freedom of the Christian man'. Thus, 'the Germans were predestined to be the bearers of the Christian principle'(p. 354). The dialectical opposition of Germanic 'Heart' and Romanic 'Head ' was being dialectically transcended (*aufgehoben*) in the constitutional monarchy of post-Napoleonic Prussia (p. 456).

The excerpts show clearly that Hegel abandons the traditional Christian notion of the love of God for every human being, or its secular equivalent, the notion of universal human rights. Although he claims that his account of history is a 'theodicy' (a term which had been used by Leibniz as a term for the justification of the way of God to men, i.e., a proof that the existence of God is compatible with the existence of evil) he declares that divine providence extends only to peoples and states, not individuals (3.D.I). States are 'actual Gods' even though disfigured by 'bad behaviour'. Only one nation is granted 'epoch-making' dominance in a given era, and those 'Gods' who are past their day are 'without rights' and 'no longer count'(3.D.VI). History is the dialectical development of one *Volk* out of another, indeed on the ruins of former cultures. History is therefore a 'slaughter bench' on which 'individuals are sacrifice and abandoned', including whole nations when their time is up. 'Moral claims are irrelevant' when it is a question of keeping the world-historical process on the march for 'world history falls outside . . . justice and virtue, wrongdoing, violence and vice' (3.D.V). Some nations never have their day: Hegel, unlike Herder, can with fullest justice be termed a racist (see the discussion of the African Negro, pp. 95–9). 'The spirit spends many races and generations of men at this labour of its self-knowledge. That it lays out a prodigious expenditure . . . matters nothing to it. It is rich enough for expenditure on that scale . . . it has nations and individuals enough to spend' (Hegel, 1985, p. 43).

Leopold von Ranke (1795–1886) published little philosophical reflection on history, but he himself protested that it was 'ridiculous' to suggest 'that I lack philosophical or religious interest . . . since it is precisely this and this alone which has driven me to history', and insisted that history is 'not a denial but the fulfilment of philosophy' (Krieger, 1977, p. 132). He even writes that history and philosophy should ideally 'fully coincide' (3.E.II). When he opposes the two, stating 'philosophy' to be the realm of the universal, whereas 'history' is that of the 'particular' (3.E.II), he means by 'philosophy' specifically the Fichtean and Hegelian and Kantian claim that a single goal of history can be known *a priori*, and that individual persons, peoples and epochs are merely means to this end. Against, this, he asserts that the individual is an end-in-itself. His stress on particularity has repeatedly been mistaken, especially in the English-speaking world, for a 'positivist' accumulation of bare facts.[11] By a being's particularity he means that the inner core of each being is unique, and must be 'intuited' by a 'spiritual apperception' which 'divines' or 'penetrates' through the outer appearance to its inner, incomparable essence. In this he echoes Humboldt, and in particular draws on the notion that each finite particular is a unique manifestation of God's infinity. This is an idea which can be traced back through Leibniz to earlier German mysticism particularly as summarized epigrammatically by Angelus Silesius (1624–77), who had recently been 'discovered' by the Early Romantic Friedrich Schlegel; thus 'No speck so tiny is, no spark can be so dim, The wise man does not see God's splendour deep within'.[12] It is this background which is a mystical spirituality drawing remotely on Duns Scotus's stress on '*haecceitas*' (see 1.I), which explains Ranke's claims that every epoch has 'an immediate relation to the divine' and has 'equal rights' (3.E.I), that 'history recognizes something infinite in every existence'; and that 'the religious foundation on which our efforts rest' is belief that 'the eternal dwells in the individual' (3.E.II). We are a world away from 'positivist' understandings of particulars merely as instances of some general kind.

Nevertheless throughout his career, Ranke reiterates the theme that the historian must concern himself with the universal as well as with the particular, and that the

---

11   For example, Southgate, 1996, pp. 22–4; Stanford, 1988, p. 54. Novick traces this 'almost total misunderstanding' of Ranke as 'an unphilosophical empiricist' to turn-of-the century American historians such as Dodd, Emerton and Adams (Novick, 1988, pp. 26–30), although Ross (1990) shows that there was not at the outset as much ignorance of Ranke's stress on 'large philosophical synthesis' as was once thought (p. 165).

12   Angelus Silesius, *The Cherubinic Wanderer*, trans. M. Shrady, New York: Paulist Press, 1986, 4.160; compare 'the more we let each voice sound forth with its own tone, The more diverse will be the chant in unison' (individual creatures in their differences rather than their similarity manifest God): 'The rose does have no why; it blossoms without reason' (individual beings reveal God not by being 'explained away' as effects or consequences of some general principle but in the irreplaceable thisness of their existence); 1: 268,1: 289.

particular can indeed only be truly known when its is related to the universal. True, in 1824, when he first makes his oft-quoted claim that the historians task is to 'indicate what actually happened' (*zeigen, wie es eigentlich gewesen*, Ranke, 1983, p. 137), he states that 'strict presentation of facts, no matter how contingent and unattractive they might be, is undoubtedly the supreme law. The development of the unity and progress of the events is next in order of importance', but when, in the 1840s virtually the same phrase recurs, he writes: 'Only from a spiritually combined series of facts does the event result. Our task is thus to inquire into which really happened (*eigentlich geschehen ist*) in the series of facts. In its sum' (Krieger, 1977, p. 142). This commitment was repeated many times; for instance, in the 1830s he wrote that 'only when we raise ourselves to a view of the whole [*of history*] can we hope to grasp the individual which in its principle and its life participates in the life of the whole' (p. 214), and that 'I am ever more confirmed in the opinion that in the final analysis nothing other than universal history can be written' (p. 160).[13] Furthermore, he frequently writes that the entire world historical process is progressive despite the apparent denial in 1833 (3.E.VI). Thus, in the 1840s he declares that 'there is objectively a world-historical general development' which 'must reveal itself to the simple conscientious, and attentive procedure of research,' and that 'the axiom of the progress of the human race . . . often misunderstood, has its truth' (p. 142). This was essentially the message of his 1880 statement in the preface to his *Universal History* (3.A.VII), where he specifies as the ultimate purpose of history, that the great European powers, whatever their wasteful conflicts, and though they supplant one another over time, hand on to humanity in general an every-increasing wealth of higher culture. Thus the common complaint (see, for instance, Burke, 1990, pp. 36–44) that Ranke substituted for the interest in culture evident in earlier historians a narrowly political emphasis is an oversimplification; his concentration on political history was partly the result of the sources which were at hand, and partly his conviction that the nation state was a key feature in the preservation of national culture . Each of his national histories contains sections on culture.

He repeatedly ascribes 'necessity' to the world historical process, and frequently terms it divine 'Providence' (Krieger, 1977, p. 106), so that it is quite wrong to associate him with Popper, on the assumption that both believed that 'the course of history is not determined; there is no necessity about it' and to imply that he believed that 'words like Fate, Fortune, and Destiny are empty air' (Stanford, 1998, p. 78). Yet there is a need to explain how Ranke can be so confident of the providential course of history when he rejects the 'progress' of Condorcet or Hegel, and frequently insists that history consists of irresolvable conflicts. The answer is that he enthusiastically

13   The idea of a 'universal history' has a long history, going back through the Enlightenment to Judeo-Christianity but also to Polybius. Many of Ranke's remarks about it seem to owe more to Polybius than anyone else, e.g.: 'He . . . who believes that by studying isolated histories, he can acquire a fairly just view of history as a whole, is, as it seems to me, much in the case of one who, after having looked at the dissevered limbs of an animal once alive and beautiful, fancies he has been as good as any eyewitness of the creature itself in all its action and grace . . . For we can get some idea of a whole from a part, but never knowledge of the whole and conviction of its truth. It is indeed by study of the interconnection of all the particulars, their resemblances and differences that we are enabled at least to make a general survey, and thus derive both benefit and pleasure from history.' Kelley, 1991, pp. 38–9.

appropriated the Principle of Polarity which we have just met in Hegel, though he understands it differently. Actually, the idea that the cosmos has a rationale hidden in eternal strife goes back to the pre-Socratic Heraclitus,[14] to whom Ranke approvingly refers more than once (e.g., Ranke, 1983, p. 97). The contrast with Hegel, also a Heraclitus enthusiast, is that for Ranke polarity may be the end of the story, while Hegel seeks claim that it is ultimately dialectically *aufgehoben*.

Once the pervasiveness of the *Polaritätsprinzip* in Ranke is appreciated, his many shrugs of the shoulders over unresolved historical conflicts appear not as denials of providence, but as expressions of the conviction that they are God's ways of orchestrating history. In 1861 the wrote that 'it is no constant development, it is an unending struggle between forces that permeate the world. The Romanic and the Germanic world, Islam and Christendom, the papacy and Imperial power, Protestant and Catholics, revolutionary and conservative tendencies resist one another, yet their conflict draws them together, they are inseparably linked' (Schulin, 1990, p. 75). Pelikan suggests that there are 'perhaps hundreds' of such 'oppositions' in Ranke's German Reformation history and discusses some of them (Pelikan, 1990, pp. 91–8). This polarity-thinking explains why he could write that in all history 'the clash of the antagonistic principles of freedom and necessity' is at work (see 3.E.IV), that history is nothing other than the 'earthly, real meshing' of 'the general and the particular' (Krieger, 1977, p. 348, cf. pp. 153, 166–7, 189, 273), and that on this opposition 'all European history is based' (p. 241).

Finally, two critical comments: first, Ranke gives no indication of *how* intuition of particulars is to emerge out of the unremittingly industrious pursuit of historical research, upon which he always insisted; that is, he fails to show how the 'spiritual apperception' of particulars could be the central element of the public, institutionalized, international discipline of History, which he personally did so much to establish. Secondly, the ultimate reason for his resort to the polarity principle with such frequency is that it allows him to believe in divine providence despite the apparent counter-evidence. But though there may be a case for looking at things this way *if* on independent grounds one has reason for believing in a providential God (and the vitality and depth of Ranke's own Lutheran faith in God can scarcely be doubted because of the abundant evidence for it in personal correspondence), it is much more questionable to argue *from* the empirical evidence of conflict to the reality of divine providence as did Ranke. Thus he wrote in 1833, concerning the balance of power in Europe, that 'in great danger one can safely trust in the guardian spirit (*Genius*) which always protects Europe from domination by any one-sided and violent tendency, which always meets pressure on the one side with resistance on the other, and through a union of the whole which grows firmer from decade to decade, has happily preserved the freedom and separate existence of each state' (Ranke, 1983, p. 73). But what then would then be his explanation for the complete disappearance of a large nation-state such as Poland a few years before his birth? Or what of the fate of Serbia, about which he had

---

14 For example, 'An unapparent connexion is stronger than an apparent one' (207). 'The real constitution is accustomed to hide itself' (208). 'They do not apprehend how being at variance it agrees with itself: there is a back-stretched connexion, as in the bow and the lyre' (209). 'It is necessary to know that war is common and right is strife and that all things happen by strife and necessity' (211). 'War is the father and king of all' (212); Kirk, Raven and Schofield, 1983, pp. 192–3.

written, or Ireland, his wife's homeland? Is there no room for unremedied injustice or tragic loss in Ranke's world-historical view? Is everything always just as it should be? If so, Ranke's faith in divine Providence might not be so far from the Hegel's 'slaughterbench' view of history after all. In particular his moral condemnation of Hegel for allowing some generations to be merely 'means' to the end of others is difficult to reconcile with his own apparent indifference to the fate of countless nations, let alone individual human beings, who have fallen victim to the power struggles of history, and whereas Hegel, for example, does give the Asian nations a low but necessary place on the dialectical ladder towards his Germanic *telos* of history, Ranke excludes them entirely, in view of the 'eternal repose' (p. 162) of their cultures.

Selected Texts

Edited by Robert M. Burns

3.A Johann Gottfried Herder, 1744–1803

3.A.1 History: The Exploration of Human Difference[1]

. . . No one in the world feels the weakness of general characterisation more than I do. If one depicts a whole people, an age, an area, whom has one depicted? If one groups into one mass the peoples and periods which succeed each other eternally like the waves of the sea, what has one described? To whom does the descriptive term apply? Finally, one brings all of it together into nothing but *a general word*, whereby each individual thinks and feels as he will. How imperfect the means of description! How great the ease of misunderstanding!

Have you noticed how inexpressible is the individuality of one man, how difficult it is to know distinctly what distinguishes him, how he feels and lives, how differently his eyes see, his soul measures, his heart experiences, everything? What depth there is in the character of a single nation which, even after repeated and probing observation, manages to evade the word that would capture it and render it recognizable enough for general comprehension and empathy. If this is so, how then can one survey an ocean of entire peoples, times and countries, comprehend them in one glance, one sentiment or one word, a weak incomplete silhouette of a word? A whole *tableau vivant* of manners, customs, necessities, particularities of earth and heaven must be added to it, or precede it; you must enter the spirit of a nation before you can share even one of its thoughts or deeds. . . .

. . .

. . . Do not limit your response to a word, but penetrate deeply into this century, this region, this entire history, plunge yourself into it all and feel it all inside yourself – then only will you be in a position to understand; then only will you give up the idea of comparing everything, in general or in particular, with yourself. For it would be manifest stupidity to consider yourself to be the quintessence of all times and all peoples.

. . .

. . . That no people long remained, or could remain, what it was, that each, like the arts and sciences and everything else in the world, had its period of growth, flowering

---

1   From *Yet Another Philosophy of History* (1774) in Herder, 1969, pp. 181–3.

and decay; that each of these modifications has lasted only the minimum of time which could be given to it on the wheel of human destiny; that, finally, no two moments in the world were ever identical and that therefore the Egyptians, the Romans and the Greeks have not stayed the same through all time . . .

. . . How can you order them, follow their course, distinguish the essential effect in each scene, quietly trace the influences and finally give a name to it all? But if you cannot do all this, history just flickers and wavers before your eyes like a confusion of scenes, peoples and times. . . .

3.A.II   No Single Ideal of Human Perfection[2]

. . . Each form of human perfection [*is*] in a sense, national and time-bound and con-sidered most specifically, individual. Nothing develops, without being occasioned by time, climate, necessity, by world events or the accidents of fate. Tendencies or talents slumbering in the heart, therefore, may never become actual accomplishments. A na-tion may have the most sublime virtues in some respects and blemishes in others, show irregularities and reveal the most astonishing contradictions and incongruities . . . for him who wants to understand the human heart within the living elements of its cir-cumstances, such irregularities and contradictions are perfectly human. . . .

What right justifies the arbitrary verdicts of praise and blame which we heap on all the earth on account of a favourite people of antiquity with which we have become infatuated? . . . Defects and virtues . . . always dwell together under one human roof. . . .

. . . A learned society of our time proposed, doubtless with the best of intentions, the following question: 'Which was the happiest people in history?' If I understand the question aright, and if it does not lie beyond the horizon of a human response, I can only say that at a certain time and in certain circumstances, *each* people met with such a moment or else there never was one. Indeed, human nature is not the vessel of an absolute, unchanging and independent happiness, as defined by the philosopher; eve-rywhere it attracts that measure of happiness of which it is capable: it is a pliant clay which assumes a different shape under different needs and circumstances. Even the image of happiness changes with each condition and climate . . . Basically, therefore, all comparison is unprofitable . . . Each nation has its centre of happiness within itself, just as every sphere has its centre of gravity.

Mother Nature has taken good care of this . . . She has put tendencies towards diversity in our hearts; she has placed part of the diversity in a close circle around us; she has restricted man's view so that by force of habit the circle became a horizon, beyond which he could not see nor scarcely speculate. All that is akin to my nature, all that can be assimilated by it, I hanker and strive after, and adopt; beyond that, kind nature has armed me with insensibility, coldness and blindness, which can even turn into contempt and disgust. Her aim is only to force me back on myself so that I find satisfaction in my own centre. The Greek adopts as much of the Roman, the Roman of the Greek, as he needs for himself; he is satisfied, the rest falls to the earth and he no longer strives for it. If, in this development of particular national tendencies towards

Ibid., pp. 184–7.

particular forms of national happiness, the distance between the nations grows too great, we find prejudices arising. The Egyptian detests the shepherd and the nomad and despises the frivolous Greek. Similarly prejudices, mob judgment and narrow nationalism arise when the dispositions and spheres of happiness of two nations collide. But prejudice is good, in its time and place, for happiness may spring from it. It urges nations to converge upon their centre, attaches them more firmly to their roots, causes them to flourish after their kind, and makes them more ardent and therefore happier in their inclinations and purposes. . . .

3.A.III   Cultural Relativism versus Progress[3]

The general, philosophical, philanthropical tone of our century wishes to extend 'our own ideal' of virtue and happiness to each distant nation, to even the remotest age in history. But can one such single ideal act as an arbiter praising or condemning other nations or periods, their customs and laws; can it remake them after its own image? Is good not dispersed over the earth? Since one form of mankind and one region could not encompass it, it has been distributed in a thousand forms, changing shape like an eternal Proteus throughout continents and centuries. . . .

Those who have so far undertaken to explain the progress of the centuries have mostly cherished the idea that such progress must lead towards greater virtue and individual happiness. In support of this idea they have embellished or invented facts, minimized or suppressed contrary facts, and in this way invented the fiction of the 'general, progressive amelioration of the world' which few believed, least of all the true student of history and the human heart.

Others, who saw the harmfulness of this dream without knowing a better one, saw vices and virtues alternating like climates, perfections sprouting and dying like spring leaves, human customs and preferences strewn about like leaves of fate. No plan! No progress, but an endless revolution! Weaving and unravelling like Penelope! They fell into a whirlpool of scepticism about all virtue, about all happiness and the destiny of man . . . Doubt in a hundred forms. . . .

Does this mean there can be no manifest progress, and development, in some higher sense than we usually think? . . . Each age is different, but each has the centre of happiness within itself. The youth is not happier than the innocent, contented child: nor is the peaceful old man unhappier than the energetic man in his prime. . . . And yet the strivings never cease. No one lives in his own period only; he builds on what has gone before and lays a foundation for what comes after. . . . The Egyptian could not have existed without the Oriental, nor the Greek without the Egyptian; the Roman carried on his back the whole world. This indeed is genuine progress, continuous development, however little it may prosper the individual! Becoming on a grand scale! History may not manifestly be revealed as the theatre of a directing purpose on earth – of which our shallow histories boast so much – for we may not be able to espy its final end. But it may conceivably offer us glimpses of a divine theatre through the openings and ruins of individual scenes . . .

3   Ibid., pp. 187–8.

3.A.IV   Defence of the Medieval[4]

The spirit of 'Nordic chivalry' has been compared to the heroic age of the Greeks –
and, to be sure, points of comparison do exist – but it seems to me that it is really
unique in the sequence of the centuries, resembling nothing but itself. Because it
comes between the Romans and us – *quanti viri* – some have treated it with derision;
others, somewhat adventurously minded, have exalted it above everything, but it seems
to me that it is neither more nor less than a 'particular state of the world', whose
advantages and disadvantages should not be compared with those of preceding ages: it
took its point of departure from these ages, but by ceaseless transformation and aspira-
tion became uniquely itself – on a grand scale!

   We can read of the dark sides of this period in any book. Every classical litterateur
who takes our regimented century for the *ne plus ultra* of mankind finds occasion to
reproach whole centuries for barbarism, wretched constitutional law, superstition and
stupidity, lack of manners and taste, and to mock their schools, country seats, temples,
monasteries, town halls, guilds, cottages and houses . . . [*But*] Europe was populated
and built up; generations and families, master and servant, king and subject, interacted
more strongly and closely with one another; what one is wont to call 'simple country
seats' prevented the luxuriant, unhealthy growth of the cities, those slagheaps of human vitality and energy, whilst the lack of trade and sophistication prevented ostenta-
tion and the loss of human simplicity in such things as sex and marriage, thrift and
diligence, and family life generally. The mediaeval guilds and baronies engendered
pride in the knights and craftsmen, self-confidence, steadfastness and manliness in
their spheres of activity, and checked the worst torment of mankind, the enslavement
of lands and souls under a yoke which now, apparently, since the earlier social enclaves
have been disbanded, everyone accepts readily and wholeheartedly. How could so
many warring republics, so many strong and independent cities, spring up later on?
Because the vital forces, on whose sad remains we now live, were planted, nourished
and nurtured in the rougher climate of an earlier period. . . .

   . . . I am by no means disposed to defend the perpetual migrations and devastations,
the feudal wars and attacks, the armies of monks, the pilgrimages, the crusades. I only
want to explain them; to show the spirit which breathed through it all, the fermenta-
tion of human forces. . . .

3.A.V   The Essence of Enlightenment: Mechanism[5]

. . A large part of this so-called new civilization is actually a piece of mechanism. More
closely examined, this mechanism is in fact the essential characteristic of the new spirit. . . .
   . . . The new philosophy . . . in more than one way . . . is nothing but a mechanism.
With all their philosophy and their knowledge, how ignorant and anaemic our enlightened men often are in matters of life and common sense! . . . If there is one thing in the
world you want to see badly done, entrust it to the philosopher. On paper, everything

4 Ibid., pp. 191–3.
5 Ibid., pp. 196–209.

is neat, smooth, beautiful and great; in performance it is a disaster. At every step he is astonished and petrified before unforeseen obstacles and consequences. . . .

. . . What indeed, could be more mechanical than the new philosophy itself! It has forced its way into the sciences, the arts, customs and ways of living and is considered the sap and blossom of our century. Old traditions, prejudices in favour of painstaking scholarship, slow maturing, searching inquiry, and cautious judging have been thrown off like a yoke from the neck! . . . We have dictionaries and philosophies about all subjects, but, even with these tools in our hands, we do not understand any of them. These digests and summaries of preceding pedantry are nothing but abstractions, a kind of instant philosophy produced by a mechanical process from a couple of general ideas.

. . .

. . . Ideas of universal love for humanity, for all nations, and even enemies, are exalted, whilst warm feelings of family and friendship are allowed to decay. Principles of liberty, honour and virtue are commonplace; they are loudly acknowledged, and in certain countries everyone down to the lowest pays lip service to them, whilst at the same time lying in chains of cowardice, shame, luxury, servility and miserable desultoriness. . . .

Is this then the ideal state into which we are being fashioned, to which all Europe, perhaps even the whole world, increasingly aspires? Is it the ultimate aim to organize, plan and control everything in order to create human beings, citizens, entities with their own *raison d'être*? And if so, surely this can only be determined by applying a most careful political calculus to the numbers involved, to the needs and to the purposes. . . .

. . .

. . . Unless all I have written has been in vain, it should now be clear that the emergence and further development of a nation is never other than a work of destiny, the result of a thousand concurrent causes and, in a way, of the entire element in which it lives. And this being so, is it not childish to base this development on a few bright ideas and to imagine that this constitutes a scientific revolution? Should this or that book, author, or whole library, further this development? Should the product of them all, the philosophy of our century, do likewise? . . .

. . .

. . . How inundated we are with fine principles, elaborations, systems, interpretations . . . The head and the heart are completely separated: man has unfortunately reached a point where he acts not according to what he knows but according to what he desires. . . .

. . .

This is a time when the art of legislation is considered the sole method of civilizing nations. Yet this method has been employed in the strangest fashion to produce mostly general philosophies of the human race, rational axioms of human behaviour . . . Views of all time and peoples for all times and peoples. For all times and peoples? That means, alas, precisely *not* for the very people whom the particular code of law was meant to fill like clothing . . .

What an abyss there is between even the finest general truth and the least applications to a given sphere, to a particular purpose and in one specific manner! . . .

. . .

This is a time when everyone enthuses about education, interpreted as meaning good knowledge of the exact sciences, instruction, enlightenment, clarification, and the polishing of manners. As if all that could change and develop dispositions! No thought is given to ways of restoring or creating afresh the attitudes and even prejudices, the practices and energies, whereby alone it possible to build a 'better world'. . . .

When, in former times, nations were so much more parochial, they thought quite differently about these matters. Every cultural development originated from particular individual needs and in turn fostered other such needs; the process was one of genuine experience, achievement and practical life in a circumscribed sphere. . . .

. . .

And so, it would appear there is an ever-growing progress. Soon there will be European colonies everywhere! Savages all over the world will become ripe for conversion as they grow fonder of our brandy and our luxuries; soon they will approach our culture and become, so help me God, good, strong and happy men, just like us!

. . .

. . . 'Ways of living and mores!' How wretchedly primitive was the age in which nationality and national character still existed; and with it, hatred and hostility towards the foreigner, self-centered parochialism, prejudice, attachment to the soil where one was born and in which one was buried; a native mentality, a narrow span of idea, – eternal barbarism! With us thank God, national character is no more! We love each and every one, or rather, we can dispense with love; we simply *get on* with one another, being all equally polite, well-mannered and even-tempered. To be sure, we no longer have a fatherland or any kinship feelings; instead we are all philanthropic citizens of the world. The princes speak French, and soon everybody will follow their example; and then, behold, perfect bliss: the golden age, when all the world will speak one tongue, one universal language, is dawning again! There will be one flock and one shepherd! National cultures, where are you?

3.A.VI The Truth of History[6]

As a rule the philosopher is never more of an ass than when he confidently wishes to play God; when with remarkable assurance he pronounces on the perfection of the world. . . .

The philosopher has not considered that . . . [*man*] . . . this elusive double creature . . . can be modified in a thousand ways and almost has to be, given the structure of our earth. . . .

. . .

He has not considered – this omniscient philosopher – that there can be a great, divine plan for the whole human race which a single creature cannot survey, since it is not he, philosopher or monarch of the eighteenth century though he be, who matters in the last resort. While each actor has only one role in each scene, one sphere in which to strive for happiness, each scene forms part of a whole, a whole unknown and invisible to the individual self-centered actor. . . .

See the entire universe from heaven to earth! What are the means, what are the

Ibid., pp. 214–19.

ends? Is not everything a means to a million ends? Is not everything an end for a million means? The chain of an almighty and omniscient goodness is twisted and tangles a thousand times: but each link in the chain has its own place – it is attached to the chain, but is unaware of the end to which the chain is finally attached. Everyone is under the illusion that he himself is the centre, is sensitive to everything around him only so far as it directs its rays or its waves onwards this centre. . . .

. . . The history . . . of the human race . . . is an unending drama with many scenes, God's epic through all the centuries, continents and generations, a fable with a thousand variations full of immense meaning. . . .

. . .

The passage of God over the nations! The spirit of laws, times, manners, and arts and how they succeed each other, prepare for each other, develop from each other, and disperse each other! If only one had a mirror of the human race to reveal all his with the fidelity, completeness and perception of a divine revelation. There is no lack of preliminary attempts, but these are as yet crude and unsystematic, enclosed, as it were, in husks and confusion. We have ransacked and rummaged through almost all nations of our present age and through the history of all previous ages, almost without knowing what we were looked for. Historical facts and research, descriptions of discoveries and travels, are available in plenty, but who will sort them out and sift them?

. . .

Who will restore for us the temple of God, which is being built continuously through all the centuries? . . .

. . .

Our age will soon open more eyes: before very long we will be impelled to seek spiritual springs to quench the thirst of the deserts – we will learn to value the epochs we now despise – the sentiment of general humanity and happiness will be stimulated; vistas of a higher than human existence will emerge out of this ruin-crammed history, and reveal to us a design where we found only confusion: everything will be found in its proper place – a history of mankind in the noblest meaning of the term!

3.B   Wilhelm von Humboldt, 1767–1835

3.B.1   The Mystery of Language[7]

. . . *Language* . . . is the organ of inner being, this being itself, as it successively attains to inner knowledge and outward expression. It therefore strikes with all the most delicate fibres of its roots into the national mentality; and the more aptly the latter reacts upon it, the more rich and regular its development. . . .[8]

. . . Language indeed, arises from a depth of human nature which everywhere forbids us to regard it as a true product and creation of peoples. It possesses an autonomy that visibly declares itself to us, though inexplicable in its nature, and seen from this aspect, is no production of activity, but an involuntary emanation of the spirit, no

7   From Humboldt, 1988.
8   Ibid., p. 21.

work of nations, but a gift fallen to them by their inner destiny. They make use of it without knowing how they have fashioned it[9]. . . .

The *individual man* is always connected with a whole, with that of his nation, of the race to which the latter belongs, and of the entire species. From whatever aspect one may look at it, his life is necessarily tied to *sociality*. . . . In the merely vegetative existence, as it were, of man on the soil, the individual's *need for assistance* drives him to combine with others, and calls for understanding through *language* so that common undertakings may be possible. But *mental cultivation*, even in the loneliest seclusion of temperament, is equally possible only through language, and the latter requires to be directed to an external being that understands it. . . .

. . . This connection of the individual with his nation lies right at the centre from whence the total mental power determines all thinking, feeling, and willing. For *language* is related to everything therein, to the whole as to the individual, and nothing of this ever is, or remains, alien to it.[11]

. . . Although languages are the work of nations . . . they still remain the self-creation of individual, in that they can be produced solely in each individual, but only in such fashion that each presupposed the understanding of all.[12]

. . . Language is, as it were, the outer appearance of the spirit of a people; the language is the spirit and the spirit their language; we can never think of them sufficiently as identical. How they actually conjoin with each other in one and the same source, beyond reach of our conception, remains inexplicably hidden from us . . . Though *we* may separate intellectuality and language, no such division in fact exists. . . .[13]

Language, regarded in its real nature, is an enduring thing, and at every moment a transitory one. Even its maintenance by writing is always just an incomplete, mummylike preservation, only needed again in attempting thereby to product the living utterance, In itself it is no product (*Ergon*) but an activity (*Energeia*).[14]

Language is the formative organ of *thought*. *Intellectual activity*, entirely mental, entirely internal, and to some extent passing without trace, becomes, through *sound*, externalized in speech and perceptible to the senses. Thought and language are therefore one and inseparable from each other. But the former is also intrinsically bound to the necessity of entering into a *union* with the verbal sound, thought cannot otherwise achieve clarity, nor the idea become a concept. The inseparable bonding of *thought*, *vocal apparatus*, and *hearing* to language is unalterably rooted in the original constitution of human nature, which cannot be further explained. . . .

. . .

. . . Quite regardless of communication between man and man, speech is a necessary condition for the thinking of the individual in solitary seclusion. In appearance, however, language develops only *socially*, and man understands himself only one has tested the intelligibility of his word by trial upon others.[15] . . .

    Ibid., p. 24.
0   Ibid., p. 41.
1   Ibid., p. 43
2   Ibid., p. 44
3   Ibid., p. 46.
4   Ibid., p. 49.
5   Ibid., p. 54–56.

. . . Only in the individual does language receive its ultimate determinacy. Nobody means by a word precisely and exactly what his neighbour does, and the difference, be it ever so small, vibrates, like a ripple in water through the entire language, Thus all understanding is at the same time a non-understanding, all occurrence in thought and feeling at the same time a divergence.[16]

3.B.II   Historical Imagination[17]

An event . . . is only partially visible in the world of the senses; the rest has to be added by intuition, inference, and guesswork . . . For observation can pierce circumstances which either accompany or follow one another, but not their inner causal nexus, on which, after all, their inner truth is solely dependent. . . .

One has . . . scarcely arrived at the skeleton of an event by a crude sorting out of what actually happened. What is so achieved is the necessary basis of history, its raw material, but not history itself. To stop here would be to sacrifice the actual inner truth, well-founded within the causal nexus, for an outward, literal, and seeming truth. . . .

. . . If the historian . . . can only reveal the truth of an event by presentation, by filling in and connecting the disjointed fragments of direct observation, he can do so, like the poet, only through his imagination. The crucial difference, which removes all potential dangers, lies in the fact that the historian subordinates his imagination to experience and the investigation of reality. In this subordination, the imagination does not act as pure fantasy, and is, therefore, more properly called the intuitive faculty or connective ability . . . The historian must therefore seek the necessity of events; he must not, like the poet, merely impose on his material the appearance of necessity. rather, he must keep constantly in mind the ideas which are the laws of necessity . . .

. . .

Thus two methods have to be followed simultaneously in the approach to historical truth; the first is the exact, impartial, critical investigation of events; the second is the connection of the events explored and the intuitive understanding of them which could not be reached by the first means. . . .

. . . The vast, serried turmoil of the affairs of this world, in part arising out of the nature of the soil, human nature, and the character of nations and individuals, in part springing up out of nowhere as if planted by a miracle, dependent on powers dimly perceived and visibly activated by eternal ideas rooted deeply in the soul of man – all this composes an infinitude which the mind can never press into a single form, but which incites the historian to try just that again and again and gives him the strength to achieve it in part. . . .

. . .

. . . Historical truth is, generally speaking, much more threatened by philosophical than by artistic handling . . . Philosophy dictates a goal to events . . . Teleological history . . . never attains the living truth of universal destiny because the individual

16   Ibid, p. 63
17   From Wilhelm von Humboldt, 'On the Historian's Task' (1821) Ranke, 1983, pp. 5–15 taken from the translation in *History and Theory*, VI (1967), pp. 57–71.

always has to reach the pinnacle of his development within the span of his fleeting existence. . . .

3.B.III   'Ideas' in History[18]

. . . All understanding presupposes in the person who understands, as a condition of its possibility, an analogue of that which will actually be understood later: an original, antecedent congruity between subject and object. Understanding is not merely an extension of the subject, nor is it merely a borrowing from the object, it is rather both simultaneously. Understanding always is the application of a pre-existent general idea to something new and specific. When two beings are completely separated by a chasm, there is no bridge of communication between them; and, in order to understand each other, they must, in some other sense, have already understood each other . . . In the case of history that antecedent of understanding is quite obvious, since everything which is active in world history is also moving within the human heart . . . The more deeply, therefore, the soul of a nation feels everything human . . . the greater will be its chances to produce historians in the true sense of the word.

[*Although all historical events are in 'space and time' and governed by 'laws of nature', according to Humboldt, and the historian must attend to these, it is not enough to view history as 'like a dead clockwork, moved by mechanical forces and governed by inexorable laws' (Ranke, 1983, p. 16) for*] it has long been recognized that the exclusive pursuit of his method would lead directly away from an insight into the truly creative forces, that the central element in every activity containing something of life, is precisely what defies calculation, and that seemingly mechanical determination is nevertheless fundamentally subject to free and active impulses . . .

. . .

The psychological forces of multiple, intermeshing human abilities, emotions inclinations, and passions . . . are little subject to discernible laws and can be captured only by certain analogies. Above all other things, they concern the historian as the most direct mainsprings of action and the most immediate causes of the events resulting from action; and they are most frequently appealed to in the explanation of events. It is precisely this point of view, however, which requires the greatest care. It is furthest from having world-historic dimensions; it diminishes the tragedy of world history to a banal drama of mediocrity, tempts one all too easily to tear individual occurrences out of the total context and puts petty commotions of personal motives in the place of universal destiny . . . [*It*] locates everything in the individual, and yet fails to recognize the uniqueness and depth, the essential nature of the individual. . . .

. . .

. . . Ideas . . . by their very nature lie outside the compass of the finite, and yet pervade and dominate every part of world history. . . .

. . .

. . . Every human individuality is an idea rooted in actuality, and this idea shines forth so brilliantly from some individuals that it seems to have assumed the form of an individual merely to use it as a vehicle for expressing itself. When one traces human

18   Ibid., pp. 15–23.

activity, after all its determining causes have been subtracted there remains something original which transforms these influences instead of being suffocated by them; in this very element there is an incessantly active drive to give outward shape to its inner, unique nature. It is the same with the individuality of nations. . . .

. . .

. . . The goal of history can only be the actualization of the idea which is to be realized by mankind in every way and in all shapes in which the finite form may enter into a union with the idea. . . .

. . . The historian's task is the presentation of the struggle of an idea to realize itself in actuality. For the idea will not always be successful in its first attempt; not infrequently it will become perverted because it is unable to master completely the actively resisting matter.

There are two things which the course of this inquiry has attempted to keep firmly in mind; that there is an idea, not itself directly perceptible, in everything that happens, but that this idea can be recognized only in the events themselves. The historian must, therefore, not exclude the power of the idea from his presentation by seeking everything exclusively in his material sources; he must at least leave room for the activity of the idea. Going beyond that, moreover, he must be spiritually receptive to the idea and actively open to perceiving and appropriating it. Above all, he must take great care not to attribute to reality arbitrarily created ideas of his own, and not to sacrifice any of the living richness of the parts in his search for the coherent pattern of the whole. . . .

3.C   Friedrich Schleiermacher, 1768–1834

3.C.I   The Interplay of Divination and Comparison[19]

From the moment it begins, technical interpretation involves two methods: a divinatory and a comparative. Since each method refers back to the other, the two should never be separated.

By leading the interpreter to transform himself, so to speak, into the author, the divinatory method seeks to gain an immediate comprehension of the author as an individual. The comparative method proceeds by subsuming the author under a general type. It then tries to find his distinctive traits by comparing him with the others of the same general type. Divinatory knowledge is the feminine strength in knowing people; comparative knowledge, the masculine.

Each method refers back to the other. The divinatory is based on the assumption that each person is not only a unique individual in his own right, but that he has receptivity to the uniqueness of every other person.

This assumption in turn seems to presuppose that each person contains a minimum of everyone else, and so divination is aroused by comparison with oneself. But how is it possible for the comparative method to subsume a person under a general type

---

19   From Schleiermacher, 1977, pp. 150–1.

Obviously, either by another act of comparison (and this continues into infinity) or by divination.

The two methods should never be separated. Divination becomes certain only when it is corroborated by comparisons. Without this confirmation, it always tends to be fanatical. But comparison does not provide a distinctive unity. The general and the particular must interpenetrate, and only divination allows this to happen.

3.C.II   The Hermeneutical Circle[20]

. . . Wherever the understanding of a series of sentences and their interconnection is in question, one must first and foremost know the whole to which they belong . . . In fact, every highly coherent set of sentences is governed by a dominant concept, though the way this concept 'governs' the text will vary according to the type of work. This concept, just as a word in a given sentence, can be fully determined only when it is read in its context. That is, any set of sentences, large or small, can be understood correctly only in terms of the whole to which it belongs. And just as the shorter sets of sentences are conditioned by larger sets, so, too, these larger sets are conditioned by still larger ones. Thus the obvious conclusion is that any part can be completely understood only through the whole.

When we consider the task of interpretation with this principle in mind, we have to say that our increasing understanding of each sentence and of each section, an understanding which we achieve by starting at the beginning and moving forward slowly, is always provisional. It becomes more complete as we are able to see each larger section as a coherent unity. But as soon as we turn to a new part we encounter new uncertainties and begin again, as it were, in the dim morning light. It is like starting all over, except that as we push ahead the new material illumines everything we have already created, until suddenly at the end every part is clear and the whole work is visible in sharp and definite contours.

. . .

It must first be said that not every text is a whole in the same sense. Some texts are only loose series of statements. In these cases understanding a particular part in terms of the whole is not possible at all. Other texts are only a loose succession of smaller units. In these cases particular points must be understood from the units of which they are a part. Which of these is the case with a given discourse or text depends on the genre to which it belongs, and of course even within a given genre there are numerous gradations. One author will develop his work in strict adherence to the specifications of a genre, whereas another will be extremely flexible in his use of those specifications. Our first inkling of how an author deals with a genre is gained from our general acquaintance with the author and his way of writing. In the case of speeches which are not available to us in written form and so can be heard only once, our provisional grasp of the whole cannot extend beyond what we gather from our general knowledge of the genre and from our acquaintance with the speaker and his habits, unless the speaker himself gives an overview of what he is going to say. . . .

20   Ibid., pp. 197–203.

It follows from what I have said that for both speeches and written texts our initial grasp of the whole is only provisional and imperfect . . . We must shift from the ending back to the beginning and improve our initial grasp of the work by starting all over again. . . .

. . .

Yet . . . just as a word relates to a sentence, a sentence to a section, and a section to a world as a particular to a totality or a part to a whole, so, too, every speech and every text is a particular or part that can be completely understood only in relation to a still larger whole. It is easy to see that every work represent just such a particular or part in two respects. First, each work is a part of the sphere of literature to which it belongs, and together with other works of similar merit forms a body of literature. This body of literature helps one to interpret each work with reference to the language. Second, each work is also a part of the author's life, and together with his other facts it forms the totality of his life. This it is to be understood only from the totality of the person's acts inasmuch as it is of influence upon his life, and is in keeping with it, throughout his entire life up to the appearance of the work. . . .

Even after we have revised our initial concept of a work, our understanding is still only provisional, and a text is placed in an entirely different light when, after reading through all the literature related to it and after acquainting ourselves with other, even quite different works by the same author and, as much as possible, with his entire life, we return to the work in question. . . .

3.D   Georg Wilhelm Friedrich Hegel, 1770–1831

3.D.1   Reason, Sovereign of the World[21]

The only Thought which Philosophy brings with it to the contemplation of History is the *simple* conception of *Reason*; that Reason is the Sovereign of the World; that the history of the world, therefore, presents us with a rational process . . . [*that*] Reason is the *substance* of the universe; viz. that by which and on which all reality has its being and subsistence. On the other hand, it is the *Infinite Energy* of the Universe . . . Reason is not . . . a mere ideal, a mere intention – having its place outside reality, nobody knows where; something separate and abstract, in the heads of certain human beings. It is *the infinite complex of things*, their entire Essence and Truth . . .

To *explain* History is to depict the passions of mankind, the genius, the active powers, that play their part on the great stage; and the providentially determined process which they exhibit constitutes what is generally called the 'plan' of Providence . . . Pious persons are encouraged to recognize in particular circumstances, something more than mere chance; to acknowledge the guiding hand of God; e.g. when help has unexpectedly come to an individual in great perplexity and need . . . But in the history of the World, the Individuals we have to deal with are *Peoples*; Totalities that are States. We cannot therefore be satisfied with what we may call this peddling view of Providence . . .

21   Hegel, 1956, pp. 9–14.

3.D.II   The World-Historical Dialectic[22]

Universal history . . . shows the development of the consciousness of Freedom on the part of Spirit, and of the consequent realisation of that Freedom. This [*dialectical*] development implies a gradation – a series of increasingly adequate expressions or manifestations of Freedom, which result from its Idea . . . It assumes successive forms which it successively transcends; and by this very process of transcending its earlier stages, gains an affirmative, and in fact a richer and more concrete shape . . . Every step in the process . . . has its determinate peculiar principle. In history this principle is idiosyncrasy of Spirit   peculiar National Genius. That such or such a specific quality constitutes the peculiar genius of a people, is the element of our inquiry which must be derived from experience, and historically proved. . . .

. . .

   It is the concrete spirit of a people which we have distinctly to recognise, and since it is Spirit it can only be comprehended spiritually, that is, by thought. It is this alone which takes the lead in all the deeds and tendencies of that people, and which is occupied in realizing itself, – in satisfying its ideal and becoming self-conscious – for its great business is self-production. . . . This it must and is also destined to accomplish; but the accomplishment is at the same time its dissolution, and the rise of another spirit, another world-historical people, another epoch of Universal History. . . .

   History in general is therefore the development of Spirit in *Time*. . . .

   If . . . we cast a glance of the World's History generally, we see a vast picture of changes and transactions; of infinitely manifold forms of peoples, states, individuals in unresting succession. . . .

   The general thought . . . is that of *change* at large. The sight of the ruins of some ancient sovereignty directly leads us to contemplate this thought of change in its negative aspect . . . to sadness at the thought of a vigorous and rich life now departed . . . but, . . . that change while it imports dissolution, involves at the same time the rise of *new life* – that while death is the issue of life, life is also the issue of death. This is a grand conception; one which the Oriental thinkers attained and which is perhaps the highest in their metaphysics . . . the *Phoenix* as a type of the life of *Nature*, eternally preparing for itself its funeral pile, and consuming itself upon it; but so that from its ashes it produced the new, renovated, fresh life. But this image is only Asiatic; oriental not occidental. Spirit – consuming the envelope of its existence – does not merely pass into another envelope, nor rise rejuvenescent from the ashes of its previous form; it comes forth exalted, glorified, a purer spirit. It certainly makes war upon itself – consumes its own existence; but in this very destruction it works up that existence into a new form, and each successive phase becomes in turn a material working on which it exalts itself to a new grade.

   . . . The abstract conception of a mere change give place to the thought of Spirit manifesting, developing and perfecting its powers in every direction. . . .

2   Ibid., pp. 63–4 and 71–3.

3.D.III   Reason = Spirit (*Geist*) = Freedom[23]

The nature of *Spirit* may be understood by a glance at its direct opposite – *Matter*. As the Essence of Matter is Gravity, on the other hand we may affirm that the substance, the essence of Spirit is Freedom . . . Matter possesses gravity in virtue of its tendency towards a central point. It is essentially composite; consisting of parts that *exclude* each other . . . Spirit on the contrary may be defined as that which has its centre in itself . . . Matter has its essence outside itself; Spirit is *self-contained existence* . . . It may be said of Universal History, that it is the exhibition of Spirit in the process of working out the knowledge of that which it is potentially . . . The Orientals have not attained the knowledge that Spirit – Man *as such* – is free; and because they do not know this, they are not free. They only know that *one is free*. But on that very account, the freedom of that one is only caprice . . . That one is therefore only a Despot; not a *free man*. The consciousness of Freedom first arose among the Greeks and therefore they were free; but they, and the Romans likewise, know only that *some* are free – not man as such . . . The Greeks, therefore, had slaves, and their whole life and the maintenance of the splendid liberty was implicated with the institution of slavery . . . The German nations, under the influence of Christianity, were the first to attain the consciousness, that man, as man, is free; that it is the *freedom* of Spirit which constitutes its essence . . . The History of the World is none other than the progress of the consciousness of Freedom.

. . . That the Eastern nations knew only that one is free; the Greek and Roman world only that *some* are free; while we know that all men absolutely are . . . free, – supplies us the with the natural division of Universal History . . .

. . . *The final cause of the World at large*, we allege to be the *consciousness* of its own freedom on the part of Spirit . . . This result it is, at which the process of the World's History has been continually aiming; and to which the sacrifices that have ever and anon been laid on the vast altar of the earth, through the long lapse of ages, have been offered. . . .

3.D.IV   Theodicy: The Cunning of Reason[24]

[*Concerning*] the question of the *means* by which Freedom develops . . . the first glance at History convinces us that the actions of men proceed from . . . their needs, passion . . . and interests. [*which are*] the sole springs of actions . . . Among these may, perhaps, be found aims of a liberal or universal kind – benevolence it may be, or noble patriotism . . . but they bear only a trifling proportion to the mass of the human race . . . Passions, private aims, and the satisfaction of selfish desires, are, . . . the most effective spring of actions . . . When we look at this display of passions, and the consequences of their violence . . . the evil, the vice, the ruin that has befallen the most flourishing kingdoms . . . we can scarce avoid being filled with sorrow at this universal taint of corruption . . . We endure in beholding it a mental torture . . . But even regarding History as the slaughter-bench at which the happiness of peoples, the wisdom

23   Ibid., pp. 17–19.
24   Ibid., pp. 20–33.

of States, and the virtue of individuals have been victimized – the question involuntarily arises – to what principle, to what final aim these enormous sacrifices have been offered . . .

. . .

We assert . . . that nothing has been accomplished without interest on the part of the actors; and – if interest be called passion, inasmuch as the whole individuality, to the neglect of all the actual or possible interest and claims, is devoted to an object with every fibre of volition, concentrating all its desire and power upon it – we may affirm absolutely that *nothing great in the World* has been accomplished without *passion*.

. . .

This may be called the *cunning of reason*, – that it sets the passions to work for itself, while that which develops its existence through such impulses pays the penalty, and suffers loss . . . The particular is for the most part of too trifling value compared with the general; individuals are sacrificed and abandoned . . .

3.D.V   World-Historical Individuals[25]

. . . Caesar was contending for the maintenance of his position, honour, and safety, [*whilst his*] enemies – who were at the same time pursuing their personal aims – had the form of the constitution, and the power conferred by an appearance of justice on their side . . . His victory secured for him the conquest of that entire Empire; and thus he became – though leaving the form of the constitution – the Autocrat of the State. That . . . was, however, at the same time an independently necessary feature in the history of Rome and of the world. It was not then, his private gain merely, but an unconscious impulse that occasioned the accomplishment of that for which the time was right. Such are all great historical men – whose own particular aims involve those large issues which are the will of the World-Spirit. They may be called Heroes inasmuch as they have derived their purposes and their vocation, not from the calm, regular course of things, sanctioned by the existing order; but from a concealed fount . . . from that inner Spirit, still hidden beneath the surface, which, impinging on the outer world as on a shell, bursts it in pieces, because it is another kernel than that which belonged to the shell in question. . . .

Such individuals had no consciousness of the general Idea they were unfolding, while prosecuting those aims of theirs; on the contrary, they were practical, political men. But at the same time they were thinking men who had an insight into the requirements of the time – *what was ripe for development*. This was the very Truth for their age, for their world . . . It was theirs to know this nascent principle . . . World-historical men – the Heroes of an epoch – must therefore be recognized as its clear-sighted ones; *their* deeds, *their* words are the best of that time . . . If we go on to cast a look at the fate of these World-Historical persons, whose vocation it was to be the agents of the World-Spirit – we shall find it to have been no happy one. They attained no calm enjoyment; their whole life was labour and trouble; their whole nature was naught else but their master passion. When their object is attained they flail off like

5   Ibid., pp. 29–32, 66–7.

empty hulls from the kernel. They die early, like Alexander; they are murdered, like Caesar; transported to St. Helena, like Napoleon. This fearful consolation – that historical men have not enjoyed what is called happiness, and of which only private life . . . is capable – this consolation those may draw from history who stand in need of it; and it is craved by Envy – vexed at what is great and transcendent – striving, therefore to depreciate it, and to find some flaw in it . . . The Free Man, we may observe is not envious, but gladly recognizes what is great and exalted, and rejoices that it exists.

. . . They are *great* men, because they willed and accomplished something great; not a mere fancy, a mere intention, but that which met the case and fell in with the needs of the age. This mode of considering them also excluded the so-called 'psychological' view . . . that their authors appear to have done everything under the impulse of some passion – *morbid craving* – and on account of these passions and cravings to have been not moral men. Alexander of Macedon partly subdued Greece, and then Asia; therefore he was possessed by a *morbid craving* for conquest . . . What pedagogue has not demonstrated of Alexander the Great – of Julius Caesar – that they were instigated by such passions, and were consequently immoral men? . . .

. . . But so might a form must trample down many an innocent flower – crush to pieces many an object in its path.

. . .

. . . The History of the World occupies a higher ground than that on which morality has properly its position; which is personal character – the conscience of individuals . . . these have a value, imputation, reward and punishment proper to themselves. What the absolute aim of Spirit requires and accomplishes – what Providence sees – transcends the obligations and liability to imputation and the ascription of good or bad motives, which attach to individuality in virtue of its social relations . . . It is only a formal rectitude – deserted by the living Spirit and by God – which those who stand upon ancient right and order maintain . . . Moral claims that are irrelevant must not be brought into collision with world-historical deeds and their accomplishment. The Litany of private virtues – modesty, humility philanthropy and forbearance must not be raised against them . . .

3.D.VI   The Nation State[26]

[258] . . . The state in and for itself is the ethical whole, the actualization of freedom, and it is the absolute end of reason that freedom be actual . . . Any discussion of freedom must begin not with individuality, or the individual self-consciousness, but only with the essence of self-consciousness; for whether human beings know it or not this essence realizes itself as a self-sufficient power of which single individuals are only moments. The state consists in the march of God in the world. In considering the Idea of the state, we must not have any particular states or particular institutions in mind, instead we should consider the Idea, this actual God, in its own right. Any state even if we pronounce it bad in the light of our own principles, and even if we discover this or that defect in it, invariably has the essential moment of its existence within itself (provided that it is one of the more advanced states of our time). But since it is easier to

26   From Hegel, 1991, pp. 279 and 373 and 374. The numbers at the beginning of the paragraph refer to these numbers in the original text.

discover deficiencies than to comprehend the affirmative, one may easily fall into the mistake of overlooking the inner organism of the state in favour of individual aspects. The state is not a work of art; it exists in the world, and hence in the sphere of arbitrariness, contingency and error, and bad behaviour may disfigure it in many respects. . . .
. . .

[345] Justice and virtue, wrongdoing, violence and vice . . . World history falls outside these points of view; it is, that necessary moment of the Idea of the world spirit which constitutes *its* current stage attains its *absolute right*, and the nation [*Volk*] which lives at this point and the deeds of that nation, achieve fulfilment, fortune and fame.
. . .

[347] The nation to which such a moment is allotted . . . is the *dominant* one in world history for this epoch, *and only once in history can it have this epoch-making role*. In contrast with the absolute right which it possesses as bearer of the present stage of the world spirit's development, the spirits of other nations are without rights, and they, like those whose epochs have passed, no longer count in world history. . . .
. . .

. . . The Constitutions under which World-Historical Peoples have reached their culmination are peculiar to them; and therefore do not present a generally applicable political basis . . . Nothing is so absurd as to look to Greeks, Romans, or Orientals, for models for the political arrangements of our time. . . .[27]

3.D.VII The *Volksgeist* and Religion[28]

. . . The definite *substance* . . . [*which*] exists in that concrete reality which is the State – is the Spirit of the People (*Volksgeist*) itself. The actual State is animated by this spirit, in all its particular affairs, its Wars, its Institutions etc. But man must also attain a conscious realization of this . . . The mind must give itself an express consciousness of this; and the focus of this knowledge is *Religion* . . . In considering Religion, the chief point of inquiry, is whether it recognizes, the True, – the Idea only in its separate abstract form, or in its true unity; in *separation* – God being represented in an abstract form as the Highest Being. Lord of Heaven and Earth, living in a remote region far from human actualities – or in its *unity* – God as unity of the Universal and the Individual . . . the Individual itself assuming the aspect of positive and real existence in the idea of the Incarnation. Religion is the sphere in which a nation gives itself the definition of that which it regards as the True . . . The conception of God, therefore, constitutes the general basis of a people's character.
. . .

. . . In affirming that the State is based on Religion – that it has its roots in it – we virtually assert that the former has proceeded from the latter; and that this derivation is going on now and will always continue . . .

. . . Religion is by no means a thing to be produced [*i.e. artificially by the state*]; its self-production, lies much deeper.

27 Final paragraph from Hegel, 1956, p. 47.
28 Ibid., pp. 50–2.

3.E Leopold von Ranke, 1795–1886

3.E.1 Universal Progress[29]

. . . The question arises: what is progress? Where is the progress of mankind noticeable? . . .
. . .

. . . The real substance of the continuous movement of mankind . . . is based on the fact that the great spiritual tendencies which govern mankind sometimes go separate ways and at other times are closely related. In these tendencies there is, however, always a certain particular direction which predominates and causes the others to recede. So, for example, in the second half of the sixteenth century, the religious element predominated inasmuch that the literary receded in the face of it. In the eighteenth century, on the other hand, the striving for utility gained so much ground that art and related activities had to yield before it.

Thus in every epoch of mankind a certain great tendency manifests itself; and progress rests on the fact that a certain movement of the human spirit reveals itself in every epoch, which stresses sometimes the one and sometimes the other tendency, manifesting itself there in a characteristic fashion.

If in contradiction to the view expressed here, however, one were to assume that this progress consisted in the fact that the life of mankind reaches a higher potential in every epoch – that is, that every generation surpasses the previous one completely and therefore the last epoch is always the preferred, the epochs preceding it being only stepping stones to ones that follow – this would be an injustice on the part of the deity. Such a generation, which, as it were, had become a means would not have any significance for and in itself. It would only have meaning as a stepping stone for the following generation and would not have an immediate relation to the divine. But I assert: every epoch is immediate to God, and its worth is not at all based on what derives from it but rests in its own existence its own self. In this way the contemplation of history, that is to say of individual life in history, acquires its own particular attraction, since now every epoch must be seen as something valid in itself and appears highly worthy of consideration.

The historian thus has to pay particular attention first of all to how people in a certain period thought and lived. Then he will find that, apart from certain unchangeable eternal main ideas, for instance those of morality, every epoch has its own particular tendency and its own ideal. But although every epoch has its justification and its worth in and by itself, one must still not overlook what came forth from it. The historian must therefore secondly, perceive the differences between the individual epochs, in order to observe the inner necessity of the sequence. One cannot fail to recognize a certain progress here. But I would not want to say that this progress moves in a straight line, but more like a river in which in its own way determines its course. If I may dare to make this remark, I picture the deity – since no time lies before it – as surveying all of historical mankind in its totality and finding it everywhere of equal value. There is, to be sure, something true in the idea of the education of mankind, but before God all generations of men appear endowed with equal rights, and this is how the historian must view matters.

---

29   From '*Über die Epochen der neuren Weltgeschichte*' in *Weltgeschichte*, Theil IX Ab. 2, pp. 1–9 transl. Wilma A. Iggers in Ranke, 1983, pp. 52–6.

Insofar as we can follow history, unconditional progress, a most definite upward movement, is to be assumed in the realm of material interests in which retrogression will hardly be possible unless there occurs an immense upheaval. In regard to morality, however, progress cannot be traced. Moral ideas can, to be sure, progress extensively; and so on can also assert in cultural (*geistige*) matters that, for example, the great works which art and literature have produced are enjoyed today by larger number than previously. But it would be ridiculous to want to be a greater writer of epic than Homer or a greater writer of tragedies than Sophocles.

. . . The [*Hegelian*] doctrine according to which the world spirit produces things, as it were, through deceit and uses human passions to achieve its goals is based on an utterly unworthy idea of God and mankind. Pursued to its logical conclusion consist ently, this view can lead only to pantheism. Mankind is then God in the process of becoming, who gives birth to himself through a spiritual process that lies in his nature.

I can therefore understand by the 'leading ideas' only the ruling tendencies in every century. These tendencies can only be described, but in the last analysis they cannot be subsumed under one concept. Otherwise we would again return to that which we have rejected above.

The historian must differentiate the great tendencies of the centuries and unroll the great history of mankind, which is just the complex of these various tendencies. From the standpoint of the divine idea, I cannot think of the matter differently but that mankind harbors within itself an infinite multiplicity of developments which manifest themselves gradually according to laws which are unknown to us and are more mysterious and greater than one thinks.

. . .

. . . I believe that every generation is equal in moral greatness to every other generation and that there is no higher potential of moral greatness – we cannot, for example, surpass the moral greatness of the ancient world. It often happens in the spiritual world that intensive greatness stands in inverse relation to extensive greatness. We need only compare our present literature with classical literature to see this.

. . .

The cosmo-political hypothesis [*of a single goal for mankind*] . . . cannot be proved historically . . . From a general human standpoint it would appear probable to me that the idea of mankind, which historically has been represented only in the great nations, will gradually embrace all of mankind, and this would then be inner moral progress. Historical science is not opposed to this view but provides no proof for it. We must especially guard against making this view into a principle of history. Our task is merely to keep to the facts.

3.E.II History versus Philosophy[30]

. . We shall consider history in its struggle with philosophy. We are speaking of that type of philosophy which has reached its results by way of speculation and which claims to dominate history.

30 Excerpted from '*Idee der Univeral Historie*' a manuscript of the 1830s, edited by Eberhard Kessel in *Historische Zeitschrift*, CLXXVIIII (1954) (pp. 290–301) as translated by Wilma A. Iggers, and published with the permission of Professor Kessel and the *Historische Zeitschrift*. Compared with Professor Walther Peter Fuch's unpublished reading of the manuscript and published in Ranke, 1983 (pp. 33–46), pp. 35–44.

. . .

It turns out that the philosopher, starting from a truth, which has been found elsewhere and in a way peculiar to him as a philosopher, constructs all of history for himself: how it must have taken place according to his concept of mankind . . .

Were this procedure correct, . . . history would become dependent, without an inherent interest of its own, and . . . the wellspring of its life would dry up. It would hardly be worthwhile to devote study to history since it would already be implicit in the philosophic concept.

. . .

. . . Philosophy always reminds us of the claim of the supreme idea. History, on the other hand, reminds us of the conditions of existence. The former lends weight to the universal interest, the latter to the particular interest. The former considers the development (*Fortgang*) essential and sees every particular only as a part of the whole. History turns sympathetically also to the particular. Philosophy is forever rejecting: it places the state of which it would approve into the remote future. By its nature philosophy is prophetic, forward-directed. History sees the good and the beneficent in that which exists. It tries to comprehend them and looks to the past.

Indeed, in this opposition one science directly attacks the other. While, as we have seen, philosophy is intent on subjecting history to itself, history at times makes similar claims. It does not want to consider the results of philosophy as absolute, but only as phenomena in time. It assumes that the most exact philosophy is contained in the history of philosophy, i.e., that the absolute truth recognizable to the human race is inherent in the theories which appear from time to time, no matter how much they contradict each other. History goes still one step further here; it assumes that philosophy, especially when it engages in definitions, is only the manifestation of national knowledge inherent in language. It thus denies philosophy any validity and comprehends it in its other manifestation. In this, even the philosophers side with the historians for, as a rule, they accept all former systems only as steps, only as relative phenomena, and ascribe absolute validity only to their own systems.

I do not mean to say that the historian is right in so viewing philosophy; I only want to show that in the historic view of things there is an active principle which is always opposed to the philosophic view and which constantly expresses itself. The question is what this principle is that lies at the basis of such expression.

While the philosopher, viewing history from his vantage-point, seeks infinity merely in progression, development, and totality, history recognises something infinite in every existence: in every condition, in every being, something eternal, coming from God; and this is its vital principle.

How could anything be without the divine basis of its existence?

Therefore, as we have said, history turns with sympathy to the individual; therefore it insists on the validity of the particular interest. It recognises the beneficent, the existing, and opposes change which negates the existing. It recognises even in error its share in truth. For this reason, it sees in the former rejected philosophies a part of eternal knowledge.

It is not necessary for us to prove at length that the eternal dwells in the individual. This is the religious foundation on which our efforts rest. We believe that there is nothing without God, and nothing lives except through God. By freeing ourselve from the claims of a certain narrow theology, we do, nevertheless profess that all our efforts stem from a higher, religious source.

. . .

[*But the historian should be interested not merely in the particular but in the 'totality' of which the particular is part*]

. . . Just as there exists the particular, the connection of the one to the other, so there finally exists totality . . . There is . . . something total in each life; it becomes, it exerts an effect, it acquires influence, it passes away. This totality is as certain at each moment as every expression. We must devote all our attention to it. If we are dealing with a people, we are not interested only in the individual moments of its living expressions. Rather, from the totality of its development, its deeds, its institutions, and its literature, the idea speaks to us so that we simply cannot deny our attention. The farther we go, the harder it is, of course, to get at the idea – for here, too, we can accomplish something only through exact research, through step-by-step understanding, and through the study of documents . . . What an infinite amount of material! What diverse efforts! How difficult it is only to grasp the particular. Since, moreover, there is much that we do not know, how are we to understand the causal nexus everywhere, not to mention getting to the bottom of the essence of totality? I consider it impossible to solve this problem entirely. God alone knows world history. We recognise the contradictions – 'the harmonies,' as an Indian poet says, 'known to the Gods, but unknown to men'; we can only divine, only approach from a distance. But there exists clearly for us a unity, a progression, a development.

So by way of history we arrive at a definition of philosophy's task. If philosophy were what it ought to be, if history were perfectly clear and complete, then they would fully coincide with each other. Historical science would permeate its subject matter with the spirit of philosophy . . .

3.E.III   Against Fichte and Hegel[31]

. . . A philosophy has arisen . . . attempted by Fichte, and then with greater vigor by Hegel. This view . . . starts from the assertion that reason rules the world. The advocates of this position, however, immediately proceed to explain more precisely that the purpose of the spiritual world, which is the substantial world – therefore the final purpose of the world altogether – is the spirit's consciousness of its freedom, the reality of its freedom . . . They establish the steps by which the development of the spirit accomplishes itself . . . The world spirit follows its course through a necessary development by sacrificing the individuals. It uses, as Hegel says, a kind of cunning against the world historical individuals; it lets them carry out their own purposes with all the force of passion while it, the spirit, thereby produces itself. This is not the place to mention all the details of this method, but even for someone who does not agree with us it is

31   From '*Einleitung zu einer Vorlesung über Universalhistorie*' edited by Eberhard Kessel in *Historische Zeitschrift* LXXVIII, 1954 (pp. 304–307), translated by Wilma A. Iggers and published with the permission of Professor Kessel and the *Historische Zeitschrift*, compared with the unpublished reading of the manuscript by Professor Walther, in Ranke 1983 (pp. 47–50), pp. 48–50

undeniable that there is something extremely grandiose in this effort – indeed something gigantic, if we consider the energy which the originator of the system applies – and which therefore deserves great respect.

. . . This view runs counter to the truth of individual consciousness. If this view were correct, the world spirit alone would be truly alive. It would be the sole actor; even the greatest men would be instruments in its hand and would carry out what they themselves neither understood nor wanted. History from this standpoint is actually the history of a developing God. As for myself, gentlemen, I believe in the one who was and is and will be, and in the essential immortal nature of individual man, in the living God and in the living man.

3.E.IV   The Particular and the General[32]

Two qualities are necessary to form a true historian. The first is a feeling for and a joy in the particular in and by itself. If he has a real fondness for the race of these manifold creatures of which we ourselves are a part – for this being which is always the same and yet forever different, which is so good and so evil, so noble and so beastly, so cultured and so coarse, so very much directed toward eternity and so subjected to the moment, so happy and so miserable, satisfied with little and full of desire for all – and if he has a fondness for the living phenomenon of man in general, then he will enjoy observing how man has always sought to live, regardless of the course of events. He will try to follow attentively the virtues which man has sought, the deficiencies which can be seen in him, his fortune and misfortune, the development of his nature under such diverse circumstances, and his institutions and mores. He will try to comprehend all – also the kings under whom the generations have lived, the sequence of events, and the development of major enterprises – without any purpose other than joy in individual life, as one takes joy in flowers without thinking to which of Linné's classes or of Oken's families they belong; briefly put, without thinking how the whole appears in the particular.

This, however, is not all. It is necessary that the historian keep his eyes open for the general. He will not have preconceived ideas as does the philosopher, but rather while he observes the particular, the course which the development of the world in general has taken will be revealed to him. This development, however, does not relate to general concepts which may have predominated in this or that age, but to entirely different things. There is no people on earth which has remained without contact with others. In this relationship, which depends on its own peculiar character, a people enters world history, and it is this relationship which must be stressed in general history . . . No state has ever existed without a spiritual basis and a spiritual content. In power itself a spiritual essence manifests itself. An original genius, which has its own life, fulfils conditions more or less peculiar to itself and creates a circle of effective activity for itself. It is the task of history to observe this life, which cannot be characterized through only one idea or one word. The spirit that manifests itself in the

---

32   From a manuscript of the 1830s published in Alfreed Dove's Vorwort in *Weltgeschichte*, The IX, Abt. 2, pp. vii–xi, transl Wilma A. Iggers in Ranke, 1983 (pp. 29–32), pp. 30–2.

world cannot be circumscribed by a concept. Rather its presence fills all the limits of its existence. Nothing is accidental to it. Its appearance has its foundation in everything.

3.E.V The Freedom – Necessity Polarity in Universal History[33]

History admittedly can never have the unity of a philosophical system; but history is not without inner connection. We see before us a series of events which follow and condition each other. To say condition does not, of course, denote absolute necessity. Rather, the important point is that human freedom is everywhere brought into play. Historical writing traces the scenes of freedom; this is the source of its greatest attraction . . . Nothing is absorbed entirely in the reality of the other. But still a deep inner relationship exists from which nobody is entirely free and which enters into everything. Freedom and necessity exist side by side. Necessity lies in that which has already been formed and cannot be overturned again, which is the basis of all newly emerging activity. What has developed in the past constitutes the connection with what is in the process of becoming . . . Universal history encompasses the past life of the human race in its fullness and totality, not in its individual relationships and directions.

The science of universal history is distinguished from specialised research in this way: that universal history investigating the particular remains always aware of the great whole on which it is working. The investigation of the particular, even of a single point, is of value if it is done well. If devoted to things human, it will always reveal something worth knowing in itself. It is instructive even when applied to petty detail, for the human is always worth knowing. But the investigation of the particular is always related to a larger context. Local history is related to that of a country; a biography is related to a larger event in state and church, to an epoch of national or general history. But all these epochs themselves are, as we have said, again part of the great totality which we call universal history. The greater scope of its investigation has correspondingly greater value. The ultimate goal, yet unattained, will always remain the conception and composition of a history of mankind . . . For one does not study history only for school: the knowledge of the history of mankind ought to be the common property of mankind and, above all, should benefit the nation to which we belong and without which our studies would not even exist . . .

  . . .

Comprehending the whole and yet doing justice to the requirements of research will, of course, always remain an ideal. It would presuppose an understanding on a firm foundation of the totality of human history . . . Relating the particular to the general cannot harm research. Without a general view, research would become sterile; without exact research, the general view would deteriorate into fantasy.

---

33 From Alfred Dove's Vorwort to *Weltgeschichte*, Theil IX, Abt. 2, pp. xiii–xvi, transl Wilma A. Eggers, in Ranke, 1983, pp. 57–9.

3.E.VI   The Secret of World History: Heraclitean Unity Through Difference (1833)[34]

World history does not present such a chaotic tumult, warring, and planless succession of states and peoples as appear at first sight. Nor is the often dubious advancement of civilization its only significance. There are forces and indeed spiritual, life-giving, creative forces, nay life itself, and there are moral energies, whose development we see. They cannot be defined or put in abstract terms, but one can behold them and observe them. One can develop a sympathy for their existence. They unfold, capture the world, appear in manifold expressions, dispute with and check and overpower one another. In their interaction and succession, in their life, in their decline or rejuvenation, which then encompasses an ever greater fullness, higher importance, and wider extent, lies the secret of world history . . .

. . .

But, so people will reply, is not the world developing at this moment into an ever closer community? Would not this tendency be impeded and limited by the contrast between different peoples with their national ways or different states with their individual principles?

Unless I delude myself, there is a close analogy with literature. No one spoke of a world literature at the time that French literature dominated Europe. Only since then has this idea been conceived, expressed, and propagated, in other words, only after most of the principal peoples of Europe had developed their own literature independently and often in sharp contrast . . . There would be only a disagreeable monotony if the different literatures should let their individual characters he blended and melted together. No, the union of all must rest upon the independence of each single one. Then they can stimulate one another in lively fashion and forever, without one dominating or injuring the others.

It is same with states and nations. Decided, positive prevalence of one would bring ruin to the others. A mixture of them all would destroy the essence of each one. Out of separation and independent development will emerge the true harmony.

3.E.VII   Universal Progress: A Final Statement (1880)[35]

. . . A collection of national histories, whether on a larger or a smaller scale, is not what we mean by Universal History, for in such a work the general connection of things is liable to be obscured. To recognize this connection, to trace the sequence of those

34   The concluding paragraphs of Ranke's *Die Großen Mächte* (1833) transl. Hildegarde Hunt Von Laue, from Theodore H. Von Laue *Leopold Ranke: The Formative* Years (Princeton University Press 1950) pp. 181–218. Reprinted by permission of Princeton University Press and the translator in Ranke (1983) pp. 100–1.

35   From *Universal History: The Oldest Historical Group of Nations and the Greeks*, ed. G. W. Prothero (New York: Charles Scribner's Sons, 1884), pp. xi–xiv as revised by Georg Iggers and reprinted in Ranke, 1983, pp. 162–3.

great events which link all nations together and control their destinies is the task which the science of Universal History undertakes. . . .

. . . The nations can be regarded in no other connection than in that of the mutual action and reaction involved by their successive appearance on the stage of history and their combination into one progressive community.

. . .

. . . Historical development does not alone rest on the tendency toward civilization. It arises also from impulses of a very different kind, especially from the rivalry of nations engaged in conflict with each other for the possession of the soil or for political supremacy. It is in and through this conflict, which always also affects the domains of culture, that the great powers of history are formed. In their unceasing struggle for dominion the peculiar characteristics of each nation are modified by universal tendencies, but at the same time resist and react upon them.

. . . There is a general historical life that moves progressively from one nation or group of nations to another. In the conflict between the different national groups Universal History comes into being, and the nationalities become conscious of themselves, for nations are not entirely products of nature. Nationalities so powerful and distinct as the English or the Italian are not so much the offspring of the soil and the race as of the great events through which they have passed.

But what does it require to investigate and to understand the universal life of mankind and the peculiarities of at least the more prominent nations? In this attempt the laws of historical criticism, called for in every detailed inquiry, may on no account be neglected, for it is only the results of critical investigation which can be dignified with the title of history at all. Our gaze must indeed be always fixed on the universal, but from false premises false conclusions would be drawn. Critical inquiry, on the one hand, and intelligent synthesis can only but support each other.

. . .

In the course of centuries the human race has won for itself a sort of heirloom in the material and social progress which its has made but still more in its religious development. One portion of the heritage, the most precious jewel of the whole, consists of those immortal works of genius in poetry and literature, in science and art, which, while they originated under local conditions, yet represent what is common to all mankind. With this possession are inseparably combined the memories of the event, the institutions, and the great mean of the past. One generation hand on the tradition to another, which may again and again be revived and recalled to the mind of men, as I have the courage and confidence to do.

4 Positivism

Robert M. Burns

Introduction

The term 'positivism' is now particularly associated with the 'logical positivism' of the Vienna Circle, a group of philosophers including Moritz Schlick and Rudolf Carnap centred in Vienna in the post-World War I period, with associates in Prague, Berlin and Scandinavia, and with figures such as Ludwig Wittgenstein and Karl Popper on the margins. Most migrated to the English-speaking world in the Nazi period where their message had already been very effectively presented in 1936 by A. J. Ayer's *Language, Truth and Logic* (1946), which helped to ensure that its challenge largely dominated the English-speaking philosophical agenda for many years. The logical positivists maintained that a single scientific method applies in all fields, including human nature, which is simply the discernment of regular sequences in empirical phenomena, whilst any capacity to gain insight into what lies behind the phenomena is denied. From these assumptions a criterion of meaningfulness was forged, named the 'Verification Principle', which supposedly was to be applied to propositions rather like a litmus test, allowing meaningless propositions to be discarded without further examination. It stated that meaningful propositions were either tautologies, which included the propositions of pure mathematics, or factual, in which case they had to be empirically verifiable. From this 'the meaninglessness of all metaphysics' (Carnap in Ayer, 1959, pp. 69–75) inevitably followed. Theological propositions were obviously meaningless, and ethical propositions, too, had to be regarded as non-factual: 'emotive' was one suggested classification. To the reader of chapter 1, section IV, this will have a familiar ring, and indeed Ayer acknowledged that Hume had provided 'an excellent statement of the positivist's position' (Ayer, 1959, p. 10), the Principle itself being anticipated in the memorable closing words of Hume's first *Enquiry*: 'When we run over libraries, persuaded, of these principles, what havoc must we make? If we take in our hand any volume; of divinity or school metaphysics, for instance; let us ask, *Does It contain any abstract reasoning concerning quantity or number?* No. *Does it contain any experimental reasoning concerning matter of fact and existence?* No. Commit it then to the flames: for it can contain nothing but sophistry and illusion' (Hume, 1975, p. 165).

The movement collapsed not as the result of the onslaught of critics but because, despite their early confident and aggressive optimism, its advocates never found it possible to define 'verification' in ways which did not allow in far too many propositions or too few. At an early stage the criterion's demand was changed to verifiability 'in principle' rather than 'in fact', but no *general* empirical proposition (and all theories and laws in natural science make general claims) could ever be exhaustively verified for an exception to an experienced regularity can always turn up, such as the black swans Captain Cook discovered in Australia. Popper suggested that the concern to establish a universally applicable criterion of meaning should be abandoned, and the principle reversed, and merely regarded as a way of distinguishing scientific propositions from others, namely that they must be in principle empirically *falsifiable*, but this less ambitious proposal also ran into logical difficulties. Eventually the requirement was reduced to the suggestion that meaningful propositions must be empirical conformable or disconfirmable but this left claims about 'God' and virtually every traditional metaphysical proposition unscathed: beautiful sunsets could be said to confirm God's existence to some degree, whilst earthquakes to disconfirm it; a movement which had begun with a bold, brash claim to be able to rid the world of the interminable disputes of traditional philosophy ended in inconclusiveness and indeed incoherence.

The impact of logical positivism on philosophy of history was considerable, owing to a series of articles by Carl Hempel beginning in 1940, which generated seemingly inexhaustible interest for several years, although anyone acquainted with 2.A.I and II will experience a sense of *déjà vu*. Their impact is indicated by the fact that one or other of them was nearly always reproduced in the anthologies of articles on philosophy of history published in the subsequent three decades (e.g., Gardiner, 1959, pp. 344–56; Nash, 1969, pp. 79–106; Dray, 1966, pp. 95–126). Numerous journal articles supporting or challenging it were published, and several books (e.g., Dray, 1957; Gardiner, 1952). Hempel argued that scientific explanation in general is 'deductive-nomological' (or 'covering-law': *nomos* is Greek for 'law') in nature, aiming to deduce particular facts from 'uniformities expressed by general laws' (Hempel, 1962, pp. 96–7). A weaker form of explanation was termed 'probabilistic-statistical' (p. 100), in which the explanation is provided by a statement of the relative frequency of the sequence of the phenomena. Both scientific and every-day life explanations confirm to this ideal but 'elliptically' or 'partially', as 'explanation sketches', with non-controversial gaps fillable on demand (pp. 103ff). Hempel argues that historical explanations conform entirely to the norm, even though nearly all are elliptically formulated. This includes 'genetic' or 'narrative explanation' (p. 111), which some had viewed as implying that 'historical understanding is of a basically different kind from that achieved in the natural sciences' (Gallie, 1964, p. 126)[1] for Hempel argues that 'in a genetic explanation each stage in what is otherwise straight description must be known to "lead" to the next . . . by virtue of some general principle' (Hempel, 1962, p. 113). He also maintained that explanations of human actions in terms of motives are also nomological for they are essentially appeals to generalizations founded on experience about how either rational persons normally act, or human types, e.g., how fearless persons normally act in similar situations.

The thinkers discussed in this section differ in many respects from the twentieth

---

1 The distinction between narrative and causal explanation goes at least as far back as the young Dilthey; in his 1862 review of the German translation of Buckle's *History* Dilthey wrote: 'Even before the spread of enquiry awakens in the child, which leads it to ask for the why and then the why of the why behind every event, another kind of curiosity takes shape, which can be satisfied only by the telling of stories and by the assurance that all these stories are true' (Dilthey, 1996, p. 261).

century positivists who took over the label from Auguste Comte through something of a historical accident (see Kolakowski, 1969, p. 102). Comte is certainly responsible for bringing the term 'positivist' into widespread use, applying the phrase *'philosophie positiviste'* as the standard term for his own philosophy, although traces of its use can be found in the circle of Saint-Simon to which he belonged in his youth. The short definition offered by Comte of 'the exact nature of positive philosophy' does however embrace the later common understanding of the term: 'it is . . . to regard all phenomena as subject to invariable natural *laws*, the discovery of which and their reduction to the least possible number, is the aim and end of all our efforts, while causes, either first or final, are considered to be absolutely inaccessible, and the search for them meaningless' (Comte, 1974, p. 24). But, in important respects, Comte does not conform to 'positivism' as later understood. Mill conforms more clearly to it, but not as fully as Buckle. Of the three only Buckle actually wrote history as distinct from theorizing about it. For two classical instances of nineteenth-century positivist historians see the Frenchman Hippolyte Taine and the German Karl Lamprecht (see Cassirer, 1944, ch. X for a useful discussion of them).

The author of the most informative recent account of **Auguste Comte** (1798–1857) claims that he is 'among the dozen most important figures in modern European history' (Pickering, 1993, p. 1). His impact on academic vocabulary has certainly been outstanding: he invented the word 'sociology,' virtually invented 'positivism' and 'positivist' (p. 581), and was to a considerable extent responsible for the adoption of the term 'biology', all as part of his audacious attempt to produce a systematic account of the sciences as a totality in his six-volume *Cours de Philosophie Positive* (1830–42). At its core is the claim that human knowledge develops through three stages, first theological, than metaphysical, and finally positive (4.A.I), a 'law' which he claimed to have discovered in 1822 after two nights of continuous meditation from 7.00 p.m. to 10 a.m., although it certainly echoes earlier thinkers, especially Turgot (pp. 198–9). Each stage is a necessary precondition of the following stage. Thus 'theology' is not merely an intellectual and moral perversion obstructing progress as in Condorcet, but itself constitutes progress, each of its three successive sub-stages (fetishism, polytheism and monotheism) having valuable aspects (for example, the art of polytheism). The climax of the monotheistic stage is Medieval Catholicism, which, by engendering scholastic philosophy prepared the way for it own supersession by metaphysics. It is applauded by Comte for having constituted a single moral authority throughout Western Europe capable of checking political rulers, a function Comte saw as being fulfilled by the future positivist intellectual élite (4.A.VII). Protestantism destroyed this achievement, by fusing secular and spiritual power. In general he is far more sympathetic to religion, and especially to Catholicism, than most secular humanists. The permanent need for religion is so great, in his view, that after the completion of the *Cours* he increasingly turned his attention to the formation of a 'Positivist Church' embodying a new Religion of Humanity, complete with rituals and hierarchy, thereby alienating a number of his original followers.

His account of the sciences placed them in a scale of increasing complexity and differentiation in phenomena, the 'higher' sciences presupposing and building upon the results of the 'lower' which reached the 'positive' stage first (4.A.II) . Apart from mathematics, the five fundamental theoretical sciences, each with subdivisions and associated technologies are, in order of ascent, astronomy, physics, chemistry, physiology, and, finally, 'social physics', or 'sociology'. This will have two interdependent and complementary subdivisions, social statics and social dynamics. The latter and, in large part, the former, is largely positivist history, which will form the basis of political science (4.A.VI) . But sociology does not yet exist in a properly 'positive' form (he thought it would take 'two or three generations' to realize; Pickering, 1993, p. 253) so that his often confident descriptions of it (4.A.VII) can by his own account be merely speculative projections. The scale was, as 'a schema of positive conceptions covering all the great orders of natural phenomena', intended to become the '*sine qua non* of general education' and thereby the means for the 'regeneration of our intelligence . . . even for the masses, the permanent basis of all planning; it will form the mentality of our descendants' (Comte, 1974, p. 35) for, in contrast to the Marxist understanding of ideology (see chapter 8) 'ideas govern and revolutionize the world . . . the entire social machinery rests in the last resort on opinion' (p. 37) and the 'present mental disorder', caused by 'intellectual anarchy', will cease which is to say 'the revolutionary fever which torments civilized peoples will be at an end' (pp. 35–9).

Perhaps the most striking aspect of Comte's hierarchy of the sciences is the omission of 'psychology,' which one might expect to find between physiology and sociology. It is the result of Comte's rejection of the phenomenalist notion of the immediate infallible presence to itself of the human consciousness held by Hume, British empiricism generally (including Mill; 4.B.I), and very many French thinkers (such as his contemporary Victor Cousin). It brings him closer to German historicists in understanding the individual human person to be a socio-historical product. He declared the notion of a unified ego 'purely fictive'. The 'general feeling of the self' was derived from 'the fundamental unity of the animal organism' and not the mental side of man; the inner personality was a congeries of 'essentially multiple' (Pickering, 1993, p. 598) powers between which equilibrium is only 'established very painfully', a view comparable to that of Nietzsche. Later in the century, through Comte's influence, it became a basic presupposition of Durkheim's sociology.

Certainly this distinguishes him sharply from many forms of empiricist positivism, which has tended to phenomenalism (although some logical positivists broke with it) as does his repeated insistence that it is unrealistic to think of perception as the registering of bare facts and the regular conjunctions between them. Rather, items can only be perceived when interpreted by a *theory* embraced in advance, so that scientific explanation originates always in what Schleiermacher called a hermeneutical circle (4.A.I, V). He insists above all that 'entirely empirical observation' is useless in social science because every item is always modified by its relations to the social whole. Accordingly he condemns historians who merely pile up 'facts', a tendency routinely termed 'positivist', but the antithesis of Comte's expressed position. Yet another deviation from typically 'positivist' trends is his repeated discounting of Condorcet's claims of the value of statistical calculations as a basis for social science (see also 4.B.VII and 4.C.IV); indeed he maintained that not only social but biological phenomena were too complex and variable to be subject to 'calculable and precise laws' (Pickering, 1993, p. 216). Likewise he rejected Hume's advocacy of the calculus of probabilities as a basis for judgements of historical credibility on the grounds that 'absurd consequences' follow from it, such as rejecting 'as numerically unlikely events that are, nevertheless, going to happen' (p. 579).

His acute sense of the operation of 'consensus' and solidarity' as fundamental features of all societies led him to view all societies as 'organisms' which require 'holistic' explanation, each component understandable only in terms of its function in the whole: for example, he held that, in the Middle Ages, kingship, land-tenure and Catholicism mutually modified one another in their historical concreteness. Accordingly, political rulers should never presume that they can successfully to tinker with, or abolish given structures of their society according to abstract blueprints (4.A.IIa). One might have expected him to conclude, like Montesquieu or Herder, that widely divergent social structures might evolve in different milieux which would maintain themselves indefinitely if not destroyed by outside forces, but in fact he maintains, like Condorcet, that there is in history a 'total movement of humanity' in a 'fixed order' resulting in an 'evolution of humanity' (4.A.IIIb) into a single 'collective organism' (4.A.VII), forming 'one immense social unit'. The consequent sense of human solidarity will become 'the rational basis of positive morality' (4.A.IIIb and c). These confident prophecies are hard to square with his claim elsewhere that our imagination remains necessarily dependent on our social milieu, so that 'the conception of a political system radically different from the one that surrounds us is quite beyond the dreams of our intelligence', and even those who consider themselves emancipated from such conditioning nevertheless 'all unconsciously . . . faithfully reflect in their dreams . . . this necessity' (Comte, 1974, p. 136). There is tension too between his claims about the *concreteness* of social relations and the demand, based on his notion that the individual is nothing more than a function of society, that history must be 'without names of men, even without names of peoples' (4.A.VI).

So convinced is he that he has discovered the direction of the historical process that he decrees that scientific historians are obliged to arranging human events in a 'co-ordinated series', in order to show it as 'directed towards one single goal'. This requires limiting their research to the 'élite of humanity', in which progress is to be found in its 'full manifestation', which is to say 'the white race or the European nations', and, more specifically 'the peoples of Western Europe' (4.A.VI). He is sure that historians will soon be recording 'collaboration' among the great European nations and eventually, under French leadership, 'actual combination'. There is a strongly authoritarian streak in Comte. Once the 'invariable natural laws' governing social phenomena (p. 144) have been fully determined scientifically the individual has no other role than to conform. There is no need for diffusion of power beyond the notion of an ultimate duality of scientists and political rulers. It has often been remarked that the totalitarianism of the Soviet Union or Maoist China is far closer to the vision of Comte than anything Marx envisaged.

John Stuart Mill (1806–1873) was a classic British empiricist in the lineage of Hume, as mediated particularly through the thinking of his father James Mill, the leading Utilitarian, even though Mill never describes himself as an 'empiricist', reserving the term for unreflective, and unsystematic learning from experience, as opposed to its methodical exploration, the logic of which it was the aim of his major philosophical work, the *System of Logic* (first edition 1843) to expound. Actually, he is a more extreme empiricist than any other leading figure in the British empiricist tradition, arguing – unlike Hume or twentieth-century logical positivists – that all mathematical axioms are 'experimental truths; generalizations from experience . . . inductions from

---

2 'Induction' means here the process of inferring a general law from experiences of regularities in phenomena.

the evidence of our senses'[2] (*System of Logic* II.V.4), which is to say that it is an 'illusion' that the truths of geometry and arithmetic have the 'character of necessity'. There exist no 'real things exactly conformable to the definitions of geometry', that is, 'there exist no points without magnitude; no lines without breadth, nor perfectly straight; no circles with all their radii exactly equal . . . the points, lines, circles and squares which anyone has in his mind are simply copies of the points, lines, circles and squares which he has known in experience' (*System* II.V.1). He even maintains that the principle of the uniformity of nature is itself inductively 'gained from experiences' (*System* III.III.1), which Hume never suggests but rather claims is a presupposition instilled in us by nature, and which has to be assumed in inductive reasoning. He is also a thoroughgoing nominalist; according to him all real beings are particular; that is, there are no real 'common essences' or universal truths of things which particular beings merely exemplify, so that that all general propositions are 'mere formulae for inferring particulars from particulars' (*System* II.IV.3) and their 'real premises' are always 'individual observations' (*System* III.V.2). He is also a phenomenalist; all truths of experience are traceable back to 'immediate consciousness', that is 'our own bodily sensations and mental feeling'. These are the 'original data' of all our knowledge. We need no logical or scientific method for knowing these data, which are known 'directly' through 'Intuition or Consciousness' which is' beyond possibility of question' (*System*, Introduction, 4). All other knowledge develops from them by 'inference'. It follows that my belief that any other consciousnesses exist is inferred by noting similarities between their bodies and my own.

For a time Mill was extremely enthusiastic about Comte's thinking: for a brief period he was even prepared to suggest to Comte that he was virtually his disciple, but initial enthusiasm was replaced by a considerable disillusionment. Traces of his admiration remain in the *System of Logic*: Comte's notion of 'sociology' and its division into 'statics' and 'dynamics' is fully endorsed, supported with a long quotation from Comte (*System* VI.X.V). It is acknowledged that the scientific investigation of societies and their progress 'has been systematically attempted, up to the present time by Comte alone'. The Law of the Three Stages throws 'a flood of light on the whole course of history' (4.B.VI) 'M. Comte alone', up until now, 'has seen the necessity of . . . connecting all our generalizations from history with the laws of human nature' (*System* VI.X.3).

Yet, by the time of the completion of his *System*, Mill had become painfully aware of the gulf between himself and Comte. He declares that, in rejecting introspective psychology, 'no writer . . . is chargeable in a higher degree with . . . aberration from the true scientific spirit than M. Comte' (*System* VI.IV.4). He maintains that the universal science of human nature based on immediately intuited mental phenomena as originated by Hume and developed with a 'masterly hand' by Mill's own father (4.B.I) is the only possible ultimate foundation for all the 'moral sciences' (his general term for the human sciences, current in Britain since the eighteenth century). It follows almost inevitably that Mill should embrace what in the twentieth century has become known as 'methodological individualism' (see 4.B.III). Yet this is hard to reconcile with his acknowledgement that 'there is no social phenomenon which is not more or less influenced by every other part of the condition of the same society' (which seems to be evidence of the impact of Comte's stress on social 'solidarity' and 'consensus'), without assuming that, after all, the social aspects of human beings are at most superficial, secondary accretions, i.e., there are no irreducibly 'social facts'. The same tension is evident in his discussion of 'hypothetical or abstract sciences'(IX.B.IV) which seems to imply that the modification of individuals by the 'consensus' operative in their society, is limited. Nevertheless, his travels in Europe had convinced him that the insular British and their isolated North American cousins, tended to underestimate cultural difference: for instance, British and American economists mistakenly projected Anglo-American attitudes to money on humanity in general. He therefore calls for the establishment of a new science of the causes of national character which he termed 'Ethology'. It will accumulate empirical generalizations which will in turn eventually be explained by ultimate causal laws securely known through introspective psychology, at which point scientific comprehension of human nature will be complete. The basic view, therefore, is hardly distinguishable from that Hume's uniformitarianism, although Hume never distinguishes between 'empirical laws' and ultimate causal laws as does Mill with perhaps scanty justification in terms of his overall nominalist phenomenalism.

The great difference between Mill and Comte on the question of whether or not human nature is essentially social comes to the fore in his treatment of the individual in history. There is no question for Mill of minimizing the importance in history of the contingent decisions of those in power, or of individual intellectual geniuses (contrast 4.B.VIII with 4.A.IIb). Nevertheless in the end he seeks to reconcile this with the inevitability of progress by suggesting that the presence or absence of the right persons at the right times merely determines the speed of progress. But nothing could reconcile the liberal individualist Mill with Comte's politics. In *Liberty* he writes: 'M. Comte . . . aims at establishing . . . a despotism over the individual, surpassing anything contemplated in the political ideals of the most rigid disciplinarian among the ancient philosophers' (Ryan, 1974, p. 129). Eventually Mill gave a full account of his differences with Comte in 1865 in *Auguste Comte and Positivism* (Mill, 1961), stating in particular that Comte's 'second career' leads one to 'weep at the melancholy decadence of a great intellect' (p. 185) not only because of his totalitarianism but his 'ineffably ludicrous' (p. 153) notions of a positive religion.

Henry Thomas Buckle's (1821–62) *History of Civilization in England* (vol. I, 1857, vol. II, 1861[3]) was without question mainly responsible for the spread of positivist historical ideas among the English reading public for several decades, because of its forceful and vivid style, and impressively wide-ranging scholarship. It also had a major impact in Germany: Dilthey's 1862 review of Buckle is now available in English (Dilthey 1996, pp. 261–9) and Droysen's critique has been available in English since 1893, as an Appendix to his *Outlines of the Principles of History* (Droysen, 1893, pp. 61–89) containing perhaps the first expression of what was to becomes a standard distinction between positivist and historicist explanation; namely that history contains 'things which demand not to be "explained" but understood' (p. 76). Section 4.B.VII is Mill's testimony to the enormous impact of Buckle on intellectual life at the time, taken from an additional chapter to the *System* written largely to take account of Buckle, who had however given Mill short shrift: there is just one vague footnoted reference to Mill' 'profound' *System of Logic* in Buckle's *History* (vol. I, p. 224). The reason is that Buckle is entirely in agreement with Comte concerning the 'fundamental error' of assuming that we can discover 'mental laws' by the 'observation of our own minds'; rather, they

---

3   The 1861 edition, which was the third edition of vol. I is cited here.

are to be ascertained by discovering them in history (vol. 1, pp. 150–1). Among much else which also echoes Comte is his contemptuous dismissal of most historians (he approvingly quotes Comte's description of them as 'piling up disconnected facts') and an enthusiastic progressivism which contrasts rather markedly with Mill's reservations (4.B.VII). However although he wrote that Comte 'has done more any other to raise the standard of history' (vol. 1, p. 5), he is far from being uncritical of him: his stress on the importance of statistics is unComtean, and he also rejects the notion which he finds in Comte that mental progress can occur through the hereditary transmission of acquired characteristics (vol. I, pp. 160–1).

Buckle had originally planned to write a comprehensive multi-volume history of world civilization, but decided to limit himself to English civilization justifying it by making a virtue of the cultural isolation of England (4.C.IV) which he arguably exaggerates considerably. But, despite publishing two volumes of his *History*, the first 854 pages, and the second 651 pages long, he never reached the topic of English civilization except for a rambling and very patchy survey of the history of the British intellect from 1550 to the end of the eighteenth century (vol. I, ch. 7). The first five chapters of volume 1 outline his understanding of the aims of and principles of historical explanation, the rest of the volume discussing the history of France. Volume II is devoted entirely to a history of Spain and Scotland, intended in both cases to be object-lessons in the deplorable effects of religious persecution, except for the final chapter which surveys some leading thinkers of what we would now call the Scottish Enlightenment. The second volume lacks the ebullient confidence of the first volume; the truth was, as Buckle admits half way through the volume, that he had misjudged the difficulty of his task; the project was foundering, so that his untimely death in the Near East was not the main reason for its abortive state. Although, in volume I, he had disparaged the 'imagination' as opposed to the scientific pure intellect, he now confesses that his vision of scientific progress had been largely the product of his imagination. Essentially his standpoint is that of Hume of whom he states that 'his theory of miracles, in connection, on the one hand, with the principles of evidence, and on the other hand, with the laws of causality is worked out with consummate skill' and remains 'the foundation on which the best inquirers into these matters take their stand' (vol. II, p. 460), and his stress on statistics seems to be a development of Hume. But his great hero is Adam Smith upon whose *Wealth of Nations* he lavishes praise in both volumes: it was, he says, 'probably the most important book which has ever been written whether we consider the amount of original thought it contains, or its practical influence . . . No single man ever took so great a step upon so important a subject' (vol. II, p. 443; see also 4.C.III). Hume by contrast had not Smith's 'invaluable quality of imagination' (vol. II, p. 458) and he is accused in his *History* of 'using facts not to demonstrate his conclusions, but to illustrate them' (vol. II, p. 473).

The excerpts from Buckle have been restricted because of lack of space. The essential steps in Buckle's argument are sufficiently indicated by them if the following points are borne in mind. Section 4.C.I speaks of human history as the outcome or the 'reciprocal interaction' of two basic law-governed realities: namely Nature and the human mind. As the human mind discovers Nature's laws they become ever less important in determining human events, because humanity thereby gains the means to subjugate it. It was in north-western Europe, due largely to the right climatic and physical conditions, that the human mind was stimulated into activity, instead of cowering before

Nature in ignorant fear, and seeking to propitiate it religiously. Mental laws are not to be discovered by introspection but by empirical, statistical surveys (4.C.II). Mental laws subdivide into moral and intellectual laws. The former are essentially identical throughout human history. It is intellectual laws which are genuinely progressive; without access to intellectual truth even moral purity can produce great evil (4.C.III). English history is a necessary and sufficient field for research into the laws of progress (4.C.IV). It can surely be only with wry amusement that the modern reader finds Hegel convinced that the axis of world history runs through Germany, Comte that it runs through France, and Buckle that it runs through England.

Selected Texts

Edited by Robert M. Burns

4.A   Auguste Comte, 1798–1857

4.A.1   The Law of the Three Stages[1]

. . . I believe I have discovered a fundamental law [*of*] the development of human intelligence . . . to which it is subjected from an invariable necessity, and which seems to me to be solidly established, either by rational proof drawn from a knowledge of our nature, or by the historical test, an attentive examination of the past. This law is that each of our principal conceptions, each branch of our knowledge, passes successively through three different theoretical states: the theological or fictitious, the metaphysical or abstract, and the scientific or positive. In other words, the human mind, by its nature, employs in all its investigations three methods of philosophising, of an essentially different and even opposed nature: first the theological, then the metaphysical, and finally the positive. Hence there are three mutually exclusive kinds of philosophy, or conception systems regarding the totality of phenomena: the first is the necessary starting-point of human intelligence, the third its fixed and final state; the second is only a means of transition.

In the theological state, the human mind, directing its search to the very nature of being, to the first and final causes of all the effects that it beholds, in a word, to absolute knowledge, sees phenomena as products of the direct and continuous action of more or less numerous supernatural agents, whose arbitrary intervention explains all the apparent anomalies of the universe.

In the metaphysical state, which at bottom is a mere modification of the theological, the supernatural agents are replaced by abstract forces, veritable entities (personified abstractions) inherent in the various types of being, and conceived as capable in themselves of engendering all observed phenomena, the explanation of which consists in assigning to each its corresponding entity.

Finally, in the positive state, the human mind, recognising the impossibility of attaining to absolute concepts, gives up the search for the origin and destiny of the universe, and the inner causes of phenomena, and confines itself to the discovery, through reason and observation combined, of the actual laws that govern the succession and similarity of phenomena. The explanation of the facts now reduced to its real

From Comte, 1974, pp. 19–24.

terms, consists in the establishment of a link between various phenomena and a few general facts, which diminish in number with the progress of science.

The theological system arrived at the highest perfection of which it is capable when it substituted the providential action of a unique being for the interplay of the numerous independent divinities that had been imagined in the beginning. In the same way the metaphysical system reaches its consummation in the idea not of different particular entities, but of one great general entity, *nature*, as the unique source of all phenomena. The perfection of the positive system, towards which it toils unwearied, though destined probably never to attain it, would consist in seeing all observable phenomena as the particular cases of one single fact, as for instance the fact of gravitation.

. . .

Since Bacon, intelligent people are agreed that there is no real knowledge save that which rests on observed facts. As applying to the full grown state of our intelligence, this principle is evidently incontestable. But if we look at its formative stage, it is no less certain that the human mind then could not, and should not, think in this way. For if on the one hand every positive theory is necessarily based on observation, on the other it is no less certain that in order to devote itself to observation the mind needs some kind of theory. If in contemplating phenomena we had no principles to which to attach them, not only would we find it impossible to combine isolated observations, and therefore to profit from them, but we would not be able to remember them, and most of the time the facts themselves would pass unperceived before our very eyes.

Thus between the necessity of observation for the formation of general theories, and the not less pressing necessity of constructing theories for the pursuit of observation, the human mind must have found itself trapped in a vicious circle, from which it could never have escaped, had not a natural way out been provided by the spontaneous development of theological conceptions, which offered a rallying point for its efforts and material for its activity. Such is the fundamental motive – apart from the weighty social ones which are not to be entered into at this stage – of the theological character of primitive philosophy, and the proof also if its logical necessity.

. . .

. . . It is the nature of positive philosophy to regard all phenomena as subject to invariable natural *laws*, the discovery of which, and their reduction to the least possible number, is the aim and end of all our efforts, while causes, either first or final, are considered to be absolutely inaccessible, and the search for them meaningless . . . We do not pretend to expound the generative *causes* of phenomena . . . but rather to analyse the circumstances in which the phenomena are produced, and to link them one to another by the relations of succession and similarity.

4.A.II   The Hierarchy of Fundamental Sciences: The Encyclopaedic Ladder[2]

We propose to classify the fundamental sciences. It will soon become apparent that, all things considered, it is not possible to reduce them to less than six . . .

. . .

2   Ibid., pp. 52–7.

. . . The order is determined by the degree of simplicity, or what amounts to the same thing, of generality in the phenomena, resulting in successive dependencies, and consequently greater or less difficulty in study.

A priori we can decide that the most simple phenomena, those least complicated by others, are necessarily the most general . . . Hence it is by the study of the most general or most simple phenomena that we must begin, proceeding by successive degrees to the most particular and the most complex . . .

. . .

When we first consider natural phenomena in their totality, we find ourselves dividing them, in conformity with the principle we have just established, into two great classes, the first comprising all the phenomena of inorganic, the second of organic bodies.

The second class are obviously more complicated and highly individualised than the first; they depend on the first, while the first are not at all dependent on the second. Hence the necessity of studying physiological phenomena only after those of inorganic bodies. In whatever way we explain the differences of these two kinds of bodies, what is certain is that all the phenomena, mechanical or chemical, of inorganic bodies are to be observed in organic bodies, with in addition a quite special order of phenomena, the vital phenomena properly so called, those that belong to *organism*. . . .

. . .

As a result of this discussion positive philosophy splits up into five fundamental sciences, the sequence of which is determined by a necessary subordination, independent of any hypothesis, and based on the comparison of the corresponding phenomena. These sciences are: astronomy, physics, chemistry, physiology, and social physics. The first of these sciences considers the most general phenomena, the most simple, the most abstract, the most removed from humanity; these phenomena influence all the others, without being influenced by them. The phenomena considered by the last are, on the contrary, the most peculiar, the most complex, the most directly interesting to man; they depend, more or less, on all the preceding ones, without exercising any influence on them. . . .

4.A.III   Social Physics or Sociology: Social Statics and Social Dynamics (i.e., History)[3]

. . . The Theory . . . of social phenomena . . . has not yet issued from the theologico-metaphysical prison, to which thinkers appear to condemn it, as a fatal exception, for all time . . . Our present task is to create a whole order of scientific conceptions that no previous philosopher has so much as outlined, and which had never even been glimpsed before as a possibility . . .

. . .

. . . We must extend to social phenomena a scientific distinction that is truly fundamental, and applicable by its nature to any phenomena, above all to those of living bodies: that between the *static* and the *dynamic* state of every subject of positive study. In biology, i.e. in the study of individual life, this dichotomy gives rise to the distinc-

Ibid., pp. 120–77.

tion between the anatomical point of view, which relates to organisation, and the physiological point of view, which is proper to life: in sociology the splitting up must be effected in a similar manner, and not less definitely, by distinguishing in every political subject between the conditions of existence of a society and the laws of its movement. The difference is sufficiently marked for its natural development to give rise perhaps eventually to two sciences within social physics, which might be called social statics and social dynamics, as essentially distinct from one another as anatomy and physiology for the individual. . . .

The better to characterise this dichotomy and show at once its practical importance, let me say here that it corresponds perfectly to the double notion of order and progress in politics, which we can now regard as accepted in public life. Obviously the study of the static social organism coincides at bottom with the positive theory of order, and this can only consist in a just harmony of the various elements of human society; in the same way we see that the study of the dynamic life of humanity yields the positive theory of social progress, which by thrusting aside all vain thoughts of absolute and unlimited perfection, reduces itself to the simple idea of development. . . .

(a) Social Statics

Defining according to this conception the static laws of the social organism, we shall find that their philosophic principle is a general consensus, such as characterises any and all phenomena of living bodies, and which social life manifests in the highest degree. Thus understood, the social anatomy which constitutes static sociology must have as its permanent object the positive study, at once experimental and rational, of the various parts of the social system in their action and reaction upon one another, abstracting for the time being as much as possible the movement which is always modifying them. . . .

. . .

. . . The most advanced thinkers, of France and Germany especially [*realize*] that there is a constant and necessary solidarity of political power and civil power, which means, in positive language, that the predominant social forces become in the end also the ruling forces . . .

. . . Even in revolutionary epochs, with their insufficient realisation of this funda-mental harmony, it continues to make itself felt, for it could not be entirely dissolved except with the dissolution of the social organism itself, of which it is the principal attribute. . . .

In vulgar estimation the legislator has the power to break up the harmony we are considering, if only he possesses sufficient authority: which amounts to a complete negation of the solidarity we are considering. [*But*] . . . we can say that . . . any [*politi-cal*] power whatsoever is constituted by the assent, spontaneous or considered, explicit or implicit, of the various individual wills which have decided in accordance with cer-tain convictions, to co-operate in a common action, of which the said power is first of all the instrument, and afterwards the regulator. Thus authority derives really from co-operation, and not co-operation from authority . . . It is true, no intelligent person can deny the great influence plainly exercised by a political regime on a system of civilisa-tion . . . The usual mistake is to exaggerate it beyond all reason . . .

. . . Thus a political regime is never to be considered except in its continuous relation, sometimes general, sometimes special, to the corresponding state of civilisation, apart from which it cannot be properly judged, and by the gradual pressure of which it is produced and modified. . . .

. . . Every mind that is properly organised and rationally prepared, in a word worthy of such a destiny, will know how to avoid confusing the scientific notion of order with the systematic apology for existing order . . . Positive philosophy always teaches that in accordance with the natural laws of the phenomena a certain necessary order invariably establishes itself; but never claims that such an order does not offer numerous disadvantages that can be modified to a certain extent by wise human intervention. . . .

. . .

. . . Since social phenomena are closely interconnected, their study cannot be undertaken separately, hence the necessity of always considering the various aspects of society simultaneously, whether in social statics or in social dynamics . . . No social phenomenon by whatsoever means it has been explored, as long as it is viewed in isolation . . . can be introduced into the science. . . . Thus every isolated study of social elements is from the very nature of social science quite irrational, and will remain sterile . . .

. . .

(b) Social Dynamics

The static conception of the social organism must constitute the basis of all sociology, but social dynamics is the part of most direct interest, especially today; also it gives to the new science its most outstanding characteristic, it brings to the fore the idea that most distinguishes sociology from biology, the idea of the continuous progress, or rather of the gradual development of humanity. . . .

In the true spirit of dynamic sociology, each of the consecutive social states is seen as the necessary result of the preceding one, and the necessary cause of the following one, according to the axiom of the great Leibniz. *The present is big with the future.* To discover the laws of this continuity becomes the aim of science, for it is the continuity that determines the direction of human development. In a word, social dynamics studies the laws of movement, while social statics seeks out those of coexistence. . . .

. . .

. . . At all times and in all places notable modifications have been seen taking place in the social state, even in the brief lifetime of the individual. The most ancient descriptions of human existence bear testimony to these changes, though without explanation. It is the slow and gradual but continuous accumulation of these successive changes that constitutes the social movement of which each generation marks a step . . . In an age in which the average speed of this progression seems notably increased, whatever moral opinion one may have about it, one cannot deny its reality, felt even by those who wish it to hell. Controversy therefore only arises over the subordination of these great dynamic phenomena to invariable natural laws . . . But if our observation is at all complete, we shall realise that, from whatever angle one regards society its successive modifications are always subject to a definite order, of which the explanation, in terms of human nature, is possible in a sufficient number of cases for us to expect it to be confirmed in those that remain. This order has a remarkable fixity, and can be seen in the parallel developments of populations quite distinct and independent of one another. Since on the one hand the existence of the social movement is undeniable, and since on the other the order of succession of the various states of society is never arbitrary, we must certainly regard this great continuous phenomenon as subject to natural laws not less positive, though more complex, than those of any other class of phenomena . . .

   . . . From whatever point of view one regards the total movement of humanity, from the most ancient historic times right up to our own day it can easily be seen that the various steps have followed one another in a fixed order. Here I will confine myself to the example of intellectual evolution, the clearest and most irrefutable of all . . . In the development of the scientific spirit . . . no enlightened mind could doubt today that in this long succession of efforts and discoveries, the human mind has followed an exactly determined course, so that, with previous knowledge of this course, it would have been possible to predict before it was realised, the progress marked out for each epoch . . . Men of genius, to whom this progress has been exclusively attributed, were but the organs of a predetermined movement which, if they had not been there, would have found other outlets; this history confirms in the most striking manner, for it shows us several eminent minds about to make the same discovery at once; the discovery therefore must have had but one single organ . . . As for the part of this great movement which seems today the least amenable to natural laws, the political movement, which we still look on as governed arbitrarily by people of sufficiently strong will, everyone will be able to recognise with the same certainty at least as in any other case, that the various political systems have succeeded one another historically in an exactly determined order . . .

   . . .

(c) Conclusion

. . . As a promoter of social feeling to the highest degree, this new science . . . represents men in the mass constituting in the present, past and future, both in place and in time, one immense social unit, whose various individual or national organs, in their intimate and universal solidarity, necessarily contribute each according to its mode and degree to the evolution of humanity. This supremely important and quite modern conception is destined to become the rational basis of positive morality. . . .

4.A.IV   Rejection of Introspective Psychology[4]

. . . From an ineluctable necessity the human mind observes all phenomena directly except its own. For who could conduct such a type of observation? One can understand that a man might be able to observe moral phenomena in the passions that inflame him, for the anatomical reason that the organs that are the seat of these passions are different from the organs of observation. But . . . the best way to know the passions will always be to observe them as a spectator: for every pronounced state of passion, that is every state essential to this very study, is necessarily incompatible with the state of observation. But as for examining in the same manner intellectual phe-

4   Ibid., pp. 32–3.

nomena as they appear, this is manifestly impossible. A thinking individual cannot divide himself into two, one half reasoning, and the other watching it reason. The observed and the observing organ become identical in this case. How could observation take place?

The so-called psychological method therefore is in principle invalid. And consider to what absolutely contradictory antics it leads! On the one hand you are told to insulate yourself, as much as possible, from every external sensation, above all you must refrain from intellectual work; for if you were to do the simplest sum, what would become of *internal* observation? On the other hand, after having by dint of precautions attained to the state of intellectual sleep, you must busy yourself contemplating the operations taking place in your mind, when nothing at all is taking place in it! Our posterity will doubtless one day see these pretensions transferred to the comic stage.

The results of so strange a method are in perfect conformity with its principle. In the space of two thousand years that metaphysicians have been cultivating psychology, they have not been able to agree on a single intelligible and solidly established proposition. Even today they are split into a multitude of schools in constant debate over the first elements of their doctrine. *Internal observation* engenders almost as many divergent opinions as there are individuals to pursue it.

4.A.V The Hermeneutical Circle: The Indispensability of Theory[5]

. . . The systematic empiricism that people endeavour to impose on social and above all historical observation [*outlaws*] under the pretext of impartiality, the employment of any theory. It would be difficult to imagine a dogma more radically opposed to the true spirit of positive philosophy, as also to the character it must assume in the study of social phenomena. . . . We now know that from the scientific point of view any isolated, entirely empirical observation, is essentially idle and even uncertain; science can only employ observations that are attached, at least hypothetically, to some law. . . . and the more complex the phenomena become, the more stringent is this logical requirement; without the guidance of a previous theory, the more realistic the better, the observer would not know what he should look for in what is taking place before his eyes . . . Social observation, whether static or dynamic, relating as it does to the highest degree of complexity in natural phenomena, must demand more than any other type of observation, the continuous employment of fundamental theories directed towards linking facts in process of accomplishment with those already accomplished, contrary to the irrational precept so magisterially propounded in our day and age, the application of which floods us with perfectly useless descriptions . . . I admit that this logical requirement in relation to such phenomena augments the difficulty, already considerable, of founding positive sociology, for one is obliged in some sort to create simultaneously both observations and laws in a kind of vicious circle, out of which one breaks only by using ill-prepared material and ill-conceived doctrines. Obviously it is the absence of any positive theory that renders social observation today so vague and so

Ibid., pp. 180–3.

incoherent. There is no lack of facts . . . but they remain sterile, and even unperceived, although we are immersed in them, for lack of the intellectual attitudes and speculative signposts indispensable to their scientific exploration. In view of the excessive complexity of the phenomena, static observation of them cannot become efficient unless directed by an at least rudimentary knowledge of the laws of social solidarity; and this is still more obviously true of dynamic facts, which would have no fixed sense, were they not attached, if only by provisional hypothesis, to the fundamental laws of social development. Thus a grasp of the whole is indispensable in social physics, not only in order to conceive and propound the proper questions . . . but also to direct investigation . . . The new political philosophy, far from proscribing true erudition in all its aspects . . . will exclude only aimless work, work without any guiding principle or character . . . No doubt that with this as with any other kind of phenomena – and even more than with any other, because of the greater complexity – there is a danger that continuous use of scientific theories may distort real observation, reading into it the confirmation of speculative prejudices that have no real basis . . . [*But*] positive theories must of their nature expose the observer less than any others to reading into facts what is not there. As the chief characteristic of positive theories is the continuous and systematic subjection of imagination to observation, the exclusive use of them puts the observer habitually on his guard against the inclination to read into facts what is not there, and . . . the habit of positive theories is the best prophylactic against such a speculative menace . . .

   We see then that from the very nature of social science, observation needs to be subordinated, more than in any other case, to positive speculation on the laws of solidarity and sequence that hold good for these complex phenomena. No social fact can have any real scientific significance unless it is immediately associated with some other social fact; isolated, it necessarily remains in the sterile state of mere anecdote capable at the most of satisfying a vain curiosity, but incapable of meeting any rational need. . . .

4.A.VI   History: The Principal Tool and Basis of Positivist Political Science[6]

The historical comparison of the various consecutive states of humanity is not only the principal scientific tool of the new political philosophy: developed, it will prove to be the very basis of the science . . .

   . . . From now on we can point to this historical method as offering the most natural proof and the most extensive application of that characteristic trait of sociological method, which is, to go from the whole to the parts. This indispensable condition of the rationality of social studies manifests itself unmistakably in all truly historic research, which otherwise would degenerate into the compilation of raw material, however skilfully presented . . . The irrational spirit of narrow specialism that has today attained to such bad eminence would end by reducing history to an accumulation of detached monographs, where every idea of organic and necessarily simultaneous connection of events would lose itself in the multiplicity of description. Hence it is t

6   Ibid., pp. 192–204.

social evolution as a whole that we must relate the historical comparisons of the various ages of civilisation, if they are to have a true scientific character . . .

. . . The preponderance of the historical method in social studies has the advantage also of developing social feeling, for it is the continuous demonstration of the necessary interconnection of human events which inspires immediate interest today even in the most distant of these events, and is a continual reminder of the influence that they have exercised on the gradual emergence of our own civilisation . . . Only it is important not to confuse the feeling of social solidarity with that sympathetic interest that all depictions of human life are bound to evoke, even those of fiction. . . . It does not develop through popular history, which has remained at the descriptive stage, but entirely through logical and positive history, history as a genuine science, arranging human events in co-ordinated series that show their sequence, [*will eventually engender*] . . . a more noble conception of human unity, showing the successive generations of humanity directed towards one final goal . . .

. . . One only learns to predict the future after having in some sort predicted the past . . . Arrived at the modern epoch with all the intellectual authority derived from the gradual co-ordination of all the preceding epochs, the historical method, and the historical method alone, can analyse the modern epoch, estimating each element exactly for what it is, according to the sociological series to which it belongs. Vainly do statesmen insist on the necessity of political observation: as their observation is only of the present, or at most of the recent past, the maxim they distil from it proves abortive on application. From the nature of the phenomena, observation of the present is radically insufficient; it acquires true scientific value, and becomes a source of logical prediction, only from comparison with the past, and the past in its totality. Isolated, the observation of the present would become a very powerful cause of political illusion, for it leads one to confuse principal with secondary facts, to overestimate noisy and ephemeral demonstrations in comparison with the fundamental tendencies which as a rule are not very noisy . . .

. . .

The most important of the restrictions appertaining to the historical method, a restriction that implicitly includes all the others, is the confining of scientific analysis to one social series only, that is to say to the development of the most advanced peoples, and the scrupulous avoidance of every digression to other centres of civilisation, whose evolution has so far been, for some cause or other, arrested at a more imperfect stage, unless the examination of these accessory series can throw a useful light on the principal subject. Historical exploration must therefore be limited to the élite vanguard of humanity comprising the greater part of the white race or the European nations, and even in the interests of accuracy, especially in modern times, it must be confined to the peoples of Western Europe. In any epoch study will mainly concern the political ancestors of this privileged population, whatever be their country . . . One cannot hope to grasp the true progress of human society except by the exclusive consideration of the most complete and distinctive evolution, to the elucidation of which all collateral observations relating to less complete and less notable progressions must be subordinated. Whatever interest attach to the latter, appreciation of them must be systematically adjourned until the principal laws of social movement have been ascertained in the case most favourable to their full manifestation, then it will become possible and even useful to proceed to an explanation of the modifications these laws have undergone among populations that for various reasons have lagged behind the main type of development. Till then, the puerile and inept display of sterile, ill-directed erudition at present tending to hamper the study of social evolution by the intermixture of the history of populations such as those of India and China etc., which have never exercised any real influence on our past, must be stigmatised as a source of inextricable confusion, as far as the discovery of the laws of human sociability is concerned . . .

. . . It is only when we have determined what belongs to the élite of humanity that we can regulate our intervention in the development of more or less backward peoples . . .

. . .

In the search for the true laws of sociability, the exceptional events and minute details that the anecdote-monger seeks out with insatiable curiosity must nearly always be ignored as essentially insignificant . . .

. . . However indispensable the part of history in nourishing and guiding the speculations of sociology, that part must remain abstract. It can only be a history without names of men, even without names of peoples, except that one must avoid the puerile affectation of abstaining from the use of names that may illuminate the exposition of a subject, or even facilitate and consolidate thought, especially in these initial stages of sociological science. . . .

4.A.VII   The Future[7]

None of the preceding revolutions of humanity, even the greatest one of all, the transition from the polytheistic society of antiquity to the monotheistic one of the Middle Ages, has been able to modify the whole of human existence, both individual and social, as profoundly as will the necessary advent in the near future of a fully positive society which, as we have recognised, is the sole issue possible to the immense crisis that has agitated the élite peoples of the earth for the last half century. . . .

The principal intellectual feature of the positive state will certainly be its capacity to determine and to maintain a complete mental coherence such as has never before existed even in the best ordered and most advanced minds . . . The new regime is destined to imprint on all our conceptions without distinction, from the most elementary to the most transcendent, a completely positive character, without the least admixture of any heterogeneous philosophy. . . .

. . .

. . . That great evolution which has scarcely begun to emerge from a lengthy preparatory development is bound to remains still for many centuries in a progressive state, beyond which it would be as uncalled for as irrational to speculate at present. But is very important for the further development of the true philosophic genius to recognise on principle, as clearly as possible, that the collective organism is subject as much as the individual organism to decline, even independently of alterations in the environments . . . There is nothing at all to prevent the collective life of humanity from suffering a similar destiny. This philosophical prospect, while dissipating all metaphysic

7   Ibid., pp. 210–33.

illusions about infinite progress, would not discourage energetic attempts at judicious improvement . . .

. . .

. . . Positive morality, properly organised, will produce far better moral results than religious morality, even in the monotheistic stage, has ever been able to obtain in spite of the powerful means at its disposal . . . Permanent advantages must result, under wise philosophic direction, from concentrating human effort on real life, individual and collective . . . A sound estimate of our own nature, in which vicious or excessive inclinations predominate, will secure widespread acceptance of the obligation to exercise a wise discipline over our inclinations, stimulating or restraining them as the need demands. Finally the general idea, at once scientific and moral, of the true situation of man, as natural head of the real order of things, will always underline the necessity of ceaselessly developing by their judicious exercise, the noble attributes, not less of feeling than of intellect, which place us at the summit of the living hierarchy . . . Hence a noble audacity in developing the greatness of man in every direction, secure from oppressive terrors and knowing no limit but that imposed by the collective force of the real. . . .

. . .

. . . When a true education has familiarized modern minds with the notions of solidarity and perpetuity that the positive contemplation of social evolution suggests in so many cases, then will be felt the essential moral superiority of a philosophy that binds each one of us to the whole existence of humanity, seen against a background of all times and places. . . .

. . .

. . . The great political task, prematurely attempted in the Middle Ages, and which the future alone will be able to accomplish, is that of reconciling in one milieu, and with quite different aims and principles the distinct properties of these two regimes, the one conferring social preponderance on theoretical power and the other on practical power. . . .

. . .

. . . Immediate destination of the movement will be the European occident, and the five essential elements of that noble élite of our species will each participate in the terms of its own proper genius, collaboration intimating future actual combination. Under the salutary predominance, both philosophic and political which is assured to the French spirit by the general tendencies of the modern transition, the English spirit will assert its predilection for reality and utility, the German spirit will apply its native aptitude for systematic generalisation, the Italian spirit will permeate the whole with its admirable aesthetic spontaneity, and finally the Spanish spirit will introduce its feeling both for personal dignity and universal fraternity.

4.B　John Stuart Mill, 1806–1873

4.B.I　Introspective Psychology the Fundamental Science of Human Nature[8]

M. Comte . . . not only denies to Psychology or Mental Philosophy properly so called the character of a science, but places it, in the chimerical nature of its objects and pretensions, almost on a par with astrology.

But . . . it remains incontestable that there exist uniformities of succession among states of mind, and that these can be ascertained by observations and experiment. Further, that every mental state has a nervous state for its immediate antecedent and proximate cause, though extremely probable, cannot hitherto be said to be proved . . . The successions, therefore, which obtain among mental phenomena do not admit of being deduced from the physiological laws of our nervous organisation; and all real knowledge of them must continue, for a long time at least, if not always to be sought in the direct study, by observation and experiment, of the mental successions themselves. . . . Therefore . . . there is a distinct and separate Science of Mind.

. . . To reject the resource of psychological analysis, and construct the theory of the mind solely on such data as physiology at present affords, seems to me [a] great . . . error in principle, and an even more serious one in practice. . . .

. . . I refer the reader to works professedly psychological, in particular to James Mill's *Analysis of the Phenomena of the Human Mind*, where the principal laws of association, along with many of their applications, are copiously exemplified, and with a masterly hand.

4.B.II　Ethology: Science of the Formation of Character[9]

The laws of mind . . . compose the universal or abstract period of the philosophy of human nature; and all the truths of common experience . . . must . . . be results or consequences of these. Such familiar maxims . . . collected á *posteriori* from observation of life occupy among the truths of the science the place of what, in our analysis of Induction, have so often been spoken of under the title of Empirical Laws.

An Empirical Law . . . is an uniformity, whether of succession or of co-existence which holds true in all instances within the limits of observation, but is not of a nature to afford any assurance that it would hold beyond those limits . . .

. . . The really scientific truths, then, are not these empirical laws, but the causal laws which explain them. . . .

. . .

Although, however, there is scarcely any mode of feeling or conduct which is, the absolute sense, common to all mankind; and though the generalizations which asse

---

8　John Stuart Mill, *System of Logic* (1967) Book VI, ch. IV, sections 2–3, p. 556–7.
9　Ibid., Book VI, ch. V, pp. 562–70.

that any given variety of conduct or feeling will be found universally will be considered as scientific propositions by no one at all fam[ar] with scientific investigation; yet all modes of feeling and conduct met with among mankind have causes which produce them; and in the propositions which assign those causes will be found the explanations of the empirical laws . . . Human beings do not all feel and act alike in the same circumstances; but it is possible to determine what makes one person, in a given position, feel or act in one way, another in another . . . In other words, mankind have not one universal character, but there exist universal laws of the Formation of Character. . . .

. . .

If the differences which we think we observe between French and English, or between men and women, can be connected with more general laws; if they be such as might be expected to be produced by the differences of government, former customs, and physical peculiarities in the two nations, and by the diversities of education, occupations . . . social privileges [etc.] . . . between the two sexes; then, indeed, the coincidence of the two kinds of evidence justifies us in believing that we have both reasoned rightly, and observed rightly. . . .

. . .

A science is thus formed, to which I would propose to give the name Ethology, or the Science of Character . . .

. . .

. . . Ethology stands to Psychology in relations very similar to that in which the various branches of natural philosophy stand to mechanics. . . .

. . .

Ethology is still to be created. But its creation has at length become practicable. The empirical laws, destined to verify its deductions, have been formed in abundance by every successive age of humanity, and the premises for the deductions are now sufficiently complete . . . I believe most competent judges will agree that the general laws of the different constituent elements of human nature are even now sufficiently understood to render it possible for a competent thinker to deduce from these laws with a considerable approach to certainty, the particular type of character which would be formed in mankind generally by any assumed set of circumstances. A science of Ethology, founded on the laws of Psychology, is therefore possible, though little has yet been done, and that little not at all systematically, towards forming it. . . .

4.B.III   Methodological Individualism[10]

The laws of the phenomena of society are, and can be, nothing but the laws of the actions and passions of human beings united together in the social state. Men, however in a state of society, are still men; their actions and passions are obedient to the laws of individual human nature. Men are not, when brought together, converted into another kind of substance, with different properties: as hydrogen and oxygen are different from water . . . Human beings in society have no properties but those which are derived from, and may be resolved into, the laws of the nature of individual man. . . .

10   Ibid., Book VI, Ch. VII, section 2; ch. 87 section 1, p. 573.

4.B.IV Consensus[11]

. . . The mode of production of all social phenomena is one great case of Intermixture of Laws. We can never either understand in theory or common in practice the condition of a society in any one respect, without taking into consideration its condition in all other respects. There is no social phenomenon which is not more or less influenced by every other part of the condition of the same society, and therefore by every cause which is influencing any other of the contemporaneous social phenomena. There is, in short, which physiologists term a *consensus*, similar to that existing among the various organs and functions of the physical frame of man and the more perfect animals . . . It follows from this *consensus*, that unless two societies could be alike in all the circumstances . . . no one cause will produce exactly the same effects in both . . . We can never, therefore affirm with certainty that a cause which has a particular tendency in one people or in one age will have exactly the same tendency in another . . .

4.B.V **Hypothetical or Abstract Sciences**[12]

Notwithstanding the universal *consensus* of the social phenomena . . . it is not the less true that different species of social facts are in the main dependent, immediately and in the first resort, on different kinds of causes; and therefore not only may with advantage, but must, be studied apart . . .

. . .

There is, for example one large class of social phenomena in which the immediately determining causes are principally those which act through the desire of wealth, and in which the psychological law mainly concerned is the familiar one that a greater gain is preferred to a smaller . . . A department of science may thus be constructed which has received the name of Political Economy.

. . .

Political Economy, as I have said on another occasion, concerns itself only with 'such of the phenomena of the social state as take place in consequence of the pursuit of wealth. It makes entire abstraction of every other passion or motive . . . [*It*] aims at showing what is the course of action into which mankind would be impelled if that motive . . . were absolute ruler of all their actions . . . It shows mankind accumulating wealth . . . sanctioning by mutual agreement the institution of property; . . . adopting various contrivances for increasing the productiveness of their labour (*etc. etc. etc.*) . . . All these operations, though many of them are really the result of a plurality of motives, are considered by political economy as flowing solely from the desire of wealth . . . In order to judge how [*man*] will act under the variety of desires and aversion which are concurrently operating upon him, we must know how he would act under the exclusive influence of each one in particular . . . In this way a nearer approximation is obtained than would otherwise be practicable to the real order of human affairs in those departments. . . .'

11   Ibid., Book VI, Ch. IX, section 2, p. 586.
12   Ibid., Book VI, Ch. IX, sections 3, 4, pp. 587–91

. . .

I would not here undertake to decide what other hypothetical or abstract sciences similar to Political Economy may admit of being carved out of the general body of the social science . . . There is, however, among these separate departments, one which cannot be passed over in silence, being of a more comprehensive and commanding character than any of the other branches into which the social science may admit of being divided. . . . I allude to what may be termed Political Ethology, or the theory of the causes which determine the type of character belonging to a people or to any age. Of all the subordinate branches of the social science, this is the most completely in its infancy. The causes of national character are scarcely at all understood . . .

Yet . . . the laws of national (or collective) character are by far the most important class of sociological laws. . . .

The omission [*of ethological considerations*] is no defect in . . . the separate sciences . . . as abstract or hypothetical sciences, but it vitiates them in their practical application as branches of a comprehensive social science. In political economy, for example, empirical laws of human nature are tacitly assumed by English thinkers, which are calculated only for Great Britain or the United States. Among other things, an intensity of competition is constantly supposed, which as a general mercantile fact, exists in no country in the world except these two. An English political economist . . . has seldom learned that is possible that men, should care more about their ease or their vanity than about their pecuniary gain. Yet those who know the habits of the Continent of Europe, are aware whose apparently small a motive often outweighs the desire of money getting, even in the operations which have money-getting as their direct object. . . .

4.B.VI **Progress**[13]

One of the thinkers who earliest conceived the succession of historical events as subject to fixed laws . . . Vico . . . conceived the phenomena of human society as revolving in an orbit; as going through periodically the same series of changes. Though there were not wanting circumstances tending to give some plausibility to this view, it would not bear a close scrutiny; and those who have succeed Vico in this kind of speculation have universally adopted the idea of a trajectory or progress in lieu of an orbit or cycle.

The words Progress and Progressiveness are not here to be understood a synonymous with improvement and tendency to improvement . . . It is my belief indeed that the general tendency is, and will continue to be, saving occasional and temporary exceptions, one of improvement . . . [*But*] for our purpose it is sufficient that there is a progressive change . . . that in each successive age the principal phenomena of society are different from what they were in the age preceding, and still more different from any previous age . . .

The progressiveness of the human race is the foundation on which a method philosophizing in the social science has been of late years erected . . . This method, which is now generally adopted by the most advanced thinkers on the Continent, consists in attempting by a study and analysis of the general facts of history, to discover (what

13 Ibid., Book VI, ch. X, sections 3–8, pp. 596–606.

these philosophers term) the law of progress; which law, once ascertained, must according to them enable us to predict future events, just as after a few terms of an infinite series in algebra we are able to detect the principle of regularity in their formation, and to predict the rest . . . The principal aim of historical speculation in France, of late years, has been to ascertain this law. But . . . the succession of states of the human mind and society cannot have an independent law of its own; it must depend on the psychological and ethological laws which govern the action of circumstances on men and of men on circumstances. It is conceivable that those laws might . . . determine the successive transformations of man and society to one given and unvarying order. . . .

. . .

. . . [*But*] the most erroneous generalizations are continually being made from the course of history . . . The only check or corrective is constant verifications by psychological and ethological laws. . . .

. . .

. . . The evidence of history and that of human nature combine . . . to show that there really is one social element which is . . . predominant, and almost paramount among the agents of social progression. This is the state of the speculative faculties of mankind . . .

It would be a great error . . . to assert that speculation, intellectual activity, the pursuit of truth, is among the more powerful propensities of human nature, or hold a predominating place in the lives of any, save decidedly exceptional, individuals. But notwithstanding the relative weakness of this principle among other sociological agents, its influence is the main determining cause of the social progress . . . The state of the speculative faculties . . . essentially determines the moral and political state of the community . . .

. . . Every considerable change historically know to us in the condition of any period of mankind, when not brought about by external force, has been preceded by a change of proportional extent in the state of their knowledge or in their prevalent beliefs . . . Polytheism, Judaism, Christianity, Protestantism, the critical philosophy of modern Europe and its positive science . . . each of these has been a primary agent in making society what it was at each successive period, while society was but secondarily instrumental in making *them* . . .

From this accumulated evidence, we are justified in concluding that the order of human progression in all respects will mainly depend on the order of progression in the intellectual convictions of mankind, that is, on the law of the successive transformations of human opinions. . . .

The investigation . . . has been systematically attempted, up to the present time, by M. Comte alone . . . I shall confine myself to mentioning one important generalisation, which M. Comte regards as the fundamental law of the progress of human knowledge. Speculation he conceives to have, on every subject of human inquiry, three successive stages; in the first of which it tends to explain the phenomena by supernatural agencies, in the second by metaphysical speculation, and in the third or final state confines itself to ascertaining their laws of succession and similitude. This generalisation appears to me to have that high degree of scientific evidence which is derived from the concurrence of the indications of history with the probabilities derived from the constitution of the human mind. Nor could it be easily conceived, from the mere enunciation of such a proposition, what a flood of light it throws on the whole course of history, when its consequences are traced . . .

4.B.VII   Buckle on Statistics: A Critique[14]

That the collective series of social phenomena, in other words, the course of history, is subject to general laws, which philosophy may possibly detect, – has been familiar for generations to the scientific thinkers of the Continent, and has over the past quarter of a century passed out of their peculiar domain into that of newspapers and ordinary political discussion . . . In our own country, however, at the time of the first publication of this Treatise, it was almost a novelty. Since then a great change has taken place, and has been eminently promoted by the important work of Mr. Buckle, who, with characteristic energy, flung down this great principle, together with many striking exemplifications of it, into the arena of popular discussion . . . Hence has arisen a considerable amount of controversy, tending not only to make the principle rapidly familiar to the majority of cultivated minds, but also to clear it from the confusions and misunderstanding by which it was but natural that it should for a time be clouded . . .

   . . . The most fundamental continues to be that which is grounded in the doctrine of Free Will or in other words, on the denial that the law of invariable Causation holds true of human volitions.

   . . . The support which this *à posteriori* verification affords to the law is the part of the case which has been most clearly and triumphantly brought out by Mr. Buckle.

   [*A long summary and broad endorsement of Buckle's account of statistics follows, and then the following criticism*]

   . . . Some, . . . (among whom is Mr. Buckle himself) have inferred or allowed it to be supposed that they inferred, from the regularity in the recurrence of events which depend on moral qualities, that the moral qualities of mankind are little capable of being improved, or are of little importance in the general progress of society, compared with intellectual or economic causes. But to draw this inference is to forget that the statistical tables from which the invariable averages are deduced were compiled from facts occurring within narrow geographical limits, and in a small number of successive years . . . If we compare one age with another, or one country with another, or even one part of a country with another, . . . the crimes committed within a year no longer give the same, but a different numerical age aggregate.

4.B.VIII   The Individual in History[15]

. . . The theory of the subjection of social progress to invariable laws is often held in conjunction with the doctrine that social progress cannot be materially influenced by the exertions of individual person or by the acts of government . . . [*But*] . . . though the varieties of character among ordinary individuals neutralize one another on any large scale, exceptional individuals in important positions do not in any given age

14   Ibid., Book VI, ch. XI, section 1, pp. 607–10.
15   Ibid., Book VI, ch. XI, sections 3, 4, pp 611–13.

neutralize one another; there was not another Themistocles, or Luther, or Julius Caesar . . .

. . . I believe that if Newton had not lived, the world must have waited for the Newtonian philosophy until there had been another Newton or his equivalent . . . I will not go the length of saying what Newton did in a single life might not have been done in successive steps by some of those who followed him, each singly inferior to him in genius. But even the least of those steps required a man of great intellectual superiority. Eminent men do not merely see the coming light from the hill-top; they mount on the hill-top and evoke it, and if no one had ever ascended thither, the light in many cases might never have risen upon the plain at all . . .[16] Few will doubt that had there been no Socrates, no Plato and no Aristotle there would have been no philosophy for the next two thousand years, nor in all probability then; and that if there has been no Christ and no St. Paul, there would have been no Christianity.

The point in which above all, the influence of remarkable individuals is decisive, is in determining the celerity of the movement. In most states of society it is the existence of great men which decides even whether there shall be any progress . . .

. . . We cannot foresee the advent of great men. Those who introduce new speculative thoughts or great practical conceptions into the world cannot have their epoch fixed beforehand. What science can do is this. It can trace through past history the general causes which had brought mankind to that preliminary state, which, when the right sort of great man appeared, rendered them accessible to his influence. . . .

4.C   Henry Thomas Buckle, 1821–1862

4.C.1   The Historian's Aim: Discovery of Fixed and Universal Laws[17]

. . . In the whole literature of Europe there are not more than three or four really original works which contain a systematic attempt to investigate the history of man according to those exhaustive methods which in other branches of knowledge have proved successful, and by which alone empirical observations can be raised to scientific truths.

. . .

. . . I hope to accomplish for the history of man something equivalent, or at all events analogous, to what has been effected by other inquirers for the different branches of natural science. In regard to nature, events apparently the most irregular and capricious have been explained and have been shown to be in accordance with certain fixed and universal laws. . . .

. . .

[Yet] a similar regularity is in history not only not taken for granted, but is actually denied . . . [We are] told that in the affairs of men there is something mysterious and

16   Mill is referring to a metaphor employed by Macaulay to the opposite effect against Carlyle who had emphasized the role of 'great men' in history.
17   From Buckle, 1861, vol. 1, pp. 3–19.

providential, which makes them impervious to our investigations, and which will always hide from us their future course. [*But*] such an assertion is gratuitous . . .

. . .

When we perform an action, we perform it in consequence of some motive or motives . . . those motives are the result of some antecedents, and . . . therefore, if we were acquainted with the whole of the antecedents, and with all the laws of their movement, we could with unerring certainty predict the whole of their immediate results. . . .

. . .

. . . The materials out of which a philosophical history can alone be constructed [*are*] on the one hand . . . the human mind obeying the laws of its own existence, and when uncontrolled by external agents, developing itself according to the conditions of its organization. On the other hand . . . what is called Nature, obeying likewise its laws; but incessantly coming into contact with the minds of men, exciting their passions, stimulating their intellect, and therefore giving to their actions a direction which they would not have taken without such disturbance. Thus we have man modifying nature, and nature modifying man; while out of this reciprocal modification all events must necessarily spring . . .

The problem . . . is to ascertain the method of discovering the laws of this double modification . . .

4.C.II   The Historian's Method: Statistics[18]

Of all offences, it might well be supposed that the crime of murder, is one of the most arbitrary and irregular . . . The fact is, that murder is committed with as much regularity and bears as uniform a relation to certain known circumstances as do the movements of the tides, and the rotations of the seasons . . .

. . . Still more striking, among public and registered crimes there is none which seems so completely dependent on the individuals as suicide . . . It may therefore be very naturally be thought impracticable to refer suicide to general principles, or to detect anything like regularize in an offence which is so eccentric, so solitary, so impossible to control by legislation . . . [*But*] all the evidence we possess respecting it points to one great conclusion, and can leave no doubt in our minds that suicide is merely the product of the general condition of society . . . In a given state of society, a certain number of persons must put an end to their own life. . . .

. . .

Nor is it merely the crimes of men which are marked by this uniformity in sequence. Even the number of marriages annually contracted, is determined, not by the temper and wishes of individual, but by large general facts . . . [*by*] a fixed and definite relation to the price of corn . . . Instead of having any connection with personal feeling, they are simply regulated by the average earnings of the great mass of the people.

To those who have a steady conception of the regularity of events, and have firmly seized the great truth that the actions of men, being guided by their antecedents, are in reality never inconsistent, but however capricious they may appear, only form part of one vast scheme of universal order . . . This . . . is at once the key and the basis of

18   Ibid., pp. 22–31.

history . . . Indeed, the progress of inquiry is becoming so rapid, and so earnest, that I entertain little doubt that before another century has elapsed, the chain of evidence will be complete, and it will be as rare to find an historian who denies the undeviating regularity of the moral world, as it is now to find a philosopher who denies the regularity of the material world.

4.C.III Mental Laws (Moral and Intellectual) and Progress[19]

[*Mental laws are either moral or intellectual*] . . . Double movement moral and intellectual, is essential to the very idea of civilization, and includes the entire theory of mental progress . . .

A question, therefore now arises of great moment: namely, which of these two parts or elements of mental progress is the more important. . . .

. . .

. . . There is, unquestionably, nothing to be found in the world which has undergone so little change as those great dogmas of which moral systems are composed. To do good to others; to sacrifice for their benefit your own wishes; to love your neighbour as yourself; to forgive your enemies; to restrain your passions; to honor your parents; to respect those who are set over you; these, and a few others, are the sole essentials of morals but they have been known for thousands of years . . .

. . .

. . . The deeper we penetrate into this question, the more clearly shall we see the superiority of intellectual acquisitions over moral feeling. There is no instance on record of an ignorant man who having good intentions and supreme power to enforce them, has not done for more evil than good . . . An overwhelming majority of religious persecutors have been men of the purest intentions, of the most admirable and unsullied morals . . . Diminish the sincerity, and you will diminish the persecution . . .

. . . Hypocrites are for the most part too supple to be cruel . . .

. . . The great antagonist of intolerance is not humanity, but knowledge. It is to the diffusion of knowledge, and to that alone, that we owe the comparative cessation of what is unquestionably the greatest evil men have ever inflicted on their own species [*that is*] religious persecution . . . [*but*] not so much from the enormous and almost incredible number of its known victims [*as from the resultant forced*] practice of a constant and humiliating hypocrisy. It is this which is the real curse of religious persecution. For in this way, men being constrained to mask their thoughts, there arises a habit of securing safety by falsehood and of purchasing impunity with deceit. In this way fraud becomes a necessary of life; insincerity is made a daily custom; the whole tone of public feeling is vitiated, and the gross amount of vice and error fearfully increased . . . Compared to this, all other crimes are of small account . . .

. . . The second greatest evil known to mankind is unquestionably the practice of war . . . It surely will not be pretended that the moderns have made any discoveries concerning the moral evils of war . . .

19 Ibid., pp. 158–207.

[*But*] every great increase in the activity of the human intellect, has been a heavy blow to the war-like spirit. . . .

. . .

[*Buckle argues at some length that war is disappearing because of scientific advance, partly because discoveries such as gunpowder have led to reductions in the size, and therefore power of the warrior class, and partly because the steam-engine has led to increased travel which breaks down nationalistic prejudices. A third important cause is the discovery of the laws of political economy because* 'Commercial jealousy . . . was formerly one of the most conspicuous . . . causes of war']

In the year 1776, Adam Smith published his *Wealth of Nations*, which, looking at its ultimate results, is probably the most important book which has ever been written, and is certainly the most valuable contribution ever made by a single man towards establishing the principles on which government should be based. . . .

. . . At the present day, eighty years after the publication of Smith's *Wealth of Nations*, there is not to be found anyone one of tolerable education who is not ashamed of holding opinions which, before, the time of Adam Smith, were universally received.

Such is the way in which great thinkers control the affairs of men and by their discoveries regulate the march of nations . . . This solitary Scotsman has, by the publication of one single work, contributed more toward the happiness of man, than has been effected by the united abilities of all the statesmen and legislators of whom history has preserved an authentic account.

. . . [*The Wealth of Nations demonstrated*] that it would be as absurd to attempt to impoverish a people with whom we trade as it would be in a tradesman to wish for the insolvency of a rich and frequent customer. The result is that the commercial spirit, which formerly was often warlike, is now invariably pacific. And although it is perfectly true that not one merchant out of a hundred is familiar with the argument on which these economical discoveries are founded, that does not prevent the effect which the discoveries themselves produce on his own mind . . . for an immense majority of men always follow with implicit submission the spirit of their own time and the spirit of the times is merely its knowledge . . . Most assuredly it is also true that this same intellectual movement has lessened the chance of war, by asserting the principle which ought to regulate our commercial relations with foreign countries; by proving, not only the inutility, but the positive mischief, caused by interfering with them; and . . . [*thus*] by exploding those long-established errors [*which induced*] men to believe that the nations are the natural enemies of each other. . . .

. . . Whatever theologians may choose to assert, it is certain that mankind at large has far more virtue than vice, and that in every country good actions are more frequent than bad ones . . . An enlarged experience proves that mankind is not so radically bad as we from our infancy are taught to believe . . . It is the solitary misanthrope who is most prone to depreciate the good qualities or our nature, and exaggerate its bad ones . . . Or else it is some foolish and ignorant monk, who dreaming away his existence in idle solitude, flatters his own vanity by denouncing the vices of others; and thus declaiming against the enjoyments of life, revenges himself on that society from which by his own superstition he is excluded. . . .

. . .

. . . In what may be called the innate and original morals of mankind, there is, so far as we are aware, no progress. Of the different passions with which we are born . . .

experience tells us that, as they are always antagonistic, they are held in balance by the force of their own opposition. The activity of one motive is corrected by the activity of another . . . Cruelty is counteracted by benevolence (*etc.*) . . . This is the ebb and flow of history, the perpetual flux to which by the laws of our nature we are subject. Above all this, there is a far higher movement; and as the tide rolls on, now advancing, now receding, there is amid its endless fluctuations, one thing, and one thing alone, which endures for ever. The actions of bad men produce only temporary evil, the actions of good men only temporary good; and eventually the good and the evil altogether subside, are neutralized by subsequent generations . . . But the discoveries of great men never leave us; they are immortal, they continue those eternal truths which survive . . . They are essentially cumulative, and . . . and after the lapse of centuries produce more effect than they were able to do even at the moment of their promulgation.

[*We have*] . . . resolved the study of the dynamics of society into the study of the laws of the mind . . . As the progress of civilization is marked by the triumph of the mental laws over the physical, just so it is marked by the triumph of the intellectual laws over the moral ones. . . .

The intellectual principle, is not only far more progressive than the moral principle, but is also far more permanent in its results. The acquisitions made by the intellect . . . become the heirlooms of mankind.

4.C.IV English History the Key to World History[20]

. . . History has been written by men so inadequate to the great task they have undertaken, that few of the necessary materials have yet been brought together. Instead of telling us those things which alone have any value – instead of giving us information respecting the progress of knowledge, and the way in which mankind has been affected by the diffusion of that knowledge . . . the vast majority of historians fill their works with the most trifling and miserable details; personal anecdotes of kings and courts; interminable relations of what was said by one minister, and what was thought by another; and what is worse than all, long accounts of campaigns, battles and sieges, very interesting to those engaged in them, but to us utterly useless, because they neither furnish new truths, nor do they supply the means by which new truths may be discovered . . . The consequence is, whoever now attempts to generalize historical phenomena, must collect the facts, as well as conduct the generalization. He finds nothing ready to his hand. He must be the mason, as well as the architect; he must not only scheme the edifice; but likewise excavate the quarry. The necessity of performing these double labours entails upon the philosopher such enormous drudgery, that the limits of an entire life are unequal to the task . . .

On account of these things, I have long since abandoned my original scheme; and I have reluctantly determined to write the history, not of general civilization, but of the civilization of a single people. . . . The reasons which have induced me to select the history of England as more important then any other [*are that*] . . .

. . . It is evident that, inasmuch as the great advantage of studying past events consists in the possibility of ascertaining the laws by which they are governed, the history

20   Ibid., pp. 209–21.

of any people will become more valuable in proportion as their movements have been least disturbed by agencies not arising from themselves. Every foreign or external influence which is brought to bear upon a nation is an interference with its natural development, and therefore complicates the circumstances we seek to investigate . . .

. . . The history of such a people . . . would present a condition of normal and inherent development; it would show the laws of progress acting in a state of isolation; it would be in fact an experiment ready-made, and would possess all the value of that artificial contrivance to which natural science is so much indebted. . . .

. . . The duty of the philosophic historian is, to select for his especial study the country in which the conditions have been most closely followed. Now it will be readily admitted, not only by ourselves, but by intelligent foreigners, that in England during, at all events, the last three centuries these conditions have been most closely followed . . . Of all European countries, England is the one where, during the longest period, the government has been most quiescent, and the people most active; where popular freedom has been settled on the widest basis; where each man is most able to say what he thinks, and do what he likes; where religious persecution, being little known, the play and flow of the human mind may be clearly seen . . . where that meddlesome doctrine called Protection was first attacked, and where alone it has been destroyed . . .

. . . [*None*] of our great thinkers [*were*] influenced by the intellect of France . . . Although we have been, and still are, greatly indebted to the French for our improvement in taste, in refinement, in manners, and indeed in all the amenities of life, we have borrowed from them nothing essential, nothing by which the destinies of nations are permanently altered. On the other hand, the French have not only borrowed from us some very valuable political institutions, but even the most important event in French history, is due, in no small degree, to our influence. Their Revolution of 1789 was, as is well known, brought about, or, to speak more properly, was mainly instigated, by a few great men. . . . What is less well known, and nevertheless is certainly true, is, that these eminent leaders learnt in England that philosophy and those principles by which, when translated into their own country, such fearful and yet such salutary results were effected.[21]

It will not, I hope, be supposed, that by these remarks I mean to cast any reflection on the French; a great and admirable people; a people in many respects superior to ourselves; a people from whom we have still much to learn, and whose deficiencies, such as they are, arise from the perpetual interference of a long line of arbitrary rulers. But, looking at this matter historically, it is unquestionably true that we have worked out our civilization with little aid from them, while they have worked out their with great aid from us. At the same time, it must also be admitted, that our governments have interfered less with us than their governments have interfered with them. And without in the least prejudging the question as to which is the greatest country, it is solely on these grounds that I consider our history more important than theirs . . .

. . . It seems scarcely necessary to examine the claims which may be put forward for other countries. Indeed, there are only two in whose favour any thing can be said: I mean Germany, considered as a whole, and the United States of North America. As to the Germans, it is undoubtedly true, that since the middle of the eighteenth century

---

21   A demonstration of this thesis was a major aim of chapters VIII to XIV of Volume I of Buckle's *History*.

they have produced a greater number of profound thinkers than any other country, I might perhaps say, than all other countries put together. But the objections which apply to the French are still more applicable to the Germans. For the protective principle has been, and still is stronger in Germany than in France. Even the best of the German governments are constantly interfering with the people . . . Besides this, the German literature, though now the first in Europe, owes it origin . . . to that great sceptical movement, by which in France, the Revolution was preceded. Before the middle of the eighteenth century, the German, notwithstanding a few eminent names, such as Kepler and Leibnitz, had no literature of real value; and the first impetus, which they received, was caused by the influence of those eminent French men, who, in the reign of Frederick the Great, flocked to Berlin, a city which has ever since been the head-quarters of philosophy and science . . . The German intellect, stimulated by the French in a sudden growth, has been irregularly developed; and thus hurried into an activity greater than the average civilization of the country requires. The consequence is, that there is no nation in Europe in which we find so wide and interval between the highest minds and the lowest minds. The German philosophers possess a learning, and a reach of thought, which places them at the head of the civilized world. The German people are more superstitious, more prejudiced, and notwithstanding the care which the government takes of their education, more really ignorant, and more unfit to guide themselves, than are the inhabitants either of France or England . . . The highest intellects, have, in Germany, so outstripped the general progress of the nation, that there is no sympathy between the two parties . . . The great authors address themselves, not to their country, but to each other . . . They turn their mother-tongue in a dialect eloquent indeed and very powerful, but so difficult, so subtle, and so full of complicated inversions, that to their own lower classes it is utterly incomprehensible. . . . From this, there has arisen, some of the most marked peculiarities of German literature . . . it is cut from the influence of ordinary prejudice; and hence, it has displayed, a boldness of inquiry, a recklessness in the pursuit of truth, and disregard of traditional opinions, which entitle it to the highest praise. But, on the other hand, this same circumstance has produced that absence of practical knowledge, and that indifference to material and physical interests, for which the German literature is justly ensured. . . .

In America, on the other hand, we see a civilization precisely the reverse of this . . . In no other other [*nation*] are there so few men of great learning, and so few men of great ignorance. In Germany, the speculative classes and the practical classes are altogether united, in America, they are altogether fused. . . . Since the time of Jonathan Edwards, no great metaphysician has appeared; little attention has been paid to physical science and, with the single expectation of jurisprudence, scarcely any thing has been done for those vast subjects on which the Germans are incessantly laboring. [*Therefore*] in Germany there is a serious failure in the diffusion of knowledge; and, in America, a no less serious one of accumulation . . . [*Thus*] there have arisen in America and in Germany . . . great but opposite evils, which is, it is to be feared, will not be easily remedied.[22]

---

22   Buckle's remarks on Germany and America are heavily dependent, as he acknowledges, on S Laing's *Notes on the Social and Political State of Europe* (London 1842), and A. de Toqueville's *De l* *Démocratie en Amérique* (Bruxelles, 1840).

5 Suprahistory

Hugh Rayment-Pickard

Introduction

To a strongly individualist mind, grand philosophies of history like Hegel's could be seen as a threat to personal human existence, dissolving the individual into the ocean of the universal-historical process. It was indeed Ranke's concern that the individual should not become a mere link in the chain of history. This suspicion of the historical process combined with a fierce belief in the value of the individual, inspired the radical reactions that we find in Schopenhauer, Kierkegaard and Nietzsche. Against the world-historical perspective, they assert the absolute priority of the individual viewpoint. Nietzsche called his reaction to world-history a 'suprahistorical' [*Ubergeschichtlich*] approach: a sublime view of history as random moments of intensity, which are ends in themselves. We shall adopt the term 'suprahistory' for all the thinkers discussed in this chapter.

The 'suprahistorical' view is antagonistic, not only to speculative philosophy of history, but also to Enlightenment rationalism. Although some would say that the secularism of Schopenhauer and Nietzsche was typical of the Enlightenment, their critique of Enlightenment reason certainly was not. Schopenhauer makes the point succinctly when he says that 'the foundation upon which all knowledge and science rests is the unexplained [*Unerklärliche*]' (Schopenhauer, 1965, vol. 5, p. 9). This is because the underlying reality in Schopenhauer is the non-rational, cosmic 'will'. For Nietzsche the human will to knowledge and the will to truth must be superseded by the will to power. What he calls the world of 'becoming' will never be understood because 'knowledge and becoming exclude one another' (Nietzsche, 1968, p. 280). In a rather different spirit, Kierkegaard posits the idea that a complete, rational explanation of things is always frustrated by fundamental paradoxes between time and eternity, history and chance, faith and reason.

Suprahistory is distinguishable both from speculative philosophy of history with its preoccupation with grand master narratives, and from empirical history with its concern for 'facts'. Suprahistory does not progress, and its moments do not reveal any plan or purpose. The completion of history is not teleological but poetic, made possible in singular artistic achievements which, as Kierkegaard puts it, 'transfigure' the 'prosaic actuality' of events. (Kierkegaard, 1970, p. 231). These ephemeral transfigurations come and go, but never in any direction or to any cumulative purpose.

Since grand schemes of history are irrelevant to the suprahistorical perspective a key concept for the thinkers in this chapter is the notion of a 'momentary present' in which history is completed. In *Thus Spoke Zarathustra* Nietzsche depicts the moment [*Augenblick*] as a gateway between the eternities of past and future (5.C.V). In Kierkegaard the moment [*Øiblikket*] is the intersection of eternity and temporality (Kierkegaard, 1980, p. 87f). For Schopenhauer the 'present [*Gegenwart*] alone is the form of all life' lying (as he puts it) like 'a tangent' across the spinning sphere of history (Schopenhauer, 1966, vol. 1, p. 278). By making the moment the absolute basis of meaning, the writers in this chapter resist the attempt to integrate everything into 'history'. So whereas for Hegel the moments of life are grounded in history, for the 'suprahistorists' true history is grounded in life's moments. Since these moments can only be accessed from within the living experience of the individual subject, any attempt to situate the meaning of history 'out there' as an objective 'fact' is necessarily in error.

Philosophers of time, at least since Augustine, have observed that the idea of the 'present' or the 'moment' is problematic. It is not easy to say, for example, how long 'the present' lasts. It is also questionable, as Schopenhauer and Kierkegaard both note, whether the present really exists at all since it appears merely to be the intersection of past and future (Schopenhauer, 1966, p. 7; Kierkegaard, 1980, p. 83). The thinkers in this chapter try to get around these difficulties by defining the present not as a unit of time, but as a kind of *opportunity* or *opening*.[1] So Schopenhauer defines the present not as a period of duration but as 'the form of the phenomenon of the will' (Schopenhauer, 1966, p. 279). Similarly, Kierkegaard says that 'the moment' is a 'figurative' expression to indicate the occasion of existential decision and resolution, which is a reflection of eternity in time (Kierkegaard, 1980, p. 87).[2] For Nietzsche the 'moment' is essentially a phenomenon of *change* rather than *time*: to be in the moment is to immerse oneself in the *becoming* of the world and its transience (Nietzsche, 1968, p. 293; Nietzsche, 1961, p. 176f). Describing how this 'becoming' of the world takes place, Nietzsche uses the Greek word *pathos*. (Nietzsche, 1968, p. 339). The sense here is not one of pity, but the original Greek meaning of 'incident' or 'event'. The world for Nietzsche is not made up of units of time, but moments of *pathos* (5.C.VIII). For all three thinkers, time needs to be understood from the perspective of the individual's engagement with life, and not as an objective order that can be measured by clocks and calendars.

Suprahistorism does not end with Nietzsche. We see the legacy of nineteenth-century suprahistorism variously in the priority given to 'the moment' in Jaspers and Heidegger; in Walter Benjamin's vision of the blasting open of the 'continuum of history' (8.C.I); and in Michel Foucault's view of historical discontinuity (10.A.II).

Arthur Schopenhauer (1788–1860) was not an academic philosopher and, like Nietzsche and Kierkegaard, he had contempt for professional philosophers, who he saw as mediocre careerists more concerned with making a living than in speaking the truth: 'Truth is no harlot who throws her arms around the neck of him who does not desire her; on the contrary, she is so coy a beauty that even the man who sacrifices everything to her can not be sure of her favours.' Following Plato, Aristotle and the

---

1 As Heidegger pointed out in early lectures this view of time is implicit in the New Testament concept of *kairos*. *Kairos* is the Greek word for time as 'the right moment' as opposed to *Chronos* which is time as a succession of measured units.

2 Kierkegaard is credited by Heidegger with the philosophical rediscovery of the 'moment' and, on these grounds, with the inauguration of a 'new epoch' in Western thought (Heidegger, 1983, p. 224).

Western philosophical tradition, Schopenhauer believed that ultimate truth must be timeless and universal. Since it deals with both time and particularity, Schopenhauer thought that history must be an inferior discipline.

Although Schopenhauer's low valuation of history was the dominant view of premodern philosophy (as chapter 1 has emphasized), he makes two particularly important contributions to philosophical thinking about history. First, Schopenhauer introduces the idea that the cosmic will is the basis of history. Secondly, Schopenhauer's pessimism stands out both against the secular Enlightenment belief in progress, and against the premodern religious belief in the possibility of salvation.

Schopenhauer most clearly expresses his views on history in one of the supplementary essays to *The World as Will and Representation* (5.A.I and 5.A.II). For Schopenhauer the discipline of history was caught in a paradox. The more history seeks to fulfil its vocation to describe the character of individual events, the more it is reduced to narration. This narration does not have the virtue of art or poetry which manages to disclose the universal in the singular, but consists of a dreary list of events. Yet the more history seeks to describe patterns in world-events, the more it must contradict what Schopenhauer (using Aquinas's terminology) calls the *principium individuationis* or 'principle of individuation', which asserts the particularity of every world event. History proper is thus the opposite of philosophy, since history concerns the particular and philosophy the universal. History can only chronicle the mundane sequence of the transience of the world, and as such is hardly worth the bother because 'the human mind should select for consideration that which is destined never to pass away' (Schopenhauer, 1966, vol. 2, p. 442). Philosophy by contrast can see the truth to which history is blind: that 'the chapters of the history of nations are at bottom different only through the names and dates; the really essential content is everywhere the same' (vol. 2, p. 442). The only honourable role for the historian is to furnish culture with its own story by serving as the 'rational self-consciousness of the human race' (vol. 2, p. 445).

The roots of Schopenhauer's thinking lie in the philosophies of Kant and Plato. Schopenhauer admired the way in which Kant, in *The Critique of Pure Reason*, had distinguished between 'things-in-themselves' and the way in which they appear as a manifold' of 'phenomena' structured by time and space. What was unacceptable to Schopenhauer, however, was Kant's insistence that 'things-in-themselves' could not be known, and that human perception was restricted to the mere *appearance* of things. A world of appearance 'would inevitably pass us by like an empty dream and would not be worth our consideration'. This 'dream' is precisely the condition in which historical study finds itself (vol. 1, p. 99). For Schopenhauer, the appearance of the world begged the question of why the world exists at all. To answer that question we must shift our perspective from appearance or, as he called it, 'representation' (*Vorstellung*) to an intuitive 'perception' (*Anschauung*) based on our personal experience of also being things' in the world. By examining our own existence Schopenhauer believed that we would see that the thing-in-itself is in fact a universal *will to life*, a vital life-force that maintains every object in existence.

The world as will is not a happy place. The restlessness of the will is a kind of torture from which death is a blessed release. The will to life can find no resolution in the world: desire is never satisfied and happiness is never achieved. Such pointlessness results from the divided structure of history:

What gives life its strange and ambiguous character is that in it, two fundamental purposes, diametrically opposed, are constantly crossing each other. One purpose is that of the individual will, directed to chimerical happiness in an ephemeral, dream-like and deceptive existence . . . the other purpose is that of fate, directed obviously enough to the destruction of our happiness, and thus to the mortification of our will. (Schopenhauer, 1966, vol. 2, p. 638f)

The only release from this condition is to turn the will against itself, to will *not to will*, and find respite from the will's remorseless quest after satisfaction. Only when we do this can we obtain an adequate idea (in the Platonic not the Kantian sense) of the world as will. Thomas Mann, who was heavily influenced by Schopenhauer, portrays this process in final pages of *Buddenbrooks* when the sick young Hanno improvises on the piano for the last time. Hanno's music is an expression of the will: 'a wild relentless longing, abruptly broken by startling, arresting *pianissimi* . . . like a sudden abandonment into a gulf of desire.' Eventually the music quells desire into 'a mournful lingering away'. A page or two later, Hanno is dead having completed the artistic sublimation of the will: the exchange of the musical expression of life for the reality of life itself. This exchange is much more than the production of a representation of life. Art takes us to the very *Idea* of life itself, removing as Schopenhauer puts it, the 'mist of objective and subjective contingencies' (vol. 2, p. 407).[3] This is where art and philosophy exceed history, which *represents* life, but cannot *express* it.

This is an aesthetic resolution of the tragic historical order: art is the moderation of the world's tragedy, seizing from the flux of the world 'the pure rapture of the moment' (vol. 2, p. 409). For a moment at least, we are awakened from the dream of existence and a suprahistorical view comes into focus. The tormented writhing of life is frozen into an expression of the idea of the will, which is the true idea of the historical order. Although the artist is, for Schopenhauer, an heroic figure, a secular saint, even he cannot redeem history. Art is 'not the way out of life, but only an occasional consolation in it', a momentary epiphany in the meaningless parade of historical events (vol 1, p. 267).

With such a negative view of history, it may seem strange that Schopenhauer inspired one of the most brilliant cultural historians of the nineteenth century, Jacob Burckhardt, who was also a good friend of Nietzsche. Burckhardt saw in Schopenhauer's philosophy the materials for constructing not so much a new kind of history as a new kind of discipline altogether: 'the study of the *historical*', in other words the study of the *idea* of history which Schopenhauer had characterized as 'will' and which Burckhardt called 'spirit'. Using Schopenhauer's word for perception, Burckhardt tried to offer an *Anschauung*, or general picture, of history from the perspective of what he called 'an Archimedean point outside events'. From this vantage point the past could be seen *supra*historically as 'the condensation of the historical process' in great individuals (Burckhardt, 1943, p. 15). It was this study of the *historical* that Burckhardt sought to pursue in his particular studies of the ages of Constantine and the Renaissance.

Unlike the other thinkers in this chapter, **Søren Kierkegaard** (1813–1855) was Christian philosopher. For Kierkegaard history concerns individual human existence

---

3 Music is a special case in that it goes beyond even the expression of the idea of the will to the actuality of the will itself.

and its relationship with a God, the Absolute, who must lie beyond rational grasp. Each individual person must engage with his or her own existential history, but History with a capital 'H' can never be 'understood' as a complete system. Indeed, Kierkegaard believed that the modern, 'enlightenment' attempt to systematize existence had lead to a dismal 'levelling' down of life: 'The present age,' he once remarked 'is essentially the rational, reflecting, *unimpassioned age.*' For Kierkegaard the recovery of a proper historical perspective required a personal effort from each individual to 'become subjective'.

We know from Kierkegaard's dairy entries of 1854 that he was aware of Schopenhauer's philosophy and that 'in spite of a total disagreement', he was 'surprised' to find an author who affected him so much (Kierkegaard, 1975, p. 26). Kierkegaard's disagreement concerned Schopenhauer's ethical dependence upon the inspiration of genius rather than upon absolute moral obligation. However, Schopenhauer's insistence on the individual and his fierce anti-Hegelianism must have struck a chord with Kierkegaard. Kierkegaard also detected a paradox in Schopenhauer's pessimism: 'to choose pessimism can easily be a kind of optimism – from a temporal point of view the smartest thing to do' (p. 33). In other words, by removing the illusion of historical improvement, pessimism may in fact dispel anxiety and intensify our existential attention on the moment. Although Schopenhauer's pessimism almost certainly wasn't strategic, Kierkegaard does make an interesting point: that pessimism may be an antidote to a false faith in history. Certainly, Kierkegaard and Schopenhauer were agreed on this: that historical progress was an illusion.

Kierkegaard was as vehemently opposed to Hegelianism as Schopenhauer. Hegel's assertion that truth resides in the rational totality of history was the antithesis of Kierkegaard's belief that truth is intuitive, subjective and inward. Hegel's philosophy presupposed the ultimate coincidence of the historical, the rational and the ethical, so that when we look at history we can see the logical progression of cultural structures towards a necessarily good end (3.D.I; 3.D.II; 3.D.III). We may object that many episodes in history look profoundly irrational; but, says Hegel, this is only because 'the cunning of reason' uses the irrational to rational ends (3.D.IV). This means that the individual human life, or any individual moment in history, can be interpreted only with reference to the developing historical system and its goal.

In the *Concluding Unscientific Postscript* [1846], Kierkegaard uses his narrator 'Johannes Climacus' to venture a number of arguments against Hegel. These centre round Kierkegaard's belief that it is impossible for existence to be part of Hegel's dialectical view of history. Existence is always given as singular, subjective experience which cannot be systematized (5.B.I). The Hegelian (speculative) philosopher must 'absent-mindedly' forget that he is an existing being in order to construct an abstract view of history. This, says Kierkegaard, is patently absurd. Hegel's system must also be a system *of something*, Kierkegaard argues. This means that the *existence* of something must logically precede dialectics. If existence stands outside dialectics, then Hegel's claim that *Geist* is the historical totality cannot be true. Existence is also *motion* (*kinesis*) which is the underlying dynamic of time and history (5.B.II). Yet Hegel's abstraction of motion into an idea of historical change is the very denial of motion and of existence, and therefore the denial of history itself.

Against Hegel, Kierkegaard develops a view of history that begins with human existence, as he puts it: 'history first becomes true when it becomes internal history'. History proper is not the vast spectacle of Hegel's 'world history' but an inward drama of personal existence (5.B.I). We will inevitably overlook this subjective history if we fix our gaze at the external procession of events. A so-called 'dialectic of inwardness' is called for in order that we can access the conditions of our own existence. Internal history has a structure which Kierkegaard calls the 'stages on life's way', a transition through aesthetic, ethical and religious phases of selfhood. However, this personal development does not take place as a once-and-for-all progression like Hegelian history, but stands as an axis of personal possibility which may be traversed in either direction. What are crucial to the kinesis of this internal history, which takes place in a separate version for each and every person, are the 'either/or' existential choices made by the individual. At every turn the individual is confronted with a moment of decision. For Hegel these decisions can have no ethical significance since all choices, good or bad, have an equal role to play in history. For Kierkegaard the outcome of every moment really matters for our internal history. But the history of our decisions is a patch-work of moments which does not represent a progression towards personal perfection. Good decisions cannot be stored up, as if in the bank, to accumulate personal moral capital. The correct existential decisions must be taken and retaken. Thus internal existential history demands an ethic of endless *patience* and bears the character of resolute *repetition*. It is this repetition which gives existence its continuity and its true ethical-historical perspective.

We need to be careful not to confuse this patience with a waiting for some calculated end, because for Kierkegaard patience is an end in itself, which is disinterested in though not unconcerned with, the future. In this respect at least, Kierkegaard's patience is perhaps comparable with Schopenhauer's pessimism: 'the smartest thing to do from a temporal point of view'. Such patience-for-its-own-sake, which never expects to be resolved in time, naturally opens up the question of the eternal – but does so *within* the temporal. This is Kierkegaardian suprahistory: the historical order momentarily transfigured by the eternal. The end of history is not at 'The End' at all, but in the midst of the historical order.

The consequence of Kierkegaard's philosophy for historical studies (5.B.III) is that objective historical knowledge can never be final and definitive. This is because the absolute can only be accessed introspectively. The best that the historian can hope for is approximate knowledge. Even then, he will find that his historical research and his personal existence remain in a tension which cannot be resolved.

Friedrich Nietzsche (1844–1900), is most famous for proclaiming the 'death of God' and for his attack on Christianity as a life-sapping religion of 'pity'. Although he started out as a professional philosopher he soon became, like Kierkegaard, an isolated thinker who relished his solitude and who had contempt for 'professional' philosophy. Nietzsche was also despairing of his own era, seeing the nineteenth century as the age of the 'last man': self-satisfied, repressed and having lost touch with the will to life. Nietzsche prophesied the emergence of a new form of humanity, the 'over-man', who would transcend the mediocre culture of the herd. The 'over-man' would understand his own existence in terms of the 'will to power' and history as a 'tragic' play of forces.

As with Kierkegaard, it was Schopenhauer's *pessimism* which attracted the early Nietzsche, who saw Schopenhauer as a 'dragon-slayer' whose tragic historical view had won a 'most difficult victory' over Enlightenment rationalism and historical improvement (Nietzsche, 1993, pp. 87ff). Schopenhauer's attempt to refer philosophy back to questions of life, rather than knowledge, also met with Nietzsche's approval. However, Schopenhauer's Platonism and his asceticism – his 'cadaverous perfume' – were quite unacceptable to Nietzsche (Nietzsche, 1992, p. 78f). To the late Nietzsche, Schopenhauer is a moralist who develops a metaphysics of the will in order to justify a conventional Christian ethic (Nietzsche, 1968, p. 15). The fundamental difference, as he vividly puts it in *The Will to Power* (written in the late 1880s), is that Schopenhauer saw the tragedy of history as a problem to be overcome, whereas Nietzsche viewed tragedy as a '*tonic*' (p. 449):

> I grasped that my instinct went into the opposite direction from Schopenhauer's; towards a justification of life, even at its most terrible, ambiguous, and mendacious; for this I had the formula '*Dionysian*'. (p. 521)

In *The Birth of Tragedy* [1872], Nietzsche pictures history as a mythic tension between two gods: Dionysos whose chaotic, vital powers call 'the whole phenomenal world into existence'; and Apollo whose directed, plastic powers structure the phenomenal world as a panorama of knowable entities. Life and history, in their proper state, are joined by 'a fraternal bond' between the two: Dionsyos transfigured by Apollo, 'a visualization of Dionysiac wisdom by means of Apolline artifices' (Nietzsche, 1993, p. 105). If however, in a quest for ever-more perfect knowledge, history takes the side of Apollo it rapidly becomes lifeless and merely theoretical. In Nietzsche's view this is precisely what has happened both in the age of Socrates and in contemporary German culture (5.C.II). The historian becomes theoretical man at his worst: 'the "critic" without pleasure or strength, Alexandrian man, at bottom a librarian and a corrector of proofs, wretchedly blinded by the dust of his tomes and by printing errors' (p. 89).

This theme is taken up in 'The Uses and Disadvantages of History for Life' in which Nietzsche provides a schematic classification of genres of historical writing – Monumental, Antiquarian and Critical – in an effort to show how history may either serve or poison life. Monumental history is a celebration of the great figures and events of the past. Monumental history may serve life by inspiring us with past glories; but it may also sap life with a deadening nostalgia for lost greatness. Antiquarian history is the collection of the facts and artifacts of former times. The Antiquarian historian may be life-giving if he shows us how the past has developed into the present; but he may also become a merely obsessive collector of historical data. Critical history may, by making an analysis of the past, serve life by illustrating former errors; but the critical historian may also become cynical about the human condition. The point in all cases is that history must serve life.

In *The Birth of Tragedy* (which should be read alongside 'The Uses and Disadvantages of History for Life') Nietzsche had argued that the accommodation of the Apollonian and Dionysian powers is mythic rather than logical, and a product of wisdom rather than reason. Nietzsche's talk of myth does not mean that history is fiction. Myth touches that which is beyond the grasp of a merely factual history, namely the 'Dionysiac substratum of the world' (p. 117). Myth is the 'home' or 'womb' within which the Monumental, Antiquarian and Critical disciplines of history can flourish. Nietzsche repeatedly speaks of myth as a horizon which allows us to orientate our way in the flux of life (5.C.II). If history operates without this mythic horizon, the result is an aimless intellect which has lost its reason for being.

   The recovery of the mythic horizon requires us to uncover the pre-historical ground of history. This is a task that can take us in two directions: towards what Nietzsche calls the *unhistorical* and the *suprahistorical* (5.C.I). The unhistorical ground of history is nature, the ongoing present of animal consciousness that exists only in the horizon of its immediate happening. The suprahistorical is the unhistorical writ large – the unhistorical viewed from the perspective of eternity. The unhistorical and suprahistorical inscribe two horizons (or one horizon viewed from two perspectives) the horizon of the 'moment'; and the horizon of the eternal repetition of the 'moment' through history. Having secured these horizons, historical culture can be re-appropriated in a healthy and life-giving form.

   The question of an horizon for human existence and culture is the bridge that links these early reflections on history with Nietzsche's later doctrines of eternal return and 'genealogy', both of which date from the 1880s. Passages in *The Gay Science* [1882], *Thus Spoke Zarathustra* [1883–5] and *The Will to Power* [1901] offer a mythological description of suprahistory as the eternal return of historical events (5.C.V). *Human all too Human* [1878], *Beyond Good and Evil* [1886] and *The Genealogy of Morals* [1887] illustrate how this suprahistorical myth can be applied as a form of historical study (5.C.IV; 5.C.VII).

   'Eternal Return' distills the unhistorical and suprahistorical into a single idea: the thought that every moment, even this very moment, will be repeated endlessly. In his parable of the madman in *The Gay Science*, Nietzsche speaks of the death of God having 'wiped away the horizon' leaving the universe without bearings (5.C.VI). The horizon that appears after the death of God is the carousel of eternal return, and this for Nietzsche is the final ground of history: everything spinning in a spiral of meaningless singularities. To most people eternal return, like suprahistory, is an unbearable thought (Nietzsche, 1974, p. 273f; cf. Nietzsche, 1983, pp. 60–7).[4] But to the over-man 'the ring of recurrence' appears as a joyous dance, the perfect transfiguration of Dionysos into form. The over-man, having freed himself from the idea that there must be a structural or moral coherence to history, is able to affirm history as 'a play of forces . . . at the same time one and many . . . eternally changing, eternally flooding back, with tremendous years of recurrence' (5.C.VIII).

   Practical suprahistorical study might seem to be impossible since the historical order exhibits no pattern or meaning. However, Nietzsche argues that a genealogical history of singularities is possible (5.C.VII). In a nutshell, genealogy is a way of tracing the production of values within culture and history. Genealogical history attempts to illustrate that all human ideas and values are not timeless but *have a history*. The meaning of values, indeed the values themselves, are *datable*. Values, for Nietzsche, do not get handed down to us from the heavens but are human creations. For example, in *Human all too Human* [1878], Nietzsche argues that human rights are not absolute, but can 'be traced back to tradition, tradition to some agreement' (Nietzsche, 1986, p. 319). This is history as *provenance*, following lines of descent [*Herkunft*] and noting the emergence [*Entstehung*] of values. When Nietzsche uses the word *Entstehung* he means something quite different from a first cause [*Ursprung*]. *Entstehung* is always an origination *from* some other situation, implying generation and growth from one thing to the next. Thus Nietzsche distinguishes genealogy from the traditional historical

4 Cf. Hume (2.A.III) for whom the idea of a cyclical history was not such a terrible thought.

investigation of origins and progression, whether scientific or historical. For example, in a passage from *The Will to Power* entitled 'Anti-Darwin', Nietzsche accepts Darwin's *Origin of Species* as a history of mutation, but flatly rejects it as a theory of natural progression.

It is important to note that genealogy is concerned with *values* rather than *facts*. This is not because Nietzsche is a non-realist, but because Nietzsche sees facts *as* value-judgements (5.C.III). In maxims from *The Will to Power*, Nietzsche asserts that 'there are no facts, everything is in flux, incomprehensible, elusive; what is relatively most enduring is – our opinions'. And elsewhere he repeats that 'facts are precisely what there is not, only interpretations'; and 'interpretation', he elaborates later, is 'an affect'. Value is thus *more real* than fact. But this is no restriction to history, because the genealogy of value opens up a rich dimension of unresearched territory – as Nietzsche says in *The Gay Science*: 'where could you find a history of love, of avarice, of envy, of conscience, of pious respect for tradition, or of cruelty?' (5.C.IV).

Genealogy reduces history to singularity in every aspect. Historical laws cannot explain historical moments, since every moment is complete in itself and the totality of moments is only the swirl of recurring history. Each moment originates from an earlier moment in endless regression and succession. Our perspectives on the moments of history do not furnish final knowledge but are in themselves further transitory moments. Investigation of these moments will not reveal a hidden foundation, but only the play of forces which is life itself, a procession of 'values of the briefest and most transient, the seductive flash of gold on the serpent *vita*' (Nietzsche, 1968, p. 310. See also p. 267, p. 302 and p. 327).

An important advance that Nietzsche makes on the suprahistory of Schopenhauer and Kierkegaard, is that his genealogical analysis acknowledges that history proceeds in a particular direction and that life's moments are *successive*. Schopenhauer and Kierkegaard take little account of the fact that the order in which things happen effects our valuation and interpretation of events. If the arrow of time is reversed – as Martin Amis and Kurt Vonnegut have both imagined in their fiction – the meaning of history changes entirely. The *order* of events is crucial to their meaning.

The suprahistorical reduction of life to 'moments' faces a logical difficulty which casts doubt on its claim to have overcome the world-historical perspective. If suprahistory is to escape world-history it must declare singularity to be a universal category. But a categorical view of the historical condition is precisely what is meant by world-history. The difficulty arises from the inherent contradiction of making a category out of the arbitrary and singular. Anything truly singular is necessarily unclassifiable. This leaves the suprahistorists with two options: either not to venture any categorical description of the world in general (which would leave them no way of contradicting the Hegelian model of world-history) or to risk colluding with the Hegelians, since to say that history is nothing but a collection of singular events is in fact to make a categorical claim of fundamentally the same kind as the Hegelian counter-claim that history is an organic totality.

Nietzsche attempts to overcome the difficulty by positing the essential *infinitude* of the world's arbitrariness in eternal return. The category 'world history' never gets absolutely decided because it just keeps expanding. Thus history remains a secret, *istoria abscondita*, since 'there is no way of telling what yet may become part of istory' (5.C.IV). Similarly Kierkegaard argues that history never gets closed off, like a discussion that rambles on until the original issue is forgotten. In a memorable jotting, Kierkegaard refers to 'the infinite tangential possibilities of the periphery' which leave the category of history undetermined. (Kierkegaard, 1970, p. 232). Schopenhauer offers a different solution based upon his idiosyncratic version of Platonism. On the one hand Schopenhauer asserts what he calls 'the principle of individuation' which determines the world as an ephemeral, dream-like procession of one-off entities and events, 'a kingdom of chance and error', 'transitory, finite and subject to annihilation' (Schopenhauer, 1966, vol. 1, p. 112f; vol. 1, p. 324; vol. 2, p. 484) (5.A.II). On the other hand, every individual thing is also the expression of an eternal Idea: the will-to-live which is 'the kernel of life itself' (vol. 2, p. 351). Schopenhauer argues that the idea of the will does not contradict the 'principle of individuation' or reduce the complexity and incoherence of history. On the contrary the will explains the possibility of an eternally arbitrary world. This is because the will is a 'blind urge, an impulse wholly without ground or motive' (vol. 2, p. 357).

In response it may be argued that the appeal to infinitude, uncertainty or a universal idea of incoherence effectively concedes the possibility of world history: 'infinity' is still a totalization, even if, as Hegel says, it is a 'bad' infinity that never comes to anything; 'uncertainty' by its very nature leaves open the possibility of a world-historical perspective; and, as Nietzsche himself pointed out, Schopenhauer's universal idea of the will, however conceived, is a world-historical idea with a vengeance.

What we encounter here is the paradox that Paul Ricoeur has called 'the contradiction of all historicity'. History is both *system* and *event*, *singularity* and *generality* (cf Rickert, 6.C.I). Thus there are *two* ends to history, the world-historical *and* the suprahistorical: 'The system is the end of history because history becomes nullified in Logic; singularity too is the end of history since all history is repudiated in it' (Ricoeur 1965, p. 75f). The historian attempts to interpret history between these poles. But whichever starting point he choses – the general picture or the singular event – the historian will have made a philosophical prejudgement, or pre-interpretation of history. This dilemma opens up the general problem of hermeneutics.

Selected Texts

Edited by Hugh Rayment-Pickard

5.A Arthur Schopenhauer, 1788–1860

5.A.1 History is not a Science[1]

In every class and species of things the facts are innumerable, the individual beings infinite in number, and the multiplicity and variety of their differences beyond our reach. With one look at all this, the curious and inquisitive mind is in a whirl; however much it investigates, it sees itself condemned to ignorance. But then comes *science*; it separates out the innumerable many, collects them under generic concepts, and these in turn under specific concepts, and so opens the way to a knowledge of the general and the particular. This knowledge comprehends the innumerable *individuals*, since it holds good of all without our having to consider each one by itself. In this way it promises satisfaction to the inquiring mind. All the sciences then put themselves together and over the real world of individual things which they have parceled out among themselves. But philosophy excels them all as the most universal, and thus the most important, knowledge, promising information for which the others have only prepared the way. *History* alone cannot properly enter into this series, since it cannot boast of the same advantage as the others, for it lacks the fundamental characteristic of science, the subordination of what is known; instead of this it boasts of the mere coordination of what is known. Therefore there is no system of history, as there is of every other branch of knowledge; accordingly, it is rational knowledge indeed, but not a science. For nowhere does it know the particular by means of the universal, but it must comprehend the particular directly, and continue to creep along the ground of experience, so to speak. The real sciences, on the other hand, excel it, since they have attained to comprehensive concepts by means of which they command and control the particular, and, at any rate within certain limits, foresee the possibility of things within their province, so that they can be reassured even about what is still to come. As the sciences are systems of concepts, they always speak of species; history speaks of individuals. History would accordingly be a science of individual things, which implies a contradiction. It follows also from the first statement that the sciences all speak of that which always is; history, on the other hand, speaks of that which is only once, and then

Arthur Schopenhauer, *The World as Will and Representation*, (New York: Dover Publications, 1966), vol. 2, pp. 439, 442. trans. E. Payne.

no more. Further, as history has to do with the absolutely particular and with individ
als, which by their nature are inexhaustible, it knows everything only imperfectly ar
partially. At the same time, it must allow itself to be taught by the triviality of eve
new day that which as yet it did not know at all. If it should be objected that in histo
subordination of the particular under the universal also takes place, since the periods
time, the governments, and the other main and political changes, in short, everythir
to be found in historical tables, are the universal to which the special is subordinate
this would rest on a false understanding of the concept of the universal. For the unive
sal here referred to is in history merely *subjective*, that is to say, its generality sprin;
merely from the inadequacy of the individual *knowledge* of things; it is not *objective*,
other words, a concept in which the things would actually be thought together. Eve
the most universal in history is in itself only something individual and particular, name
a long epoch or a principal event. . . .

Now in so far as history always has for its object only the particular, the individu
fact, and regards this as the exclusively real, it is the direct opposite and counterpart
philosophy, which considers things from the most universal point of view, and has th
universal as its express object . . . Whereas history teaches us that at each time som
thing different has been, philosophy endeavours to assist us to the insight that at a
times exactly the same was, is, and will be. In truth, the essence of human life, as
nature everywhere, exists complete in every present time, and therefore requires on
depth of comprehension in order to be exhaustively known. History, however, hop
to make up for depth by length and breadth; every present time is for it only a fra;
ment that must be supplemented by the past. But the length of the past is infinite, ar
joined to it again is an infinite future. On this rests the opposition between philosoph
cal and historical minds; the former want to fathom and find out, the latter try
narrate to the end. History shows on every side only the same thing under differe:
forms; but he who does not recognize such a thing in one or a few forms, will hard
attain to a knowledge of it by running through all the forms. The chapters of th
history of nations are at bottom different only through the names and dates; the real
essential content is everywhere the same.

5.A.II The Long, Heavy and Confused Dream of Mankind[2]

The material of history is the transient complexities of a human world moving lil
clouds in the wind, which are often entirely transformed by the most trifling accider
From this point of view, the material of history appears to us as scarcely an obje
worthy of the serious and arduous consideration of the human mind. Just because it
so transitory, the human mind should select for its consideration that which is destine
never to pass away.

. . . As regards the attempt specially introduced by the Hegelian pseudo-philosopl
that is everywhere so pernicious and stupefying to the mind, the attempt, namely
comprehend the history of the world as a planned whole, or, as they call it, 'to col
struct it organically,' a crude and shallow *realism* is actually at the root of this. Suc

2   ibid., vol. 2, p. 442, p. 444.

realism regards the *phenomenon* as the *being-in-itself* of the world, and imagines that it is a question of this phenomenon and of its forms and events. It is still secretly supported in this by certain, mythological, fundamental views which it tacitly assumes; otherwise it might be asked for what spectator such a comedy was really being enacted. For since only the individual, not the human race, has actual, immediate unity of consciousness, the unity of this race's course of life is a mere fiction. . . .

Only the events of our *inner* life, in so far as they concern the *will*, have true reality and are actual occurrences, since the will alone is the thing-in-itself. In every microcosm lies the macrocosm, and the latter contains nothing more than is contained in the former. Plurality is phenomenon, and external events are mere configurations of the phenomenal world; they therefore have neither reality nor significance directly, but only indirectly, through their relation to the will of the individuals. Accordingly, the attempt to explain and expound them is like the attempt to see groups of persons and animals in the forms of clouds. What history relates is in fact only the long, heavy, and confused dream of mankind.

The Hegelians, who regard the philosophy of history as even the main purpose of all philosophy, should be referred to Plato, who untiringly repeats that the object of philosophy is the unchangeable and ever permanent, not that which now is thus and then otherwise. . . .

Therefore, a real philosophy of history should not consider . . . that which is always *becoming* and never *is* (to use Plato's language), and regard this as the real nature of things. On the contrary, it should keep in view that which always is, and never becomes or passes away. Thus it does not consist in our raising the temporal aims of men to eternal and absolute aims, and then constructing with ingenuity and imagination their progress to these through every intricacy and perplexity. It consists in the insight that history is untruthful not only in its arrangement, but also in its very nature, since, speaking of mere individuals and particular events, it always pretends to relate something different, whereas from beginning to end it constantly repeats only the same thing under a different name and in a different cloak. The true philosophy of history thus consists in the insight that, in spite of all these endless changes and their chaos and confusion, we yet always have before us only the same, identical, unchangeable essence, acting in the same way today as it did yesterday and always.

5.B   Søren Kierkegaard, 1813–1855

5.B.1   The Existing Individual versus World-History[3]

Only by paying sharp attention to myself can I come to realize how a historical individuality acted when he was living, and I understand him only when I keep him alive in my understanding . . . But what it is to live I cannot learn from him as someone dead and gone. I must experience that by myself, and therefore I must understand myself not the reverse . . . World-historically, the individual subject certainly is a trifle, but the

Søren Kierkegaard, *Concluding Unscientific Postscript*, trans. H. Hong and E. Hong (Princeton: Princeton University Press, 1992), vol. 1, p. 146.

world-historical is, after all, an addendum; ethically, the individual subject is infinite
important.

Take any human passion and have it be related to the ethical in the individua
ethically viewed, this will have great significance; world-historically, perhaps none
all or perhaps very great significance, for the world-historical, viewed ethically, ente
by way of a 'perhaps.' Whereas that relation between passion and the ethical occupi
the existing individual to the utmost . . .

World-historically, to be a single individual is nothing at all, infinitely nothing- ar
yet this is a human being's only true and highest significance, and thus higher than ar
other significance, which is a phantom, not, to be sure, in itself, but always a phanto
if it is supposed to be the highest.

5.B.II   Identity through Time achieved by Passionate Decision[4]

Inasmuch as existence is motion, it holds true that there is indeed a continuity th
holds the motion together, because otherwise there is no motion. Just as the stat
ment that everything is true means that nothing is true, in the same way the stateme
that everything is in motion means that there is no motion. The motionless belongs 1
motion as motion's goal . . . both in the sense of *telos* [end, goal] and *metron* [mea
ure, criterion]; otherwise the statement that everything is in motion – if one also tak
away time and says that everything is always motion – is *eo ipso* stagnation. Aristotl
who in so many ways emphasizes motion, therefore says that God, himself unmove
moves everything. Now, whereas pure thinking summarily cancels all motion, or mea
inglessly introduces it into logic, the difficulty for the existing person is to give exis
ence the continuity without which everything just disappears. An abstract continuity
no continuity, and the existing of the existing person essentially prevents continuit
whereas passion is the momentary continuity that simultaneously has a constrainir
effect and is the impetus of motion. For an existing person, the goal of motion
decision and repetition. The eternal is the continuity of motion, but an abstract ete
nity is outside motion, and a concrete eternity in the existing person is the maximu
of passion. That is, all idealizing passion is an anticipation of the eternal in existence
order for an existing person to exist; the eternity of abstraction is gained by disregar
ing existence. An existing person can have gained admission into pure thinking only t
a dubious beginning, a dubiousness that indeed backlashes by making the existir
person's existence trivial and his parlance somewhat demented. This is just about tl
case with the majority of people in our day, when one seldom or never hears a persc
speak as if he were conscious of his being an individual existing human being, b
instead pantheistically lets himself become dizzy when *he*, too, talks about millions ar
the nations and world-historical development. For an existing person, however, pa
sion's anticipation of the eternal is still not an absolute continuity but the possibility
an approximation to the only true continuity there can be for an existing person. He
one is again reminded of my thesis that subjectivity is truth, because the objecti
truth for an existing person is like the eternity of abstraction.

4   Ibid., vol. 1, p. 312.

Abstraction is disinterested, but to exist is the highest interest for an existing person. Therefore, the existing person continually has a *telos* and it is of this *telos* that Aristotle speaks when he says (*De anima*, III, 10, 2) that . . . [theoretical thought] is different from . . . [practical thought in its end]. But pure thinking is totally in suspension and is not like abstraction, which does indeed disregard existence but still maintains a relation to it, whereas pure thinking, in mystical suspension and with no relation to an existing person, explains everything within itself but not itself, explains everything within itself, whereby the decisive explanation regarding the real question becomes impossible. When, for example, an existing person asks how pure thinking relates itself to an existing person, how he goes about being admitted into it, pure thinking gives no answer but explains existence within its pure thinking and thereby confuses everything, because that upon which pure thinking must become stranded, existence, is in a volatilized sense assigned a place within pure thinking, whereby whatever might be said within it about existence is essentially revoked. . . .

For the existing person, existing is for him his highest interest, and his interestedness in existing is his actuality. What actuality is cannot be rendered in the language of abstraction. Actuality is an *inter-esse* [between-being] between thinking and being in the hypothetical unity of abstraction. Abstraction deals with possibility and actuality, but its conception of actuality is a false rendition, since the medium is not actuality but possibility. Only by annulling actuality can abstraction grasp it, but to annul it is precisely to change it into possibility.

5.B.III   Historical Knowledge is only Approximate[5]

In regard to the historical, all learning about it and all knowledge of it is at its maximum an approximation, even in regard to the individual's own knowledge of his own historical externality. The reason is partly the impossibility of being able to identify oneself absolutely with the objective, and partly that everything historical, inasmuch as it must be known, is *eo ipso* past and has the ideality of recollection . . . I can in all eternity know absolutely, because this is an expression of the eternal within me, is myself, but the historical externality in the next moment can be reached only *approximando* [by approximation].

The historian seeks to reach the greatest possible certainty, and the historian is not in any contradiction, because he is not in passion; at most he has the research scholar's objective passion, but he is not in subjective passion. As a research scholar, he belongs to a major endeavor from generation to generation; it is at all times objectively and scientifically important for him to come as close to certainty as possible, but it is not subjectively important to him. If, for example, it suddenly became a matter of purely personal honor (which, then, is a defect in a research scholar) for a research scholar to obtain absolute certainty about this and that, he, having become liable to a righteous nemesis, would discover that all historical knowledge is only an approximation. This is no minimizing of historical research, but it illustrates the contradiction in bringing the most extreme passion of subjectivity into relation with something historical, which is the dialectical contradiction in the issue, which is not a question of some illegitimate

Ibid., vol. 1, p. 574, p. 576.

passion but of the deepest passion of all – The philosopher seeks to penetrate historical actuality with thought; he is objectively occupied with this work, and the more he succeeds the less important the historical detail becomes to him. Here, again, there is no contradiction.

The contradiction first appears when the subjective individual at the peak of his subjective passion (in his concern for an eternal happiness) is to base this on historical knowledge, of which the maximum remains an approximation. The research scholar calmly goes on living. That which occupies him objectively and scientifically makes no difference one way or the other in his subjective being and existing. If it is assumed that someone is in subjective passion in some way and then the task is to relinquish this, the contradiction will also disappear. But to require the greatest possible subjective passion, to the point of hating father and mother, and then join this together with historical knowledge that at its maximum can become only an approximation – this is the contradiction. . . .

To the person who is in the greatest possible passion, in anguish, about his eternal happiness, it is or ought to be of interest that such and such has existed; he must be interested in the slightest detail; and yet he cannot reach more than an approximation and is absolutely in contradiction. Granted that the historicity of Christianity is true – if all the historiographers of the world united to do research and to establish certainty it would still be impossible to establish more than an approximation.

5.B.IV   The Palace of World History and the Dog Kennel of Personal Existence[6]

A thinker erects an immense building, a system, a system which embraces the whole of existence and world-history etc. – and if we contemplate his personal life, we discover to our astonishment this terrible and ludicrous fact, that he himself personally does not live in this immense high-vaulted palace, but in a barn alongside of it, or in a dog kennel, or at the most in the porter's lodge. If one were to take the liberty of calling his attention to this by a single word, he would be offended. For he has no fear of being under a delusion, if only he can get the system completed . . . by means of the delusion.

5.C   Friedrich Nietzsche, 1844–1900

5.C.I   The Historical the Unhistorical and the Suprahistorical[7]

Consider the cattle, grazing as they pass you by: they do not know what is meant by yesterday or today, they leap about, eat, rest, digest, leap about again, and so from

6   Søren Kierkegaard, *The Sickness unto Death* (with *Fear and Trembling*), trans. W. Lowrie (Princeton: Princeton University Press, 1968), pp. 176–7.
7   Friedrich Nietzsche, *Untimely Meditations*, trans. R. Hollingdale (Cambridge: Cambridge University Press, 1983), pp. 60–6.

morn till night and from day to day, fettered to the moment and its pleasure or displeasure, and thus neither melancholy nor bored. This is a hard sight for man to see; for, though he thinks himself better than the animals because he is human, he cannot help envying them their happiness – what they have, a life neither bored nor painful, is precisely what he wants, yet he cannot have it because he refuses to be like an animal. . . .

. . . Thus the animal lives *unhistorically*: for it is contained in the present, like a number without any awkward fraction left over; it does not know how to dissimulate, it conceals nothing and at every instant appears wholly as what it is; it can therefore never be anything but honest. Man, on the other hand, braces himself against the great and ever greater pressure of what is past: it pushes him down or bends him sideways, it encumbers his steps as a dark, invisible burden which he would like to disown and which in traffic with his fellow men he does disown, so as to excite their envy. That is why it affects him like a vision of a lost paradise to see the herds grazing or, in closer proximity to him, a child which, having as yet nothing of the past to shake off, plays in blissful blindness between the hedges of past and future. Yet its play must be disturbed; all too soon it will be called out of its state of forgetfulness. Then it will learn to understand the phrase 'it was': that password which gives conflict, suffering and satiety access to man so as to remind him what his existence fundamentally is – an imperfect tense that can never become a perfect one. If death at last brings the desired forgetting, by that act it at the same time extinguishes the present and all being and therewith sets the seal on the knowledge that being is only an uninterrupted has-been, a thing that lives by negating, consuming and contradicting itself.

If happiness, if reaching out for new happiness, is in any sense what fetters living creatures to life and makes them go on living, then perhaps no philosopher is more justified than the Cynic: for the happiness of the animal, as the perfect Cynic, is the living proof of the rightness of Cynicism. The smallest happiness, if only it is present uninterruptedly and makes happy, is incomparably more happiness than the greatest happiness that comes only as an episode, as it were a piece of waywardness or folly, in a continuum of joylessness, desire and privation. In the case of the smallest or of the greatest happiness, however, it is always the same thing that makes happiness happiness: the ability to forget or, expressed in more scholarly fashion, the capacity to feel *unhistorically* during its duration. He who cannot sink down on the threshold of the moment and forget all the past, who cannot stand balanced like a goddess of victory without growing dizzy and afraid, will never know what happiness is – worse, he will never do anything to make others happy. Imagine the extremest possible example of a man who did not possess the power of forgetting at all and who was thus condemned to see everywhere a state of becoming: such a man would no longer believe in his own being, would no longer believe in himself, would see everything flowing asunder in moving points and would lose himself in this stream of becoming: like a true pupil of Heraclitus, he would in the end hardly dare to raise his finger. Forgetting is essential to action of any kind, just as not only light but darkness too is essential for the life of everything organic. A man who wanted to feel historically through and through would be like one forcibly deprived of sleep, or an animal that had to live only by rumination and ever repeated rumination. Thus: it is possible to live almost without memory, and to live happily moreover, as the animal demonstrates; but it is altogether impossible to live at all without forgetting. Or, to express my theme even more simply: *there is a*

degree of sleeplessness, of rumination, of the historical sense, which is harmful and ulti-
mately fatal to the living thing, whether this living thing be a man or a people or a cul-
ture.

To determine this degree, and therewith the boundary at which the past has to be
forgotten if it is not to become the gravedigger of the present, one would have to
know exactly how great the *plastic power* of a man, a people, a culture is: I mean by
plastic power the capacity to develop out of oneself in one's own way, to transform and
incorporate into oneself what is past and foreign, to heal wounds, to replace what has
been lost, to recreate broken moulds. There are people who possess so little of this
power that they can perish from a single experience, from a single painful event, often
and especially from a single subtle piece of injustice, like a man bleeding to death from
a scratch; on the other hand, there are those who are so little affected by the worst and
most dreadful disasters, and even by their own wicked acts, that they are able to feel
tolerably well and be in possession of a kind of clear conscience even in the midst of
them or at any rate very soon afterwards. The stronger the innermost roots of a man's
nature, the more readily will he be able to assimilate and appropriate the things of the
past; and the most powerful and tremendous nature would be characterized by the fact
that it would know no boundary at all at which the historical sense began to over-
whelm it; it would draw to itself and incorporate into itself all the past, its own and that
most foreign to it, and as it were transform it into blood. That which such a nature
cannot subdue it knows how to forget; it no longer exists, the horizon is rounded and
closed, and there is nothing left to suggest there are people, passions, teachings, goals
lying beyond it. And this is a universal law: a living thing can be healthy, strong and
fruitful only when bounded by a horizon; if it is incapable of drawing a horizon around
itself, and at the same time too self-centred to enclose its own view within that of
another, it will pine away slowly or hasten to its timely end. Cheerfulness, the good
conscience, the joyful deed, confidence in the future – all of them depend, in the case
of the individual as of a nation, on the existence of a line dividing the bright and
discernible from the unilluminable and dark; on one's being just as able to forget at
the right time as to remember at the right time; on the possession of a powerful instinct for sensing when it is necessary to feel historically and when unhistorically. This
precisely, is the proposition the reader is invited to mediate upon: *the unhistorical and*
the historical are necessary in equal measure for the health of an individual of a people
and of a culture.

First of all, there is an observation that everyone must have made: a man's historical
sense and knowledge can be very limited, his horizon as narrow as that of a dweller in
the Alps, all his judgements may involve injustice and he may falsely suppose that all
his experiences are original to him – yet in spite of this injustice and error he will
nonetheless stand there in superlative health and vigour, a joy to all who see him; while
close beside him a man far more just and instructed than he sickens and collapses
because the lines of his horizon are always restlessly changing, because he can no
longer extricate himself from the delicate net of his judiciousness and truth for a simple
act of will and desire. On the other hand we have observed the animal, which is quite
unhistorical, and dwells within a horizon reduced almost to a point, and yet lives in a
certain degree of happiness, or at least without boredom and dissimulation; we shall
thus have to account the capacity to feel to a certain degree unhistorically as being
more vital and more fundamental, inasmuch as it constitutes the foundation upon

which alone anything sound, healthy and great, anything truly human, can grow. The unhistorical is like an atmosphere within which alone life can germinate and with the destruction of which it must vanish, it is true that only by imposing limits on this unhistorical element by thinking, reflecting, comparing, distinguishing, drawing conclusions, only through the appearance within that encompassing cloud of a vivid flash of light – thus only through the power of employing the past for the purposes of life and of again introducing into history that which has been done and is gone – did man become man: but with an excess of history man again ceases to exist, and without that envelope of the unhistorical he would never have begun or dared to begin. What deed would man be capable of if he had not first entered into that vaporous region of the unhistorical? . . . No painter will paint his picture, no general achieve his victory, no people attain its freedom without having first desired and striven for it in an unhistorical condition such as that described. As he who acts is, in Goethe's words, always without a conscience, so is he also always without knowledge; he forgets most things so as to do one thing, he is unjust towards what lies behind him, and he recognizes the rights only of that which is now to come into being and no other rights whatever. Thus he who acts loves his deed infinitely more than it deserves to be loved: and the finest deeds take place in such a superabundance of love that, even if their worth were incalculable in other respects, they must still be unworthy of this love.

If, in a sufficient number of cases, one could scent out and retrospectively breathe his unhistorical atmosphere within which every great historical event has taken place, he might, as a percipient being, raise himself to a *suprahistorical* vantage point . . . We may use the word 'suprahistorical' because the viewer from this vantage point could no longer feel any temptation to go on living or to take part in history; he would have recognized the essential condition of all happenings – this blindness and injustice in the soul of him who acts; he would, indeed, be cured for ever of taking history too seriously . . . Historical men believe that the meaning of existence will come more and more to light in the course of *its process*, and they glance behind them only so that, from the process so far, they can learn to understand the present and to desire the future more vehemently; they have no idea that, despite their preoccupation with history, they in fact think and act unhistorically, or that their occupation with history stands in the service, not of pure knowledge, but of life. . . .

[By contrast there is] the suprahistorical man, who sees no salvation in the process and for whom, rather, the world is complete and reaches its finality at each and every moment. What could ten more years teach that the past ten were unable to teach!

Whether the sense of this teaching is happiness or resignation or virtue or atonement, suprahistorical men have never been able to agree; but, in opposition to all historical modes of regarding the past, they are unanimous in the proposition: the past and the present are one, that is to say, with all their diversity identical in all that is typical and, as the omnipresence of imperishable types, a motionless structure of a value that cannot alter and a significance that is always the same.

5.C.II   Myth is Higher than History[8]

Anyone who wishes to test himself precisely to see how closely he is related to the true aesthetic spectator or to the community of Socratic-critical men need only ask himself honestly about the feeling with which he responds to *miracles* portrayed on the stage: whether his historical sense, aimed at strict psychological causality, is insulted; whether he accepts miracles, with a benevolent concession, as a phenomenon intelligible to children but remote from himself; or whether he responds in some other way. He will thus be able to tell whether he is at all capable of understanding *myth*, the concentrated image of the world which, as an abbreviation for phenomena, cannot do without miracles. But in all likelihood almost everyone, having subjected himself to a rigorous examination, will feel so undermined by the critical-historical spirit of our culture that it is only by scholarly means and mediating abstractions that the former existence of myth can he made credible. Yet without myth all culture loses its healthy and natural creative power: only a horizon surrounded by myths can unify an entire cultural movement. Myth alone rescues all the powers of imagination and the Apolline dream from their aimless wanderings. The images of myth must be the daemonic guardians, omnipresent and unnoticed, which protect the growth of the young mind, and guide man's interpretation of his life and struggles. The state itself has no unwritten laws more powerful than the mythical foundation that guarantees its connection with religion and its growth out of mythical representations. Let us now, by way of comparison, imagine abstract man, without the guidance of myth – abstract education, abstract morality, abstract justice, the abstract state; let us imagine the lawless wandering, unchecked by native myth, of the artistic imagination; let us imagine a culture without secure and sacred primal site, condemned to exhaust every possibility and feed wretchedly on all other cultures – there we have our present age, the product of that Socratism bent on the destruction of myth. And here stands man, stripped of myth, eternally starving, in the midst of all the past ages, digging and scrabbling for roots, even if he must dig for them in the most remote antiquities. What is indicated by the great historical need of unsatisfied modern culture, clutching about for countless other cultures, with its consuming desire for knowledge, if not the loss of myth, the loss of the mythical home, the mythical womb? Let us consider whether the feverish and sinister agitation of this culture is anything other than a starving man's greedy grasping for food – and who would wish to give further nourishment to a culture such as this unsatisfied by everything it devours, which transforms the most powerful, wholesome nourishment into 'history and criticism'?

5.C.III   On Truth[9]

What is truth?

What then is truth? A movable host of metaphors, metonymies and anthropomorphisms, in short, a sum of human relations which have been poetically and rhetorically intens

---

8   Friedrich Nietzsche, *The Birth of Tragedy*, trans. S. Whiteside (Harmondsworth: Penguin, 199?, pp. 109–10.

fied, transferred and embellished, and which, after long usage, seem to people to be fixed, canonical and binding. Truths are illusions which we have forgotten are illusions; they are metaphors that have become worn out and have been drained of sensuous force, coins which have lost their embossing and are now considered as metal and no longer as coins.

Perspectivism

All evaluation is made from a definite perspective: that of the preservation of the individual, a community, a race, a state, a church, a faith, a culture – Because we forget that valuation is always from a perspective, a single individual contains within him a vast confusion of contradictory valuations and consequently of contradictory drives. This is the expression of the diseased condition in man, in contrast to the animals in which all existing instincts answer to quite different tasks.

5.C.IV   Unwritten and Secret History[10]

Something for the industrious'. – Anyone who now wishes to make a study of moral matters opens up for himself an immense field of work. All kinds of individual passions have to be thought through and pursued through different ages, peoples and great and small individuals; all their reason and all their evaluations and perspectives on things have to be brought into the light. So far, all that has given colour to existence still lacks a history. Where could you find a history of love, of avarice, of envy, of conscience, of pious respect for tradition, or of cruelty?

Historia abscondita [secret history]. – Every great human being exerts retroactive force: for his sake all of history is placed in the balance again, and a thousand secrets of the past crawl out of their hiding places – into *his* sunshine. There is no way of telling what yet may become part of history. Perhaps the past is still essentially undiscovered! So many retroactive forces are still needed.

5.C.V   Eternal Return[11]

The greatest weight. – What, if some day or night a demon were to steal after you in your loneliest loneliness and say to you: 'This life as you now live it and have lived it, you will have to live once more and innumerable times more; and there will be nothing

First extract (What is Truth?): Friedrich Nietzsche, 'On Truth and Lies in a Nonmoral Sense', *Philosophy and Truth: Selections from Nietzsche's Notebooks of the early 1870s*, trans. D. Breazeale, Atlantic Highlands, NJ: Humanities Press); (Hassocks: Harvester, 1979), p. 84. Second extract (Perspectivism): Friedrich Nietzsche, *The Will to Power*, trans. Kaufmann and Hollingdale (New York: Vintage, 1968), p. 150.

10 Friedrich Nietzsche, *The Gay Science*, trans. Kaufmann, New York; Vintage, 1974) First extract (Something for the industrious), p 81; second extract (Secret History), p. 104.

11 First extract (The Greatest Weight): Ibid., pp. 273–4. Second extract (Of the vision and the riddle): Friedrich Nietzsche, *Thus Spoke Zarathustra*, trans. R Hollingdale (Harmondsworth: Penguin, 1969), pp. 176–8.

new in it, but every pain and every joy and every thought and sigh and everything unutterably small or great in your life will have to return to you, all in the same succession and sequence . . . The question in each and every thing: 'Do you desire this once more and innumerable times more?'

Of the Vision and the Riddle. – Lately I walked gloomily through deathly-grey twilight . . . through boulders and rubble . . . a mountain path crunched under my foot's defiance . . . Upward – despite the spirit that drew it downward, drew it towards the abyss, the Spirit of Gravity, my devil and arch enemy. Upward – although he sat upon me, half dwarf, half mole: crippled, crippling; pouring lead-drops into my ear, leaden thoughts into my brain . . . Then something occurred which lightened me: for the dwarf jumped from my shoulder, the inquisitive dwarf! And he squatted down on a stone in front of me. But a gateway stood just where we had halted. Behold this gateway, dwarf!' I went on: 'it has two aspects. Two paths come together here: no one has ever reached their end. This long lane behind us: it goes on for an eternity. And the lane ahead of us – that is another eternity. They are in opposition to one another, these paths; they about one another: and it is here at this gateway that they come together. The name of the gateway is written above it "Moment".'

5.C.VI Nihilism[12]

The Future

What I relate is the history of the next two centuries. I describe what is coming, what can no longer come differently: the advent of nihilism. This history can be related now; for necessity itself is at work here. This future speaks even now in a hundred signs, this destiny announces itself everywhere; for this music of the future all ears are cocked even now. For some time now, our whole European culture has been moving as toward a catastrophe, with a tortured tension that is growing from decade to decade; . . . like a river that wants to reach the end, that no longer reflects, that is afraid to reflect.

The Death of God

Have you not heard of that madman who lit a lantern in the bright morning hours, ran to the market place and cried incessantly: 'I seek God! I seek God!'? – As many of those who did not believe in God were standing around just then, he provoked much laughter. Has he got lost? asked one. Did he lose his way like a child? asked another. Or is he hiding? Is he afraid of us? Has he gone on a voyage? emigrated? – Thus they yelled and laughed.

The madman jumped into their midst and pierced them with his eyes. 'Wither is God?' he cried. 'I will tell you. *We have killed him* – you and I. All of us are his murderers. But how did we do this? How could we drink up the sea? Who gave us the sponge to wipe away the entire horizon? What were we doing when we unchained this earth

12   First extract, (The Future): Friedrich Nietzsche, *The Will to Power*, trans. Kaufmann and Hollingdale (New York: Vintage, 1968), p. 3. Second extract (The Death of God): Friedrich Nietzsche, *The Gay Science*, trans. Kaufmann (New York: Vintage, 1974), pp. 181–2.

from its sun? Whither is it moving now? Whither are we moving? Away from all suns? Are we not plunging continually? Backward, sidewards, forward, in all directions? Is there still any up or down? Are we not straying as though through an infinite nothing? Do we not feel the breath of empty space? Has it not become colder? Is not night continually closing in on us? Do we not need to light lanterns in the morning? Do we hear nothing as yet of the noise of the gravediggers who are burying God? Do we smell nothing as yet of the divine decomposition? Gods, too, decompose. God is dead. God remains dead. And we have killed him.

'How shall we comfort ourselves, the murderers of all murderers? What was holiest and mightiest of all the world has yet owned has bled to death under our knives: who will wipe this blood off us? What water is there for us to clean ourselves? What festivals of atonement, what sacred games shall we have to invent? Is not the greatness of this deed too great for us? Must we not ourselves become gods simply to appear worthy of it? There has never been a greater deed: and whatever is born after us – for the sake of this deed he will belong to a higher history than all history hitherto.'

Here the madman fell silent and looked again at his listeners; and they, too, were silent and stared at him in astonishment. At last he threw his lantern to the ground, and it broke into pieces and went out. 'I have come too early, my time is not yet. This tremendous event is still on its way, still wandering; it has not yet reached the ears of men. Lightning and thunder require time; the light of the stars requires time; deeds, though done, still require time to be seen and heard. This deed is still more distant from them than the most distant stars – *and yet they have done it themselves.*'

5.C.VII   Genealogy[13]

There is no set of maxims more important for an historian than this: that the actual causes of a thing's origin and its eventual uses, the manner of its incorporation into a system of purposes, are worlds apart; that everything that exists, no matter what its origin, is periodically reinterpreted by those in power in terms of fresh intentions; that all the processes in the organic world are processes of outstripping and overcoming means reinterpretation, rearrangement, in the course of which the earlier meanings are necessarily either obscured or lost. No matter how well we understand the utility of a certain physiological organ (or of a legal institution, a custom, a political convention, an artistic genre, a cultic trait) we do not thereby understand anything of its origin . . . Thus the whole history of a thing, an organ, a custom, becomes a continuous *chain* of reinterpretations and rearrangements, which need not be causally connected among themselves, which may simply follow one another. The 'evolution' of a thing, a custom, an organ is not its *progressus* towards a goal, let alone the most logical and shortest *progressus*, requiring the least energy and expenditure. Rather, it is a sequence of more or less profound, more or less independent processes of appropriation, including the resistances used in each instance, the attempted transformations for purposes of defence or reaction, as well as the results of successful counterattacks.

13 Friedrich Nietzsche, *The Genealogy of Morals*, trans. F. Golffing, New York: Anchor/ Doubleday; 1956), pp. 209–10.

5.C.VIII   The Nature of the World[14]

If the world had a goal, it must have been reached. If there were for it some unintended final state, this must also have been reached. If it were in any way capable of pausing and becoming fixed, of 'being', if in the whole course of its becoming it possesses even for a moment this capability of 'being', then all becoming would long since have come to an end, along with all thinking, all 'spirit'. The fact of 'spirit' as a form of becoming proves that the world has no goal, no final state, and is incapable of being.

The old habit, however, of associating a goal with every event and a guiding, creative God with the world, is so powerful that it requires an effort for a thinker not to fall into thinking of the very aimlessness of the world as intended. This notion – that the world intentionally avoids a goal and even knows artifices for keeping itself from entering into a circular course – must occur to all those who would like to force on the world the ability for eternal novelty.

Do you know what 'the world' is to me? . . . This world: a monster of energy, without beginning, without end . . . enclosed by 'nothingness' as by a boundary; not something blurry or wasted . . . but set in a definite space as a definite force . . . as a play of forces . . . at the same time one and many . . . eternally changing, eternally flooding back, with tremendous years of recurrence, with an ebb and flood of its forms . . . the play of contradictions . . . blessing itself as that which must return eternally . . . this, my Dionysian world of the eternally self-creating, the eternally self-destroying.

14   Friedrich Nietzsche, *The Will to Power*, trans. Kaufmann and Hollingdale (New York: 1968), Vintage. First extract (If the world had a goal), p. 546; second extract (Do you know what the world is to me?), pp. 549–50.

6 Secular Historicism

Robert M. Burns

Introduction

The period from about 1880 until the aftermath of the German defeat in the First World War saw a sustained attempt to provide a philosophical justification for German historicism. Its prime mover was **Wilhelm Dilthey** (1831–1911) who made his life's work the provision, as he put it in 1883, of a 'philosophical foundation' (Dilthey, 1985, p. 49) for the work of the 'German Historical School', which he considered had 'achieved . . . the definitive constitution of history as a science . . . and of the human sciences in general' (Dilthey, 1996, p. 387; cf. Dilthey, 1985, p. 147) even though it had never 'scientifically developed' an account of its 'explanatory method' so that it 'could only protest ineffectually[1] against the impoverished, superficial, but analytically refined results' of positivists such as Comte, Mill and Buckle who 'seemed to me to truncate and mutilate historical reality in order to assimilate it to the concepts and methods of the natural sciences' (Dilthey, 1985, pp. 48–9). Dilthey sought to demonstrate that a quite distinct scientific method must be applied in the *Geisteswissenschaften* (sciences of the Mind or Spirit). He is particularly associated with the promotion of the use of this term, which subsequently became a standard term for all those disciplines dealing with human nature as opposed to the natural sciences (*Naturwissenschaften*), even though Dilthey himself said it gave only an 'imperfect indication' (p. 58) of their subject matter. Ironically it appears to have been introduced into German by the translator of Mill's *System of Logic* for the term 'moral sciences'. It has been variously translated into English but we shall use the term 'human sciences', although often also, as did Dilthey, using the term 'History' in a comprehensive sense to refer to them.

Dilthey's efforts fall into two major phases, which in some respects are quite distinct and contrasting, which difference has been confusingly ignored or underacknowledged by too many commentators, the first from about 1880 to the end of the century , and the second up to his death. The major event of the first phase was the publication of the first of two projected volumes entitled *Introduction to the Human Sciences* (1883) which was meant to offer a 'Critique of Historical Reason,' that is, 'an epistemological

---

[1] This remark and several others seem unjustly to neglect the work of Johann Gustav Droysen (1808–84) who anticipated the explanation/understanding distinction Dilthey later made much of, who had published a book on historical method, *Grundriss der Historik* in 1868, and who is unquestionably an important link between earlier and later historicism. Droysen's own critique of Buckle was in fact more detailed and sharper than Dilthey's.

foundation for the human sciences . . . i.e., a critique of the capacity of man to know himself and the society and history which he has produced' (p. 165). But these promises were never substantiated; the second volume in which a 'descriptive psychology' was to deliver them in full, never appeared. Instead, becoming known as 'the man of first volumes', he merely repeatedly revised drafts which were published only posthumously, which, however, together with the preliminary account in volume 1 and a few published articles make its nature clear enough in outline.

At its core was to be a purely 'descriptive psychology' which would merely exhibit the 'facts of consciousness' (6.A.I) infallibly present in the minds of all human beings. Scientific knowledge of the external world could by contrast only be a matter of '*second-order concepts*' (p. 96) to be vindicated by being 'analyzed' and 'traced back to first–order psychic facts' (p. 118). There is an extremely persistent emphasis in the early Dilthey on the irreducibility of the individuality at the core of every human being: 'there is . . . in each individual a point where he can by no means be classified in terms of the co-ordination of his activities with those of others' (p. 100) such that even in 'the family, the world's most concentrated form of volitional unity binding individuals [*they*] . . . are not completely absorbed in it; the individual is ultimately for and by himself'(p. 123). Socio-cultural facts are 'systems of interactions' which individuals 'carry or support', and not *vice versa*, since 'only in self-reflection do we discover within ourselves the unity and continuity of life which maintains and supports their relationships' (p. 136). This very unComtean, Mill-like individualism (see, e.g., p. 135 and pp. 377–8) leads Dilthey to question not only the legitimacy of 'sociology' or a 'special science of society' (pp. 133–4), but many assumptions common in the earlier German historicist tradition; 'mystical expressions' such as '*Volksseele* (soul of a people), *Nation, Volksgeist* (spirit of a people)' are, he says, 'no more usable in history than is the concept of life-force in physiology' (p. 92). Of a piece with this individualism is an attack on the 'pretensions' of teleological philosophy of history, whether Comtean or Hegelian. This hang-over from theology should 'wither and decay' together with the latter's demise in the face of the '*boundless ambiguity* of the *material of history*' (pp. 44, 47).

Clearly, very like British phenomenalists such as Mill, he is convinced that my 'privileged access' to my own psychic interior provides the indispensable source of the rigorous infallible certitude which he wished to establish for historical reason. Yet he sharply distinguishes himself from them, accusing them of 'contradicting inner experience' in assuming that the mind merely passively registers atomic 'impressions' and their conjunctions. Rather the human 'psychic unit' is a 'life-process' in which an interpenetrating triad, 'willing, feeling, and thinking', continually interact to form a psychic 'nexus' (*Zusammenhang*: literally 'together-hanging'). In particular, I am always active, animated by my 'will' ('hoping and striving, wishing and willing', p. 227) which is to say I am essentially characterised by purposiveness (*Zweckmässigkeit*), intent on forging my life into a purposive whole (*Zweckganzes*). It is my 'will' not my intellect which forms my purposes (although puzzlingly Dilthey sometimes attributes the positing of my values to my 'feeling' side) and my volitions are ultimately rationally unfathomable. Accordingly, he approves of the trend in later medieval scholasticism to separate will from the intellect, citing Duns Scotus's view that 'the will is free precisely inasmuch as in it the search for a reason ends,' and William of Occam's claim that 'no matter how much reason may dictate something, the will can nonetheless choose this or not choose it' (Dilthey, 1988, p. 250).

My purposiveness means that I notice and therefore 'perceive' objects as *present* in my sensory field only insofar as they are relevant to my *future*-oriented aims, and likewise my memory recalls only those *past events* somehow linked to *present* preoccupations. Therefore, far from being essentially changeless, and so timeless and eternal, as traditional metaphysical psychology had claimed of the soul, it is *entirely* 'temporal' (*zeitlich*):

> Whatever Heraclitus says about the stream of reality has complete validity concerning psychic life . . . we find no constant state of consciousness, no constant inner fact . . . Our ego-consciousness . . . precisely this 'me' . . . is the most changeable of all that is changeable. One cannot even say that it is identical with itself. (Dilthey, 1985, p. 370–1)

His view of the coequal role of will, feeling, and intellect allows him to overcome the doubts about the existence of the external world expressed by Hume and Descartes for it is sensed external resistance to the will and the feelings, not thoughts per se which makes 'external reality' as certain to a self as its own existence (6.A.II). Nevertheless, this certainty is not equal to the knowledge of the inner self, for we 'know perhaps *that* [the outer world] is there, yet are not sure *what* it is' (Dilthey, 1985, p. 202). In fact, three-quarters of the 408 pages of the first volume of the *Introduction*, are devoted to demonstrating that for 2000 years Western metaphysics has been perpetuating the 'colossal error' (p. 281) of pursuing the 'impossible' (p. 224) dream of knowing the 'real' nature of the external world, whereas even modern natural science provides 'only a calculated and highly artificial abstraction from what is given in experience' (p. 203). Indeed, Dilthey repudiates 'realism':

> The *concept of correspondence,* that is, of the correspondence between perception and thought on the one hand and of reality and being on the other had . . . is *completely obscure.* No one can imagine how something we think could correspond to something actually existing outside us. We can define what similarity means in mathematical terms: but here a similarity is maintained which is completely indefinite. Indeed, one can say that if the phenomenon of mirroring did no exist in nature and by imitation in human art, such an idea could scarcely have arisen at all. (Dilthey, 1988, p. 196)

However, the assumption is that in *Innewerden* (immediate awareness of my own inner states) no 'correspondence' of my thought to some opposed reality occurs, and so no problem arises.

One can understand Heidegger's fascination (see chapter 7) for Dilthey's highly original descriptions of the 'inner life' of the human being, but they are questionable as indubitable 'foundations' for scientific historical knowledge. It seems self-defeating to insist on the infallibility of 'inner' lived experience *as opposed to* the 'outer' world, including public historico-cultural realities, and yet to claim that the former can somehow scientifically 'ground' the latter, and, indeed, even in his earliest days, there seems to be another, opposite view in Dilthey, that the individual person is *constituted* by his social relations so that treating him as an isolated individual always involves a distorting 'abstraction':

> It is only by means of abstraction that psychology can be separated from the overall study of socio-historical reality, and it can be developed only through constant reference to that whole. To be sure, the psychophysical unit is self-contained . . . However this self-con-

tained whole . . . has, on the other hand, emerged only within the context of social reality . . . The whole content of psychic life is only an ephemeral specific form within the more encompassing content of spirit in history and society. Indeed the highest feature of its being is that it lives in something which is not itself. The object of psychology is thus always merely the individual who has been singled out from the living context of socio-historical reality . . . Neither in experience nor through inference can psychology find man as he is apart from interactions with society – man as *prior* to society as it were. (Dilthey, 1985, pp. 81–2)

There are also implausibilities in Dilthey's descriptions. For example, the distinction between the will and the intellect seems exaggerated. What 'purpose' or 'meaning' would ever satisfy a human being if he considered it completely opaque to his own intelligence? Do not human beings frequently seek to clarify their own motives, and discard or modify precisely those which seem to be irrational or pointless? Moreover, how can 'purpose' be ascribed to 'will', but the 'values' which form the purposes to 'feeling'? Furthermore, if *everything* is in flux in the 'sea of *Innewerden*', how could it possibly provide a 'firm anchor' for the human sciences? Indeed, Dilthey sometimes says that *any* attempt to fix the psychic flux in thought is distorting: 'The psychophysical life-unit that we find our-selves to be can be investigated only by means of artificial analysis. The stream of life never stands still for observation, but courses ceaselessly towards the ocean. We can neither grasp nor express it as it is, but we fix its partial contents. We break up what is flowing into firm discrete parts' (p. 282). True, elsewhere, he insists that we experience in ourselves not only flux but also our 'endurance' through time. But that can only mean that not everything in us is in Heraclitean flux. Indeed unless *some* structures endure there could be no content whatever to Dilthey's descriptive psychology. And how can Dilthey be sure that the structures he perceives in his *own* self apply to all human beings? Again, if phenomenal knowledge is infallible how could Hume and Mill have arrived at contrary accounts of it, which really raises the question of whether 'immediate aware-ness' is not a delusion, as Humboldt, Hegel, Comte and Buckle believed. Section 6.A.III, from of one of the drafts of the 1880s, shows that Dilthey was aware of the objection, but he states it only to brush it aside dogmatically, making things easier for himself by addressing only the problem that in order to think of what is 'immediately experienced' one has to express it in purely logical forms, when in fact we have to express it in a concrete, historical language.

It was almost certainly persistent self-doubts along these lines which led to the re-peated failures to carry his project forward. Heidegger too flatteringly suggests that the failure simply manifests the 'elemental restlessness' (Heidegger, 1962, p. 450) of a genius. The moment of truth seems to have been an 1894 attack by the Berlin psy-chologist Ebbinghaus centring on the point that every 'description' of psychic states must contain a hypothetical interpretation of data which in themselves are ambiguous and fragmentary. This stunned Dilthey who ceased to lecture or write on psychology for several years. There were also criticisms from the Windelband and Rickert, and towards the end of the decade from Husserl. The upshot was that Dilthey recon-structed his approach essentially by connecting it up with Schleiermachean hermeneutics which he had studied early in his career,[2] although there are virtually no references to

2   This early work is indispensable for serious study of Schleiermacher's hermeneutics, and has re-cently been translated into English in Dilthey, 1996, pp. 33–227.

it in his earlier discussions of 'historical reason'. The first clear indication of the shift appeared in the 1900 article 'The Rise of Hermeneutics' (6.A.IV). It begins with the understated acknowledgement that 'inner experience' far from being an epistemological panacea raises 'great difficulties', and it is flatly stated that I experience myself only through comparison with *others*. True, others are known only through 're-creation' (*Nachbildung*) on the basis of 'our own sense of life' but obviously we are in the realms of hermeneutical paradox: there is no straightforward movement from 'inside' to 'outside' but only a fallible, never completed, moving to-and-fro. The misleading impression is given, by ignoring Gustav Droysen, that after Schleiermacher the topic had slumbered until its revival by Dilthey.[3]

The remaining excerpts are all taken from an unfinished work entitled *The Construction of the Historical World*. Section 6.A.V expresses one of his most characteristic emphases in later years: that knowledge of one's own and other minds, emerges out of an interdependent triad of inner experience (*Erlebnis*), outer expression (*Ausdruck*) and understanding (*Verstehen*), which is to say that self-knowledge can be achieved only through a 'round-about' journey into the outer, public world. Then, in 6.A.VI Dilthey insists that I can understand both myself and others only because we share a 'common background' of objectified intelligent purposiveness embracing not only language, but the arrangements of houses, parks, and so forth, for which he used the Hegelian term 'Objective Spirit'. 6.A.VII contains some of the terms most characteristically associated with Dilthey's accounts of *Verstehen*: empathy and re-experiencing (*Nachfühlen*, *Nacherleben*) the feelings of others, transposition (*Hineinversetzen*) of oneself into the other's mind recreating (*Nachbildung*) and reconstructing (*Nachkonstruieren*) the thoughts of others which is essentially, and at its most general, a matter of understanding the 'meaning' which others are seeking to embody in their lives.

Finally, 6.A.VIII contains an extended description of 'Meaning' which Dilthey regarded as the fundamental characteristic of human life, and is clearly a carrying forward of his early emphasis on the purposiveness of the self. Each self seeks to 'organize' itself in terms of a meaning which is always incomplete, provisional, approximate, an effort for which Dilthey now adopts the Nietzschean term 'will to power'. We might say the self is forever trying to weave the various threads of its life into a 'plot'. The self is seeking to turn its passage through life into a story worth telling, giving it a narrative unity, and so it constantly interprets and reinterprets the fragments of its life to turn them into a coherent whole.[4] But each self is also in interaction with others who are

---

3   Droysen wrote that while we can classify Nature and explain it by laws, 'real understanding' which illuminates 'acts of volition' in contrast to 'the mechanics of atoms', is 'the most perfect form of cognition which is humanly possible' and is 'like an act of creation like a spark of light between two electrophoric bodies, like an act of conception' (Iggers, 1983, pp. 109–11).
4   So Dilthey is a 'narrativist'; for him the human self and every cultural group is trying to tell its own story, is *constituted* by the story it tells, and is moreover continually *retelling* its story as it reassesses itself in the light of new experiences, and new reflections on itself. The human consciousness is therefore a text which is continually rewriting itself. Moreover, as the later Dilthey in particular emphasizes, the texts which individual human beings weave are always interwoven with those which have been, and are being, woven by others. Therefore, for Dilthey (and the same is true for Heidegger's analysis of Dasein's 'historicality', which owes so much to Dilthey; see chapter 7) it is not that the historian imposes narrative form on a raw material originally non-narrational. Rather, human life is narrative 'all the way down'; historians may radically transform the narratives they investigate, but they do not impose an alien form on something which was not originally a story.

intent on the same task, the interaction often leading to conflict. The post-religious Dilthey refuses to consider that the pursuit of meaning could succeed by the traditional move of positing some overall transcendent meaning into which we can integrate our lives, so borrowing a ready-made meaning, as it were. The only meaning in life is rather that which is 'inherent' in life. Life itself is a 'chaos of harmonies and dissonances' with no possibility of taking up the latter in some higher harmony; there is no 'progress' towards a final integrating consummation. In the end each human individual fails to achieve a full integration: he pits himself in vain against limits, so that life is tragic.

During Dilthey's career there developed a widely diffused conviction among German philosophers that the only way forward must lie in pursuing the path pioneered by Kant. Although 'back to Kant' became a well-known slogan for this 'Neo-Kantianism' (Willey, 1978), there was in most cases no question of slavish imitation of Kant; it was just that his basic approach was being seen as more adequate than, on the one hand, positivism or materialism, and one the other the totalizing metaphysics of Hegel. It has been suggested that one can distinguish seven different types of 'Neo-Kantianism' in this period. Dilthey himself was without question a 'Neo-Kantian' as is evident in his repeated use of the term 'Critique of Historical Reason' to describe his project: consider also the following radical remark:

> the main difference between Kant and myself [*is that for me*] the intellect also transforms its own conditions of consciousness through its engagement with things. Kant's a priori is fixed and dead; but the real conditions of consciousness and its presuppositions, as I grasp them, constitute a living historical process, a development; they have a history . . . they can never be abrogated, because we think by means of them, but they are a product of development. (Dilthey, 1985, pp. 500–1)

It was this sort of remark which led Husserl to classify Dilthey as a sceptical relativist (see chapter 7).

Two main Neo-Kantian schools developed, one associated with Baden or South–Western Germany (Freiburg, Heidelberg, and Strassburg), and the other with Marburg. The latter was mainly preoccupied with analyzing the *a priori* presuppositions of natural science whilst a major concern of the former was the vindication of history as a science methodologically distinct from natural science. **Wilhelm Windelband** (1848–1915) is regarded as its founder, with Heinrich Rickert his successor. Windelband's 1894 Strassburg Rectorial address (6.B.I) should be readily intelligible, provided that one is familiar with the *Geistes/Naturwissenschaften* distinction which Windelband rejects, pleading that the needed distinction should instead be *methodological*, between 'nomothetic' science and 'idiographic' science, i.e., the study of the repetitive and regular on the one hand, and the individual and unique on the other.

Heinrich Rickert (1863–1936) published in 1902 a vast elaboration of Windelband's distinction in the form of a defence of the notion of history as an objective, rigorous science of the individual. It runs to almost 700 pages, with more added in later editions, and must have been the longest book in philosophy of history ever published until it was rivalled by Troeltsch's 777–page *Historicism and its Problems* (1922). It is tediously long-winded, and the extracts provided here are misleading in the degree to which they condense it. Almost all critics agree that its argument is flawed. However Rickert makes points of abiding significance. Any serious student needs to familiarise himself with the gist of Rickert's position since Max Weber's discussions of the methodology of history and the social sciences, which have been much more influential in the English-speaking world than Rickert's, take much from him and are far more understandable after an exposure to him. The title *The Limits of Concept Formation in Natural Science* might seem inappropriate for a book on history as opposed to natural science, but the opening pages make clear that the claim is that natural science and history mutually delimit one another's spheres, that is, are 'interdefinable' (Rickert, 1986, p. 113) in that since natural science aims at discovering universal laws or generalisations, it is incapable of dealing with individuality or uniqueness in things, whilst history is the science of 'the unique and individual configuration of the real event' (p. 47). There is therefore a 'radical logical opposition' between the aims of the two, but they are also complementary, so that in practice the two diametrically opposed sciences manifest '*interpenetration* and *concomitance*' (ibid., p. 35), and any historical treatment will make use of natural science's generalizations in innumerable ways.

Rickert starts by rejecting the 'picture theory' of knowledge (pp. 42–3), that is, the assumption that to know something is to construct a mental 'copy' (p. 45) of the real thing on the grounds that by 'reality' is meant 'the immediately experienced or given reality in which we live our sentient existence' (p. 214), and this is an 'infinite manifold' (p. 43), which could therefore never be comprehensively be reproduced in the mind. This point is one raised already in essence in chapter 1, section III: that in sense perception we focus on an infinitesimally small portion of what is potentially given in our sensory field. Rickert maintains that we *experience* infinity because we sense that the interconnected real things which confront us in experience stretch out in all spatio-temporal directions endlessly ('extensive infinity'), whilst, if we focus on any particular thing, we find the aspects of it which could be explored are also infinite ('intensive infinity', p. 50).[5] Rickert dwells on these considerations to drive home the point that that science can deal with 'reality' *only* by applying *a priori* criteria of selectivity, in terms of some specific 'scientific *interest*' (p. 49). Thus science always '*transforms . . . reality*' (p. 46). A thought, will be 'true' if it is '*valid*' in terms of the particular criteria of selectivity applied, not because it fully represents its object. Natural-scientific concepts abstract the general aspects of things leaving behind their 'uniqueness and individuality' and therefore cause a 'fissure' or 'gap' (p. 39) between reality and themselves. Nevertheless 'in our practical conduct we would stand helpless before reality' (p. 42) without this 'simplification' of it. History 'views reality from a completely different logical perspective' by concerning itself with the 'unique, real event' (p. 50) thereby 'filling the gap that natural science inevitably leaves in our knowledge' (p. 54).

Rickert even claims that history is 'more closely related to the real' (p. 53) than natural science, because 'only the individual and unique *really happened*' (p. 48); that is, natural science discards 'the very properties that are essential to . . . real entities' (p. 39). He seems unwarrantably one-sided here; the logic of his own position rather implies that an exclusive focus on individuality would be just as distorting of reality as focusing on generality, *both* approaches, if applied in isolation, producing a 'fissure' between themselves and realities. Indeed, elsewhere he maintains that 'although the concepts of natural science encompass only a bit of the content of the immediately

5   This Baden Neo-Kantian stress on the infinity of experience is no doubt the source for much of what Walter Benjamin says about this.

given and infinitely diverse empirical reality, it is obvious that these concepts stand i
a most intimate *relationship* to reality' so that 'the general it represents holds *valid*
for individual reality' (pp. 43–4).

The most obvious objection to Rickert's position is that general terms have to b
used to render anything whatever intelligible, which he concedes at the beginning c
6.C.I, but pleads that they can be assembled to form a concept of a complex whol
which is, as such, individual and unique. Yet to admit that 'the concrete singularity c
everything real eludes every science' so that 'mere heterogeneity' is for ever exclude
from the realm of science is surely already to abandon Rickert's dramatically bol
opening claims. This, however, is only the first of a series of such admissions whic
repeatedly narrow the reach of historical science, as the need for additional forms c
essential generalisation are acknowledged. As a first step he says that by a historic
individual we should mean not something simply 'unique' but rather '*indivisible*
illustrating this by referring to the Koh-I-Noor diamond. But this makes clear that b
'indivisible' he does *not* mean non-splittable, but that division would result in loss c
value, which is to admit that the essential ingredient in the perception of such ind
viduality is a human valuation to which 'reality' in itself is indifferent. Next follows
discussion of whether the human soul is intrinsically valuable on the grounds, allege
by traditional metaphysical psychology, of its indivisible unity. Rickert's answer, couche
in the language of Diltheyan psychology, is that that the psyche is unified only by th
purpose it embraces, which is to say a *value*. Nevertheless, Rickert argues that th
cannot be sufficient to explain the nature of historical science, since no historian eve
treats all human beings as equally interesting, but invariably selects only a few as sig
nificant.

The question therefore, is whether this selectivity flows merely from arbitrary preju
dices. Rickert denies this; although conceding that history must always be 'value-rela
tive', because it is always about historical individuals, who are constituted by the value
adopted, he maintains that this does not imply that the historian should himself *evalu
ate*. To use one of his examples; writing about Luther because he established 'value
which became deeply embedded in subsequent German culture, does not mean tha
one must slant the account in terms of one's own particular religious or anti-religiou
or political commitments. But it rapidly becomes clear that Rickert does not mean tha
the historian operates without values, but only that his values are '*valid for everyone*
and so of 'general significance': 'What is historically essential must be *important* nc
only for this or that particular historian, but for *all*' and it is these general values whic
'constitute the primary basis of . . . the objectivity . . . of the historical sciences' (Ricker
1962, p. 97). Even Rickert's most sympathetic critics, from Ernst Troeltsch in 190
(Iggers, 1968, p. 180) onwards considered that his assertion that there are universa
transcultural values is unjustifiable. It is obvious from Rickert's example of Goeth
that he is far from holding that the historian operates only with values held by every
one in all times and places, since this evaluation is restricted to recent generations c
the German educated élite.[6] But if Rickert's argument fails here then the historian'
criteria are themselves culturally relative as Weber and Simmel were ready to admit.

---

6   Even relatively well-educated non-Germans find the adulation of classically educated Germans fc
Goethe difficult to comprehend: the composer, Richard Strauss, wrote in March 1945, after Goethe
house in Weimar had been hit by an Allied bomb: 'Goethe's house, the world's holiest place destroyed

Section 6.C.II corrects any misapprehension that by historical individuals Rickert means only individual persons: he means also historic wholes such as the Renaissance or Romanticism, and 6.C.III shows him maintaining that the historian is never interested in an individual person *per se* but only those whom he terms 'historical centres' that is, those who have had an impact on the values historically held by a community, and this leads him to argue that the sphere of the 'historical' is in fact the sphere of 'culture'. He is arguing that if a general term is required for all the human sciences it should be *Kulturwissenschaft* rather than Dilthey's *Geisteswissenschaft* with its inappropriate 'psychological' connotations (Rickert, 1986, p. 117). Cultures are differentiated from one another by common allegiance to 'values', which, however, according to Rickert, invariably develop historically. Rickert then introduces (6.C.IV) the term 'non-real meaning configurations' for these values. This seems to generate a comic paradox: Rickert has insisted that history is a 'science of reality' unlike natural science because of its concern for individuality, but now he asserts that the very basis of this individuality is 'non-real'. But Rickert does address this challenge, and uses the notion not only to provide an account of the nature of historical general terms such as 'the Renaissance' or 'Enlightenment' (compare Weber's 'ideal types'; see 6.E.III and the last paragraphs of 6.E.II), but also in 6.C.V showing how grasping 'non-real mental configurations' can be used as the indispensable means of 're-creating' the *real* mental life of others.

Georg Simmel (1858–1918) financed his life of wide-ranging scholarship by private means until finally awarded his first salaried professorship in 1914. Perhaps this explains why he was frequently more radical at least in mood and tone than Rickert and Weber, standing in some respects closer to Dilthey, following him in making 'Life' the central category of his philosophy (see the later part of 6.D.IV) and being still ready to follow him in defining history as a branch of 'psychology' and very much embracing Dilthey's version of 'neo-Kantianism', i.e., namely with a frank recognition that the *a priori* categories or forms of historical thought are themselves historically conditioned and transient 'forms of life' (*Lebensformen*).[7] His *The Problems of Philosophy of History*, from which all but one of our excerpts are taken, was first published in 1892 and then republished in a radically revised form in 1905 (Simmel, 1977).

Section 6.D.I makes clear that he shares the Neo-Kantian rejection of 'epistemological realism' or 'epistemological naturalism' i.e., the assumption that in knowledge the mind copies or reproduces reality; like Rickert, Simmel maintains that it is impossible for the historian to *reproduce* the historical event 'as it really was' (which Rankean phrase he frequently quotes dismissively); rather the historian produces a 'transformation' of it by applying his own categories. Nevertheless, he discards Rickert's argument for rejecting the 'copy' theory on the grounds of the infinity of experience, maintaining merely that a form of knowledge not rooted in a limited, finite '*point of view*' or *problematic*' (p. 82) is inconceivable.[8] He considers that this implies a refutation of

---

[7]   One assumes that Wittgenstein's use of the term to describe language games came directly or indirectly from Simmel.

[8]   Simmel writes: 'Historical truth is not a mere reproduction; it is an intellectual activity. Historical truth produces something new out of its raw material . . . This does not simply amount to an abridged summary of details. On the contrary, history proceeds by posing questions to its raw material and ascribing meaning to singular phenomena . . . History reveals meanings and values in its raw material. These meanings and values structure the past in such a way that a new construct is produced, a construct which satisfies the criteria that *we* impose', (p. 78).

'historicism' (defined as the notion that the self is merely 'constrained or coerced' by history understood as a 'a superpersonal force . . . alien to the self'), because the thesis that the self 'constitutes' history by applying its own categories proves its autonomy. Here again he echoes Dilthey. Consider for example the following passage from a 1903 talk:

> An apparently irreconcilable antithesis arises when historical consciousness is followed to its last consequences. The finitude of every historical phenomenon – be it is a religion or an ideal or a philosophical system – accordingly, the relativity of every kind of human apprehension of the totality of things, is the last word of the historical world-view. Everything passes away in the process; nothing remains. And over against this both the demand of thought and the striving of philosophy for universally valid knowledge assert themselves. The historical world-view liberates the human spirit from the last chains that natural science and philosophy have not yet broken. But where are the means to overcome the anarchy of opinions that then threatens to befall us? To the solution of the long series of problems that are connected with this, I have devoted my whole life. I see the goal. If I fall short along the way, then I hope my young travelling companions, my students will follow it to the end. (Dilthey, 1996, p. 389)

Any evaluation of Simmel must surely address the question of whether the 'counter-relativism' which has been attributed to him (Mandelbaum, 1967, ch. IV), is not relativism in disguise, because according to him the individual 'ego' does not itself freely invent its categories, but absorbs them from the wider cultural milieu in which it participates. Indeed, the historian must acknowledge the 'necessity' and 'constraint' of conforming to them, if his work is to be distinguished from arbitrary subjective caprice. Moreover not only are the categories *themselves* repeatedly transformed in the historical 'Life' process, but they vary from one type of history to another, each having its own internal criterion of 'truth'. 'Universal history' is therefore rejected as impossible except in the sense of a 'at best the simultaneous application of a variety of these different problematics.' Here, the logic of his analysis clearly makes room for a 'new historicism' seeking 'to convey the complexity of multiple viewpoints'; that is, instead of the 'traditional Western male hegemonic outlook' (Berkhofer, 1995, pp. 178–9) the writing of history from the point of view of women, blacks, gays and so forth. Simmel himself seems, however, merely to have had in mind the different types of history practised within the German academic establishment of his day. But he is certainly rejecting the purely 'formal' logical approach to history that Rickert was trying to develop, and replacing it with the notion of an indefinite variety of concrete institutionalised, historically-conditioned forms of historical practice clustered round varying categories expressing different interests. This raises the question of whether such an apparently purely descriptive approach (which seems similar to Wittgenstein's declaration '*This language-game is played!*'[9]) could ever adjudicate between categories being applied by would-be historians, and so distinguish genuine forms of history from fraudulent or inadequate ones.

Nevertheless, he does discuss the nature of historical significance in general, provoked by Eduard Meyer who, in his *On the Theory and Method of History* (1902), had

---

9 Wittgenstein, 1967, para. 654, with the implication that, 'It is clear that every sentence in our language "is in order as it is" ', para. 98.

argued that the significance or importance of historical events lay in the magnitude of their consequences. Simmel's position is that Meyer's suggestion evades the issue because even trivial events 'cause' innumerable future events. In fact, the consequences themselves must be judged significant if significance is to be attributed to their causes, and on the contrary all 'significant' events have causes or preconditions judged not in themselves to be significant. Nevertheless, after pointing up a number of criteria which seem to operate in accepted forms of historical judgement, he does acknowledge the importance of quantity in judgements of history, by emphasising the operation of 'quantum thresholds' in such evaluations. He continues to make the point that the historian needs to show not only a significant content to the objects of his concern but that they *exist* (p. 138). Yet he is silent about how the historian is to come to an assured 'knowledge of single, direct empirical relationships' as he puts it, prior to applying 'truly' to them his 'abstract historical concepts', perhaps not surprisingly because this seems to raise once more 'realist' notions of a 'correspondence' between the mind and known external facts, which he had been apparently eager to reject. But he seeks to circumvent the problem by claiming that historical facts are 'mental' and therefore are 'already formed or constituted in some way' by the human being 'prior to its historical investigation' (pp. 138–9). Section 6.D.III is a discussion of the value and status of Marxist historical materialism, which is comparable both with 4.B.V and 6.E.III.

Simmel devotes much space in *The Problems of the Philosophy of History* to the question of the nature of understanding other minds, writing of the 'intuitive recreation' (p. 63) or 'empathetic reconstruction of an historical, mental event ' (p. 73), which he declares is a 'basic psychological and epistemological problem of historical understanding'. The account is, however, confused and ambivalent and it is hardly surprising that Simmel apologetically characterizes it as 'only a preliminary effort' (p. 6) at understanding. On the one hand, he seems to suggest that (p. 76) that such recreations can possess 'trans-subjective or super-personal validity' (p. 76), speculating that this might be possible because of 'evolutionarily transmitted interpretive faculties' (p. 97), in other words that we all share in a kind of collective unconscious upon which we can draw in understanding each other (p. 76). His language frequently suggests that in fact we do somehow 'copy' the mental contents of others' minds in knowing them, but elsewhere he rejects the notion of a 'mechanical copy' in the historian's 'mental states' of the 'mental states of the historical person' (p. 93) and also disowns the 'the naïve idea of "projection"' (p. 76). He also in this connection rejects the suggestion he attributes to Ranke that the historian must suppress his own personality in order to know the mind of the other; rather one must in some way *intensify* one's own subjectivity if empathy with the other is to be achieved (p. 88).

Because of these confusions Section 6.D.IV is taken from a later effort at discussing this issue (Simmel, 1980). Here he rejects the notion that there must be some sort of 'identity' between myself and others in order for understanding to occur: it is, rather, just that if there is too much dissimilarity, understanding will fail. Simmel then boldly insists that I do not infer the presence of other minds by judging that their bodily gestures and sounds are similar to those which, in my own case, I have learned to associate with my own mental activity. Behind such a view, he suggests, lies an unacceptably crude body–mind dualism. Rather we encounter others through a *gestalt* intuition of 'the whole person'. Towards the end of the essay, Simmel justifies this in terms of a vitalist as opposed to a mechanical-materialist world view: knowledge of others and all forms of historical science are 'forms of life' (*Lebensformen*), and are ultimately justified because they are manifestations of 'Life', or rather need no such justification. Elsewhere[10] he describe this 'Life' as 'the metaphysical basic fact, as the essence of all being' (Simmel, 1971, pp. 386–7). It is an infinite surge which needs continually to create boundaries or forms for itself in which it can contain itself, and yet can never tolerate such 'crystallizations' for long, because they frustrate it, or bottle it up, as it were, so that Life is 'at once flux without pause and yet something enclosed in bearers and contents, formed about midpoints, individualized, and therefore always a bounded form which continually jumps its bounds' (p. 363), 'at once fixed and variable; of finished shape, and developing further; formed, and ever breaking through its forms' (p. 364), so that 'life in the absolute sense is something which includes life in the relative sense and its respective opposite', which is to say that life is essentially characterised by 'contradiction' (p. 370) and 'self-alienation' (p. 372). Obviously, this idea of a dynamic polarity at the heart of things is not new; Simmel refers to Schopenhauer and Nietzsche (p. 364), that is to 'Will's production of its opposite Idea' in the former, and the oscillation between Apollo and Dionysus in the latter, suggesting that in the former the boundless pole is more prominent, whilst in the latter the major stress is on 'individuality cased in form' (p. 368) but we have earlier seen that the 'polarity principle' goes back though Ranke and Hegel, to Herder and Goethe, and indeed to Empedocles, the Pythagoreans, and Heraclitus. In Simmel, *Life* is not meant to be a new kind of God but arguably it functions somewhat in this way, and it is difficult to understand it as other than a reference to a new kind of cosmic first principle of a pantheist kind more in tune with, for example, evolutionary notions than previous versions of pantheism.

Simmel deploys it illuminatingly at many different levels. He sees it in the restlessness of all human beings who both long for stability and at the same time resent the boredom and frustration which stability brings. He argues that it is the main factor in social changes from variations in fashion in clothing to moral and political revolutions. He sees all forms of knowledge as specific forms of life which transcend the individual and which will mutate and finally disintegrate as Life breaks these bounds and moves on to something else. The ultimate question however is whether this metaphysical or ontological vision is the overcoming of 'historicism' (historical determinism) or a capitulation to it; if the historical process, and activities of historians are all simply momentary flashes produced by a blind, pulsating, unending cosmic drive, where is truth and what could it be?

The attention received by the economic historian and sociologist *Max Weber* (1864–1920) has long eclipsed the other thinkers represented in this section at least in the English-speaking world. His methodological discussions have been very widely read but are often embedded in polemical criticism of mostly long forgotten opponents and are thick with complicated syntax and needless obscurity, due to failure to spend time revising the style of his hastily produced articles. He takes many of Rickert's ideas for granted (see 6.E.I) , and a lack of familiarity with these is one further cause of the difficulties students often have in reading him; for instance, the notion that the infinit

---

10   In his essays 'The Transcendent Character of Life', and 'The Conflict in Modern Culture' (1918 in Simmel, 1971, pp. 353–74, pp. 375–93.

of experienced reality renders *a priori* criteria of selectivity essential in any science, and that the human sciences have an essentially 'value-related' subject matter which is, at its core, individual 'meanings' which cannot in the last analysis be understood nomologically, but only by some sort of 'empathic' reconstruction of the minds of others (see 6.E.I). Despite this, he differs from Rickert in some respects, above all, in abandoning Rickert's attempt to maintain that that scientific history can be objective because based on 'general values'; he says that it is 'meaningless' to expect that the cultural sciences can ever come to operate within some 'permanently and universally valid' set of presuppositions (6.E.I, 6.E.VI).

Section 6.E.II contains basic definitions by Weber of what he understands by the 'meanings' which he makes the central objects of historical science. 6.E.III is the classic statement by Weber of a notion with which he is always associated, although the first sentence of the excerpt indicates that he did not consider that he had invented it; In general we can say that this is Weber's explanation of how 'general' concepts can be used to build up an intuition of an individual reality. He suggests that their role is 'limiting' or negative in that, when the individual reality is measured against or compared with them they highlight the extent of its deviation from the artificial, simplified norms expressed by them. 'Types' have been employed as a means of understanding human nature at least since Aristotle, whose *Ethics* contain descriptions of the 'miser,' the 'magnanimous' man and so forth, with no suggestion that they are ever empirically encountered in a pure form. Weber is very insistent that ideal types are 'utopian,' that is, not meant to be reports of actual reality. Thus, when medieval historians use the term 'Christianity' they can only be referring to an artificially constructed ideal type never fully instantiated. Nevertheless, such concepts are sometimes employed to express judgments based on the historian's personal values, a practice of which Weber disapproves, though perhaps questionably in terms of the ultimate relativism already noted. We also find him approving of Marxist theory when understood as a set of imaginative heuristic[11] concepts but not as accounts of what is 'empirically valid and real'. 6.E.IV is taken from a critique of Meyer's account of historical significance which should be compared with 6.D.III: Weber frequently acknowledged his debts not only to Rickert but also to Simmel.

Section 6.E.V expresses some of Weber's double-edged convictions concerning professional academic research. Clearly he believes that in the last analysis the only acceptable motive for research can be pursuit of truth; everything must be 'rooted' in this ultimate commitment, which explains Weber's references elsewhere in these extracts to the 'conscience' and 'duty' of the historian. He notes, however, that, in an 'age of specialisation', this is frequently lost sight of by those who, whether as 'fact-greedy' specialists, or as wide-ranging dilettantish theoreticians, relentlessly pursue their worldly careers, and he even says 'It is well that should be so'. We are also to hold in mind that this goal of truth will never be reached and that there will not even be the consolation of progress towards this ultimate goal, because the goalposts will shift for ever as the 'standpoints of science' shift. The life of the authentic modern scholar, who does not lose his soul to specialisation treated idolatrously as an end rather than a means, is therefore described in bleakly heroic, even tragic terms.

1   That is, helpful as guides to research, from the Greek *eurisko*, I seek (the past tense is *eureka*, I have found).

Weber never sought to articulate the position philosophically at any length, but his young, fervent admirer Karl Jaspers (1883–1969) made it fundamental to his entire philosophical position. According to Jaspers every human effort to reach the truth, or indeed realize any ideal, will reach a limit at which point it founders (*scheitert*) in contradiction and antinomy. He describes Weber as for ever 'foundering'. But experience of defeating limits can be the beginning of wisdom: out of these limit-situations (*Grenzensituationen*) a 'philosophical faith' might develop which will continue to pierce the encompassing darkness with longing for truth, wresting some consolation from achieving what seem to be fragmentary anticipations or 'ciphers' of the ultimate goal. For Jaspers, transforming this secular 'faith' into something approaching religious faith in a God of Truth, was not a live possibility, and likewise not for Weber, but Weber's nostalgia for religious belief is evident in his extensive studies of world religions, and particularly in his argument against Marxism that Western capitalism was causally dependent on the emergence of a set of values he terms 'the Protestant Ethic' (see Weber, 1992), rather than the latter being a function of the former.

There is no trace left in Weber of any belief that history is progressing to a final consummation, and specifically not that Western scientific development is a source of such progress. In fact, Weber comes to argue that the specific form of rationality developed in the West is corrupting humanity because it has produced obsessions with mean-end rationality (*Zweckrationalität*) which absurdly, men had attempted to transform into an end in itself, but which is becoming a mere treadmill deflecting them from concern for the ultimate end of human existence which has been the theme of all the great world religions. The modern 'disenchanted' industrialised, bureaucratised world is therefore simply a 'cage' in which trapped individuals hopelessly long for their own individual 'meaning' in a culture with no common ideals or purposes beyond that of pursuit of money: Section 6.E.V shows Weber even applying this analysis to modern research in the humanities. This now famous indictment of the 'mechanized petrifaction' to which modern culture is leading, clearly carries forward Herder's indictment of the Enlightenment. The only escape from this misery could be the emergence of an entirely new 'prophet' or 'a great rebirth of old ideas and ideals' (Weber, 1992, p 182), but Weber seems to hold out little hope for either possibility. He nowhere developed these world-historical themes at any length, but they permeate a great deal of his work. (They are usefully surveyed in Brubaker, 1984). Many later thinkers have been influenced by this pessimistic reversal of the old Enlightenment optimism; it clearly is echoed in the later Heidegger's argument that modern technology with its 'reckoning' thinking 'entraps' and disguises the truth (see Heidegger, 1977 and chapter 7).

Selected Texts

Edited by Robert M. Burns

6.A   Wilhelm Dilthey, 1831–1911

6.A.1   The Principle of Phenomenality[1]

The expression 'consciousness' (*conscientia*) cannot be defined; we can only exhibit [*what it denotes*] as an ultimate datum incapable of further analysis. . . .

Objects as well as acts of will – indeed, the whole immense external world as well as my self which differentiates itself from it – are, to begin with, lived experiences (*Erlebnisse*) in my consciousness which I here refer to as 'facts of consciousness'. The most general claim that can be made about things as well as thoughts or feelings is that they are facts of consciousness. For this designates the all-pervasive and uniform essential character-istic of all of them – to be given in consciousness, and thus to be a content of con-sciousness. This universal relation to consciousness is the most general condition of everything which exists for us. . . .

We can call what has just been set forth *the principle of phenomenality*. . . .

. . .

The certainty with which existence is established in this realm differs from that which can be ascribed to any other fact or proposition in that it is not only immediate but unshakeable . . . The relation by which reality immediately attaches to all that is given in consciousness – namely the reality of the facts of consciousness – is fully transparent and clear to us, and we neither feel a need to go behind it nor see any possibility of doing so. . . .

. . .

. . . Whenever there is reflexive awareness (*Innewerden*) or self-possession of a fact of consciousness the problem of knowledge does not exist. For the latter consists in the question how consciousness of a thing can arise can in me, given that I myself am not the thing, that its properties are not my properties. . . .

From Dilthey, 1989, pp. 246–9, trans. J. Barnouw and F. Schreiner. This excerpt (with the two following ones) is from the 'Breslau Draft' for the projected Book Four of *Introduction to the Human Sciences*.

6.A.II   Certainty of Existence of the External World[2]

. . . Our will, which has a reflexive awareness of itself in feelings of movement – in the hand that touches, in the foot that walks – experiences resistances, and thus finds itself forced to posit perceptions as things. Reality is nothing more than this lived experience. Our feelings which stand in a ordered relation to the will, involve pain and pleasure connected with the coming and going of these perceptions. These feelings are independent of the will and allow us to experience the pressure of the external world in another way than by the sense of touch. . . .

This is the continuous fact which is the basis of self-consciousness: without a world we would have no self-consciousness, and without self-consciousness there would be no world present for us. What transpires in this act of contact, so to speak is life – not a theoretical process, but what we call *lived experience*: pressure and counter-pressure, positing oneself over against things that are themselves posited, forces of life in us and around us that are continually experienced . . . [*Life is*] not [*the act of*] a spectator, the I, sitting before the stage of the world, but rather action and counteraction in which, whether the characters are kings or clowns and fools, the same facticity is overpoweringly experienced. This is why no philosopher has ever succeeded in persuading those who participate in life that everything is [*mere*] representation, that the world is a stage and not real. . . .

6.A.III   A Purely Descriptive Psychology[3]

But I am still far from finding myself convinced of the evidentness of such an experiential science, based on the facts of consciousness. I must not let my strong conviction about an experiential science of the human, social, and historical world, which looms before me, and constitutes my life's work, guide my thinking and writing here, but must cautiously consider each link in the chain of fact and the inferences that they support. . . .

To be sure the point of departure and the object of analysis, namely, the fact of consciousness which I possess in reflexive awareness, provides immediate certainty. My hoping, fearing, wishing, feeling, and wanting – this inner world held together by the continuity of my self-consciousness – *is* immediate certainty; it is the very thing itself. On the other hand, as soon as one tries to obtain clear knowledge of what it is one possesses in the immediate way, and tries to communicate it to others [one sees that] the judgements one pronounces are valid only on a further condition. A statement about what is given in inner perception, the articulation or analysis of it does not have the same validity as the given itself; rather, its validity rests on a presupposition. And what is this condition or presupposition? The fact of consciousness as given in inner perception is different from the statement that expresses it. But is 'express' the right word? Regarding a phrase such as 'I am very sad,' most people would agree that no more is expressed or pronounced in it than is already tacitly

2   Ibid., pp. 330–1.
3   Ibid., pp. 271–4.

contained in the reflexive awareness of this state [of sadness]. But this assumption is not justified, not even in this very simple instance . . . – the processes of separating and connection, judging and inferring – place these facts only under new conditions of consciousness, without adding anything which would alter their content or bring their truth into question.

. . .

Even the principle of phenomenality and its positive core, which as we said constitutes the secure foundation of philosophical thinking, is not a fact but rather a general proposition arrived at through a process of thought. [*My previous conclusions concerning the 'primary and immediate evidentness of the facts of consciousness' therefore*] seem to be swallowed up altogether in this circle of my thought.

. . . I must also ask the question whether the immediate evidentness of the fact of consciousness might not itself be derivative and therefore dependent on the conditions of thought.

. . . If we answer affirmatively, then . . . there could be no immediate knowledge. The evidentness of the forms and laws of thought would be for us the only unconditioned thing, and would initially establish the presence of reality. Thus the laws of thought would rule over our mental life like a primordial fate. Reality would be derived from logical necessity and would be subordinate to it as an expression of it . . . On the other hand, the denial of this assumption implies, as we have already argued, that there must be an immediate knowledge, self-sufficient and self-contained, of the reality of the facts of consciousness. . . .

This second alternative corresponds to the truth. It can in fact be shown that knowledge of the reality of the facts of consciousness needed not be gained by way of reasoning, but rather that we have an immediate knowledge of it. . . .

When someone laboriously climbs the stairs of a tower, seeing the view from the top, the stairs have merely served to raise his eye to the vantage point from which the broad landscape becomes visible. Our reasoning has as little to do with producing knowledge as the stairs have with seeing . . . All our reasoning thus merely provided directions for carrying out, in a wide variety of circumstances, the psychic act in which the facts of consciousness are there for me and are experienced as reality . . .

5.A.IV   Hermeneutics[4]

. . We have now to deal with the problem of the *scientific* knowledge of individuals . . Is such knowledge possible, and what means are at our disposal to attain it?

It is a problem of the greatest significance . . . The entire science of philology and of history is based on the presupposition that such reunderstanding of what is singular can be raised to objectivity. The historical consciousness developed on this basis has enabled modern man to hold the entire past of humanity present within himself: Beyond the limits of his own time he peers into past cultures, appropriating their energies and taking pleasure in their charm, with a consequent increase in his own happiness . . .

Human sciences have indeed the advantage over the natural sciences that their object is not sensory appearance as such, not reflection of reality within consciousness,

From 'The Rise of Hermeneutics' (1900) in Dilthey, 1996, pp. 235–50.

but is rather first and foremost an inner reality, a nexus experienced from within. Yet the very way in which this reality is given in inner experience raises great difficulties for its objective apprehension . . . Moreover, the inner experience through which I attain reflexive awareness of my own condition can never by itself bring me to a consciousness of my own individuality. I experience the latter only through a comparison of myself with others; at that point alone I become aware of what distinguishes me from others . . . But the existence of other people is given us at first only from the outside, in facts available to sense, that is, in gestures, sounds, and actions. Only through a process of re-creation of that which is available to the senses do we complete this inner experience. Everything – material, structure, the most individual traits of such a completion – must be carried over from our own sense of life. Thus the problem is: How can one quite individually structured consciousness bring an alien individuality of a completely different type to objective knowledge through such re-creation? What kind of process is this, in appearance so different from the other modes of conceptual knowledge?

. . .

Such understanding ranges from grasping the babblings of children to *Hamlet* or the *Critique of Pure Reason*. Through stone and marble, musical notes, gestures, words, and texts, actions, economic regulations and constitutions, the same human spirit addresses us and demands interpretation. . . .

. . .

Such *rule-guided understanding of fixed and relatively permanent objectifications of life is what we call exegesis or interpretation . . .*

That is indeed the immeasurable significance of literature for our understanding of spiritual life and of history, for only in language does human inner life find its complete, exhaustive, and objectively understandable expression. That is why the art of understanding centres on the exegesis or interpretation of those remains of human reality preserved in written form.

. . .

Because hermeneutics determines the possibility of universally valid interpretation on the basis of an analysis of understanding, it ultimately arrives at a solution to the quite general problem with which the present essay began. . . .

[*Dilthey then traces the history of hermeneutics from ancient Greece, through Christian theologians, up to an art critics such as Winkelmann and 'Herder's congenial empathic projection into the soul of other peoples and ages' to its climax in Schleiermacher who had achieved 'the definitive foundation of a scientific hermeneutics (p. 246). He notes that this was within the approach of 'German transcendental philosophy that seeks a creative capacity underlying what is given in consciousness – a capacity that is unconscious of itself but functions in a unified fashion to produce the overall form of the world in us' and that this achievement was part of a broader movement: with Schiller, Wilhelm von Humboldt, the Schlegel brothers, 'German culture had turned its attention from literary production to a reunderstanding of the historical world' (p. 247) and that this had influenced Hegel, Ranke, Savigny and others.*]

. . . In understanding, the individuality of the exegete and that of the author are not opposed to each other like some incomparable facts. Rather, both have been formed upon the substrate of a general human nature, and it is this which makes possible the commonality of people with each other for speech and understanding . . . The interpreter tentatively projects his own sense of life into another historical milieu . . . thus making possible within himself a re-creation of an alien form of life.

6.A.V Lived Experience, Expression and Understanding[5]

We can now mark off the human sciences from the natural sciences by quite clear criteria . . . Mankind, if apprehended only by perception and perceptual knowledge, would be for us a physical fact, and as such it would be accessible only to natural-scientific knowledge. It becomes an object for the human sciences only in so far as human states are consciously lived, in so far as they find expression in living utterances, and in so far as these expressions are understood. Of course this relationship of life, expression, and understanding embraces not only the gestures, looks, and words in which men communicate, or the enduring mental creations in which the depths of the creator's mind open themselves to the spectator, or the permanent objectifications of mind in social structures, through which the common background of human nature shines and is permanently visible and certain to us. The mind-body unit of life is known to itself through the same double relationship of lived experience and understanding, it is aware of itself in the present, it rediscovers itself in memory as something that once was; but when it tries to hold fast and to apprehend its states, when it turns its attention upon itself, the narrow limits of such an introspective method of self-knowledge make themselves felt. Only from his actions, his fixed utterances, his effects upon others, can man learn about himself; thus he learns to know himself only by the round-about way of understanding. What we once were, how we developed and became what we are, we learn from the way in which we acted, the plans which we once adopted, the way in which we made ourselves felt in our vocation, from old dead letters, from judgments on us which were spoken long ago. In short, it is through the process of understanding that life in its depths is made clear to itself, and on the other hand we understand ourselves and others only when we transfer our own lived experience into every kind of expression of our own and other people's life. Thus everywhere the relation between lived experience, expression, and understanding is the proper procedure by which mankind as an object in the human sciences exists for us. The human sciences are thus founded on this relation between lived experience, expression, and understanding. Here for the first time we reach a quite clear criterion by which the delimitation of the human sciences can be definitively carried out. A science belongs to the human sciences only if its object becomes accessible to us through the attitude which is founded on the relation between life, expression, and understanding.

From this common nature of the sciences in question follow all the peculiarities which have been emphasised in discussions on the sciences, or cultural science, or history, as constituting their nature. Thus the peculiar relation in which the unique, singular, individual stands here to universal regularities. . . .

Hodges 1944, pp. 141–3. Translated from chapter 1 of *The Construction of the Historical World*. In this and other excerpts using Hodges' translations, 'human studies' is replaced by 'human sciences', and 'Cultural Studies' by 'Cultural Sciences'.

6.A.VI Objective Mind[6]

I understand by [*objective mind*] . . . the manifold forms in which the common background subsisting among various individuals has objectified itself in the sensible world.
In this objective mind the past is for us a permanent enduring present. Its realm extends from the style of life and the forms of economic intercourse to the whole system
of ends which society has formed for itself, to morality, law, the State, religion, art,
science and philosophy. For the work of genius too represents a common stock of
ideas, mental life, and ideals at a particular time and in a particular environment. From
earliest childhood our self receives its nourishment from this world of objective mind.
It is also the medium in which the understanding of other persons and their expressions takes place. For everything in which the mind has objectified itself contains in
itself a factor common to the I and the Thou. Every square planted with trees, every
room in which chairs are arranged, is intelligible to us from our infancy, because every
square and every object in the room has had its place assigned to it by the common
human activities of planning, arranging, and value-determining. The child grows up
among the regular life and habits of a family, which it shares with other members, and
the mother's injunctions are accepted by it in this context. Before it learns to speak, it
is already deeply immersed in the medium of a common background. And it learns to
understand gestures and looks, movements and exclamations, words and sentences
only because they confront it always in the same form and in the same relation to that
which they mean and express. Thus the individual gets his bearings in the world of
objective mind.

6.A.VII Empathy, Re-creating and Re-living[7]

On the basis of this empathy or transposition there arises the highest form of understanding in which the totality of mental life is active – recreating or re-living. Understanding as such moves in the reverse order to the sequence of events. But full empathy
depends on understanding moving with the order of events so that it keeps step with
the course of life. It is in this way that empathy or transposition expands. Re-experiencing follows the line of events. We progress with the history of a period, with an
event abroad or with the mental processes of a person close to us. Re-experiencing is
perfected when the event has been filtered through the consciousness of a poet, artist
or historian and lies before us in a fixed and permanent work.

. . .

But what does this re-experiencing consist of? We are only interested in what the
process accomplishes; there is no question of giving a psychological explanation. So
we shall not discuss the relation of this concept to those of sympathy and empathy,
though their relevance is clear from the fact that sympathy strengthens the energy of
re-living. . . .

6   Hodges, 1944, pp. 118–19. Translated from *The Understanding of Other Persons and their Expressions, an* essay written for inclusion in the *Critique of Historical Reason* and published posthumously.
7   From drafts for 'A Critique of Historical Reason', in Dilthey, 1976, pp. 226–7.

This re-living plays a significant part in the acquisition of mental facts, which we owe to the historian and the poet. Life progressively limits a man's inherent potentialities. The shaping of each man's nature determines his further development. In short, he always discovers, whether he considers what determines his situation or the acquired characteristics of his personality, that the range of new perspectives on life and inner turns of personal existence is limited. But understanding opens for him a wide realm of possibilities which do not exist within the limitations of his real life. The possibility of experiencing religious states in one's own life is narrowly limited for me as for most of my contemporaries. But, when I read through the letters and writings of Luther, the reports of his contemporaries, the records, of religious disputes and councils, and those of his dealings with officials, I experience a religious process, in which life and death are at issue, of such eruptive power and energy as is beyond the possibility of direct experience for a man of our time. But I can re-live it. I transpose myself into the circumstances; everything in them makes for an extraordinary development of religious feelings. . . .

5.A.VIII Meaning: The Comprehensive Human Category[8]

. . . Understanding the nature of life involves categories which have nothing to do with nature. The decisive point is that these categories are not applied to life *a priori* as something strange but lie in its nature . . . We cannot delimit the number of these categories or formalize their relationship logically. Meaning, value, purpose, development and ideal are such categories. But the totality of a life, or any section of the life of mankind, can only he grasped in terms of the category of the meaning which the individual parts have for the understanding of the whole. All the other categories depend on this. Meaning is the comprehensive category through which life can he understood.

. . . A deeper look reveals organisation even in the poorest soul. We see it most clearly where great men have a historical destiny; but no life, is so poor that its course does not contain some organisation . . .

The category of meaning designates the relationship, inherent in life, of parts of a life to the whole. The connections are only established by memory, through which we can survey our past. Here meaning takes the form of comprehending life. We grasp the meaning of a past moment. It is significant for the individual because in it an action or an external event committed him for the future. Or, perhaps, the plan for the future conduct of life was conceived then. It is significant for communal life because the individual intervened in the shaping of mankind and contributed to it with his essential being. In all these and other cases the particular moment gains meaning from its relationship with the whole, from the connection between past and future, between individual and mankind. But in what does the particular kind of relationship of parts to the whole in a life consist of?

It is a relationship which is never quite complete. One would have to wait for the end

Ibid., pp. 235–45.

of a life, for only at the hour of death could one survey the whole from which the relationship between the parts could be ascertained. One would have to wait for the end of
history to have all the material necessary to determine its meaning. On the other hand,
the whole is only there for us when it becomes comprehensible through its parts. Understanding always hovers between these two points of view. Our view of the meaning of life
changes constantly. Every plan for your life expresses a view of the meaning of life. The
purposes we set for the future are determined by the meaning we give to the past. The
actual formation of life is judged in terms of the meaning we give to what we remember

. . .

Meaning is the special relationship which the parts have to the whole in a life. We
recognise this meaning as we do that of words in a sentence, through memory and
future potentialities. The nature of the meaning-relationships lies in the pattern of life
formed in time by the interaction between a living structure and its environment.

What is it, then, which, in the contemplation of one's life, constitutes the pattern
which links the parts into a whole and makes the life comprehensible? An experience is
a unit made up of parts linked by a common meaning. The narrator achieves his effect
by emphasising the significant elements of a course of events. The historian describes
certain human beings as significant and certain turning-points in life as meaningful . .
The parts of a life have a certain meaning for the whole . . .

Every expression has a meaning in so far as it is a sign which signifies or points to
something that is part of life. Life does not mean anything other than itself. There is
nothing in it which points to a meaning outside it.

. . . Life is like a melody the notes of which are not the expressions of hidden realities
within. Like notes in a melody, life expresses nothing but itself.

. . . The simplest case in which meaning occurs is the understanding of a sentence.
Each word had a meaning and, by joining them, we arrive at the meaning of a sentence.
Here understanding of the sentence results from the meaning of individual words. But
there is an interaction between the whole and the parts through which ambiguities of
meaning are eliminated and the meaning of individual words determined.

. . . The same relation holds between the parts and the whole of a life and here, too,
the understanding of the whole, the significance of life, is derived from the meaning of
the parts.

. . .

. . . We are looking for the kind of connection which is inherent in life itself, and we are
looking for it in the individual events. In each of these which contributes to the pattern something of the meaning of life must be contained . . .

We can only reach an approximate understanding of life; it lies in the nature of both
understanding and life that the latter reveals quite different sides to us according to the
point of view from which we consider its course in time . . . From the point of view of
value life appears as an infinite wealth of existential, negative or positive intrinsic values. It is a chaos of harmonies and dissonances – where the dissonances do not dissolve
into harmonies. . . .

. . .

Life itself contains the grief over its finitude and the desire to overcome it, striving
for realisation and objectification, denial or removal of existing limits, separation, and
combination.

. . .

. . . Life and its course form a pattern which develops through the constant absorption of new experiences on the basis of the older ones: I call this the acquired mental structure . . . This makes up the character of every life, and we must try to grasp it without prejudices. . . .

. . . The existence of a person constitutes his individuality. It limitations cause suffering and a desire to overcome them. Finitude is tragic and we feel impelled to transcend it. Limitation expresses itself externally as the pressure of the world on the subject. Through the power of circumstances and the character of the mind this can become so strong that it impedes progress. But in most cases finitude makes man try to overcome the pressure of new circumstances and new human relationships. As every state is equally finite is produced the same will to power which springs from being conditioned, the same will to inner freedom which results from inner limitations . . . This inwardly-determined pattern of life, which promotes the restless progress of change, I call development.

This concept is quite different from the speculative fantasies about progress to ever higher stages. It means that the subject becomes clearer and more differentiated. But the life of an individual like the lower forms of life, can lack the realisation of a higher meaning and remain tied to the natural basis of plant-like growth, of rise and decline between birth and death. It can decline early or move upwards until the end.

5.B Wilhelm Windelband, 1848–1915

5.B.1 History an Idiographic not Nomothetic Science[9]

At present, a certain classification of the disciplines which attempt to establish knowledge of reality is regularly employed. They are distinguished into natural sciences [*Naturwissenschaften*] and sciences of the mind [*Geisteswissenschaften*]. Stated in this particular form, I regard the dichotomy as unfortunate . . . Recent epistemological critique has . . . provided strong grounds for doubting the justifiability of accepting a form of 'inner perception' as a special, autonomous form of knowledge. In addition, this view holds that there is no sense in which it can be acknowledged that the facts of the so-called sciences of the mind are established exclusively on the basis of inner perception. . . .

. . . What is the source of the methodological relationship between psychology and the natural sciences? It evidently lies in the consideration that both psychology and the natural sciences establish, collect, and analyze facts only from the viewpoint and for the purpose of understanding the general nomological relationship to which these facts are subject . . . From this perspective, however, the distance between psychology and chemistry is hardly greater than the distance between mechanics and zoology. . . .

In contrast to these sciences, the majority of the disciplines that are usually called sciences of the mind have a distinctively different purpose: they provide a complete

From Windelband, 1980, taken from pp. 173–85.

and exhaustive description of a single, more or less extensive process which is located within a unique, temporally defined domain of reality . . . The sciences of the mind are concerned with a single event or a coherent sequence of acts or occurrences; the nature and life of an individual person or an entire nation; the definitive properties and the development of a language, a religion, a legal order, an artifact of literature, art, or science. . . .

At this point, we have before us a purely methodological classification of the empirical sciences that is grounded, upon sound logical concepts. . . .

. . . The former disciplines are nomological sciences. The latter disciplines are sciences of process or sciences of the event. The nomological sciences are concerned with what is invariably the case. The sciences of process are concerned with what was once the case. If I may be permitted to introduce some new technical terms, scientific thought it *nomothetic* in the former case and *idiographic* in the latter case. . . .

. . . This methodological dichotomy classifies only modes of investigation, not the contents of knowledge itself. It is possible – and it is in fact the case – that the same subjects can be the object of both a nomothetic and an idiographic investigation . . .

. . .

. . . Natural science and history are both empirical sciences. In other words, the foundations of both sciences – or, from a logical perspective, the premises of their arguments – lie in experience, the data of perception. Both disciplines also agree that what the naive man usually means by experience is not sufficient to satisfy the requirements of either discipline. The foundation of both disciplines rests upon a scientifically refined and critically disciplined form of experience which has been subjected to conceptual analysis. Consider the problems of identifying differences in the structure of intimately related organisms; the correct use of a microscope; the certain interpretation of simultaneity in the amplitude of a pendulum, and the position of a needle on meter. In each of these cases, the perceptions must be scrupulously educated. For the same reason, the laborious techniques of identifying the characteristic features of certain handwriting, observing the style of a writer, or comprehending the intellectual horizon and the range of interest of an historical source must also be learned . . . Up to now, logic[10] has been much more interested in the nomothetic sciences than in the idiographic sciences. There are exhaustive logical investigations concerning the methodological significance of precision instruments, the theory of experimentation, the determination of probability on the basis of multiple observations of the same phenomenon, and other similar questions. However, philosophical concern with parallel problems in the methodology of history does not ever remotely approximate its interest in the methodological problems of the natural sciences . . . And yet from the perspective of the theory of knowledge in general, it would be of the greatest interest to discover the logical forms according to which the critique of observations in historic research proceeds . . .

. . . Natural science seeks laws; history seeks structural forms. In the natural science thought moves from the confirmation of particulars to the comprehension of gener

10   Windelband and his successors, Rickert and Weber use the term 'logic' more broadly than it currently used by English-speaking philosophers (who tend to restrict its usage to Aristotelian syllogistic logic and symbolic logic) to refer to methodological and epistemological presuppositions of t sciences; in other words much as Mill had employed it to refer to 'the science of proof or evidence (Mill, 1967, p. 7). [RMB]

relationships; in the historical sciences, it is devoted to the faithful delineation of the particulars. From the perspective of the natural scientist, the single datum of observation never has any intrinsic scientific value. The datum is scientifically useful only to the extent that the scientist believes he is justified in representing the datum as a type, a special case of a general concept which is developed on the basis of the datum. He is concerned only with the properties of the datum which provide insight into a general nomological regularity. The historian's task, on the other hand, is to breathe new life into some structure of the past in such a way that all of its concrete and distinctive features acquire an ideal actuality or contemporaneity. His task, in relation to what really happened, is similar to the task of the artist, in relation to what exists in his imagination. . . .

. . .

. . . The comparison of research in the natural sciences and history will establish even more clearly the predominance of abstraction in natural science and of perceptuality in history. Consider the conceptual apparatus which historical criticism requires in order to analyze the historical tradition. These analytical techniques may be extremely refined and sophisticated. Nevertheless, the ultimate aim of history is always to extract and reconstruct from the raw material of history the true shape of the past in robust and vital clarity. History produces images of men and human life in the total wealth and profusion of their uniquely peculiar forms and with their full and vital individuality preserved intact . . . The world which the natural sciences construct is completely different. No matter how perceptually concrete and graphic the starting points of the natural sciences may be, their cognitive goals are theories – in the final analysis, mathematical formulations of laws of motion . . . From the colorful world of the senses, the natural sciences construct a system of abstract concepts . . . Utterly indifferent to the past, the natural sciences drop anchor in the sea of being that is eternally the same. They are not concerned with change as such, but rather with the invariable form of change.

If the dichotomy between the two kinds of empirical science is so profound, we can understand why a conflict must break out between natural science and history for the decisive influence upon our general world view and philosophy of life. The question is: from the perspective of our total cognitive purposes, which is more valuable, knowledge of laws or knowledge of events? Is it more important to understand the general, atemporal nature of things or to understand individual, temporal phenomena? . . .

At this point, I shall only touch superficially on the extraneous resolution of this question from the standpoint of utility. From this standpoint, both forms of knowledge are equally justifiable. Knowledge of general laws always has the practical value of making possible both predictions of future states and a purposeful human intervention in the course of events . . . All purposeful activity in human social life, however, is no less dependent upon the experience acquired as a result of historical knowledge . . . For these reasons alone, the human race is obliged to carry the immense school bag of history. . . .

However we are not really concerned with utility in this sense. We are more interested in the immanent value of knowledge. . . .

. . .

. . . The commitment to the generic is a bias of Greek thought, perpetuated from the Eleatics[11] to Plato, who found not only real being but also real knowledge only in the general. From Plato this view passed to our day. Schopenhauer makes himself a spokesman for this prejudice when he denies history the value of a genuine science because its exclusive concern is always with grasping the specific, never with comprehending the general. It is no doubt correct that there is a great deal that the human understanding can grasp only by comprehending the common content of diffuse and fragmented particulars. But the more we strive for knowledge of the concept and the law, the more we are obliged to pass over, forget, and abandon the singular fact as such. We can see this disposition in the characteristically modern attempt 'to make history into a natural science' – the project of the so-called positivist philosophy of history. In the final analysis, what is the product of such an inductive system of laws of the life of a people? A few trivial generalities which can be excused only on the basis of a careful analysis of their numerous exceptions.

In opposition to this standpoint, it is necessary to insist upon the following: every interest and judgment, every ascription of human value is based upon the singular and the unique. Simply consider how swiftly our emotions abate whenever their object is multiplied or becomes nothing more than one case among thousands of others of the same sort. 'She is not the first,' we read in one of the most terrifying texts of *Faust.* Our sense of values and all of our axiological sentiments are grounded in the uniqueness and incomparability of their object. . . .

Every dynamic and authentic human value judgment is dependent upon the uniqueness of its object. It is, above all, our relationship to personalities that demonstrate this. It is not an unbearable idea that yet another identical exemplar of a beloved or admired person exists? Is it not terrifying, and inconceivable that we might have second exemplar in reality with our own individual peculiarities? This is the source of horror and mystery in the idea of the *Doppelgänger* – no matter how great the temporal distance between the two persons may be. It has always been painful to me that people as refined and sensitive as the Greeks could tolerate one of the doctrines which persists throughout their entire philosophy. According to this doctrine, the personality itself – with all its actions, afflictions, and passions – will also return in the periodic recurrence of all things. Life is debased when it has already transpired in exactly the same way numerous times in the past and will be repeated again on numerous occasions in the future. Consider the dreadful idea that as the same person I have already lived and suffered, striven and struggled, loved and hated, thought and desired exactly the same things and that when the great cosmic year has elapsed and time returns shall have to play exactly the same role in the same theater over and over. This point concerning, individual human life has even more force when it is applied to the total historical process: this process has value only if it is unique. This is the principle which the Christian philosophy of the Church Fathers successfully maintained against Hellenism. From the outset, the fall of man and the salvation of the human race had the status of unique facts situated at the focal point of the world view of the Church Fathers. This was the first significant and powerful insight into the inalienable met

11 Parmenides and Zeno were active as philosophers in the fifth century BC in Elea, a Greek colony in Southern Italy. They argued (reaching a position in some ways comparable to Advaita Vedanta Indian Philosophers such as Sankara) that reality must be an absolutely universal, changeless unity, that the multiplicity of particular changing beings we apparently experience could only 'seem' exist. [RMB]

physical right of historiography: to maintain the past in its unique and unrepeatable reality for the recollection of mankind.

On the other hand, general propositions are necessary at every stage of inquiry in the idiographic sciences. And these they can borrow only – with perfect legitimacy – from the nomothetic disciplines. Every causal explanation of any historical occurrence presupposes general ideas about the process of things on the whole. When historical proofs are reduced to their purely logical form, the ultimate premises will always include natural laws of events, in particular, laws of mental events or psychological processes. Consider someone who has no idea at all concerning how men in general think, feel, and desire. It would not only be impossible for him to comprehend individual happenings in order to acquire knowledge of events and processes. He would already have failed in the critical determination of historical facts. . . .

. . . [*But*] In the total synthesis of knowledge, which is the ultimate aim of all scientific research, these two cognitive moments remain independent and juxtaposed. . . .

[*They*] cannot be derived from a common source. Consider the causal explanation of the single phenomenon as the reduction of this phenomenon to general laws. . . .

. . . A description of the present state of the universe follows from the general laws of nature only if the immediately preceding state of the universe is presupposed. But this state presupposes the state that immediately precedes it, and so on. Such a description of a particular, determinate state of the arrangement of atoms, however, can never be derived from the general laws of motion alone. The definitive characteristics of a single point in time can never be immediately derived from any 'cosmic formula' . . .[12]

General laws do not establish an ultimate state from which the specific conditions of the causal chain could ultimately be derived. It follows that all subsumption under general laws is useless in the analysis of the ultimate causes or grounds of the single, temporally given phenomenon. Therefore, in all the data of historical and individual experience a residuum of incomprehensible, brute fact remains, an inexpressible and indefinable phenomenon. Thus the ultimate and most profound nature of personality resists analysis in terms of general categories. From the perspective of our consciousness, this incomprehensible character of the personality emerges as the sense of the indeterminacy of our nature – in other words, individual freedom. . . .

. . .

In fact, thought can contribute nothing further to the resolution of these questions . . . The law and the event remain as the ultimate, incommensurable entities of our world view. This is one of the boundary conditions where scientific inquiry can only define problems and only pose questions in the clear awareness that it will never be able to solve them.

12   Hegel, as we have seen, sought to demonstrate that the 'particular' is derived from the 'general', and in a sense the general from the particular, or rather that these opposites are dialectically dependent on one another, the opposition being '*aufgehoben*' in the 'concrete universal'. Windelband implicitly rules out the possibility of such a reconciliation or atonement, insisting that the general and particular, law and event are 'ultimate incommensurables' (compare Ranke: 3.E. IV, 3. E. V). The Eleatics (see the preceding footnote) sought to solve the problem by ruling out the reality of the particular. Nominalists such as William of Ockham (see 1.1) moved to the opposite extreme, acknowledging the reality only of particular things, and maintaining that that the apparently general aspects of things are mere 'fictions' or 'names'. It was pointed out in the introduction to this chapter that Rickert veers towards this nominalist view to a greater degree than Windelband. [RMB]

6.C   Heinrich Rickert, 1863–1936

6.C.I   The Historical Individual[13]

... The *problem of concept formation in history* ... *is whether a scientific analysis and reduction of perceptual reality is possible that does not at the same time – as in the concept. of natural science – forfeit individuality* ... From the infinite manifold of the percep-tual content of reality, can certain aspects be accentuated and consolidated into scien-tific concepts in such a way that they represent not what is common to a plurality of things and processes, but, rather, only what is present in *one* individual? ...

Obviously we do not contest the indispensability of a *generality* for all scientific concept formation. Even a fleeting glance at a historical representation shows that it too almost always consists of words that have *general meanings*. It could not be other-wise, for these are the only words intelligible to everyone. ...

. . .

... Does it follow that the *use* of words with general meanings as elements of con-cepts is possible only in the *one* direction that we find in natural science? ...

Each of the elements of a scientific concept must be intrinsically general [*but*], their combination [*may result in a*] ... complex of general elements as a *whole* [*which*] has a content that occurs only in one unique and specific object. ...

... In natural science, the general – which is already present in the most elementary meanings of words – is also what the science endeavours to develop further ... Even the most restricted law of nature must always hold for an indefinite number of things and processes if it is to deserve the name of a 'law.' Although history also *uses* the general so that it can think and judge scientifically, the general is nothing more than *means* for history. In other words, it forms the indirect path on which history attempts to return to the individual as its real object ...

. . .

... At this point, we stress that [*the*] word [*individual*] does not have only the meaning to which we limited our account in the foregoing, namely, that of the unique, the specific, and the singular. On the contrary, it also includes the *indivisible*. The concept of indivisibility indicates a *unity* that arouses our logical interest ... Has the expression 'individual' lost its meaning when it is used to designate unique manifolds and is only the simple atom indivisible? ...

. . .

Initially, the principle that is the basis of the unity of the indivisibility that arises from uniqueness can be clarified by the comparison of two *bodies* ...

Let us employ [*as an illustration*] a particular lump of coal and a particular large diamond, such as the famous Koh-i-noor ... As regards *uniqueness* ... both can split apart. A blow of the hammer would shatter one individual as well as the other. But while the splitting of a lump of coal is the most indifferent matter imaginable, the diamond will be scrupulously protected from this. Moreover, we do not want to see the diamond split, *because* it is unique ... Although another lump of coal can always

13   From Rickert, 1986, pp. 78–98.

be substituted for this one, another Koh-i-noor can never be produced. As a result, the difference between the two kinds of individuals must be clear. The unique is always necessarily indivisible as well – or an individual [*In-dividuum*] in the strict sense of the word – when its uniqueness acquires an irreplaceable *significance*. In this sense, it is incontestable that not only minds, but also bodies, form individual unities . . .

. . .

. . . The mode of unity in indivisibility just characterized can arise only if its uniqueness is *related to a value*.

. . .

. . . Because we find this unity of indivisibility in all human mental life, we are easily lead to believe that it is tied to the nature of the psychic itself. But that is a mistake . . . Individual unity as the indivisibility of a personality is grounded on no other consideration but the following: We associate a *value* with this unity, and as a result, the aspects that are irreplaceable or essential with reference to this value form a whole that *should* not be divided. In short, the individual unity or indivisibility of the unique personality is no different from unity of the individual as such that is related to a value.

On the basis of this consideration, the concept of the 'psychic structural nexus' [*des psychischen Strukturzusammenhanges*] also becomes intelligible. The *historical* unity of a personality is not constituted by an 'experienced' unity. On the contrary, as long as we have not grasped its nature, the indivisible unity of the personality that is related to a *value* leads us to the mistaken conclusion that an *individual* unity may already be discovered in the experienced unity of the real psychic structural nexus as such. This becomes especially clear when the structural nexus is also characterized as a *purposive nexus* [*Zweckzusammenhang*]. That is because a *value* is implicit in the concept of a purpose, and the unity of individuality rests on this value alone . . . There is no person whose individuality is so indifferent to us as that of a lump of coal. It follows from this, however, that the indivisible unity of uniqueness is still not tied to the psychic as such. Independent of value, we . . . can easily *conceive* a unique mental life that possesses no individual unity – even though it always has to have the unity of the psychic structural nexus . . .

. . .

. . . The historian as a scientist is not practical but theoretical. Thus his mode of activity is always *representational*, and not *judgmental*. In other words, he shares the perspectives of considering something with the practical person, but not the activity of willing and valuing itself. This can also he expressed in the following way: History is *not a valuing science* but a *value-relevant* science. . . .

. . .

. . . The inadequacy of the concept of the historical individual obtained thus far is demonstrated by the fact that in practical life, we regard *all* persons as individuals. History, however, never represents the individuality of all persons. What is the basis for limiting it to a part of them?

Obviously it is based on the consideration that history is interested only in what – as we usually put it – has a *general* significance. This must mean that for history, the value with reference to which objects become historical individuals must be a general value: in other words, a value that is *valid for everyone*. All persons become individuals in the strict sense by virtue of the fact that we relate every human individual to some sort of value . . . If we compare a personality such as Goethe with any average person, and if we ignore the consideration that even the individuality of this average person means something with reference to some value or other, it follows that Goethe is related to such a person in the same way the Koh-i-noor diamond is related to a lump of coal . . . The significance of Goethe, on the other hand, lies precisely in what distinguishes him from all other instances of the concept of a person. There is no general concept under which he can be subsumed. Thus the individual Goethe is an in-dividual in the same sense as the individual Koh-i-noor: His distinctive status as an individual is valued by *everyone* for its individuality. . . .

History, therefore, represents objects that become individuals from this perspective by replacing practical valuation with the purely theoretical value relationship. In this way, history as a science distinguishes the essential from the inessential in a *generally valid fashion* . . .

. . .

. . . Precisely *because* it gives an account of what is related to a *general* value, history has to give an account of the individual and the distinctive. So the historical individual is significant for *everyone* by virtue of that in which it is *different from everything else* . . .

Thus it is true that historical representation requires something general as a principle of selection, but this second[14] generality of history is not the *goal* for which its formations of concepts strive, no more than is the case for the elements of concepts. It is rather the *presupposition* on the sole basis of which a generally valid representation of what is unique and individual can be undertaken. . . .

. . .

. . . It is simply not the business of historical science to offer positive or negative *valuations*: in other words, to assert that the individual realities they represent are either good or bad, valuable or antagonistic to value. For in that case, how is history to arrive at *generally* valid value judgments? It is rather the case that we have to scrupulously distinguish what we mean by the 'relation' of an individual to a value from the direct positive or negative *valuation* of this individual . . . Insofar as the value perspective is decisive for history, this concept of the 'value relation' – in opposition to 'valuation' – is actually *the* essential criterion for history as a pure science.

But what does it mean to relate an object to a value theoretically, without valuating it as good or bad, as valuable or antagonistic to values? In order to understand this, let us . . . consider two persons who have pronounced disagreements in what they love and hate – in other words, in what they value. . . .

One of the two may be a radical democrat and a free trader, the other an extreme aristocrat and a protectionist. In that event, there will certainly be few cases in which they agree in their valuations or value judgments about political events of their own time or the past, in their own country or in other nations. In other words, they will regard very different things as good or bad. But does this mean that one of them will be interested only in those individual political events that are indifferent to the other? Of course not. Even among politicians who take the most diverse positions imaginable, *the same* individual events form the object of *interest*. . . .

. . .

. . . For example, we can regard the personality of Luther as either a good thing or

14 Rickert's 'first generality' is the one of general concepts to describe an individual in its unique complexity. [RMB]

bad thing. In other words, we can believe that it was a stroke of luck for the cultural development of Germany or that it brought misfortune. On this point, the opinions of historians will probably always be in disagreement. But no one who knows the facts will doubt that Luther had some sort of *significance* with reference to generally acknowledged values, and it can never occur to a historian to claim that Luther's personality is historically *unimportant*. . . .

. . .

. . . The belief that we could ever maintain an absolutely value-free standpoint in history – in other words, that we could not only avoid practical positive or negative value judgments, but also theoretical value relations – amounts to self-deception.

Everyone will freely admit that history has to represent only the 'essential.' When the historian does not follow this rule and incorporates inessential matters into his representations, we raise a serious objection against him. But the word 'essential' – and the words 'interesting,' 'characteristic,' 'important,' and 'significant' as well, which must always be applicable to the historical – loses all specifiable meaning if there is no relation between the objects designated in this way and some sort of value. Fundamentally, therefore, the claim that every object that falls within the domain of history must be related to a value only articulates in *logically useful* terms the quite trivial truth that everything history represents is interesting, characteristic, important, or significant. The interesting, the characteristic, and the important can be good as well as bad, but the question of whether it is good or bad does not have to be considered at all. To this extent, its *valuation* is unimportant. But everything immediately loses the quality of the interesting, the important, and the characteristic when every sort of *relation* to values is terminated. . . .

. . .

. . . Logically . . . the concept of history can now be formulated as follows. It is a science of *reality* insofar as it is concerned with unique, individual realities as such, the only realities of which we have any knowledge at all. It is a *science* of reality insofar as it adopts a standpoint in which we merely consider something, a standpoint that is valid for everyone; thus it is solely by means of a relation to a general value that history constitutes significant or essential individual realities or historical individuals as the object of its representation. . . .

5.C.II   The Historical Nexus[15]

. . What we have said thus far about the representation of individual realities by history is still not sufficient to define the logical concept of historical science. [*For the sake of simplicity – we have so far articulated the concept of the historical individual as if it were*] self-contained and thus *isolated*. But we should not regard the individual or the singular as what is isolated. In the real events of the empirical world, nothing is ever isolated . . . From the perspective of our presuppositions, isolation would be unhistorical. . . . [*Historical science's*] work is done only when it places every object that it considers in the *nexus* in which this object actually exists.

. . . In opposition to the single historical individuals, the nexus in which they belong

5   Ibid., pp. 107–8.

must be called *general* . . . Here again, we in fact encounter a 'generality,' and in addition to the general *elements* of concepts and general values, it is the *third generality* that appears in every history. . . . [But] The 'general' historical nexus is a comprehensive *whole*, and the single individuals are its parts. Generality in the sense of natural science, on the other hand, is the general content of a *concept* under which single individuals are subsumed as *instances* . . . The historical individual considered in the foregoing is always articulated in a historical whole. But there is no sense in which such an articulation coincides with *subsumption* under a general concept or a natural law.

. . . The concrete class [*Gattung*] the nexus – or however we propose to describe a historical *whole* – is individual and distinctive, just like each of its parts. In other words, it is more comprehensive and extensive, but not conceptually more general, than the single individuals of which it consists. The Italian Renaissance, for example, is just as much a historical individual as Machiavelli, the romantic school just as much as Novalis

. . . For history, therefore, Machiavelli and Novalis are not instances but constituents. Their inclusion in the 'general' historical nexus of the Renaissance or romanticism signifies the inclusion of one individual in another more comprehensive individual.

6.C.III   History: The Science of Cultural Development[16]

. . . The next . . . step on the path to the definition of the concept of history is taken when we reflect on the following fact: General values – and this holds true for values that are in fact generally acknowledged as well as for normatively general values – obtain only among human beings who live together in some sort of *community*, in other words, *social* beings in the broadest sense of the term. We know that there are no isolated individuals at all in empirical reality. Moreover, human mental life that has developed to the point of recognizing general values can only be a life with other human beings, or a social life.

. . .

. . . The general values governing historical concept formation . . . must always be a common concern of the members of a community . . . For example . . . the values of the church, the nation, law, the state, marriage, the family, economic organization, religion, science, art and so on. Thus only human beings who become in-dividual with respect to goods of this sort and the values attached to them are possible historical centers for the science of history. . . .

Suppose we try to find a common *name* for these values that are attached to good of this sort . . .

. . . The name can only be culture. This expression, therefore, will be important for us

This word, originally used for the cultivation of the soil, is now conventionally employed as the name for all those goods that the members of a community take seriously, or whose 'cultivation' can be required of them. For this reason, the normatively general social values we have discussed should be designated as *cultural values*, and th opposition of nature and culture finally makes it possible to develop conclusively th

16   Ibid., pp. 131–7.

substantive[17] concept of historical science in opposition to the *substantive* concept of natural science. Culture is the common concern in the life of peoples. Thus it is also the good with reference to whose values individuals acquire their *historical* significance as something that everyone acknowledges. . . .

But if normatively general cultural values are the governing principles of every historical representation, we have gone one step farther in the definition of the concept of the historical center. In the first place, it is self-evident that *those* persons become preeminently important for history who themselves have taken a real value position on the normatively general social values of the state, law, the economy, art, and so on, persons whose individuality has acquired essential significance for the real course of history in this way. All other real existence remains historical only to the extent that its individuality has an influence on human cultural activity and its results. But this concept of the historical center is still not entirely sufficient for our purposes . . . We also have to consider that history – to the extent that this is possible – always has to represent the development of its objects, that is, *sequences of changes*, whose successive stages are fundamentally different from each other.

. . . Real culture exists only where value-related or historical-teleological *development either exists or has existed* . . . *We speak of 'natural peoples'* [*Naturvölker*] and juxtapose them to 'historical' peoples as well as to 'civilized' or 'cultural peoples' [*Kulturvölker*]. Again we can leave undecided the question of whether there are absolutely unhistorical beings who have no culture at all. But if a people really exhibits no historically essential changes in the entire course of its known development, then in fact we could subsume it only under general concepts of recurrence. In this respect, therefore, we could conceive it only as 'nature,' in the logical sense. A people exhibits historically essential changes only if it manifests a historical development with reference to its cultural values . . . As a result, it is again clear that historical peoples must always be cultural peoples, and culture can exist only in historical peoples. The concepts of culture and history condition each other reciprocally. In a certain sense, they are interdependent: It is cultural values alone that make history as a science possible, and it is historical development alone that brings forth real cultural goods to which cultural values are attached.

Now we have finally defined the concept of the *central processes of history* to the extent that this seems necessary for our purposes. . . .

5.C.IV   Non Real Meaning Configurations[18]

. . . There are configurations (*Gebilde*) that are neither corporeal nor mental events. Thus they simply cannot be conceived as empirical realities that occur temporally.

---

7 'Substantive' is implicitly opposed here to 'formal'. The 'formal' difference between natural and historical science has already been dealt with: natural science develops generalizations, history is an individualizing science. But Rickert is addressing here the criticism that this mode of distinguishing them is too abstract. He therefore offers a more concrete means of distinguishing them in terms of the object' or 'substance' of their research rather than their formal methodological approach; he maintains that natural science deals with 'nature', history with 'culture'. Here there is an implied criticism of Dilthey: Rickert is arguing that '*Kultur*' should be regarded as the object of historical science rather than '*Geist*'. [RMB]

8 Ibid., 139–51.

Nevertheless, we are all directly acquainted with them, which is why they also cannot be relegated to a metaphysical beyond. In every respect, this domain is *nonreal*. In it we would have to include, for example, the 'meaning' of a word or the theoretical 'content' of a judgment. Every thinking person who 'understands' such a configuration at all, understands it as *the same*. Conversely, we will later see that a nonreal 'object' necessarily belongs to 'understanding,' assuming that the word is not to lose its exact meaning. At the outset, it is important to see that the real mental acts of understanding – or of 'meaning' as well – are *different* in every individual, in spite of the identity of the object of understanding. In other words, they can at best *resemble* one another – to the extent that realities can in general resemble one another. But they can never be *identical*, like the common object of understanding. . . .

. . . On the assumption that such configurations are nonreal, that which constitutes the 'spiritual' sort of culture as *culture* – namely, its value relevance – also seems to be a nonreal world. But if this is the case, it seems we cannot call the material of history 'culture,' for the historical sciences propose to represent real events, not nonreal objects. Or is it perhaps false that the historian always attempts to understand real temporal events? Is history – precisely insofar as it is a cultural science – possibly a science of nonreal configurations? That is, in addition to its real material, does it also have a nonreal 'material'?

. . .

. . . Values as such are never real. On the contrary, they hold validly. In other words, the values themselves cannot be real, but rather only the goods in which they are 'realized' and in which we discover them. In the same way, the *meaning* reality acquires with reference to a value does not itself fall within the domain of real existence. On the contrary, it obtains only in relation to a valid value. In this sense, the meaning itself is unreal. In consequence, by culture we understand, first, real historical *life* to which a meaning is attached that constitutes it as culture. In addition, we can also understand by culture the nonreal 'content' itself, conceived as the meaning of such a life that is detached from all real existence and is interpreted with reference to cultural values. In 'meaningful life' itself, both of these senses interpenetrate. In the theory of such a life, they must be distinguished.

. . . In other words, art and science – and even religion, law, politics, and so on – designate, first, meaningful realities and, second, configurations that are no more real than the valid content of scientific truths. For this reason, we will always explicitly refer to the latter as *nonreal configurations* of cultural *meaning*. Without exploring the differences between these configurations in more detail, we do this to scrupulously distinguish them from the *historical realities of culture* to which they are attached.

. . .

. . . The distinction between meaningful and nonmeaningful realities actually forms the real core of Dilthey's theory of the human sciences, especially as it is developed in his last writings . . . There can be no question of a fundamental opposition between Dilthey's ideas and those set out here. It is only that Dilthey, as we saw earlier, unfortunately did not succeed in providing a *clear conceptual* analysis of the essential features of his principle of demarcation. This is because he too always remained too preoccupied with the difference between bodies and mental processes . . . Dilthey confuses the nonreal, meaningful content of culture that is situated in the realities of history with the real psychic existence that actually occurs in the mental life of single individuals.[19] Thus it remains concealed that it is not the real spirit [*Geist*] but, rather, the nonreal meaning that forms the genuinely decisive factor in *substantively* distinguishing history from every natural science . . . As a result, that which, in spite of this, is valuable in his theories, remains ad hoc and unsystematic. It stems more from a powerful historical 'instinct' than from conceptual clarity concerning the nature of history. . . .

. . .

. . . The nonreal actually stands in opposition to psychic existence to the extent that, unlike real mental processes, it never need directly pertain to a single individual alone. On the contrary, it can always be 'experienced' in common by many – indeed, in principle by all – real subjects. For this reason it should also be called 'general,' in addition to the four[20] kinds of generality differentiated earlier. . . .

Here it will be best to employ an example. . . .

Let us assume that a number of people are gathered in a church for a worship service. The realities we identify include, first of all, bodies such as the building with its pews, pulpit, and organ; and also a plurality of psychophysical individuals – the clergyman, the organist, and the members of the congregation who listen to both the sermon and the church music. But it is obvious that what is actually present is not yet *exhausted* by such a complex of real physical and psychic objects. Indeed, in these realities, insofar as they are *merely* real, we simply do not yet have what we can call the worship service of a *congregation*. In this context, we will disregard completely an interplay of any divine or supernatural factors whatsoever. Because they would always remain inaccessible to any treatment by an empirical science, we have to do this. We will focus only on what cannot be denied even by someone who sees in the worship service the expression of a crass superstition.

In that case, we are obliged to claim the following: The people gathered in the church constitute the 'unity' of a congregation only because they understand *the meaning* of the sermon and the sacred music that the preacher and the organist bring to expression by means of words or tones. This meaning consists neither in the real sounds of the words or organ tones with which it is connected nor in the mental realities by means of which it is grasped. On the contrary, it is a nonreal configuration built from theoretical, religious, and aesthetic factors, and perhaps from others as well. Without exception, however, they are nonreal. The different real individuals 'experience' this meaning in common as the same. It is on its basis alone that the members constitute *one* congregation. Perhaps no one of them grasps this meaning in an absolutely complete fashion. Some may find the preacher too difficult to understand, and others may be unmusical. As a result, only one aspect of the entire meaning configuration that belongs to the worship service will be accessible to them. However, the real psychophysical individuals gathered in the church become the members of the religious congregation only *to the extent* that they participate in the nonreal meaning configurations expressed by the sermon and the music; or – as this may also be put – only to the extent that the meaning of the words and tones somehow becomes 'truly vital' in their mental life.

19 Actually 6.A.VI. shows that this criticism is not entirely fair. [RMB]

20 For the passage concerning the fourth generality of history, not excerpted here, see Rickert, 1986, pp. 115–16. It occurs when one can identify a group of historical individuals each of which is significant for the same reason. [RMB]

This meaning, which is more or less completely realized in the different members of the congregation, can also be called the 'spirit' of the congregation, assuming that we want to use this word for the totality of nonreal meaning configurations. . . .

. . . Entities such as the 'zeitgeist' and the 'folk soul' must be regarded as wholly problematic as long as they are understood as psychic realities. This is because only what takes place temporally in single individuals is mentally real. Thus a real general zeitgeist or a real general folk soul cannot exist, except as a thoroughly problematic metaphysical reality. The problems posed by such concepts, however, assume a new aspect when entities such as the 'spirit' of a religious community described earlier are considered. Without being corporeal, they are vested in many individuals in common. Thus they also lie beyond the only opposition between general and particular we have considered so. It is true that the conceptually abstracted *meaning* of historical culture is not a general reality. But it does not coincide with the individual mental life of single individuals either . . .

. . . Terms such as 'Greek,' 'German,' 'Renaissance,' and 'romanticism,' are first of all, to be understood as names for concepts of unreal meaning configurations that can be more or less completely grasped in common by many persons within a people or an age. . . .

6.C.V Explanation, Understanding and Re-Creation[21]

There have been repeated attempts to differentiate two groups of sciences or two kinds of representation within the same science in such a way that one 'explains' its objects and the other 'understands' them. The concept of historical understanding, which is often linked with that of 'reexperiencing', has actually been made the focal point of a theory of the human sciences. In this context, it is usually regarded as self-evident that the object of understanding or reexperiencing is the real mental life of historical personalities or mass movements. Because psychology deals with the reality of mental life, the attempt to make a 'psychology' the foundation of historical science again comes into play, and this time apparently with justification. . . .

. . . [*But*] the significance of 'psychology as a human science' conceived as a 'foundation' of historical science remains thoroughly problematic . . . We have to ask . . . how does the concept of historical understanding and reexperiencing, as correctly understood, fit into our theory of individualizing concept formation in cultural science?

. . .

The expression 'to understand' has many meanings, which will not be enumerated here. . . .

The grasp of a nonreal meaning configuration is what is usually meant by understanding . . . This is the only way the expression 'understanding' acquires a thoroughly precise meaning. Meaningful wholes can be understood only as unities or totalities . . . The object of understanding as a nonreal meaning configuration always remains a whole or a unity. Realities, on the other hand, are decomposed into their parts for

21   Ibid., pp. 156–70.

the purpose of explanation. Or, in explanation, the path leads from the parts to the whole; in understanding, it proceeds in the opposite direction, from the whole to the parts. . . .

. . .

[*However*] we are primarily concerned with the historian's representation of *real* meaningful mental life. If we want to call this representation as well 'understanding,' we cannot restrict the expression to the comprehension of detached nonreal meaning configurations. On the contrary, we are obliged to say that the historian wants to 'understand' real mental life itself.

. . . But the understanding of real historical material can never be concerned with a *merely* real – and thus value-free and nonmeaningful – mental life. In its pure reality – given that we want to assume it actually exists – mental life remains just as 'incomprehensible' for us as a purely real material object, such as a stone lying in the street. Otherwise, there is no objection to the use of the expression 'understanding' for the comprehension of real, meaningful mental life. In that case, the real is an object of understanding in the sense that and to the extent that it is the 'bearer' of a nonreal meaning. . . .

. . .

. . . [*But*], . . . nothing psychic that really transpires in other individuals can ever be *directly* accessible to the historian . . .

. . . We will make the following terminological distinction. Provisionally, we will call only the comprehension of the unreal *meaning* of the mental life of other persons 'understanding.' The comprehension of the *real* mental existence of other persons, however, we will call 're-creation' . . . Historical understanding, therefore, must be a matter of the interpretive re-creation of the meaningful mental life of other persons. As we can now claim, it is both 're-created' in the individuality of its real existence and 'understood' in the individuality of its nonreal meaning . . .

. . . We will speak of a 're-creation', of the mental life of another person only where history is more or less successful in transcending the purely conceptual content of its representation . . .

. . .

Meaning . . . has a property that can never be ascribed to psychic existence: It can be directly grasped by us in common with other persons as *the same* nonreal meaning and, as we have seen, not as an entity that has a general content but, rather, in its *individuality* . . . This opens up the possibility that meaning erects the *bridge* that leads us from our own mental life to that of another person, even in its real individuality. From this perspective, we proceed to the problem of re-creative understanding. . . .

. . .

Suppose someone tells us something the meaning of which we understand completely. To this extent we can also make it 'our own.' At the same time, however, it may strike us as quite 'alien.' This would certainly be the case if a German, after the World War, expressed his satisfaction with the 'Peace' of Versailles. What happens inside us? In this way at least one aspect of the problem of interpretive re-creation can be clarified. In our terminology, what is at stake here can be formulated in the following way. We 'understand' the nonreal meaning of the alien words, but we cannot 're-create' the real, alien mental processes of the person who expresses this meaning. In such a case, we say that although we have understood the words completely, the other person remains 'unintelligible' to us, meaning thereby that we are unable to re-create his real mental life. . . .

Suppose, however, we do not regard our contemporary as 'insane,' and therefore as permanently 'incomprehensible.' Then we can attempt to penetrate his real mental life on the basis of the meaning of his words that we have understood. In other words, we can ask what must have occurred in his mind that was responsible for the fact that he could really intend and express these words with precisely this meaning that we have understood. In such a case, it will at least become evident how we use the understanding of nonreal meaning to build the *bridge* from our own mental life to another mental life that is not directly accessible to us. . . .

. . .

. . . In this case . . . we also attempt to 'empathize' with a mental life in which this meaning is really vital, a mental life that really lives in this meaning. That can happen if we ask the following question: Assuming we spoke these words and merely understood their meaning, how would our mental life have to be constituted for these words to be really vital in it? In this case we will say that we are 'transposed' into the psyche of another. . . .

6.D   Georg Simmel, 1858–1918

6.D.1   Refutation of Historical Realism[22]

How does the theoretical construct that we call history develop from the material of immediate, experienced reality? That question is the subject of this book. It will establish that this transformation of immediate, experienced reality is more radical than the naive consciousness usually supposes. In this sense, the book is a critique of historical realism: the view according to which historical science is simply a mirror image of the event 'as it really happened.' The error committed here seems to be no less significant than the error of aesthetic realism. According to the latter thesis, the purpose of art is to copy or reproduce reality. This thesis fails to recognize how completely any 'reproduction' actually forms the contents of reality. The constitutive power of the intellect in relation to nature is generally acknowledged.[23] However the point that the intellect has the same constitutive power in relation to history is obviously more difficult to grasp. This is because mind is the material of history. Consider the formative categories of the mind, their general autonomy, and the sense in which the material of history satisfies the requirements of these categories. Consider also the distinction between these categories and the material of history itself. If mind constitutes history, then this distinction is not so clear as it is in the case of the natural sciences. The purpose of this book, therefore, is to establish – not in detail, but only in principle – the a priori of historical knowledge. For historical realism, history is a simple reproduction of the event. Any discrepancy between history and the event is merely the result of an abridge-

22   Simmel, 1977, pp. vii–ix and pp. 76–85.
23   Simmel takes for granted that everyone acknowledges that Kant was right that the categories 'constitute' Nature, See 1.V. [RMB]

ment that is purely quantitative. In opposition to this standpoint, we shall establish the legitimacy of the Kantian question: how is history possible?

Consider *Kant's* question: how is nature possible? As a contribution to our weltanschauung, the value of Kant's answer to this question lies in the freedom which the self or ego achieves in its relationship to everything that falls within the domain of mere nature. The self produces nature as its own idea. The general, constitutive laws of nature are simply the forms of our mind. Nature is thereby subjected to the sovereign self; not, of course, to the capriciousness of the self and its concrete vacillations, but rather to *the existence* of the self and the conditions necessary for its existence. The origin of these conditions is not independent of the self. On the contrary, they constitute its own immediate life. Consider the two forces which threaten modern man: nature and history. In Kant's work, the first of these forces is destroyed. Both seem to suffocate the free, autonomous personality. Nature has this property because mechanism subjects the psyche – like the falling stone and the budding plant – to blind necessity. History has this property because it reduces the psyche to a mere point where the social threads woven throughout history interlace. The entire productivity of the psyche is analyzed as a product of evolution. In the work of Kant, the autonomous mind escapes the imprisonment of our empirical existence by nature. The concept of nature formed by consciousness, the intelligibility of the forces of nature, what nature can be in relation to the psyche – all this is an achievement of the psyche itself. The mind frees the self from enslavement by nature. But this enslavement is now transformed into another: the mind enslaves itself. On the one hand, the personality is analyzed as an historical phenomenon. History, on the other hand, is the history of mind. In consequence, the personality seems to remain free from the tyranny of historical inevitability. But actually, history as a brute fact, a reality, and a superpersonal force threatens the integrity of the self quite as much as nature. In reality, therefore, history represents constraint or coercion by a force alien to the self. In this case, however, the temptation to conceive necessity as freedom is much more subtle. This is because the force which constrains us has the same essential nature that we have. It is necessary to emancipate the self from historicism[24] in the same way that Kant freed it from naturalism, Perhaps the same epistemological critique will succeed here too: namely, to establish that the sovereign intellect also forms the construct of *mental existence* which we call history only be means of its own special categories. Man as an object of knowledge is a product both of nature and history But man as a knowing subject produces both nature and history.

. . . Consider the stream of existence in which the mind discovers itself. It is the mind itself which maps out the shores of this stream and determines the rhythm of its waves. Only under these conditions does the mind constitute itself as 'history.' The definitive purpose of the ensuing investigations may, therefore, be described as follows: they attempt to emancipate the mind – its formative power – from historicism, in the same way that Kant freed it from nature.

. . .

In this context, it is most essential to dispose of historical realism. This doctrine has retreated from the theory of the external world to the philosophy of mind. Consider

---

24   Simmel is using this term in the sense of 'historical determinism', and not in the sense in which 'Historicism' is employed in this book, according to which Simmel himself is a historicist. [RMB]

the epistemological realism which explains truth as a correspondence – in the sense of a mirror image – between thought and its object, an object which is necessarily external to its corresponding thought. Insofar as the natural sciences are concerned, this view has been refuted.[25] Moreover it is relatively easy to see that the description of a real event in terms of mathematical formulae or atoms, in terms of a mechanism or dynamism, is only a set of symbols, a construct built of mental categories. It is only a system of tokens that represent the object of knowledge. It is easy to see that there is no sense in which this sort of description qualifies as an exact reproduction of the object itself. In the sociohistorical sciences, however, the essential identity of knowledge and its object – for both lie within the domain of the mental – still leads us to the same mistaken conclusion: that form of naturalism which holds that knowledge is possible as a simple reproduction of its object and conceives the faithfulness of this reproduction as the criterion for knowledge itself. The task of enabling us to see the event 'as it really happened' is still naively imposed upon history. In opposition to this view, it is necessary to make clear that every form of knowledge represents a translation of immediately given data into a new language, a language with its own intrinsic forms, categories, and requirements. In order to qualify as a science, the facts – inner, unobservable facts as well as external, observable facts – must answer certain questions, questions which they never confront in reality and in their form as brute data. In order to qualify as objects of knowledge, certain aspects of the facts are thrown into relief and others are relegated to the background. Certain specific features are emphasized. Certain immanent relations are established on the basis of ideas and values. All this – as we might put it – transcends reality. The facts as objects of knowledge are formed into new constructs that have their own laws and their own peculiar qualities.

. . .

. . . The decisive point to keep in mind here is the refutation of epistemological naturalism. On this view, knowledge is supposed to be a mirror image of reality. But knowledge is a novel construct, a self-sufficient, autonomous construct that follows its own laws according to its own peculiar categories. Consider the thesis that no science can completely express the complexity and the qualitatively infinite profusion of real existence. There is no sense in which this thesis provides an adequate view of the definitive form of knowledge. This is a purely quantitative viewpoint. Ultimately, it is grounded on the inadequacy of our cognitive faculties, and it is not sufficient to refute naturalism in principle. This thesis fails to recognize that even under these ideal conditions – even if a qualitatively and quantitatively complete description of reality were actually possible – the discipline of history would still be different form a mirror image of reality. Just as a portrait would retain its peculiar nature and value even if colour photography could reproduce a phenomenon with absolute accuracy.

Suppose, however, we grant what this viewpoint mistakenly supposes: that the impossibility of a quantitative description of the infinite complexity of real existence poses the definitive problem of knowledge. Even in this case, it would still follow that historical science is obliged to produce a complete *transformation* of concrete existence. Consider the points of concentration and importance, the characteristic tendencies

---

25   Again Simmel takes entirely for granted the Neo-Kantian view that the theories and mathematical laws of natural science are mental constructs which do not directly reflect or correspond with the nature of reality. [RMB]

and moments to which historical knowledge reduces the manifold of existence. They must be constituted as *unified entities* that exhibit a continuous process, an intelligible structure, and a character that can be empathetically reconstructed. They must be represented as a collection of phenomena that can be comprehended from their focal point. History weaves a fabric from fragments of material that have been transformed by the process of emphasis and omission. Its threads and categories are very different from those exhibited by concrete reality. Even the quantitative changes involved produce other changes that are formal and purely functional.

Consider, by way of example, the political biography of a ruler. The politically important ideas and activities are distinguished within the continuity of a rich, multifaceted, and expansive life. They make up his political career, the course of which is intrinsically continuous. However it is hardly the case that any moment of his political life transpires in the artificial isolation that this historical construct requires ... His political life is completely intelligible only in relation to his life as a whole. Knowledge of his life as a whole, however, is impossible for any science; so the historian constructs a new, synthetic concept: politics. In view of the generality and abstract precision required by this historical concept, it is possible that politics never enters the consciousness of the ruler. ...

. . .

Consider the sort of picture sketched by the history of politics, art, religion, and economics. And consider an exhaustive representation of the totality of the event, the only possible object of a history which would describe things 'as they really were.' In principle, the relationship between the two is no different from the relationship between the portrait or the landscape painting and the complete reality of the subject matter. It is impossible to describe the individual event as it really was because it is impossible to describe the event as a whole. A science of the total event is not only impossible for reasons of unmanageable quantity: it is also impossible because it would lack a *point of view* or *problematic* ... Given a criterion for knowledge that is perfectly general, it would be impossible to identify or distinguish any element of reality. This is the deeper reason why there are only histories, but no history as such. What we call universal history or world history can at best be the simultaneous application of a variety of these differential problematics. Or, on the other hand, it may be the sort of history which throws into relief the aspects of the event which are most significant or important from the perspective of a sense of value.

If we are sufficiently careful about how the import of this remark should be understood, we can say that each history – each individual branch of historical science – has its own peculiar criterion of truth.

. . .

[*For instance*] ... compare the history of art with ecclesiastical history. The subject matter of art history is composed of works that are discontinuously related; this is because each work of art is a complete, self-contained entity. The history of art constructs a coherent process from these disconnected works of art. It represents them as if a process of organic evolution joined them together like the annual rings of a tree. Here the relationship between the given raw material of history and the form it assumes as an object of historical knowledge is altogether different from the relationship between the facticity of the life of a religious community and its representation in the form of history. This is because ecclesiastical or religious life really is continuous. The acts of a single religious virtuoso are not only extraordinary moments within religious life: insofar as they occur at all, they almost never have the insularity of works of art. We might say that they are implicated in the homogeneous substance which evolves within the history of religion. The essential point here is the following: in order to write or understand the history of art, a much more spontaneous functioning of personal or subjective synthesis is required than in ecclesiastical history . . . Nevertheless, historical truth – in the objective sense – can be ascribed to propositions in both branches of history. . . .

These examples are sufficient to establish the following conclusion: there is no sense in which historical truth qualifies as a mirror image of historical reality. . . .
. . .

[*The following passage is inserted in the third edition at this point*[26]]
. . . In the foregoing, I made reference to a 'subjective factor.' Here we must keep in mind the distance and detachment which any science requires, in contrast to the free play of the artistic imagination . . . It is one and the same complex of contents that we comprehend under the great forms of mental life: the forms of the empirical and the religious, the aesthetic and the practical, the conceptual and the emotional. But a form has certain specifications. It is never absolutely comprehensive; it is always historically determined and subject to historical variations. It follows that certain contents seem to have a predisposition for a certain form; other contents fall under this form only with difficulty or in a fragmentary fashion, and some contents simply do not fall under it all . . . Any form only comprehends reality in an incomplete fashion.

. . . Suppose that the historian confronts an existential totality. Its properties appear differently, as if they were reflected by different mirrors, each with its own characteristic angle of refraction: politics, artistic accomplishment, religiosity, and epochs of specific types provide examples of these differences in perspective. In relation to the totality of real life, each of the images produced in this way is subjective. Each is determined by the purpose of historical knowledge. But the purpose of historical knowledge cannot be derived from reality; nevertheless, certain aspects of reality tend to fall under some forms but not others. The historical perspective is only applicable to certain aspects of reality; it only applies to certain modes of classifying these aspects. The objective properties of the elements of reality are not, as such, historical. It does not follow from this that history is capricious. . . .

. . . The 'subjectivity' of history as a form does not entail that historical concepts are employed in an arbitrary fashion – just to the contrary . . . The ambiguity of the concept of 'objectivity' has created misunderstanding . . .

6.D.II Criteria of Historical Significance[27]

We describe certain phenomena as 'significant' or 'important' quite independent of the position they occupy in a genuine scale of values. Of course they have such a status and this could be a reason they are felt to be 'significant.' However the import of this concept is different from the import of the concept of value;[28] the valuable and the

---

26 Simmel, 1977, pp. 207–8.
27 Ibid., pp. 155–73.
28 There is surely an implicit criticism of Rickert's stress on value here. [RMB]

significant imply two different emphases, even if the difference is more a matter of feeling than of precise description. They refer to properties that are purely intrinsic to a phenomenon. And they also refer to properties which a phenomenon acquires by virtue of its effects upon other phenomena and as a result of its comparative relationships with the remainder of historical existence. . . .

. . . The attribution of morality or immorality, beauty or ugliness can endow the bearer of these predicates with the quality of being 'significant' to us. But the latter invariably remains a novel and autonomous category. The same degree of a value which on one occasion is regarded as significant or important may, on another occasion, not fall under this category at all.

. . . On the hand, we ascribe a *meaning* to historical existence insofar as historical phenomena do not unfold in the monotony and uniformity of mediocre or average qualities, but rather approach extremes of all sorts. On the other hand, we also ascribe meaning to historical phenomena insofar as they are not completely incomparable and qualitatively different from one another, insofar as they possess an ideal structure that transforms individual men, actions, and circumstances into representatives of types of men, actions, and circumstances. A metaphysics of history can find elements of significance and importance in facts of both kinds; they lie, of course, beyond the purely empirical construct of history. From the standpoint of this construct, the extreme phenomena as well as the average, the typical as well as the unique, are produced with the same indifferent, intrinsically homogenous necessity, Consider the fact that the phenomena discussed here have this function. They transcend history as mere fact. The facts of history provide a point of departure for a more profound picture, a new taxonomy or tendency. . . .

. . .

. . . What is 'objectively' important? If we limit the application of the concept of importance to the concrete event, or whatever qualifies as the basic element of history, then the following point is obvious. If something is important, then importance must be 'ascribed' or 'attached' to it; in other words, it is important because the historian is interested in it. 'Intrinsically' an item may be moral or corrupt, gigantic or idyllic, brilliant or profound. It is *important*, in the sense that it is a point of orientation or organization for historical inquiry, exclusively because of the interest that it acquires as a result of the feelings or sentiments of the historical observer. The following seems to be the most plausible method for establishing an objective criterion of historical importance. Importance is not a property of the individual element itself, but rather a property of its *consequences*. But suppose that historical importance cannot be ascribed to these consequences; in that case, it is difficult to see why it should be ascribed to their cause. *Suppose*, however, that they exhibit this property. Then their objective structure would also lend historical importance to their cause. However this would not make the ascription of historical importance any less subjective than it is in the first case. We might also attempt to establish an objective status for historical importance in the following way. It is not the qualitative properties of the consequences which determine historical importance, but only the number of these consequences, which would determine whether importance can be ascribed to their cause. In this case, it is simply the number of the consequences as such that has historical importance. Consider the isolated entity the energies or potencies of which are exhausted in its own production. Suppose that no further consequences can be attributed to it: then it would qualify as insignificant or unimportant. This feeling, of course, will always remain subjective; however this sort of subjectivity would be objectively grounded. As a constant presupposition, it would at least eliminate purely individual or arbitrary differences of interpretation . . .

. . . Consider the mere quantum – the weight or the number – of these effects as we consciously or unconsciously estimate it. Perhaps this provides the criterion for the feeling of historical interest with which we react to certain causal factors. The causal factors that we designate as 'important' are precisely those which have consequences that are, in comparison with 'unimportant' events, more observably determinable or quantitatively estimable . . . We would ascribe historical interest only to those knowable sequences of mental events to which a certain quantum of effects can be clearly or intuitively attributed. There is no reason why each of these events must have some intrinsic historical importance . . . Here it would be legitimate to speak of a *threshold of the historical consciousness*, whose location is determinable by reference to these quanta of effects, reactions, or consequences. It is necessary to emphasize the importance of this concept of a threshold of historical consciousness. It is one of those metatheoretical assumptions of historical theory that is decisively repudiated by historical realism and naturalism. . . .

All of the more abstract strata of the mind exhibit threshold phenomena. Consider aesthetic forms. Many of them, perhaps even all of them, can acquire this status only if they have reached certain minimal dimensions. Objects smaller than this may have reached the threshold of perception or observation, but they have not crossed the threshold of the aesthetic. Many facts that are indifferent or amusing on a small scale cross the threshold of tragic phenomena as soon as they appear in larger or fuller dimensions and are revealed as types of a more universal human experience. The consciousness of justice or legality produces its characteristic reactions only if processes have attained a certain breadth or scope. The theft of a pin is, of course, still theft. It lies within the threshold of this concept, but it lies beyond the point or threshold at which the practical, legal prosecution of a thief would begin. The same point holds invariably. Consider the elements which produce reactions on a given plane of feeling. They have this effect only if they have attained certain minimum dimensions. . . .

Suppose we read in the diary of some otherwise unknown person of the eighteenth century that he has befriended one of his equally unknown contemporaries. Or suppose we find that he was filled with active sympathy for the French Revolution. From a logical or conceptual point of view, these are historical facts, but in the substantively important sense of the concept, they are not. This is because they have no historical interest. If they have no historical interest, this is not because they are lacking in human dignity or interest. Suppose we discovered that both of these facts were motivated by the most profound moral impulses and expressed emotions and a spiritual refinement of the highest order: it would not follow that they fall within the threshold of historical significance. The reason for this might possibly be the following. The number of the consequences of these facts that lies within our grasp or comprehension is simply of insufficient weight and importance . . . An event qualifies as history to the extent to which we can ascribe effect-sequences to it. These sequences are infinitely diverse and they intersect at innumerable points; ultimately, they form that compact mass which we call 'history.'

. . . There is a definitive difference between . . . the feeling or sense of historical significance . . . and all other kinds of value or significance. The strength or weakness with which this feeling is associated with a phenomenon is a function of the extent to which its consequences are interwoven into this complex of effect-sequences. The limits of this complex may be imprecise – in many relatively specialized provinces of history, they may even be indeterminate – but its core or center is identifiable in a completely unambiguous fashion. This plurality of identifiable effects does not *constitute* historical significance as an objective property which can be ascribed to the event itself, but insofar as it is the cause or source of a specific mental energy, it *produces* this property in us. It is like all other threshold effects. At a certain point, quantitative changes in the number of causal elements produce a qualitative change in their effects. This may be one reason we feel that persons and events of the recent past lack historical depth or perspective: they have not yet had the opportunity to generate extensive consequences. . . .

. . .

[*But in addition*] there are countless things that interest us not because their content has value, significance, or originality, but simply because they are *there*, because they *exist* and have the form of reality. However as a mere idea, no matter how clearly its content may be imagined, things of this sort would arouse no interest. In the foregoing we were concerned with things to which we always respond with the same feelings, even though they are purely imaginary and fall under the category of the mere idea. But there are many other things that immediately lose whatever significance and value they have as soon as we learn that they are 'not true.' In this context, reality might be compared to an elixir which flows through the mere contents of ideas. When it evaporates, they are left behind as uninteresting and insubstantial shells, all that remains of the identifiable or expressible logical content of such an idea. . . .

. . .

This existential interest, an interest in facticity that is independent of any metaphysical consideration, is the essential feature of all history. . . .

. . . This interest is essential to the historical interest but is not sufficient to constitute it. There is no sense in which everything that exists is historically important. . . .

. . .

In consequence, the threshold of historical consciousness can be grounded on a new basis. This threshold is located where the existential interest intersects with the interest in the significance of content, which has its own peculiar threshold. In the foregoing, I ventured the hypothesis that this threshold is determined by reference to the quantum – the number or weight – of the effects of a given event. Where these two criteria mesh – the existential interest and the interest in content – we find the specific interest in the facticity of certain distinctive sequences of events, persons, circumstances and states that provides the foundation for history. [*Simmel concludes the discussion by stressing, like the other thinkers considered in this chapter that the interest of the historian lies specifically in appreciation of the unique individuality of historical phenomena.*]

5.D.III   Marx's Historical Materialism[29]

. . . According to this theory, the properties of economic life and the structures and processes of group life, which are a function of the production and distribution of the

29   Ibid., pp. 185–91.

means of existence, determine the whole of historical life: both domestic and foreign policy, religion and art, law and technology. To what extent has this principle been applied to the facts of history with some plausibility? . . .

. . .

Consider . . . the problem of the *selection or choice* which historical materialism has made from the range of possible ultimate motives or causes of history. As regards its actual empirical appearance, human life presents a bewildering complexity of sequential series of interests. Like strands of different thread in a fabric, they are interwoven through consciousness, the relations of power, and the external phenomenon itself. Each interest, considered independent of all the others, is homogeneous and continuous, but only limited aspects of any given interest appear on the actual surface of life. The interest functions at a deeper level, beneath the aspects that intermittently appear on the surface. On the level of human life as it is actually experienced, no interest is independently identifiable. Religion and the economy, individual life and the constitution of the state, art and law, sciences and forms of marriage – all are inextricably interwoven. This is the source of what we call history. Its moments are continuous, and each moment is identifiable in all of the others. These moments exhibit the following variation. At different points in space and time and at different levels of consciousness, a given moment may acquire a dominant interest . . . Although there are only partial and specialized histories, but no history as such, there is, nevertheless, an 'idea'[30] of 'history in 'general' that transcends all these fragmentary histories. This idea provides a synthesis of the spatio-temporal interrelations of all these sequences. 'History as such' is a unified entity that we cannot grasp directly; however the idea of this entity prevents our construct of history from collapsing into incoherent splinters and fragments.

We owe to historical materialism a novel and partial realization and a cogent demonstration of this a priori, ideal entity. Historical materialism has made it plausible to suppose that the evolution of the economy and the development of ideal values which seem to be utterly unrelated, are intimately connected, at least at many points . . . In other words, the history of the economy is the symbol of history in general. Any approximation to this theoretical possibility may, of course, be very significant. However this possibility entails the following presupposition. The role of the ultimate explanans[31] of the totality of history may be ascribed with equal legitimacy to every historical moment. In this respect, the economy is no different from all the other sequences that make up history. Consider the history of forms of government or customs of social intercourse, intellectual cultivation or criminal law. There is complete continuity of relationship between each of these histories and every other history, even though this relationship may be indirect and more or less remote. Therefore each of these histories could function as the ultimate epistemic basis for complete or universal history. . . . Therefore this particular thesis of historical materialism seems to be a premature and dogmatic foreshortening of our historical perspective.

. . . Therefore the moment with which we terminate an historical explanation – the moment to which we ascribe the ultimate cause of all subsequent historical phe-

30   Simmel is using the word 'Idea' in the Kantian sense discussed earlier *supra*, p. 62. [RMB]
31   'Explanans' means 'that which explains.' [RMB]

nomena – is quite arbitrary. *Each* moment that bear upon a given historical sequence is obviously a condition for the development of ensuing sequences.

. . .

Suppose . . . we see history as an interwoven fabric in which qualitatively different kinds of event-sequences are interconnected. Given this picture of history, we must admit that historical materialism has achieved a hitherto unattained synthesis of the totality of historical data. In a reduction of extraordinary simplicity, the whole of history is tuned to a single key-note. But consider the claim that historical materialism provides a naturalistic reproduction of reality. This is a methodological error of the first class. It confuses the conceptual construct of the event – a product of our theoretical interests – with the immediacy of the actual, empirical occurrence of the event itself. It also confuses a principle that has an heuristic import, and should always be employed in an exploratory fashion, with a constitutive principle, an assumption from which the facts of history are derived . . . Therefore only one possible sense remains as the import of the thesis of historical materialism: events occur *as if* the economic motive governed human behaviour . . . It is only an heuristic principle from which facts of other categories can be *explained or derived*, facts which could also be explained or derived from other principles . . . The formation of the raw material of history by means of our *epistemic* requirements is most emphatically not a realistic reproduction of objects by the mind. On the contrary, the mind constitutes these items as the objects of a scientific investigation.

. . . For historical materialism, the economy, which is located in the most basic historical stratum, is the permanent and self-sufficient condition for all other developments. It is an undercurrent which does not alternate with the currents of other developments. It is the source from which they flow. In relation to other historical phenomena, the economy might be called the historical thing-in-itself. . . .

. . . [*But*] let us suppose that the development of morals and law, religion and art, etc. follow the curve of economic development without influencing economic changes in any essential way. In that case, I simply do not see how the transformations of economic life itself can be explained. We are told that the invention of firearms, the discovery of America, and the intellectual fertility that distinguished the close of the Middle Ages do not provide the cause of the transition from feudal and natural forms of economy to the economic forms of the modern era. On the contrary, the economic changes in question demand and produce these intellectual, technological, and territorial expansions. But why do human beings not remain permanently satisfied with a natural or feudal economy? At least originally, there was supposed to be an absolute correspondence between every form of production and its age, but 'the age' in which any form of production is located is defined exclusively by reference to the form of production itself. Therefore it is not at all clear how subsequent contradictions – between the forces of production and the forms of production – could develop from this initial state of correspondence. Facts of other categories are supposed to have no role in producing changes in the form of production. It follows that every stage of economic development must contain the forces responsible for its own transformation – a self-generating process. It takes place without cross-fertilization of any sort, a kind of parthenogenesis of the economy . . . The forms of production in a given epoch are said to have become 'outdated' or 'antiquated', new forces of production are said to have 'developed'; new societal forms are said to be in a state of 'evolution.' These expressions are only empty phrases, not much better than an explanation of these changes by reference to the 'force of time.' It is almost as if an initial quantity of vital energy were granted to every economic epoch, a quantity that gradually exhausts itself. But suppose that *reciprocal causal relationships* between all historical factors are excluded in principle. Then *what* can be responsible for the exhaustion of one form of production, the increasing tensions and contradictions, and the birth of new economic forms? It seems that this question can be answered only on the basis of an obscure metaphysics, a metaphysics in which the concept of the 'autonomous movement of the idea' still survives.

However it is not our purpose to engage in a fruitless polemic against historical materialism . . . Perhaps the rigorous internal consistency which is the hallmark of historical materialism only exhibits with a peculiar clarity the metaphysics implied in every other theory of history. It is impossible for us to gain a perspicuous view of the reciprocal causal relations of all historical factors; however this reciprocal causal nexus is the only genuinely unified entity in history. It follows that any coherent construct of the total historical process is possible only as a result of an artificial, one-sided partiality or bias. . . .

6.D.IV   Understanding Other Minds[32]

. . . Since the mind of the other person cannot be read like a book that lies open before me, is there not only one possible source of this material: namely, my own mind? . . .

. . . Certain observations may be adduced in support of this apparently necessary condition for historical interpretation. Experience seems to show that a person who has never loved or hated cannot understand the lover or the person filled with hatred. The sober pragmatist cannot understand the conduct of the idealistic dreamer . . . It follows that the historian who is a pedantic philistine and accustomed to the life of the petit bourgeois will not be able to understand the expression of the lives of Mirabeau or Napoleon, Goethe or Nietzsche – no matter how profuse and perspicuous these manifestations may be. . . .

Nevertheless, the conclusion that understanding rests upon an identity between the subject and the object would be premature . . . A certain degree of disparity or dissimilarity between the nature of the historian and the nature of historical persons makes understanding impossible. But . . . we are only justified in making the following claim. Given certain dimensions of psychic *difference* or *dissimilarity* in nature the understanding of the expressions and manifestations of the latter is obstructed. . . .

[*Against the hypothesis that*] we are obliged to *infer* the mental states of another person from the appearance of certain external symbols and signs . . . I shall only adduce a single empirical counterinstance. One of the observations which reveals the frame of mind of another person most forcefully and unambiguously is the look in his eye. But such an observation is not based on any analogy derived from self-observation. Suppose that I am not an actor and have not rehearsed the visual expressions of anger and affection, lassitude and ecstasy, terror and desire before a mirror. Then

32   From 'On the Nature of Historical Understanding'; in Simmel, 1980, pp. 99–107 and pp. 122–6.

have practically no opportunity to observe these expressions in my own case. Consider, therefore, the association between my own inner experience and my observation of its expression, the association on which the inference from the observed behavior of another person to the interpretation of his mental states is allegedly grounded. In this case, there can be no such association. This fact alone, it seems to me, proves conclusively that the relationship between my mental life and its observable expression cannot provide the key to the relationship between the observable behaviour of another person and his mental life.

But why is such a key necessary? Only because of the unfortunate split of the human being produced by the mind–body dichotomy. On this view, the body is identifiable by reference to a form of observation that is alleged to be purely physical, public, and concrete. The identification of the mind, on the other hand, requires a projection of my mental states into another person, a transposition mediated by the process of association discussed above. This act of projection is complex, even mystical ... I am convinced, contrary to this view, that we observe *the whole person*. The isolation of his corporeality is a product of subsequent abstraction. . . . This sort of perception of total existence may be obscure and fragmentary ... Nevertheless, it is the fundamental and uniform mode in which one person affects another. It is a total impression which cannot really be analyzed in a rational fashion. Although open to considerable revisions and corrections, it is the first piece of knowledge-and usually the decisive piece of knowledge – which we have concerning another human being.

. . .

The dubious consequences of [*the projection*] theory of interpretation have their origin in realism – the thesis according to which knowledge produces things 'as they really are.' According to this concept of knowledge, my own experience constitutes immediate reality. Only if the experience of the other person can be represented as identical to my own, so this naive theory would have us believe, can I be certain in identifying his mental processes on the basis of his observable behavior ... In opposition to this theory, I hold that the other person or the Thou – like the ego or self – is an ultimate, irreducible entity. The projection theory of knowledge is no more valid for the domain of the Thou than it is for the world of external objects. . . .

. . .

The category of the Thou has roughly the same crucial status in the world of praxis and history that the category of substance or causality occupies in the world of natural science. The category itself is incommensurable. The concept of the Thou does not have the same status as all the other objects of my ideas. I am obliged to ascribe a being-for-itself to the Thou. It is the same integrity that I experience exclusively in my own ego – the self, which must be distinguished from everything that is properly an object. Here is the explanation of the fact that we experience the other person, the Thou, both as the most alien and impenetrable creature imaginable, and also as the most intimate and familiar. On the one hand, the ensouled Thou is our only peer or counterpart in the universe ... On the other hand, the Thou also has an incomparable autonomy and sovereignty. It resists any decomposition or analysis into the subjective representation of the ego. It has that absoluteness of reality which the ego ascribes to itself.

The concept of the Thou or the other person and the concept of understanding express the same ultimate, irreducible phenomenon of the human mind. The Thou, as we might put it, is its substance, and understanding is its function . . . The Thou, or understanding, is the transcendental[33] presupposition of the fact that man is by nature a political animal . . . It only appears in the later or more advanced stages of our development. Most often, it lacks the precision of its content. Further, its appearance presupposes the satisfaction of extremely complex psychological conditions. However acts of consciousness that present themselves as primary also require the satisfaction of earlier, more primitive conditions. They require a period of development too. The issue here only concerns a difference of degree . . . The view that mental phenomena like the concepts of the Thou or understanding cannot be intrinsically simple and primary because they only appear imperfectly, in advanced states of our development, and only given the satisfaction of many different conditions . . . is completely mistaken. . . .

. . .

. . . The rhythm and the constant dynamic of life is the formal agent of understanding . . . It could be said that we see ourselves as examples of this super-individual form of animation. Within the perpetual interplay of events and fluctuations that transpire within us, we perceive, more or less certainly, an end or purpose that is at least formal a realization of predispositions, a blossoming of buds which lie within us – or, more accurately, which we are . . . [For instance] I examine the philosophical theories of the eighteenth century until the critical philosophy of Kant appears as its result. I observe Italian art, from the Byzantine rigidity and the manifold uncouthness of the trecento to the individualistic disorder of the quattrocento and its result, the harmonious and comprehensive unity of High Renaissance composition. In each of these cases, I feel my spirit – insofar as it experiences these fulfillments as its own – gradually expand. Its powers of perception are increasingly actualized. As my mind experiences these sequences of contents and traverses them, it is aware of itself as being not merely moved but rather endowed with a specific value: a process of development.

From this perspective, development may be an original and irreducible concept which is not accessible to further analysis. Nor is it dependent upon some pre-existing end o purpose. On the contrary it is only a rhythm or movement of mental life itself, a specific form of inner growth. . . .

. . .

. . . Understanding is an irreducible, primitive phenomenon in which a universal relationship between man and the world is expressed . . . This is because life is the ultimate authority of the spirit, its court of last resort. Therefore the form of life ultimately determines the forms in which life can be intelligible. Life can only be understood by life. . . .

. . . Mechanism cannot comprehend the unity and totality of life. On the mechanistic view, life can only be pieced together from its fragments. But those parts, from the standpoint of an organic conception, are only the products of an ex post facto analysis of the unity of life. Mechanism, therefore, cannot comprehend understanding as a primitive, irreducible phenomenon, a process that transpires between one whole person and another whole person. From the standpoint of mechanism, this process is only a derivative synthesis of separate factors.

For the same reasons, the mechanistic view cannot grasp what could be called the

33   For the Kantian meaning of this term, chapter 1, section 5. [RMB]

creative aspect of the process of understanding, the aspect which makes it possible for one person to produce the image of another mind within his own experience from alien and remote phenomena which he has not experienced ... [*According to*] the mechanistic conception ... historical interpretation is a mere copy or impression of the event 'as it actually happened.' But actually historical understanding is an activity of the subject, the historian. It is dependent upon the categories and forms which are employed to represent the object of interpretation ... The truth of an interpretation is a vital and functional relationship between the interpretation and its object. It is the result of an active process, not a mechanical reproduction of a photographic plate. ...

In these divergent interpretation of the process of understanding, the entire antithesis between a mechanistic and an organic or vitalistic perspective becomes clear. Like every intellectual controversy which is pursued to its ultimate source, the conclusions which we reach concerning this antithesis are dependent upon the most profound and comprehensive commitments of our world view.

6.E   Max Weber, 1864–1920

6.E.1   A Science of Real Individual Cultural Configurations[34]

The type of social science in which we are interested is an *empirical science* of concrete reality (*Wirklichkeitswissenschaft*). Our aim is the understanding of the characteristic uniqueness of the reality in which we move. We wish to understand on the one hand the relationships and the cultural significance of individual events in their contemporary manifestations and on the other the causes of their being historically *so* and not *otherwise*. Now, as soon as we attempt to reflect about the way in which life confronts us in immediate concrete situations, it presents an infinite multiplicity of successively and coexistently emerging and disappearing events, both 'within' and 'outside' ourselves ... All the analysis of infinite reality which the finite human mind can conduct rests on the tacit assumption that only a finite portion of this reality constitutes the object of scientific investigation, and that only it is 'important' in the sense of being 'worthy of being known.' But what are the criteria by which this segment is selected? It has often been thought that the decisive criterion in the cultural sciences, too, was in the last analysis, the regular recurrence of certain causal relationships. The 'laws' which we are able to perceive in the infinitely manifold stream of events must – according to this conception – contain the scientifically 'essential' aspect of reality ... Accordingly, even among the followers of the Historical School we continually find the attitude which declares that the ideal which all the sciences, including the cultural sciences, serve and towards which they should strive even in the remote future is a system of propositions from which reality can be 'deduced'. ...

... [*But*] As far back as we may go into the grey mist of the far-off past, the reality to which the laws apply always remains equally *individual*, equally *undeducible* from

34   From pp. 72–85 of ' "Objectivity" in Social Science and Social Policy' (1904), in Weber, 1949, pp. 49–112. A number of typographical errors have been corrected.

laws. A cosmic 'primeval state' which had no individual character or less individual character than the cosmic reality of the present would naturally be a meaningless notion . . .

The social-scientific interest has its point of departure, of course, in the *real*, i.e. concrete, individually-structured configuration of our cultural life in its universal relationships which are themselves no less individually-structured, and in its development out of other social cultural conditions, which themselves are obviously likewise individually structured. . . .

. . .

. . . We arrive at the decisive feature of the method of the cultural sciences. We have designated as 'cultural sciences' those disciplines which analyze the phenomena of life in terms of their cultural significance . . . The concept of culture is a *value-concept*. Empirical reality becomes 'culture' to us because and insofar as we relate it to value ideas. It includes those segments and only those segments of reality which have become significant to us because of this value-relevance. . . . We cannot discover, however, what is meaningful to us by means of a 'presuppositionless' investigation of empirical data. Rather perception of its meaningfulness to us is the presupposition of its becoming an *object* of investigation. Meaningfulness naturally does not conclude with laws as such, and the more general the law the less the coincidence. For the specific meaning which a phenomenon has for us is naturally *not* to be found in those relationships which it shares with many other phenomena.

The focus of attention on reality under the guidance of values lend it significance and the selection and ordering of the phenomena which are thus affected in the light of their cultural significance is entirely different from the analysis of reality in terms of laws and general concepts. Neither of these two types of the analysis of reality has any necessary logical relationship with the other. They coincide in individual instances but it would be most disastrous if their occasional coincidence caused us to think that they were not distinct in *principle* . . . And the decisive element in this is that only through the presupposition that a finite part alone of the infinite variety of phenomena is significant, does the knowledge of an individual phenomenon become logically meaningful . . . A chaos of 'existential judgments' about countless individual events would be the only result of a serious attempt to analyze reality 'without presuppositions.' . . . Order is brought into this chaos only on the condition that in every case only a part of concrete reality is interesting and *significant* to us, because only it is related to the *cultural values* with which we approach reality. Only certain sides of the infinitely complex concrete phenomenon, namely those to which we attribute a general, *cultural significance* – are therefore worthwhile knowing. They alone are objects of causal explanation. And even this causal explanation evinces the same character; an *exhaustive* causal investigation of any concrete phenomena in its full reality is not only practically impossible – it is simply nonsense. We select only those causes to which are to be imputed in the individual case, the 'essential' feature of an event. Where the *individuality* of phenomenon is concerned, the question of causality is not a question of *laws* but of concrete causal *relationships*; it is not a question of the subsumption of the event under some general rubric as a representative case but of its imputation as a consequence of some constellation. It is in brief a *question of imputation*. Wherever the causal explanation of a 'cultural phenomenon' – an 'historical individual' is under consideration, the knowledge of causal *laws* is not the end of the investigation but only a *means*. . . .

What is the consequence of all this?

Naturally, it does not imply that the knowledge of *universal* propositions, the construction of abstract concepts, the knowledge of regularities and the attempt to formulate '*laws*' have no scientific justification in the cultural sciences. Quite the contrary, f the causal knowledge of the historians consists of the imputation of concrete effects o concrete causes, a *valid* imputation of any individual effect without the application of '*nomological' knowledge* – i.e., the knowledge of recurrent causal sequences – would n general be impossible. Whether a single individual component of a relationship is, in a concrete case, to be assigned causal responsibility for an effect, the causal explanation of which is at issue, can in doubtful cases be determined only by estimating the effects which we *generally* expect from it and from the other components of the same complex which are relevant to the explanation. . . .

The conclusion which follows from the above is that an 'objective' analysis of cultural events, which proceeds according to the thesis that the ideal of science is the reduction of empirical reality of (sic)[35] 'laws,' is meaningless. It is not meaningless, as is often maintained, because cultural or psychic events for instance are 'objectively' less governed by laws. It is meaningless for a number of other reasons. Firstly, because the knowledge of social laws is not knowledge of social reality but is rather one of the various aids used by our minds for attaining this end; secondly, because knowledge of *cultural* events is inconceivable except on a basis of the *significance* which the concrete constellations of reality have for us in certain *individual* concrete situations. In *which* ense and in *which* situations this is the case is not revealed to us by any law; it is decided according to the *value-ideas* in the light of which we view 'culture' in each individual case. 'Culture' is a finite segment of the meaningless infinity of the world process, a segment on which human *beings* confer meaning and significance. . . . The transcendental[36] presupposition of every *cultural science* lies not in our finding a certain culture or any 'culture' in general to *be valuable* but rather in the fact that we are *cultural beings*, endowed with the capacity and the will to take a deliberate attitude towards the world and to lend it *significance* . . . When we speak here of the conditioning of cultural knowledge through *evaluative* ideas (*Wertideen*) (following the terminology of modern logic), it is done in the hope that we will not be subject to crude misunderstandings such as the opinion that cultural significance should be attributed only to *valuable* phenomena. Prostitution is a cultural phenomenon just as much as religion or money. . . .

All knowledge of cultural reality, as may be seen, is always knowledge from *particular points of view*. When we require from the historian and social research worker as an elementary presupposition that they distinguish the important from the trivial and that he should have the necessary 'point of view' for this distinction, we mean that they must understand how to relate the events of the real world consciously or unconsciously to universal 'cultural values' and to select out those relationships which are significant for us. If the notion that those standpoints can be derived from the 'facts themselves' continually recurs, it is due to the naive self-deception of the specialist

---

*   The correct preposition most surely be 'to'. [RMB]
*   Again the use of this Kantian term indicates that Weber takes for granted the Neo-Kantians' rejection of the possibility that any science could be a purely presuppositionless discovery of empirically given facts. [RMB]

who is unaware that it is due to the evaluative ideas with which he unconsciously approaches his subject matter, that he has selected from an absolute infinity a tiny portion with the study of which he *concerns* himself. . . .

. . .

Undoubtedly, all evaluative ideas are 'subjective.' Between the 'historical' interest in a family chronicle and that in the development of the greatest conceivable cultural phenomena which were and are common to a nation or to mankind over long epochs there exists an infinite gradation of 'significance' arranged into an order which differs for each of us. And they are, naturally, historically variable in accordance with the character of the culture and the ideas which rule men's minds. But it obviously does not follow from this that research in the cultural sciences can only have results which are 'subjective' in the sense that they are *valid* for one person and not for others. Only the degree to which they interest different persons varies. In other words, the choice of the object of investigation and the extent or depth to which this investigation attempts to penetrate into the infinite causal web, are determined by the evaluative ideas which dominate the investigator and his age. In the *method* of investigation, the guiding 'point of view' is of great importance for the *construction* of the conceptual scheme which will be used in the investigation. In the mode of their *use*, however, the investigator is obviously bound by the norms of our thought just as much here as elsewhere. For scientific truth is precisely what is *valid* for all who *seek* the truth.

However, there emerges from this the meaninglessness of the idea which prevails occasionally even among historians, namely, that the goal of the cultural sciences, however far it may be from realization, is to construct a closed system of concepts, in which reality is synthesized in some sort of *permanently* and *universally* valid classification and from which it can again be deduced. The stream of immeasurable events flows unendingly towards eternity. The cultural problems which move men form themselves ever anew and in different colors, and the boundaries of that area in the infinite stream of concrete events which acquires meaning and significance for us, i.e., which becomes an 'historical individual,' are constantly subject to change. The intellectual contexts from which it is viewed and scientifically analyzed shift. The points of departure of the cultural sciences remain changeable throughout the limitless future as long as a Chinese ossification of intellectual life does not render mankind incapable of setting new questions to the eternally inexhaustible flow of life. A systematic science of culture, even only in the sense of a definitive, objectively valid, systematic fixation of the problems which it should treat, would be senseless in itself. Such an attempt could only produce a collection of numerous, specifically particularized, heterogeneous and disparate viewpoints in the light of which reality becomes 'culture' through being significant in its unique character.

6.E.II   The Nature of Meaning[37]

(1) The 'meaning' to which we refer may be either (a) the meaning actually intended either by an individual agent on a particular historical occasion or by a number of

37   From 'The Nature of Social Action', in Weber 1978, pp. 7–9. From the original *Wirtschaft und Gesellschaft*, originally published 1922.

agents on an approximate average in a given set of cases, or (*b*) the meaning attributed to the agent or agents, as types, in a pure type constructed in the abstract. In neither case is the 'meaning' to be thought of as somehow objectively 'correct' or 'true' by some metaphysical criterion. This is the difference between the empirical sciences of action, such as sociology and history, and any kind of *a priori* discipline, such as jurisprudence, logic, ethics, or aesthetics whose aim is to extract from their subject-matter its 'correct' or 'valid' meaning.

(2) No sharp dividing line can be drawn between meaningful action and what we shall call for our present purposes 'purely reactive' behaviour: that is, behaviour with which the agent does not associate any subjectively intended meaning. An extremely important part of all behaviour which is relevant to sociology, especially purely traditional behaviour (see below), straddles this dividing line. In several types of psychophysical process, action which is meaningful and so understandable is not to be found at all; in others, the meaning can only be discovered by specialists. For instance, mystical experiences which cannot be adequately expressed in words are not fully understandable by those not attuned to them. On the other hand, it is not necessary, in order to be able to understand an action, that one should be able to perform a similar action oneself; 'It is not necessary to be Caesar in order to understand Caesar.' The ability totally to 're-live' an experience is important if one is to be certain that one has understood it, but is not absolutely necessary in order to interpret its meaning. In any piece of behaviour, those elements which can be understood are often intimately bound up with those elements which can not.

(3) The aim of all interpretation of meanings is, like that of science in general, to achieve certainty. This certainty in our understanding of action may take either a rational form (in which case it may be either logical or mathematical) or the form of empathetically re-living the experience in question (involving the emotions and artistic sensibility). Rational certainty is achieved above all in the case of an action in which the intended complex of meanings can be *intellectually* understood in its entirety and with complete clarity. Empathetic certainty is achieved when an action and the complex of feelings experienced by the agent is completely re-lived in the imagination. Rational intelligibility, which here implies the possibility of achieving an immediate and unambiguous intellectual grasp of meaning, is to be found in its highest degree in those complexes of meaning which are related to each other in the way in which mathematical or logical propositions are . . . The same is true when someone in his actions derives from 'empirical facts' which we recognize to be the case and from the ends which he has set himself the conclusions which (in our experience) clearly follow as to the kind of 'means' which he should adopt . . . We can, however, also achieve a degree of certainty which, although not as high, is quite adequate for the needs of explanation, in our understanding of those 'errors', including the confusion of one problem with another, to which we ourselves are especially liable or whose genesis we are able empathetically to re-live.

On the other hand, there are a number of ultimate 'goals' or 'values' towards which man's actions may, as a matter of empirical fact, be directed which we very often cannot understand with complete certainty, though in some cases we can grasp their meaning at an intellectual level. In such cases, however, the more radically these ultimate values diverge from our own, the more difficult it is for us to understand them by re-living them through an act of empathetic imagination. Indeed, depending on the

particular case, we may have to be content either with a merely intellectual understanding or, where even that proves to be unattainable, with a simple acceptance of
them as brute facts . . . Examples of this kind include attempts by those who are not
themselves sympathetic to them to understand many acts of extreme religious devotion or charity . . . The more we ourselves are susceptible to them, the more certainly
we can re-live such emotional states as anxiety, anger, ambition, envy, jealousy, love,
enthusiasm, pride, vengefulness, devotion, submissiveness, lust of all kinds, and the
reactions which result from them (irrational though they are from the point of view of
rationally purposive action). In every case, however, even when such emotions far
exceed anything of which we ourselves are capable, we can gain some understanding
of their meaning by empathy and we can intellectually allow for their influence on the
direction taken, by the action and the means used in performing it.

   When we adopt the kind of scientific procedure which involves the construction of
types, we can investigate and make fully comprehensible all those irrational, effectively
determined, patterns of meaning which influence action, by representing them as 'deviations' from a pure type of the action as it would be if it proceeded in a rationally
purposive way. For example, in explaining a panic on the stock exchange, it is first
convenient to decide how the individuals concerned would have acted if they had not
been influenced by irrational emotional impulses; then these irrational elements can be
brought in to the explanation as 'disturbances'. Similarly, when dealing with a political
or military enterprise, it is first convenient to decide how the action would have proceeded if all the circumstances and all the intentions of those involved had been known
and if the means adopted had been chosen in a fully rationally purposive way, on the
basis of empirical evidence which seems to us valid. Only then does it become possible
to give a causal explanation of the deviations from this course in terms of irrational
factors. . . .

6.E.III   Ideal Types[38]

We have in abstract economic theory an illustration of those synthetic constructs which
have been designated as '*ideas*' of historical phenomena. It offers us an ideal picture of
events on the commodity-market under conditions of a society organized on the principles of an exchange economy, free competition and rigorously rational conduct. This
conceptual pattern brings together certain relationships and events of historical life
into a complex, which is conceived as an internally consistent system. Substantively
this construct in itself is like a *utopia* which has been arrived at by the analytical accentuation of certain elements of reality. Its relationship to the empirical data consists
solely in the fact that where market-conditioned relationships of the type referred to
by the abstract construct are discovered or suspected to exist in reality to some extent
we can make the *characteristic* features of this relationship pragmatically *clear* and
understandable by reference to an *ideal-type*. This procedure can be indispensable for
heuristic as well as expository purposes. The ideal typical concept will help to develop
our skill in imputation in *research*: it *is* no 'hypothesis' but it offers guidance to the
construction of hypotheses. It is not a *description* of reality but it aims to give unam-

---

38   From 'Objectivity in Social Science and Social Policy', – Weber, 1949, pp. 89–103.

biguous means of expression to such a description . . . Quite the same logical principles . . . are used in constructing the idea of the medieval 'city economy' as a 'genetic'
concept. When we do this, we construct the concept 'city economy' not as an average
of the economic structures actually existing in all the cities observed but as an *ideal-
type*. An ideal type is formed by the one-sided *accentuation* of one or more points of
view and by the synthesis of a great many diffuse, discrete, more or less present and
occasionally absent *concrete individual* phenomena, which are arranged according to
those one-sidedly emphasized viewpoints into a unified *analytical* construct
(*Gedankenbild*). In its conceptual purity, this mental construct (*Gedankenbild*) cannot
be found empirically anywhere in reality. It is a *utopia*. Historical research faces the
task of determining in each individual case, the extent to which this ideal-construct
approximates to or diverges from reality, to what extent for example, the economic
structure of a certain city is to be classified as a 'city-economy.' When carefully applied,
those concepts are particularly useful in research and exposition. In very much the
same way one can work the 'idea' of 'handicraft' into a utopia by arranging certain
traits, actually found in an unclear, confused state in the industrial enterprises of the
most diverse epochs and countries, into a consistent ideal-construct by an accentuation of their essential tendencies . . . Furthermore, one can juxtapose alongside the
ideal typical 'handicraft' system the antithesis of a correspondingly ideal-typical capitalistic productive system, which has been abstracted out of certain features of modern
large scale industry. On the basis of this, one can delineate the utopia of a 'capitalistic'
culture, i.e., one in which the governing principle is the investment of private capital
. . It is possible, or rather, it must be accepted as certain that numerous, indeed a very
great many, utopias of this sort can be worked out, of which *none* is like another, and
none of which can be observed in empirical reality as an actually existing economic
system, but *each* of which however claims that it is a representation of the 'idea' of
capitalistic culture. *Each* of these can claim to be a representation of the 'idea' of
capitalistic culture to the extent that it has really taken certain traits, meaningful in
their essential features, from the empirical reality of our culture and brought them
together into a unified ideal-construct . . . Inasmuch as the 'points of view' from which
they can become significant for us are very diverse, the most varied criteria can be
applied to the selection of the traits which are to enter into the construction of an
ideal-typical view of a particular culture.

. .

    Whoever accepts the proposition that the knowledge of historical reality can or should
be a 'presuppositionless' copy of 'objective' facts, will deny the value of the ideal-type
. . The construction of abstract ideal-types recommends itself not as an end but as a
means. Every conscientious examination of the conceptual elements of historical exposition shows however that the historian as soon as he attempts to go beyond the bare
establishment of concrete relationships and to determine the *cultural* significance of
even the simplest individual event in order to 'characterize' it, *must* use concepts which
are precisely and unambiguously definable only in the form of ideal types. Or are
concepts such as 'individualism,' 'imperialism,' 'feudalism,' 'mercantilism,' 'conventional,' etc., and innumerable concepts of like character by means of which we seek
analytically and empathically to understand reality constructed substantively by the
'presuppositionless' *description* of some concrete phenomenon or through the abstract synthesis of those traits which are common to numerous concrete phenomena?

. . . It is a conceptual construct (*Gedankenbild*) which is neither historical reality nor even the 'true' reality . . . By means of this category, the adequacy of our imagination, oriented and disciplined by reality, is *judged*.

. . . If the historian (in the widest sense of the word) rejects an attempt to construct such ideal types as a 'theoretical construction,' i.e., as useless or dispensable for his concrete heuristic purposes, the inevitable consequence is either that he consciously or unconsciously uses other similar concepts without formulating them verbally and elaborating them logically or that he remains stuck in the realm of the vaguely 'felt.'

Nothing, however, is more dangerous than the *confusion* of theory and history stemming from naturalistic prejudices. This confusion expresses itself firstly in the belief that the 'true' content and the essence of historical reality is portrayed in such theoretical constructs or secondly, in the use of these constructs as a procrustean bed into which history is to be forced or thirdly, in the hypostatization of such 'ideas' as real 'forces' and as a 'true' reality which operates behind the passage of events and which works itself out in history.

This latter danger is especially great since we are also, indeed primarily, accustomed to understand by the 'ideas' of an epoch the thoughts or ideals which dominated the mass or at least an historically decisive number of the persons living in that epoch itself and who therefore significant as components of its culture . . . An ideal type of certain situations, which can be abstracted from certain characteristic social phenomena of an epoch, might – and this is indeed quite often the case – have also been present in the minds of the persons living in that epoch as an ideal to be striven for in practical life or as a maxim for the regulation of certain social relationships. . . .

. . . The causal relationship between the historically determinable idea which governs the conduct of men and those components of historical reality from which their corresponding ideal-*type* may be abstracted, can naturally take on a considerable number of different forms. The main point to be observed is that *in principle* they are both fundamentally different things. There is still another aspect: those 'ideas' which govern the behavior of the population of a certain epoch i.e., which are concretely influential in determining their conduct, can, if a somewhat complicated construct is involved, be formulated precisely only in the form of an ideal type, since empirically it exists in the minds of an indefinite and constantly changing mass of individuals and assumes in their minds the most multifarious nuances of form and content, clarity and meaning. Those elements of the spiritual life of the individuals living in a certain epoch of the Middle Ages, for example, which we may designate as the 'Christianity' of those individuals, would, if they could be completely portrayed, naturally constitute a chaos of infinitely differentiated and highly contradictory complexes of ideas and feelings. This is true despite the fact that the medieval church was certainly able to bring about unity of belief and conduct to a particularly high degree. If we raise the question as to what in this chaos was the 'Christianity' of the Middle Ages (which we must nonetheless use as a stable concept) and wherein lay those 'Christian' elements which we find in the institutions of the Middle Ages, we see that here too in every individual case, we are applying a purely analytical construct created by ourselves. It is a combination of articles of faith, norms from church law and custom, maxims of conduct, and countless concrete interrelationships which we have fused into an 'idea'. . . .

. . . All expositions for example of the 'essence' of Christianity are ideal types enjoying only a necessarily very relative and problematic validity when they are intended be regarded as the historical portrayal of empirically existing facts. On the other hand, such presentations are of great value for research and of high systematic value for expository purposes when they are used as conceptual inttsruments for *comparison* with and the *measurement* of reality. They are indispensable for this purpose.

There is still another even more complicated significance implicit in such ideal-typical presentations. They regularly seek to be, or are unconsciously, ideal-types not only in the *logical* sense but also in the *practical* sense, i.e., they are *model types* which – in our illustration – contain what, from the point of view of the expositor, *should* be and what to him is 'essential' in Christianity *because it is enduringly valuable*. If this is consciously or – as it is more frequently – unconsciously the case, they contain ideals to which the expositor *evaluatively* relates Christianity. These ideals are tasks and ends towards which he orients his 'idea' of Christianity and which naturally can and indeed, doubtless always will differ greatly from the values which other persons, for instance, the early Christians, connected with Christianity . . . Here it is no longer a matter of the purely theoretical procedure of treating empirical reality with respect to values but of *value-judgments* which are integrated into the concept of '*Christianity*.' Because the ideal type claims empirical validity here, it penetrates into the realm of the evaluative *interpretation* of Christianity. The sphere of empirical science has been left behind and we are confronted with a profession of faith, not an ideal-typical construct. As fundamental as this distinction is in principle, the confusion of these two basically different meanings of the term 'idea' appears with extraordinary frequency in historical writings . . . The modern relativistically educated historian . . . on the one hand seeks to 'understand' the epoch of which he speaks 'in its own terms,' and on the other still seeks to 'judge' it, feels the need to derive the standards for his judgment from the subject-matter itself, i.e., to allow the 'idea' in the sense of the *ideal* to emerge from, the 'idea' in the sense of the 'ideal-type.' The esthetic satisfaction produced by such a procedure constantly tempts him to disregard the line where these two ideal types diverge – an error which on the one hand hampers the value-judgment and on the other, strives to free itself from the responsibility for its own judgment. In contrast with this the *elementary duty of scientific self-control* and the only way to avoid serious and foolish blunders requires a sharp, precise distinction between the logically *comparative* analysis of reality by ideal-*types* in the logical sense and the *value-judgment* of reality on *the basis of ideals*. An 'ideal-type' in our sense, to repeat once more, has no connection at all with *value-judgments*, and it has nothing to do any type of perfection other than a purely *logical* one. . . .

. . .

We have intentionally avoided a demonstration with respect to that ideal-typical construct which is the most important one from our point of view; namely, the Marxian theory. This was done in order not to complicate the exposition any further . . . We will only point out here that naturally all specifically Marxian 'laws' and developmental constructs – insofar as they are theoretically sound – are ideal types. The eminent, indeed unique, *heuristic* significance of these ideal types when they are used for the assessment of reality is known to everyone who has ever employed Marxian concepts and hypotheses. Similarly, their perniciousness, as soon as they are thought of as empirically valid or as real (i.e. truly metaphysical) 'effective forces,' 'tendencies,' etc. is likewise known to those who have used them.

6.E.IV Objective Possibility: (Counterfactuals)[39]

The judgment that, if a particular historical fact were thought of as absent from a set of historical conditions, or as present in a modified form, this would have caused historical events to proceed in ways which were different in certain definite, historically important respects . . . seems to be of considerable value in determining the 'historical significance' of that fact . . . We shall attempt to get a little clearer on this question.
. . .

The theory of 'objective possibility', as it is called, to which I am referring here, is based on the work of the distinguished physiologist von Kries . . .

. . . When it is said that history has causally to understand the concrete reality of an 'event' in its individuality, that does not of course mean, as we have seen already, that it must 'reproduce' the event, leaving nothing out, in the totality of its individual qualities and causally explain the event in that form: such an undertaking would be not only practically impossible, but absurd in principle. Rather, history has to do exclusively with the causal explanation of those 'elements' and 'aspects' of the event in question which are, from certain points of view, of 'general significance' and on that account of historical interest. In just the same way, the judge in his deliberations concerns himself, not with the total individual course of the events, but with those elements which are essential if the events are to be subsumed under norms. He is not interested in the infinity of 'absolutely' trivial details; nor, leaving that aside, is he interested in everything which might be of interest for other approaches . . . For him all that is relevant is whether the causal chain linking thrust to death was of such a kind and whether the subjective attitude of the agent and his relationship to his act was such that a particular norm of criminal law became applicable. The historian, on the other hand, in dealing with, for example, the death of Caesar, is interested neither in the criminological nor in the medical problems which the 'case' might have presented [*etc.*]; . . . Rather, he is concerned primarily simply with the circumstance that the death occurred precisely at that time, in a concrete political situation, and he discusses the connected question whether this circumstance has had any definite 'consequence of any importance for the course of 'world history'.
. . .

The real question which we have to ask, however, is this: through what logical operations do we arrive at, and demonstratively support, the insight that such a causal relationship exists between these 'essential' constituents of the effect and certain constituents selected from the infinity of determining factors? . . . The attribution of cause takes the form of a thought process which encompasses a series of acts of abstraction . . . Let us take an example from Eduard Meyer's own practice. No one has expounded as formatively and clearly as he has the significance, in terms of world history, of the Persian Wars for the development of Western civilisation. But how does he do this from the logical point of view? Essentially, he develops the following argument. There were two 'possibilities': on the one hand, there was the further development of

39   From 'Critical Studies in the Logic of the Cultural Sciences' (1905), as translated in Web 1978, pp. 113–21. The term 'counterfactual' is now standard in English-speaking philosophy for what Weber terms 'objective possibility'. [RMB]

theocratic religious culture whose origins lay in the mysteries and oracles, under the aegis of the Persian protectorate, which as far as possible always used the national religion, as in the case of the Jews, as an instrument of domination; on the other, there was the victory of the free culture of Greece, with its this-worldly concerns, which has given us those cultural values by which we still live today. Between these two possibilities the 'decision' was made by a skirmish of the miniscule proportions of the so-called 'battle' of Marathon, which in turn was the indispensable 'precondition' of the growth of the Athenian fleet and so of the further course of the struggle for freedom, the preservation of the independence of Greek civilisation, the positive stimulus to the beginnings of specifically Western historiography and the perfection of the drama and of all that unique cultural life which ran its course on this stage of world history, tiny as it was in purely quantitative terms.

Moreover, the fact that that battle 'decided' between those 'possibilities', or had a very important bearing on that decision, is obviously the one and only reason why our historical interest (since we are not Athenians) is in general engaged by it. Without some evaluation of those 'possibilities' and of the irreplaceable cultural values which, to our retrospective gaze, 'hung' on that decision, it would be impossible to determine its 'significance' and to see any reason in fact why it should not equate it with a scuffle between two Kaffir or Indian tribes . . .

But what, then, does it mean to speak of several 'possibilities' between which these battles are supposed to have 'decided'? First of all, it means all events the formation of (let us say it calmly) imaginary models by means of the elimination of one or several of the constituents of the 'concrete situation' which were actually present in reality and by means of the construction in thought of an event altered in respect of one or a number of 'conditions'. The very first step towards an historical judgment is thus (and this is the point to be emphasised here) a process of abstraction, which proceeds by means of analysis and isolation in thought of the constituents of what is immediately given, seen as a complex of possible causal relationships, and which should result in a synthesis of the 'real' causal connexions. Already, therefore, this first step transforms the given 'actuality' into an intellectual construct, so as to make it into an historical 'fact': following Goethe, we may say that 'fact' involves theory.

. . .

When . . . Eduard Meyer judges that a theocratic religious development in Greece at the time of the Battle of Marathon was 'possible' or, given certain eventualities, 'probable', this implies the proposition that certain elements of what was historically given were objectively present (in other words, could be determined by objectively valid methods), and that these were such that, if we think away the Battle of Marathon (and, of course, a considerable number of other constituents of the actual course of events) or think of it as having happened differently, they were, to adapt an expression first used in criminal law, 'capable' of causing such a development in accordance with general empirical rules. The 'knowledge' on which such a judgment relies in order to prove the 'significance' of the Battle of Marathon is, in accordance with all that has been said so far, on the one hand knowledge of certain 'facts' belonging to the 'historical situation', which can be demonstrated from the sources ('ontological' knowledge), and on the other hand, as we have already seen, knowledge of certain familiar empirical rules, especially concerning the way in which men tend to react to given situations ('nomological' knowledge) . . . At all events, it is established that, to prove his crucial thesis about the 'significance' of the Battle of Marathon, Meyer had, in case of dispute, to analyse that 'situation' into its 'constituents' to such a point that our 'imagination' could apply to this 'ontological' knowledge our empirical 'nomological' knowledge, derived from our own practical experience of life and our knowledge of the behaviour of others. Then we could make a positive judgment to the effect that the joint working of those facts 'could' – in the circumstances thought of as altered in a certain way – have caused the effect claimed to be 'objectively possible'; but that means simply that if we were to 'think' of it as having actually happened, we should recognise the facts so altered in our minds as 'sufficient causes'.

In the interests of avoiding ambiguity, this simple matter has been formulated in a necessarily somewhat laborious way; but this formulation shows not only that the establishment of causal connexions in history involves abstraction in its twin senses of isolation and generalisation, but also that the simplest historical judgment about the historical 'significance' of a 'concrete fact' is far from being a mere matter of registering what is 'given'. Rather, not only does it represent a categorially formed intellectual construct, but also its content can only be validated if we bring to the 'given' reality the whole store of our empirical 'nomological' knowledge.

6.E.V   History and Truth[40]

The attempts to determine the 'real' and the 'true' meaning of historical concepts always reappear and never succeed in reaching their goal . . . None of those systems of ideas, which are absolutely indispensable in the understanding of those segments of reality which are meaningful at a particular moment, can exhaust its infinite richness. They are all attempts, on the basis of the present state of our knowledge and the available conceptual patterns, to bring order into the chaos of those facts which we have drawn into the field circumscribed by our *interest*. The intellectual apparatus which the past has developed through the analysis, or more truthfully, the analytical rearrangement of the immediately given reality, and through the latter's integration by concepts which correspond to the state of its knowledge and the focus of its interest, is in constant tension with the new knowledge which we can and *desire* to wrest from reality. The progress of cultural science occurs through this conflict. Its result is the perpetual reconstruction of those concepts through which we seek to comprehend reality. The history of the social sciences is and remains a continuous process passing from the attempt to order reality analytically through the construction of concepts – the dissolution of the analytical constructs so constructed through the expansion and shift of the scientific horizon – and the reformulation anew of concepts on the foundations thus transformed . . . This process shows that in the cultural sciences concept construction depends on the setting of the problem, and the latter varies with the content of culture itself. The relationship between concept and reality in the cultural sciences involves the transitoriness of all such syntheses. . . .

. . .

. . . The *objective* validity of all empirical knowledge rests exclusively on the ordering of the given reality according to categories which are *subjective* in a specific sense,

40   From 'Objectivity' in Social Science and Social Policy', Weber, 1949, pp. 104–12.

namely, in that they present the *presuppositions* of our knowledge and are based on the presupposition of the *value* of those *truths* which empirical knowledge alone is able to give us. The means available to our science offer nothing to those persons to whom this truth is of no value. It should be remembered that the belief in the value of scientific truth is the product of certain cultures and is not a product of man's original nature . . . In the empirical social sciences, as we have seen, the possibility of meaningful knowledge of what is essential for us in the infinite richness of events is bound up with the unremitting application of viewpoints of a specifically particularized character, which, in the last analysis, are oriented on the basis of evaluative ideas. These evaluative ideas are for their part empirically discoverable and analyzable as elements of meaningful human conduct, but their validity can *not* be deduced from empirical data as such. The 'objectivity' of the social sciences depends rather on the fact that the empirical data are always related to those evaluative ideas which alone make them worth knowing and the significance of the empirical data is derived from these evaluative ideas. But these data can never become the foundation for the empirically impossible proof of the validity of the evaluative ideas. The belief which we all have in some form or other, in the metaempirical validity of ultimate and final values, in which the meaning of our existence is rooted, is not incompatible with the incessant changefulness of the concrete viewpoints, from which empirical reality gets its significance. Both these views are, on the contrary, in harmony with one another. Life with its irrational reality and its store of possible meanings is inexhaustible. The *concrete* form in which value-relevance occurs remains perpetually in flux . . .

Now all this should not be misunderstood to mean that the proper task of the social sciences should be the continual chase for new viewpoints and new analytical constructs. . . .

There are, to use the words of F. Th. Vischer, 'subject matter specialists' and 'interpretative specialists.' The fact-greedy gullet of the former can be filled only with legal documents, statistical worksheets and questionnaires, but he is insensitive to the refinement of a new idea. The gourmandise of the latter dulls his taste for facts by ever new intellectual subtleties. . . .

All research in the cultural sciences in an age of specialization, once it is oriented towards a given subject matter through particular settings of problems and has established its methodological principles, will consider the analysis of the data as an end in itself. It will discontinue assessing the value of the individual facts in terms of their relationships to ultimate value-ideas. Indeed, it will lose its awareness of its ultimate rootedness in the value-ideas in general. And it is well that should be so. But there comes a moment when the atmosphere changes. The significance of the unreflectively utilized viewpoints becomes uncertain and the road is lost in the twilight. The light of the great cultural problems moves on. Then science too prepares to change its standpoint and its analytical apparatus and to view the streams of events from the heights of thought. It follows those stars which alone are able to give meaning and direction to its labors:

> The newborn impulse fires my mind,
> I hasten on, his beams eternal drinking,
> The Day before me and the Night behind,
> Above me Heaven unfurled, the floor of waves beneath me.
> > Goethe's *Faust*, Act 1, Scene II (translated by Bayard-Taylor)

7 Hermeneutics

Robert M. Burns

Introduction

We have seen how Schleiermacher developed the modern discipline of 'hermeneutics' (3.C.I and 3.C.II), and Dilthey made it the central concept of his later philosophy of history (6.A.IV–VIII), after he had abandoned his earlier dream of establishing historical science on the basis of a purely 'descriptive psychology'. Even when the term 'hermeneutics' was not explicitly used, the notion of all historical knowledge as essentially interpretive activity in which specific facts become intelligible only when understood as parts within a wider whole, which, however, paradoxically can be understood only through its parts, was recognized not only by historicists such as Humboldt, Ranke and Simmel, but even Comte (4.A.V). These thinkers were also alert to the fact that even the historian's own changing efforts at understanding were themselves part of the wider, dynamic historical whole which he was seeking to understand (e.g., Dilthey see p. 164). One eminent philosopher in early twentieth-century Germany, namely Edmund Husserl, fought against Dilthey (Husserl, 1965, pp. 122–47) to vindicate the notion that human beings could achieve an 'absolute', non-relative, transhistorical standpoint. Nevertheless, many of those considerably influenced by him moved over to the hermeneutical camp. This chapter therefore begins with a consideration of Husserl's account of the nature of historical consciousness from his own standpoint. I then surveys three thinkers, each of whom was permanently influenced by Husserl to some degree but who embraced hermeneutics, and sought to show in different ways that a radical acceptance of the historically relative nature of human consciousness need not lead to despair concerning the possibility of knowledge.

Edmund Husserl* is regarded by some as the most influential philosopher of the twentieth century (Bernet et al., 1993, p. xv) yet his philosophy is not very well known in the English-speaking world. A knowledge of Husserl is certainly important if one is to understand the development of the thinking of Heidegger, Gadamer and Ricoeur all of whom react against Husserl.

Heidegger, Gadamer and Ricoeur in various ways believed that human existence must always be *interpreted*, and that this interpretation will always be conditioned by our cultural and historical perspectives. By contrast Husserl tried to show that despite the contingencies of history and culture, it is possible to avoid the need for interpretation by adopting the correct 'transcendental' attitude to the world. Under these con-

---

* The introductory text on Edmund Husserl is by Hugh Rayment-Pickard.

ditions interpretation is not required because the meaning of things would show itself to us without ambiguity.[1]

Although there is a basic difference here, Paul Ricoeur urges us to note a fundamental link between Husserl's philosophy and the hermeneutic tradition: 'Beyond the simple opposition there exists, between phenomenology and hermeneutics, a mutual belonging . . . On the one hand . . . *phenomenology remains the unsurpassable presupposition of hermeneutics*. On the other hand, phenomenology cannot constitute itself without a *hermeneutical presupposition* (Ricoeur, 1981, p. 101). It is for this reason that Paul Ricoeur can credit Husserl with a twofold 'contribution' to hermeneutics (Ricoeur, 1974, pp. 8–10): First, Husserl raised the question of the interpretation of existence by seeking to describe the relationship that the existing subject has to the world. It is this relationship that Heidegger investigated in a more radical way through his analysis of human existence as 'being-in-the-world'. Secondly, the later Husserl devised the concept of 'lifeworld' as a way of describing the world *before* we make any interpretation of it, the world prior to 'every predicating, theorizing activity' (Husserl, 1977, p. 59). This is an essential concept for hermeneutics. If there is no pre-interpreted world, then this raises the problem of what exactly is being interpreted when interpretation takes place. Furthermore, hermeneutics needs the idea of a common lifeworld if it is to explain 'intersubjectivity', in other words how our various perspectives connect up (Husserl, 1970, p. 128).

In Husserl's estimation twentieth-century philosophy faced two main threats: On the one hand was naïve empiricism, which tried to reduce the world to facts without bothering to offer a theory of knowledge to explain how facts are possible. On the other hand was relativism, which had given up hope of ever finding certain knowledge. In the development of his own thinking, Husserl looked back to Descartes, Hume and Kant – all of whom believed in the possibility of absolute knowledge.

Husserl's alternative was a 'new' kind of philosophy called 'phenomenology', a form of thinking based upon Descartes' insight, three hundred years earlier, that philosophy must begin with the certainty of individual consciousness. One's consciousness must be certain, Husserl argued, since *consciously* to deny one's own consciousness would be what philosophers call 'a performative contradiction'. Phenomenology (from the Greek verb *phaino* meaning 'to appear') aimed to strengthen our consciousness of reality by suspending or 'bracketing' our prejudices and misconceptions about the world. From the perspective of a purified consciousness, the meaning of things in the world would become 'self-evident'. The significant advance that Husserl made on Descartes was his characterization of all consciousness as 'intentional', by which he meant that there is no such thing as 'empty' consciousness because consciousness is always consciousness *of* something.

It is possible to make the mistake of thinking that philosophy of history was not one

Yet for all the difference, Heidegger, Gadamer and Ricoeur stand in a tradition which is broadly phenomenological. This is why the early Heidegger says that he is trying to bring phenomenology back to its 'ownmost and purest possibility' (Heidegger, 1992, p. 135). See also Heidegger, 1962, p. 49–64). Gadamer says that his *Truth and Method* is 'phenomenological in its method' (Gadamer, 1979, p. xxiv) and that one of his objectives was to measure up to the 'conscientiousness of phenomenological description which Husserl has made a duty for us all' (Gadamer, 1979, p. xv). Ricoeur argues that phenomenology is indispensible to any understanding of twentieth-century hermeneutics (Ricoeur, 1981, pp. 101–28).

of Husserl's concerns. This is because Husserl understood the question of history essentially to be one of *time*, and our *consciousness* of time. The problem of time is not, for Husserl, one among others, but the fundamental issue in the constitution of consciousness itself. Husserl's reflections on this subject are a central theme of his writing from *The Philosophy of Internal Time Consciousness* [1905] to *The Crisis of the European Sciences* [1936].

In the 1930s Husserl was forced into a more direct engagement with history per se, when Heidegger's writings started to attract widespread attention. Heidegger's *Being and Time* [1927] had brought to the fore the question of history not only in relation to individual human existence but also in relation to the development of Western culture. Husserl's response in *The Crisis of the European Sciences* was to argue: (a) that culture develops historically as the expansion of shared human knowledge; and (b) that shared human knowledge requires the existence of a common human consciousness. The structure of this consciousness is what Husserl (7.A.I) refers to as 'the historical *a priori*'. In other words, although the contents of consciousness is continually changing, the condition of possibility of conscious experience remains the same through time and space: consciousness – whenever or wherever it happens – must always take place in the present moment. Although the present moment is always on the move, it remains *structurally* consistent as a 'flowing vital horizon' of conscious awareness. Husserl described this horizon of perception as the common 'lifeworld' [*Lebenswelt*] within which the various contingent 'worlds' of culture and knowledge take place. In order to demonstrate the coherence of knowledge in the lifeworld, Husserl takes geometric knowledge (a rather well-worn illustration), arguing that the perception of a triangle must be the same for all people at all times. But he extends this argument to include historical knowledge as well: 'Every establishment of an historical fact which lays claim to unconditioned objectivity . . . presupposes this invariant or absolute a priori' (Husserl, 1970, p. 377). Husserl saw this as an antidote *both* to the sceptical historicist tendency to describe all historical knowledge as relative, *and* to the naive empiricist tendency to talk about 'facts' without ever asking how facts are made possible. Thus Husserl tried to square the circle of 'relative' and 'absolute' knowledge by offering two complementary arguments: first, that absolute knowledge has a necessarily relative grounding in subjective human perspectives; and secondly, that our relative perspectives have an absolute structure: the flowing horizon of conscious awareness.

Husserl's philosophy of history faces many objections, in particular the criticism that phenomenology ends up in solipsism, with individual human minds cut off both from other persons and historical change. Yet critics must themselves contend with Husserl's central argument: that all philosophy – philosophy of history included – always presupposes individual human consciousness.

Martin Heidegger (1889–1976) was one of the most original and influential, but also most controversial philosophers of the twentieth century. Of pious Catholic country town origins he first studied scholastic philosophy while training for the priesthood but abandoned this aim in 1909, studying Catholic philosophy and theology at Freiburg University, dropping theology in 1912, and gradually losing his faith. His *Habilitationschrift* (roughly, second doctoral thesis) on Duns Scotus embraced the *haecceitas* doctrine that 'what really exists is an individual something. . . . Everything that really exists is a "this-now-here"' (Safranski, 1998, p. 66) and was submitted to Rickert, who however soon left Freiburg for Heidelberg, and was succeeded by Husserl.

Heidegger, who had earlier been attracted to Husserl's philosophy but remained sceptical of its claims to 'transcendentality',[2] established himself as Husserl's favourite collaborator.

Husserl made impressive promises[3] concerning his projected science of 'phenomenology'; it would be a 'science founded in itself, and standing absolutely on its own basis . . . the one science that stands absolutely on its own ground'. It would do this by 'taking possession of the absolute ground of pre-conceptual experience', and then 'create original concepts, adequately adjusted to this ground' by an 'absolutely transparent method' devoid of 'unclear, problematic concepts' and 'paradoxes' (Husserl, 1931, p. 20). It would 'include all sciences and all forms of knowledge' in its scope, providing 'the definitive criticism of every fundamentally distinct science' and deciding on all questions of their 'meaning and legitimacy', in this way fulfilling 'the secret longing of the whole philosophy of modern times' (p. 166).

It would accomplish all this by developing a 'scientific essential knowledge of . . . *consciousness in general*' (p. 102), its aim being to 'describe and determine with *rigorous* conceptual precision the generic essence of perception in general . . . of memory, empathy, will, and so forth' (p. 192). To achieve this the phenomenologist had to 'bracket' or 'disconnect' himself from the 'natural standpoint', which '*completely bars me from using any judgment that concerns spatio-temporal existence (Dasein)*' (p. 100). This 'self-suspending of the phenomenologist', in which he mentally detaches himself from his own 'empirical ego', 'nullifies the world' in a 'phenomenological reduction' or 'transcendental transposition', and assumes the role of the 'transcendental ego' or 'pure consciousness' (pp. 11, 136), opens up a field of pure essential truths, i.e., 'transcendental experience'. These bold claims all turn on an elaboration of the distinction already essentially encountered in Rickert (6.C.IV) between non-real or 'irreal' meanings and psychological 'facts', for phenomenology '*will be established not as a science of facts, but as a science of essential Being . . .* [with] *absolutely no facts*' (p. 40). It is this which Husserl thinks distinguishes his position from the otherwise comparable 'psychological' (i.e., merely factual or 'real') phenomenalism of Hume or Dilthey, providing it with the unassailable certainty which is beyond that of mere 'facts'. By 'essences' he means the general structural forms exemplified in any factual psychical states. One such 'essential' truth is supposedly that there is no non-temporal consciousness, i.e., 'Temporality' . . . is a *necessary form binding experiences with experiences*. Every real experience . . . is necessarily one that endures' (p. 217). Despite this emphasis on time, Husserl is concerned to reject the 'historicist' relativism he considered that he found in Dilthey according to which 'the ideas of truth, theory, and science' would lose their absolute validity' (Husserl, 1965, p. 125).

One can readily understand why so many students, not only in Germany but France, Poland and elsewhere, should have been attracted by phenomenology's promise of making a radical fresh start in philosophy and achieving definitive solutions to its hitherto apparently irresolvable disputes. Heidegger had been one such, but the core of his

---

[2]   As he acknowledges with coy understatement in Heidegger, 1972, pp. 74–82. For the meaning of the term 'transcendental', see p. 27.

[3]   In the Preface to the English edition (1931) to his *Ideas* which had been published in German in 1913 he compares himself to Moses: he 'sees the infinite open country of the true philosophy, the promised land" on which he himself will never set foot', acknowledging that 'this confidence may make a smile' (Husserl, 1962, p. 21).

dissent from Husserl was the rejection of the idea of a 'pure' transcendental ego, which he saw, under Nietzsche's influence, as a relic of the 'dead' God which modern philosophy must discard. Reading Dilthey convinced him that human consciousness was always located, and essentially temporal, striving to turn itself into a meaningful 'happening' (*Geschehen*; he stresses in *Being and Time* the etymological relationship with *Geschichte 'History'*, Heidegger, 1962, p. 41), and that the analysis of *this* non-transcendental, radically temporal and historically relative consciousness must be philosophy's central task. Reading Kierkegaard, newly fashionable in Germany, also reinforced his conviction that the attempt to divorce thinking from existence (5.B.I, II, IV) was a self-defeating absurdity.

Heidegger owed much to Husserl: it was with his support that Heidegger gained in 1923 his first professorial appointment at Marburg University, where he consolidated his reputation as the 'secret king of philosophy' because of his charismatic lecturing style. Then in 1927 *Being and Time* was published in the phenomenological periodical which Husserl edited, and finally in 1928 he was appointed Husserl's successor at Freiburg with Husserl's vigorous support. However, when Husserl came to read *Being and Time* he experienced 'one of the bitterest blows of my life'; he felt that only his own 'blind infatuation' for Heidegger had prevented his recognition that Heidegger was 'embarked on the development of a systematic philosophy of the kind that I have always throughout it my life's work to render permanently impossible' (Ott, 1993, p. 181). Heidegger had been less than candid to Husserl: in 1923 he had written to Karl Jaspers: 'Husserl has completely lost his marbles . . . uttering banalities to make one cringe . . . obsessed with his mission as the "founder of phenomenology". Nobody knows what that is' (p. 182).[4]

The aim of *Being and Time* was to provide an 'existential analytic' of *Dasein* (therebeing, Existence: a replacement for the term 'human being' in order to avoid the latter's misleading associations, but also implicitly rejecting Husserl's claim to transcend '*Dasein*'). The term 'phenomenological' (Heidegger, 1962, pp. 38–9)[5] is retained, but emptied of its Husserlian meaning since the notion of pure, presuppositionless description is excluded; the analytic can therefore only be a 'hermeneutic' (p. 62) which, like all interpretations, is never a 'presuppositionless apprehending', and 'must be 'founded essentially upon fore-having, fore-sight, and fore-conception', which Dasein will have 'grown up both into and in a [*historical*] traditional way' (p. 41). It

4   After the estrangement, Husserl's publications reasserted very strongly his original positions, (e.g. the *Cartesian Meditations* of 1929), but he also came to try to take more serious account of an essentially historical *Lebenswelt* or life-world in apparent response to *Being and Time*. 7.A.1 is an instance of this. But Husserl does not abandon the notion of a 'transcendental ego' which would discover truths of absolute universal validity ; in fact in many ways the emphasis becomes starker: ' I cannot follow . . . the opinion of those who want to see an "overcoming" of the foundation of the transcendental ego in this latest work of Husserl . . . His old battle for philosophy as rigorous science which had led him earlier to a sharp demarcation against historicism (1911) appears now, as the end of his life, in a new phase. . . . The *Crisis* attempts to give an implicit answer to *Being and Time* (Gadamer, 1976, pp. 158, 161). The 'historical a priori' is in effect developed from his long expressed view that consciousness is essentially temporal.

5   As Gadamer delicately expresses it, *Being and Time* 'preserved the external form of an affiliation with the transcendental phenomenology' of Husserl. But 'it was not really basically a continuation and detailed extrapolation of a program of phenomenological research' (Gadamer, 1976, pp. 138, 140).

must be emphasized, however, that, in *Being and Time* Heidegger continues to share with Husserl the conviction that philosophy can achieve a definitive standpoint foundational for all the sciences. He claims to have articulated the final 'primordial' (p. 275) truth about Dasein as a 'whole' (p. 276), which, since all truth is Dasein-relative (see 1.II), must be foundational for the specific sciences since they 'are ways of Being in which Dasein comports itself towards entities which it need not be itself' (p. 30). They are therefore entirely produced by Dasein for Dasein, not means by which it can align its consciousness with that of a divine Absolute. Obviously, Heidegger needs somehow to show how Dasein, despite being presupposition-loaded, need not remain trapped in a vicious hermeneutical circle in its self-understanding. The need, he declares, 'is not to get out of the circle but to come into it in the right way. In the circle is hidden a positive possibility of the most primordial kind of knowing' (p. 19). What we have to do is 'leap into the "circle", primordially and wholly', so that 'we have a full view of Dasein's circular being' (p. 365).

However, he does not seek to perform this feat at the outset of the book, claiming at first only 'provisionality' for his interpretation. Much of it is, he acknowledges, 'a matter of appropriating the labours of Dilthey' (p. 449), but it is often expressed in fresh, arresting, and memorable terminology, such as his description of the 'thrownness' (*Geworfenheit*) of Dasein. It is not however as if, having been hurled into the world like a stone, Dasein is at rest and free to gaze around with surprised but disinterested curiosity. Rather it remains impelled *forward*, pro-jected towards the future, entangled in concernful involvements so that in the first instance it becomes conscious of things only insofar they bear upon its preoccupied anxiety about future outcomes, so that it is fundamentally *'Sorge'* (Care), and is *irreducibly* 'Being-in-the world'.

What might seem at first sight impossible to reconcile with the achievement of a 'primordial' understanding of Dasein is Heidegger's insistence that it is ordinarily *Undurchsichtig*, untransparent to itself (pp. 186–7), because it hides itself from itself, burying itself in everyday distractions, falling away into 'inauthenticity', alienating itself from itself, despite an inner voice, conscience, which would call it to take heed, pull itself together, and take charge of its own destiny. Why is Dasein in flight from itself, that is, from its own destiny (*Geschick*), and therefore from its own *historicity* (*Geschichtlichkeit*)? Ultimately, because it is *'fleeing in the face of death'* (p. 298). Heidegger insists that we know about our impending death not through hearsay or an empirical survey but *a priori*, in the form of a basic state-of-mind or mood, namely anxiety (pp. 295, 301–2). Dasein's usual means of remaining 'in denial' is to engage in a conspiracy of mutual escapism with other Daseins; I know all along the vague general truth which 'everyone' knows, that we all die 'someday', but it is not real for me, because it is 'not yet', it is not 'present-at-hand', the criterion of reality for the average man.

Heidegger's good news, however, is that this dreadful secret, once confronted, provides the very solution to our problem at two levels. First, 'owning up' to its impending death is the key to each Dasein's achieving its own authentic (*eigentlich*, 'owned')[6] 'existence' because it renders it 'wholly transparent' (p. 354) to itself, *'hellsichtig'* (pre-

---

[6] *Eigentlich*: compare Ranke's *'wie es eigentlich gewesen'*. The word can mean 'essentially' or 'actually' but *'eigen'* means 'own'' which is clearly close to the notion of what is 'essential' to something.

ternaturally insightful, p. 436) inducing a 'moment of vision' (*Augenblick*, p. 387).[7] Secondly, we reach the ultimate realm of 'primordial and authentic truth' (p. 364) concerning Dasein's essence in general; once we face death with 'anticipatory *resoluteness*' we experience '*in a phenomenally primordial way . . . Dasein's authentic Being-a-whole*' (p. 351).

These are large claims. Contrast Dilthey's assessment that although our overall aim is to make our life a meaningful whole, death invariably frustrates this, causing unsurmountable 'grief' so that life, it is simply 'tragic', and we must accept that 'Life is just a chaos of harmonies and dissonances.' (6.A.VIII).[8] Two points need to be borne in mind when assessing Heidegger's thesis. First, the truism that a brush with death can shock one into an illuminating reassessment of one's priorities was much remarked upon in post-World War I Germany, often in connection with 'going over the top' in the trenches; Karl Jaspers in particular had made much of the notion that 'boundary situations', whether death, sickness, loss of job, breakdown of marriage or philosophico-scientific failure (see supra, p. 168) can jolt human beings out of their illusions (see Heidegger, 1962, footnote vi, pp. 494–5). Secondly, there is a kind of finitized form of Hegelian dialectic here, or at least of the 'polarity principle' (supra, p. 65); the realization of my own impending death highlights my current existence by contrasting my nothingness with it. Once I have faced up to my death I have foreseen my 'End', my limits, and now see my Dasein in its 'totality'.

Facing up resolutely to my own death brings about the 'Moment of Vision' which bestows genuine 'enlightenment' (p. 439) because it makes me authentically Present to myself for the first time (p. 387). Inauthentic Dasein thinks that only the 'present' is real because the future is not yet and the past dead and gone, but in fact the authentic Present is the holding together of Past and Future. Inauthentic Dasein is therefore obsessed with 'today'. The main thing is to be '*aktuell*', which in German has all the overtones of being up-to-date, fashionable, trendy, current, relevant, 'modern'. Pathetically, the *aktuell* values which fallen Dasein embraces are all culturally conditioned, i.e., dictated by a 'past' which is unrecognized. But authentically temporal or 'historical' Dasein faces up to its future (i.e., its Death), and is then thrown back to the authentic Present which '*deprives* the "today" of its character *as present*' (p. 444) and produces a '*moment of vision . . .* a *disavowal* of that which in the "today" is working itself out as the "past"'' (p. 438). For the first time Dasein can 'pull itself together' (p. 442) to discern the genuine possibilities which come to it from its past, seize them, and resolutely move to actualize them into the future. But the 'hidden basis' of this, which is Dasein's 'authentic historicality' (p. 428), is facing death, which allows Dasein to 'have its roots . . . essentially in the future' (p. 438). In short, inauthentic Dasein

---

7   '*Augenblick*', literally flash of the eye, is a modification of Kierkegaard's claim that for the man of faith there comes a 'moment' in which time and eternity are fused. For Heidegger there is no eternity but the three dimensions of time, past, present, and future, are supposedly integrated in this moment. Heidegger acknowledges that this echo of Kierkegaard is derived from Jaspers (Heidegger, 1962, p. 497ftn.iii).

8   Simmel's analysis is also worth noting: 'I am convinced . . . death is immanent in life from the outset . . . Life stretches out toward the absolute of life . . . but it stretches out towards nothingness as well . . . To climb beyond oneself in growth and reproduction, to sink below oneself in old age and death – these are not additions to life, but such rising up and spilling over the boundaries of the individual condition constitutes life itself' (Simmel, 1971, p. 369).

'temporalizes itself in terms of making present. The moment of vision, however, temporalizes itself in quite the opposite manner – in terms of the authentic future' (p. 388) Thus '*the primary meaning of existentiality is the future . . . The primary phenomenon of primordial and authentic temporality is the future*' (pp. 376, 378).

Many philosophical and religious traditions make much of facing up to death, but notions of its significance vary widely. The contrast of Heidegger's account with Christianity is particularly illuminating. According to the latter, death is evil (contrast Epicureanism, Platonism, or Buddhism), but the Christian approaches death by begging for mercy, 'denying himself' and 'taking up' his Cross in obedient, passive submission to divine providence, in the hope that participation in Christ's death will also be participation in his resurrection. For Heidegger likewise death is a real affront to mankind: '*Death is something that stands before us – something impending*' (p. 294). There is, however, no begging for mercy, and no hope of resurrection, because there is no miracle-working divine lover of mankind to whom one can entrust oneself. Annihilation is unavoidable: '*Death is not to be outstripped*' (p. 308). Heidegger's descriptions of authentic consciousness of death use terms of *confrontation* (conveyed in the use of the prepositions, prefixes and suffixes *vor* and *bevor* largely lost in the English translation), and even, at times, of a *violent power struggle*. Dasein passes 'under the eyes of death', 'shatters itself against death' and is 'thrown back' (7.B.III); 'death *lays claim*' to Dasein (p. 308). The moment of vision is a '*capturing* of Dasein's entity 'in spite of this entity's own tendency to cover things up. Existential analysis, therefore, constantly has the character of doing violence [*Gewaltsamkeit*]' (p. 359). 'Anticipatory resoluteness . . . frees for death the possibility of acquiring *power* over Dasein's existence and of basically dispersing all fugitive Self-concealments' (p. 357). But, of course, Dasein's Death is not another living entity over against it, but simply its own annihilation, so that the power struggle is in reality internal to it and the violence is self-inflicted. It alone, however, brings authentic self-knowledge and self-possession. Thus, Dasein is 'forced into the possibility of taking over from itself it ownmost Being' (p. 308) and 'Dasein, by anticipation, lets death become powerful in itself, then, as free for death, Dasein understands itself in its own *superior power*' (p. 436). One might say that despite the overwhelming defeat which it will eventually suffer, it wins a *temporary* victory, thereby gaining the trophy of *Selbstständigkeit* (self-subsistence, autonomy, firmness of self, p. 369). It is its own redeemer: Dasein 'snatches' for itself its own possibilities, 'taking them over' and 'handing them down to itself'; thus 'Dasein *hands* itself down *to* itself, free for death, in a possibility which it has inherited and yet has chosen' (p. 435). In short Dasein takes charge of its own fate which in this deeply paradoxical understanding is defined as 'powerless superior power', which puts Dasein in readiness for adversities' (p. 436), but it bestows on Dasein 'unshakable joy', blended with 'sober anxiety' (p. 358).

What have these strange claims got to do with the academic discipline of history? Not necessarily very much: Heidegger's attitude to professional academic historians is at best ambivalent and frequently contemptuous, owing much to Nietzsche's second *Untimely Meditation*. But one can say, first, that the philosopher who gains 'primordial' insight into Dasein by resolutely anticipating his own death endows himself with 'productive logic' which 'leaps ahead as it were' into every field awaiting scientific exploration uncovering its basic ontological structures. He can therefore develop the 'authentic' basic concepts for it, and then make them available to historical researchers as 'transparent assignments for their inquiry' (pp. 30–1). Accordingly, in 7.B.I and II we see Heidegger rejecting any suggestion that philosophy of history should take for granted the present status quo in the practices of professional historians, and then invent ad hoc justifications for them, 'limping along after, investigating the status of some science as it chances to find it, in order to discover its "method"' (p. 30) which is what he implies Rickert and Simmel had done. Secondly, the science of history ('historiology' as the English translation oddly puts it), *should* be more intimately related to Dasein's nature than any other specific science, because Dasein is essentially 'historicality'. Because 'Dasein is its past, whether explicitly or not', inauthentic Dasein is constantly 'falling prey to the tradition of which it has more or less explicitly taken hold', which 'keeps it from providing its own guidance' because 'tradition take what has come down to us and delivers it over to self-evidence' i.e., makes it spuriously 'obvious' to us. So, the authentic historian's central task is 'to discover this tradition, preserve it and study it explicitly' disclosing 'what it "transmits" and how this is trans-mitted and thus overcome the fact that 'this elemental historicality of Dasein may remain hidden from Dasein' (p. 41). In this way, Dasein will be enabled to 'take over' the 'heritage' which has been handed down to it, 'but not necessarily *as* handed down' (7.B.III). Finally, it should be noted that though Heidegger at one point declares Dasein is characterized by '*Mitsein*' (p. 308), Being-with-Others, his descriptions of Dasein are extremely individualistic; authentic Dasein is above all characterized by 'non-relational' 'ownness'; it is inauthentic Daseins who are lost in the 'they'. *Being and Time* contains no detailed discussions whatever of authentic familial or sexual relationships, or of friendships, or civil or political relationships. 'Historicity' is repeat-edly described as a character of Daseins in isolation from one another. Yet Heidegger does make a distinction between 'fate' and 'destiny', the former appertaining to indi-vidual, the latter to nations (7.B.III).[9] Clearly he is trying to make room for political

9   The idea of national destiny (often fused with the idea of personal fate in the case of 'world historical' leaders) had been an ingredient of German historicism at least since Humboldt and Hegel and had become a key feature of the German historical tradition in the work of nationalist historian such as Heinrich von Treitschke (1834–96), Ranke's successor in Berlin. But it was central also to the thesis of *The Decline of the West* (1918, 1922) by Oswald Spengler (1880–1936) which had an enor-mous impact in post-World War I Germany, and no doubt influences what Heidegger says concern-ing destiny. Spengler characterizes his work as a contribution to '*the philosophy of destiny* – indeed the first of its kind' (Spengler, 1932, vol. I, p. xiv). The notion of Destiny is for him opposed to '*the Causality Principle*', i.e., natural scientific explanation in terms of laws and is the constitutive categor of true historical science: 'the destiny idea demands life experience not scientific experience, the powe of seeing and not that of calculating, depth and not intellect . . . Real history is heavy with fate but fre of laws. One can divine the future . . . but one cannot reckon it' (pp. 117–18). It is integral to th concept of 'Time' the '*counter-conception to Space*' and therefore 'birth and generation in oppositio to death' (pp. 126–7). Clock-time is an attempt to spatialize time as opposed to 'living *historica* Time' (p. 124). The causality principle lies behind 'the kind of history that is commonly writter which 'even if it does not lose itself in compilation of data, comes to a halt before the *superficial* incidental . . . Nature and history mingle in a cheap unity . . . The secret logic of history is . . . replace by a causal . . . The anecdotal foreground of history [*is*] the arena of all the scientific causality-hunte . . . And even the social or economic interpretation of political development, to which present-da historical work is trying to rise as to a peak-ideal . . . is still exceedingly shallow and trivial' (pp. 143 4). Natural science is about the '*continuously possible*' (p. 158) whilst 'History carries the mark of th *singular-factual*' (p. 158) which is 'the deep logic of world-becoming' (p. 144) or 'the actualizing c a soul' (p. 147) such as that of Napoleon who wrote: ' "I feel myself driven towards an end that I d

action, and for national history, but the theme is left entirely undeveloped, and one can only surmise what the political implications might be: one might reasonably speculate, however, that Heidegger would be not at all interested in Western mass democracy, but would hold that 'authentic' nations would be led by either a single Dasein somewhat akin to Hegel's world historical figure, with something of Nietzsche's *Übermensch* about him, or at most, some small élite group of such individuals.

If so, in 1927 Heidegger could but hope that his nation, recently sure of its unique destiny among the nations, not only because of its cultural superiority but its economic and military might, could be restored to its greatness by such a leader. By the early 1930s, Heidegger seems to have become very confident that he could identify him. On 20 April 1933, Hitler's birthday, the Nazis engineered the resignation of the just recently installed Rector of Freiburg University, and Heidegger was unanimously elected as his successor on the following day, delivering his now notorious *Rektoratsrede* (Wolin, 1993, pp. 29–39) on 27 April, and 'ostentatiously' (Ott, 1993, p. 136) becoming a member of the Nazi party on 1 May, the 'Day of National Labour'. He proceeded enthusiastically to implement the *Gleichschaltung* (coordination) of the university with the *Volk* by the implementation of the *Führerprinzip*, and made speeches complaining that 'research' had 'got out of hand and concealed its uncertainty behind the ideas of international scientific and scholarly progress' and 'aimless teaching' (Wolin, 1993, p. 44) and declaring that in the future everything must be 'interlocked with the whole through its rootedness in the *Volk*' (p. 45). Near the end of lectures delivered in 1935 is a meditation on the words of a chorus from Sophocles' *Antigone* in which a man is described, whom Heidegger clearly regards as 'authentic' man par excellence. He not only manifests 'power' but is violent (*gewalttätig*) provoking the revulsion of those who think in terms of 'conventional compromise and mutual aid' and who therefore 'disparage all violence' (Heidegger, 1961, p. 126). He 'breaks out and breaks up, captures and subjugates' both the natural environment and, it is implied, his fellow citizens. He deploys 'power against the overpowering' (*Überwältigende*), a term used in this period by Heidegger to describe the essence of things or Being. It will eventually claim him in death (p. 133), but, showing impious boldness (*tolma*), he fights heroically against this to the end. His violence expresses the fundamental nature of Dasein which is a 'breach' in the solidity of Being, which Being posits so that consciousness can arise: 'Man is forced into being-there (*Dasein*), hurled into the afflic-

---

ot know"' or Bismarck through whom 'the epoch of German national union accomplished itself' (p. 44). History and therefore destiny is identified with Western European 'Faustian' culture (the culture of 'Will') as opposed to Eastern or classical Greek culture: 'The Indians . . . have no history, no life, memories, no care . . . *Western history was willed and Indian history happened* . . . Classical man willed to have no history, no duration, neither past nor future (pp. 133–4), which is really 'masked cowardice' (p. 204). Spengler calls for a new kind of historian who can interpret 'world-happening': will be 'the business of quite a new kind of "judge of men" (*Menschenkenner*)' (p. 160). In effect this is to say that 'all genuine historical work is philosophy, unless it is mere ant-industry' (p. 41). Nevertheless 'all the philosophers of the newest age are open to a serious criticism. What they do not possess is real standing in actual life. Not one of them has intervened in higher politics . . . in economics, or in any other *big* actuality, with a single act or a single compelling idea . . . How poor their personalities, how commonplace their political and practical outlook . . . A doctrine that does not attack and affect the life of the period in its inmost depths is not doctrine and had better not be taught' (pp. 41–2). One feels that the Heidegger of the 1920s and 1930s was striving to respond to this challenge.

tion (*Not*) of such being, because the overpowering as such, in order to appear in its power, requires a place, a scene of disclosure . . . Being itself hurls man into this break-ing-away . . . The being-there of the historical man is the breach through which the being . . . in the essent can open' (p. 137). Who is he, whose hubris, and ruthless cruelty Heidegger celebrates as that of the ideal 'authentic', truly historical man? It is Creon, the impious dictator of the polis of Thebes. Since, in the same lectures Heidegger extols the 'inner truth and greatness of Nazism' (p. 166) I think there can be not very much doubt that Creon is intended to symbolize Hitler.[10]

Heidegger eventually realized he had made a mistake. He resigned his Rectorship within a year, began to express what can be understood as implicit criticism of Nazism in lectures, and a new philosophy gradually emerges which in some respects is the opposite of earlier views, although there are, of course, many elements of continuity, which sometimes Heidegger later overemphasizes in an effort to create an appearance of greater consistency over time than is warranted.[11] All the claims about the effect of 'anticipatory resoluteness' towards death disappear: he wrote to Sartre on 28 October 1945 that he accepted his dismissive criticisms of them (see Sartre, 1956, pp. 545–6; Safranski, 1998, p. 349). All traces of the rhetoric of violence, the stress on 'authentic' Dasein's self-grounding resolve, and role as the source of truth disappear. Instead 'man of himself has no power over truth and it remains independent of him' (Heidegger, 1966, p. 84) and it may come only if he waits receptively for it in *Gelassenheit* (calm openness) and 'lets thing be'. The only way in which one can speak of the relevance of 'resolve' is in terms of the 'steadfastness hidden in *Gelassenheit*' (Heidegger, 1966, p. 81). The term *Gelassenheit* has its origins in the medieval Rhineland mystical tradition, and this is one of a series of echoes of Christian Neoplatonism in the later Heidegger's descriptions of the relation between man and 'Being', which together with other features frequently give Heidegger's later texts an atmosphere of mystical religiosity.[12] For instance, he uses the word *Andenken* of the kind of thinking that is required which literally means 'thinking on' but is commonly used for religious 'devotions'.[13] He also emphasizes the etymological relation between 'thinking' and 'thanking' (*Denken* and *Danken*); that is, true thinking comports itself toward the thing 'with the thanks owed for being' (Heidegger, 1968, p. 141). Genuinely to think of something means 'to love it, to favour it' (Heidegger, 1993, p. 220). Man's vocation is not to be 'the

10   In 1944 in occupied Paris Anouilh was to make Antigone, the opposer of Creon, the symbol of resistance against Nazism, and Brecht's 1948 production identifies Creon with Hitler (see the intro-duction to Sophocles, 1984.) Heidegger quotes from the translation of Hölderlin, the German Ro-mantic poet who came to have a central place in his meditations. Hölderlin's translations of Sophocles and other works, emphasizes the theme that prideful violence can 'force God to appear' (Constantine 1988, p. 295). Those who would object to such an interpretation need to explain why Heidegger does not explicitly dissociate himself from it.

11   After the war Heidegger had to face a Denazification Tribunal, and it was several years before he was granted permission once more to teach in public. It was very much in his interests in these years to suggest that the contrasts in his thinking with what could be understood as akin to Nazism could be traced back to earlier work.

12   The most adequate philosophical term for God is 'Being itself', according to Thomas Aquinas and much of the medieval scholastic philosophical tradition.

13   Hegel had made exactly the opposite move: stating that a thinking that thought it was depend-ent on a transcendent God for its ability to know (*Andenken*) was inferior to the true *Denken* which was aware of its identity with the Absolute.

tyrant of Being' but is destined by Being to 'guard the truth of Being. Man is the shepherd of Being' (p. 234). The opposite of this kind of thinking is the *'rechnendes Denken'* the calculative thinking which lies behind the technology which is dehumanizing mankind. There is an echo of Weber's *Zweckrationalität* here, but Heidegger says that even those cultural scientists who pride themselves on adherence to *Wertrationalität* as opposed to *Zweckrationalität* are in the grip of calculative thinking, for when a thing is 'evaluated' it is always 'robbed of its worth' (p. 251). Yet, despite this religiosity he persists in saying that the 'Being' of which he speaks is 'not God and not a cosmic ground' (p. 234).

This quietist mysticism is often expressed in terms of contemplative communing with nature: Heidegger writes of walks along woodland paths, savoring the silence and light of a clearing, and of 'learning to exist in the nameless' (p. 223). But this is somewhat misleading; in heavy dependence on Humboldt whose 'deep dark insights into the nature of language . . . we must never cease to admire' (Heidegger, 1982, p. 136), he stresses that it is in language that Being reveals itself (Heidegger, 1993, p. 246), although not in our current language, in which we find the 'devastation' and 'downfall' of language' (p. 222). Consequently philosophizing is meditating on the revelation of Being in language. This is 'History' as he now understands it, which 'does not consist in the happenings and deeds of the world, nor in the cultural achievements of man' (Heidegger, 1966, p. 79). It is historical because it is related to his claim that the whole of the Western linguistic tradition was deeply imprinted with the original insights into Being of pre-Socratic philosophers which needs to be retrieved and transcended, or from German poets such as Hölderlin, although Heidegger is now careful to add that ' "German" is not spoken to the world so that the world might be reformed through the German essence; rather, it is spoken to the German so that from a fateful belongness to the nations they might become world-historical along with them' (Heidegger, 1993, p. 342).

Hans-Georg Gadamer (b. 1900) can use Heideggerian language to present his own views even when they do not seem very closely related to Heidegger, whom he had known as a student at Marburg. If his ideas approach those of any previous thinker treated in this book, it is perhaps Simmel with his notion of a single unending interplay of minds within one milieu which transcends them, which is the 'super-individual . . . formal agent of understanding' (6.D.IV). Attention was paid to Gadamer in 1.II, and two points only will be added here. First, a major feature which underlies all that is said in the excerpts but is not made explicit in our selections, is that, like Heidegger, he is influenced by the thinking on language of Herder and above all by Humboldt who became the founder of . . . the philosophy of language . . . and modern linguistic science' (Gadamer, 1976, p. 61) revealing language as the 'generative and creative power' of understanding, the 'all-encompassing' and 'sustaining medium of all . . . manifestations of the spirit' (p. 77) 'toward which philosophy is ever more clearly directed' (p. 75): 'As I often tell my students, when you take a word in your mouth you must realize that you have not taken a tool that can be thrown aside if it won't do the job, but you are fixed in a direction of thought which comes from afar and stretches beyond you' (Gadamer, 1979, p. 496).

Secondly, both the challenge and perhaps limitation of Gadamer's approach seems revealed above all in a controversy between himself and Habermas which emerged following the publication of his major work *Truth and Method*. For Gadamer, 'history' always seems to mean the humanist cultural tradition of the educated European élite engaged in the endless process of reinterpreting great texts from the past. It seems far removed from the pressures of existence of the masses whose labour sustained the élite in being throughout the history of the West, but were effectively excluded from the great hermeneutical conversation. Moreover, no notice is taken of the view that, according to Marx, the thoughts of this élite have in fact been 'ideologies' functioning as attempts to legitimize an exploitative socio-economic system. Habermas, acknowledging the value in many respects of Gadamer's hermeneutics, argues that he nevertheless fails to acknowledge the presence of 'systematically distorted patterns of communication' (Habermas, 1970a, p. 302) in Western intellectual history. Gadamer's approach is inadequate in such cases of 'pseudo-communication' and 'false consensus', which need to be 'explained' by factors 'outside' the conversation for,

> the objective framework of social action is not exhausted by the dimension of intersubjectively intended and symbolically transmitted meaning. The linguistic infrastructure of a society is part of a complex that, however symbolically mediated, is also constituted by the constraints of reality – by the constraint of outer nature that enters into procedures for technical mastery and by the constraint of inner nature reflected in the repressive character of social power relations . . . *Social actions can only be comprehended in an objective framework that is constituted conjointly by language, labor, and domination.* The happening of tradition . . . in fact is relative to systems of labor and domination. (Habermas, 1970b, p. 361)

Here it is Marxist criticism of ideology which Habermas has chiefly in mind. Elsewhere he raises the question of 'neurotic' distortions of consciousness as posited in Freudian psychoanalysis. Gadamer makes the classic idealist response (see the remarks on Hegel pp. 64ff) that Marxist critique of ideology, and the psychoanalytical therapy which Habermas advocates, are both 'linguistic acts of reflection', so that hermeneutical reflection must be regarded 'universal and basic to all interhuman experience' (Gadamer 1976, p. 30), inescapably occupying the role of ultimate critical interpreter of the claims of all sciences of whatever kind (p. 39). Nor will he allow that the hermeneutic specialist will be 'eunuch-like' in his political disengagement for he is 'so little separated from the ongoing tradition (for example, those of his nation) . . . that he is really *himself engaged in* contributing to the growth and development of the national state (p. 28). But in admitting that 'we have no universal criterion at our disposal which would tell us when we are caught up in the false consciousness of a pseudo-understanding' (Habermas, 1970a, p. 303), Habermas seems close to admitting that hermeneutics, as Gadamer understands it, must indeed have the last word.

Paul Ricoeur (b. 1913) is an astonishingly wide-ranging and prolific philosophe and theologian, long almost as much at home in the United States as in his native France. He first established his reputation in post-war France as an expert on phenomenology and existentialism, publishing a translation into French and commentary of Husserl's *Ideas I* in 1950 at a time when Husserlian phenomenology was becoming major preoccupation of French philosophy. Note that in section 7.D.I he means by 'phenomenology' the analysis of ideal or *irreal* meanings, as in Husserl, and by 'hermeneutics' the understanding of meanings in the minds of real, individual historically conditioned beings. In part 1 of 7.D.I he acknowledges that he is attracted by Heidegger's notion (which perhaps he attributes too readily to the later Husserl) that the human 'understanding' is grounded in deeper pre-conscious ontological structures, and it becomes evident that this is because he has read Marx, Nietzsche and Freud, whom he terms three 'masters of suspicion' who have so 'heightened' modern consciousness that we are coming to recognize that 'it is not consciousness which is the original given, but false consciousness, prejudice, illusion, and for this reason consciousness must be interpreted'. There is obviously similarity here with Habermas except that for Ricoeur this recognition calls not for interweaving extra-hermeneutical explanation with hermeneutical understanding but the broadening of the latter, and indeed the recognition that its primary function must be 'deciphering the hidden meaning in the apparent meaning' (see part 3 of 7.D.I) of human discourse, i.e., 'symbolic' 'indirect, secondary' structures of significance in human utterance. 'Symbol' is not a symptom of 'distorted communication' which should be eliminated, but rather our sole and abiding means of access not only to the transcendent heights of the 'sacred' but to the correlative depths of 'evil': our awareness of these fundamental dimensions of reality only 'erupt' into our consciousness through 'primary symbols' (Ricoeur, 1969, p. 9). For Ricoeur the 'death of God' was announced prematurely, and humanity's most intractable problem is the evil inclination in every human heart, which (like Kant) he believes is not ultimately explicable or removable by any known science or technique. Moreover, even our conceptual grasp of reality makes progress through new insights which first enter consciousness in symbols. In this programmatic essay, Heidegger is perhaps given short shrift: in *Being and Time* he too is a 'master of suspicion' in his insistence that for the most part, Dasein's consciousness is 'false' and 'corrupted' (*verfallen*). Ricoeur remains entirely silent about the role that anticipatory encounter with death plays in Heidegger in supposedly inducing 'primordial' insight into Dasein's nature, and pays no attention to the fact that the later Heidegger's philosophy of language very much centres on what Ricoeur would term 'symbolic' disclosures of Being.

Selected Texts

Edited by Robert M. Burns

7.A Edmund Husserl, 1859–1938*

7.A.1 The Historical A-priori[1]

We stand within the horizon of human civilization, the one in which we now live. We are constantly, vitally conscious of this horizon, and specifically as a temporal horizon implied in our given present horizon. To the one human civilization there correspond essentially the one cultural world as the surrounding life-world with its [peculiar] manner of being; this world for every historical period and civilization, has its particular features and is precisely the tradition. We stand, then, within the historical horizon in which everything is historical, even though we may know very little about it in a definite way. But it has its essential structure that can be revealed through methodological inquiry. . . .

Every explication and every transition from making explicit to making self-evident (even perhaps in cases where one stops much too soon) is nothing other than historical disclosure; in itself, essentially, it is something historical, and as such it bears, with essential necessity, the horizon of its history within itself. . . .

Making geometry self-evident, then, whether one is clear about this or not, is the disclosure of its historical tradition. But this knowledge, if it is not to remain empty talk or undifferentiated generality, requires the methodical production, proceeding from the present and carried out as research in the present, of differentiated self-evidences of the type discovered above (in several fragmentary investigations of what belongs to such knowledge superficially, as it were). Carried out systematically, such self-evidences result in nothing other and nothing less than the universal a priori of history with all its highly abundant component elements.

We can also say now that history is from the start nothing other than the vital movement of the coexistence and the interweaving of original formations and sedimentation of meaning. Anything that is shown to be a historical fact, either in the present through experience or by a historian as a fact in the past, necessarily has its *inner structure of meaning*; but especially the motivational interconnections established about it in term

* The selected text section on Edmund Husserl has been prepared by Hugh Rayment-Pickard.
1 Edmund Husserl, 'The Origin of Geometry', Appendix VI to *The Crisis of the European Science and Transcendental Phenomenology* (Evanston: Northwestern University Press, 1970), pp. 369–78

of everyday understanding have deep, further and further-reaching implications which must be interrogated, disclosed. All [merely] factual history remains incomprehensible because, always merely drawing its conclusions naively and straightforwardly from facts, it never makes thematic the general ground of meaning upon which all such conclusions rest, has never investigated the immense structural a priori which is proper to it. Only the disclosure of the essentially general structure lying in our present and then in every past or future historical present as such, and, in totality, only the disclosure of the concrete, historical time in which we live, in which our total humanity lives in respect to its total, essentially general structure-only this disclosure can make possible historical inquiry [*Historie*] which is truly understanding, insightful, and in the genuine sense scientific. This is the concrete, historical a priori which encompasses everything that exists as historical becoming and having-become or exists in its essential being as tradition and handing-down. . . .

From the historicism which prevails extensively in different forms [today] I expect little receptivity for a depth-inquiry which goes beyond the usual factual history . . . especially since, as the expression 'a priori' indicates, it lays claim to a strictly unconditioned and truly apodictic self-evidence extending beyond all historical facticities. One will object: what naïveté, to seek to display, and to claim to have displayed, a historical a priori, an absolute, supertemporal validity, after we have obtained such abundant testimony for the relativity of everything historical, of all historically developed world-apperceptions, right back to those of the 'primitive' tribes. Every people, large or small, has its world in which, for that people, everything fits well together, whether in mythical-magical or in European-rational terms, and in which everything can be explained perfectly. Every people has its 'logic' and, accordingly, if this logic is explicated in propositions, 'its' a priori.

However, let us consider the methodology of establishing historical facts in general, thus including that of the facts supporting the objection; and let us do this in regard to what such methodology presupposes. Does not the undertaking of a humanistic science of 'how it really was' contain a presupposition taken for granted, a validity-ground never observed, never made thematic, of a strictly unassailable [type of] self-evidence, without which historical inquiry would be a meaningless enterprise? All questioning and demonstrating which is in the usual sense historical presupposes history [*Geschichte*] as the universal horizon of questioning, not explicitly, but still as a horizon of implicit certainty, which, in spite of all vague background-indeterminacy, is the presupposition of all determinability, or of all intention to seek and to establish determined facts.

What is historically primary in itself is our present. We always already know of our present world and that we live in it, always surrounded by an openly endless horizon of unknown actualities. This knowing, as horizon-certainty, is not something learned, not knowledge which was once actual and has merely sunk back to become part of the background; the horizon-certainty had to be already there in order to be capable of being laid-out thematically; it is already presupposed in order that we can seek to know what we do not know. . . .

It is of particular importance now to bring into focus and establish the following insight: Only if the apodictically general content, invariant throughout all conceivable variation, of the spatiotemporal sphere of shapes is taken into account in the idealization can an ideal construction arise which can be understood for all future time and by all coming generations of men and thus be capable of being handed down and reproduced with the identical intersubjective meaning. This condition is valid far beyond geometry for all spiritual structures which are to be unconditionally and generally capable of being handed down. . . .

It is a general conviction that geometry, with all its truths, is valid with unconditioned generality for all men, all times, all peoples, and not merely for all historically factual ones but for all conceivable ones. The presuppositions of principle for this conviction have never been explored because they have never been seriously made a problem. But it has also become clear to us that every establishment of a historical fact which lays claim to unconditioned objectivity likewise presupposes this invariant or absolute a priori.

Only [through the disclosure of this a priori] can there be an a priori science extending beyond all historical facticities, all historical surrounding worlds, peoples, times, civilizations; only in this way can a science as *aeterna veritas* appear. Only on this fundament is based the secured capacity of inquiring back from the temporarily depleted self-evidence of a science to the primal self-evidences. . . .

We can now recognize from all this that historicism, which wishes to clarify the historical or epistemological essence of mathematics from the standpoint of the magical circumstances or other manners of apperception of a time-bound civilization, is mistaken in principle. For romantic spirits the mythical-magical elements of the historical and prehistorical aspects of mathematics may be particularly attractive; but to cling to this merely historically factual aspect of mathematics is precisely to lose oneself to a sort of romanticism and to overlook the genuine problem, the internal-historical problem, the epistemological problem. Also, one's gaze obviously cannot then become free to recognize that facticities of every type, including those involved in the [historicist] objection, have a root in the essential structure of what is generally human, through which a teleological reason running throughout all historicity announces itself. With this is revealed a set of problems in its own right related to the totality of history and to the full meaning which ultimately gives it its unity.

If the usual factual study of history in general, and in particular the history which in most recent times has achieved true universal extension over all humanity, is to have any meaning at all, such a meaning can only be grounded upon what we can here call internal history, and as such upon the foundations of the universal historical a priori

7.B   Martin Heidegger, 1889–1976

7.B.1   The Nature of Historiology (*Geschichtswissenschaft*)[2]

We need not discuss the Fact that historiology, is, as a kind of Being of Dasein, factically 'dependent' at any time on the 'prevailing world view'. Beyond this, we must inquire into the ontological possibility of how the sciences have their source in Dasein's state of Being. . . .

If Dasein's Being is in principle historical, then every factical science is always man

2   Heidegger, 1962, pp. 444–8.

festly in the grip of this historizing. But historiology still has Dasein's historicality as its presupposition in its own quite special way.

. . . The issue here is not one of 'abstracting' the concept of historiology from the way something is factically done in the sciences today, nor is it one of assimilating it to anything of this sort. For what guarantee do we have in principle that such a factical procedure will indeed be properly representative of historiology in its primordial and authentic possibilities? . . . On the other hand the existential idea of historiology is not given a higher justification by having the historian affirm that his factical behaviour is in agreement with it. Nor does the idea become false if he disputes any such agreement.

. . .

. . . The question of whether the object of historiology is just to put once-for-all 'individual' events into a series, or whether it also has 'laws' as its objects, is one that is radically mistaken. The theme of historiology is neither that which has happened just once for all nor something universal that floats above it, but the possibility which has been factually existent. . . .

. . . In no science are the 'universal validity' of standards and the claims to 'universality' which the "they" and its common sense demand, *less* possible as criteria of 'truth' than in authentic historiology.

Only because in each case the central theme of historiology is the *possibility* of existence which has-been-there, and because the latter exists factically in a way which is world-historical, can it demand of itself that it takes its orientation inexorably from the facts' . . . If the historian 'throws' himself straightaway into the 'world-view' of an era, he has not proved as yet that he understands his object in an authentically historical way, and not just 'aesthetically'. And on the other hand, the existence of a historian who 'only' edits sources, may be characterized by a historicality which is authentic.

Thus the very prevalence of a differentiated interest even in the most remote and primitive cultures, is in itself not proof of the authentic historicality of a 'time'. In the end the emergence of a problem of 'historicism' is the clearest symptom that historiology endeavours to alienate Dasein from its authentic historicality. Such historicality does not necessarily require historiology. It is not the case that unhistoriological eras as such are unhistorical also.

7.B.II   Dasein and Time[3]

Dasein does not exist as the sum of the momentary actualities of Experiences which come along successively and disappear. Nor is there a sort of framework which this succession gradually fills up. For how is such a framework to be present-at-hand, where in each case, only the Experience one is having 'right now' is 'actual', and the boundaries of the framework – the birth which is past and the death which is only oncoming lack actuality? . . .

Dasein does not fill a track or stretch 'of life' – one which is somehow present-at-hand – with the phases of its momentary actualities. It stretches *itself* along in such a way that its own Being is constituted in advance as a stretching-along. The 'between'

Ibid., pp. 426–9

which relates to birth and death already lies *in the Being* of Dasein. On the other hand, it is by no means the case Dasein 'is' actual in a point of time, and that, apart from this, it is 'surrounded' by the non-actuality of its birth and death. Understood existentially, birth is not and never is something past in the sense of something no longer present-at-hand; and death is just as far from having the kind of Being of something still outstanding, not yet present-at-hand but coming along. Factical Dasein exists as born; and as born, it is already dying, in the sense of Being-towards-death. As long as Dasein factically exists, both the 'ends' and their 'between' *are*, and they *are* in the only way which is possible on the basis of Dasein's Being as *care*. Thrownness and the Being towards death in which one either flees it or anticipates it, form a unity, and in this unity birth and death are 'connected' in a manner characteristic of Dasein. As care Dasein *is the* 'between'.

. . . The movement [Bewegtheit] of existence is not the motion [Bewegung] of something present-at-hand. It is definable in terms of the way Dasein stretches along. The specific movement in which Dasein is *stretched along and stretches itself along*, we call its "*historizing*". The question of Dasein's 'connectedness' is the ontological problem of Dasein's historizing. To lay bare *the structure of historizing*, and the existential temporal conditions of its possibility, signifies that one has achieved an *ontological* understanding of *historicality*.

. . .

[*Thus*] . . . the *locus* of the problem of history has already been decided. This *locus* is not to be sought in historiology as the science of history. Even if the problem of 'history' is treated in accordance with a theory of science, not only aiming at the 'epistemological' clarification of the historiological way of grasping things (Simmel) or the logic with which the concepts of historiological presentation are formed (Rickert), but doing so with an orientation towards the 'side of the object', then, as long as the question is formulated this way, history becomes in principle accessible only as the *Object* of a science. Thus the basic phenomenon of history, which is prior to any possible thematizing by historiology and underlies it, has been irretrievably put aside. How history can become a possible *object* for historiology is something that may be gathered only from the kind of Being that belongs to the historical – from historicality and from the way it is rooted in temporality.

. . .

. . . The existential–ontological constitution of historicality has been covered up by the way Dasein's history is ordinarily interpreted; we must get hold of it *in spite of* all this. . . .

. . .

. . . The existential Interpretation of historiology as a science aims solely at demonstrating its ontological derivation from Dasein's historicality. . . .

In analysing the historicality of Dasein we shall try to show that this entity is not 'temporal' because it 'stands in history'; but that, on the contrary, it exists historically and can so exist only because it is temporal in the very basis of its Being.

Nevertheless, Dasein must also be called 'temporal' in the sense of Being 'in time'. Even without a developed historiology, factical Dasein needs and uses a calendar and clock. Whatever may happen 'to Dasein', it experiences it as happening 'in time' . . . The historical is ordinarily characterized with the help of the time of within-time-ness. But if this ordinary characterization is to be stripped of its seeming self-evidence and exclusiveness, historicality must first be 'deduced' purely in terms of Dasein's primordial temporality . . .

7.B.III   Authentic Historicity and Death[4]

Dasein factically has its 'history', and it can have something of the sort because the Being of this entity is constituted by historicality . . . The Being of Dasein has been defined as care. Care is grounded in temporality. Within the range of temporality, therefore, the kind of historizing which give existence its definitely historical character, must be sought. Thus the Interpretation of Dasein's historicity will prove to be, at bottom, just a more concrete working out of temporality. We first revealed temporality with regard to that way of existing authentically which we characterized as anticipatory resoluteness. How far does this imply an authentic historizing of Dasein?

We have defined 'resoluteness' as a projecting of oneself upon one's own Being-guilty – a projecting which is reticent and ready for anxiety. Resoluteness gains its authenticity as *anticipatory* resoluteness. In this Dasein understands itself with regard to its potentiality-for being, and it does so in such a manner that it will go right under the eyes of Death in order to take over in its thrownness that entity which it is itself, and to take it over wholly. The resolute taking over of one's factical 'there', signifies at the same time that the Situation is one which has been resolved upon. In the existential analysis we cannot, in principle, discuss what Dasein *factically* resolves in any particular case . . . Nevertheless, we must ask whence, *in general*, Dasein can draw those possibilities upon which it factically projects itself. One's anticipatory projection of oneself on that possibility of existence which is not to be outstripped – on death – guarantees only the totality and authenticity of one's resoluteness. . . .

As thrown, Dasein has indeed been delivered over to itself and its potentiality-for-Being, *but as Being-in-the-world*. As thrown, it has been submitted to a 'world', and exists factically with Others. Proximally and for the most part the Self is lost in the "they". It understands itself in terms of those possibilities of existence which 'circulate' in the 'average' public way of interpreting Dasein today. These possibilities had mostly been made unrecognizable by ambiguity; yet they are well known to us . . .

The resoluteness in which Dasein comes back to itself discloses current factical possibilities of authentic existing, and discloses them *in terms of the heritage* which that resoluteness, as thrown, *takes over*. In one's coming back resolutely to one's thrownness, there is hidden a *handing down* to oneself of the possibilities that have come down to me, but not necessarily *as* having thus come down . . . The more authentically Dasein resolves – and this means that in anticipating death it understands itself unambiguously in terms of its ownmost distinctive possibility – the more unequivocally does it choose and find the possibility of its existence, and the less does it do so by accident. Only by the anticipation of death is every accidental and 'provisional' possibility driven out. Only Being-free *for* death, gives Dasein its goal outright and pushes existence into its finitude. Once one had grasped the finitude of one's existence, it snatches one back from the endless multiplicity of possibilities which offer themselves as closest to one – those of comfortableness, shirking, and taking things lightly – and brings Dasein into

Ibid., pp. 434–43.

the simplicity of its *fate* [*Schicksals*]. This is how we designate Dasein's primordial historizing, which lies in authentic resoluteness and in which Dasein *hands* itself *down* to itself free *for* death, in a possibility which it has inherited and yet has chosen.

Dasein can be reached by the blows of fate only because in the depths of its Being Dasein *is* fate in the sense we have described . . . Fate does not first arise from the clashing together of events and circumstances. Even one who is irresolute gets driven about by these – more so than one who has chosen; and yet he can 'have' no fate.

If Dasein, by anticipation, lets death become powerful in itself, then, as free for death, Dasein understands itself in its own *superior power*, the power of its finite free dom, so that in this freedom, which 'is' only in its having chosen to make such choice, it can take over the *powerlessness* of abandonment to its having done so, and can thus come to have a clear vision for the accidents of the Situation that has been dis closed. But if fateful Dasein, as Being-in-the-world, exists essentially in Being-with Others, its historizing is a co-historizing and is determinative for it as *destiny* [*Geschick*] This is how we designate the historizing of the community, of a people. Destiny is not something that puts itself together out of individual fates, any more than Being-with one-another can be conceived as the occurring together of several Subjects. Our fate have already been guided in advance, in our Being with one another in the same world and in our resoluteness for definite possibilities. Only in communicating and in strug gling does the power of destiny become free. Dasein's fateful destiny in and with its 'generation' will go to make up the full authentic historizing of Dasein.

. . . Fate requires as the ontological condition for its possibility, the state of Being of care – that is to say, temporality. Only if death, guilt, conscience, freedom and finitude reside together equiprimordially in the Being of an entity as they do in care, can that entity exist in the mode of fate; that is to say, only than can it be historical in the very depths of its existence.

Only an entity which, in its Being, is essentially **futural**, *so that it is free for its death and can let itself by thrown back up its factical 'there' by shattering itself against death that is to say, only an entity which, as futural, is equiprimordially in the process of* **having been**, *can, by handing down to itself the possibility it has inherited, take over its own thrownness and be* **in the moment of vision** (*Augenblick*) *for 'its time'. Only authentic temporality which is at the same time finite, makes possible something like fate – that is say, authentic historicality.*

. . . The resoluteness which comes back to itself and hands itself down . . . become the *repetition*[5] of a possibility of existence that has come down to us. *Repeating*

---

5 'Repetition' is a theme which had been developed by Kierkegaard (see p. 136); for him it was 'the new [*philosophical*] category which has to be brought to light' to replace 'foolish patter' about 'me diation in Hegelian philosophy' (Kierkegaard, 1941, p. 52). It was an expression of his insistence that the individual could achieve 'self-identity' only through 'passionate decision' (see 5.C.II); that one's personal identity is not a given, but a task (not a *Gabe* but an *Aufgabe*, as it is often put German) to be achieved through an act of *will* which amounts to reaffirming or *repeating* oneself the same in the past, present and future. Yet he is clear that the individual human being is powerless to make this act of will on his own; the grace of God, given in personal relationship with Him, indispensable; that is, the 'self is 'constituted' only in and by its relation to God (Kierkegaard, 1954 p. 147). Otherwise it is attempting to 'constitute itself' by trying to 'relate itself to itself' (p. 146). But it can only 'attain and remain in equilibrium and rest by itself' (p. 147) through a saving relationship with God when the 'self is no longer merely the human self' but 'the self directly in the eyes of God so that the self acquires self-identity 'by being before God'. Thus 'the more conception of God, the

anding down explicitly – that is to say, going back into the possibilities of the Dasein *hat has-been-there*. The authentic repetition of a possibility of existence that has been – the possibility that Dasein may choose its hero – is grounded existentially in anticipa-*ory resoluteness*; for it is in resoluteness that one first chooses the choice which makes *one free for the struggle of loyally following in the footsteps of that which can be *epeated . . . Arising, as it does, from a resolute projection of oneself, repetition doe *not let itself be persuaded of something by what is 'past', just in order that this, as *omething which was formerly actual, may recur. Rather the repetition, makes a *eciprocative rejoinder* to the possibility of that existence which has-been-there. But *when such a rejoinder is made to the possibility in a resolution, it is made in a *moment *f vision; and as such* it is at the same time a *disavowal* of that which in the "today", is *orking itself out as the 'past'. Repetition does not abandon itself to that which is *ast, nor does it aim at progress. In the moment of vision authentic existence is indif-*erent to both these alternatives . . .

   . . . History has its essential importance neither in what is past nor in the "today" *nd its 'connection' with what is past, but in that authentic historizing of existence *which arise from Dasein's *future*. As a way of Being for Dasein, history has its roots so *essentially in the future that death, as the possibility of Dasein which we have already *haracterized, throws anticipatory existence back upon its *factical* thrownness, and so *or the first time imparts to *having-been* its peculiarly privileged position in the histori-*al. *Authentic Being – towards – death, that is to say, the finitude of temporality – is the *idden basis of Dasein's historicality*. Dasein does not first become historical in repeti-*on; but because its is historical is temporal, it can take itself over in its history by *epeating. For this, no historiology is as yet needed.

   Resoluteness implies handing oneself down by anticipation to the "there" of the *noment of vision; and this handing down we call "fate". This is also the ground for *estiny, by which we understand Dasein's historizing in Being-with-Others. In repeti-*on, fateful destiny can be disclosed explicitly as bound up with the heritage which has *ome down to us. . . .

---

*ore self; the more self, the more conception of God' (pp. 210–11) It is 'faith' which allows 'the self being itself and in willing to be itself to be 'grounded transparently in God' (p. 211). Sin, by *ntrast is 'disobedient . . . self-assertion . . . willfulness' fired ('potentiated') by an unacknowledged *espair' (pp. 211–21) through unconscious awareness of the self's weakness, i.e., its powerlessness to *onstitute' itself. This is 'quite universal' (p. 155) in man. The root of despair is anxiety or 'dread of *thing' (p. 158): the awareness that, left to oneself, one is 'nothing' and is doomed to trying, and *ling, to create oneself out of nothing. The 'maximum of despair' is 'absolute defiance' (p. 175). *eidegger's account of Dasein as achieving 'authenticity' (i.e., 'salvation') through 'anticipatory reso-*teness' towards its own Death, is, point-by-point a reversal of all that Kierkegaard says. The 'Self' *alizes itself not by standing before the eyes of God but 'going under the eyes of Death' i.e. unflinch-*gly facing up to its own nothingness, and wresting self-identity out of the situation by its own *soluteness' thereby '*handing* itself *down* to itself.' 'Fateful repetition' is identified with individual *asein's 'pulling itself together' thereby achieving the '*loyalty* of existence to its own Self' (Heidegger, *62, p. 443). Elsewhere (in the passage from which section 7.A.I. is extracted) it is stated that 'the *storiological disclosure of the 'past' is based on fateful repetition' and that 'it alone guarantees the *bjectivity' of historiology'. (p. 447). In the present passage, however, there is mention of Dasein's *ing engaged in repetition of a 'hero'. The reference is left unclarified but seems to imply identifica-*n with another Dasein from the past or present, and therefore may well be read as carrying political *ertones. [RMB]

7.C   Hans-Georg Gadamer, b. 1900

7.C.1   Interpretation of Works of Art is not 'Re-Creation' but 'Ontological Expansion'[6]

No matter how much the variety of the performances or realisations of such a struc ture[7] goes back to the conception of the players – it also does not remain enclosed in the subjectivity of what they think, but it is embodied there. Thus it is not at all a question of a mere subjective variety of conceptions, but of the possibilities of being that the work itself possesses, which lays itself out in the variety of its aspects.

This is not to deny that here there is a possible starting-point for aesthetic reflection. In different performances of the same play, say, one can distinguish between one kind of mediation and another, just as one can conceive the conditions of access to works of art of a different kind in various ways, eg when one looks at a building from the point of view of how it would look on its own or how its surroundings ought to look. Or when one is faced with the question of the restoration of a painting. In all these cases the work itself is distinguished from its 'representation'. But one fails to appreciate the compelling quality of the work of art if one regards the variations possible in the rep resentation as free and optional, In fact they are all subject to the supreme criterion of the 'right' representation.

We know this in the modern theatre as the tradition that stems from a production the creation of a role, or the practice of a musical performance. Here there is no ran dom succession, a mere variety of conceptions, but rather from the constant following of models and from a productive and changing development there is cultivated a tradi tion with which every new attempt must come to terms. The interpretative artist too has a sure consciousness of this. The way that he approaches a work or a role is always related in some way to models which did the same. But it has nothing to do with blind imitation. Although the tradition that is created by a great actor, producer, or musi cian remains effective as a model, it is not brake on free creation but has become so one with the work that the concern with this model stimulates the creative interpretative powers of an artist no less than the concern with the work itself. The reproductive arts have this special quality that the works with which they are concerned are explicitly left open to this kind of re-creation and thus have visibly opened the identity and continu ity of the work of art towards its future.

Perhaps the criterion that determines here whether something is 'a correct represen tation' is a highly mobile and relative one. But the compelling quality of the represen tation is not lessened by the fact that it cannot have any fixed criterion. Thus we do not allow the interpretation of a piece of music or a drama the freedom to take the fixed 'text' as a basis for a lot of ad-lib effects, and yet we would regard the canonisation of a particular interpretation, e.g. in a gramophone recording conducted by the com poser, or the detailed notes on performance which come from the canonised first performance, as a failure to understand the actual task of interpretation. A 'correct

---

6   Gadamer, 1979, pp. 106–7.
7   That is, a play or drama. [RMB]

ness', striven for in this way, would not do justice to the true binding nature of the work, which imposes itself on every interpreter in a special and immediate way and does not allow him to make things easy for himself by simply imitating a model.

It is also, as we know, wrong to limit the 'freedom' of interpretative choice to externals or marginal phenomena and not rather to think of the whole of an interpretation in a way that is both bound and free. Interpretation is probably, in a certain sense, recreation, but this re-creation does not follow the process of the creative act, but the lines of the creative work which has to be brought to representation in accord with the meaning the interpreter finds in it. Thus, for example, performances of music played on old instruments are not as faithful as they seem. Rather they are an imitation of an imitation and in danger 'of standing at a third remove from the truth' (Plato).

In view of the finite nature of our historical existence there is, it would seem, something absurd about the whole idea of a uniquely correct interpretation. . . .

7.C.II 'Play' as the Clue to the Nature of Interpretation[8]

. . . The work of art is not an object that stands over against a subject for itself. Instead the work of art has its true being in the fact that it becomes an experience changing the person experiencing it. The 'subject' of the experience of art, that which remains and endures, is not the subjectivity of the person who experiences it, but the work itself. This is the point at which the mode of being of play becomes significant. For play has its own essence, independent of the consciousness of those who play. Play also exists – indeed, exists properly – when the thematic horizon is not limited by any being-for-self of subjectivity, and where there are no subjects who are behaving 'playfully'.

The players are not the subjects of play; instead play merely reaches presentation through the players. We can see this first from the use of the word, especially from its multiple metaphorical applications. . . .

. . .

If we examine how the word 'play' is used and concentrate on its so-called transferred meanings we find talk of the play of light, the play of the waves, the play of a component in a bearing-case, the inter-play of limbs, the play of forces, the play of gnats, even a play on words. In each case what is intended is the to-and-fro movement which is not tied to any goal which would bring it to an end. This accords with the original meaning of the word spiel as 'dance', which is still found in many word forms (e.g., in Spielmann, jongleur) The movement which is play has no goal which brings it to an end; rather it renews itself in constant repetition. The movement backwards and forwards is obviously so central for the definition of a game that it is not important who or what performs this movement. The movement of play as such has, as it were, no substrate. It is the game that is played – it is irrelevant whether or not there is a subject who plays. The play is the performance of the movement as such. Thus we speak of the play of colours and do not mean only that there is one colour, that plays against another, but that there is one process or sight, in which one can see a changing variety of colours.

Ibid., pp. 92–4.

. . . Thus we say that something is 'playing' somewhere or at some time, that something is going on (sich abspielt, im Spiele ist).

This linguistic observation seems to me to be an indirect indication that play is not to be understood as a kind of activity. As far as language is concerned, the actual subject of play is obviously not the subjectivity of an individual who among other activities also plays, but instead the play itself. . . .

. . .

. . . Play obviously represents an order in which the to-and-fro motion of play follows of itself. It is part of play that the movement is not only without goal or purpose but also without effort. It happens, as it were, by itself. The ease of play, which naturally does not mean that there is any real absence of effort, but phenomenologically refers only to the absence of strain, is experienced subjectively as relaxation. The structure of play absorbs the player into itself, and thus takes from him the burden of the initiative, which constitutes the actual strain of existence. . . .

7.C.III The Rehabilitation of Prejudice[9]

. . . The romantic critique of the enlightenment ends itself in enlightenment, in that it evolves as historical science and draws everything into the orbit of historicism. The basic discrediting of all prejudices, which unites the experiential emphasis of the new natural sciences with the enlightenment, becomes, in the historical enlightenment universal and radical.[10]

This is the point at which the attempt to arrive at an historical hermeneutics has to start its critique. The overcoming of all prejudices, this global demand of the enlightenment, will prove to be itself a prejudice, the removal of which opens the way to an appropriate understanding of our finitude, which dominates not only our humanity but also our historical consciousness.

Does the fact that one is set within various traditions mean really and primarily that one is subject to prejudices and limited in one's freedom? Is not, rather, all human existence, even the freest, limited and qualified in various ways? If this is true, then the idea of an absolute reason is impossible for historical humanity. Reason exists for us only in concrete, historical terms, i.e. it is not its own master, but remains constantly dependent on the given circumstances in which it operates . . . That man is concerned here with himself and his own creations (Vico) is only an apparent solution of the problem set by historical knowledge. Man is alien to himself and his historical fate in a quite different way from that in which nature, that knows nothing of him, is alien to him.

. . . Long before we understand ourselves through the process of self-examination we understand ourselves in a self-evident way in the family, society, and state in which

9 Ibid., pp. 244–6.
10 By 'Romantic' Gadamer means the notion, which we found above all in Schleiermacher, but also in Humboldt and Ranke, of understanding the past, or the mind of a past historical agent, 'as essentially was'. Gadamer is suggesting that despite the usual understanding of Romanticism as a reaction against the Enlightenment, Romantic hermeneutics, because of its ideal of purely objective understanding, is in fact a continuation and intensification of the Enlightenment 'prejudice against prejudice'. [RMB]

e live. The focus of subjectivity is a distorting mirror. The self-awareness of the indi-
dual is only a flickering in the closed circuits of historical life. That is why the preju-
ces of the individual, far more than his judgments, constitute the historical reality of
s being.

. . . That which presents itself, under the aegis of an absolute self-construction by
ason, as a limiting prejudice belongs, in fact, to historical reality itself. What is neces-
ry is a fundamental rehabilitation of the concept of prejudice and a recognition of
e fact that there are legitimate prejudices, if we want to do justice to man's finite
storical mode of being. Thus we are able to formulate the central question of a truly
storical hermeneutics, epistemologically its fundamental question, namely: where is
e ground of the legitimacy of prejudices? What distinguishes legitimate prejudices
om all the countless ones which it is the undeniable task of the critical reason to
ercome?

C.IV   The Fusion of Horizons[11]

ffective-historical consciousness is primarily consciousness of the hermeneutical situ-
ion. To acquire an awareness of a situation is, however, always a task of particular
fficulty. The very idea of a situation means that we are not standing outside it and
nce are unable to have any objective knowledge of it. We are always within the
uation, and to throw light on it is a task that is never entirely completed. This is true
so of the hermeneutic situation, i.e. the situation in which we find ourselves with
gard to the tradition that we are trying to understand. The illumination of this situ-
ion – effective-historical reflection – can never be completely achieved, but this is not
ie to a lack in the reflection, but lies in the essence of the historical being which is
irs. To exist historically means that knowledge of oneself can never be complete. All
lf-knowledge proceeds from what is historically pre-given . . .

Every finite present has its limitations. We define the concept of 'situation' by saying
at it represents a standpoint that limits the possibility of vision. Hence an essential
rt of the concept of situation is the concept of 'horizon'. The horizon is the range of
sion that includes everything that can be seen from a particular vantage point. Apply-
g this to the thinking mind, we speak of narrowness of horizon, of the possible
pansion of horizon, of the opening up of new horizons etc. The word has been used
philosophy since Nietzsche and Husserl to characterise the way in which thought is
d to its finite determination, and the nature of the law of the expansion of the range
vision. A person who has no horizon is a man who does not see far enough and
nce overvalues what is nearest to him. Contrariwise, to have an horizon means not
be limited to what is nearest, but to be able to see beyond it. A person who has an
orizon knows the relative significance of everything within this horizon, as near or
r, great or small. Similarly, the working out of the hermeneutical situation means the
hievement of the right horizon of enquiry for the questions evoked by the encounter
th tradition.

In the sphere of historical understanding we also like to speak of horizons, especially
ien referring to the claim of historical consciousness to see the past in terms of its

Ibid., 268–74

own being, not in terms of our contemporary criteria and prejudices, but within its own historical horizon. The task of historical understanding also involves acquiring the particular historical horizon, so that what we are seeking to understand can be seen in its true dimensions. If we fail to place ourselves in this way within the historical horizon out of which tradition speaks, we shall misunderstand the significance of what it has to say to us. To this extent it seems a legitimate hermeneutical requirement to place ourselves in the other situation in order to understand it. We may ask, however, whether this does not mean that we are failing in the understanding that is asked of us. The same is true of a conversation that we have with someone simply in order to get to know him, i.e. discover his standpoint and his horizon. This is not a true conversation in the sense that we are not seeking agreement concerning an object, but the specific contents of the conversation are only a means to get to know the horizon of the other person. . . .

. . .

. . . Are there, then, two different horizons here, the horizon in which the person seeking to understand lives, and the particular historical horizon within which he places himself? Is it a correct description of the art of historical understanding to say that we are learning to place ourselves within alien horizons? Are there such things as closed horizons, in this sense? We recall Nietzsche's complaint against historicism that it destroyed the horizon bounded by myth in which alone a culture is able to live. Is the horizon of one's own present time ever closed in this way, and can a historical situation be imagined that has this kind of closed horizon?

. . . Just as the individual is never simply an individual, because he is always involved with others, so too the closed horizon that is supposed to enclose a culture is an abstraction. The historical movement of human life consists in the fact that it is never utterly bound to any one standpoint, and hence can never have a truly closed horizon. The horizon is, rather, something into which we move and that moves with us. Horizons change for a person who is moving. . . .

When our historical consciousness places itself within historical horizons, this does not entail passing into alien worlds unconnected in any way with our own, but together they constitute the one great horizon that moves from within and, beyond the frontiers of the present, embraces the historical depths of our self-consciousness. It is, in fact, a single horizon that embraces everything contained in historical consciousness. . . .

. . .

This placing of ourselves is not the empathy of one individual for another, nor is the application to another person of our own criteria, but it always involves the attainment of a higher universality that overcomes, not only our own particularity, but also that of the other . . . Hence it is constantly necessary to inhibit the overhasty assimilation of the past to our own expectations of meaning. Only then will we be able to listen to the past in a way that enables it to make its own meaning heard . . .

. . .

In fact the horizon of the present is being continually formed, in that we have continually to test all our prejudices. An important part of this testing is the encounter with the past and the understanding of the tradition from which we come. Hence the horizon of the present cannot be formed without the past. There is no more an isolated horizon of the present than there are historical horizons. Understanding, rather s always the fusion of these horizons which we imagine to exist by themselves. . . .

. . . Every encounter with tradition that takes place within historical consciousness involves the experience of the tension between the text and the present. The hermeneutic task consists in not covering up this tension by attempting a naive assimilation but consciously bringing it out . . . Historical consciousness is aware of its own otherness and hence distinguishes the horizon of tradition from its own. On the other hand, it is itself, as we are trying to show, only something laid over a continuing tradition, and hence it immediately recombines what it has distinguished in order, in the unity of the historical horizon that it thus acquires, to become again one with itself.

. . . In the process of understanding there takes place a real fusing of horizons, which means that as the historical horizon is projected, it is simultaneously removed. We described the conscious act of this fusion as the task of the effective – historical consciousness . . .

7.D Paul Ricoeur, b. 1913

7.D.1 Existence and Hermeneutics[12]

My purpose here is to explore the paths opened to contemporary philosophy by what could be called the graft of the *hermeneutic problem* onto *the phenomenological method*. . . .

The Origin of Hermeneutics

. . The Hermeneutic problem . . . was first raised within the limits of *exegesis*.[13]

. . .

But exegesis could lead to a general hermeneutics only by means of a second development, the development of classical philology and the *historical sciences* that took place at the end of the eighteenth century and the start of the nineteenth century. It is with Schleiermacher and Dilthey that the hermeneutic problem becomes a philosophic problem . . . The hermeneutic problem [*for Dilthey*] is . . . seen from the perspective of psychology: to understand, for a finite being, is to be transported into another life. Historical understanding thus involves all the paradoxes of historicity: how can a historical being understand history historically? These paradoxes, in turn, lead back to a much more fundamental question: in expressing itself, how can life objectify itself, and, in objectifying itself, how does it bring to light meanings capable of being of being taken up and understood by another historical being, who overcomes his own historical situation? . . .

Grafting Hermeneutics onto Phenomenology

There are two ways to ground hermeneutics in phenomenology . . . The short route is the one taken by an *ontology of understanding*, after the manner of Heidegger . . .

From, 'Existence and Hermeneutics' translated K. McLaughlin, In Ricoeur, 1974, pp. 3–24.
'Exegesis' usually means interpretation of Scripture. [RMB]

Instead of asking: On what condition can a knowing subject understand a text or history? one asks: What kind of being is it whose being consists of understanding? The hermeneutic problem thus becomes a problem of the Analytic of this being, Dasein which exists through understanding.

Before saying why I propose to follow a more roundabout, more arduous path starting with linguistic and semantic considerations, I wish to give full credit to this ontology of understanding. If I begin by giving due consideration to Heidegger' philosophy, it is because I do not hold it to be a contrary solution, that is to say, his Analytic of Dasein is not an alternative which would force us to choose between an ontology of understanding and an epistemology of interpretation . . . The doubt express toward the end of this section is concerned only with the possibility of the making of a direct ontology, free at the outset from any methodological requirement and consequently outside the circle of interpretation whose theory this ontology for mulates. But it is the *desire* for this ontology which animates our enterprise and which keeps it from sinking into either a linguistic philosophy like Wittgenstein's or a reflec tive philosophy of the neo-Kantian sort. . . .

. . .

I fully accept the movement toward this complete reversal of the relationship be tween understanding and being; moreover it fulfills the deepest wish of Dilthey's phi losophy, because for him life was the prime concept . . . The relationship between life and its expressions was rather the common root of the double relationship of man to nature and of man to history. . . .

If the problem of hermeneutics is posed in these ontological terms, of what help is Husserl's phenomenology? . . . What we first encounter on the way back is, of course, the later Husserl, the Husserl of the *Crisis*; it is in him first of all that we must seek the phenomenological foundation of this ontology. His contribution to hermeneutics is twofold . . . Husserl's final phenomenology joins its critique of objectivism to a posi tive problematic which clears the way for an ontology of understanding. This new problematic has as its theme the *Lebenswelt*, the 'life-world,' that is, a level of experi ence anterior to the subject-object relation, which provided the central theme for all the various kinds of neo-Kantianism.

If, then, the later Husserl is enlisted in this subversive undertaking, which aims at substituting an ontology of understanding for an epistemology of interpretation, the early Husserl, the Husserl who goes from the *Logical Investigations* to the *Cartesian Meditations*, is held in grave suspicion. . . .

. . . If the later Husserl points to this ontology, it is because his effort to reduce being failed and because, consequently, the ultimate result of phenomenology escapes the initial project. It is in spite of itself that phenomenology discovers, in place of an idealist subject locked within its system of meanings, a living being which from all time has, as the horizon of all its intentions, a world, the world.

. . . There is operative life, which Husserl sometimes calls anonymous, not because he is returning by this detour to an impersonal Kantian subject, but because the sub ject which has objects is itself derived from this operative life.

. . . The question of historicity is no longer the question of historical knowledge

---

14   That is, the 'transcendental reduction' (see p. 221). Ricoeur may well be exaggerating the differ ence between the later and earlier Husserl (see p. 222n.4). [RMB]

conceived as method. Now it designates the manner in which the existent 'is with' existents . . ., it involves a manner of being akin to being, prior to the encounter with particular beings. At the same time, life's ability to freely stand at a distance in respect to itself, to transcend itself, becomes a structure of finite being . . . What was a paradox – namely, the relation of the interpreter to his object – becomes an ontological trait.

[*But Ricoeur complains that Heidegger does not show how historical understanding, properly speaking is derived from this primordial understanding*[15]]

[*Secondly*] . . . The difficulty in passing from understanding as in mode of knowledge to understanding as a mode of being consists in the following: the understanding which is the result of the Analytic of Dasein is precisely the understanding through which and in which this being understands itself as being. Is it not once again *within language* itself that we must seek the indication that understanding is a mode of being?

These two objections also contain a positive proposition: that of substituting, for the short route of the Analytic of Dasein, the long route which begins by analyses of language . . . This semantics will be organized around the central theme of meanings with multiple or multivocal senses or what we might call symbolic senses. . . .

II The Level of Semantics

t is first of all and always in language that all ontic or ontological understanding arrives at its expression. . . . Everywhere, from exegesis to psychoanalysis, is a certain architecture of meaning, which can be termed 'double meaning' or 'multiple meaning,' whose role in every instance, although in a different manner, is to show while concealing. . . .

. . . I propose to call these multivocal expressions 'symbolic.' Thus, I give a narrower sense to the word 'symbol' than authors who, like Cassirer, call symbolic any apprehension of reality by means of signs, from perception, myth, and art to science; but I give it a broader sense than those authors who, starting from Latin rhetoric or the neo-Platonic tradition, reduce, the symbol to analogy. *I define 'symbol' as any structure of signification in which a direct, primary, literal meaning designates, in addition, another meaning which is indirect, secondary, and figurative and which can be apprehended only through the first*. This circumscription of expressions with a double meaning properly constitutes the hermeneutic field.

. . . *Interpretation, we will say, is the work of thought which consists in deciphering the hidden meaning in the apparent meaning in unfolding the levels of meaning implied in the literal meaning* . . . Symbols and interpretation thus become correlative concepts. . . .

. . . Interpretation gives rise to very different, even opposing methods. [*For instance: phenomenology of religion and psychoanalysis. These two*] are as radically opposed as possible. There is nothing surprising in this: interpretation begins with the multiple determinations of symbols – with their overdetermination as one says in psychoanalysis; but each interpretation, by definition, reduces this richness, this multivocity, and 'translates' this symbol according to its own frame of reference . . .

---

5   Here, it seems to me, Ricoeur fails to acknowledge sufficiently that Heidegger maintains that primordially Dasein *is* 'temporality' or 'historicality', so that there is nothing to 'derive'. [RMB]

IV   The Level of Reflection

. . . A semantics of expression with multiple meanings is not enough to qualify hermeneutics as philosophy. A linguistic analysis which would treat these significations as a whole closed in on itself would ineluctably set up language as an absolute. This hypostasis of language, however, repudiates the basic intention of a sign, which is to hold 'for', thus transcending itself and suppressing itself in what it intends. . . .

By making this admission we join Heidegger again. . . .

Yet how can semantics be integrated with ontology without becoming vulnerable to the objections we raised earlier against an Analytic of Dasein? The intermediary step in the direction of existence is reflection . . . It is in the self that we have an opportunity to discover an existent.

In proposing to relate symbolic language to self-understanding, I think I fulfil the deepest wish of hermeneutics. The purpose of all interpretation is to conquer a re-moteness, a distance between the past cultural epoch to which the text belongs and the interpreter himself. By overcoming this distance, by making himself contemporary with the text, the exegete can appropriate its meaning to himself . . . Every hermeneutics is thus, explicitly or implicitly, self-understanding by means of understanding others.

. . . Why is the self that guides the interpretation able to recover itself only as a result of the interpretation? . . .

[Because] the celebrated Cartesian *cogito*, which grasps itself directly in the experi-ence of doubt, is a truth as vain as it is invincible . . . Reflection is blind intuition if it is not mediated by what Dilthey called the expressions in which life objectifies itself . . . The *cogito* can be recovered only by the detour of a decipherment of the documents of its life. . . .

. . . We have indeed learned, from all the exegetic disciplines and from psychoanaly-sis in particular, that so-called immediate consciousness is first of all 'false conscious-ness'. Marx, Nietzsche, and Freud have taught us to unmask its tricks

. . .

. . . It is always necessary to rise by means of a corrective critique from misunder-standing to understanding.

V   The Existential Level

. . . The ontology of understanding . . . can be, for us who proceed indirectly and by degrees, only a horizon, an aim rather than a given fact. A separate ontology is beyond our grasp: it is only within the movement of interpretation that we apperceive the being we interpret. . . . It is only in a conflict of rival hermeneutics that we perceive something of the being to be interpreted . . .

. . . Freud invites us . . . to ask anew the question of the relationship between signi-fication and desire, between meaning and energy, that is . . . between language and life . . . Existence, we can now say it, is desire and effort. We term it effort in order to stress its positive energy and its dynamism; we term it desire in order to designate its lack and poverty . . .

. . . It is in deciphering the tricks of desire that the desire at the root of meaning and reflection is discovered . . . It is behind itself that the *cogito* discovers, through the work of interpretation, something like an *archaeology of the subject*. Existence is glimpsed in the archeology, but it remains entangled in the movement of deciphering to which it give rise.

. . . Another hermeneutics – that of the philosophy of the spirit, for example – suggests another manner of shifting the origin of sense, so that it is no longer behind the subject but in front of it . . . In the final analysis, this is what animates Hegel's *Phenomenology of the Spirit*.[16] I mention it here because its mode of interpretation is diametrically opposed to Freud's. Psychoanalysis offered us a regression towards the archaic; the phenomenology of the spirit offers us a movement in which each figure finds its meaning, not in what precedes but in what follows. . . .

[*He also mentions as a possibility theological hermeneutics i.e., an interpretation based on the 'sacred'*]

Can one proceed any further? Can these different existential functions be joined in a unitary figure, as Heidegger tried to do in the second part of *Being and Time*? . . . In the dialectic of archaeology, teleology, and eschatology an ontological structure is manifested, one capable of reassembling the discordant interpretations on the linguistic level. But this coherent figure of the being which we ourselves are, in which rival interpretations are implanted is given nowhere but in the dialectic of interpretations. In this respect, hermeneutics is unsurpassable. . . .

In this way, ontology is indeed the promised land for a philosophy that begins with language and with reflection; but, like Moses, the speaking and reflecting subject can only glimpse this land before dying.

16   That is, as we saw, Hegel sees the human mind as starting always with a partial, one-sided grasp of the truth, and moving dialectically towards a more adequate grasp of it. [RMB]

8 Kulturkritik

Hugh Rayment-Pickard

Introduction

Marxism had from the beginning functioned as a form of critique, exposing the historic power-relations between the working and ruling classes. In his early period Marx had spoken about a necessary 'reform of consciousness' and of the need for a 'reckless critique of all that exists, reckless in the sense that the critique is neither afraid of its own results nor of conflicting with the powers that be' (Marx, 1977, p. 36). Marx and the other thinkers in this chapter – all of whom belong in their various ways to the Western Marxist tradition – attempt to develop an understanding of the critical role of philosophy with respect to the history of culture and society. The key issue at stake concerns the relationship between theory and practice: whether theory, in the guise of historical discourse or otherwise, should not merely reflect history but play a role within history.

The origins of this debate lie in an area of ambiguity in Marx's writing. In the classic statement of his theory of history, 'The Preface' to *The Critique of Political Economy*, Marx distinguished between the 'economic base' of society and its legal, political, religious, aesthetic, or philosophic 'superstructure'. In this text however, there is a lack of clarity about the precise relationship between the superstructure and the base. Although Marx argued that the base was the engine of historical development, he did not make it clear whether culture, philosophy and art had any active role to play in history. Some crude interpreters of Marx took this to mean that the superstructure could initiate nothing in history because culture merely reacted to changes in material economic circumstances. Other thinkers, notably the twentieth-century Marxists Gramsci and Lukács, took inspiration from other texts such as the *Theses on Feuerbach* (written in 1845), where Marx had asserted the importance of something he called 'practical-critical activity' or praxis. Praxis implied that culture could have a positive 'revolutionary' role in history when harnessed to the underlying thrust of the historical process.

The Italian Marxist Antonio Gramsci was one of the first thinkers to produce a fully worked-out rejection of the view that the superstructure was merely an expression of the real material processes of history. For Gramsci history was an organic whole, a totality of cultural and material realities. To talk of 'culture' in the abstract was as meaningless as the idea of an abstract 'materialism'. In contradiction of much Marxist orthodoxy, Gramsci saw pure materialism as a form of metaphysics. At any stage in history the relevance and truth of culture depended upon its integration within the prevailing historical totality. Gramsci described this using Croce's phrase 'absolute historicism'. Seen this way, as an essential part of the concrete historical picture, culture could be understood as a potent force in historical change. Indeed Gramsci argued that revolution could only be achieved once the workers had secured what he called cultural 'hegemony' – in other words control over the 'legal, political, religious, aesthetic, or philosophic' superstructure.

Although he was in many ways an original thinker, Gramsci was also a party intellectual seeking to develop Communist doctrine. A more independent, radical and searching development of Marxist thinking came from the members of the Frankfurt Institute of Social Research or 'Frankfurt School', which incorporated thinkers such as Theodor Adorno, Max Horkheimer, Herbert Marcuse and Walter Benjamin. Although the Institute was established in 1923 with the aim of developing Marxism as a social science it was not until the 1930s, when Max Horkheimer became its Director, that the Frankfurt School developed the distinctive neo-Hegelian philosophy that is often called 'critical theory'.[1] The Frankfurt School members were more adventurous and eclectic in their approach than either Gramsci or Lukács, combining Marxist analyses with social theory, psychoanalysis and existentialism. Herbert Marcuse, for example, brought the thinking of Husserl and Heidegger to bear on the problems of materialist history. In an early article, 'Contributions to a Phenomenology of Historical Materialism' Marcuse, 1928),[2] Marcuse followed Heidegger in seeing Dasein as the basis of history, but supplemented the analysis of Dasein with a Marxist analysis of class and the historic role of the proletariat.

For the thinkers of the Frankfurt School the Marxian problematic of theory and practice was of central importance. Their particular concern was the defence of 'theory' as a tool of social knowledge and historical change. The School followed Lukács in rejecting the 'positivist' model of historical and social knowledge which, so they argued, could produce lists of facts but could not explain the underlying processes of history. In order to understand history, argued Horkheimer, one requires an adequate 'social theory'. An adequate social theory must be concerned not merely with the description but with the critique of culture. In this way, theory becomes *critical* – an agent and not merely an observer of history.

A more radical defence of theoretical criticism came from Theodor Adorno in his *Negative Dialectics* [1973]. Adorno's thinking was intensely affected by the Holocaust and he famously declared that there could be no more poetry after Auschwitz. The events of the Second World War confirmed Adorno in his pessimistic view of history: that hope is an illusion and that the so-called 'progress' of history in fact leads to barbarism and oppression. 'No universal history leads from savagery to humanitarianism' he said in *Negative Dialectics*, 'but there is one from the slingshot to the megaton bomb.' Adorno called this view *Zerfallsgeschichte* ('the history of decay'). For him modern history was the story of ever-increasing forms of oppression culminating politically in the Third Reich and philosophically in the decadence of Nietzsche and de Sade: 'The fallen nature of man cannot be separated from social progress' (Adorno and Horkheimer, 1997, p. xiv). The classic text of *Zerfallsgeschichte* is Adorno's joint work with Horkheimer, *The Dialectic of Enlightenment* [1944], in which it is argued that

The original vision of the School is set out in Horkheimer (1972).
For a fuller examination of Marcuse's early philosophy of history see Jay (1973).

the true effect of Enlightenment was not the ascent of humanity as described by Condorcet and Kant (2.B.IV and 2.C.I), but the development of reason as a form of totalitarianism. Although the Enlightenment claimed to be freeing humanity from repressive myths, it was in fact a myth itself: the myth of human sovereignty over nature, of the unity of knowledge and above all of historical progress. In the face of *Zerfallsgeschichte*, Adorno saw the role of the theorist as an ever-vigilant critic of prevailing circumstances and claims for truth. Adorno called this attitude a 'negative dialectic', which unlike Hegel's positive dialectic never reaches a final *Aufhebung*. Negative dialectics is a never-ending critique which must even turn its critical power upon itself:

> Dialectics is obliged to make a final move. It must now turn even against itself. The critique of every self-absolutizing particular is a critique of the shadow which absoluteness casts upon the critique; it is a critique of the fact that critique itself, contrary to its own tendency, must remain within the medium of the concept. It destroys the claim of identity by testing and honouring it; therefore, it can reach no further than that claim. The claim is a magic circle that stamps critique with the appearance of absolute knowledge. It is up to the self-reflection of critique to extinguish that claim, to extinguish it in the very negation of negation that will not become a positing . . . It lies in the definition of negative dialectics that it will not come to rest in itself as if it were total. This is its form of hope. (Adorno, 1973, p. 406)

Although Adorno speaks about hope, it is hard to see what hopeful outcome could result from negative dialectics since his view of *Zerfallsgeschichte* denied the possibility of progress. Without the possibility of progress, human action becomes pointless and fatalism inevitable. It was on just such grounds that Lukács criticized Adorno's apparent passivity in the face of *Zerfallsgeschichte*, saying that Adorno had gone to live in the 'Grand Hotel of the Abyss' where the catastrophe of history would be observed but not challenged (cited in Jarvis, 1998, p. 188).

Jürgen Habermas, the best-known successor to Adorno and the Frankfurt School, makes a different but complementary criticism of negative dialectics. Habermas argues that negative dialectics is too sceptical about Enlightenment reason but not sceptical enough about scepticism itself. This leaves Adorno stranded in 'the relentless unfolding of paradox' (Habermas, 1987, pp. 119–20; 128–9). Habermas himself, as is shown below, tries to advance 'critical theory' in a new direction: towards a positive defence of reason.

Although **Karl Marx** (1818–1883) wrote during the middle decades of the nineteenth century, many of his most important writings, particularly those concerned with the philosophy of history, were not published until a century later. Two important texts from 1844/5 – Marx and Engels' *The German Ideology* and Marx's 'Economic and Philosophical Manuscripts' (sometimes called 'The Paris Manuscripts') were not published until 1932.[3] *The German Ideology* contains the most detailed account of historical materialism and the *Manuscripts* offered arguments about human nature, alienation and Hegelian dialectic. The *Grundrisse*, Marx's outline of a planned six-part study of economics (and the most comprehensive expression of Marx's mature thought), was written in the 1850s but not published until 1941. This publication

---

3   Although *The German Ideology* did appear in an incomplete edition in 1903.

history has had consequences for the reception of Marx's work and the interpretation of his view of history. Early interpreters had to depend primarily upon Marx's brief paragraphs on history in *The Communist Manifesto* (1848) and in 'The Preface to the Critique of Political Economy' (1859). Some critics, notably Lukács, intuitively grasped the deeper philosophical grounding of Marx's writing before seeing the 1844 *Manuscripts*. In general, however, Marx's writing was not well understood until the second half of the twentieth century.

Marx believed that he was making a radical break with Hegelian philosophy. Whereas Hegel had understood the real substance of history to be the logical development of consciousness (3.D.II), Marx believed that history was really the development of the material forces of human life. For Marx, history is grounded in the 'vital activity' (8.A.I) of human existence: the physical business of satisfying basic needs, reproducing and cooperating with others (8.A.II). This base of material history – the human body seeking its survival – also features human consciousness. But human consciousness is dependent upon the material base of the individual species being: 'The phantoms formed in the brain are . . . necessarily sublimates of their material life processes' (Marx, 1977, p. 164). As the individual human has thoughts, so societies possess a superstructure of laws, political systems and administrative structures. But this superstructure has no living body of its own, it is a parasite which takes its life from the dynamic forces of living humanity. It is therefore a mistake to see history simply as the evolution of laws and political systems – as for example Hegel viewed the evolution of civil society. Real history, for Marx, is the history of the human production and re-production of life (8.A.I). This is not to say that consciousness has no historical role, merely that it cannot act on its own (8.A.II) and must be understood in relation to prevailing material circumstances.

However, when Marx speaks of 'material', he clearly means something more complex than physical substances. The 'material' base is also described as 'the *relations* of production' (8.A.III), in other words as social organization. In *The German Ideology* (8.A.II), Marx speaks about the importance of language or 'practical consciousness' in the development of social 'relations'. And in the *Manuscripts* (8.A.I) Marx defines human nature as 'species-being', which is characterized by the way in which man 'practically and *theoretically*' relates to his world through '*conscious* vital activity'. Thus the so-called *material* base already includes human consciousness, theory and social structures. As Lukács and other 'Hegelian' Marxists observed, Marx is in fact closer to Hegel than his own protestations would often have us believe.

Within the material base and within species-being so-called 'productive forces' are operating to create human history. At their most primitive level the productive forces are identical with the will to live. Primeval production is sexual reproduction and biological survival. Marx has a number of terms for these primitive forces: 'essential powers' (*Wesenskräfte*), 'life-powers' (*Lebenskräfte*) and 'species-powers' (*Gattungskräfte*) Marx, 1977, pp. 101–4). The forces of production are not to be thought of in any abstract sense, but as physical labour acting upon the natural world. 'Labour', writes Marx in *Capital*, 'is . . . a process . . . in which man of his own accord starts, regulates and controls the material relations between himself and Nature. He opposes himself to Nature as one of her own forces, setting in motion his arms and legs, head and hands, the natural forces of his body, in order to appropriate Nature's productions in a form adapted to his own wants' (Marx, 1956, p. 88). This appropriation may be aided by technology or by the organization of labour, and these too are productive forces.

The tragedy of the human condition is that the more successfully species-being realizes itself in productive activity, the more alienated humanity becomes from its own nature. Human society originates as a kind of 'primitive communism' in which the workers live directly from the fruits of their own labour. However, the natural human urge is towards greater productivity. Through specialization (the so-called 'division of labour') and the development of 'classes', production becomes more efficient. But at the same time the worker is alienated from the objects of his labour, which not only become commodities to be exchanged but are also abstracted into what Marx calls 'surplus-value' or 'capital'.

Alienation takes its most acute form in the separation of humanity into 'classes'. But these class divisions also provide the social mechanism by which human history can progress dialectically. In ancient and feudal societies Marx finds numerous forms of class division. But with the emergence of capitalism the class system becomes simplified into the bourgeoisie and the proletariat: two irreconcilably separate classes, the one brutally oppressing the other, and whose differences can only be resolved by conflict. The outcome of this conflict is already sealed, as the slave – following Hegel's rule – will overcome the master and the proletariat establishes itself as the only class.[4] In doing so the proletariat effectively abolishes class altogether. Both the bourgeoisie and the proletariat have historic missions. The mission of the bourgeoisie is to create the proletariat as a cohesive alienated mass, ready for revolt. The mission of the proletariat is to force the hand of history by overcoming the bourgeois through revolution.

However, revolution requires theory. The proletariat must become conscious of its historic role. It is one of the functions of communism to provide the workers with historical self-understanding. But this understanding is not *merely* theoretical, but is rooted in material social conditions. Thus in *The Communist Manifesto* [1848] Marx describes the 'theoretical conclusions of the communists' as 'in no way based on ideas or principles that have been invented, or discovered, by this or that would-be universal reformer. They merely express, in general terms, actual relations springing from an existing class struggle.' Such a theory would not merely *reflect* or *interpret* the world; the point of philosophy, as Marx says elsewhere, is to *change* the world.

The end of historical change, for Marx, is the emergence of communist society. As the workers re-appropriate control of production, alienation evaporates. Without the tension of alienation or the antagonism of classes, history loses its dynamism and settles into a stable state. From the perspective of a communist state the interpretation of history would at last become a definite science, since the material success of communism would be the proof of its historical theory.

Before his conversion to Marxism in 1918, *Georg Lukács'* (1885–1971) intellectual concerns were primarily in the domain of culture, rather than economics or politics. In these early years, Lukács came under the influence of the writings of Dilthey and attended lectures by Simmel, Rickert and Windelband. His early philosophy of history bears the marks of a pessimistic *Lebensphilosophie*. Lukács saw modernity in decline from a 'Homeric' ideal of a unified culture in which the life of the individual was integrated into the epic and self-contained narrative of history. In his early writings *Soul and Form* [1910] and *The Theory of the Novel* [1916], Lukács's view is that history

---

4   See also chapter 10, where Fukuyama takes up the theme of the master and slave.

is tragic and formless, an endless expenditure of life-energies that never resolves itself into a pattern or consummation. After 1918 Lukács' philosophy of history became a self-conscious defence of the Leninist interpretation of historical materialism. Although his critics are quick to label him as a mere dogmatist, Lukács's writing had a considerable influence on the most undogmatic and unorthodox of Marxist thinkers, including Walter Benjamin who described *History and Class Consciousness* [1923] as one of the four most important books of the early twentieth century.

History and Class Consciousness, which is excerpted below, is Lukács' best-known work. In this collection of essays he tried to redefine Marx's theory of history against its more 'vulgar' materialist and positivist interpretations.[5] Marxism was not, for Lukács, a scientific description of history unfolding according to natural laws, but a theory of history as a dynamic whole. The facts of history, meaningless in themselves, become 'concrete' realities when they are understood as part of the totality of the historical process. This includes the subject of history, the revolutionary proletariat, which must become conscious of its own role in relation to the completion of history. 'Only when the consciousness of the proletariat is able to point out the road along which the dialectics of history is objectively impelled . . . will the proletariat become the identical subject-object of history whose praxis will change reality' (Lukács, 1971, p. 197).

Lukács read Marx as a Hegelian who takes from Hegel the machinery for integrating the subject of history into history's objective completion. For Marx, of course, this subject was not *Geist* but the social reality of the proletariat. However, the Hegelian *method* of dialectic permits Marx to realize the means of the proletariat's integration into history. Hegel's cardinal error was that he 'failed to discover the identical subject-object in history' and was therefore 'forced to go out beyond history' into the 'empire of reason'. From this vantage point, the evolution of history would inevitably appear as 'the cunning of reason' (p. 147).

A key concept imported from Hegel into Lukács' Marxism is the idea of concretion (p. 142). Hegel argued that every finite entity only attains meaning by becoming part of a concrete totality. Whereas Marx caricatured Hegel as an idealist, Lukács recognized that Hegel's totality must be both an ideal and a material state of affairs. If Hegel's concept of totality excluded matter, it would not be a true totality. This totalizing integration is what Lukács means by the idea of the concrete. It follows then that the Marxian totality must also include *thought*. 'The "relativization" of truth in Hegel means that the higher factor is always the truth of the factor beneath it in the system. This does not imply the destruction of "objective" truth at the lower stages but only that it means something different as a result of being integrated in a more concrete and comprehensive totality. When Marx makes dialectics the essence of history, the movement of thought also becomes just a part of the overall movement of history' (p. 188). The achievement of 'class consciousness' by the proletariat is an historic moment of concretion. It is on the basis of this consciousness that society as a whole can understand the truth of history: 'The self-understanding of the proletariat is . . . simultaneously the objective understanding of the nature of society' (p. 149).

The historical self-awareness of the proletariat 'begins with knowledge of the present' and views history as the process by which the present is structured (p. 159). 'The

---

5 After criticism from the Communist Party, in 1933, Lukács recanted some of his views in *History and Class Consciousness*.

essence of history lies precisely in the changes undergone by those *structural forms* which . . . determine the objective nature of both . . . [man's] . . . inner and his outer life' (p. 153). The searching out of these 'structural forms' is the true task of the historian and the route to an understanding of the totality of the historical process. By contrast, the detached, 'contemplative' attitude of bourgeois historiography ignores the historian's 'standpoint' which is historically 'conditioned' in the present. Bourgeois history 'reifies' the true subject of history, the structural evolution of the proletariat, by trying to reduce history to objective knowledge of laws or facts. What Lukács called 'reification' can only be undone when the 'subject' of history (the proletariat) thinks through its situation and thus becomes its own 'object'.

Walter Benjamin (1892–1940) was the most quixotic member of the Frankfurt School. He classified himself as a Marxist historical materialist. Yet against all Marxist orthodoxy he argued that history could not be understood without theology: 'My thinking is related to theology like a blotter is to ink. It is full absorbed by it' (Benjamin, 1972, I(3), p. 1235). In Benjamin's philosophy there are also elements of nineteenth-century suprahistory, Nietzschean nihilism, Kant's analytic of experience and a Cabalistic Judaism based on riddles and the failure of human reason. One consequence of this unlikely fusion of components is that Benjamin's philosophy of history is all but impossible to classify.

Benjamin's theory of history is most clearly evident in two texts: *The Theses on the Philosophy of History* [1940] and the section on knowledge and progress in the *Arcades Project* (written between 1927 and 1940). Although he was little known in his own lifetime, Benjamin has come to be regarded, in some circles at least, as one of the most important thinkers of the twentieth century

Benjamin, rather like Schopenhauer, developed his own philosophy through a re-working of Kant's theory of knowledge. Although Kant had elaborated in great detail the transcendental structures of mind which make knowledge possible, he neglected to explore the condition of the 'naked, primitive, self-evident experience' upon which perception is based. In his early writing, particularly his essay 'On the Programme of the Coming Philosophy' [1918], Benjamin sets himself the task of devising a 'superior concept of experience': a dynamic and plural encounter with the visible 'surfaces' of the world. Experience thus comes to us not in the form of concepts but images: surface 'configurations' of inscription and colour. These configurations do not stabilize experience for us (as Kant's transcendental aesthetic does) but expose us to an infinity which is immanent in experience itself. By contrast with Kant who had argued that 'the absolute' cannot be experienced as a thing-in-itself, Benjamin declares the infinitude of configuration in experience to be absolute.[6] So whereas Kant had advocated metaphysics within the limits of reason alone, Benjamin asserts a metaphysics within the limits of experience: 'To say that knowledge is metaphysical means in the strict sense: it is related via the original concept of knowledge to the concrete totality of experience, i.e. *existence*' (ed. Smith, 1989, p. 11).

Benjamin also challenges the priority which Kant, and his 'Enlightenment' successors, gave to the self. For Kant the (transcendental) self, the so-called 'synthetic unity of apperception', is at the centre of the organization of knowledge. In Benjamin'

6   These remarks cannot do justice to Benjamin's complex reworking of Kant. For an excellent analysis see Caygill (1998).

reckoning this Kantian self is a piece of 'mythology'. 'The task of future epistemology is to find for knowledge the sphere of total neutrality in regard to the concepts both of subject and object' (p. 5). What we mean by 'the self' is, for Benjamin, constituted within this 'sphere of neutrality', which is the process of experience itself.

This recasting of Kant's epistemology is important in Benjamin's understanding of the historian's task. The past like everything else comes to us as experience: 'The true picture of the past flits by. The past can be seized only as an image which flashes up at the instant when it can be recognized and is never seen again' (8.C.I). This 'flashing up' is an historical event in itself, a phenomenon generated in a particular 'now-time' and graspable only at that moment. There is no continuum to history, no order, no progression, and no pattern – only a multitude of moments each with its own potential for historical disclosure.

It follows from such an epistemology, that human beings can never see the whole of history, since 'knowledge exists in lightening flashes' (p. 43). Yet Benjamin attempts to *imagine* the viewpoint of a cosmic observer by borrowing an image from a picture by Paul Klee, *Angelus Novus*. Klee depicts what Benjamin calls an 'angel of history' who can see the past as a whole and is blasted into the future by the storm of so-called 'progress'. From the human perspective, says Benjamin, we see history as a causal and progressive sequence of development. Yet from the angelic perspective, history appears as wreckage, decay and debris. This is an arresting image, but it is also a total description of history of the kind that Benjamin declares impossible. Benjamin, like his suprahistorist predecessors, gets caught in the paradoxes of reflection that accompany any denial of totality.[7]

In the early 1930s, Benjamin's thinking takes a Marxist turn. However, the label 'Marxist' needs to be applied to Benjamin with caution since, as Hannah Arendt has put it, he was 'the most peculiar Marxist ever produced . . . [by the Frankfurt School] . . . which God knows had its share of oddities' (Benjamin, 1973, p. 11). Benjamin's very particular view of historical materialism may be understood as a development of his theory of the image. For Benjamin the 'image' is the 'primal phenomenon' of history, and is *material* in the sense that it forms the unit of concrete experience. It follows therefore that history is subject to the same limitations as experience itself, which takes the form of a 'continuous multiplicity'. As such, history can never come together as a continuous story or as a total description. In the notes Benjamin left for his so-called *Arcades Project* he says that 'history breaks down into images, not stories' (ed. Smith, 1989, p. 67). This separation of image and narrative means that history does not follow in a progressive sequence like the frames of a film: 'a continuity of historical presentation is unattainable' (p. 60).

Although the imagistic condition of history results in narrative discontinuity, Benjamin's understanding of the image allows for the possibility of 'a univocal sense of historicity' attainable through the analysis of oppression and guilt.

> In order to guarantee a univocal sense of historicity [*Geschehens*], the highest category of World-history is Guilt. Every world-historical moment creates debt and blame. Cause and effect can never be decisive categories for the structure of world-history, since they are incapable of delivering totality. (Benjamin, 1972, VI, p. 92)

See chapter 5, pp. 139f.

As Benjamin puts it elsewhere, 'the continuum of history is that of the oppressor' which means that the 'subject of history' is not humanity but the oppressors (I(3), p. 1244). This continuum of oppression only appears to us in flashes when, by means of a 'telescoping of the past through the present' (ed. Smith, 1989, p. 60), the 'constellation' of a previous era impinges on the 'constellation' of the present, thereby unmasking both the true condition of the present and its revolutionary potential.

The revolutionary moment is not a rational juncture, but a 'shock' in history, a 'state of emergency' which shatters our view of history as a rational system. For Benjamin. this moment can only be understood *theologically* as a non-rational, cosmically-given. messianic appearance. The messianic view of time gives a name at least to the random flashes of historical knowledge, even if it does not explain them. Such flashes are not the result of another divine world breaking in on this one, but a fundamental feature of the ordinary human world: 'The messianic world is the world of comprehensive and integral actuality' (Benjamin, 1972, I(3), p. 1238). This actuality is not only a feature of the present, but the basis both of a promise of future freedom from oppression and of the consummation of history. Since there can be no *progression* towards this future it must simply 'flash up':

> Only the Messiah himself consummates all history, in the sense that he alone redeems, completes, creates its relation to the Messianic. For this reason nothing historical can relate itself on its own account to anything Messianic. Therefore the Kingdom of God is not the telos of the historical dynamic; it cannot be set as a goal. From the standpoint of history it is not the goal, but the end. (Benjamin, 1978, p. 313)

Critics disagree about the level of importance to give to Benjamin's messianism. However, it is at least clear that Benjamin's historical materialism cannot be understood without taking into account his theology. The first Thesis vividly depicts the 'automaton' of historical materialism under the necessary control of the 'hunchback' of theology. The last Thesis quotes approvingly the Jewish practice of regarding 'every second of time' as 'the strait gate through which the Messiah might enter.'

Jürgen Habermas (b. 1929) is probably the most influential German philosophe of the late twentieth century. Although he was a member of the Frankfurt School who worked as an assistant to Adorno in the 1950s, his work is perhaps best thought of a 'neo-critical theory', an extension of the critical-theoretical project. Habermas' work has centred on a defence of enlightenment reason against modern and post-modern relativism. In undertaking this defence Habermas draws upon ideas from the social sciences, notably the theory of 'rationalization' in Max Weber (6.E.II) and the 'systems theory' of Niklas Luhmann.

In his more recent writing, Habermas has argued that even our most basic efforts at 'communication' demand common norms of understanding and reason. Without such norms communication would break down and even ordinary forms of civil agreement would become impossible: 'What raises us out of nature is the only thing whose nature we can know: language. Through its structure autonomy and responsibility are posited for us. Our first sentence expresses unequivocally the intention of universal and unconstrained consensus' (cited in Bottomore, 1984, p. 59). This view of language has important implications for our view of truth: whilst you or I may speak from historically-conditioned circumstances, our use of language presupposes the possibility of universal truth beyond history. Although there is no direct access to such truth, Habermas argues in *Towards the Reconstruction of Historical Materialism* [1976] that it is possible to engage in what he calls 'universal pragmatics': 'the research programme aimed at reconstructing the universal validity basis of truth.' The key concept in universal pragmatics is 'the ideal speech situation', an imaginary state of affairs in which all the parties to a conversation would have equal, unrestricted opportunity of participation. In reality our involvement in conversations is always restricted, but in contributing to dialogue we assume that some of the conditions of 'ideal speech' will be fulfilled, and in doing so we validate 'ideal speech' as the basis of truth.

Although Habermas defends Enlightenment reason, he is also a critic of Enlightenment subjectivity – whether the transcendental human subject of Descartes, Kant and Husserl, or the collective social subject described by Horkheimer and Adorno. Habermas tries to replace 'subject-centred reason' with what he calls 'systems rationality': a view of reason generated in the inter-personal, linguistic realm of human interactions. As Terry Eagleton puts it: 'There is, in other words, a kind of "deep" rationality built into the very structures of our language, regardless of what we actually say, and it is this which provides Habermas with the basis for a critique of our actual verbal practices. In a curious sense, the very act of enunciation can become a normative judgement on what in enunciated' (Eagleton, 1991, p. 130).

In the 1960s – notably in the essays in *Theory and Practice* – Habermas started to rethink Marxism in the light of twentieth-century circumstances, arguing that the base-superstructure distinction could not be maintained, that 'the proletariat as proletariat' had 'dissolved', that 'alienation' had been 'deprived of its palpable economic form as misery' and that 'today Marx would have to abandon his hope that theory can become material force, once it had taken hold of the masses' (Habermas, 1974, p. 196f). Later, in the 1970s, Habermas used his theory of communication to undertake a more radical 'reconstruction' ('taking a theory apart and putting it back together in a new form') of Marx's historical materialism. We have already seen how, in the *Paris Manuscripts* and elsewhere, Marx's view of materialism was more complex than is often thought, involving social structures, theoretical perspectives and language. It is these aspects of historical materialism that Habermas was seeking to bring to the fore. Marx had already defined species being in terms of social productivity and 'conscious vital activity'. Habermas redefines species being as a combination of social labour and *language*. Relations of production depend upon language, and therefore a revised version of historical materialism may be offered: The subject of history is humanity as a linguistic and labouring reality and historical materialism concerns not only the history of social labour but also the history of communicative action. The reconstruction of Marx's philosophy of history helps Habermas to develop communications theory into a theory of social evolution. History takes the shape of the evolution of communicative freedom and rationality. Like the 'ideal speech situation' the concept of an ideal society is a necessary presupposition. Yet it is not merely a presupposition since in any given society at any given stage in history one may see the ideal more or less *realized* in the prevailing social circumstances.

Habermas' defence of reason and norms in history has provided an important counter-voice to the often fashionable 'postmodern' consensus that it is no longer possible to disentangle truth from fiction (see chapters 9 and 10). The distinctiveness of Habermas' perspective comes into focus in his debate with Gadamer. Habermas argues against Gadamer that the truth cannot be determined through hermeneutics but only by *critique*. We must find a *meta*-hermeneutical standpoint from which to sift out false and distorted aspects of tradition. Tradition and prejudice cannot form this standpoint since they are internal to the hermeneutical process and complicit with the object of critique (on Gadamer, see chapter 1; on the Gadamer–Habermas debate, see chapter 7). Later, in the *Philosophical Discourse of Modernity*, Habermas makes a critique of Michel Foucault's philosophy of history (see chapter 10) arguing that Foucault is unable to supply an adequate model of truth and without such a model is unable to argue effectively for the truth of his own theory of history. As a result, according to Habermas, Foucault ends up in 'unholy subjectivism' (Habermas, 1998, p. 276). The failure of 'postmodern' theories such as Foucault's to provide any basis for objective judgements also robs history of any critical power.

Selected Texts

Edited by Hugh Rayment-Pickard

8.A   Karl Marx, 1818–1883

8.A.1   **Human Species-life and Alienation**[1]

Man is a species-being not only in that practically and theoretically he makes both his own and other species into his objects, but also, and this is only another way of putting the same thing, he relates to himself as to the present, living species, in that he relates to himself as to a universal and therefore free being.

Both with man and with animals the species-life consists physically in the fact that man (like animals) lives from inorganic nature, and the more universal man is than animals the more universal is the area of inorganic nature from which he lives. From the theoretical point of view, plants, animals, stones, air, light, etc. form part of human consciousness, partly as objects of natural science, partly as objects of art; they are his intellectual inorganic nature, his intellectual means of subsistence, which he must first prepare before he can enjoy and assimilate them. From the practical point of view, too, they form a part of human life and activity. Physically man lives solely from these products of nature, whether they appear as food, heating, clothing, habitation, etc. The universality of man appears in practice precisely in the universality that makes the whole of nature into his inorganic body in that it is both (i) his immediate means of subsistence and also (ii) the material object and tool of his vital activity. Nature is the inorganic body of a man, that is, in so far as it is not itself a human body. That man lives from nature means that nature is his body with which he must maintain a constant interchange so as not to die. That man's physical and intellectual life depends on nature merely means that nature depends on itself, for man is a part of nature.

While alienated labour alienates (1) nature from man, and (2) man from himself, his own active function, his vital activity, it also alienates the species from man; it turns his species-life into a means towards his individual life. Firstly it alienates species-life and individual life, and secondly in its abstraction it makes the latter into the aim of the former which is also conceived of in its abstract and alien form. For firstly, work, vital activity, and productive life itself appear to man only as a means to the satisfaction of a need, the need to preserve his physical existence. But productive life is species-life. It is

Karl Marx, 'The Economic and Philosophical Manuscripts', in *Karl Marx: Selected Writings*, ed. D. McLellan (Oxford: Oxford University Press, 1977), pp. 81–3.

life producing life. The whole character of a species, its generic character, is contained in its manner of vital activity, and free conscious activity is the species-characteristic of man. Life itself appears merely as a means to life.

The animal is immediately one with its vital activity. It is not distinct from it. They are identical. Man makes his vital activity itself into an object of his will and consciousness. He has a conscious vital activity. He is not immediately identical to any of his characterizations. Conscious vital activity differentiates man immediately from animal vital activity. It is this and this alone that makes man a species-being. He is only a conscious being, that is, his own life is an object to him, precisely because he is a species-being. This is the only reason for his activity being free activity. Alienated labour reverses the relationship so that, just because he is a conscious being, man makes his vital activity and essence a mere means to his existence. The practical creation of an objective world, the working-over of inorganic nature, is the confirmation of man as a conscious species-being, that is, as a being that relates to the species as to himself and to himself as to the species. It is true that the animal, too, produces. It builds itself a nest, a dwelling, like the bee, the beaver, the ant, etc. But it only produces what it needs immediately for itself or its offspring; it produces one-sidedly whereas man produces universally; it produces only under the pressure of immediate physical need, whereas man produces freely from physical need and only truly produces when he is thus free; it produces only itself whereas man reproduces the whole of nature. Its product belongs immediately to its physical body whereas man can freely separate himself from his product. The animal only fashions things according to the standards and needs of the species it belongs to, whereas man knows how to produce according to the measure of every species and knows everywhere how to apply its inherent standard to the object; thus man also fashions things according to the laws of beauty.

Thus it is in the working over of the objective world that man first really *affirms* himself as a species-being. This production is his active species-life. Through it nature appears as his work and his reality. The object of work is therefore the objectification of the species-life of man; for he duplicates himself not only intellectually, in his mind, but also actively in reality and thus can look at his image in a world he has created. Therefore when alienated labour tears from man the object of his production, it also tears from him his species-life, the real objectivity of his species and turns the advantage he has over animals into a disadvantage in that his organic body, nature, is torn from him.

8.A.II   History and Human Consciousness[2]

We must begin by stating the first premise of all human existence and, therefore, of all history, the premise, namely, that men must be in a position to live in order to be able to 'make history'. But life involves before everything else eating and drinking, a habitation, clothing, and many other things. The first historical act is thus the production of the means to satisfy these needs, the production of material life itself. And indeed

2   Karl Marx, *The German Ideology*, in *Karl Marx: Selected Writings*, ed. D. McLellan (Oxford: Oxford University Press, 1977), pp. 165–8.

this is an historical act, a fundamental condition of all history, which today, as thousands of years ago, must daily and hourly be fulfilled merely in order to sustain human life. . . . Therefore in any interpretation of history one has first of all to observe this fundamental fact in all its significance and all its implications and to accord it its due importance. . . .

The second point is that the satisfaction of the first need (the action of satisfying, and the instrument of satisfaction which has been acquired) leads to new needs; and this production of new needs is the first historical act. . . . The third circumstance which, from the very outset, enters into historical development, is that men, who daily remake their own life, begin to make other men, to propagate their kind: the relation between man and woman, parents and children, the family. . . . These three aspects of social activity are not of course to be taken as three different stages, but just as three aspects or . . . three 'moments', which have existed simultaneously since the dawn of history and the first men, and which still assert themselves in history today.

The production of life, both of one's own in labour and of fresh life in procreation, now appears as a double relationship: on the one hand as a natural, on the other as a social, relationship. By social we understand the co-operation of several individuals, no matter under what conditions, in what manner, and to what end. It follows from this that a certain mode of production, or industrial stage, is always combined with a certain mode of co-operation, or social stage, and this mode of co-operation is itself a 'productive force'. Further, that the multitude of productive forces accessible to men determines the nature of society, hence, that the 'history of humanity' must always be studied and treated in relation to the history of industry and exchange. . . . Thus it is quite obvious from the start that there exists a materialistic connection of men with one another, which is determined by their needs and their mode of production, and which is as old as men themselves. This connection is ever taking on new forms, and thus presents a 'history' independently of the existence of any political or religious nonsense which in addition may hold men together.

Only now, after having considered four moments, four aspects of the primary historical relationships, do we find that man also possesses 'consciousness', but, even so, not inherent, not 'pure' consciousness. From the start the 'spirit' is afflicted with the curse of being 'burdened' with matter, which here makes its appearance in the form of agitated layers of air, sounds, in short, of language. Language is as old as consciousness, language is practical consciousness that exists also for other men, and for that reason alone it really exists for me personally as well; language, like consciousness, only arises from the need, the necessity, of intercourse with other men. Where there exists a relationship, it exists for me: the animal does not enter into 'relations' with anything, it does not enter into any relation at all. For the animal, its relation to others does not exist as a relation. Consciousness is, therefore, from the very beginning a social product, and remains so as long as men exist at all. Consciousness is at first, of course, merely consciousness concerning the immediate sensuous environment and consciousness of the limited connection with other persons and things outside the individual who is growing self-conscious. At the same time it is consciousness of nature, which first appears to men as a completely alien, all-powerful, and unassailable force, with which men's relations are purely animal and by which they are overawed like beasts, it is thus a purely animal consciousness of nature (natural religion) just because nature is as yet hardly modified historically. . . . On the other hand, man's consciousness of the necessity of associating with the individuals around him is the beginning of the consciousness that he is living in society at all. This beginning is as animal as social life itself at this stage. It is mere herd-consciousness, and at this point man is only distinguished from sheep by the fact that with him consciousness takes the place of instinct or that his instinct is a conscious one. This sheep-like or tribal consciousness receives its further development and extension through increased productivity, the increase of needs, and, what is fundamental to both of these, the increase of population. With these there develops the division of labour, which was originally nothing but the division of labour in the sexual act, then that division of labour which develops spontaneously or 'naturally' by virtue of natural predisposition (e.g., physical strength), needs, accidents, etc. etc. Division of labour only becomes truly such from the moment when a division of material and mental labour appears. . . . From this moment onwards consciousness can really flatter itself that it is something other than consciousness of existing practice, that it really represents something without representing something real; from now on consciousness is in a position to emancipate itself from the world and to proceed to the formation of 'pure' theory, theology, philosophy, ethics etc. But even if this theory theology, philosophy, ethics, etc, comes into contradiction with the existing relations this can only occur because existing social relations have come into contradiction with existing forces of production. . . .

Moreover, it is quite immaterial what consciousness starts to do on its own: out of all such muck we get only the one inference that these three moments, the forces of production, the state of society, and consciousness, can and must come into contradiction with one another, because the division of labour implies the possibility, nay the fact, that intellectual and material activity – enjoyment and labour, production and consumption – devolve on different individuals, and that the only possibility of their not coming into contradiction lies in the negation in its turn of the division of labour It is self-evident, moreover, that 'spectres', 'bonds', 'the higher being', 'concept', 'scruple', are merely the idealistic, spiritual expression, the conception apparently of the isolated individual, the image of very empirical fetters and limitations, within which the mode of production of life and the form of intercourse coupled with it move.

8.A.III   The Overall Scheme of History[3]

In the social production of their life, men enter into definite relations that are indispensable and independent of their will, relations of production which correspond to a definite stage of development of their material productive forces.

The sum total of these relations constitutes the economic structure of society, the real foundation, on which rises a legal and political superstructure and to which correspond definite forms of social consciousness. The mode of production of material life conditions the social, political and intellectual life processes in general. It is not the consciousness of men that determines their being, but, on the contrary, their social being which determines their consciousness.

At a certain stage of their development, the material productive forces of society

3   Karl Marx, 'The Preface to A Critique of Political Economy', in *Karl Marx: Selected Writings*, ed. D. McLellan (Oxford: Oxford University Press, 1977), pp. 389–90.

come in conflict with the existing relations of production, or with the property relations within which they have been at work hitherto. Then begins an epoch of social
revolution.

In considering such transformations a distinction should always be made between
the material transformation of the economic conditions of production and the legal,
political, religious aesthetic or philosophic – in short, ideological forms in which men
become conscious of this conflict and fight it out. Just as our opinion of an individual
is not based upon what he thinks of himself, so can we not judge of such a period of
transformation by its own consciousness; on the contrary, this consciousness must be
explained rather from the contradictions of material life, from the existing conflict
between the social productive forces and the relations of production.

No social order ever perishes before all the productive forces for which there is room
in it have developed; and new, higher relations of production never appear before the
material conditions of their existence have matured in the womb of the old society
itself. Therefore mankind always sets itself only such tasks as it can solve; since it will be
always found that the task itself arises only when the material conditions for its solution already exist or are at least in the process of formation.

In broad outlines Asiatic, ancient, feudal, and modern bourgeois modes of production can be designated as progressive epochs in the economic formation of society.
The bourgeois relations of production are the last antagonistic form of the social process of production arising from the social conditions of the life of the individuals. The
productive forces developing in the womb of bourgeois society create the material
conditions for the solution of that antagonism. This social formation brings, therefore,
the prehistory of human society to a close.

3.B   Georg Lukács, 1885–1971

3.B.1   The Dialectics of History[4]

Thus man has become the measure of all (societal) things. . . . At the conceptual level
the structure of the world of men stands revealed as a system of dynamically changing
relations in which the conflicts between man and nature, man and man (in the class
struggle, etc.) are fought out. The structure and the hierarchy of the categories are the
index of the degree of clarity to which man has attained concerning the foundations of
his existence in these relations, i.e. the degree of consciousness of himself.

At the same time this structure and this hierarchy are the central theme of history.
History is no longer an enigmatic flux *to which* men and things are subjected. It is no
longer a thing to be explained by the intervention of transcendental powers or made
meaningful by reference to transcendental values. History is, on the one hand the
product (albeit the unconscious one) of man's own activity, on the other hand it is the
succession of those processes in which the forms taken by this activity and the relations
of man to himself (to nature, to other men) are overthrown. So that if . . . the catego-

Georg Lukács, *History and Class Consciousness*, tr. R. Livingstone (London: Merlin Press, 1971),
p. 185–8.

ries describing the structure of a social system are not immediately historical, i.e. if the empirical succession of historical events does not suffice to explain the origins of a particular form of thought or existence, then it can be said that despite this, or better, because of it, any such conceptual system will describe in its totality a definite stage in the society as a whole.

And the nature of history is precisely that every definition degenerates into an illusion: *history is the history of the unceasing overthrow of the objective forms that shape the life of man*. It is therefore not possible to reach an understanding of particular forms by studying their successive appearances in an empirical and historical manner. This is not because they transcend history, though this is and must be the bourgeois view with its addiction to thinking about isolated 'facts' in isolated mental categories. The truth is rather that these particular forms are not immediately connected with each other either by their simultaneity or by their consecutiveness. What connects them is their place and function in the totality and by rejecting the idea of a 'purely historical' explanation the notion of history as a universal discipline is brought nearer. When the problem of connecting isolated phenomena has become a problem of categories, by the same dialectical process every problem of categories becomes transformed into a historical problem. Though it should be stressed: it is transformed into a problem of universal history which now appears – more clearly than in our introductory polemical remarks – simultaneously as a problem of method and a problem of our knowledge of the present.

From this standpoint alone does history really become a history of mankind. For it contains nothing that does not lead back ultimately to men and to the relations between men. It is because Feuerbach gave this new direction to philosophy that he was able to exercise such a decisive influence on the origins of historical materialism. However, by transforming philosophy into 'anthropology' he caused man to become frozen in a fixed objectivity and thus pushed *both* dialectics and history to one side. And precisely this is the great danger in every 'humanism' or anthropological point of view. For if man is made the measure of all things, and if with the aid of that assumption all transcendence is to be eliminated without man himself being measured against this criterion, without applying the same 'standard' to himself or – more exactly – without making man himself dialectical, then man himself is made into an absolute and he simply puts himself in the place of those transcendental forces he was supposed to explain, dissolve and systematically replace. At best, then, a dogmatic metaphysics is superseded by an equally dogmatic relativism.

This dogmatism arises because the failure to make man dialectical is complemented by an equal failure to make reality dialectical. Hence relativism moves within an essentially static world. As it cannot become conscious of the immobility of the world and the rigidity of its own standpoint it inevitably reverts to the dogmatic position of those thinkers who likewise offered to explain the world from premises they did not consciously acknowledge and which, therefore, they adopted uncritically. For it is one thing to relativise the truth about an individual or a species in an ultimately static world (masked though this stasis may be by an illusory movement like the 'eternal recurrence of the same things' or the biological or morphological 'organic' succession of periods). And it is quite another matter when *the concrete, historical function and meaning* of the various 'truths' is revealed within a unique, concretised historical process. Only in the former case can we accurately speak of relativism. But in that case inevitably becomes dogmatic. For it is only meaningful to speak of relativism where an 'absolute' is in some sense assumed. The weakness and the half-heartedness of such 'daring thinkers' as Nietzsche or Spengler is that their relativism only abolishes the absolute in appearance.

For, from the standpoint of both logic and method, the 'systematic location' of the absolute is to be found just where the apparent movement stops. The absolute is nothing but the fixation of thought, it is the projection into myth of the intellectual failure to understand reality concretely as a historical process. Just as the relativists have only appeared to dissolve the world into movement, so too they have only appeared to exile the absolute from their systems. Every 'biological' relativism, etc., that turns its limits into 'eternal' limits thereby involuntarily reintroduces the absolute, the 'timeless' principle of thought. And as long as the absolute survives in a system (even unconsciously) it will prove logically stronger than all attempts at relativism. For it represents the highest principle of thought attainable in an undialectical universe, in a world of ossified things and a logical world of ossified concepts. So that here both logically and methodologically Socrates must be in the right as against the sophists, and logic and value theory must be in the right as against pragmatism and relativism.

What these relativists are doing is to take the present philosophy of man with its social and historical limits and to allow these to ossify into an 'eternal' limit of a biological or pragmatic sort. Actuated either by doubt or despair they thus stand revealed as a *decadent version* of the very rationalism or religiosity they mean to oppose. Hence they may sometimes be a not unimportant *symptom* of the inner weakness of the society which produced the rationalism they are 'combating'. But they are significant only as symptoms. It is always the culture they assail, the culture of the class that has not yet been broken, that embodies the authentic spiritual values.

Only the dialectics of history can create a radically new situation. This is not only because it relativises all limits, or better, because it puts them in a state of flux. Nor is it just because all those forms of existence that constitute the counterpart of the absolute are dissolved into processes and viewed as concrete manifestations of history so that the absolute is not so much denied as endowed with *its concrete historical shape and treated as an aspect of the process itself.*

3.C   Walter Benjamin, 1892–1940

3.C.1   The True Picture of the Past[5]

The story is told of an automaton constructed in such a way that it could play a winning game of chess, answering each move of an opponent with a countermove. A puppet in Turkish attire and with a hookah in its mouth sat before a chessboard placed on a large table. A system of mirrors created the illusion that this table was transparent

Walter Benjamin, 'Theses on the Philosophy of History', in *Illuminations*, ed. H. Arendt (London: Fontana, 1973), pp. 255–66, omitting theses as follows: VII–VIII (pp. 258–9); X–XII (pp. 260–2); XIV–XV (pp. 263–4); thesis XVII (from p. 265).

from all sides. Actually, a little hunchback who was an expert chess player sat inside and
guided the puppet's hand by means of strings. One can imagine a philosophical counterpart to this device. The puppet called 'historical materialism' is to win all the time.
It can easily be a match for anyone if it enlists the services of theology, which today, as
we know, is wizened and has to keep out of sight.

II

'One of the most remarkable characteristics of human nature,' writes Lotze, 'is, alongside so much selfishness in specific instances, the freedom from envy which the present
displays toward the future.' Reflection shows us that our image of happiness is thoroughly colored by the time to which the course of our own existence has assigned us.
The kind of happiness that could arouse envy in us exists only in the air we have
breathed, among people we could have talked to, women who could have given themselves to us. In other words, our image of happiness is indissolubly bound up with the
image of redemption. The same applies to our view of the past, which is the concern of
history. The past carries with it a temporal index by which it is referred to redemption.
There is a secret agreement between past generations and the present one. Our coming was expected on earth. Like every generation that preceded us, we have been
endowed with a *weak* Messianic power, a power to which the past has a claim. That
claim cannot be settled cheaply. Historical materialists are aware of that.

III

A chronicler who recites events without distinguishing between major and minor ones
acts in accordance with the following truth: nothing that has ever happened should be
regarded as lost for history. To be sure, only a redeemed mankind receives the fullness
of its past – which is to say, only for a redeemed mankind has its past become citable in
all its moments. Each moment it has lived becomes a *citation á L'ordre du jour* – and
that day is Judgement Day.

IV

Seek for food and clothing first, then
the Kingdom of God shall be added unto you.

Hegel, 1807

The class struggle, which is always present to a historian influenced by Marx, is a fight
for the crude and material things without which no refined and spiritual things could
exist. Nevertheless, it is not in the form of the spoils which fall to the victor that the
latter make their presence felt in the class struggle. They manifest themselves in this
struggle as courage, humor, cunning, and fortitude. They have retroactive force and
will constantly call in question every victory, past and present, of the rulers. As flowers
turn toward the sun, by dint of a secret heliotropism the past strives to turn toward
that sun which is rising in the sky of history. A historical materialist must be aware of
this most inconspicuous of all transformations.

V

The true picture of the past flits by. The past can be seized only as an image which flashes up at the instant when it can be recognized and is never seen again. 'The truth will not run away from us': in the historical outlook of historicism these words of Gottfried Keller mark the exact point where historical materialism cuts through historicism. For every image of the past that is not recognized by the present as one of its own concerns threatens to disappear irretrievably. (The good tidings which the historian of the past brings with throbbing heart may be lost in a void the very moment he opens his mouth.)

VI

To articulate the past historically does not mean to recognize it 'the way it really was' (Ranke). It means to seize hold of a memory as it flashes up at a moment of danger. Historical materialism wishes to retain that image of the past which unexpectedly appears to man singled out by history at a moment of danger. The danger affects both the content of the tradition and its receivers. The same threat hangs over both: that of becoming a tool of the ruling classes. In every era the attempt must be made anew to wrest tradition away from a conformism that is about to overpower it. The Messiah comes not only as the redeemer, he comes as the subduer of Antichrist. Only that historian will have the gift of fanning the spark of hope in the past who is firmly convinced that *even the dead* will not be safe from the enemy if he wins. And this enemy has not ceased to be victorious.

. . .

X

My wing is ready for fight,
I would like to turn back.
If I stayed timeless time,
I would have little luck.

Gerhard Scholem, 'Gruss vom Angelus'

A Klee painting named 'Angelus Novus' shows an angel looking as though he is about to move away from something he is fixedly contemplating. His eyes are staring, his mouth is open, his wings are spread. This is how one pictures the angel of history. His face is turned toward the past. Where we perceive a chain of events, he sees one single catastrophe which keeps piling wreckage upon wreckage and hurls it in front of his feet. The angel would like to stay, awaken the dead, and make whole what has been smashed. But a storm is blowing from Paradise; it has got caught in his wings with such violence that the angel can no longer close them. This storm irresistibly propels him into the future to which his back is turned, while the pile of debris before him grows skyward. This storm is what we call progress.

. . .

XIII

Every day our cause becomes clearer and people get smarter.
Wilhelm Dietzgen, *Die Religion Der Sozialdemokratie*

Social Democratic theory, and even more its practice, have been formed by a concep
tion of progress which did not adhere to reality but made dogmatic claims. Progress a
pictured in the minds of Social Democrats was, first of all, the progress of mankin
itself (and not just advances in men's ability and knowledge). Secondly, it was some
thing boundless, in keeping with the infinite perfectibility of mankind. Thirdly, progres
was regarded as irresistible, something that automatically pursued a straight or spira
course. Each of these predicates is controversial and open to criticism. However, whe
the chips are down, criticism must penetrate beyond these predicates and focus o
something that they have in common. The concept of the historical progress of man
kind cannot be sundered from the concept of its progression through an homogene
ous, empty time. A critique of the concept of such a progression must be the basis c
any criticism of the concept of progress itself.

. . .

XVI

A historical materialist cannot do without the notion of a present which is not a trar
sition, but in which time stands still and has come to a stop. For this notion defines th
present in which he himself is writing history. Historicism gives the 'eternal' image c
the past; historical materialism supplies a unique experience with the past. The histor
cal materialist leaves it to others to be drained by the whore called 'Once upon a time
in historicism's bordello. He remains in control of his powers, man enough to bla
open the continuum of history.

XVII

Historicism rightly culminates in universal history. Materialistic historiography diffe
from it as to method more clearly than from any other kind. Universal history has n
theoretical armature. Its method is additive; it musters a mass of data to fill the homc
geneous, empty time. Materialistic historiography, on the other hand, is based on
constructive principle. Thinking involves not only the flow of thoughts, but their a
rest as well. Where thinking suddenly stops in a configuration pregnant with tension
it gives that configuration a shock, by which it crystallizes into a monad. A historic
materialist approaches a historical subject only where he encounters it as a monad. I
this structure he recognizes the sign of a Messianic cessation of happening, or, p
differently, a revolutionary chance in the fight for the oppressed past. He takes cogn
zance of it in order to blast a specific era out of the homogeneous course of history
blasting a specific life out of the era or a specific work out of the lifework. . . .

XVIII

'In relation to the history of organic life on earth,' writes a modern biologist, 't
paltry fifty millennia of *homo sapiens* constitute something like two seconds at the clo

f a twenty-four-hour day. On this scale, the history of civilized mankind would fill ne-fifth of the last second of the last hour.' The present, which, as a model of Messianic ime, comprises the entire history of mankind in an enormous abridgment, coincides xactly with the stature which the history of mankind has in the universe.

A

Historicism contents itself with establishing a causal connection between various mo- ients in history. But no fact that is a cause is for that very reason historical. It became istorical posthumously, as it were, through events that may be separated from it by housands of years. A historian who takes this as his point of departure stops telling the equence of events like the beads of a rosary. Instead, he grasps the constellation which is own era has formed with a definite earlier one. Thus he establishes a conception of ie present as the 'time of the now' which is shot through with chips of Messianic me.

B

he soothsayers who found out from time what it had in store certainly did not expe- ence time as either homogeneous or empty. Anyone who keeps this in mind will erhaps get an idea of how past times were experienced in remembrance – namely, in ist the same way. We know that the Jews were prohibited from investigating the iture. The Torah and the prayers instruct them in remembrance, however. This stripped ie future of its magic, to which all those succumb who turn to the soothsayers for ilightenment. This does not imply, however, that for the Jews the future turned into omogeneous, empty time. For every second of time was the strait gate through which ie Messiah might enter.

.D   Jürgen Habermas, b. 1929

.D.I   The Reconstruction of Historical Materialism[6]

he word *restoration* signifies the return to an initial situation that had meanwhile en corrupted; but my interest in Marx and Engels is not dogmatic, nor is it histori- l-philological. *Renaissance* signifies the renewal of a tradition that has been buried r some time; but Marxism is in no need of this. In the present connection, *recon- ruction* signifies taking a theory apart and putting it back together again in a new rm in order to attain more fully the goal it has set for itself. This is the normal way (in y opinion normal for Marxists too) of dealing with a theory that needs revision in any respects but whose potential for stimulation has still not been exhausted.

Not by chance . . . I have been working on a theory of communicative action. Al- ough the theory of communication is intended to solve problems that are rather of

Jürgen Habermas, *Communication and the Evolution of Society, The Habermas Reader*, ed. W ithwaite (Cambridge: Polity Press, 1996), pp. 225–7.

a philosophical nature – problems concerning the foundations of the social sciences – I see a close connection with questions relating to a theory of social evolution. Thi assertion might appear somewhat off the track; I would like, therefore, to begin b recalling the following circumstances:

(1) In the theoretical tradition going back to Marx the danger of slipping into bac philosophy was always especially great when there was an inclination to suppress philo sophical questions in favor of a scientistic understanding of science. Even in Mar himself the heritage of the philosophy of history sometimes came rather unreflectedl into play. . . . Thus special care is called for if we are today to take up once again th basic assumptions of historical materialism in regard to social evolution. . . .

(2) From the beginning there was a lack of clarity concerning the normative founda tion of Marxian social theory. This theory was not meant to renew the ontologica claims of classical natural law, nor to vindicate the descriptive claims of nomologic; sciences; it was supposed to be 'critical' social theory but only to the extent that could avoid the naturalistic fallacies of implicitly evaluative theories. Marx believed h had solved this problem with a *coup de main*, namely with a declaredly materialisti appropriation of the Hegelian logic. Of course, he did not have to occupy himse especially with this task; for his practical research purposes he could be content to tak at its word, and to criticize immanently, the normative content of the ruling bourgeo: theories of modern natural law and political economy – a content that was, moreove incorporated into the revolutionary bourgeois constitutions of the time. In the mear time, bourgeois consciousness has become cynical; as the social sciences – especiall legal positivism, neo-classical economics, and recent political theory – show, it ha been thoroughly emptied of binding normative contents. However, if (as become even more apparent in times of recession) the bourgeois ideals have gone into retire ment, there are no norms and values to which an immanent critique might appeal . . On the other hand, the melodies of ethical socialism have been played through with out result. A philosophical ethics not restricted to meta-ethical statements is possib today only if we can reconstruct general presuppositions of communication and proc dures for justifying norms and values.

In practical discourse we thematize one of the validity-claims that underlie speech its *validity-basis*. In action oriented to reaching understanding, validity-claims (to th comprehensibility of the symbolic expression, the truth of the propositional conten the truthfulness of the intentional expression, and the rightness of the speech act wit respect to existing norms and values) are set in the general structures of possible con munication. In these validity-claims communication theory can locate a gentle b obstinate, a never silent although seldom redeemed claim to reason, a claim that mu be recognized de facto whenever and wherever there is to be consensual action. If th is idealism, then idealism belongs in a most natural way to the conditions of reprodu tion of a species that must preserve its life through labour and interaction, that is, a by virtue of propositions that can be true and norms that are in need of justificatior

(3) Not only are there connections between the theory of communicative actic and the foundations of historical materialism; in examining individual assumptions evolutionary theory, we run up against problems that make communications-theoret cal reflections necessary. Whereas Marx localized the learning processes important fc evolution in the dimension of objectivating thought – of technical and organization knowledge, of instrumental and strategic action, in short, of *productive forces* – the

are good reasons meanwhile for assuming that learning processes also take place in the dimension of moral insight, practical knowledge, communicative action, and the consensual regulation of action conflicts – learning processes that are deposited in more mature forms of social integration, in new *productive relations*, and that in turn first make possible the introduction of new productive forces. The rationality structures that find expression in world-views, moral representations, and identity formations, that become practically effective in social movements and are finally embodied in institutional systems, thereby gain a strategically important position from a theoretical point of view. The systematically reconstructible patterns of development of normative structures are now of particular interest. These structural patterns depict a *developmental logic* inherent in cultural traditions and institutional change. This logic says nothing about the *mechanisms* of development; it says something only about the range of variations within which cultural values, moral representations, norms, and the like – at a given level of social organization – can be changed and can find different historical expression. In its developmental *dynamics*, the change of normative structures remains dependent on evolutionary challenges posed by unresolved, economically conditioned, system problems and on learning processes that are a response to them. In other words, culture remains a superstructural phenomenon, even if it does seem to play a more prominent role in the transition to new developmental levels than many Marxists have heretofore supposed. This prominence explains the contribution that communication theory can, in my view, make to a renewed historical materialism.

9 Narrativism

Hugh Rayment-Pickard

Introduction

Although the idea that histories are structured as stories seems rather obvious, it has only been in the past fifty years that philosophers of history have tried in earnest to explore the relationship between history and narrative.[1] The initiative for this exploration has not come exclusively from philosophers of history but has also taken its impetus from developments in linguistic and narrative theory: in the Anglo-American world from cultural theorists like Northrop Frye and Frank Kermode; and on the continent from the French 'structuralist' thinkers Lévi-Strauss and Roland Barthes.

In the Anglo-American world, the development of a narrativist view of history began in the mid 1960s with the appearance of Arthur Danto's *Analytic Philosophy of History* [1965] and W.B Gallie's *Philosophy and the Historical Understanding* [1968]. Danto was responding to the controversial 'analytic' philosophy of history advanced by Carl Hempel (see also chapter 4). Hempel, in his essay 'The Function of General Laws in History' [1942], had argued that the validity of historical study must depend upon its ability to produce quasi-scientific 'laws'. Danto argued that even 'general laws' must employ narratives and that history is an essentially narrative exercise. Gallie for his part was astonished that the narrative quality of history had not received more philosophical attention. He attempted to produce an account of historical consciousness as narrative, claiming that 'all history is, like saga, basically a narrative of events in which human thought and action play a predominant part' (Gallie, 1964 p. 69). In order to read the text of history we follow the story in the same way that we follow games, in other words by understanding sets of rules and expectations. However, the most comprehensive and influential Anglo-American defence of narrativism has come from Hayden White, who is examined in more detail below. White not only supplied a systematic classification of historical narratives, but he was prepared to push narrativism towards its non-realist extreme, remaining agnostic about the relationship between historical narratives and historical events. White

1   There have been many thinkers strongly critical of narrative history. The French Annales School of the 1930s fiercely rejected narrative or as they called it 'event' history in favour of the more 'scientific' approach of identifying problems and developing hypotheses. Carl Hempel and Karl Popper in the '40s and '50s argued that narrative explanations were insufficient and that history could only be a serious discipline if it could develop general laws.
2   For an excellent description of the development of narrativism see Richard Vann's essay in e Ankersmit and Kellner (1995).

magisterial and lucid *Metahistory* [1973] still dominates the field of narrativist philosophy of history.

The Anglo-American developments in narrativism of the 1960s and 70s took place in more or less complete isolation from the rise of structuralism in linguistics and the human sciences which became so influential in France over the same period. It was not until the mid 1980s when Paul Ricoeur published his three-volume study *Time and Narrative*, that anyone had attempted properly to integrate these two strands of thought.

On the continent the emergence of structuralism had provided the philosophical basis for a new way of looking at the relationship between history and language. In the 1920s Ferdinand de Saussure, the father of structuralism, presented a view of language as a self-referential system of signs which does not depend for its meaning upon a correspondence with the world. For Saussure, the meanings of words were merely conventions written into a system of rules which he called *langue* (the hidden grammar of language). We never encounter *langue* as such but only the application of *langue* in particular instances of language-use (which Saussure called *parole*). Saussure's structuralist successors applied the *langue/parole* distinction beyond linguistics into an analysis of culture in general. As Lévi-Strauss pointed out, the structuralist implication for historiography was that the *langue* or mythic structure of history would be the true subject of historical studies. The *parole* of history – i.e., events themselves – would only have meaning only as the particulars of general systems of history. The structuralists emphasized *system* rather than *happening* as the essence of history.

Earlier thinkers – most notably Hegel and Marx – had already offered descriptions of the 'system' of history as a logical progression through necessary epochs. What crucially distinguished structuralist systematic history from its predecessors was its view of history as system of signs rather than a system of events. The structuralists endeavoured to decipher the 'codes' of the texts of history rather than to uncover the logical structure of historical happening. In his seminal essay *The Discourse of History* [1967] Roland Barthes attacks what he called 'the prestige attached to *it happened*':

> Historical discourse does not follow the real, it can do no more than signify the real, constantly repeating that *it happened*, without the assertion amounting to anything but the signified 'other side' of the whole process of historical narration. (Barthes, 1970, p. 154)

In fact for Barthes the entire 'other side' of narration (in other words the idea of a 'real world' represented in narrative) is an irrelevance since narrative forms an object complete in itself. 'Claims concerning the "realism" of narrative are . . . to be discounted . . . The function of narrative is not to represent, it is to constitute a spectacle . . . not of a mimetic order' (Barthes, 1977, p. 123f).

This separation of historical narration from happening had significant consequences: first, the reduction of history to its discourses had the effect of levelling the distinction between 'history' and 'literature'. Thus Barthes defines the historian as 'not so much a collector of facts as a collector and relater of signifiers; that is to say, he organizes them with the purpose of establishing positive meaning and filling the vacuum of pure, meaningless series' (Barthes, 1970, p. 153). Secondly, Barthes (and others) would argue that the narrative structures of history are in fact fixed sets of relations and therefore essentially static. Unlike the dynamic system of say Hegel, which evolved in time, the structuralists saw the narrative systems of history as timeless diagrams. Thus Lévi-Strauss described the narrative of history as an 'a-temporal matrix' detached from historicity; and Barthes has argued that in narrative 'temporality only exists in the form of a system' and that 'true' time is merely 'a reality effect' of language (see Barthes, 1977, p. 98).

For a while structuralism was regarded as a radical and new departure in philosophy. However, its point of view was broadly-speaking idealist in that it stressed the primacy of linguistic structures of cognition. These structures were seen to be *logically* prior to any kind of historical event, since events without cognition – what Barthes terms 'the other side' of historical narration – are necessarily unknowable. Although the structuralist moment in post-war philosophy was not long-lived, and in itself perhaps not all that significant, the question of the epistemological status of narration developed into a key issue for the philosophy of history.

A central task for any narrativist view of history is to describe the relationship between the text of history and the happening of the world; and it is here that a division opens up among narrativist philosophers of history. On the one hand there are what may be called the 'high' narrativists – for example, Roland Barthes and Hayden White – who take the view that the correlation between text and world is impossible to determine, since all culture is inside language. On the other hand, there are the 'low' narrativists – Paul Ricoeur and David Carr, for example – who admit that the world-text relationship is complex, but still insist upon a link between what takes place in narrative and what happens in the world.

For the high narrativists the world always presents itself to us as text, so that the relationship between an historical text and any other presentation of the world only concerns a distinction of genre. As Hayden White argues, 'history has no stipulatable subject matter uniquely its own; it is always written as part of a contest between contending poetic figurations of what the past *might* consist of' (White, 1978, p. 98).[3] the world always appears inside language, we can have no non-linguistic experience of history against which to judge the descriptive accuracy of historical narration. 'We cannot refer to events as such,' argued Mink, 'but only to events under a description' (Mink, 1978, p. 145).[4] Consequently the representational power of narrative may exist but it can never be *demonstrated*. Thus one significant outcome of the 'high' narrativist perspective is that it undermines the basis for determining what would ordinarily be thought of as the 'objective truth' of history.

By contrast the 'low' narrativist view contends that there is some congruence between the narrative of history and the world's happening. Put otherwise, we could say that the low narrativists take seriously the question of *time*. In his famous essay 'Structure, Word, Event' (1968) Paul Ricoeur makes a case against the high narrativist (or 'structuralist') view, arguing that high narrativism must reduce history to a static diagram of textual components and their relationships (Ricoeur, 1974, pp. 79–86). This can never do justice to the dynamic and time-bound character of narrative itself, and requires the exclusion of the constitutive subject of history: the happening events. By contrast Ricoeur characterizes narrative as a dynamic system, itself stretched

3   For an elaboration of the high narrativist position see Mink (1978).
4   For a similar viewpoint see, White (1981).

out in time, which exists symbiotically with the happening of the world out of which historical texts are generated. Furthermore, says Ricoeur, historical narratives are themselves historical acts that play their part in the happening of the world. The success of Ricoeur's argument is a matter of debate. David Carr, in *Time, Narrative and History* [1991] discounts Ricoeur's claim to have connected 'life' with 'narration', arguing that Ricoeur never quite manages to show that narrative structures resemble the patterns of history. In response, Carr offers his own argument for a 'community of form' between narrative and history. Against structuralism, Carr defines narrative structure as essentially *temporal* with a 'beginning–middle–end' structure. Drawing on Husserl's analysis of 'internal time consciousness', Carr argues that the world actually appears to us as episodes of experience. Husserl had stated that moment by moment our perceptions contain both memory and anticipation, thereby structuring experience as 'a field of occurrence' containing a mini-narrative of past, present and future. Carr concludes that all 'action, life and historical existence are themselves structured narratively, independently of their presentation in literary form, and that this structure is practical before it is aesthetic or cognitive' (Carr, 1991, p. 85).

The success of Carr's argument depends upon whether history is the same thing as lived experience. If one were to take Croce's view that the occurrence of events is not the same thing as our perception of them, then we might have to conclude as a number of thinkers have that the world appears to take place as a chronicle, 'one damned thing after another', a succession of events without beginning or end. If this were the case then a narrative structure would have to be *imposed* in order for history to appear as story. This would confirm the 'high' narrativist view of history as a literary construct.

As an anthropologist, **Claude Lévi-Strauss** (1908–) is an unlikely figure to have risen to significance in the philosophy of history. However, Lévi-Strauss elevated anthropology into a study of culture in general, thereby crossing the field of *Geistwissenschaft* opened up by nineteenth century historicism from Herder to Dilthey. The issue he sought to explore was the historico-philosophical question of the character of '*l'esprit humain*': how humans understand themselves in relation to the worlds of nature, culture and the cosmos.

Lévi-Strauss applied structuralism in social anthropology to understand how myth and symbol function not only as the codes of any given culture, but as the codes of human culture in general. Although Levi-Strauss conducts detailed analyses of particular myths, such as 'The Story of Asdiwal' [1960], he also attempts to uncover the primal structures of myth across culture. The crucial unit of mythic structure is the 'mytheme' which is 'a bundle of relations'; and at the root of all relations are 'binary oppositions', simple pairings of contrasting ideas. The fundamental example of this is the distinction between Nature and Culture. Other binarisms include: human/animal, human/god, this world/other world, and life/death. Myths organize themselves complex elaborations of the tensions between opposites.

Lévi-Strauss's view of the 'mythic' extends far beyond the formal definition of myth as story or legend. For him the whole of culture operates mythologically and this is precisely why myth is so important. In his four-volume study of American Indian mythology, *Mythologiques* [1964. 1966, 1968, 1972], Lévi-Strauss applies a mythological analysis to all aspects of human life: clothing, food, beliefs, music, speech, sexual behaviour and social relationships. Indeed any aspect of human life is possible material

for such a mytho-structural analysis. Lévi-Strauss's crucial presupposition is that al
though analysis must always use local examples, the deep structure of this coding is no
merely local, but operates between cultures and across history. Hence in *The Savag*
Mind [1962], Lévi Strauss observes:

> No anthropologist can fail to be struck by the common manner of conceptualizing initia-
> tion rites employed by the most diverse societies throughout the world. Whether in Af-
> rica, America, Australia or Melenasia, the rites follow the same pattern: first, the novices,
> taken from their parents, are symbolically 'killed' and kept hidden in the forest of bush
> where they are put to test by the Beyond; after this they are 'reborn' as members of the
> society. (Lévi Strauss, 1966, p. 264)

This synthetic approach to myth has earned Lévi-Strauss criticism: fellow anthropolo
gists have found the connections he makes interesting but fanciful; and Jonathan Culle
has argued that Lévi-Strauss' identification of patterns of myth does not in itself pro
vide any explanation of what these patterns mean (Culler, 1975, p. 54).

There are important philosophical-historical implications to Lévi-Strauss' work. H
method effectively cuts across history by offering a structural analysis of culture at th
level of myth. Although the objects under consideration are apparently datable tex
drawn from given cultures at given times, Lévi-Strauss' ultimate focus of enquiry – th
primal binary structure of myth – is a non-historical and abstract entity which operate
across culture and time. Thus in *The Savage Mind*, Lévi-Strauss argues for an underly
ing coherence of perspective between primitive humanity and our modern scientif
intellect.

At the end of *The Savage Mind* Lévi Strauss offers some direct remarks on the sub
ject of history, arguing that historian *must* always seek to identify form and structur
A history which imposes no structure, but which catalogues every event will collap
under the infinite weight of material. 'What makes history possible is that a sub-set
events is found, for a given period, to have approximately the same significance for
contingent of individuals who have not necessarily experienced the events and ma
even consider them at an interval of several centuries' (Lévi Strauss, 1966, p. 257
Although Lévi-Strauss allows for the fact that the interpretation of 'sub-sets' is plura
he insists that the process of historical writing is unified in its use of 'chronologic
codes' organized around the binarism 'before/after'. Each historical code must b
calibrated to perform its task, so that a history of Europe would be coded in centuri
or millennia, whereas a history of the First World War would require sequencing
months and years. Although the codes in themselves are coherent wholes, they cann
be meshed together to produce a total history. So historical discourse takes the form
a set of discontinuous codes. The resolution of these discontinuities – Lévi-Strau
does not say this as such, but the implication is clear enough – could only be achieve
outside history at the level of myth.

Although **Roland Barthes** (1915–1980) was not an historian, his concern with t
production of culture inevitably generated an interest in history. The history that Bart
was eager to uncover was not the history of things that have happened, but history
a textual construct. This approach was evident in one of Barthes' earliest works *Wr
ing Degree Zero* [1953], an analysis of the history of 'literature' by considering t
structural conditions underlying the appearance of literature as a cultural pheno

enon. Barthes's point is that for a text to appear as a work of literature it must be coded as 'literature'. The task he sets himself is to trace historically how this coding has taken place. Before the mid-nineteenth century, Barthes argues, literature was naively realist, taking for granted that language operates by producing pictures of the world. This so-called 'classical writing' gives way in the mid nineteenth century to a more self-conscious literature, which has an eye not only to its own artifice and interests but also to its self-justification. The consequence of this self-awareness is the break-up of the unified 'classical' view of literature, which falls apart as 'Literature' seeks its destiny in an ever-expanding range of genres and styles. History, for Barthes is just another kind of literature. Hence he argues that historical narratives function like novels: 'in both we find the construction of an autarkic world which elaborates its own dimensions and limits, and organizes within these its own Time, its own Space, its population, its own set of objects and its myths' (Barthes, 1967, p. 26). The historico-philosophical principle underlying the logic of this essay is that, for Barthes, language itself and its structural transformations are the substance of history.

The textual character of history foregrounds the activities of writing and reading. The writer of history is not a free agent open to express any kind of meaning, but someone who is confined by the horizon of literary possibility handed on from the past. What gets written is 'a tissue of quotations drawn from the innumerable centres of culture' (Barthes, 1977, p. 146). However, the disaggregated sources of writing find a unity on the side of reading, since the reader is 'the space on which the quotations that make up a writing are inscribed without any of them being lost; a text's unity lies not in its origin but its destination' (p. 148). The reader, and what Barthes calls his 'pleasure' in reading, constitute the true 'historical subject' (Barthes, 1990, p. 62).

What makes an *historical* narrative is not that such texts faithfully represent the past, but that they produce what could be called a 'history-effect', an arrangement of codes and voices within the text which signal to the reader that an historical narration is in progress. In *S/Z* Barthes identifies five narrative codes: The hermeneutic, the semetic, the symbolic, the proairetic and the cultural. Each of the elements of a narration can be assigned to one of the codes, which 'weave' and intertwine in the text to produce its overall structural character.

Two codes have a particular relevance for the interpretation of an historical narration: the proairetic and the hermeneutic. The proairetic code (from the Greek *proairesis* meaning the purpose, plan or scope of action) concerns the sequencing of narrative. In themselves, Barthes argues, the actions of a narrative are simply given and follow no necessary logic. A sequence of action – say, 'meeting', 'greeting' and 'shaking hands' – requires meaning because of the proairetic code of manners which the reader will bring to the text. The hermeneutic code concerns the way in which narration – through suggestion, suspense and delay – signals to the reader that the truth is being disclosed. The hermeneutic code is closely linked with the reader's desire (another Barthian theme) to uncover the meaning of the narrative. Between them, the proairetic and hermeneutic voices form what Barthes calls the 'melody' and 'harmony' of a narration. For Barthes, both these codes are essentially plural: sequences of actions may take on a number of meanings and the question of the truth of a narration never gets resolved but is, necessarily, left in suspense.

Whether Barthes' attitude to 'structuralism' undergoes a transformation in the late 1960s is a much-debated issue (but not one that can be discussed here). What seems to be clear, at least, is that Barthes increasingly emphasizes the plurality of structural possibilities in a text over and against any reductive structural model. In *S/Z* [1970] Barthes emphasizes the 'infinitude' of meaning in a text which cannot be reduced 'to a narrative structure, a grammar or a logic'. In an earlier essay 'The Death of the Author' (1968) Barthes had argued that the 'structure' of a narrative does not provide any ultimate ground for interpretation. The idea that narrative structures take their meaning from an underlying 'history' is a 'theological' presupposition. 'History' is a false foundation ('hypostasis' in Barthes' terminology) which cannot be implicit to a narrative but is an interpretation imposed by the reader. So the text – whether the narrative of history or any other – is not the site of definitive meaning, but 'a multi-dimensional space in which a variety of writings, none of them original, blend and clash' (Barthes, 1977, p. 147).

The effect of Barthes' abandonment of history to literature was the sacrifice of historical realism. The texts of history must effectively be read like novels and the question of 'truth' is replaced by the question of the reader's pleasure. To some this might seem like the ruin of history. To others, such as Hayden White, the 'French' emphasis on the literary character of philosophy and history was not a problem. Indeed for White the salvation of historical writing was seen to lie in literature. In 1976 White wrote that 'history is in bad shape today because it has lost sight of its origins in the literary imagination' (White, 1978, p. 99).

Over the past thirty years, **Hayden White** (b. 1928) has established himself as the most articulate and persuasive proponent of what we have called the 'high' narrativist position. For White, the function of history is to produce stories which will disclose the condition of the present time. The 'truth' of these stories is for him not the issue. The point is to enliven our vision of the world by offering new perspectives and for the historian 'to participate positively in the liberation of the present from the *burden of history*' (p. 41). The sentiment comes directly, and self-consciously, from Nietzsche who lamented the 'malady of history' in his own time and advocated 'history in the service of life' (see chapter 5). In our case White says that history must disclose discontinuity: 'for discontinuity, disruption, and chaos is our lot' (White, 1978, p. 50).

Among the Structuralists, Lévi-Strauss is the most quoted and approved in White's writing.[5] Lévi-Strauss' mythic view of history resonates with that of Northrop Frye, another profound influence on White. Frye was a literary critic who argued that history, like all other forms of narration, must derive its structures from archetypal forms of myth. In particular, Frye identified four types of historical myth: Romantic myth based upon the quest for a utopian future; Comic myths of historical development by evolution or revolution; Tragic myths of 'decline and fall' and Ironic myths of recurrence and disaster (Frye, 1957). Frye observed, as Lévi-Strauss would, that historical writing is caught between the need to explain and the need to describe. The more that history describes the world the less it explains; the more it explains the less it describes. Furthermore, the explanatory function of history also drives it in the direction of myth since the more comprehensive an explanation becomes, the more mythic and poetic becomes its structure.

5   As Richard Vann observes, Barthes's essay 'The Discourse of History' (Barthes, 1970) had little impact on the English speaking world, despite being available in translation from 1970.

In his ground-breaking work, *Metahistory* [1973], White develops and elaborates Frye's typology of historical myth, producing a table setting out the formal possibilities of historical narration.[6] White sees historical narration operating in three modes: the modes of emplotment, argument and implication. White reclassifies Frye's mythic types as four 'modes of emplotment': Romance, Tragedy, Comedy and Satire. These determine how the story of history will be told. The 'mode of argument' controls how a given history will explain what is happening in the story. White lists four modes of argument: the Formist which explains every historical detail in its own terms without regard for the whole; the Mechanistic which construes history as the operation of laws; the Organicist which subsumes parts into wholes; and the Contextualist which balances the Formist tendency with the Organicist. Finally, the four 'modes of ideological implication' – Anarchist, Radical, Conservative and Liberal – determine the 'lesson' or 'message' which will be implied by a history. So White sees Burckhardt as Satirical-Contextualist-Conservative and Hegel (who is difficult to pin down at the best of times) as a committed Organicist but Comic and Tragic by turns and open to either a Radical or Conservative reading. White sets out the whole scheme in the form of a table that echoes some of the diagrammatic reductions of structuralism. Although White denies that *Metahistory* is a *structuralist* exercise, there are very clear affinities between his own morphology of historical narrative and the narrative models devised by, say Greimas and Barthes.

To this already elaborate scheme, White adds a further deep-structural layer of concepts aimed at explaining the temperamental disposition that determines the choice of one mode over any other.

> Before the historian can bring to bear upon the data of the historical field the conceptual apparatus he will use to represent and explain it, he must first *pre*figure the field – that is to say, constitute it as an object of mental perception . . . That is to say, before a given domain can be interpreted, it must first be construed as a ground inhabited by discernable figures. The figures, in turn, must be conceived to be classifiable as distinctive orders, classes, genera, and species of phenomena. (White, 1973, p. 30)

White says that we find the source of our historical predilections in the fundamental rhetorical structures of language: the four 'master tropes' of Metaphor, Metonym, Synecdoche and Irony. The metaphorical disposition points history towards art and myth, as in Nietzsche. The metonymic disposition encourages reductive and schematic classification, as in Marx. The synecdochic disposition is predisposed to see the whole of history represented in its parts, as in Ranke. The ironic disposition, which White sees as the disposition of all philosophy of history, is a sceptical attitude towards questions of historical truth and reality. In this way, White attempts to map both the surface structures and the deep grammar of historical consciousness.

White's analysis of tropes begs the obvious question of a still-deeper level of structure, which prefigures the disposition to a given trope. White persistently resists the temptation to pursue this question into the realms of psychology or biography. However, the question opens up a weakness in White's analysis: Since the tropes do not explain the choice of any given historical consciousness, but only describe the condi-

---

*   The reader will find a clear and concise summary of White's scheme in his essay 'Interpretation in History', (in White, 1978).

tions of possibility of historical writing, the final question of how and why historical consciousness arises remains unanswered.

Paul Ricoeur's (b. 1913) philosophy does not fit into any obvious 'school'. He is not an existentialist like Sartre, or a phenomenologist like Merleau-Ponty, or a structuralist like Barthes, or a post-structuralist like Foucault, yet in Ricoeur's thought we can see components of all these. He is a religious philosopher, but he doesn't write traditional Christian apologetics like Barth, Bultmann or Rahner. His writing branches out in many directions – biblical criticism, political theory, ethics, metaphysics, the theory of language, psychoanalysis, hermeneutics – always building more or less explicit links and hinting at underlying strata of thinking that transcend the academic disciplines. Ricoeur's thought has followed its own path, between dualisms and extremes, with a kind of independence and integrity, which has earned him a singular kind of respect in philosophy.

Although Ricoeur arrives at a fully-worked out narrativist position in the 1980s, we can trace the primary concerns and motives of his narrativism back through earlier phases of his career. From the beginning we can see Ricoeur's concern with the relationship between 'structure' and 'history'. In his early Husserlian writings, collected in *History and Truth* [1955], Ricoeur tried to forge a link between the structure of human subjectivity and the possibility of historical objectivity. In his later hermeneutic writings of the 1960s and 70s Ricoeur turned his attention to the relationship between history and the structure of language. Lately in *Time and Narrative* [1983], Ricoeur has argued that narrative is the essential structure connecting subjectivity, language and history.

In his early career, Ricoeur – like many other thinkers of his generation – came under the influence of Husserl who had argued that all forms of understanding are grounded in individual human consciousness (7.A.I). In *History and Truth* Ricoeur emphasizes the subjective, creative activity of the historian who must employ the imagination in order to *construct* the objectivity of history. In other words, the historian is not passive, but actively builds historical objectivity through 'observation', 'explanation' and 'understanding' (Ricoeur, 1965).[7] The historian *observes* documents and other traces in an attempt to 'reconstruct' the past as historical 'fact'; he *explains* where and how these traces belong in various narrative sequences; and he attempts to *understand* the 'organic bonds' which give the sequences of traces their coherence. But the objectivity of history is conditioned by four subjective contingencies: the *choice* that the historian must make about which data are important; the fact that the historian must employ *theories of explanation* which require their own philosophical justification; the *imagination* that must be used to bridge the 'historical distance' between 'now' and 'then'; and finally, *the subjective experience of the historian* which is the basis for understanding the human protagonists of history. The philosophy of history must uncover the *subjective* basis of historical awareness, argues Ricoeur, since 'there is no history . . . without an . . . *epoché* of everyday subjectivity' (Ricoeur, 1965, p. 31).[8] The subjectivity in question not only involves the historian's subjectivity, but includes the subjectivity of the readers of history. This means that the interpretation of history is

---

7   Here Ricoeur takes his lead from Bloch's theory of 'historical observation' and Dilthey's distinction between understanding and explanation.
8   The word 'epoché' is Husserl's term for the way in which we can analyse subjective experience by 'reducing' it down to its essential character.

irreducibly *intersubjective* and therefore generates 'an irradiation of meanings from a multiplicity of organizing centres' (p. 39). As Ricoeur puts in another essay, 'a certain pluralism is inherent in the preconception of the drama of history and historical work' (p. 74).

Subjectivity and the phenomenon of plural meaning continued to be central interests of Ricoeur's writings of the 1970s. In these texts, however, language rather than consciousness is foregrounded as the key issue in historical understanding. In 7.D.I, for example, Ricoeur argues that the problem of hermeneutics arises because language speaks simultaneously at different levels and in different senses. This is owing to the 'symbolic' character of language. Ricoeur defines a symbol as a 'structure of signification' that generates both a literal and a figurative meaning. Such problems of interpretation are constantly thrown up for the historian since the resources for historical study are linguistic: documents, artifacts and other 'historical traces'. The hermeneutic challenge for the historian is to use historical traces to bridge the 'distance' between past cultures and his own. Elsewhere Ricoeur calls this the 'hermeneutic arc' that connects 'text' with 'life', historical trace with lived experience. Interpretation operates in both directions across the hermeneutic arc. We interpret the traces of the past, but the traces of the past also act upon us (Ricoeur, 1981, p. 162). Thus interpretation leads to a new 'self-understanding' which Ricoeur calls 'appropriation' (7.D.I). In 9.D.I Ricoeur connects this notion of appropriation with Gadamer's hermeneutic of fused horizons' (7.C.IV).

A decade later in *Time and Narrative* (1983–5), Ricoeur developed his understanding of the text-life relationship by arguing that narrative is the literary genre that provides the best analogy for the actuality of life. This is because life and narrative both take place in *time*. Ricoeur is not claiming that narratives mirror history in any naive, literal way. For him the relationship between narrative and the happening of history is *metaphorical* (Ricoeur, 1988, p. 154); and metaphor, as Ricoeur had argued in *The Rule of Metaphor* [1975] is not merely rhetorical but *ontological* since the metaphor has the quality of 'being-as' its analogue.

The temporal identity of historical narrative is characterized by three 'connectors' which make historical time conceivable: (1) The calendar which (like Lévi-Strauss' chronological code – 9.A.I) gives time a scale calibrated at one end to 'zero' and divided into measurable units; (2) the concept of generational succession which sees time as a connected series of living historical agents; and (3) the fact of the historical trace enables us to 'reckon' with time as a succession of datable documents (Ricoeur, 1988, pp. 104–26). In this way historical narrative is able to connect up the various orders of time: 'History . . . reinscribes the time of narrative within the time of the universe. This is a "realist" thesis in the sense that history locates its chronology on the single scale of time common to what is called the "history" of living species, the "history" of the solar system and the galaxies' (p. 181f). Fiction, by comparison with history, works by 'neutralizing' the connectors between the phenomenological (apparent) and cosmological (actual) orders of time and opening up a 'treasure trove of imaginative variations' (p. 128).

Having said this, Ricoeur does not want to dissolve the difference between fiction and history; instead he argues for an inevitable 'interweaving' of the two. When we try to think historically, we inevitably have to construct the past in our minds like a novel. Thus our historical thinking calls upon the device of fiction. On the other hand, when we make up a story our narration inevitably proceeds 'historically' *as if* we were describing an actual past. In this way our fictive thinking calls upon the device of history. 'By the interweaving of fiction and history I mean the fundamental structure, ontological as well as epistemological, by virtue of which history and fiction each concretize their respective intentionalities only by borrowing from the intentionality of the other' (p. 181).

Selected Texts

Edited by Hugh Rayment-Pickard

9.A Claude Lévi-Strauss, b. 1908

9.A.1 The Codes of History[1]

The anthropologist respects history, but he does not accord it a special value. He conceives it as a study complementary to his own: one of them unfurls the range of human societies in time, the other in space. And the difference is even less great than it might seem, since the historian strives to reconstruct the picture of vanished societies as they were at the points which for them corresponded to the present, while the ethnographer does his best to reconstruct the historical stages which temporally preceded their existing form.

This symmetry between history and anthropology seems to be rejected by philosophers who implicitly or explicitly deny that distribution in space and succession in time afford equivalent perspectives. In their eyes some special prestige seems to attach to the temporal dimension, as if diachrony were to establish a kind of intelligibility not merely superior to that provided by synchrony, but above all specifically human.

It is easy to explain, if not to justify, this preference. The diversity of social forms, which the anthropologist grasps as deployed in space, present the appearance of a discontinuous system. Now, thanks to the temporal dimension, history seems to restore to us not separate states, but the passage from one state to another in a continuous form. And as we believe that we apprehend the trend of our personal history as a continuous change, historical knowledge appears to confirm the evidence of inner sense. History seems to do more than describe beings from the outside, or at best give us intermittent flashes of insight into internalities, each of which are so on their own account while remaining external to each other: it appears to re-establish our connection, outside ourselves, with the very essence of change.

There would be plenty to say about this supposed totalizing continuity of self which seems to me to be an illusion sustained by the demands of social life – and consequently a reflection of the external on the internal – rather than the object of an apodictic experience. But there is no need to resolve this philosophical problem in order to perceive that the proposed conception of history corresponds to no kind of reality. As historical knowledge is claimed to be privileged, I feel entitled (as I would not other-

1 Claude Lévi-Strauss, *The Savage Mind* (London: Weidenfeld & Nicholson, 1966), pp. 256–62.

wise feel) to make the point that there is a twofold antinomy in the very notion of an historical fact. For, *ex hypothesi*, a historical fact is what really took place, but where did anything take place? Each episode in a revolution or a war resolves itself into a multitude of individual psychic movements. Each of these movements is the translation of unconscious development, and these resolve themselves into cerebral, hormonal or nervous phenomena, which themselves have reference to the physical or chemical order. Consequently, historical facts are no more *given* than any other is. It is the historian, or the agent of history, who constitutes them by abstraction and as though under the threat of an infinite regress.

What is true of the constitution of historical facts is no less so of their selection. From this point of view, the historian and the agent of history choose, sever and carve them up, for a truly total history would confront them with chaos. Every corner of space conceals a multitude of individuals each of whom totalizes the trend of history in a manner which cannot be compared to the others; for any one of these individuals, each moment of time is inexhaustibly rich in physical and psychical incidents which all play their part in his totalization. Even history which claims to be universal is still only a juxtaposition of a few local histories within which (and between which) very much more is left out than is put in. And it would be vain to hope that by increasing the number of collaborators and making research more intensive one would obtain a better result. In so far as history aspires to meaning, it is doomed to select regions, periods, groups of men and individuals in these groups and to make them stand out, as discontinuous figures, against a continuity barely good enough to be used as a backdrop. A truly total history would cancel itself out – its product would be nought. What makes history possible is that a sub-set of events is found, for a given period, to have approximately the same significance for a contingent of individuals who have not necessarily experienced the events and may even consider them at an interval of several centuries. History is therefore never history, but *history-for*. It is partial in the sense of being biased even when it claims not to be, for it inevitably remains partial – that is, incomplete – and this is itself a form of partiality. When one proposes to write a history of the French Revolution one knows (or ought to know) that it cannot, simultaneously and under the same heading, be that of the Jacobin and that of the aristocrat. *Ex hypothesi*, their respective totalizations (each of which is anti-symmetric to the other) are equally true. One must therefore choose between two alternatives. One must select as the principal either one or a third (for there are an infinite number of them) and give up the attempt to find in history a totalization of the set of partial totalizations; or alternatively one must recognize them all as equally real: but only to discover that the French Revolution as commonly conceived never took place.

History does not therefore escape the common obligation of all knowledge, to employ a code to analyse its object, even (and especially) if a continuous reality is attributed to that object. The distinctive features of historical knowledge are due not to the absence of a code, which is illusory, but to its particular nature: the code consists in a chronology. There is no history without dates. To be convinced of this it is sufficient to consider how a pupil succeeds in learning history: he reduces it to an emaciated body, the skeleton of which is formed by dates. Not without reason, there has been a reaction against this dry method, but one which often runs to the opposite extreme. Dates may not be the whole of history, nor what is most interesting about it, but they are its *sine qua non*, for history's entire originality and distinctive nature lie in apprehending the relation between *before* and *after*, which would perforce dissolve if its terms could not, at least in principle, be dated.

Now, this chronological coding conceals a very much more complex nature than one supposes when one thinks of historical dates as a simple linear series. In the first place, a date denotes a moment in a succession: $d2$ is after $d1$ and before $d3$. From this point of view dates only perform the function of ordinal numbers. But each date is also a cardinal number and, as such, expresses a *distance* in relation to the dates nearest to it. We use a large number of dates to code some periods of history; and fewer for others. This variable quantity of dates applied to periods of equal duration are a gauge of what might be called the pressure of history: there are 'hot' chronologies which are those of periods where in the eyes of the historian numerous events appear as differential elements, others, on the contrary, where for him (although not of course for the men who lived through them) very little or nothing took place. Thirdly and most important, a date is a *member* of a class. These classes of dates are definable by the meaningful character each date has within the class in relation to other dates which also belong to it, and by the absence of this meaningful character with respect to dates appertaining to a different class. Thus the date 1685 belongs to a class of which 1610, 1648 and 1715 are likewise members; but it means nothing in relation to the class composed of the dates: 1st, 2nd, 3rd, 4th millennium, nor does it mean anything in relation to the class of dates: 23 January, 17 August, 30 September, etc.

On this basis, in what would the historian's code consist? Certainly not in dates, since these are not recurrent. Changes of temperature can be coded with the help of figures, because the reading of a figure on the thermometer evokes the return of an earlier situation: whenever I read 0°C, I know that it is freezing and put on my warmest coat. But a historical date, taken in itself, would have no meaning, for it has no reference outside itself: if I know nothing about modern history, the date 1613 makes me none the wiser. The code can therefore consist only of classes of dates, where each date has meaning in as much as it stands in complex relations of correlation and opposition with other dates. Each class is defined by a frequency, and derives from what might be called a corpus or a domain of history. Historical knowledge thus proceeds in the same way as a wireless with frequency modulation: like a nerve, it codes a continuous quantity – and as such an asymbolic one – by frequencies of impulses proportional to its variations. As for history itself, it cannot be represented as an aperiodic series with only a fragment of which we are acquainted. History is a discontinuous set composed of domains of history, each of which is defined by a characteristic frequency and by a differential coding of *before* and *after*. It is no more possible to pass between the dates which compose the different domains than it is to do so between natural and irrational numbers. Or more precisely: the dates appropriate to each class are irrational in relation to all those of other classes.

It is thus not only fallacious but contradictory to conceive of the historical process as a continuous development, beginning with prehistory coded in tens or hundreds of millennia, then adopting the scale of millennia when it gets to the 4th or 3rd millennium, and continuing as history in centuries interlarded, at the pleasure of each author, with slices of annual history within the century, day to day history within the year or even hourly history within a day. All these dates do not form a series: they are of different species. To give just one example, the coding we use in prehistory is not preliminary to that we employ for modern and contemporary history. Each code refers to a system of meaning which is, at least in theory, applicable to the virtual totality of human history. The events which are significant for one code are no longer so for another. Coded in the systems of prehistory, the most famous episodes in modern and contemporary history cease to be pertinent; except perhaps (and again we know nothing about it) certain massive aspects of demographic evolution viewed on a worldwide scale, the invention of the steam-engine, the discovery of electricity and of nuclear energy.

Given that the general code consists not in dates which can be ordered as a linear series but in classes of dates each furnishing an autonomous system of reference, the discontinuous and classificatory nature of historical knowledge emerges clearly. It operates by means of a rectangular matrix:

. . . .
. . . .
. . . .
. . . .
. . . .
. . . .

Where each line represents classes of dates, which may be called hourly, daily, annual, secular, millennial for the purposes of schematization and which together make up a discontinuous set. In a system of this type, alleged historical continuity is secured only by dint of fraudulent outlines. Furthermore, although the internal gaps in each class cannot be filled in by recourse to other classes, each class taken as a whole nevertheless always refers back to another class, which contains the principle of an intelligibility to which it could not itself aspire. The history of the 17th century is 'annual' but the 17th century, as a domain of history belongs to another class, which codes it in relation to earlier and later centuries; and this domain of modern times in its turn becomes an element of a class where it appears correlated with and opposed to other 'times': the middle ages, antiquity, the present day, etc. Now, these various domains correspond to histories of different power.

Biographical and anecdotal history, right at the bottom of the scale, is low-powered history, which is not intelligible in itself and only becomes so when it is transferred *en bloc* to a form of history of a higher power than itself; and the latter stands in the same relation to a class above it. It would, however, be a mistake to think that we progressively reconstitute a total history by dint of these dove-tailings. For any gain on one side is offset by a loss on the other. Biographical and anecdotal history is the least explanatory; but it is the richest in point of information, for it considers individuals in their particularity and details for each of then the shades of character, the twists and turns of their motives, the phases of their deliberations. This information is schematized, put in the background and finally done away with as one passes to histories of progressively greater 'power'. Consequently, depending on the level on which he places himself, the historian loses in information what he gains in comprehension or vice versa, as if the logic of the concrete wished to remind us of its logical nature by modelling a confused outline of Gödel's theorem in the clay of 'becoming'. The historian's relative choice, with respect to each domain of history he gives up, is always confined to the choice between history which teaches us more and explains less, and history which explains more and teaches less.

9.B   Roland Barthes, 1915–1980

9.B.1   The Structural Analysis of Narratives[2]

The narratives of the world are numberless. Narrative is first and foremost a prodigious variety of genres, themselves distributed amongst different substances – as though any material were fit to receive man's stories. Able to be carried by articulated language, spoken or written, fixed or moving images, gestures, and the ordered mixture of all these substances; narrative is present in myth, legend, fable, tale, novella, epic, history, tragedy, drama, comedy, mime, painting (think of Carpaccio's *Saint Ursula*), stained glass windows, cinema, comics, news item, conversation. Moreover, under this almost infinite diversity of forms, narrative is present in every age, in every place, in every society; it begins with the very history of mankind and there nowhere is nor has been a people without narrative. All classes, all human groups, have their narratives, enjoyment of which is very often shared by men with different, even opposing, cultural backgrounds. Caring nothing for the division between good and bad literature, narrative is international, transhistorical, transcultural: it is simply there, like life itself.

Must we conclude from this universality that narrative is insignificant? Is it so general that we can have nothing to say about it except for the modest description of a few highly individualized varieties, something literary history occasionally undertakes? But then how are we to master even these varieties, how are we to justify our right to differentiate and identify them? How is novel to be set against novella, tale against myth, drama against tragedy (as has been done a thousand times) without reference to a common model? Such a model is implied by every proposition relating to the most individual, the most historical, of narrative forms. It is thus legitimate that, far from the abandoning of any idea of dealing with narrative on the grounds of its universality, there should have been (from Aristotle on) a periodic interest in narrative form and it is normal that the newly developing structuralism should make this form one of its first concerns – is not structuralism's constant aim to master the infinity of utterances [*paroles*] by describing the 'language' ['*langue*'] of which they are the products and from which they can be generated. Faced with the infinity of narratives, the multiplicity of standpoints – historical, psychological, sociological, ethnological, aesthetic, etc. – from which they can be studied, the analyst finds himself in more or less the same situation as Saussure confronted by the heterogeneity of language [*langage*] and seeking to extract a principle of classification and a central focus for description from the apparent confusion of the individual messages. Keeping simply to modern times, the Russian Formalists, Propp and Lévi-Strauss have taught us to recognize the following dilemma: either a narrative is merely a rambling collection of events, in which case nothing call be said about it other than by referring back to the storyteller's (the author's) art, talent or genius – all mythical forms of chance – or else it shares with other narratives a common structure which is open to analysis, no matter how much patience its formulation requires. There is a world of difference between the most complex random-

Roland Barthes, 'Introduction to the Structural Analysis of Narratives', *Image Music Text*, ed. S. Heath (London: Fontana, 1977), pp. 79–82.

ness and the most elementary combinatory scheme, and it is impossible to combine (to produce) a narrative without reference to an implicit system of units and rules.

Where then are we to look for the structures of narrative? Doubtless, in narratives themselves. *Each and every* narrative? Many commentators who accept the idea of a narrative structure are nevertheless unable to resign themselves to dissociating literary analysis from the example of the experimental sciences; nothing daunted, they ask that a purely inductive method be applied to narrative and that one start by studying all the narratives within a genre, a period, a society. This commonsense view is utopian. Linguistics itself, with only some three thousand languages to embrace, cannot manage such a programme and has wisely turned deductive, a step which in fact marked its veritable constitution as a science and the beginning of its spectacular progress, it even succeeding in anticipating facts prior to their discovery. So what of narrative analysis, faced as it is with millions of narratives? Of necessity, it is condemned to a deductive procedure, obliged first to devise a hypothetical model of description (what American linguists call a 'theory') and then gradually to work down from this model towards the different narrative species which at once conform to and depart from the model. It is only at the level of these conformities and departures that analysis will be able to come back to, but now equipped with a single descriptive tool, the plurality of narratives, to their historical, geographical and cultural diversity.

Thus, in order to describe and classify the infinite number of narratives, a 'theory' (in this pragmatic sense) is needed and the immediate task is that of finding it, of starting to define it. Its development can be greatly facilitated if one begins from a model able to provide it with its initial terms and principles. In the current state of research, it seems reasonable that the structural analysis of narrative be given linguistics itself as founding model.

9.B.II   Narratives and Time[3]

Structurally narrative institutes a confusion between consecution and consequence, temporality and logic. This ambiguity forms the central problem of narrative syntax. Is there an atemporal logic lying behind the temporality of narrative? Researchers were still quite recently divided on this point. Propp, whose analytic study of the folktale paved the way for the work going on today, is totally committed to the idea of the irreducibility of the chronological order: he sees time as reality and for this reason is convinced of the necessity for rooting the tale in temporality. Yet Aristotle himself, in his contrast between tragedy (defined by the unity of action) and historical narrative (defined by the plurality of actions and the unity of time), was already giving primacy to the logical over the chronological. As do all contemporary researchers (Lévi-Strauss, Greimas, Bremond, Todorov), all of whom (while differing on other points) could subscribe to Lévi-Strauss's proposition that 'the order of chronological succession is absorbed in an atemporal matrix structure'.

Analysis today tends to 'dechronologize' the narrative continuum and to 'relogicize' it, to make it dependent on what Mallarmé called with regard to the French language 'the primitive thunderbolts of logic'; or rather, more exactly (such at least is our wish

3   Ibid., pp. 98–9.

the task is to succeed in giving a structural description of the chronological illusion – it is for narrative logic to account for narrative time. To put it another way, one could say that temporality is only a structural category of narrative (of discourse), just as in language [*langue*] temporality only exists in the form of a system; from the point of view of narrative, what we call time does not exist, or at least only exists functionally, as an element of a semiotic system. Time belongs not to discourse strictly speaking but to the referent; both narrative and language know only a semiotic time, 'true' time being a 'realist', referential illusion. . . . It is as such that structural analysis must deal with it.

9.C   Hayden White, b. 1928

9.C.I   The Fictions of Factual Representation[4]

In order to anticipate some of the objections with which historians often meet the argument that follows, I wish to grant at the outset that *historical events* differ from *fictional events* in the ways that it has been conventional to characterize their differences since Aristotle. Historians are concerned with events which can be assigned to specific time-space locations, events which are (or were) in principle observable or perceivable, whereas imaginative writers – poets, novelists, playwrights – are concerned with both these kinds of events, and imagined, hypothetical, or invented ones. The nature of the kinds of events with which historians and imaginative writers are concerned is not the issue. What should interest us in the discussion of 'the literature of fact' or, as I have chosen to call it, 'the fictions of factual representation' is the extent to which the discourse of the historian and that of the imaginative writer overlap, resemble, or correspond with each other. Although historians and writers of fiction may be interested in different kinds of events both the forms of their respective discourses and their aims in writing are often the same. In addition, in my view, the techniques or strategies that they use in the composition of their discourses can be shown to be substantially the same, however different they may appear on a purely surface, or dictional, level of their texts.

Readers of histories and novels can hardly fail to be struck by their similarities. There are many histories that could pass for novels, and many novels that could pass for histories, considered in purely formal (or, I should say, formalist) terms. Viewed simply as verbal artifacts histories and novels are indistinguishable from one another. We cannot easily distinguish between them on formal grounds unless we approach them with specific preconceptions about the kinds of truths that each is supposed to deal in. But the aim of the writer of a novel must be the same as that of the writer of a history. Both wish to provide a verbal image of 'reality.' The novelist may present his notion of this reality indirectly, that is to say, by figurative techniques, rather than directly, which is to say, by registering a series of propositions which are supposed to correspond point by point to some extratextual domain of occurrence or happening, as the historian claims to do.

Hayden White, 'The Fictions of Factual Representation' in *Tropics of Discourse* Baltimore: Johns Hopkins University Press, 1978), pp. 121–2.

But the image of reality which the novelist thus constructs is meant to correspond in its general outline to some domain of human experience which is no less 'real' than that referred to by the historian. It is not, then, a matter of a conflict between two kinds of truth (which the Western prejudice for empiricism as the sole access to reality has foisted upon us), a conflict between the truth of correspondence, on the one side, and the truth of coherence, on the other. Every history must meet standards of coherence no less than those of correspondence if it is to pass as a plausible account of 'the way things *really* were.' For the empiricist prejudice is attended by a conviction that 'reality' is not only perceivable but is also coherent in its structure. A mere list of confirmable singular existential statements does not add up to an account of reality if there is not some coherence, logical or aesthetic, connecting them one to another. So too every fiction must pass a test of correspondence (it must be 'adequate' as an image of something beyond itself) if it is to lay claim to representing an insight into or illumination of the human experience of the world. Whether the events represented in a discourse are construed as atomic parts of a molar whole or as possible occurrences within a perceivable totality, the discourse taken in *its* totality as an image of some reality bears a relationship of correspondence to that *of which* it is an image. It is in these twin senses that all written discourse is cognitive in its aims and mimetic in its means. And this is true even of the most ludic and seemingly expressivist discourse, of poetry no less than of prose, and even of those forms of poetry which seem to wish to illuminate only 'writing' itself. In this respect, history is no less a form of fiction than the novel is a form of historical representation.

9.C.II   The Mode of Emplotment[5]

Providing the 'meaning' of a story by identifying, the *kind of story* that has been told is called explanation by emplotment. If, in the course of narrating his story, the historian provides it with the plot structure of a Tragedy, he has 'explained' it in one way; if he has structured it as a Comedy, he has 'explained' it in another way. Emplotment is the way by which a sequence of events fashioned into a story is gradually revealed to be a story of a particular kind.

Following the line indicated by Northrop Frye in his *Anatomy of Criticism*, I identify at least four different modes of emplotment: Romance, Tragedy, Comedy, and Satire. There may be others, such as the Epic, and a given historical account is likely to contain stories cast in one mode as aspects or phases of the whole set of stories emplotted in another mode. But a given historian is forced to emplot the whole set of stories making up his narrative in one comprehensive or *archetypal* story form. For example Michelet cast all of his histories in the Romantic mode, Ranke cast his in the Comic mode, Tocqueville used the Tragic mode, and Burckhardt used Satire. The Epic plot structure *would* appear to be the implicit form of chronicle itself. The important point is that every history, even the most 'synchronic' or 'structural' of them, will be emplotted in some way. The Satirical mode provided the formal principles by which the supposedly 'non-narrative' historiography of Burckhardt can be identified as a 'story' of particular sort. For, as Frye has shown, stories cast in the Ironic mode, of which Satire is the fictional form, gain their effects precisely by frustrating normal expectation

5   Hayden White, *Metahistory*, (Baltimore: Johns Hopkins University Press, 1973), pp. 7–11.

about the kinds of resolutions provided by stories cast in other modes (Romance, Comedy, or Tragedy, as the case may be).

The Romance is fundamentally a drama of self-identification symbolized by the hero's transcendence of the world of experience, his victory over it, and his final liberation from it – the sort of drama associated with the Grail legend or the story of the resurrection of Christ in Christian mythology. It is a drama of the triumph of good over evil, of virtue over vice, of light over darkness, and of the ultimate transcendence of man over the world in which he was imprisoned by the Fall. The archetypal theme of Satire is the precise opposite of this Romantic drama of redemption; it is, in fact, a drama of diremption, a drama dominated by the apprehension that man is ultimately a captive of the world rather than its master, and by the recognition that, in the final analysis, human consciousness and will are always inadequate to the task of overcoming definitively the dark force of death, which is man's unremitting enemy.

Comedy and Tragedy, however, suggest the possibility of at least partial liberation from the condition of the Fall and provisional release from the divided state in which men find themselves in this world. But these provisional victories are conceived differently in the mythic archetypes of which the plot structures of Comedy and Tragedy are sublimated forms. In Comedy, hope is held out for the temporary triumph of man over his world by the prospect of occasional *reconciliations* of the forces at play in the social and natural worlds. Such reconciliations are symbolized in the festive occasions which the Comic writer traditionally uses to terminate his dramatic accounts of change and transformation. In Tragedy, there are no festive occasions, except false or illusory ones; rather, there are intimations of states of division among men more terrible than that which incited the tragic agon at the beginning of the drama. Still, the fall of the protagonist and the shaking of the world he inhabits which occur at the end of the Tragic play are not regarded as totally threatening to those who survive the agonic test. There has been a gain in consciousness for the spectators of the contest. And this gain is thought to consist in the epiphany of the law governing human existence which the protagonist's exertions against the world have brought to pass.

The reconciliations which occur at the end of Comedy are reconciliations of men with men, of men with their world and their society; the condition of society is represented as being purer, saner, and healthier as a result of the conflict among seemingly unalterably opposed elements in the world; these elements are revealed to be, in the long run, harmonizable with one another, unified, at one with themselves and the others. The reconciliations that occur at the end of Tragedy are much more somber; they are more in the nature of resignations of men to the conditions under which they must labor in the world. These conditions, in turn, are asserted to be inalterable and eternal, and the implication is that man cannot change them but must work within them. They set the limits on what may be aspired to and what may be legitimately aimed at in the quest for security and sanity in the world.

Romance and Satire would appear to be *mutually exclusive* ways of emplotting the processes of reality. The very notion of a Romantic Satire represents a contradiction in terms. I can legitimately imagine a Satirical Romance, but what I would mean by that term would be a form of representation intended to expose, from an Ironic standpoint, the fatuity of a Romantic conception of the world. On the other hand, however, I can speak of a Comic Satire and a Satirical Comedy, or of a Satirical Tragedy and a Tragic Satire. But here it should be noted that the relation between the genre (Tragedy or Comedy) and the mode in which it is cast (Satirical) is different from that which obtains between the genre of Romance and the modes (Comic and Tragic) in which it may be cast. Comedy and Tragedy represent *qualifications* of the Romantic apprehension of the world, considered as a process, in the interest of taking seriously the forces which *oppose* the effort at human redemption naively held up as a possibility for mankind in Romance. Comedy and Tragedy take conflict seriously, even if the former eventuates in a vision of the ultimate *reconciliation* of opposed forces and the latter in a *revelation* of the nature of the forces opposing man on the other. And it is possible for the Romantic writer to assimilate the truths of human existence revealed in Comedy and Tragedy respectively within the structure of the drama of redemption which he figures in his vision of the ultimate victory of man over the world of experience. But Satire represents a different kind of qualification of the hopes, possibilities, and truths of human existence revealed in Romance, Comedy, and Tragedy respectively. It views these hopes, possibilities, and truths ironically, in the atmosphere generated by the apprehension of the ultimate inadequacy of consciousness to live in the world happily or to comprehend it fully. Satire presupposes the *ultimate inadequacy* of the visions of the world dramatically represented in the genres of Romance, Comedy, and Tragedy alike. As a phase in the evolution of an artistic style or literary tradition, the advent of the Satirical mode of representation signals a conviction that the world has grown old. Like philosophy itself, Satire 'paints its gray on gray' in the awareness of its own inadequacy as an image of reality. It therefore prepares consciousness for its repudiation of all sophisticated conceptualizations of the world and anticipates a return to a mythic apprehension of the world and its processes. These four archetypal story forms provide us with a means of characterizing the different kinds of explanatory affects a historian can strive for on the level of narrative emplotment. And it allows us to distinguish between *diachronic*, or processionary, narratives of the sort produced by Michelet and Ranke and the *synchronic*, or static, narratives written by Tocqueville and Burckhardt. In the former, the sense of structural transformation is uppermost as the principal guiding representation. In the latter, the sense of structural continuity (especially in Tocqueville) or stasis (in Burckhardt) predominates. But the distinction between a synchronic and diachronic representation of historical reality should not be taken as indicating mutually exclusive ways of emplotting the historical field. This distinction points merely to a difference of emphasis in treating the relationship between continuity and change in a given representation of the historical process as a whole.

Tragedy and Satire are modes of emplotment which are consonant with the interest of those historians who perceive behind or within the welter of events contained in the chronicle an ongoing structure of relationships or an eternal return of the Same in the Different. Romance and Comedy stress the emergence of new forces or conditions out of processes that appear at first glance either to be changeless in their essence or to be changing only in their phenomenal forms. But each of these archetypal plot structures has its implication for the cognitive operations by which the historian seeks to 'explain' what was 'really happening' during the process of which it provides an image of its true form.

9.C.III   The Table of Modes[6]

In my view, a historiographical style represents a particular *combination* of modes of emplotment, argument, and ideological implication. But the various modes of emplotment, argument, and ideological implication cannot be indiscriminately combined in a given work. For example, a Comic emplotment is not compatible with a Mechanistic argument, just as a Radical ideology is not compatible with a Satirical emplotment. There are, as it were, elective affinities among the various modes that might be used to gain an explanatory affect on the different levels of composition. And these elective affinities are based on the structural homologies which can be discerned among the possible modes of emplotment, argument, and ideological implication. The affinities can be represented graphically as follows:

Mode of Emplotment	Mode of Argument	Mode of Ideological Implication
Romantic	Formist	Anarchist
Tragic	Mechanistic	Radical
Comic	Organicist	Conservative
Satirical	Contextualist	Liberal

These affinities are not to be taken as *necessary* combinations of the modes in a given historian. On the contrary, the dialectical tension which characterizes the work of every master historian usually arises from an effort to wed a mode of emplotment with a mode of argument or of ideological implication which is inconsonant with it. For example, as I will show, Michelet tried to combine a Romantic emplotment and a Formist argument with an ideology that is explicitly Liberal. So, too, Burckhardt used a Satirical emplotment and a Contextualist argument in the service of an ideological position that is explicitly Conservative and ultimately Reactionary. Hegel emplotted history on two levels – Tragic on the microcosmic, Comic on the macrocosmic – both of which are justified by appeal to a mode of argument that is Organicist, with the result that one can derive either Radical or Conservative ideological implications form a reading of his work.

But, in every case, dialectical tension evolves within the context of a coherent vision or presiding image of the form of the whole historical field. This gives to the individual thinker's conception of that field the aspect of a self-consistent totality. And this coherence and consistency give to his work its distinctive stylistic attributes. The problem here is to determine the grounds of this coherence and consistency. In my view, these grounds are poetic, and specifically linguistic, in nature.

Before the historian can bring to bear upon the data of the historical field the conceptual apparatus he will use to represent and explain it, he must first *pre*figure the field – that is to say, constitute it as an object of mental perception. This poetic act is indistinguishable from the linguistic act in which the field is made ready for interpretation as a domain of a particular kind. That is to say, before a given domain can be interpreted, it must first be construed as a ground inhabited by discernible figures. The

Ibid., pp. 29–31.

figures, in turn, must be conceived to be classifiable as distinctive orders, classes, genera, and species of phenomena. Moreover, they must be conceived to bear certain kinds of relationships to one another, the transformations of which will constitute the 'problems' to be solved by the 'explanations' provided on the levels of emplotment and argument in the narrative.

In other words, the historian confronts the historical field in much the same way that the grammarian might confront a new language. His first problem is to distinguish among the lexical, grammatical, and syntactical elements of the field. Only then can he undertake to interpret what any given configuration of elements or transformations of their relationships mean. In short, the historian's problem is to construct a linguistic protocol, complete with lexical, grammatical, syntactical, and semantic dimensions, by which to characterize the field and its elements *in his own terms* (rather than in the terms in which they come labelled in the documents themselves), and thus to prepare them for the explanation and representation he will subsequently offer of them in his narrative. This preconceptual linguistic protocol will in turn be – by virtue of its essentially *prefigurative* nature – characterizable in terms of the dominant tropological mode in which it is cast.

Historical accounts purport to be verbal models, or icons, of specific segments of the historical process. But such models are needed because the documentary record does not figure forth an unambiguous image of the structure of events attested in them. In order to figure 'what *really* happened' in the past, therefore, the historian must first prefigure as a possible object of knowledge the whole set of events reported in the documents. This prefigurative act is *poetic* inasmuch as it is precognitive and precritical in the economy of the historian's own consciousness. It is also poetic insofar as it is constitutive of the structure that will subsequently be imaged in the verbal model offered by the historian as a representation and explanation of 'what *really* happened' in the past. But it is constitutive not only of a domain which the historian can treat as a possible object of (mental) perception. It is also constitutive of the *concepts* he will use *to identify the objects* that inhabit that domain and *to characterize the kinds of relationships* they can sustain with one another. In the poetic act which precedes the formal analysis of the field, the historian both creates his object of analysis and predetermines the modality of the conceptual strategies he will use to explain it. But the number of possible explanatory strategies is not infinite. There are, in fact, four principal types, which correspond to the four principal tropes of poetic language. Accordingly, we find the categories for analysing the different modes of thought, representation, and explanation met with in such nonscientific fields as historiography in the modalities of poetic language itself. In short, the theory of tropes provides us with a basis for classifying the deep structural forms of the historical imagination in a given period of its evolution.

9.D Paul Ricoeur, b. 1913

9.D.1 Life in Quest of Narrative[7]

It has always been known and often repeated that life has something to do with narrative; we speak of a life story to characterize the interval between birth and death. And yet assimilating life to a story in this way is not really obvious; it is a commonplace that must first be submitted to critical doubt. This doubt is the work of all the knowledge acquired in the past few decades concerning narrative, a knowledge which appears to distance narrative from lived experience and to confine it to the region of fiction. We are going, first, to pass through this critical zone in an effort to rethink in some other way this oversimplified and too direct relation between history and life, in such a way that fiction contributes to making life, in the biological sense of the word, a human life. I want to apply to the relation between narrative and life Socrates' maxim that an unexamined life is not worth living.

I shall take as my starting-point, as I cross this zone of criticism, the remark of a commentator: stories are recounted and not lived; life is lived and not recounted. To clarify this relation between living and narrating, I suggest that we first examine the act of narrating itself.

The narrative theory I shall now be discussing is at once very recent, since in its developed form it dates from the Russian and Czech formalists in the twenties and thirties and from the French structuralists of the sixties and seventies. But it is also quite ancient, in that it can be seen to be prefigured in Aristotle's *Poetics*. It is true that Aristotle recognized only three literary genres: epic, tragedy and comedy. But his analysis was already sufficiently general and formal to allow room for modern transpositions. For my part, I have retained from Aristotle's *Poetics* the central concept of emplotment, which in Greek is *muthos* . . .

I shall broadly define the operation of emplotment as a synthesis of heterogeneous elements. Synthesis between what elements? *First of all*, a synthesis between the events or incidents which are multiple and the story which is unified and complete; from this first point of view, the plot serves to make *one* story out of the multiple incidents or, if you prefer, transforms the many incidents *into one* story. . . . The plot, however, is also a synthesis from a *second* point of view: it organizes together components that are as heterogeneous as unintended circumstances, discoveries, those who perform actions and those who suffer them, chance or planned encounters, interactions between actors ranging from conflict to collaboration, means that are well or poorly adjusted to ends, and finally unintended results; gathering all these factors into a single story makes the plot a totality which can be said to be at once concordant and discordant . . . *Finally*, emplotment is a synthesis of the heterogeneous in an even more profound sense. . . . We could say that there are two sorts of *line* in every story told: on the one hand, a discrete succession that is open and theoretically indefinite, a series of incidents (for we can always pose the question: and then? and then?); on the other hand, the story told

Paul Ricoeur, 'Life in Quest of Narrative' in *On Paul Ricoeur*, ed. D. Wood (London: Routledge, 1991), pp. 20–33.

presents another temporal aspect characterized by the integration, culmination and closure owing to which the story receives a particular configuration. In this sense, composing a story is, from the temporal point of view, drawing a configuration out of a succession . . . If we may speak of the temporal identity of a story, it must be characterized as something that endures and remains across that which passes and flows away.

From this analysis of the story as the synthesis of the heterogeneous, we can retain three features: the mediation performed by the plot between the multiple incidents and unified story; the primacy of concordance over discordance; and, finally, the competition between succession and configuration.

. . .

We can now attack the paradox we are considering here: stories are recounted, life is lived. An unbridgeable gap seems to separate fiction and life. To cross this gap, the terms of the paradox must, to my mind, be thoroughly revised.

Let us remain for the moment on the side of the narrative, hence on that of fiction, and see in what way it leads us back to life. My thesis is here that the process of composition, of configuration, is not completed in the text but in the reader and under this condition, makes possible the reconfiguration of life by narrative. I should say, more precisely: the sense or the significance of a narrative stems from the *intersection of the world of the text and the world of the reader*. The act of reading thus becomes the critical moment of the entire analysis. On it rests the narrative's capacity to transfigure the experience of the reader.

Allow me to stress the terms I have used here: the *world of* the reader and the *world of the text*. To speak of a world of the text is to stress the feature belonging to every literary work of opening before it a horizon of possible experience, a world in which it would be possible to live. A text is not something closed in upon itself, it is the projection of a new universe distinct from that in which we live. To appropriate a world through reading is to unfold the world horizon implicit in it which includes the actions, the characters and the events of the story told. As a result, the reader belongs at once to the work's horizon of experience in imagination and to that of his or her own real action. The horizon of expectation and the horizon of experience continually confront one another and fuse together. Gadamer speaks in this regard of the 'fusion of horizons' essential to the art of understanding a text. . . . In a word, hermeneutics is placed at the point of intersection of the (internal) configuration of the work and the (external) refiguration of life.

At this stage of the analysis, we are already able to glimpse how narrative and life can be reconciled with one another, for reading is itself already way of living in the fictive universe of the work; in this sense, we can already say that stories are recounted but they are also *lived in the mode of the imaginary*.

We must now readjust the other term of this opposition, what we call *life*. We must question the erroneous self-evidence according to which life is lived not told.

To this end, I should like to stress the pre-narrative capacity of what we call life. What has to be questioned is the overly simple equation made between life and experience. A life is no more than a biological phenomenon as long as it has not been interpreted. And in interpretation, fiction plays a mediating role. To open the way for this new phase of the analysis, we must underscore the mixture of acting and suffering which constitutes the very fabric of a life. It is this mixture which the narrative attempts to imitate in a creative way. In speaking of Aristotle, we indeed omitted the very definition he gives of the narrative; it is, he says, 'the imitation of an action' *mimesis praxeos*. We therefore have to look for the points of support that the narrative can find in the living experience of acting and suffering; and that which, in this experience, demands the assistance of narrative and expresses the need for it.

The first point of anchorage that we find for narrative understanding in living experience consists in the very structure of human acting and suffering. In this respect, human life differs widely from animal life, and, with all the more reason, from mineral existence. We understand what action and passion are through our competence to use in a meaningful way the entire network of expressions and concepts that are offered to us by natural languages in order to distinguish between *action* and mere physical *movement* and psychophysiological *behaviour*. In this way, we understand what is signified by project, aim, means, circumstances, and so on. All of these notions taken together constitute the network of what we could term the *semantics of action*. In this network we find all the components of the synthesis of the heterogeneous. In this respect, our familiarity with the conceptual network of human acting is of the same order as the familiarity we have with the plots of stories that are known to us; it is the same phronetic understanding which presides over the understanding of action (and of passion) and over that of narrative.

The second point of anchorage that the narrative finds in practical understanding lies in the symbolic resources of the practical field. This feature will decide which aspects of doing, of being-able to do, and of knowing-how-to-do belong to poetic transposition.

If indeed action can be recounted, this is because it is already articulated in signs, rules and norms; it is always symbolically mediated. This feature of action has been heavily underscored by cultural anthropology.

The third point of anchorage of the narrative in life consists in what could be called the *pre-narrative quality of human experience*. It is due to this that we are justified in speaking of life as a story in its nascent state, and so of life as an *activity and a passion in search of a narrative*. The comprehension of action is not restricted to a familiarity with the conceptual network of action, and with its symbolic mediations, it even extends as far as recognizing in the action temporal features which call for narration. It is not by chance or by mistake that we commonly speak of stories that happen to us or of stories in which we are caught up, or simply of the story of a life.

. . .

It follows that fiction, in particular narrative fiction, is an irreducible dimension of *self-understanding*. If it is true that fiction is only completed in life and that life can be understood only through the stories that we tell about it, then an *examined* life, in the sense of the word as we have borrowed it from Socrates, is a life *recounted*.

This definition of subjectivity in terms of narrative identity has numerous implications. To begin with, it is possible to apply to our self-understanding the play of sedimentation and innovation which we saw at work in every tradition. In the same way, we never cease to reinterpret the narrative identity that constitutes us, in the light of the narratives proposed to us by our culture. In this sense, our self-understanding presents the same features of traditionality as the understanding of a literary work. It is in this way that we learn to become the *narrator* and the hero *of our own story*, without actually becoming the *author of our own life*. We can apply to ourselves the concept of *narrative voices* which constitute the symphony of great works such as epics, tragedies, dramas and novels. The difference is that, in all these works, it is the author who is disguised as the narrator and who wears the mask of the various characters and, among all of these, the mask of the dominant narrative voice that tells the story we read. We can become our own narrator, in imitation of these narrative voices, without being able to become the author. This is the great difference between life and fiction. In this sense, it is true that life is lived and that stories are told. An unbridgeable difference does remain, but this difference is partially abolished by our power of applying to ourselves the plots that we have received from our culture and of trying on the different roles assumed by the favourite characters of the stories most dear to us. It is therefore by means of the imaginative variations of our own ego that we attempt to obtain a narrative understanding of ourselves, the only kind that escapes the apparent choice between sheer change and absolute identity. Between the two lies narrative identity.

In conclusion, allow me to say that what we call the *subject* is never given at the start. Or, if it is, it is in danger of being reduced to the narcissistic, egoistic and stingy ego from which literature, precisely, can free us.

So, what we lose on the side of narcissism, we win back on the side of narrative.

In place of an *ego* enamoured of itself arises a *self* instructed by cultural symbols, the first among which are the narratives handed down in our literary tradition. And these narratives give us a unity which is not substantial but narrative.

10 Posthistory

Hugh Rayment-Pickard

Introduction

Theories about the 'end of history' are sometimes thought to be a recent 'postmodern' development. However, the idea that history will end is one of the oldest in Western thought. Of particular importance is the Christian view, which developed in the first century AD out of Jewish apocalyptic beliefs. By contrast with the 'circular' views of time based on natural cycles that we find in ancient Greek thought, Christian history was conceived as linear and finite, a one-off narrative with a definite beginning and end. The linearity of history was essential to the core doctrines of Christianity, as St Augustine argued in a scathing attack on cyclical theories of history. Augustine believed that cycles implied pessimism and repetition and that only a linear history could make sense of hope and redemption (Augustine, 1972, pp. 498–502). Christian history was the story of God's purposeful activity from the creation of the world from nothing to a Last Day of divine judgement. The Christian end of history, which was called the *parousia* (meaning the 'presence' or 'coming'), was a complete winding up of the created order and the imposition of a post-historical age of divine rule. An entire section of theology, called 'eschatology' (from the Greek word *eschaton* meaning 'end'), was given over to the study of the so-called 'four last things': death, judgement, heaven and hell.

Although in the modern period the Christian apocalyptic view ceased to be a dominant cultural myth, it was replaced by a new Enlightenment view of the end of history as the self-perfection of humanity. From the Renaissance on we see the emergence of philosophies based on a belief in the human capacity for self-improvement. Many Enlightenment thinkers (but Hume is an exception) thought that the human race was on an ascending graph of improvement, that history was progressing under its own steam towards a logical goal, and that sooner or later a more or less perfect world-order would be achieved. For example, Condorcet (2.B.IV) speaks confidently of a time when the sun will shine only on free men who know no other master but their reason'.

A number of philosophers, most notably Karl Löwith (*Meaning in History: The Theological Presuppositions of the Philosophy of History*, 1949) and Rudolf Bultmann *History and Eschatology: The Presence of Eternity*, 1957), have argued that this 'enlightenment' belief in progress is in fact merely a secularized version of Christian history. Although widely supported, the so-called 'secularization thesis' has not gone uncontested. Hans Blumenberg, for example, has argued (*The Legitimacy of the Mod-*

ern Age, 1966) that the enlightenment idea of 'progress' and the Christian idea o *parousia* are quite different. Whereas the Christian *parousia* is an apocalyptic closur from outside without warning or preparation, the modern end of history is the last i a progression of logical stages. Thus belief in historical progress, for Blumenberg, i not ancient and religious, but *modern* and secular and has its origins in the stead development of scientific and cultural 'curiosity': 'there arises in the modern age a indissoluble connecting link between man's historical self-understanding and the re alization of scientific knowledge as the confirmation of the claim to unrestricted theo retical curiosity' (Blumenberg, 1983, p. 232).

Supporters and critics of the secularization thesis generally agree at least that th modern conception of the end of history is connected directly with a belief in th historical importance and uniqueness of modernity. Blumenberg argues that the theo retical curiosity of the modern age drives it to construct a theory of its own beginnin and end. This means that modern people think of history in distinct epochs: 'th Middle Ages', 'the Renaissance', 'the Enlightenment' and so on. 'The modern age writes Blumenberg, 'was the first and only age that understood itself as an epoch an in doing so simultaneously created other epochs' (p. 116). We certainly see evidenc of such epochal thinking in Hegel's and Marx's schemes of world history (3.D.II an 8.A.III) or say, in Schelling's *Philosophy of the Ages of the World*. The current concer with 'post-modernity' may also be seen, ironically, as a 'modern' preoccupation wit epochs, as modernity attempts to understand its own limits.

As this book has already illustrated, the question of the destiny of the modern c Enlightenment epoch has provoked many different responses. We have seen thos thinkers who, variously, have some degree of faith in 'the Enlightenment project' suc as Hume, Condorcet, Kant, Hegel, Marx and Habermas. Even Foucault in his essa 'What is Enlightenment?' (1983) – despite what we might expect from some of h earlier writings – remained open about the possibility of the maturation of the huma species and recognized reason as a necessary instrument of critique. For Nietzsche, o the other hand, modernity was a dead-end that must be overcome by the higher hi tory of the over-man. With Adorno anti-Enlightenment pessimism finds its most e treme form; for him modernity equals barbarism, a situation from which there is n obvious exit. Blumenberg takes the general view that epochs never end in fulfillmer but only in paradox: 'Eras exhaust themselves more in the transformation of the certainties and unquestionable axioms into riddles and inconsistencies than in the solution' (Blumenberg, 1983, p. 464).

The transformation of the modern age into 'riddles and inconsistencies' is wh Gianni Vattimo (*The End of Modernity*, 1988) calls the condition of 'posthistory 'Posthistory' arises in the late twentieth century, he argues, because we have lost o modern Enlightenment certainty in the unity and direction of culture. Vattimo tak the term 'posthistory' from Arnold Gehlen (Gehlen, 1978) who argues that althoug we still 'believe' in progress, we no longer know where progress is going. Progress h become 'routine', and we now expect almost daily announcements of new advances technology, but the *point* of this progress has been lost. For Vattimo this is a sign the end of the modern epoch, the 'dissolution of history' and the opening of posthistor

The thinkers in this section offer three views about the destiny of history and tl 'posthistorical' condition. Foucault sees history as a discontinuous series in which tl question of the ends and limits of history is constantly at stake. 'The problem', Foucau rgues, 'is no longer one of tradition, of tracing a line, but of division, of limits; it is no onger one of lasting foundations' (Foucault, 1974, p. 5). Jean Baudrillard has argued hat history has 'disappeared' because we can no longer distinguish illusion from real-y, and because events have 'accelerated' beyond our capacity to grasp them as 'his-ory'. Finally, Francis Fukuyama offers a neo-Hegelian argument for the completion f history in 'liberal democracy'. The posthistorical age is a period in which liberal emocracies will consolidate and improve.

Michel Foucault (1926–1984) has come to be regarded as one of the most impor-nt philosophers of history of the late twentieth century. Although Foucault is com-aratively unusual among philosophers of history in having actually written books of istory, his intellectual development and enduring temperament are best understood s *philosophical*. However, the historical and the philosophical are inter-linked in oucault's writing. He once described his books as 'philosophical fragments on his-orical building sites' (cited in Macey, 1994, p. 403). This tells us two important aings: first that Foucault's philosophical reflections emerge from the study of the articulars of history; and secondly, that he was not concerned with the absolute truth f history, but with forms of historical knowledge which are provisional, fragmentary nd plural.

The character of Foucault's approach is perhaps best illustrated by *The Order of hings* [1966] which is at once a study in history and a philosophy of history. Foucault ses historical research to demonstrate that in the West our way of understanding our orld and ourselves has undergone a number of radical shifts. History thus breaks own into a series of *episteme*, a technical term that Foucault uses to describe 'the total t of relations that unite at a given period the discursive practices that give rise to pistemological figures, sciences and formalized structures'. Foucault identifies three pisteme: first, the 'sixteenth-century episteme' in which the world is understood theo-gically as a divine 'text' bearing the signature of God; secondly, the 'classical episteme' a which knowledge operates by seeking to order and classify the world; and thirdly ae 'modern episteme' in which knowledge is organized into empirical sciences around nan' as the knowing subject. Foucault's underlying argument is that what we mean y 'the human being' is not given, but is created by historically-conditioned systems of nowledge. When one episteme gives way to another what it means to be human ndergoes a change. At the end of the book a further postmodern episteme is hinted , but not named (10.A.I).[1] Foucault predicts, in a now famous image, that the mod-n episteme will end with the disappearance of man like a face in the sand at the edge f the sea. This event is a necessary consequence of the logic of the modern episteme, hich has sought to reduce 'the human' to a finite, knowable entity. Foucault calls this henomenon 'the analytic of finitude': 'that fundamental death on the basis of which y empirical life is given to me' (Foucault, 1970, p. 315). This is the death of the todern idea of 'the human', an idea, which like all others 'has a history' with its own eginning and end. The end of the history of the human removes from the 'postmodern' pisteme any organizing centre of knowledge. Human posthistory will be perspectival, vithout constants', 'haphazard', 'random', 'entangled' and 'without a landmark or pint of reference' (10.A.II).

The term 'postmodern episteme' is used here with caution, since Foucault does not in fact offer y positive descriptions of the age after the end of 'man'.

Foucault's so-called 'archaeological' research method in *The Order of Things* aims to 'examine each event in terms of its own evident arrangement'. This means that Foucault' concern is with the structure of the episteme and what he calls its 'archive', or basic se of rules. However, he shows no interest in any over-arching structure. So whilst Foucau is concerned with the succession of the episteme, he is not concerned with the ques tion of their logic and progression. For Foucault, the general historical picture is on of radical discontinuity. The influence of Nietzsche here is unmistakable (5.C.VII) and in the early 1970s Foucault started to use the Nietzschean term 'genealogy' rathe than 'archaeology' to describe his approach. Still later, in the 1980s, Foucault als used the term 'problemmatization'. The enduring thought that underlies Foucault' shifts in emphasis and terminology is 'discontinuity', a concept that Foucault describe most fully in *The Archaeology of Knowledge* [1969]. Whereas traditional history seek to reveal a continuity underlying historical events, Foucault's counter-traditional his tory, which he calls 'effective history' (10.A.II), seeks to reveal history as a sequenc without underlying coherence.

So how does discontinuity impact on historical research? In the opening pages o *The Archaeology of Knowledge*, Foucault addresses this question at some length, de fending a discontinuous view of history as a positive approach to historical study. 'Dis continuity was the stigma of temporal dislocation that it was the historian's task t remove from history. It has now become one of the basic elements of historical analy sis' (Foucault, 1974, p. 8). Foucault describes three ways in which discontinuity paradoxically both the 'instrument' and the 'object' of historical research. First, di continuity is instrumental since ideas of 'period', 'era' or 'epoch' are not given i history but must be *imposed* as 'a deliberate operation of the historian'. Secondl discontinuity is instrumental since the historian *produces* discontinuity precisely in h attempt to 'discover the limits' of an historical process. Thirdly, discontinuity is th object of history since it is discontinuity that constantly requires explanation.

This 'limit attitude', as Foucault calls it (Foucault, 1991, p. 45), implies a subtle an complex understanding of the end of modernity. Instead of arguing that we have no suddenly stepped beyond Enlightenment, Foucault prefers to emphasize the reflexiv use of enlightenment reason as a means of investigating 'the events which have led t to constitute ourselves'. Thus the end of modernity is not the emergence of a ne epoch, but the 'problematization' of the constitution of the modern era. The futur must not be approached with a ready-made theory of postmodernity or of post-Er lightenment, but 'experimentally' through a 'historico-practical' testing of the limi of modernity.

In the Preface to *The Order of Things*, Foucault contrasts two ends of history: 'utc pia' and 'heterotopia', consummation and dispersion. Utopias are visions of the ha monious completion of history. Heterotopias by contrast are 'disturbing' challeng to the unity of history and the possibility of its completion. Foucault's own 'lim attitude' has just such a heterotopic quality. Whereas historians have traditionally a tempted to reveal the continuity and unity of history, how and where all the pieces f together, Foucault's aim is to expose history as 'limit', 'rupture', 'irruption', 'transfo mation', 'displacement'. A 'limit attitude', Foucault points out in *The Archaeology Knowledge*, forbids the possibility of a 'total history' with a definite 'convergence c culmination'. An example of 'total history' would be the standard enlightenment vie of 'the continuous chronology of reason' (Foucault, 1974, p. 8). Total history is re placed by what Foucault calls 'general history', the analysis of history as *series* without origin or destination. 'A total description draws all phenomena around a single centre . . . a general history . . . would deploy the space of a dispersion' (Foucault, 1974, p. 10). General history is therefore the *end* of the idea of 'the end of history' in its normal sense.

Jean Baudrillard (b. 1929) started writing in the 1960s as a Marxist sociologist who extended the critique of 'commodities' to the 'everyday' realities of fashion, sexuality and the consumer society. Under the influence of 'semiology' (the study of signs and language that had become fashionable through Lévi-Strauss and Barthes) Baudrillard steadily moved away from Marxism. In *The System of Objects* [1968] and *The Consumer Society* [1970] Baudrillard used semiology to argue that commodities are most clearly understood not as objects with economic value, but as signs within a cultural-linguistic code. However, in *The Mirror of Production* [1973] Baudrillard uses semiology to surpass Marxism, which he sees not as 'a radical critique of capitalism' but as 'its highest form of justification or ideology' (Baudrillard, 1988, p. 4). In the 1980s, notably in *Simulacra and Simulations* [1981] Baudrillard develops the view for which he is best known: the theory of late twentieth-century culture as a self-referential system of signs in which it is no longer possible to distinguish image from reality. It is this condition, which Baudrillard calls 'hyperreality' that forms the basis of his thinking about the posthistorical condition. Hyperreality comes about because of the development of modern technologies of information and communication. The modern pervasiveness of news, television, advertising, computers, video cameras has expanded and empowered the realm of images within culture. Moreover we now depend upon these images for our individual, cultural and historical self-understanding. This dependence comes at the price of the disappearance of 'real life' as it was once understood and the emergence of hyperreality: a simulation that substitutes for what we thought of as 'reality'. In this process, argues Baudrillard, we are transformed from being spectators of the media to being its products. We are 'objects transposed to the other side of the screen, mediumatized' (Baudrillard, 1997, p. 22). Although the world around looks and feels real enough to us, the appearance of the world has been conditioned for us in advance, and we have no access to the world apart from this conditioning.

Baudrillard's theory is not unprecedented. Nietzsche, whose philosophy so often pre-figures 'postmodern' thought, had predicted in *Twilight of the Idols* [1889] that the epoch of the future would be one in which the 'real world' would become 'a myth'. In the 1930s Walter Benjamin argued in his essay 'The Work of Art in an Age of Mechanical Reproduction' that the mass production of images, particularly in the cinema, had destroyed the aura of 'the real'. Marshall McLuhan in the 1960s had developed the optimistic vision that the mass media would enable a new age of communication and information. In *The Society of the Spectacle* [1967] the French theorist Guy Debord had argued that 'in societies where modern conditions of production prevail, all of life presents itself as an immense accumulation of spectacles. Everything that was directly lived has moved away into a representation.' (Debord 1983, §1) Elias Canetti (referred to by Baudrillard in 10.C.1) wrote in *The Human Province* [1973] about the importance of uncovering what he called the 'Dead Point' of modern history, when 'at a certain point, history was no longer real. Without noticing it, all mankind had suddenly left reality' (Canetti, 1978, p. 69). For Canetti the discovery of this point would be a crucial moment of posthistorical self-awareness. Without this awareness, Canetti argued, we would continue to live in a desolate age of destroyed reality.

Baudrillard's unique insight is his theory of 'simulation' and 'the simulacrum' (plural: simulacra). 'The simulacrum' is a particular way of thinking about images and representation. Images obviously existed before the mass media, but Baudrillard argues that these did not fully operate as *simulacra*. In a pre-technological culture one could laboriously make a 'counterfeit' of something, but this imitated rather than replaced the original object. In a modern industrial culture we have been able to mass-produce objects, such perfect and innumerable doubles of the original that the original is of no special significance. But in our modern media culture, we have the power to 'simulate' reality in another medium – film, TV, photography – and to do this on a vast scale. 'Simulation', says Baudrillard, 'is to feign to have what one hasn't' (Baudrillard 1988, p. 167). In other words, simulation creates reality rather than imitating or mass-producing it. In hyperreality, Baudrillard argues, such simulations replace 'reality' not only in particular instances, but in general. 'The whole of everyday political, social, historical, economic reality is incorporated into the simulative dimension of hyperrealism we already live out the "aesthetic" hallucination of reality' (Baudrillard, 1988, p. 146). This hallucination is the posthistorical condition.

How, though, does the advent of hyperreality signal what Baudrillard calls the 'disappearance' of history'? In 10.C.I, Baudrillard describes the 'acceleration' of events in hyperreality. With the aid of technology hyperreal events can happen faster, indeed so fast that we can no longer take in what is happening to us. Furthermore, technology has enabled a saturation of information. Owing to the speed and density of history historical analysis becomes impossible and, says Baudrillard, history 'vanishes'. In vanishing, history takes with it its 'end' or 'goal' leaving the accelerated events of hyperreality without purpose or rationale. This produces the posthistorical phenomenon that Baudrillard calls the 'crystallization' of time into uncertain moments that do not belong to any general pattern of purpose.

How are we to respond to this posthistorical condition? Guy Debord had argued that what he called the 'paralysis of history' in the modern 'society of the spectacle' was based upon a 'false consciousness of time' (Debord, 1983, §158); he believed that the recovery of truth would be possible through patient, Marxist 'practical critique'. By contrast Baudrillard rejects salvation through critique since there is no longer any basis for a critique of hyperreality, since hyperreality has so thoroughly contaminated our thinking and our culture (Baudrillard, 1997, p. 20). 'Good old critical and ironical judgement [is] no longer possible' (Baudrillard, 1990, p. 87). In a fatalistic situation, argues Baudrillard, one can only use what he calls 'fatal strategies': the attempt to push forward the collapse of hyperreality through excess and exaggeration. Baudrillard's infamous essays of 1991, arguing that the Gulf War 'did not happen' but was a media simulation or computer game, may be read as an example of just such a 'fatal strategy'. One of the positive effects of Baudrillard's provocation was to ignite an important debate about how far we can know the 'truth' about contemporary history in a media-saturated culture.[2]

2   On this debate see ed. Norris, 1992 and Paul Patton's essay 'This is not a War' in ed. Zurbrugg 1997.

Francis Fukuyama (b. 1952) is an American political scientist who worked as an adviser to the United States Department of State under the Regan administration. Fukuyama became internationally famous in 1989 after publishing an article called 'The End of History' which was later expanded into a book of the same title. In these texts Fukuyama launched an historical defence of Western political values, arguing that the events of the late twentieth century demonstrate a global consensus in favour of liberal democracy. This consensus constitutes the 'End of History' in the sense that there will be 'no further progress in the development of underlying principles and institutions'. There will still be events, but history – in the sense of the universal story of human development – will have reached its conclusion.

Fukuyama's understanding of universal history derives directly from Hegel, or rather from an interpretation of Hegel by Alexandre Kojève. In the 1930s Kojève had made a new reading of Hegel based upon the master–slave relationship described in *The Phenomenology of Spirit* (Hegel, 1979). Hegel imagines the beginning of history as a primal battle in which humans risk their lives in order to win 'recognition' from others. Recognition is achieved for the victor when the other person becomes enslaved. However, this master-slave relationship is unstable since on the one hand the slave also seeks recognition and on the other hand the master seeks recognition from an equal. The relationship can only reach an equilibrium when both parties benefit from the recognition of the other. Fukuyama follows Kojève in bringing the concept of 'recognition' to the centre of an understanding of the historical process. For him history is driven by our common quest for personal recognition. Only in a liberal democracy, where (theoretically, at least) everyone has equal esteem, can recognition become universal.

> Any child born on the territory of the United States or France or any number of other liberal states is by that very act endowed with certain rights of citizenship. No one may harm the life of that child, whether she is poor or rich, black or white, without being prosecuted by the criminal justice system. In time, that child will have the right to own property, which must be respected by the state and by fellow citizens ... And finally, when this child reaches adulthood, he or she will have the right to participate in the very government that establishes these rights in the first place, and to contribute to deliberations on the highest and most important questions of public policy. This participation can take the form of either voting in periodic elections, or the more active form of entering into the political process directly, for instance by running for office, or writing editorials in support of a position or person, or by serving in a public-sector bureaucracy. Popular self-government abolishes the distinction between masters and slaves: everyone is entitled to at least some share of the role of master. Mastery now takes the form of the promulgation of democratically determined laws, that is, sets of universal rules by which man self-consciously masters himself. Recognition becomes reciprocal when the state and the people recognize each other, that is, when the state grants its citizens rights and when citizens agree to abide by the state's laws. (Fukuyama, 1992, p. 203)

This, argues Fukuyama, is the end of history since we cannot conceive of a better form of government.

Fukuyama's argument begins with an assumption about human nature. We are, he says, governed by two sorts of stuff: reason and desire. As Fukuyama acknowledges, the distinction originates with Plato. In part IV of *The Republic*, Plato describes the

soul – or human nature – as having three parts: The first part (*nous*) is reason, mind o
intelligence; the second (*epithemeia*) is appetite or irrational passion: hunger, thirs
sexual desire; the third (*thymos*) is spiritedness, or the noble passions of indignation
righteous anger, the desire for esteem and value. '*Thymos*' is an interesting concep
which Plato uses to identify the uniquely human passions. Animals can be hungr
thirsty and libidinous. But only humans can long for justice or seek after a bette
society. The word *thymos* probably derives from another Greek verb *thuo*, which mean
to sacrifice; and *thymos* implies the need for sacrifice in the name of a higher goal. I
Plato the goals *thymos* strives after are abstract: love, beauty, truth, freedom, The Goo

In the Introduction to his *Philosophy of History*, Hegel uses the distinction betwee
ideas and passion in his understanding of world-history:

> Two elements, then, enter into the object of our investigation; the first the Idea, the
> second the complex of human passions; the one the warp, the other the woof of the vast
> arras-web of Universal History. The concrete mean and union of the two is Liberty,
> under the conditions of morality in a State. (Hegel, 1956, p. 23)

Hegel sees that history requires energy as well as logic, supplying 'the impelling an
actuating force for accomplishing deeds' (ibid., p. 24). Fukuyama follows Hegel
seeing history as the product of these two components: mind and *thymos*, reason an
the spirit of nobility. The spirit of nobility above all seeks recognition for the self –
wants esteem, respect and honour from other human beings. But only the mind ca
imagine the social circumstances under which *thymos* can be fulfilled; only the mir
can think of the form of state which will allow for reciprocal recognition and fre
society. History is what occurs as Mind gradually realizes this goal.

Interestingly, the posthistorical condition is not one that Fukuyama relishes. On
the struggle for recognition is over, Fukuyama worries what will happen to our thymot
drives. One fear is that *thymos* will peter out and leave humanity self-satisfied but lif
less. Here Fukuyama turns to Nietzsche who depicts the liberal democrat as 'The La
Man' – a hollow and lifeless form of humanity, emptied of the will to strive for high
values. Fukyama's other fear is that *thymos* may find 'an extreme and pathologic
expression in anti-social violence.

The initial academic reception of Fukuyama's philosophy of history was genera
critical. Many, looking about at a far from perfect world – featuring barbaric wa
oppression, totalitarianism and injustice – found Fukuyama's theory preposterous. Criti
from the left (see Norris, 1992, pp. 155–8) criticized him for crude capitali
triumphalism. Critics from the right argued that liberal democracy was by no mea
safe from global threats such as Communism. However, Fukuyama's book *The End
History and the Last Man* [1992] clearly struck a popular chord, appearing on bestsell
lists in the US, France, Japan and elsewhere. If nothing else, Fukuyama had broug
some of the fundamental questions of speculative philosophy of history into popul
discussion.

One of the most notable critiques of Fukuyama has come from the French philos
pher Jacques Derrida, who from the late 1960s developed an approach to philosop
called 'deconstruction'. Derrida's deconstruction has tried to show that absolute clai
to truth (of the kind made by Fukuyama) always contradict themselves and end up
'aporia' (a Greek word meaning a blocked-path or dead end). In *Specters of Ma*

1993], Derrida contends that Fukuyama's 'end of history' theory is fissured with fundamental contradictions. First, Derrida argues that although Fukuyama proclaims the end of history, this is in fact only the promise or prophecy of an end (Derrida, 1994, pp. 56–7; 59–61). Fukuyama cannot show us the end of history because the world is still home to regimes that have yet to embrace liberal democracy. Thus the theoretical perspective that Fukuyama presents with such confidence, is in fact a quasi-religious faith that the facts of the future will fulfill his ideal of historical completion. Secondly, Derrida argues that Fukuyama trips up in his attempt to distinguish between the *facts* and the *ideals* of history. Although there are terrible *facts* in the twentieth century, Fukuyama still argues that the *ideal* of liberal democracy has gained increasing acceptance. This is because the 'end of history' is not a state of affairs but 'a regulating ideal' that cannot be measured against any historical event or any so-called 'empirical' failure (p. 62). The fact that the 'empirical history' of the twentieth century includes many examples of totalitarianism and barbarism, argues Fukuyama, does not disprove this ideal. The problem with this, as Derrida points out, is that elsewhere Fukuyama uses other facts of history – the collapse of the eastern bloc contrasted with the economic success of the USA and the EC – to demonstrate the legitimacy, and progress, of the liberal-democratic ideal.

In making these criticisms, Derrida is not contesting all the values that Fukuyama ascribes to his version of 'the end of history'. But for him the end of history exists only in the hope or *promise* of a free and democratic society. As such the end of history never arrives. Posthistory is the endless task of hope and waiting.

Selected Texts

Edited by Hugh Rayment-Pickard

10.A   Michel Foucault, 1926–1984

10.A.1   The End of Man[1]

The impression of fulfilment and of end, the muffled feeling that carries and animate
our thought, and perhaps lulls it to sleep with the facility of its promises, and makes u
believe that something new is about to begin, something we glimpse only as a thin lin
of light low on the horizon – that feeling and that impression are perhaps not i
founded. It will be said that they exist, that they have never ceased to be formulate
over and over again since the early nineteenth century; it will be said that Hölderli
Hegel, Feuerbach, and Marx all felt this certainty that in them a thought and perhap
a culture were coming to a close, and that from the depths of a distance, which wa
perhaps not invincible, another was approaching – in the dim light of dawn, in th
brilliance of noon, or in the dissension of the falling day. But this close, this perilou
imminence whose promise we fear today, whose danger we welcome, is probably no
of the same order. Then, the task enjoined upon thought by that annunciation was t
establish for man a stable sojourn upon this earth from which the gods had turne
away or vanished. In our day, and once again Nietzsche indicated the turning-poi
from a long way off, it is not so much the absence or the death of God that is affirme
as the end of man (that narrow, imperceptible displacement, that recession in the for
of identity, which are the reason why man's finitude has become his end); it become
apparent, then, that the death of God and the last man are engaged in a contest wit
more than one round: is it not the last man who announces that he has killed Go
thus situating his language, his thought, his laughter in the space of that already dea
God, yet positing himself also as he who has killed God and whose existence includ
the freedom and the decision of that murder? Thus, the last man is at the same tin
older and yet younger than the death of God; since he has killed God, it is he himse
who must answer for his own finitude; but since it is in the death of God that h
speaks, thinks, and exists, his murder itself is doomed to die; new gods, the same go
are already swelling the future Ocean; man will disappear. Rather than the death
God – or, rather, in the wake of that death and in a profound correlation with it – wh
Nietzsche's thought heralds is the end of his murderer; it is the explosion of man's fa

---

1   Michel Foucault, *The Order of Things* (London: Tavistock Publications, 1970), pp. 384–7.

in laughter, and the return of masks; it is the scattering of the profound stream of time by which he felt himself carried along and whose pressure he suspected in the very being of things; it is the identity of the Return of the Same with the absolute dispersion of man. Throughout the nineteenth century, the end of philosophy and the promise of an approaching culture were no doubt one and the same thing as the thought of finitude and the appearance of man in the field of knowledge; in our day, the fact that philosophy is still – and again – in the process of coming to an end, and the fact that in it perhaps, though even more outside and against it, in literature as well as in formal reflection, the question of language is being posed, prove no doubt that man is in the process of disappearing.

For the entire modern *episteme* – that which was formed towards the end of the eighteenth century and still serves as the positive ground of our knowledge, that which constituted man's particular mode of being and the possibility of knowing him empirically – that entire *episteme* was bound up with the disappearance of Discourse and its featureless reign, with the shift of language towards objectivity, and with its reappearance in multiple form. If this same language is now emerging with greater and greater insistence in a unity that we ought to think but cannot as yet do so, is this not the sign that the whole of this configuration is now about to topple, and that man is in the process of perishing as the being of language continues to shine ever brighter upon our horizon? Since man was constituted at a time when language was doomed to dispersion, will he not be dispersed when language regains its unity? And if that were true, would it not be an error – a profound error, since it could hide from us what should now be thought – to interpret our actual experience as an application of the forms of language to the human order? Ought we not rather to give up thinking of man, or, to be more strict, to think of this disappearance of man – and the ground of possibility of all the sciences of man – as closely as possible in correlation with our concern with language? Ought we not to admit that, since language is here once more, man will return to that serene non-existence in which he was formerly maintained by the imperious unity of Discourse? Man had been a figure occurring between two modes of language; or, rather, he was constituted only when language, having been situated within representation and, as it were, dissolved in it, freed itself from that situation at the cost of its own fragmentation: man composed his own figure in the interstices of that fragmented language. Of course, these are not affirmations; they are at most questions to which it is not possible to reply; they must be left in suspense, where they pose themselves, only with the knowledge that the possibility of posing them may well open the way to a future thought.

One thing in any case is certain: man is neither the oldest nor the most constant problem that has been posed for human knowledge. Taking a relatively short chronological sample within a restricted geographical area – European culture since the sixteenth century – one can be certain that man is a recent invention within it. It is not around him and his secrets that knowledge prowled for so long in the darkness. In fact, among all the mutations that have affected the knowledge of things and their order, the knowledge of identities, differences, characters, equivalences, words – in short, in the midst of all the episodes of that profound history of the *Same* – only one, that which began a century and a half ago and is now perhaps drawing to a close, has made possible for the figure of man to appear. And that appearance was not the liberation of an old anxiety, the transition into luminous consciousness of an age-old concern, the entry into objectivity of something that had long remained trapped within beliefs and philosophies: it was the effect of a change in the fundamental arrangements of knowledge. As the archaeology of our thought easily shows, man is an invention of recent date. And one perhaps nearing its end.

If those arrangements were to disappear as they appeared, if some event of which we can at the moment do no more than sense the possibility – without knowing either what its form will be or what it promises – were to cause them to crumble, as the ground of Classical thought did, at the end of the eighteenth century, then one can certainly wager that man would be erased, like a face drawn in sand at the edge of the sea.

10.A.II   Effective History: 'one kingdom, without providence or final cause'[2]

'Effective' history differs from traditional history in being without constants. Nothing in man – not even his body – is sufficiently stable to serve as the basis for self-recognition or for understanding other men. The traditional devices for constructing a comprehensive view of history and for retracing the past as a patient and continuous development must be systematically dismantled. Necessarily, we must dismiss those tendencies that encourage the consoling play of recognitions. Knowledge, even under the banner of history, does not depend on 'rediscovery', and it emphatically excludes the 'rediscovery of ourselves.' History becomes 'effective' to the degree that it introduces discontinuity into our very being – as it divides our emotions, dramatizes our instincts, multiplies our body and sets it against itself. 'Effective' history deprives the self of the reassuring stability of life and nature, and it will not permit itself to be transported by a voiceless obstinacy toward a millennial ending. It will up-root its traditional foundations and relentlessly disrupt its pre-tended continuity. This is because knowledge is not made for understanding; it is made for cutting.

From these observations, we can grasp the particular traits of historical meaning as Nietzsche understood it – the sense which opposes *wirkliche Historie* to traditional history. The former transposes the relationship ordinarily established between the eruption of an event and necessary continuity. An entire historical tradition (theological or rationalistic) aims at dissolving the singular event into an ideal continuity – as a teleological movement or a natural process. 'Effective' history, however, deals with events in terms of their most unique characteristics, their most acute manifestations. An event, consequently, is not a decision, a treaty, a reign, or a battle, but the reversal of a relationship of forces, the usurpation of power, the appropriation of a vocabulary turned against those who had once used it, a feeble domination that poisons itself as it grows lax, the entry of a masked 'other.' The forces operating in history are not controlled by destiny or regulative mechanisms, but respond to haphazard conflicts. They do not manifest the successive forms of a primordial intention and their attraction is not that of a conclusion, for they always appear through the singular randomness of events. The inverse of the Christian world, spun entirely by a divine spider, and different from

---

2   Michel Foucault, 'Nietzsche, Genealogy, History', in *The Foucault Reader*, ed. P. Robinow (Harmondsworth: Penguin, 1991), pp. 87–90.

the world of the Greeks, divided between the realm of will and the great cosmic folly, the world of effective history knows only one kingdom, without providence or final cause, where there is only 'the iron hand of necessity shaking the dice-box of chance.' Chance is not simply the drawing of lots, but raising the stakes in every attempt to master chance through the will to power, and giving rise to the risk of an even greater chance. The world we know is not this ultimately simple configuration where events are reduced to accentuate their essential traits, their final meaning, or their initial and final value. On the contrary, it is a profusion of entangled events. If it appears as a 'marvellous motley, profound and totally meaningful,' this is because it began and continues its secret existence through a 'host of errors and phantasms.' We want historians to confirm our belief that the present rests upon profound intentions and immutable necessities. But the true historical sense confirms our existence among countless lost events, without a landmark or point of reference.

Effective history can also invert the relationship that traditional history, in its dependence on metaphysics, establishes between proximity and distance. The latter is given to a contemplation of distances and heights: the noblest periods, the highest forms, the most abstract ideas, the purest individualities. It accomplishes this by getting as near as possible, placing itself at the foot of its mountain peaks, at the risk of adopting the famous perspective of frogs. Effective history, on the other hand, shortens its vision to those things nearest to it – the body, the nervous system, nutrition, digestion, and energies; it unearths the periods of decadence, and if it chances upon lofty epochs, it is with the suspicion – not vindictive but joyous – finding a barbarous and shameful confusion. It has no fear of looking down, so long as it is understood that it looks from above and descends to seize the various perspectives, to disclose dispersions and differences, to leave things undisturbed in their own dimension and intensity. It reverses the surreptitious practice of historians, their pretension to examine things furthest from themselves, the grovelling manner in which they approach this promising distance (like the metaphysicians who proclaim the existence of an afterlife, situated at a distance from this world, as a promise of their reward). Effective history studies what is closest, but in an abrupt dispossession, so as to seize it at a distance (an approach similar to that of a doctor who looks closely, who plunges to make a diagnosis and to state its difference). Historical sense has more in common with medicine than philosophy; and it should not surprise us that Nietzsche occasionally employs the phrase 'historically and physiologically,' since among the philosopher's idiosyncrasies is a complete denial of the body. This includes, as well, 'the absence of historical sense, a hatred for the idea of development, Egyptianism,' the obstinate 'placing of conclusions at the beginning,' of 'making last things first.' History has a more important task than to be a handmaiden to philosophy, to recount the necessary birth of truth and values; it should become a differential knowledge of energies and failings, heights and degenerations, poisons and antidotes. Its task is to become a curative science.

The final trait of effective history is its affirmation of knowledge as perspective. Historians take unusual pains to erase the elements in their work which reveal their grounding in a particular time and place, their preferences in a controversy – the unavoidable obstacles of their passion. Nietzsche's version of historical sense is explicit in its perspective and acknowledges its system of injustice. Its perception is slanted, being a deliberate appraisal, affirmation, or negation; it reaches the lingering and poisonous traces in order to prescribe the best antidote. It is not given to a discreet effacement before the objects it observes and does not submit itself to their processes; nor does it seek laws, since it gives equal weight to its own sight and to its objects. Through this historical sense, knowledge is allowed to create its own genealogy in the act of cognition; and *wirkliche Historie* composes a genealogy of history as the vertical projection of its position.

10.B   Jean Baudrillard, b. 1929

10.B.1   The Future[3]

Several plausible hypotheses exist with regard to this disappearance of history. To our contemporary astrophysical imaginary, Canetti's phrase 'the whole human race suddenly left reality behind' irresistibly evokes the vitesse de libération, the 'escape velocity' that a body needs to free itself from the gravitational force of a star or planet. According to this image, we can suppose that the acceleration of modernity with respect to technology, current events and the media, the acceleration of all economic, political, sexual exchange – all that we designate finally by the word 'liberation' – has brought us to as escape velocity such that one day we escaped the referential sphere of the real and history (and this being the case, we can speak, following Canetti, of a 'precise' moment in history, just as in physics the point of 'liberation' can be precisely calculated). We are truly 'liberated', in every sense of the word, so liberated that our momentum (the accelerated metabolization of our societies) has taken where the event is possible because gravitation is still strong enough to enable things to reflect themselves, to turn back on themselves, and hence to have some duration and some consequence. . . .

Events no longer have consequences because they go too quickly – they are diffused too quickly, too far, they are caught up in circuits – they can never return as testimony for themselves or their meaning (meaning is always a testimony). On the other hand, each totality of events or culture must be fragmented, disarticulated in order to enter into the circuits; each language must be resolved into the binary system, 0/1, in order to circulate no longer in our memories, but in the electronic and luminous memory of computers. No human language withstands the speed of light. No historical event withstands its planetary diffusion. No meaning withstands its acceleration. No history withstands the centrifugation of facts by themselves, to the limitlessness of space-times (I would say further: no sexuality withstands its liberation, no culture withstands its promulgation, no truth withstands its verification, etc. . . . .).

This is what I call simulation. But I wish to make it clear that simulation is double-edged and that what I put forward here is nothing other than an exercise in simulation. I am no longer in a position to 'reflect' anything. I can only push hypotheses to their limit, remove them from their critical zone of reference, make them go beyond the point of no-return. I send theory as well into the hyperspace of simulation – where it

3   Jean Baudrillard, 'The Year 2000 will not take place', in *Futur*Fall: Excursions into Post-Modernity*, ed. E. A. Grosz et al., Power Institute of Fine Arts, University of Sydney, 1986, pp. 18–25.

loses all objective validity, but perhaps gains in coherence, that is to say in real affinity with the system that surrounds us.

The second hypothesis with regard to the disappearance of history is in a way the inverse of the first – it adheres no longer to the acceleration, but to the deceleration of processes. Once more it comes directly from physics.

Matter slows the passage of time. More precisely, time on the surface of a very dense body seems to go slower. The phenomenon increases as the density increases. The effect of this deceleration is to increase as the density increases. The effect of this deceleration is to increase the wavelength of light emitted by the body, as received by the external observer. Past a certain limit, time stops, the wavelength becomes infinite. The wave no longer exists. Light is extinguished.

Here, the analogical transfer is not difficult either. You only have to imagine 'masses' in place of 'matter', and 'history' in place of 'time'. You will then see that quite simply there is a deceleration of history when it approaches the astral body of 'silent majorities'. Our societies are dominated by this mass process, not so much in the demographic or sociological sense of the word as in the sense of passing, here too a critical point, a point of no-return, not through acceleration (as in our first hypothesis) but through inertia. This is the most important event in modern societies, the most subtle and profound ruse in their history: the advent, in the very course of their socialization, their mobilization, their productive and revolutionary intensification (they are all revolutionary with regard to previous centuries), the advent of a force of inertia, of an immense indifference, and of the silent power of this indifference. This is what we call mass (the masses). This mass, this inert material of the social, does not result from an absence of exchange, of information and communication; on the contrary, it results from the multiplication and saturation of exchange, information etc. It springs from the hyperdensity of cities, of commodities, of messages, of circuits. It is the cold star of the social, and around this mass history cools, it slows down, events succeed each other and vanish in indifference. Neutralized, mithridatized by information, in return the masses neutralize history and function as a screen of absorption. They have no history themselves, no meaning, no consciousness, no desire. They are the potential residue of all history, of all meaning, of all consciousness, of all desire. The deployment in our modernity of all these fine things has fomented a mysterious counterpart whose misrecognition (the misrecognition of this inertial force, this strength of inertia, this inverse energy) unhinges all current political, social, historical strategies.

The effect in this case is the opposite to that in our first hypothesis: progress, history, reason, desire are no longer able to find their 'escape velocity'. They can no longer pull away from this too dense body which irresistibly slows their progress, which slows time to the point that thereafter the perception or imagination of the future escapes us. All social, historical, temporal transcendence is absorbed by this mass in its silent immanence. We are already at the point where political, social events no longer have sufficient autonomous energy to move us, and hence unfold like a silent film of which we are not individually but collectively irresponsible. History stops here, and we see in what way: not for want of people, nor of violence (there will always be more violence, but violence should not be confused with history), nor of events (there will always be more events, thanks to the media and information), but by deceleration, indifference and stupefaction. History can no longer outrun itself, it can no longer envisage its own finality, dream of its own end; it is buried in its own immediate effect, it implodes in the here and now. Finally, we cannot even speak of the end of history, because there is no time for it to reach its own end. Its effects accelerate, but its progress ineluctably slows down. It will come to a standstill, and fade out like light and time on the edge of an infinitely dense mass. . . .

Third hypothesis, third analogy. This time I no longer derive my effects from physics but from music, but it is still the 'vanishing point' which interests me, the point of disappearance or evanescence of something – that point of which Canetti speaks, beyond which everything ceases to be true. . . .

We are all obsessed (and not only in music) with high fidelity, obsessed with the quality of musical 'reproduction'. Armed with the tuners, amplifiers and speakers of our stereo system we adjust bass and treble, we mix, we combine, we multiply tracks, in search of an impeccable technology and an infallible music. I still remember a sound booth in a recording studio where the music, broadcast on four tracks, reached you in four dimensions, so that it seemed visceral, secreted from inside, with a surreal depth . . . This was no longer music. Where is the degree of technological sophistication, where is the 'high fidelity' threshold beyond which music as such would disappear? For the problem of the disappearance of music is the same as that of the disappearance of history: it will not disappear *for want* of music, it will disappear for having exceeded that limit point, vanishing point, it will disappear in the perfection of its materiality. . . .

It is exactly the same with history. Here too we have exceeded that limit where, by the sophistication of events and information, history as such ceases to exist. . . .

By definition, this 'vanishing point' is unlocatable, this point before which there was history, there was music, there was a meaning to events, to the social, to sexuality (and even to psychoanalysis – but this too has long since so completely exceeded this point of exacerbation, of finicky perfection in the theory of the unconscious that the concept of it has vanished). Where does stereo perfection end? The boundaries are constantly pushed back, since they are those of technological obsession. Where does information end?

We leave history to enter simulation (as much, to my mind by the biological concept of genetic code as by the media, as much by space exploration, which for us functions as a space of simulation, as by the idea of the computer as a cerebral equivalent, etc.). This is by no means a despairing hypothesis, unless we regard simulation as a higher form of alienation – which I certainly do not. It is precisely in history that we are alienated, and if we leave history we also leave alienation (not without nostalgia, it must be said, for that good old drama of subject and object).

But we can just as well suppose that history itself is, or was nothing but an enormous simulation model. Not in the sense that it would have been only so much sound and fury, or that events would never have had the meaning attributed to them, or that history is nothing more than the account given of it, etc. (which is perhaps true, but of no direct interest here). No, I speak rather of the time in which it unfolds, of that linear time in which events are thought to follow one another like cause and effect, even eschatological process, Last Judgement or revolution, salvation or catastrophe, is at once the time of the end and of its unlimited suspension. This time, in which only a history can take place, i.e. a succession of facts, not senseless but all precariously balanced on the future, isn't the time of ceremonial societies, where everything is completed in the beginning and where the ceremony retraces the perfection of this original event – perfect in the sense that everything is complete. In opposition to this order in which time is *complete*, i.e. doesn't exist at all in the sense that we understand it, the liberation of real historical time (for it is precisely a question of a 'liberation', of a deliverance from the ritual universe wherein arises progressively the linearity of time and of death) can appear as a purely artificial process. What is this difference (*Aufschiebung*), what is this suspension, why must that which must be completed be completed at the end of time, at the end of history? We have here the projection of a model of reality which must have seemed perfectly fabricated, perfectly fictional, perfectly absurd and immaterial to those cultures which had no sense of a deferred payment, of waiting, of a progressive sequence, of a finality . . . A scenario which moreover imposed itself with difficulty, so much was it not obvious, so much did it contradict every fundamental exigency. The early years of Christianity were marked by a vehement resistance, even among believers, to the postponement into some indefinite future of the coming of the Kingdom of God. The acceptance of this 'historical' perspective of salvation, i.e. of its endless deferral, didn't happen without violence, and all succeeding heresies agreed on this leitmotif: the immediate demand for the Kingdom of God, the immediate fulfillment of the promise. Something like a defiance of time. We know that whole communities went so far as to suicide in order to hasten the coming of the Kingdom. Since this was promised to them at the end of time, they only had to put an end to time at once.

All history is accompanied by an age-old defiance of the temporality of history. The will to see things completed at once, and not after a long detour, is by no means a regressive childhood phantasm. It is a defiance of time which is born with time itself. Two contradictory forms arise with linear time, i.e. with the birth of time as such. The first consists in following the meanderings of this time and in constructing a history, the other consists in accelerating the course of time, or in abruptly condensing it to bring it to an end. Opposed to the historical perspective, which constantly displaces the stakes onto a hypothetical end, has always been a fatal demand, a fatal strategy of time, which is to leap ahead, to annihilate time and to short-circuit the Last Judgement. It cannot be said that either of these two forces have truly triumphed over the other, and throughout history itself the burning question remains: should we or should we not wait? Since the messianic upheaval amongst the early Christians who, tired of waiting for the promised Kingdom of Heaven, wanted to hasten the *parousia* by their own death, that is to say to end the detour of time by the short-circuit of their own destruction, beyond the heresies and controversies, there has always been the desire to anticipate the end – by death if necessary, by a kind of seductive suicide which aims to separate God from history. Ascetics had the same fatal strategy, as did the Cathars: to ensnare God by their own death, or by attaining perfection, thereby confronting him with his responsibilities, those beyond the end, those of completion.

If you think about it, terrorism is nothing else. It attempts to ensnare power by an immediate and total act, without waiting for the end of history. It puts itself in the ecstatic position of the end, thereby hoping to induce the history of the Last Judgement. Of course this never happens, but such defiance of history has a long history, and it is always fascinating, for ultimately neither time nor history have even been accepted. Even if they are not disposed to effect a fatal strategy of this kind, people remain deeply conscious of the arbitrariness, of the artificial character, namely the fundamental hypocrisy of time and history. They are never taken in by those who ask them to wait in hope.

Even beyond terrorism, isn't there a glimmer of this violent parousical demand in the global phantasm of catastrophes which hangs over the contemporary world? The demand for a violent resolution of reality, precisely when this escapes us into hyperreality? Hyperreality puts an end to the hope of a Last Judgement (or a revolution). If the envisaged ends escape us, if even history holds no possibility of bringing them about, since meanwhile it has come to an end (this is always the story of Kafka's Messiah: he arrives too late, one day too late, the delay is unbearable) then we might as well effect the precession of the end, we might as well short-circuit the coming of the Messiah. This has always been the diabolic (demonic?) temptation: to falsify ends and the calculation on ends, to falsify time and the occurrence of things, by precipitating the flow, to hasten the end – in the impatience for completion, or by the hidden intuition that the promise of completion is in any case itself false and diabolical.

The denegation of history therefore could be a tiresome and artificial duration – All *Aufhebung* is experienced as an *Aufschiebung* – a denegation of time as artifact. A denegation that is readily identified in its religious and millenarian forms, in its individual and terrorist forms, but also perceptible in the widespread refusal, the suspension of historical will, and even in the obsession, in the apparently opposite compulsion to historicize everything, to document everything, to memorize all of our past and that of all cultures. Isn't this the symptom of a collective intuition of the end of history, that events and the living time of history are finished (thus verifying Canetti's proposition), and that we must arm ourselves with the whole artificial memory, with all the signs of the past in order to confront the absence of a future and the glacial times ahead? Don't we have the impression that mental and intellectual structures are collapsing, burying themselves far form the sun in memory banks and archives, in search of a silent efficacity or an improbable resurrection? All forms of thought are buried under the wisdom of the year 2000. They already scent the terror of the year 2000. Our societies instinctively adopt the solution of those cryogenic people that are plunged into liquid nitrogen to await the discovery of a means of survival. They are like those luxurious and funereal wares buried in the underground sarcophagus of the Forum des Halles as a museum of our culture for future generations, after the catastrophe. These societies which expect nothing from any future coming and which trust less in history, these societies which bury themselves under their prospective technologies, under stockpiles of information and in vast alveolar communication networks *where time is finally annihilated by pure circulation* – these generations will perhaps never wake up, but they remain oblivious. The year 2000 will perhaps not take place, but they remain oblivious.

10.C   Francis Fukuyama, b. 1952

10.C.I   The End of History[4]

The distant origins of the present volume [*The End of History and the Last Man*] lie in an article entitled 'The End of History?' which I wrote for the journal The National

---

4   Francis Fukuyama, *The End of History and the Last Man* (London: Hamish Hamilton, 1992), pp. xi–xii.

Interest in the summer of 1989. In it, I argued that a remarkable consensus concerning the legitimacy of liberal democracy as a system of government had emerged throughout the world over the past few years, as it conquered rival ideologies like hereditary monarchy, fascism, and most recently communism. More than that, however, I argued that liberal democracy may constitute the 'end point of mankind's ideological evolution' and the 'final form of human government', and as such constituted the 'end of history'. That is, while earlier forms of government were characterized by grave defects and irrationalities that led to their eventual collapse, liberal democracy was arguably free from such fundamental internal contradictions. This was not to say that today's stable democracies, like the United States, France, or Switzerland, were not without injustice or serious social problems. But these problems were ones of incomplete implementation of the twin principles of liberty and equality on which modern democracy is founded, rather that of flaws in the principles themselves. While democracy and others might lapse back into other, more primitive forms of rule like theocracy or military dictatorship, the ideal of liberal democracy could not be improved on. . . .

Many people were confused in the first instance by use of the word 'history'. Understanding history in a conventional sense as the occurrence of events, people pointed to the fall of the Berlin Wall, the Chinese communist crackdown in Tiananmen Square, and the Iraqi invasion of Kuwait as evidence that 'history was continuing', and that I was *ipso facto* proven wrong.

And yet what I suggested had come to an end was not the occurrence of events, even large and grave events, but History: that is, history understood as a single, coherent, evolutionary process, when taking into account the experience of all peoples in all times. This understanding of History was most closely associated with the great German philosopher G. W. F. Hegel. It was made part of our daily intellectual atmosphere by Karl Marx, who borrowed this concept of History form Hegel, and is implicit in our use of words like 'primitive' or 'advanced', 'traditional' or 'modern', when referring to different types of human societies. For both of these thinkers, there was a coherent development of human societies from simple tribal ones based on slavery and subsistence agriculture, through various theocracies, monarchies, and feudal aristocracies, up though modern liberal democracy and technologically driven capitalism. This evolutionary process was neither random nor unintelligible, even if it did not proceed in a straight line, and even if it was possible to question whether man was happier or better off as a result of historical 'progress'.

Both Hegel and Marx believed that the evolution of human society was not open-ended, but would end when mankind had achieved a form of society that satisfied its deepest and most fundamental longings both thinkers thus posited an 'end of history': for Hegel this was the liberal state, while for Marx it was a communist society. This did not mean that the natural cycle of birth, life, and death would end, that important events would no longer happen, or that newspapers reporting them would cease to be published. It meant, rather, that there would be no further progress in the development of underlying principles and institutions, because all of the really big questions had been settled.

10.C.II *Thymos*: The Striving for Noble Goals[5]

The decline of community life suggests that in the future, we risk becoming secure and self-absorbed last men, devoid of thymotic striving for higher goals in our pursuit of private comforts. But the opposite danger exists as well, namely, that we will return to being first men engaged in bloody and pointless prestige battles, only this time with modern weapons. Indeed, the two problems are related to one another, for the absence of regular and constructive outlets *megalothymia* may simply lead to its later resurgence in an extreme and pathological form.

It is reasonable to wonder whether all people will believe that the kinds of struggles and sacrifices possible in a self-satisfied and prosperous liberal democracy are sufficient to call forth what is highest in man. For are there not reservoirs of idealism that cannot be exhausted – indeed, that are not even touched – if one becomes a developer like Donald Trump, or a mountain climber like Reinhold Meissner, or politician like George Bush? Difficult as it is, in many ways, to be these individuals, and for all the recognition they receive, their lives are not the most difficult, and the causes they serve are not the most serious or the most just. And as long as they are not, the horizon of human possibilities that they desires will not be ultimately satisfying for the most thymotic natures.

In particular, the virtues and ambitions called for by war are unlikely to find expression in liberal democracies. There will be plenty of metaphorical wars – corporate lawyers specializing in hostile takeovers who will think of themselves as sharks or gunslingers, and bond traders who imagine, as in Tom Wolfe's novel *The Bonfire of the Vanities*, that they are 'masters of the universe'. (They will believe this, however, only in bull markets). But as they sink into the soft leather of their BMWs, they will know somewhere in the back of their minds that there have been real gunslingers and masters in the worked, who would feel contempt for the petty virtues required to become rich or famous in modern America. How long megalothymia will be satisfied with metaphorical wars and symbolic victories is an open question. One suspects that some people will not be satisfied until they proved themselves by that very act that constituted their humanness at the beginning of history: they will want to risk their lives in violent battle, and thereby prove beyond any shadow of a doubt to themselves and to their fellows that they are free. They will deliberately seek discomfort and sacrifice because the pain will be the only way they have of proving definitely that they can *think well of themselves*, that they remain *human beings*.

Plato argued that while *thymos* was the basis of the virtues, in itself it was neither good nor bad, but had to be trained so that it would serve the common good. *Thymos* in other words, had to be ruled by reason, and made an ally of desire. The just city was one in which all three parts of the soul were satisfied and brought into balance under the guidance of reason. The best regime was extremely difficult to realize because had to satisfy the whole of man simultaneously, his reason, desire and *thymos*. But even if it was not possible for actual regimes to completely satisfy man, the best regime provided a standard by which one could measure those regimes that actually existed. That regime was best that best satisfied all three parts of the soul simultaneously.

---

5 Ibid., pp. 328–9.

By this standard, when compared to the historical alternatives available to us, it would seem that liberal democracy gives fullest scope to all three parts. If it could not qualify as the most just regime 'in speech' it might serve as the most just regime 'in reality'. For as Hegel teaches us, modern liberalism is not based on the abolition of the desire for recognition so much as on its transformation into a more rational form.

10.C.III   One Journey, One Destination[6]

Rather than a thousand shoots blossoming into as many different flowering plants, mankind will come to seem like a long wagon train strung out along a road. Some wagons will be pulling into town sharply and crisply, while others will be bivouacked back in the desert, or else stuck in ruts in the final pass over the mountains. Several wagons, attacked by Indians, will have been set aflame and abandoned along the way. There will be a few wagoners who, stunned by the battle, will have lost their sense of direction and are temporarily heading in the wrong direction, while one or two wagons will get tired of the journey and decide to set up permanent camps at particular points back along the road. Others will have found alternative routes to the main road, though they will discover that to get through the final mountain range they all must use the same pass. But the great majority of wagons will be making the slow journey into town, and most will eventually arrive there. The wagons are all similar to one another: while they are pointed different colours and are constructed of varied materials, each has four wheels and is drawn by horses, while inside sits a family hoping and praying that their journey will be a safe one. The apparent differences in the situations of the wagons will not be seen as reflecting permanent and necessary differences between the people riding in the wagons, but simply a product of their different positions along the road.

Alexandre Kojève believed that ultimately history itself would vindicate its own rationality. That is, enough wagons would pull into town such that any reasonable person looking at the situation would be forced to agree that there had been only one journey and one destination. It is doubtful that we are at that point now, for despite the recent worldwide liberal revolution, the evidence available to us now concerning the direction of the wagons' wanderings must remain provisionally inconclusive. Nor can we in the final analysis know, provided a majority of the wagons, eventually reach the same town, whether their occupants, having looked around a bit at their new surroundings, will not find them inadequate and set their eyes on a new and more distant journey.

Ibid., pp. 338–9.

Further Reading

These suggestions are made with the needs of beginners in mind, and are not meant to be comprehensive. The recommended books often contain bibliographies helpful for more advanced study. Advice offered in the course of this book will normally not be repeated here.

The Current Situation in Philosophy of History

Recent publications tend to be dominated by the discussion of 'postmodern' views of history. Earlier chapters of this present book have shown that several notions now commonly associated with postmodernism are not entirely revolutionary breaks with previous understandings: for example, the rejection of the idea that the historian can reproduce the past 'as it actually was' in favour of the notion that he or she can only shape his account in terms of his own categories, which themselves can only be historically conditioned, was fully developed in Simmel and Weber; that history should be the exploration of difference and discontinuity rather than universalities is the central theme of the tradition which can be traced back through Rickert, Windelband and Ranke to Herder, and similarly the rejection of the notion of any unilinear progressive structural trend traced back through Ranke to Herder. Nevertheless, the postmodern challenge has unquestionably livened up recent philosophy of history. An invaluable collection of articles on the topic is Jenkins (1997). In three books Jenkins has himself forcefully promoted a 'postmodernist' repudiation of the 'history' established in the Western world's academic institutions. Jenkins (1991) is a relatively restrained simple introduction, whilst Jenkins (1995) is perhaps his most carefully considered and valuable book. It contains a lively and lucid critique of Carr (1987, originally published as far back as 1961) and Elton (1967). These two books have arguably constituted the staple diet in philosophy of history in many History Departments for too long. Jenkins (1995) will be invaluable in helping to wean students and teachers away from them. Its enthusiastic promotion of the thought of Hayden White is also noteworthy. A lively attempt by a practising historian to counter the postmodernist challenge is Evans (1997). Some of Evans's barbed remarks goaded Jenkins into extremely polemical responses in his latest book (1999), which seeks to show that 'postmodern ways of thinking probably signal the end of history', understood in any way in which it has

The suggestions up to and including chapter 6, with the exception of the recommendations on Husserl in that chapter, are by Robert M. Burns and the rest by Hugh Rayment-Pickard.

been hitherto understood in academia. For an attempt to reconcile much in 'postmodernism' with a chastened 'realism', see contributions 17 and 25 by Gabriel Spiegel in Jenkins (1997). For a French historian's engagement with postmodern themes see Certeau (1988), Part One. Callinicos (1995) provides a reflective survey of recent philosophy of history from a perspective sympathetic to the Marxist tradition. In the face of postmodernism it calls for the continued deployment of Marxist theory in historiography as a 'research programme' rather than a doctrine of 'historical inevitability' (compare 6.D.III and 6.E.III). Habermas (1987) also present a post-Marxist evaluation of the contemporary predicament in philosophy of history. Both Callinicos and Habermas presume the reader's prior acquaintance with the thinkers discussed, and consequently will be hard going for the beginner. For a thorough and well-balanced advocacy of a 'middle way' between postmodernist-relativist views and traditional historical 'realism' see McCullagh (1998) which can be unreservedly recommended; its compendious discussion of recent contributions to philosophy of history in English is likely to remain invaluable to students for many years. The only journal in English devoted to philosophy of history is *History and Theory*, but the *Journal of the History of Ideas* sometimes contains important contributions to the history of the subject.

Chapter 1   On Philosophizing about History

Concerning the history of philosophical reflection on history dealt with in section 1.I, Kelley (1991) is an invaluable source of original texts. Kelley (1998) supplements this with a historical survey which functions in part as a commentary on the texts provided in the former. Concerning the discussion of Collingwood in 1.II see Mink (1968) and Mink (1972). A full-scale survey of the whole of Collingwood's philosophy of history can be found in Van Dussen (1981).

  Discussions of 'realism' are legion in recent philosophy, many of them of a forbidding technicality quite beyond the reach of the beginner. Chapter 3 of Putnam (1981) outlines his 'internal realist' position whilst chapter 9 presents a critique of Foucault's historicism. See also Putnam (1990). The professional academic philosopher who has had the broadest cultural impact in the English-speaking world in recent decades is Richard Rorty. In many publications Rorty has promoted a view which is a blend of American pragmatism (especially Dewey and William James) the 'analytic' tradition (Wittgenstein, Quine, Davidson) and what he terms 'post-Nietzschean European philosophy' (he mentions Heidegger, Gadamer, Derrida and Foucault, among others). He claims that his position overcomes the realism-relativism debate by abandoning the distinctions 'between the absolute and the relative . . . reality and appearance', which he considers is possible once one accepts the 'Darwinian' view that 'words' are simply 'tools' which the human organism uses as 'part of the interaction with its environment'. He summarizes his views in the introduction to Rorty (1999), whilst Rorty (1991) situates his position at length in relation to many leading philosophers of the 'analytic' tradition. Rorty has certainly been a major force in shifting the debate within English-speaking philosophy in 'historicist' direction. For a lucid brief presentation of the views of a leading English 'analytic' philosopher of an older generation on 'realism' and other related issues, which explicitly resists 'historicist' trends by developing 'transcendental' arguments, inspired to some degree by Kant, see Strawson (1985).

If Rorty is right, philosophy's traditional concern for the question of whether our thoughts and beliefs can ever 'correspond' with 'reality', is a pointless irrelevance, and even a pernicious linguistic trap. But for those not yet ready to embrace such a radical rejection of what has since Descartes been widely regarded as the first task of philosophers, among many introductions to Hume's epistemology see Ayer (1980), Flew (1961) or (1986), or Dicker (1998), and for a simple general introduction to Kant see Scruton (1982). Hartnack (1967) provides a clear, basic introduction to Kant's epistemology while Hartnack (1974), in a brilliant feat of lucid compression, deals with not only Kant's epistemology but also his ethics. Copleston's multi-volume *History of Philosophy* (1967) still supplies reliable basic accounts of leading figures in the Western philosophical canon although the scholarship is inevitably becoming dated in places. Oxford University Press's OPUS *History of Western Philosophy* is geared to the interests of beginners: in this series, see in connection with the thinkers covered in this book, Woolhouse (1988) and Solomon (1988). There has been an impressive expansion of work in history of philosophy in recent years. The *Routledge History of Modern Philosophy* provides ready access (see especially Brown 1995 and Solomon and Higgins 1993) There are also many useful volumes on individual philosophers in the *Cambridge Companion* series (e.g., Norton 1993 or Beiser 1993).

Chapter 2   Enlightenment

For a survey of historical treatments of the Enlightenment see Outram (1995). Gay (1969) remains invaluable as a full-length treatment, and Hampson (1968) as a briefer introductory survey. For a classic treatment of the notion of progress see Bury (1932) For a more recent survey see Nisbet (1980), and the essays in Melzer et al. (1995) Graham (1997) examines and contrasts five claims to discern overall trends in history: progressivism, decline, collapses, cultural cycles, and religious attempts to trace divine providence in history. A determinedly 'historicist' interpretation of Hume is provided by Livingston (1984). See also Livingston and Martin (1991), Danford (1990), Phillipson (1989), Pompa (1990), and Wootton (1993). For Condorcet see Baker (1975). Amongst several useful books on Kant and history see Galston (1975 and Yovel (1980). Kant (1970) contains most of Kant's texts on history. See also Kant (1963).

Chapter 3   Classical Historicism

On early German historicism in general see Meinecke (1972) and Iggers (1983). On Herder, see Barnard (1965), Koepke (1987), and Berlin (1992). There is little for beginners on Schleiermacher (but see Dilthey 1996) or Humboldt. There is an enormous secondary literature on Hegel. On his philosophy of history see Beiser (1993) the valuable discussion in Pompa (1990), and also O'Brien (1975). Pinkard (1995 never mentions Hegel's *Lectures on the Philosophy of History* in a discussion of Hegel on history which is entirely based on the early *Phenomenology of Spirit*, and develops a picture of an anti-metaphysical Hegel which is profoundly at odds with the *Lectures* Taylor (1975) provides a very full account of Hegel's philosophy as a whole, and Copleston (1967) is very good on the German Idealists in general. The best book on Ranke is Krieger (1977). There are also several invaluable essays on Ranke in Igger and Powell (1990). Droysen, whom, it has been stressed, provides an important link between the historicists of this chapter and chapter 6, is discussed in chapter V of Iggers (1983).

Chapter 4 Positivism

There is very little modern detailed scholarship in English concerning the accounts of history provided by any of the three positivists dealt with in chapter 4. For a general introduction to Mill see Ryan (1974). An account of the history of positivism is provided by Kolakowski (1969). For twentieth-century logical positivism see Ayer (1959).

Chapter 5 Suprahistory

There are a number of accessible studies of Schopenhauer: Copleston (1975), Magee (1997), Janaway (1994) and Tanner (1999). For more advanced reading see Simmel (1986) which also discusses Nietzsche. Primary reading might begin with Schopenhauer (1974) which was regarded as a sketch of the ideas in Schopenhauer's central text: *The World as Will and Representation* (Schopenhauer 1966). Kierkegaard (1940), (1978), (1980) and (1987) provide the basis for initial primary reading. For Kierkegaard's biographical and cultural background see Lowrie (1970) and Kirmmse (1990) and (1996). There are many introductions to Kierkegaard's thought including Hannay (1982), Pattison (1997) and Watkin (1997). For wider reading see Fenves (1993), Weston (1994), Furguson (1995), and ed. Hannay, ed. (1997). Kaufmann (1974) is the best known introduction to Nietzsche but Stern (1978), Danto (1980) and M. Clarke (1990) also give good overviews. 'Nietzsche, Genealogy, History' in Foucault (1991) is not only a key text for Foucault, but also summarizes Nietzsche on history. See also chapter 9 of White (1973) for a narrativist perspective; and chapter 9 of Eagleton (1990) for a 'Marxist' viewpoint. Nietzsche's 'Second Untimely Meditation' (Nietzsche 1983) and *The Birth of Tragedy* (Nietzsche 1993) are good starting points for primary reading.

Chapter 6 Secular Historicism

There is a lack of up-to-date introductory level material in English concerning thinkers explored in this chapter, but Iggers (1983) is useful, and two older treatments which may be consulted, though dated in some respects, are Mandelbaum (1967) and Antoni (1952). Carr is an important presentation of the case that 'action, life, and historical existence' is 'structured narratively . . . independent of their presentation in literary form' against 'narrativists' such as White or Mink (see chapter 9) who argued, as Mink put it, that 'stories are not lived but told . . . Narrative qualities are transferred from art to life' (Mink 1970, p. 60). Carr explores Dilthey's treatment of the opposite view compared with that of Husserl, Heidegger, and more recent thinkers. A recent survey of Dilthey scholarship is Owensby (1994), which is often too compressed to be accessible to the beginner. A work of weighty scholarship too complex for the beginner is Makkreel (1975). It seeks to show the 'essential *continuity*' of the early and later Dilthey whilst providing a detailed account 'much misunderstood transition to the hermeneutic standpoint' concerning which it seeks to substantiate the intriguing claim that Husserl was 'the single most important influence on Dilthey during the transitional decade of 1895 to 1905'. It also places an unusual stress on Dilthey's work on aesthetics and poetics as a key to an overall understanding of him. On Simmel there is next to nothing which is helpful in English on his philosophy of history except for Guy Oakes's introductions to his translations of Simmel. An up-to-date scholarly review of Simmel scholarship in general can be found in the introductions to Simmel (1977) and (1980). On Rickert see Oakes (1990), which traces the connection between Rickert's thought and Weber. On Weber's vision of historical developments see Brubacker (1984) and also Roth and Schluchter (1979). On Jaspers' evaluation of Weber see Jaspers (1989). Bambach (1995) contains useful discussions of Windelband and Rickert.

Chapter 7   Hermeneutics

For good treatments of Husserl's 'philosophy of history' see section 7 of David Carr's introduction to Husserl (1970) and the chapter on 'Husserl and the Sense of History' in Ricoeur (1967). The most authoritative general introduction to Husserl is Bernet et al. (1993), which takes account of Husserl's unpublished writings. However, Bell (1989) is more accessible. Beginners should start with Husserl's own article on 'Phenomenology' in *The Encyclopaedia Britannica* and his *Paris Lectures* (Husserl 1975).

   The literature on Heidegger is very large but much of it is unhelpful to beginners. simple, brief introductions, mainly to *Being and Time*, are Steiner (1991) and Inwood (1997) which deals at some length with Heidegger's views on time and history. Polt (1999) is lengthier, exploring Heidegger's later philosophy more fully, and is geared successfully to the beginner. Specifically on Heidegger's philosophy of history see Hoy (1978) and Carr (1991). Bambach (1995) discusses the relationship of Heidegger's thinking to Dilthey and the Neo-Kantians. For authoritative and readable biographies see Ott (1993) and Safranski (1998). The latter, unlike the former, seeks to follow the development of Heidegger's thinking. On the controversial question of Heidegger's relationship with Nazism, Young (1998) provides a thorough and scholarly survey of Heidegger's philosophy which seeks to minimize the importance of Heidegger's commitment to Nazism in evaluating his philosophy. For a comparison of Heidegger with other philosophers on the theme of death see Malpas and Solomon (1999). On Gadamer, Warnke (1987) provides a useful, well-balanced critical assessment as does chapter 4 of Hekman (1986). Bernstein (1983) provides extensive discussions of Gadamer integrated into a broader consideration of current Anglo-American philosophy. For Ricoeur see the recommendations for chapter 9 provided below.

Chapter 8   Kulturkritik

For contrasting expositions of Marx's philosophy of history see Elster (1986) and Cohen (1978). The three volumes of Kolokowski (1978) provide a far more comprehensive, polemical, analysis of Marx, his precursors and successors. McLellan (1977) contains Marx's key writings on historical materialism. McLellan also provides helpful notes and further suggestions for reading. Sim (1994) is an accessible introduction to Lukács. Jay (1986) and Feenberg (1980) present Lukács in relation to Critical Theory. For a historical study see Gluck and Gluck (1985). Lukács (1971), although excerpted in this volume, is worth much fuller exploration. Overviews of Benjamin's thinking can be found in Hannah Arendt's 'Introduction' to Benjamin (1973) and Gary Smith's 'Introductory Essay' to Smith, ed. (1989). For views on Benjamin's philosophy of history see Rolf Tiedemann's essay also in Smith, ed. (1989); chapter 12 of Eagleton (1990), pp. 325–39; Habermas (1998), pp. 11–16; and ed. Steinberg (1996). Accessible writings by Benjamin can be found in the essay collections: Benjamin (1973) and (1978) and in Smith, ed. (1989). Outhwaite (1995) is a useful and recent introduction to Habermas, but easily the best overview is McCarthy (1978). Rockmore (1989) is a substantial study of Habermas on history. For other views see Rorty (1991, pp. 164–76), and Albrecht Wellmer's essay in Bernstein (1985). Habermas is very difficult, but Habermas (1998) is a fairly accessible text and is relevant to other thinkers in this book. A good selection of texts by Habermas can be found in Outhwaite, ed (1996).

Chapter 9 Narrativism

For an introduction to Lévi-Strauss see Leach (1970) and Paz (1970). On Lévi-Strauss and structuralism see Sturrock (1981) and Boon (1972). For further primary reading see Lévi-Strauss (1974) and (1983). Barthes (1972) and (1977) are good places to start reading Barthes himself. For introductions to Barthes' thought see Lavers (1982), Culler (1983), Moriarty (1992) and Rylance (1994). Culler (1975) and Sturrock (1981) consider Barthes in the context of structuralism. Indispensable for primary reading is White (1973) – some of the arguments are summarized in chapter 2 of White (1978). For reactions to White see: *History and Theory*, Beiheft 19 (1980), Kansteiner (1993), and H. Kellner, 'Hayden White and the Kantian Discourse' in Sills and Jensen (1992). Canary and Kozicki (1978) is an early volume of discussions. Kellner (1989) is a sympathetic development of White's ideas. The three volumes of Ricoeur's *Time and Narrative* are rather hard going, although they do contain some helpful surveys of previous thinking on narrative. Ricoeur is most accessible through his essays, which are collected variously in Ricoeur (1965), (1974) and (1981). For general studies of Ricoeur see Ihde (1971) and S. Clarke (1990). For reactions see Carr (1991) and Hayden White's essay on 'The Metaphysics of Narrativity' in Wood, ed. (1991).

Chapter 10 Posthistory

For introductory studies of Foucault see Merquior (1985), Smart (1985) and Macey (1994). For further primary reading see 'Nietzsche, Genealogy, History', 'What is Enlightenment?' and 'The Preface to *The History of Sexuality* (Vol. II)' – all in Foucault (1991). The 'Introduction' to Foucault 1972 is also important. For wider reading see Megill (1985) (situating Foucault in a tradition from Nietzsche), Flynn (1997) (for an interesting analysis of Foucault and Sartre on history), and Hayden White's treatment of *The Order of Things* in *History and Theory* 12, 1 (1973). Kellner (1989) is the only comprehensive introduction to Baudrillard. Secondary analysis includes Rojek and Turner, eds. (1993), Kellner, ed. (1994), Gane (1991), and Zurbrugg, ed. (1997). For critical responses see Norris (1992) and Callinicos (1989). Poster, ed. (1998) contains a selection of primary reading. There have been a number of recent edited volumes on Fukuyama including Burns (1994). For influences on Fukuyama see Strauss (1953) and Kojève (1969). See Fukuyama (1996) and (1999) for primary reading. Jenkins (1999) is a recent contribution to the discussion of posthistory.

Bibliography

Adorno, T. 1973. *Negative Dialectics*, trans. E. B. Ashton. London: Routledge, Kegan Paul.

Adorno, T. and Horkheimer, M. 1997. *The Dialectic of Enlightenment*, trans. J. Cumming. London: Verso.

Ankersmit, F. 1983. *Narrative Logic*. The Hague: Nijhoff.

Ankersmit, F and Kellner, H. (eds). 1995. *A New Philosophy of History*. London: Reaktion.

Antoni, C. 1960. *From History to Sociology*, trans. H. White. London: Merlin Press.

Aquinas, Thomas. [1945]. *Summa Theologiae* in *Basic Writings of Thomas Aquinas*, ed. A Pegis. New York: Random House.

Arnauld, A. 1964. *The Art of Thinking* (1662), trans. J. Dickoff and P. James. New York: Bobbs-Merrill.

Augustine. 1972. *City of God*, trans. H. Bettenson. London: Penguin Books.

Ayer, A. J. 1980. *Hume*. Oxford: Oxford University Press.

Ayer, A. J. 1946. *Language, Truth and Logic* (1936), second edition. London: Victor Gollancz.

Ayer, A. J. (ed.) 1959. *Logical Positivism*. New York: Free Press.

Baker, K. M. 1975. *Condorcet: Natural Philosophy to Social Mechanics*. Chicago: Chicago University Press.

Bambach, C. R. 1995. *Heidegger, Dilthey, and the Crisis of Historicism*. Ithaca, New York: Cornell University Press.

Barnard, F. M. 1965. *Herder's Social and Political Thought*. Oxford: Clarendon Press.

Barthes, R. 1967. *Writing Degree Zero* and *Elements of Semiology*, trans. A. Lavers and C. Smith. London: Cape.

—— 1970. 'Historical Discourse', in *Introduction to Structuralism*, ed. M. Lane. New York: Basic Books.

—— 1972. *Mythologies*. trans. A. Lavers. London: Cape.

—— 1974. *S/Z*. New York: Hill and Wang.

—— 1977. *Image Music Text*, ed. S. Heath. London: Fontana.

—— 1990. *The Pleasure of the Text*. Oxford: Blackwell, Publishers.

—— 1997. *Criticism and Truth*, trans. K. Keuneman. London: Athlone.

Baudrillard, J. 1988. *Selected Writings*, ed. M. Poster. Cambridge: Polity Press.

—— 1990. *Fatal Strategies*. New York: Semiotext(e).

—— 1997. 'Aesthetic Illusion and Virtual Reality', in N. Zurbrugg (ed.), *Jean Baudrillard: Art and Artefact*. London: Sage.

—— 1994. *The Illusion of the End*, trans. C. Turner. Cambridge: Polity Press.

Beck, U. 1992. *Risk Society: Towards a New Modernity*. London: Sage.

Beiser, F. C. 1993. 'Hegel's Historicism', in *The Cambridge Companion to Hegel*, ed. F. Beiser. Cambridge: Cambridge University Press.

Bell, D. 1989. *Husserl*. London: Routledge.

Benjamin, W. 1972. *Gesammelte Schriften* (8 vols), ed. R. Tiedemann and H. Schweppenhäuser.

Frankfurt: Suhrkamp.

—— 1973. *Illuminations*, ed. H. Arendt. London: Fontana.

—— 1978. *Reflections: Essays, Aphorisms, Autobiographical Writings*, ed. P. Demetz, trans. E. Jephcott. New York: Harcourt Brace Jovanovich.

—— 1996. *Selected Writings*, ed. M. Bullock and M. Jennings. Cambridge, MA: Harvard, University Press.

Berkhofer, R. 1995. 'Viewpoints in Historical Practice', in Ankersmit and Kellner 1995, pp. 174–91.

Berlin, I. 1960. 'The Concept of Scientific History', in *History and Theory*, I, (1960).

—— 1973. 'Counter-Enlightenment', in *Dictionary of History of Ideas*. New York: Charles Scribner, Vol. II, pp. 100–12.

—— 1992. *Vico and Herder*. London: Hogarth Press.

Bernet et al. 1993. *An Introduction to Husserlian Phenomenology*. Evanston: Northwestern University Press.

Bernstein, R. J. 1983. *Beyond Objectivism and Relativism*. Oxford: Basil Blackwell.

—— 1985. *Habermas and Modernity*. Cambridge: Polity Press.

Betti, E. 1980. 'Hermeneutics as the general methodology of the *Geisteswissenschaften*', in Bleicher 1980, pp. 51–94.

Bleicher, J. 1980. *Contemporary Hermeneutics*. London: Routledge & Kegan Paul.

Blumenberg, H. 1983. *The Legitimacy of the Modern Age*, trans. Robert Wallace. Cambridge, MA: MIT Press.

Boon, J. 1972. *From Symbolism to Structuralism: Lévi Strauss in a Literary Tradition*. London: Routledge.

Bottomore, T. 1984. *The Frankfurt School*, London: Tavistock.

Brown, S. (ed.). 1995. *Routledge History of Philosophy, Volume V: British Empiricism and the Enlightenment*.

Brubaker, R. 1984. *The Limits of Rationality*. London: George Allen and Unwin.

Buckle, H. T. 1861. *History of Civilization in England* (1857 and 1861). Third edition. London: Parker, Son and Bourn.

Buckley, M. 1987. *At the Origins of Modern Atheism*. New Haven: Yale University Press.

Buck-Morss, S. 1977. *The Origin of Negative Dialectics, Theodor W. Adorno, Walter Benjamin and the Frankfurt Institute*. Brighton: Harvester Wheatsheaf.

Bultmann, R. 1957. *History and Eschatology: The Presence of Eternity*. New York: Harper and Row.

Burckhardt, J. 1943. *Reflections on History*. London: George Allen & Unwin.

—— 1990. *The Civilization of The Renaissance in Italy*, trans. S. Middlemore. London: Penguin Books.

Burns, R. M. 1981. *The Great Debate on Miracles*. Lewisburg: Bucknell University Press.

Burns, T. (ed.). 1994. *After History? Francis Fukuyama and his Critics*. Lenham: Rowman & Littlefield.

Bury, J. B. 1920. *The Idea of Progress*. New York and London: Macmillan.

Butler, J. 1961. *The Analogy of Religion* (1736). New York: Frederick Ungar.

Callinicos, A. 1989. *Against Postmodernism: A Marxist Critique*. Cambridge: Polity Press.

Canary, R. and Kozicki, H. (eds). 1978. *The Writing of History: Literary Form and Historical Understanding*. Madison: University of Wisconsin Press.

Canetti, E. 1978. *The Human Province*, tr. J. Neugroschel. New York: Seabury.

Cannon, J. et al. (eds). 1988. *The Blackwell Dictionary of Historians*. Oxford: Blackwell Publishers.

Carr, D. 1991. *Time, Narrative and History*. Bloomington: University of Indiana Press.

Carr, E. H. 1987. *What is History?* Second edition with new material by R. W. Davies of first edition (1961). Harmondsworth: Penguin Books.

Carrard, P. 1992. *Poetics of the New History*. Baltimore: Johns Hopkins University Press.
Carrithers, M. 1986. 'Montesquieu's Philosophy of History', *Journal of the History of Ideas*, Jan–March 1986, Vol. XLVIII, No. 1, pp. 61–80.
Cassirer, E. 1944. *An Essay on Man. New Haven: Yale University Press.*
—— 1950. *The Problem of Knowledge*. New Haven: Yale University Press
—— 1951. *The Philosophy of the Enlightenment*. Princeton: Princeton University Press.
Caygill, H. 1998. *Walter Benjamin*. London: Routledge.
Certeau, de M. 1988. *The Writing of History*. New York: Columbia University Press, 1988.
Clarke, M. 1990. *Nietzsche on Truth and Philosophy*. Cambridge: Cambridge University Press.
Clarke, S. 1990. *Paul Ricoeur*. London: Routledge.
Cohen, G. 1978. *Karl Marx's Theory of History: A Defence*. Oxford: Oxford University Press
—— 1988. *History Labour and Freedom: Themes from Karl Marx*. Oxford: Oxford University Press.
Collingwood, R. 1940. *Essay on Metaphysics*. Oxford: Clarendon Press.
—— 1946. *The Idea of History*. Oxford: Clarendon Press.
Comte, A. 1974. *The Essential Comte*, ed. S. Andreski, trans. Margaret Clarke. London: Croom Helm.
Condorcet 1955. *Sketch for a Historical Picture of the Progress of the Human Mind*, trans. June Barraclough, with an introduction by Stuart Hampshire. London: Weidenfeld and Nicolson
Constantine, D. 1988. *Hölderlin*. Oxford: Clarendon Press.
Copleston, F. 1975. *Arthur Schopenhauer: Philosopher of Pessimism*. New York: Harper and Row
—— 1967. *History of Philosophy*, in eight volumes. New York: Image Books.
Croce, B. 1941. *History as the Story of Liberty*. London: George Allen and Unwin.
Culler, J. 1975. *Structuralist Poetics*. London: Routledge and Kegan Paul.
—— 1976. *Saussure*. London: Fontana.
—— 1983. *Barthes*. London: Fontana.
Danford, J. 1990. *David Hume and the Problem of Reason*. New Haven: Yale University Press
Danto, A. 1965. *Analytical Philosophy of History*. Cambridge: Cambridge University Press.
—— 1980. *Nietzsche as Philosopher*. New York: Columbia University Press.
Dean, M. 1994. *Critical and Effective Histories*. London: Routledge.
Debord, G. 1983. *The Society of the Spectacle*. Detroit: Black and Red.
Derrida, J. 1973. *Speech and Phenomena*, trans. D. Allison. Evanston: Northwestern University Press.
—— 1994. *Specters of Marx*, trans. P. Kamuf. London: Routledge.
Descartes, R. 1985. *Philosophical Writings of Descartes*, Vol. I translated by J. Cottingham, R. Stoothoff and D. Murdoch. Cambridge: Cambridge University Press.
Dicker, G. 1998. *Hume's Epistemology and Metaphysics*. London: Routledge.
Dilthey, W. 1976. *Selected Writings*, ed., trans. and introduced H. Rickman. Cambridge: Cambridge University Press.
—— 1985. *Introduction to the Human Sciences* (first published 1893), ed. R. Makkreel and F. Jodi, in *Selected Works*, Volume 1, Princeton: Princeton University Press.
—— 1988. *Introduction to the Human Sciences*, trans. R. Betanzos. Detroit: Wayne State University Press.
—— 1996. *Selected Works*, Volume IV, 'Hermeneutics and the Study of History'. Princeton Princeton University Press.
Dray, W. 1957. *Laws and Explanation in History*. Oxford: Clarendon Press.
—— 1966. *Philosophical Analysis and History*. New York: Harper and Row.
Droysen, J. 1893. *Outline of the Principles of History*, trans. by E. Andrews. Boston: Ginn & Co
Dussen, W. J. van der. 1981. *History as a Science*. The Hague: Martinus Nijhoff.
Eagleton, T. 1990. *The Ideology of the Aesthetic*. Oxford: Blackwell Publishers.
—— 1991. *Ideology: An Introduction*. London: Verso.

Elster, J. 1986. *An Introduction to Karl Marx.* Cambridge: Cambridge University Press.

Elton, G. R. 1967. *The Practice of History.* London: Fontana Press.

Elton, G. R. 1991. *Return to Essentials.* Cambridge: Cambridge University Press.

Evans, C. 1992. *Passionate Reasoning: Making Sense of Kierkegaard's Fragments.* Bloomington: Indiana.

Evans, R. J. 1997. *In Defence of History.* London: Granta Books.

Feenberg, A. 1980. *Lukács, Marx and the Sources of Critical Theory.* Lenham: Rowman and Littlefield.

Fenves, P. 1993. *'Chatter': Language and History in Kierkegaard.* Stanford: Stanford University Press.

Flew, A. 1961. *Hume's Philosophy of Belief.* London: Routledge and Kegan Paul.

—— 1986. *David Hume: Philosopher of Moral Science.* Oxford: Basil Blackwell

Flynn, T. 1997. *Sartre, Foucault and Historical Reason (Volume 1: Toward an Existentialist Theory of History).* Chicago: University of Chicago.

Foucault, M. 1970. *The Order of Things,* trans. A. Sheridan Smith. London: Tavistock.

—— 1972. *The Archaeology of Knowledge,* trans. A. Sheridan Smith. London: Tavistock.

—— 1991. *A Foucault Reader,* ed. P. Rabinow. Harmondsworth: Penguin Books.

Frye, N. 1957. *The Anatomy of Criticism: Four Essays.* Princeton: Princeton University Press.

Fukuyama, F. 1992. *The End of History and The Last Man.* London: Hamish Hamilton.

—— 1996. *Trust.* New York: Free Press.

—— 1999. *The Great Disruption.* New York: Free Press.

Furguson, H. 1995. *Melancholy and the Critique of Modernity.* London: Routledge.

Gadamer, H.-G. 1976. *Philosophical Hermeneutics.* Berkeley: University of California Press.

—— 1979. *Truth and Method.* London: Sheed and Ward. Second edition, trans. from the second edition by William Glen-Doepel. Trans./ed. John Cumming and Garret Barden.

Gallie, W. B. 1964. *Philosophy and the Historical Understanding.* London: Chatto and Windus.

Galston, W. 1975. *Kant and the Problem of History.* Chicago: University of Chicago Press.

Gane, M. 1991. *Baudrillard: Critical and Fatal Theory.* London: Routledge.

Gardiner, P. 1952. *The Nature of Historical Explanation.* Oxford: Clarendon Press

—— 1959. *Theories of History.* New York: The Free Press.

Gay, P. 1966. *The Enlightenment: An Interpretation: The Rise of Modern Paganism.* Republished New York: W. W. Norton, 1977.

—— 1969. *The Enlightenment: An Interpretation: The Science of Freedom.* Republished New York: W. W. Norton, 1977.

Gehlen, A. 1978. 'Die Säkularisierung des Fortschritts', in K. Rehberg (ed.), *Enblicke,* Vol. 3. Frankfurt: Klostermann.

Gluck, M and Gluck, M. 1985. *Georg Luckács and his Generation: 1900–1918.* Cambridge, MA: Harvard University Press.

Graham, G. 1997. *The Shape of the Past: A Philosophical Approach to History.* Oxford: Oxford University Press.

Gray, J. 1995. *Enlightenment's Wake.* London: Routledge.

Guicciardini, F. 1969. *Maxims and Reflections of a Renaissance Statesman,* trans. M. Domandi. New York: Harper Torchbooks.

Habermas, J. 1970a. 'On Hermeneutics' Claim to Universality', in Mueller-Vollmer (1986) pp. 294–319.

—— 1970b. 'A Review of Gadamer's *Truth and Method*' (1970) from *Zur Logik der Sozial-wissenschaften,* pp. 251–89. Frankfurt am Main: Suhrkamp Verlag, reprinted in *Understanding and Social Enquiry,* ed. F. Dallmayr and T. McCarthy. Notre Dame: University of Notre Dame Press, pp. 335–63.

—— 1974. *Theory and Practice.* London: Heinemann.

—— 1976. *Communication and the Evolution of Society.* Boston: Beacon.

—— 1979. *Legitimation Crisis*. London: Heinemann.

—— 1987. *The Philosophical Discourse of Modernity*. Cambridge: Polity Press.

Hacking, I. 1975. *The Emergence of Probability*. Cambridge: Cambridge University Press.

Hampson, N. 1968. *The Enlightenment*. Harmondsworth: Penguin Books.

Hannay, A. 1982. *Kierkegaard*. London: Routledge.

Hannay, A. (ed.) 1997. *The Cambridge Companion to Kierkegaard*. Cambridge: Cambridge University Press.

Hartnack, J. 1967. *Kant's Theory of Knowledge*.

—— 1974. *Immanuel Kant: an Explanation of his Theory of Knowledge and Moral Philosophy* Atlantic Highlands, N.J.: Humanities Press, 1972.

Heckman, S. J. 1986. *Hermeneutics and the Sociology of Knowledge*. Cambridge: Polity Press.

Hegel, G. 1956. *The Philosophy of History*. New York: Dover Publications, unabridged and un altered republication of the last revision of the translation by J. Sibree, published by Colonia Press, 1899.

—— 1975. *Hegel's Logic*, being Part One of the *Encyclopaedia of the Philosophical Sciences* (1830) trans. W. Wallace (1873), third edition. Oxford: Oxford University Press.

—— 1979. *Phenomenology of Spirit*, trans. A. Miller. Oxford: Oxford University Press.

—— 1985. *Introduction to the Lectures on the History of Philosophy*. Oxford: Clarendon Press.

—— 1991. *Elements of the Philosophy of Right*, ed. A. Wood, trans. H. Nisbet. Cambridge Cambridge University Press.

Heidegger, M. 1961. *An Introduction to Metaphysics*, trans. R. Mannheim. New Haven: Yal University Press.

—— 1962. *Being and Time*, trans. J. Macquarrie and E. Robinson. New York: Harper an Row.

—— 1966. *Discourse on Thinking*, trans. J. Anderson and E. Freund. New York: Harper an Row.

—— 1968. *What is Called Thinking?*, trans. R. Wieck and J. Gray. New York: Harper and Row

—— 1972. *On Time and Being*, trans. J. Stambaugh. New York: Harper and Row.

—— 1975. *Poetry, Language, Thought*, trans. A. Hofstadter. New York: Harper Colophon.

—— 1977. *The Question of Technology and Other Essays*, trans. W. Lovitt. New York: Harper an Row.

—— 1982. *On the Way to Language*, trans. P. Herz and J. Stambaugh. New York: Harper an Row.

—— 1983. *Die Grundbegriffe der Metaphysik: Welt, Endlichkeit, Einsamkeit (Gesamtausgal* vol. 29/30), ed. F.-W. von Herrmann. Frankfurt: Klostermann.

—— 1993. *Basic Writings*, revised and expanded edition, ed. D. Krell. London: Routledge.

—— 1992. *History of the Concept of Time*, trans. T. Kisiel, Bloomington: Indiana Universi Press.

Held, D. 1980. *Introduction to Critical Theory: Horkheimer to Habermas*. London: Hutchinso

Hempel, C. 1962. 'Explanation in Science and History' in Dray 1966, pp. 95–126, reprinte with slight alterations from *Frontiers of Science and Philosophy*, ed. R. Colodny. Pittsburg University of Pittsburgh Press, 1962.

Herder, J. G. 1969. *J. G. Herder on Social and Political Culture*, ed. F. M. Barnard. Cambridge Cambridge University Press.

—— 1940. *God, Some Conversations* (1787), trans. F. Burkhardt. New York: Bobbs-Merrill.

Hodges, H. A. 1944. *Wilhelm Dilthey: An Introduction*. London: Routledge and Kegan Pau

Hoy, D. C. (ed.) 1986. *Foucault: A Critical Reader*. Oxford: Blackwell.

Hoy, D. C. 1978. 'Heidegger, historicity and historiography in *Being and Time*', in *Heidegge and Modern Philosophy*, ed. Michael Murray. New Haven: Yale University Press.

Horkheimer, M. 1972. 'Traditional and Critical Theory', *Critical Theory: Selected Essays*. Ne York: Herder & Herder.

Hughes, H. S. 1976. *Consciousness and Society.* New York: Octagon Books.

Humboldt, W. 1983. 'On the Historian's Task' (1821), originally published in *History and Theory VI* (1967) pp. 57–71, reprinted in Ranke 1983.

—— 1988. *On Language,* trans. P. Heath. Cambridge: Cambridge University Press.

Hume, D. 1902. *Enquiries concerning the Human Understanding and concerning the Principles of Morals,* ed. L. A. Selby-Bigge, second edition.

—— 1947. *Dialogues concerning Natural Religion,* ed. N. K. Smith. New York: Bobbs-Merrill.

—— 1978. *A Treatise of Human Nature.* Oxford: Clarendon Press

—— 1987. *Essays Moral Political and Literary.* Indianapolis: Liberty Classics.

Husserl, E. 1931. *Ideas* (London: Macmillan, 1931) trans. W. R. Boyce Gibson. New York: Collier.

—— 1964. *Cartesian Meditations,* trans. D. Cairns. The Hague: Martinus Nijhoff.

—— 1965. *Phenomenology and the Crisis of Philosophy,* trans. Q. Lauer. New York: Harper Torchbooks.

—— 1970. *The Crisis of the European Sciences,* trans. D. Carr. Evanston: Northwestern University Press.

—— 1975. *The Paris Lectures,* trans. P. Koestenbaum. The Hague: Martinus Nijhoff.

—— 1977. *Phenomenological Psychology,* trans. J. Scanlon. The Hague: Martinus Nijhoff.

Iggers, G. G. 1995. 'Historicism: The History and Meaning of the Term', *Journal of the History of Ideas,* vol. 56, no. 1, pp. 129–52.

Iggers, G. G. and Powell, J. M. (eds). 1990. *Leopold von Ranke and the Shaping of the Historical Discipline.* Syracuse: Syracuse University Press.

Iggers, G. G. 1983. *The German Conception of History.* Wesleyan University Press, second edition; first edition 1968. Hanover, NH: University Press of New England.

Ihde, D. 1971. *Hermeneutic Phenomenology. The Philosophy of Paul Ricoeur.* Evanston: Northwestern University Press.

Inwood, M. 1997. *Martin Heidegger.* Oxford: Oxford University Press.

Janaway, C. 1994. *Schopenhauer.* Oxford: Oxford University Press.

Jarvis, S. 1998. *Adorno: A Critical Introduction.* Cambridge: Polity Press.

Jaspers, K. 1989. *On Max Weber,* trans. R. Whelan. New York: Paragon House.

Jay, M 1973. *The Dialectical Imagination.* Boston: Little, Brown & Co.

—— 1984. *Adorno.* London: Fontana.

—— 1986. *Marxism and Totality.* Chicago: University of Chicago Press.

Jenkins, K. (ed.) 1997. *The Postmodern History Reader.* London: Routledge.

Jenkins, K. 1991. *Rethinking History,* London: Routledge.

—— 1995. *On 'What is History?' From Carr and Elton to Rorty and White.* London: Routledge

—— 1999. *Why History? Ethics and Postmodernity.* London: Routledge.

Kansteiner, W. 1993. 'Hayden White's Critique of the Writing of History', *History and Theory* 32 (3), pp. 273–95.

Kant, I. 1933. *Critique of Pure Reason* (1781 and 1787), trans. N. Kemp Smith. Second edition with corrections. London: Macmillan & Co.

—— 1953. *Prolegomena to any Future Metaphysics* (1783), trans. P. Lucas. Manchester: Manchester University Press.

—— 1956. *Critique of Practical Reason* (1788), translated L. W. Beck. New York: Bobbs-Merrill.

—— 1963. *On History,* ed. L. W. Beck. New York: Macmillan

—— 1970. *Immanuel Kant Political Writings,* ed H. Reiss, trans. H. Nisbet. Cambridge: Cambridge University Press. Second edition, 1991.

—— 1999. *Religion within the Boundaries of Mere Reason* (1793), trans. A. Wood and G. Di Giovanni. Cambridge: Cambridge University Press.

Kaufmann, W. 1974. *Nietzsche: Philosopher, Psychologist, Antichrist.* Princeton: Princeton University Press.

Kelley, D. R. 1988. 'The Theory of History' in *The Cambridge History of Renaissance Philoso phy*, ed. Charles B., Schmidt, Quentin Skinner, et al. *Cambridge History of Renaissance Phi losophy* Cambridge: Cambridge University Press, 1988, pp. 746–61.

—— (ed.). 1991 *Versions of History from Antiquity to the Enlightenment*. New Haven and London: Yale University Press.

—— 1998. *Faces of History*. New Haven: Yale University Press.

Kellner, D. 1989. *Jean Baudrillard: From Marxism to Postmodernism and Beyond*. Cambridge Polity Press.

—— 1994. *Baudrillard: A Critical Reader*. Oxford: Blackwell Publishers.

Kellner, H. 1989. *Language and Historical Representation: Getting the Story Crooked*. Madison University of Wisconsin Press.

Kermode, F. 1966. *The Sense of an Ending: Studies in the Theory of Fiction*. Oxford: Oxford University Press.

Kierkegaard, S. 1940. *The Present Age*. Oxford: Oxford University Press.

—— 1970. *Journals and Papers* (Volume 2), ed. and trans. H. and E. Hong. Bloomington Indiana University Press.

—— 1975. *Journals and Papers* (Volume 4), ed. and trans. H. and E. Hong. Bloomington Indiana University Press.

—— 1978. *Two Ages: The Age of Revolution and the Present Age*. Princeton: Princeton University Press.

—— 1980. *The Concept of Anxiety*. Princeton: Princeton University Press.

—— 1987. *Either/Or*. Princeton: Princeton University Press.

—— 1988. *The Stages on Life's Way*. Princeton: Princeton University Press.

—— 1992. *Concluding Unscientific Postscript*. Princeton: Princeton University Press.

Kirk, G., Raven, J. and Schofield, M. 1983. *The Presocratic Philosophers*. Cambridge: Cambridg University Press.

Kirmmse, B. 1990. *Kierkegaard in Golden Age Denmark*. Bloomington: Indiana University Pres

—— 1996. *Encounters with Kierkegaard: A Life as Seen by his Contemporaries*. Princeton Princeton University Press.

Koepke, W. 1987. *Johann Gottfried Herder*. Boston: Twayne, 1987.

Kojève, A. 1969. *Introduction to the Reading of Hegel*, trans. J Nichols. New York: Basic Book

Kolakowski, L. 1969. *The Alienation of Reason: A History of Positivist Thought*, trans. by N Guterman. New York: Doubleday and Co., Anchor Books.

—— 1978. *Main Currents of Marxism* (3 volumes). Oxford: Oxford University Press.

Krieger, L. 1977. *Ranke: The Meaning of History*. Chicago: University of Chicago Press.

von Laue, T. 1950. *Leopold Ranke: The Formative Years*. Princeton: Princeton University Pres

Lavers, A. 1982. *Roland Barthes: Structuralism and After*. London: Methuen.

Leach, E. 1970. *Lévi Strauss*. London: Fontana.

Lee, D. and Beck, R. 1954. 'The Meaning of "Historicism"' *American Historical Review*, 5 pp. 568–77

Lentricchia, F. 1989. 'Foucault's Legacy: A new Historicism?', in Veeser 1989, pp. 231–42.

Lévi-Strauss, C. 1966. *The Savage Mind*. London: Weidenfeld & Nicolson.

—— 1974. *Structural Anthropology*. New York: Basic Books.

—— 1983. *The Raw and the Cooked: Introduction to a Science of Mythology*.

Livingston, D. 1984. *Hume's Philosophy of Common Life*. Chicago: University of Chicago Pres

Livingston, D. and Martin, M. 1991. *Hume as Philosopher of Society, Politics, and Histor* Rochester: University of Rochester Press.

Löwith, K. 1948. *Meaning in History: The Theological Presuppositions of the Philosophy of Histo* Chicago: University of the Chicago Press.

Lowrie, W. 1970. *A Short Life of Kierkegaard*. Princeton: Princeton University Press.

Lukács, G. 1971. *History and Class Consciousness*, trans. R. Livingstone. London: Merlin.

—— 1980. *The Destruction of Reason*. London: Merlin.

Lyotard, J.-F. 1984. *The Post-Modern Condition*, trans. G. Bennington and B. Massumi. Manchester: Manchester University Press.

Macey, D. 1994. *The Lives of Michel Foucault*. London: Vintage.

MacIntyre, A. 1981. *After Virtue*. London: Duckworth.

Makkreel, R. A. 1975. *Dilthey: Philosopher of the Human Studies*. Princeton: Princeton University Press.

Magee, B. 1997. *The Philosophy of Schopenhauer*. Oxford: Oxford University Press.

Malpas, J. E. and Solomon, R. C. 1999. *Death and Philosophy*. London: Routledge.

Mandelbaum, M. 1967. *The Problem of Historical Knowledge*. New York: Harper Torchbooks.

—— 1971. *History, Man, and Reason*. Baltimore: Johns Hopkins Press

Marcuse, H. 1928. 'Beiträge zu einer Phänomenologie des historischen Materialismus', *Philosophische Hefte* I, 1.

Marx, K. 1956. *Selected Writings*, ed. T. Bottomore. New York: McGraw-Hill.

—— 1977. *Selected Writings*, ed. D. McLellan. Oxford: Oxford University Press.

McCarthy, T. 1978. *The Critical Theory of Jürgen Habermas*. Cambridge, MA: MIT Press.

McCullagh, C. B. 1998. *The Truth of History*. London: Routledge.

McLellan, D. 1977. *Karl Marx Selected Writings*. Oxford: Oxford University Press.

Megill, A. 1985. *Prophets of Extremity: Nietzsche, Heidegger, Foucault, Derrida*. Berkeley: University of California Press.

Meinecke, F. 1972. *Historism*, trans. J. Anderson. London: Routledge and Kegan Paul.

Melzer, A. M., Weinberger, J. and Zinman, R. (eds). 1995. *History and the Idea of Progress*. Ithaca and London: Cornell University Press.

Merquior, J. 1985. *Foucault*. London: Fontana.

Meyerhoff, H. (ed.). 1959. *The Philosophy of History in our Time*. New York: Doubleday Anchor.

Mill, J. S. 1961. *Auguste Comte and Positivism*. Ann Arbor, Mich.: Michigan University Press.

—— 1967. *A System of Logic*. London: Longman, Green and Co. New Impression.

Mink, L. O. 1965. 'The Autonomy of Historical understanding', in Dray, 1966, pp. 160–92 (also reprinted in Mink 1987, pp. 61–88).

—— 1968. 'Collingwood's Dialectic of history', reprinted in Mink 1987, pp. 246–85.

—— 1970. 'History and Fiction as Modes of Comprehension', in Mink 1987, pp. 42–60.

—— 1972. 'Collingwood's Historicism: a Dialectic of Process', reprinted in Mink 1987, pp. 223–45.

—— 1978. 'Narrative Form as Cognitive Instrument', in *The Writing of History: Literary Theory and Historical Understanding*, ed. R. Canary and H. Kozicki. Madison: University of Wisconsin Press. Also in Mink 1987, pp. 182–203.

—— 1987. *Historical Understanding*. Ithaca and London: Cornell University Press.

Moriarty, M. 1992. *Roland Barthes*. Stanford: Stanford University Press.

Mueller-Vollmer, K. 1986. *The Hermeneutics Reader*. Oxford: Basil Blackwell.

Nagel, E. 1959. 'The Logic of Historical Analysis' in Meyerhoff 1959, pp. 203–15.

Nagel, T. 1979. *Mortal Questions*. Cambridge: Cambridge University Press.

Nagel, T. 1986. *The View from Nowhere*. New York: Oxford University Press.

Nash, R. H. 1969a. *Ideas of History*. New York: E. P. Dutton and Co.

—— 1969b. *The Light of the Mind: St. Augustine's Theory of Knowledge*. Lousiville: University of Kentucky.

Nietzsche, F. 1961. *Thus Spoke Zarathustra*, trans. R. Hollingdale. London: Penguin Books.

—— 1968. *The Will to Power*, ed. W. Kaufmann. New York: Vintage.

—— 1974. *The Gay Science*, trans. W. Kaufmann. New York: Vintage.

—— 1983. *Untimely Meditations*, trans. R. Hollingdale. Cambridge: Cambridge University Press.

—— 1986. *Human All Too Human*, trans. R. Hollingdale. Cambridge: Cambridge University Press.

—— 1992. *Ecce Homo*, trans. R. Hollingdale. London: Penguin Books.

—— 1993. *The Birth of Tragedy*, trans. S. Whiteside. London: Penguin Books.

Nisbet, R. A. 1980. *History of the Idea of Progress*. New York: Basic Books.

Norris, C. 1992. *Uncritical Theory: Postmodernism, Intellectuals and the Gulf War*. London Lawrence and Wishart.

Norton, D. F. (ed.). 1993. *The Cambridge Companion to Home*. Cambridge: Cambridge University Press.

Novick, P. 1988. *That Noble Dream*. Cambridge: Cambridge University Press.

Oakes, G. 1990. *Weber and Rickert*. Cambridge, Mass.: MIT Press.

O'Brien. G. D. 1975, *Hegel on Reason and History: A Contemporary Interpretation*. Chicago Chicago University Press.

Ott, H. 1993. *Martin Heidegger*. London: HarperCollins.

Outhwaite, W. 1995. *Habermas: A Critical Introduction*. Stanford: Stanford University Press

—— 1996. *The Habermas Reader*. Cambridge: Polity Press.

Outram, D. 1995. *The Enlightenment*. Cambridge: Cambridge University Press.

Owensby, J. 1994. *Dilthey and the Narrative of History*. Ithaca and London: Cornell University Press.

Patočka, J. 1996. *Heretical Essays in the Philosophy of History*, trans. E. Kohák. Chicago: Open Court.

Pattison, G. 1997. *Kierkegaard and the Crisis of Faith*. London: SPCK.

Patton, P. 1993. *Nietzsche, Feminism and Political Theory*. London: Routledge.

Paz, O. 1970. *Lévi-Strauss: An Introduction*. London: Cape.

Pelikan, J, 1990. 'Leopold von Ranke as Historian of the Reformation', in Iggers and Powell 1990, pp. 89–98.

Phillipson, N. 1989. *Hume*. London: Weidenfeld & Nicolson.

Pickering, M. 1991. *August Comte, An Intellectual Biography*, volume 1. Cambridge: Cambridge University Press.

Pinkard, T. 1995. 'Hegel on history, self-determination, and the absolute', in Melzer, Weinberger and Zinman 1995, pp. 30–58.

Polt, R. 1999. *Heidegger: An Introduction*. London: UCL Press.

Pompa, L. 1990. *Human Nature and Historical Knowledge*. Cambridge: Cambridge University Press.

Popper, K. R. 1957. *The Poverty of Historicism*. London: Routledge and Kegan Paul.

Putnam, H. 1981. *Reason, Truth and History*. Cambridge: Cambridge University Press.

—— 1990. *Realism with a Human Face*. Cambridge, MA: Harvard University Press.

von Ranke, L. 1983. *The Theory and Practice of History*, ed. Georg G. Iggers and K. von Moltke New York: Irvington Publishers Inc. (copyright. Bobbs-Merrill Co. 1973).

Reill, P. H. 1990. 'History and the Life Sciences in the Early Nineteenth Century', in Iggers and Powell, 1990, pp. 21–35.

Rickert, H. 1962. *Science and History: a Critique of Positivist Epistemology*. Princeton: D. Van Nostrand Company. Inc.

—— 1986. *The Limits of Concept Formation in Natural Science* (abridged edition), ed. and trans. Guy Oakes. Cambridge: Cambridge University Press.

Ricoeur, P. 1965. *History and Truth*. Evanston: Northwestern University Press.

—— 1967. *Husserl: An Analysis of his Phenomenology*. Evanston: Northwestern University Press

—— 1969. *The Symbolism of Evil*. Boston: Beacon Press.

—— 1974. *The Conflict of Interpretations*, ed. D. Ihde. Evanston: Northwestern University Press

—— 1981. *Hermeneutics and the Human Sciences*, trans. J. Thompson. Cambridge: Cambridge University Press.

—— 1984. *Time and Narrative*, Volume 1. Chicago: University of Chicago Press.

—— 1985. *Time and Narrative*, Volume 2. Chicago: University of Chicago Press.

—— 1988. *Time and Narrative*, Volume 3. Chicago: University of Chicago Press.

Rockmore, T. 1989. *Habermas on Historical Materialism*. Bloomington: Indiana University Press.

Rojek, C. and Turner, B. (eds). 1993. *Forget Baudrillard?* London: Routledge.

Rorty, R. 1991a. *Essays on Heidegger and Others*. Cambridge: Cambridge University Press.

—— 1991b. *Objectivism, Relativism, and Truth*. Cambridge: Cambridge University Press.

—— 1999. *Philosophy and Social Hope*. Harmondsworth: Penguin Books.

Rose, G. 1978. *The Melancholy Science*. London: Macmillan.

Ross, D. 1990. 'On the Misunderstanding of Ranke and the Origins of the Historical Profession in America', in Iggers and Powell, pp. 154–69.

Roth, G. and Schluchter, W. 1979. *Max Weber's Vision of History*. Berkeley: University of California Press.

Ryan, A. 1974. *J. S. Mill*. London: Routledge and Kegan Paul.

Rylance, R. 1994. *Roland Barthes*. Brighton: Harvester Wheatsheaf.

Safranski, R. 1998. *Martin Heidegger: Between Good and Evil*, trans. E. Osers. Cambridge, MA: Harvard University Press.

Sartre, J.-P. 1956. *Being and Nothingness*, trans. H. Barnes. New York: Philosophical Library.

Schelling, F. 1988. *Ideas for a Philosophy of Nature*. Cambridge: Cambridge University Press.

Schleiermacher, F. 1977. *Hermeneutics: The Handwritten Manuscripts* ed. H. Kimmerle, trans. J. Duke and J. Forstmann. Missoula, Montana: Scholars Press. English translation of second German edition, Heidelberg: Carl Winter, 1974.

Schnädelbach, H. 1984. *Philosophy in Germany 1831–1933*. Cambridge: Cambridge University Press, 1984.

Schoedinger, A. 1996. *Readings in Medieval Philosophy*. Oxford: Oxford University Press, 1996.

Schopenhauer, A. 1965. *Sämtliche Werke*. Stuttgart: Cotta/Insel.

—— 1966. *The World as Will and Representation*, trans. E Payne. New York: Dover.

—— 1974. *The Fourfold Root of the Principle of Sufficient Reason*, trans. E Payne. New York: Open Court.

Schulin, E. 1990. 'Universal History and National History', in Iggers and Powell, 1990 pp. 70–81.

Scruton, R. 1982. *Kant*. Oxford: Oxford University Press.

Shapiro, B. 1969. *John Wilkins, 1614–1672*. Berkeley: University of California Press.

Sills, C. and Jensen, C. 1992. *The Philosophy of Discourse*. Portsmouth: Boynton/Cook.

Sim, S. 1994. *George Lukács*. New York: Prentice-Hall.

Simmel, G. 1971. *On Individuality and Social Forms*, ed. D. Levine. Chicago: University of Chicago Press.

—— 1977. *The Problems of Philosophy of History: An Epistemological Essay* (second edition 1905) trans. and ed. G. Oakes. New York: Free Press.

—— 1980. 'On the Nature of Historical Understanding', in *Georg Simmel Essays on Interpretation in Social Science*, trans. and ed. G. Oakes. Manchester: Manchester University Press, pp. 97–126.

—— 1986. *Schopenhauer and Nietzsche*. Amherst: University of Massachusetts Press.

Simmel, G. 1990. *The Philosophy of Money*, ed. D. Frisby, translated T. Bottomore. London: Routledge.

Smart, B. 1985. *Michel Foucault*. Chichester: Ellis Horwood.

Smith, B. and Woodruff Smith, D. (eds). 1995. *The Cambridge Companion to Husserl*. Cambridge: Cambridge University Press.

Smith, G. (ed.). 1989. *Benjamin – Philosophy, Aesthetics, History*. Chicago: University of Chicago Press.

Solomon, R. C. 1983. *In the Spirit of Hegel*. New York: Oxford University Press.

—— 1988. *Continental Philosophy since 1750: The Rise and Fall of the Self*. Oxford: Oxford University Press.

Solomon, R. C. and Higgins, K. M. (eds). 1993. *Routledge History of Philosophy, Volume VI: Th*
 Age of German Idealism. London: Routledge.
Sophocles 1984. *The Three Theban Plays*, trans. Robert Fagles. London: Penguin Classics.
Southgate, B. 1996. *History: What and Why?* London: Routledge.
Stanford, M. 1988. *An Introduction to the Philosophy of History*. Oxford: Blackwell Publishers.
—— 1994. *A Companion to the Study of History*. Oxford: Blackwell Publishers.
Steinberg, M. (ed.). 1996. *Walter Benjamin and the Demands of History*. Ithaca: Cornell Uni
 versity Press.
Steiner, G. 1991. *Heidegger*. Chicago: Chicago University Press.
Stern, J. 1978. *Nietzsche*. London: Fontana.
Strauss, L. 1953. *Natural Right and History*. Chicago: University of Chicago Press.
Strawson, P. E. 1985. *Skepticism and Naturalism*. London: Methuen.
Sturrock, J. 1981. *Structuralism and Since: From Lévi-Strauss to Derrida*. Oxford: Oxford Uni
 versity Press.
Tanner, M. 1999. *Schopenhauer*. London: Routledge.
Taylor, C. 1975. *Hegel*. Cambridge: Cambridge University Press.
Tinkler, J. 1996. 'Bacon and History', in *The Cambridge Companion to Bacon*, ed. M. Peltonen
 Cambridge: Cambridge University Press, pp. 232–59.
Van Leeuwen, H. 1963. *The Problem of Certainty in English Thought, 1630–1690*. The Hague
 Martinus Nijhoff.
Vattimo, G. 1988. *The End of Modernity*. Cambridge: Polity Press.
Vesser H. (ed.). 1989. *The New Historicism*. London: Routledge.
Vyverberg, H. 1989. *Human Nature, Cultural Diversity, and the French Enlightenment*. New
 York: Oxford University Press.
Warnke, G. 1987. *Gadamer: Hermeneutics, Tradition and Reason*. Cambridge: Polity Press.
Watkin, J. 1997. *Kierkegaard*. London: Chapman.
Weber, M. 1949. *The Methodology of the Social Sciences*, trans. and ed. (E. Shils and H. Finch
 New York: Free Press.
—— 1978. *Selections in Translation*, ed. W. Runciman, trans. E. Matthews. Cambridge: Cam
 bridge University Press.
—— 1992. *The Protestant Ethic and the Spirit of Capitalism*, trans. T. Parsons, introduction b
 A. Giddens. London: Routledge.
Weston, M. 1994. *Kierkegaard and Modern Continental Philosophy*. London: Routledge.
White, H. 1973. *Metahistory*. Baltimore: Johns Hopkins University Press.
—— 1978. *Tropics of History*. Baltimore: Johns Hopkins University Press.
—— 1981. 'The Value of Narrativity in the Representation of Reality', in *On Narrative*, ed. W
 Mitchell. Chicago: University of Chicago Press.
Willey, T. E. 1978. *Back to Kant*. Detroit: Wayne State University Press.
Windelband, W. 1980. 'History and Natural Science' (Rectorial address Straßburg, 1894), trans
 from 'Geschichte und Naturwissenschaft' Präludien (Tübingen, 1924), II, 136–60, by G
 Oakes in *History and Theory* 19, pp. 165–85.
Wittgenstein, L. 1967. *Philosophical Investigations*, third edition. Oxford: Basil Blackwell.
—— 1969. *On Certainty*, ed. G. Anscombe and G. von Wright, trans. D. Paul and G. Anscombe
 Oxford: Basil Blackwell.
Wood, D. (ed.). 1991. *On Paul Ricoeur: Narrative and Interpretation*. London: Routledge.
Woolhouse, R. S. 1988. *The Empiricists*. Oxford: Oxford University Press.
Wolin, R. 1993. *The Heidegger Controversy: A Critical Reader*. Cambridge, MA: The MIT Press
Wootton, D. 1993. 'David Hume the historian', in Noreton 1993, pp. 281–312.
Young, J. 1996. *Heidegger, Philosophy, Nazism*. Cambridge: Cambridge University Press.
Yovel, Y. 1980. *Kant and the Philosophy of History*. Princeton: Princeton University Press.
Zurbrugg, N. (ed.). 1997. *Jean Baudrillard: Art and Artefact*. London: Sage.

Index of Names

Index of Subjects and Terms

901
P5685

100099